The Complete Atlas of Britain

Published by The Automobile Association

Produced by the Cartographic Department, Publications Division of the
Automobile Association.

Based on the Ordnance Survey maps, with the permission of the Controller of
Her Majesty's Stationery Office. Crown Copyright Reserved.

Printed by Sir Joseph Causton & Sons Ltd., London and Eastleigh, England.

The contents of this book are believed correct at the time of printing.
Nevertheless, the publisher can accept no responsibility for errors or omissions,
or for changes in the details given.

Published by the Automobile Association, Fanum House, Basing View,
Basingstoke, Hampshire RG21 2EA.

ISBN 0 86145 005 1

Contents

Journey Planning

The Motoring Atlas of Great Britain combines superb maps with accurate and practical routefinding aids. These aids are designed to help the motorist complete a journey as quickly and with as little stress as possible.

ALERTNESS

Whether a journey is undertaken for business or pleasure, it is essential that the driver should set out feeling alert and confident, and that he should remain so until his destination is reached. A tired, frustrated driver is a potential danger to himself, to his passengers, and to other road users. The driver will feel more confident, and will certainly have a less troublesome journey, if he has planned his journey in advance.

MILEAGE

One of the fundamental considerations to be taken into account when planning a journey of any sort is that of the mileage involved. The mileage chart on page iii, which gives the distances between a selection of towns in Great Britain, can be used to make a rough calculation of the total journey length. From this an indication of the journey time may be gained.

ROUTE PLANNING

Once an indication of the journey length and time has been ascertained it is necessary to decide on a general route, and for this the route planning maps on pages iv-ix are an invaluable guide. They depict principal routes throughout the country, and pinpoint the larger conurbations on those routes. Detailed routes can

be worked out from the maps in the main atlas section of this book. The driver may find it useful to make a note of road numbers and route directions before setting out, as this can reduce his need to stop and consult the atlas.

MOTORAIL

If the journey involved is very long, the motorist may find it both more convenient and less exhausting to take advantage of the British Rail Motorail service. The cost of transporting a car and a family of four by rail is between 10 and 20% higher than travelling by road, but there may be considerable gains in travelling time, and savings in vehicle wear and tear. Details of the Motorail Service are given on page X.

RADIO

Frequent radio bulletins are issued by the BBC and Independent Local Radio stations on road conditions, possible hold-ups, etc, and these can be of great assistance to the driver. By tuning in to the local stations of areas being passed through it may be possible to avoid delays, and be prepared to make running changes to the route. The map and accompanying text of page XI give details of the wavelengths and reception areas of all local radio stations in Great Britain.

ROAD SIGNS

Considerable help in negotiating the nation's highways can be obtained by understanding the various types of road direction signs. They are illustrated, and their functions described, on page XII. The principal benefit of the system

is that primary route signs indicate the most straightforward route between one major town and another. It should be remembered that the shortest route is not necessarily the quickest. The driver is advised, where possible, to avoid driving through towns and built-up-areas, even if such routes appear to be more direct from the map. Delays caused by traffic lights, one-way systems, pedestrians, etc, will almost certainly be encountered in such areas.

THE NATIONAL GRID

The National Grid system, which is explained on page XIII, enables the driver to pinpoint any town or village in the atlas after having first found the reference number of that place by consulting the index. There is a separate index for London. A series of plans of principal towns and cities in Great Britain will be found between pages 153 and 191.

MOTORWAYS

When planning routes, many drivers will consider using motorways. They have several advantages over other types of road; not only are they faster, but they are also very easy to follow and allow a more consistent speed to be maintained. Drivers should, however, be fully conversant with the special rules for motorway driving, which are contained in the Highway Code. Perhaps the most ignored of these is that the outside lanes of a motorway should be used for overtaking only: there is no such thing as a 'fast lane'. Beginning on page 114 is a series of maps of the principal motorways in Great Britain.

Mileage Chart

The distances between towns on the mileage chart are given to the nearest mile, and are measured along the normal AA recommended routes. It should be noted that AA recommended routes do not necessarily follow the shortest distances between places but are based on the quickest travelling time, making maximum use of motorways or dual-carriageway roads.

Mileage chart (triangular distance matrix; each row is headed by the town named, distances read against the towns listed above it)

- **Aberdeen**
- **Aberystwyth** — 463
- **Barnstaple** — 212 594
- **Birmingham** — 176 119 423
- **Brighton** — 177 200 261 594
- **Bristol** — 151 86 98 121 504
- **Cambridge** — 154 119 101 251 218 468
- **Cardiff** — 187 44 184 106 135 110 524
- **Carlisle** — 298 256 275 368 197 364 234 230
- **Carmarthen** — 282 66 234 109 249 134 200 48 512
- **Colchester** — 282 303 216 48 183 113 165 280 261 517
- **Dorchester** — 186 186 350 120 178 62 120 161 91 198 579
- **Dover** — 199 113 299 393 233 128 201 78 202 272 308 619
- **Edinburgh** — 493 449 390 383 98 395 342 374 467 296 464 334 127
- **Exeter** — 446 246 54 235 182 347 116 231 78 172 157 40 193 576
- **Fort William** — 555 135 598 513 560 494 211 503 465 484 577 405 575 445 171
- **Glasgow** — 105 442 45 488 446 399 379 95 394 351 371 462 292 461 330 143
- **Gloucester** — 336 450 107 339 191 161 111 112 240 58 118 35 151 52 126 109 469
- **Guildford** — 101 416 531 149 422 97 99 99 206 322 140 94 107 44 125 217 174 549
- **Hereford** — 129 31 323 436 125 325 222 130 189 85 226 56 141 53 179 55 144 85 455
- **Holyhead** — 157 273 182 321 432 290 327 351 292 315 155 225 211 251 217 326 155 307 108 452
- **Hull** — 218 200 242 106 245 303 307 236 285 288 207 276 150 254 160 234 266 146 321 229 363
- **Inverness** — 400 479 485 579 498 172 66 603 160 647 561 552 542 259 533 502 532 624 451 623 493 106
- **Kendal** — 308 128 179 183 277 195 147 260 301 149 344 305 266 240 50 248 218 229 322 149 318 191 279
- **Leeds** — 71 368 59 165 169 221 181 215 331 287 206 278 291 194 227 122 236 147 216 253 135 305 178 333
- **Lincoln** — 70 143 427 78 200 154 166 133 276 390 239 271 213 228 135 231 180 206 87 165 195 94 257 197 393
- **Liverpool** — 128 74 80 381 126 106 115 228 144 221 333 253 225 297 254 258 163 126 202 196 182 271 101 269 114 354
- **Maidstone** — 257 177 239 309 611 246 315 183 55 152 450 564 204 456 42 154 78 258 356 192 89 158 50 167 230 269 582
- **Manchester** — 247 36 88 44 72 373 97 125 121 213 133 214 326 239 218 283 242 203 183 118 190 155 168 258 87 257 134 346
- **Middlesborough** — 115 295 146 122 64 87 309 88 236 236 280 232 186 304 341 146 335 324 248 295 93 288 200 271 312 182 358 246 274
- **Newcastle** — 38 144 331 173 152 96 94 270 125 265 264 312 261 150 244 370 109 367 354 273 324 58 320 231 302 342 214 386 275 238
- **Northampton** — 222 190 135 113 149 83 132 197 500 152 204 92 93 76 341 452 182 344 149 143 94 177 243 135 50 115 125 54 202 173 470
- **Norwich** — 112 259 230 184 131 234 105 175 246 529 314 312 202 151 180 379 493 293 370 170 237 59 293 284 251 62 216 167 163 312 279 498
- **Nottingham** — 123 66 162 132 72 178 104 37 72 160 432 88 176 115 153 111 281 397 217 273 212 205 130 192 187 164 84 146 188 59 236 160 399
- **Oxford** — 104 142 41 260 231 153 98 167 125 170 216 518 192 212 79 60 48 357 471 101 362 139 103 117 157 261 106 80 74 113 64 170 155 489
- **Penzance** — 271 337 411 303 488 458 358 324 370 281 406 419 722 422 407 245 267 226 562 675 120 565 366 173 353 301 465 236 352 199 292 277 111 313 694
- **Perth** — 611 406 317 413 388 154 192 261 499 269 310 252 196 117 284 367 371 467 386 60 105 491 44 534 495 433 429 146 440 384 419 512 339 510 380 83
- **Plymouth** — 534 80 194 260 337 226 410 381 281 248 292 358 329 343 651 344 330 168 191 149 484 598 43 488 290 96 276 224 388 158 275 121 217 200 67 236 617
- **Preston** — 302 232 378 174 120 226 155 131 102 33 267 30 123 68 43 344 119 136 141 235 158 183 296 258 185 302 269 267 198 86 206 197 187 280 107 278 149 315
- **Salisbury** — 223 134 456 211 63 164 196 103 313 284 202 117 214 188 229 265 568 248 253 102 60 74 406 520 91 409 161 40 146 161 311 96 137 52 83 114 116 173 540
- **Sheffield** — 201 79 283 295 360 143 45 150 105 136 106 38 212 78 45 34 119 407 68 160 138 195 135 256 372 242 247 250 241 167 215 161 188 122 169 223 83 259 167 373
- **Shrewsbury** — 93 147 89 225 319 302 106 85 203 98 214 186 68 210 64 122 117 131 431 169 105 52 167 77 271 383 183 273 245 183 210 125 174 108 143 111 223 50 202 75 403
- **Southampton** — 168 203 23 244 152 477 227 67 171 191 108 324 293 231 105 242 192 237 286 589 258 277 126 49 95 429 541 107 433 145 55 140 186 335 118 132 75 63 130 140 197 561
- **Stoke** — 185 36 52 164 63 242 294 320 110 51 174 93 191 164 43 205 57 88 91 105 406 121 124 88 171 93 248 359 200 252 241 203 208 161 149 148 141 130 217 45 218 111 381
- **Stranraer** — 263 442 285 272 421 197 499 155 576 371 297 393 353 164 204 227 465 234 291 232 161 260 265 333 337 432 351 93 192 457 126 500 461 413 395 111 404 365 385 478 305 475 346 239
- **Taunton** — 426 172 91 152 210 67 230 75 462 152 121 187 262 153 336 308 208 181 219 208 256 270 573 271 257 95 124 76 411 525 32 413 221 43 230 151 315 85 198 48 150 127 50 162 544
- **York** — 265 227 119 252 145 62 243 80 338 246 417 185 87 185 147 88 52 72 253 101 76 24 89 362 38 194 193 237 190 208 326 297 199 293 282 202 253 113 245 157 226 270 138 315 204 326
- **London** — 209 167 417 165 78 162 167 82 219 212 452 290 56 128 115 67 280 252 199 37 211 141 194 261 564 206 267 135 30 104 402 516 172 405 78 125 64 218 307 153 60 120 53 118 215 211 535

Route Planning Maps

Route Planning Maps

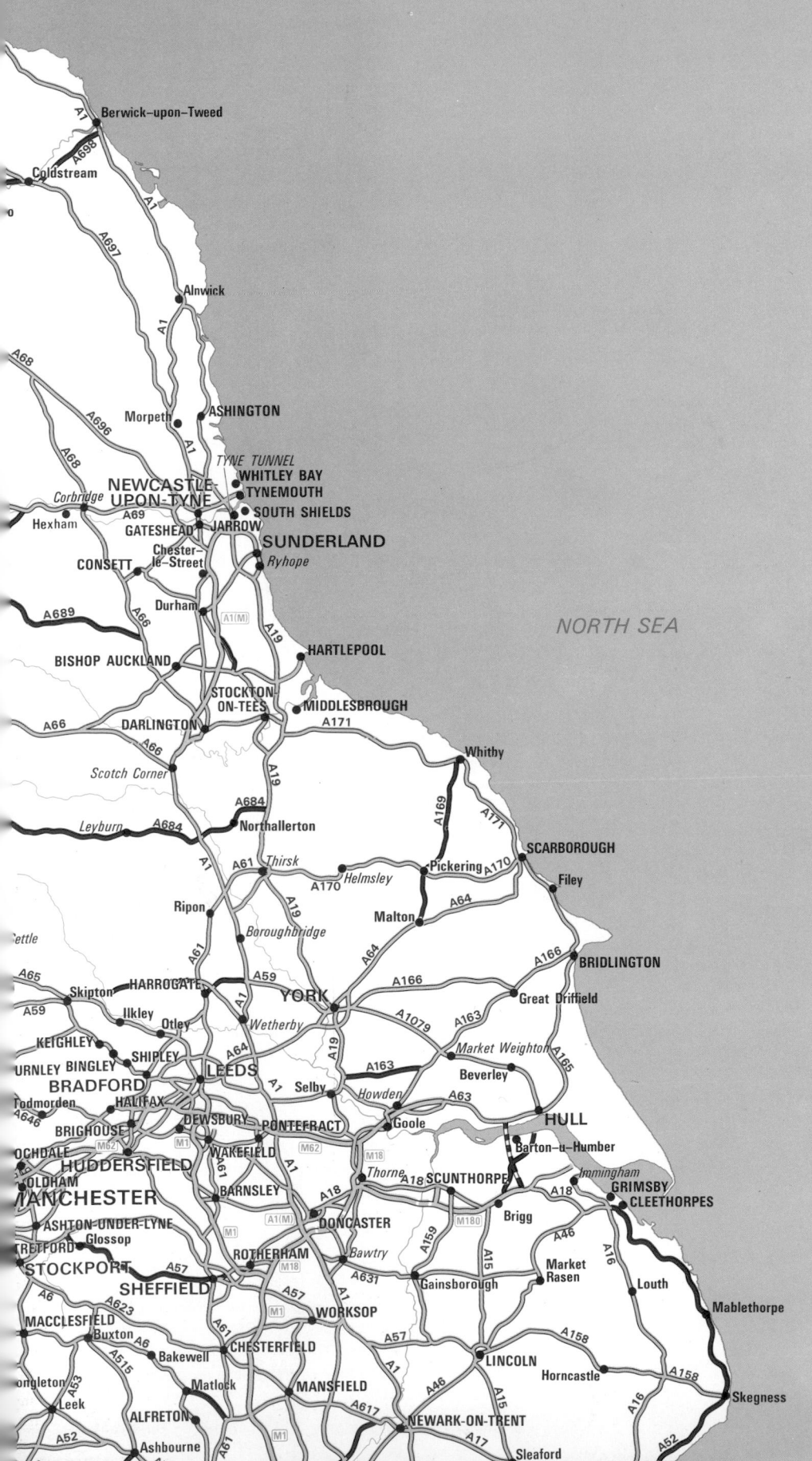

Route Planning Maps

Orkney Islands

John o'Groats

Thurso A836
Melvich A836
A9
A882
A895
A897
Wick

Helmsdale

Golspie

MORAY FIRTH

Cullen Portsoy Macduff Fraserburgh
Elgin A98 Banff A98
Nairn Forres A96 A95 Turriff Peterhead
A941 Rothes A96 A95 A92 Boddam
Aberlour Keith A952
A95 Huntly A947 Old Meldrum Ellon
A9 Grantown-on-Spey A96 A92
Carrbridge A95 Tomintoul Inverurie
Aviemore A939
A9
Kingussie ABERDEEN

Braemar A93 Ballater Banchory A93
A93 A957 A92
A94 Stonehaven
Blair Atholl Laurencekirk A92
Pitlochry Inverbervie
A827 Brechin
Aberfeldy A9 Forfar Montrose
Blairgowrie A93 A94 A929
A9 Coupar Angus A92 Arbroath
A85 DUNDEE
TAY BRIDGE
A85 Crieff Newport-on-Tay
PERTH M90 A914 Cupar St Andrews
A9 Auchterarder Auchtermuchty
Dunblane Kinross A915 A917 Crail
A91 A977 M90 Dysart Buckhaven
STIRLING Kincardine DUNFERMLINE KIRKCALDY
-on-Forth Burntisland
M9 FORTH BRIDGE Dunbar
ALKIRK EDINBURGH A1
Linlithgow Musselburgh

IX

Motorail Services

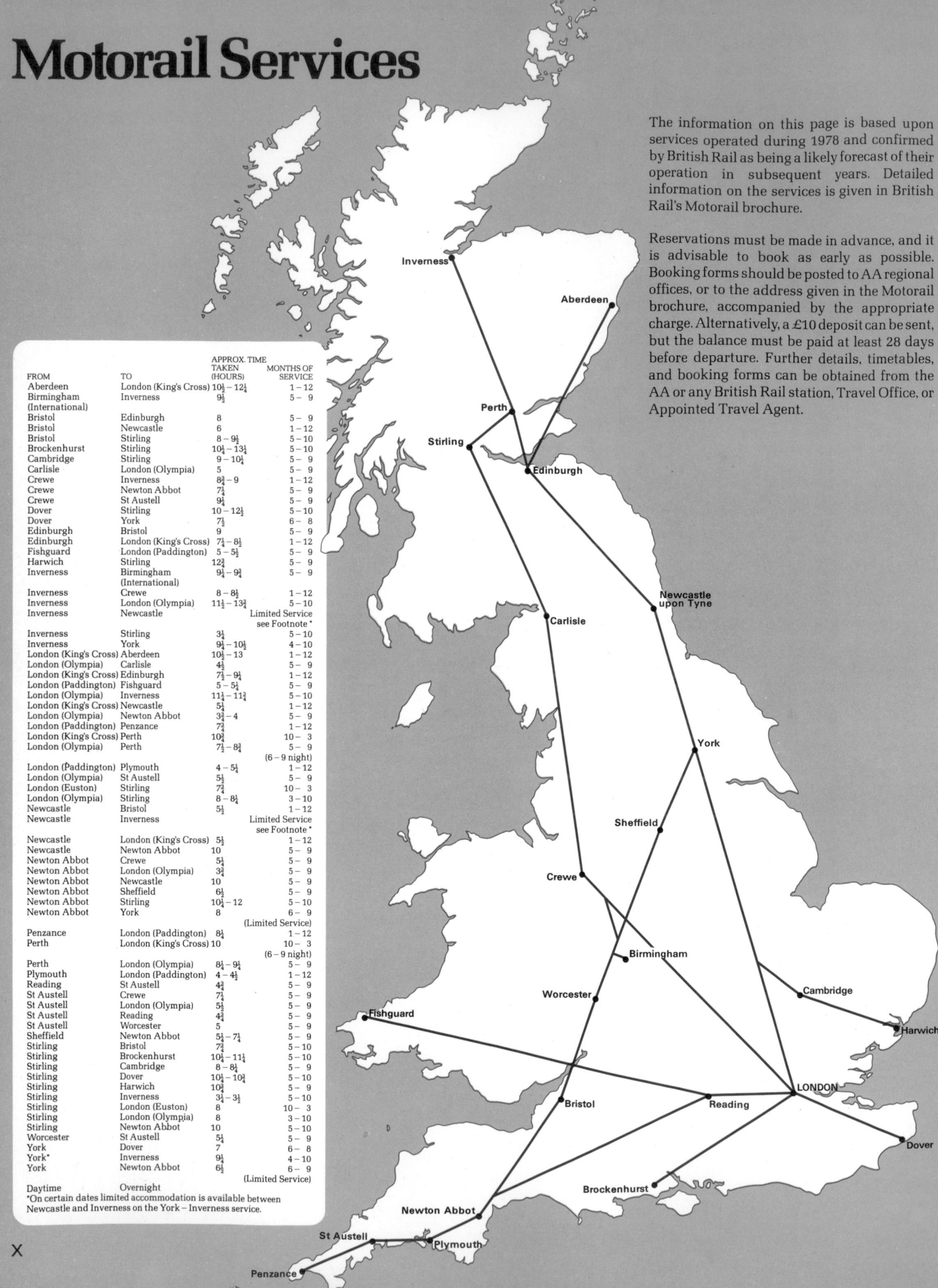

The information on this page is based upon services operated during 1978 and confirmed by British Rail as being a likely forecast of their operation in subsequent years. Detailed information on the services is given in British Rail's Motorail brochure.

Reservations must be made in advance, and it is advisable to book as early as possible. Booking forms should be posted to AA regional offices, or to the address given in the Motorail brochure, accompanied by the appropriate charge. Alternatively, a £10 deposit can be sent, but the balance must be paid at least 28 days before departure. Further details, timetables, and booking forms can be obtained from the AA or any British Rail station, Travel Office, or Appointed Travel Agent.

FROM	TO	APPROX. TIME TAKEN (HOURS)	MONTHS OF SERVICE
Aberdeen	London (King's Cross)	$10\frac{1}{4} - 12\frac{1}{4}$	1 – 12
Birmingham (International)	Inverness	$9\frac{1}{2}$	5 – 9
Bristol	Edinburgh	8	5 – 9
Bristol	Newcastle	6	1 – 12
Bristol	Stirling	$8 - 9\frac{1}{2}$	5 – 10
Brockenhurst	Stirling	$10\frac{1}{4} - 13\frac{1}{4}$	5 – 10
Cambridge	Stirling	$9 - 10\frac{1}{4}$	5 – 9
Carlisle	London (Olympia)	5	5 – 9
Crewe	Inverness	$8\frac{3}{4} - 9$	1 – 12
Crewe	Newton Abbot	$7\frac{1}{4}$	5 – 9
Crewe	St Austell	$9\frac{1}{4}$	5 – 9
Dover	Stirling	$10 - 12\frac{1}{2}$	5 – 10
Dover	York	$7\frac{1}{2}$	6 – 8
Edinburgh	Bristol	9	5 – 9
Edinburgh	London (King's Cross)	$7\frac{1}{4} - 8\frac{1}{2}$	1 – 12
Fishguard	London (Paddington)	$5 - 5\frac{1}{2}$	5 – 9
Harwich	Stirling	$12\frac{3}{4}$	5 – 9
Inverness	Birmingham (International)	$9\frac{1}{4} - 9\frac{3}{4}$	5 – 9
Inverness	Crewe	$8 - 8\frac{1}{2}$	1 – 12
Inverness	London (Olympia)	$11\frac{1}{4} - 13\frac{3}{4}$	5 – 10
Inverness	Newcastle	Limited Service see Footnote *	
Inverness	Stirling	$3\frac{1}{4}$	5 – 10
Inverness	York	$9\frac{1}{4} - 10\frac{1}{4}$	4 – 10
London (King's Cross)	Aberdeen	$10\frac{1}{4} - 13$	1 – 12
London (Olympia)	Carlisle	$4\frac{1}{2}$	5 – 9
London (King's Cross)	Edinburgh	$7\frac{1}{4} - 9\frac{1}{4}$	1 – 12
London (Paddington)	Fishguard	$5 - 5\frac{1}{2}$	5 – 9
London (Olympia)	Inverness	$11\frac{1}{4} - 11\frac{3}{4}$	5 – 10
London (King's Cross)	Newcastle	$5\frac{1}{4}$	1 – 12
London (Olympia)	Newton Abbot	$3\frac{3}{4} - 4$	5 – 9
London (Paddington)	Penzance	$7\frac{3}{4}$	1 – 12
London (King's Cross)	Perth	$10\frac{3}{4}$	10 – 3
London (Olympia)	Perth	$7\frac{1}{2} - 8\frac{3}{4}$	5 – 9 (6 – 9 night)
London (Paddington)	Plymouth	$4 - 5\frac{1}{4}$	1 – 12
London (Olympia)	St Austell	$5\frac{1}{4}$	5 – 9
London (Euston)	Stirling	$7\frac{3}{4}$	10 – 3
London (Olympia)	Stirling	$8 - 8\frac{1}{4}$	3 – 10
Newcastle	Bristol	$5\frac{1}{2}$	1 – 12
Newcastle	Inverness	Limited Service see Footnote *	
Newcastle	London (King's Cross)	$5\frac{1}{2}$	1 – 12
Newcastle	Newton Abbot	10	5 – 9
Newton Abbot	Crewe	$5\frac{1}{4}$	5 – 9
Newton Abbot	London (Olympia)	$3\frac{3}{4}$	5 – 9
Newton Abbot	Newcastle	10	5 – 9
Newton Abbot	Sheffield	$6\frac{1}{2}$	5 – 9
Newton Abbot	Stirling	$10\frac{1}{4} - 12$	5 – 10
Newton Abbot	York	8	6 – 9 (Limited Service)
Penzance	London (Paddington)	$8\frac{1}{4}$	1 – 12
Perth	London (King's Cross)	10	10 – 3 (6 – 9 night)
Perth	London (Olympia)	$8\frac{1}{4} - 9\frac{1}{4}$	5 – 9
Plymouth	London (Paddington)	$4 - 4\frac{1}{2}$	1 – 12
Reading	St Austell	$4\frac{3}{4}$	5 – 9
St Austell	Crewe	$7\frac{1}{4}$	5 – 9
St Austell	London (Olympia)	$5\frac{1}{4}$	5 – 9
St Austell	Reading	$4\frac{3}{4}$	5 – 9
St Austell	Worcester	5	5 – 9
Sheffield	Newton Abbot	$5\frac{1}{4} - 7\frac{1}{4}$	5 – 9
Stirling	Bristol	$7\frac{3}{4}$	5 – 10
Stirling	Brockenhurst	$10\frac{1}{4} - 11\frac{1}{4}$	5 – 10
Stirling	Cambridge	$8 - 8\frac{1}{4}$	5 – 9
Stirling	Dover	$10\frac{1}{4} - 10\frac{3}{4}$	5 – 10
Stirling	Harwich	$10\frac{3}{4}$	5 – 9
Stirling	Inverness	$3\frac{1}{4} - 3\frac{1}{2}$	5 – 10
Stirling	London (Euston)	8	10 – 3
Stirling	London (Olympia)	8	3 – 10
Stirling	Newton Abbot	10	5 – 10
Worcester	St Austell	$5\frac{1}{4}$	5 – 9
York	Dover	7	6 – 8
York*	Inverness	$9\frac{1}{4}$	4 – 10
York	Newton Abbot	$6\frac{1}{2}$	6 – 9 (Limited Service)

Daytime   Overnight

*On certain dates limited accommodation is available between Newcastle and Inverness on the York – Inverness service.

Local Radio

Under normal circumstances any car radio receiver should pick up the broadcasts by local radio stations in the reception areas shown on the map on this page. However, adverse conditions may effect the clarity of the signal. Exceptional atmospheric conditions and/or favourable topography (eg no hill ranges between the transmitter and the receiver) may considerably extend the reception areas.

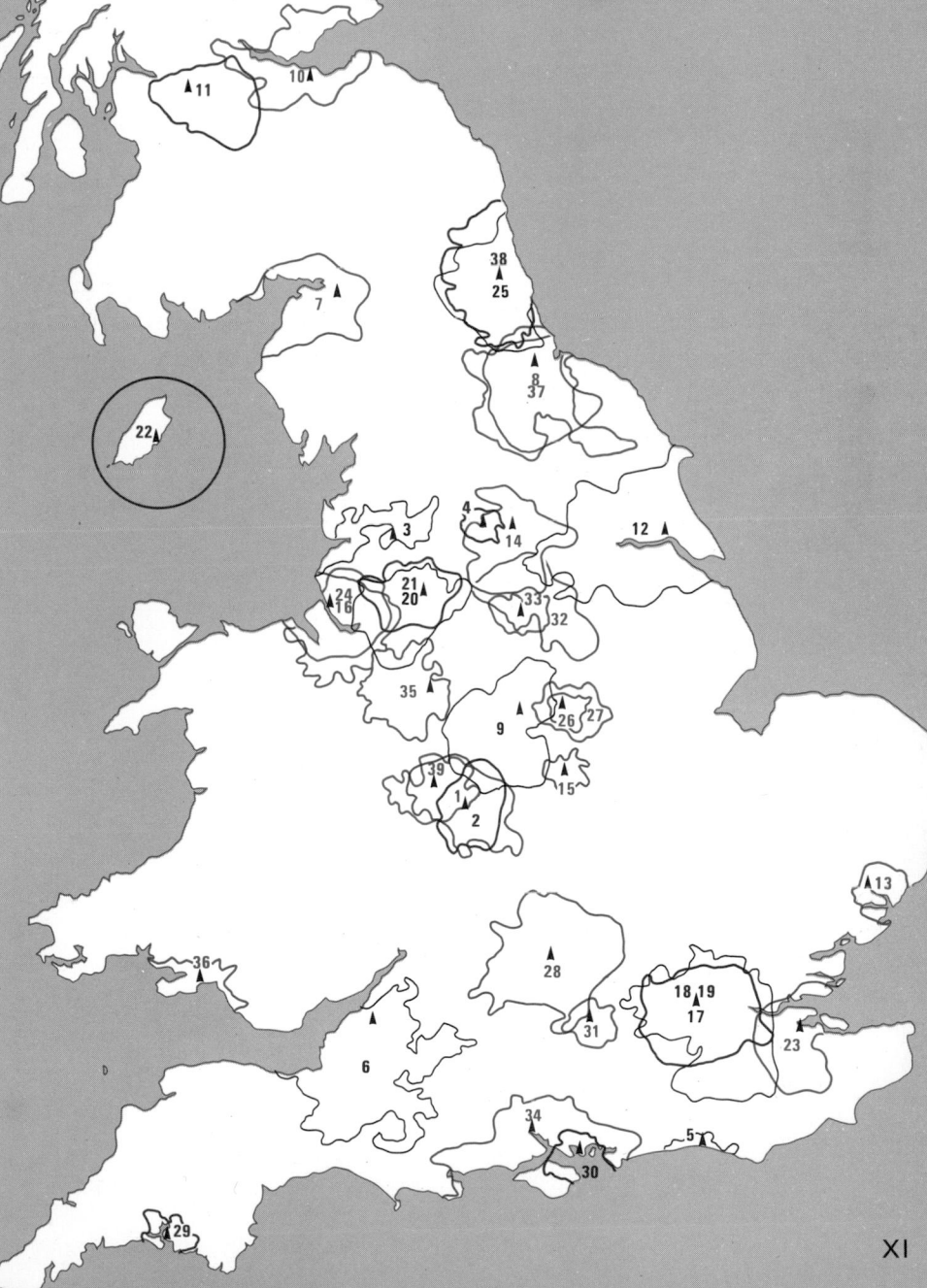

TOWN AND RADIO STATION	MEDIUM WAVE	FREQUENCY Khz	VHF
Birmingham			
1 BBC Radio Birmingham	206	1458	95.6
2 BRMB Radio	261	1152	94.8
Blackburn			
3 BBC Radio Blackburn	351	855	96.4
Bradford			
4 Pennine Radio	235	1278	96.0
Brighton			
5 BBC Radio Brighton	202	1485	95.3
Bristol			
6 BBC Radio Bristol	194	1548	95.5
Carlisle			
7 BBC Radio Carlisle	397	756	95.6
Cleveland			
8 BBC Radio Cleveland	194	1548	96.6
Derby			
9 BBC Radio Derby	269	1116	96.5/94.2
Edinburgh			
10 Radio Forth	194	1548	96.8
Glasgow			
11 Radio Clyde	261	1152	95.1
Humberside			
12 BBC Radio Humberside	202	1485	96.9
Ipswich			
13 Radio Orwell	257	1170	97.1
Leeds			
14 BBC Radio Leeds	388	774	92.4
Leicester			
15 BBC Radio Leicester	189	1584	95.1
Liverpool			
16 Radio City	194	1548	96.7
London			
17 BBC Radio London	206	1458	94.9
18 Capital Radio	194	1548	95.8
19 LBC	261	1152	97.3
Manchester			
20 BBC Radio Manchester	206	1458	95.1
21 Piccadilly Radio	261	1152	97.0
Man, Isle of			
22 Manx Radio	219	1367	89
Medway			
23 BBC Radio Medway	290	1035	96.7
Merseyside			
24 BBC Radio Merseyside	202	1485	95.8
Newcastle			
25 BBC Radio Newcastle	206	1458	95.4
Nottingham			
26 BBC Radio Nottingham	197	1521	95.4
27 Radio Trent	301	999	96.2
Oxford			
28 BBC Radio Oxford	202	1485	95.2
Plymouth			
29 Plymouth Sound	261	1152	96.0
Portsmouth			
30 Radio Victory	257	1170	95.0
Reading			
31 Thames Valley	210	1431	97.0
Sheffield			
32 BBC Radio Sheffield	290	1035	97.4/88.6
33 Radio Hallam	194	1548	95.2
Solent			
34 BBC Radio Solent	221	1359	96.1
Stoke-on-Trent			
35 BBC Radio Stoke on Trent	200	1503	96.1
Swansea			
36 Swansea Sound	257	1170	95.1
Teesside			
37 Radio Tees	257	1170	95.0
Tyne and Wear			
38 Metro Radio	261	1152	97.0
Wolverhampton			
39 Beacon Radio	303	990	97.2

Road Signs

Considerable help in negotiating the nation's highways can be obtained by understanding the various types of road direction signs illustrated on this page. The principal benefit of the sign system is that the primary route signs (green) indicate the most straightforward route between one town and another. These signs do not necessarily indicate the most direct route, but it should be remembered that direct routes may not be the quickest, or the easiest to follow.

MOTORWAYS On the map - All Motorways are blue. Motorway signposts have white lettering on a blue background. Advance Direction signs approaching an interchange generally include the junction number in a black box. On the map the junction number appears in white on a blue circle.

Midlands
(South Wales)
(London)

Severn Beach
B 4055
Bristol West
A 4018

17

A ROADS All A roads are shown in red on the map, unless part of the primary network when they are green. (as above) The signposts along these roads have black lettering on a white background. At a junction with a Primary Route the Primary Road number appears yellow in a green box.

Yeovil A 37

Bath
A 368

Weston
S·Mare
A 368

PRIMARY ROUTES On the map - all the Primary Routes are green. The sign posts on Primary roads are also green, with white lettering and yellow numbers. Apart from the Motorways, Primary Routes are the most important traffic routes in both urban and rural areas. They form a network of throughroutes connecting 'Primary Towns', which are generally places of traffic importance. Usually Primary routes are along A roads.

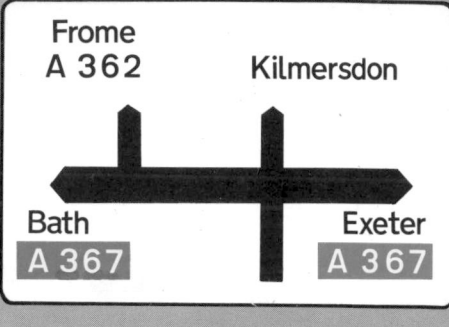

Frome
A 362   Kilmersdon

Bath   Exeter
A 367   A 367

CONFIRMATORY SIGNS These often appear after important road junctions and confirm that drivers have taken their intended route. The colour of confirmatory signs differs according to the road classification, eg blue for Motor ways, green for Primary Routes, and white for A and B roads.

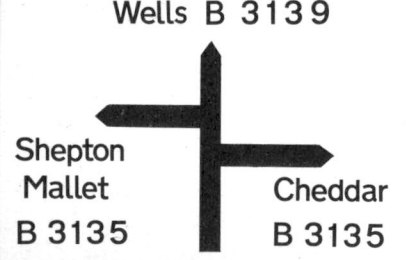

Wells B 3139

Shepton
Mallet   Cheddar
B 3135   B 3135

B ROADS On the map - all B roads not in the Primary network are signified by the colour yellow. The signs on B roads are black lettering on a white background, the same as for A roads.

M5
The Midlands
Gloucester 33

Cranmore
Station
Batcombe

Waterlip
Stoke St
Michael

UNCLASSIFIED ROADS On the map - all unclassified roads are white. New signposts along unclassified roads are usually of the Local Direction type. These have black lettering on a white background with a blue border. Local Direction signs may also appear in addition to Primary and non-Primary signs and indicate the route to local districts and amenities.

The National Grid

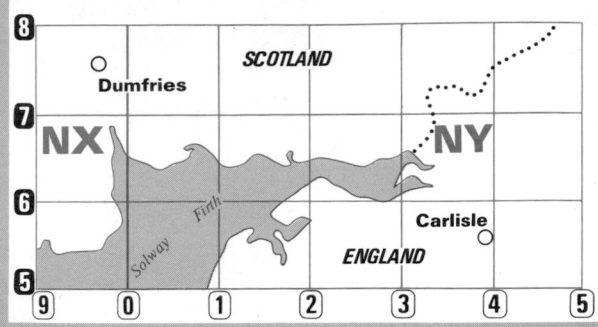

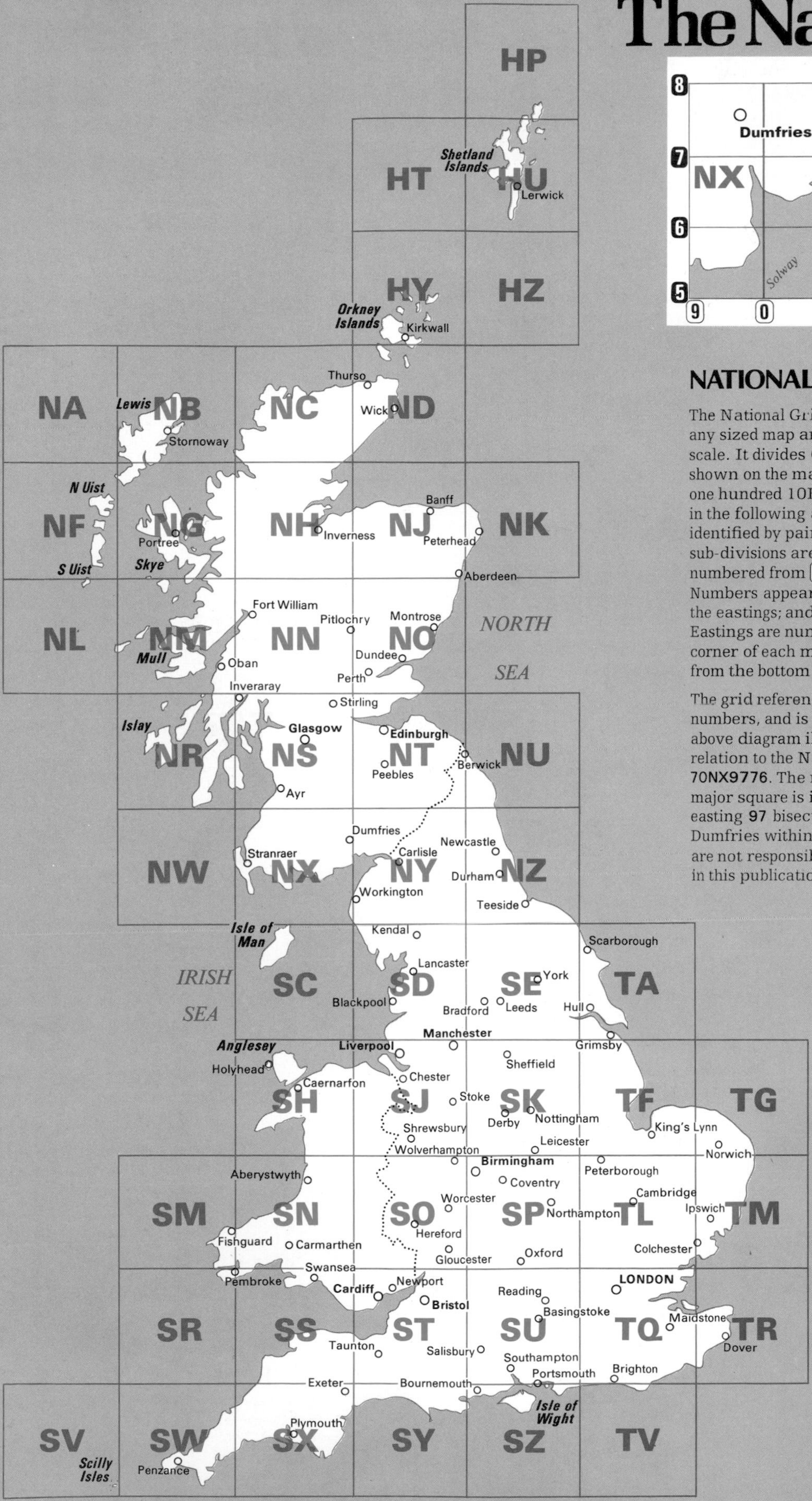

NATIONAL GRID EXPLANATION

The National Grid referencing system can be applied to any sized map and is accurate within the limitations of scale. It divides Great Britain into 100Km squares (as shown on the map), each of which is sub-divided into one hundred 10Km squares. The large squares appear in the following atlas as thick blue lines and are identified by pairs of letters *eg* NX etc; the small sub-divisions are shown as thin blue lines and are numbered from **0**..........**9** for each major square. Numbers appearing at the bottom of the map *eg* **0**, are the eastings; and those at the side *eg* **8**, the northings. Eastings are numbered from the top or bottom left-hand corner of each major square; northings are numbered from the bottom left or right-hand corner.

The grid reference comprises two letters and four numbers, and is preceded by the map page number. The above diagram illustrates the position of Dumfries in relation to the National Grid. The town's reference is **70NX9776**. The map appears on page **70**, the relevant major square is identified by the letters **NX**, and easting **97** bisects northing **76** to form the position of Dumfries within the 10Km square. The Ordnance Survey are not responsible for the accuracy of the National Grid in this publication.

Legend

Italiano	Deutsch		English	Français
N. di autostrade	Autobahn mit Nummer		Motorway with number	Autoroute avec numéro
Snodo con numero	Anschlusstelle mit Nummer		Junction with number	Echangeur avec numéro
Snodo con entrata o uscita limitata	Anschlusstelle mit beschränkter Auf oder Abfahrt		Junction with limited entry or exit	Echangeur à entrée ou sortie restreinte
Area di servizio	Tankstelle mit Raststätte		Service area	Aire de service
Autostrada e Snodo i costruzione	Im Bau befindliche Autobahn und Anschlusstelle		Motorway & Junction under construction	Autoroute et Jonction en construction
Rotta primaria	Hauptverbindungsstrasse		Primary route	Route primaire
Altre strade A	Andere A Strasse	A130	Other A roads	Autres routes A
Strade Classe B	Strasse der Klasse B	B2137	B Roads	Routes catégorie B
Non-classificate	Nicht klassifizierte Strasse		Unclassified	Non classifiée
Corsia a due piste	Strasse mit getrennten Fahrbahnen	A7	Dual Carriageway	double chaussée
In construzione	Im Bau befindliche Strasse		Under construction	En construction
Scozia : strade strette con aree di passaggio Scotland	Schottland: enge Strasse mit Uberholstellen		Scotland: narrow roads with passing places.	L'Écosse: Route étroite avec lieu de déplacement
Centro di servizio (24 ore ☎)	Dienststelle (24 Stunden ☎)	AA 24 hour	Service centre (24 hours ☎)	Station-service (24 heures ☎)
Centro di servizio (ore di lavoro normali)	Dienststelle (übliche Bürostunden)	AA	Service centre (normal office hours)	Station service (heures d'ouverture normales)
Centro di servizio autostrada	Autobahndienststelle	AA info	Motorway Information Centre	Centre-service d'autoroute
Centro di servizio strada	Strassendienststelle	AA 13	Road service centre	Centre-service de route
Centro di servizio porto	Hafendienststelle	AA	Port service centre	Centre-service de port
Telefoni AA & RAC	AA und RAC Telefonzellen	☎	AA & RAC telephones	Téléphones AA & RAC
Telefoni PTT in aree isolate	Öffentliche Telefonzellen in abgelegenen Gebieten (PO)	☎	PO telephones in isolated areas	Téléphones PTT dans endroits isolés
Area di pic-nic	Picknickplatz	PS	Picnic site	Terrain de Pique-nique
Punti di vista AA	AA-Aussichtspunkt	Bembridge Viewpoint	AA viewpoint	Points de vue AA
Inclinazione (la freccia indica in pendio)	Steigung (Pfeile weisen bergab)		Steep gradient (arrows point downhill)	Côte (la flèche est dirigée vers le bas)
Pedaggio strada	Gebührenpflichtige Strasse	Toll	Road toll	Péage de route
Passaggio a livello	Bahnübergang	LC	Level crossing	Passage à niveau
Traghetto veicoli (Gran Bretagna)	Autofähre (Grossbritannien)	V	Vehicle ferry (Gt Britain)	Bac pour véhicules (Grande-Bretagne)
Traghetto veicoli (continentale)	Autofähre (Kontinent)	CALAIS V	Vehicle ferry (continental)	Bac pour véhicules (Continental)
Aeroporto	Flughafen	✈	Airport	Aéroport
Area urbana	Stadtbezirk		Urban area	Zone urbaine
Confine nazionale	Nationale Grenze		National boundary	Frontière nationale
Confine di contea	Grafschaftsgrenze		County boundary	Frontière provinciale
Distanza in mille fra simboli	Entfernung zwischen Zeichen in Meilen	2	Distance in miles between symbols	Distance en milles entre symboles
A.S.M. in piedi	Ortshöhe nach Füssen	2137 ▲	Spot height in feet	Altitude en pieds anglais
Fiume e lago	Fluss und See		River and lake	Rivière et lac
Numeri di pagine di seguito	Hinweiszahlen für Anschlusskarten	13	Overlaps and numbers of continuing pages	Chiffres de guide pour cartes voisines
Spiaggia Sabblosa	Sandstrand		Sandy Beaches	Plage de Sable
Luogo da vedere	Sehenswürdigkeit	•	Place of Interest	Endroit à voir
Luogo preistorico	Vorgeschichtliche Stätte		Prehistoric Site	Lieu préhistorique
Castello	Schloss/Burg		Castle	Château
Giardini notevoli	Bemerkenswerter Garten	❋	Notable Gardens	Jardins renommés
Casa rimarchevole	Bemerkenswertes Landhaus		Notable House	Maison remarquable
Luogo archeologico industriale	Industriestatte von historischem Interesse		Industrial Archaeological Site	Lieu archéologique industriel
Collezioni di animali Giardini zoologici	Tiersammlung Zoologischer Garten		Animal Collection Zoos	Collection d'Animaux Jardins zoologiques

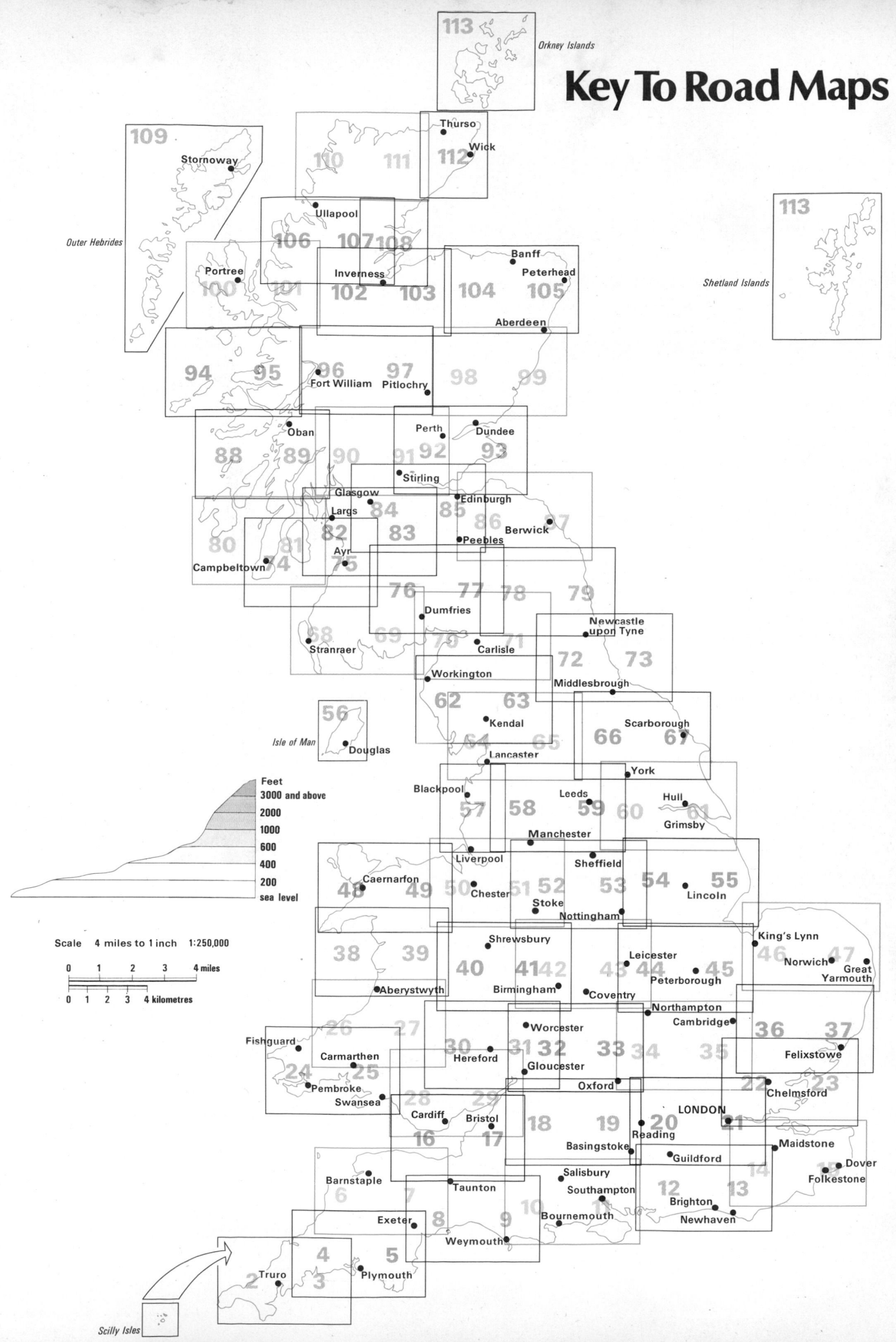

Key To Road Maps

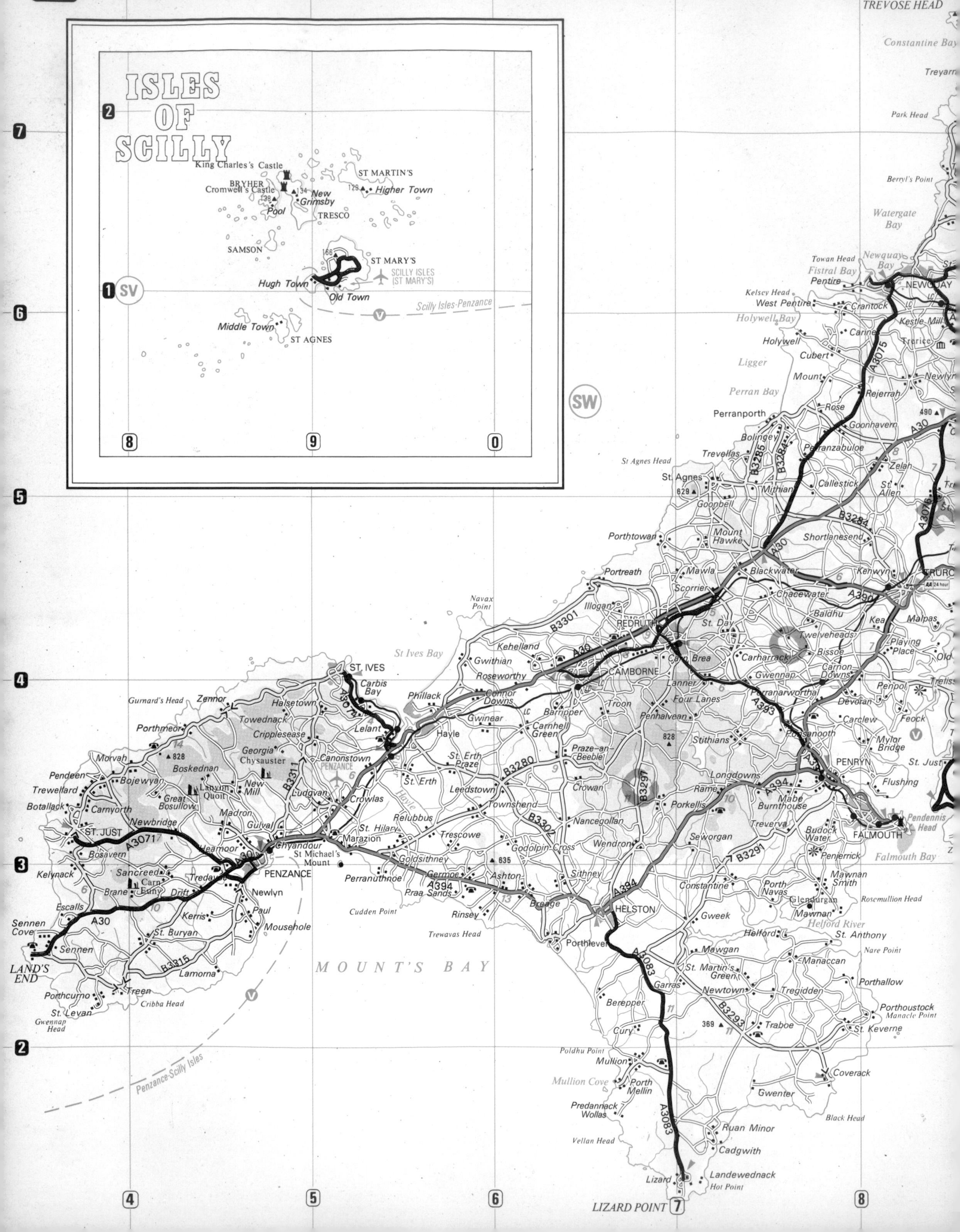

TREVOSE HEAD

Constantine Bay

Treyarnon

Park Head

ISLES OF SCILLY

Berryl's Point

Watergate Bay

King Charles's Castle

ST MARTIN'S

BRYHER
Cromwell's Castle ▲134 New
▲138 Grimsby
Pool

▲129 *Higher Town*

TRESCO

Towan Head Newquay
Fistral Bay Bay
Pentire NEWQUAY

SAMSON

▲168 ST MARY'S

ST MARY'S
SCILLY ISLES
(ST MARY'S)

Kelsey Head
West Pentire Crantock LC
Holywell Bay

Hugh Town

Old Town

Scilly Isles-Penzance

Holywell
Cubert
Mount Newlyn

Ligger Rejerrah 490▲

Middle Town
ST AGNES

SW

Perran Bay Rose Goonhaven A30
Perranporth Goonhaven

Bolingey
Perranzabuloe
St Agnes Head Trevellas

St Agnes
▲629 B3285 B3284 Zelah
Goonbell Callestick St
Allen

Mithian

Porthtowan Mount B3284
Hawke Shortlanesend

Portreath Mawla Kenwyn TRURO
Scorrier AA 24 hour
Blackwater A30
Navax B3301 Illogan Chacewater
Point Baldhu Kea Malpas

Illogan REDRUTH Twelveheads Old
St. Day
St Ives Bay Kehelland Carn Brea Bissoe Playing
Gwithian CAMBORNE Carharrack Place
ST IVES Roseworthy Gwennap Carnon
Carbis Connor Downs Downs
Bay Phillack Barripper Lanner Penpol
Gurnard's Head Zennor Downs Troon Four Lanes Penhalvean Devoran Carclew
Halsetown Gwinear Carnhell Feock
Porthmeor Towednack Hayle Green Praze-an- Stithians 828▲ Perranarworthal Mylor
Cripplesease Beeble Bridge St. Just
Georgia St. Erth B3297 Longdowns PENRYN
Morvah ▲828 Chysauster Praze Rame Flushing
Boskednan Canonstown B3280 Chowan Porkellis A394 Mabe Burnthouse
Pendeen Lanyon PENZANCE Townshend B3302 Treverva Budock Pendennis
Trewellard Quoit New Mill St. Erth Nancegollan Water FALMOUTH Head
Bojewyan Ludgvan B3331 Leedstown Sewardan Penjerrick Falmouth Bay
Botallack Great Bosullow Madron Crowlas Relubbus Godolphin Cross Wendron
Carnyorth Newbridge Gulval St. Hilary Trescowe Constantine Mawnan
ST. JUST A30 711 Heamoor Marazion Goldsithney Sithney Smith
Bosavern Treen 635▲ Germoe B3291 Gweek Glendurgan
Kelynack Ghyandour Ashton Breage Mawnan
Sancreed Carn St Michael's Praa Sands Helford River
Brane Euny Mount Perranuthnoe A394 HELSTON Helford Rosemullion Head
Drift Newlyn Rinsey Mawgan St. Anthony
Escalls Kerris Paul A3083 Gweek Manaccan
Sennen A30 Mousehole Cudden Point Trewavas Head St. Martin's Nare Point
Cove Porthleven Green Porthallow
Sennen MOUNT'S BAY Berepper Newtown Tregidden
LAND'S Garras Porthoustock
END Porthcurno Treen Cribba Head Cury Traboe Manacle Point
St. Levan 369▲ B3293 St. Keverne
Gwennap Poldhu Point
Head Mullion Coverack
Mullion Cove Porth Gwenter
Predannack Mellin Black Head
Wollas
Vellan Head Ruan Minor
Lizard Cadgwith
Landewednack
Hot Point

LIZARD POINT

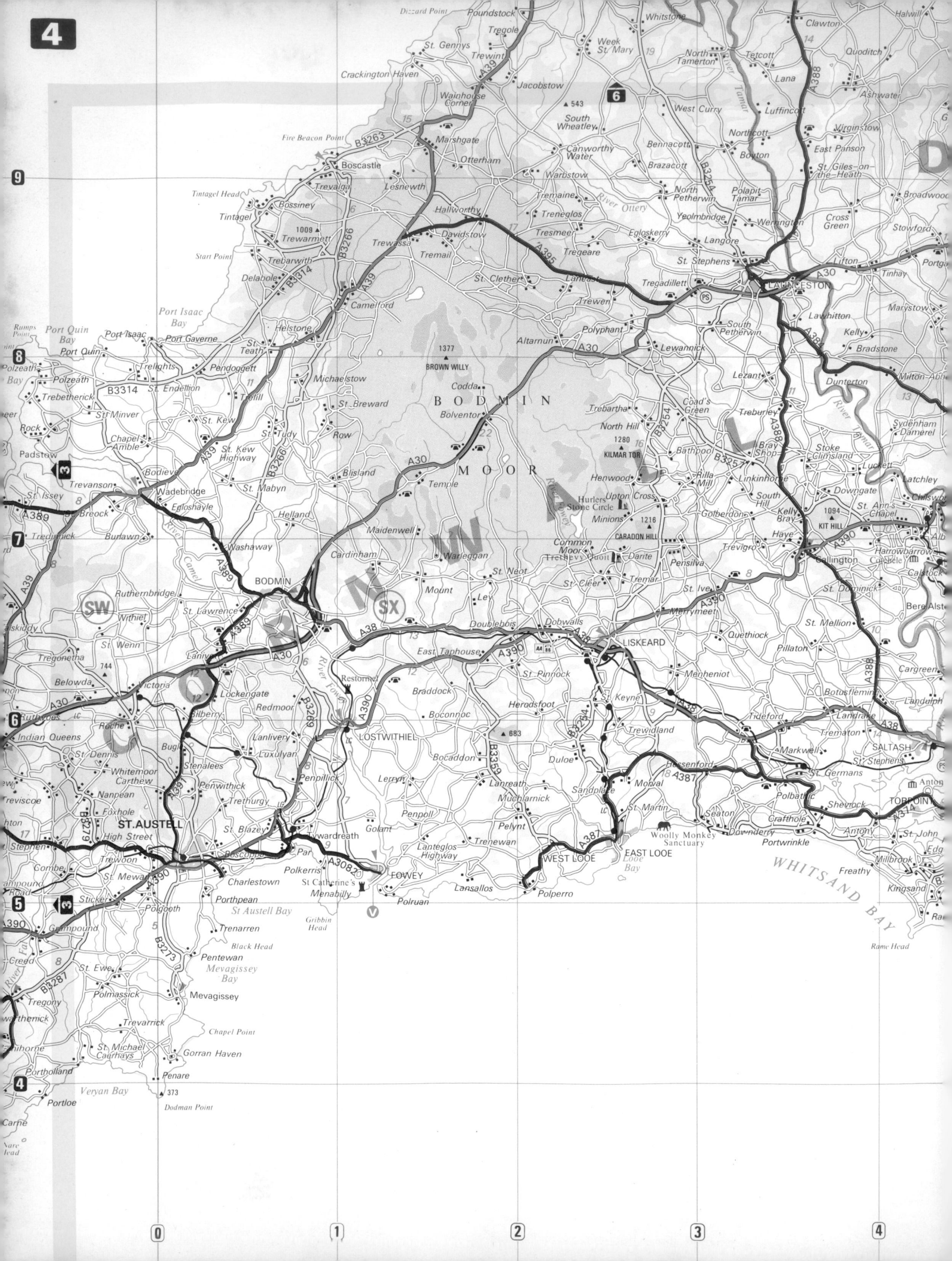

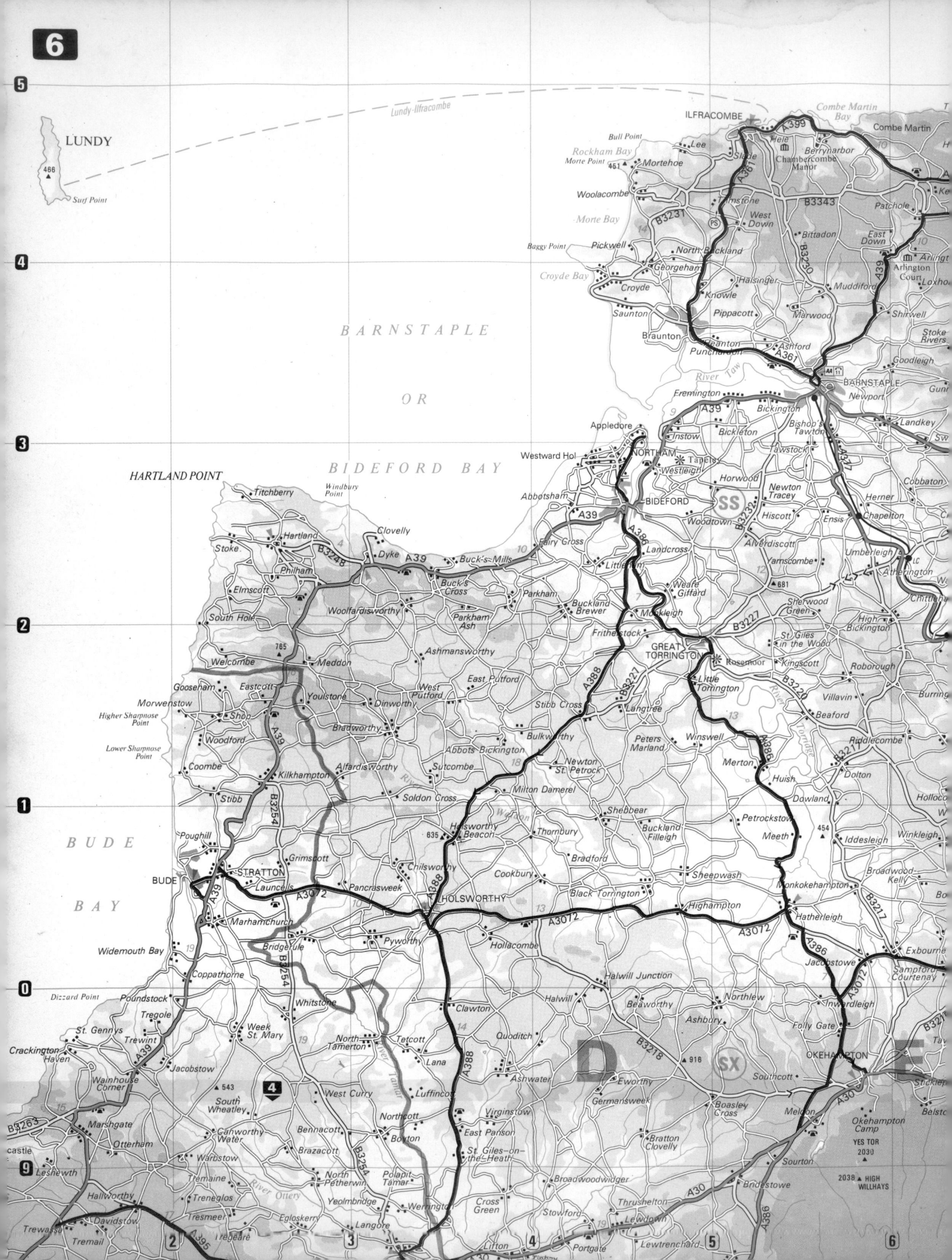

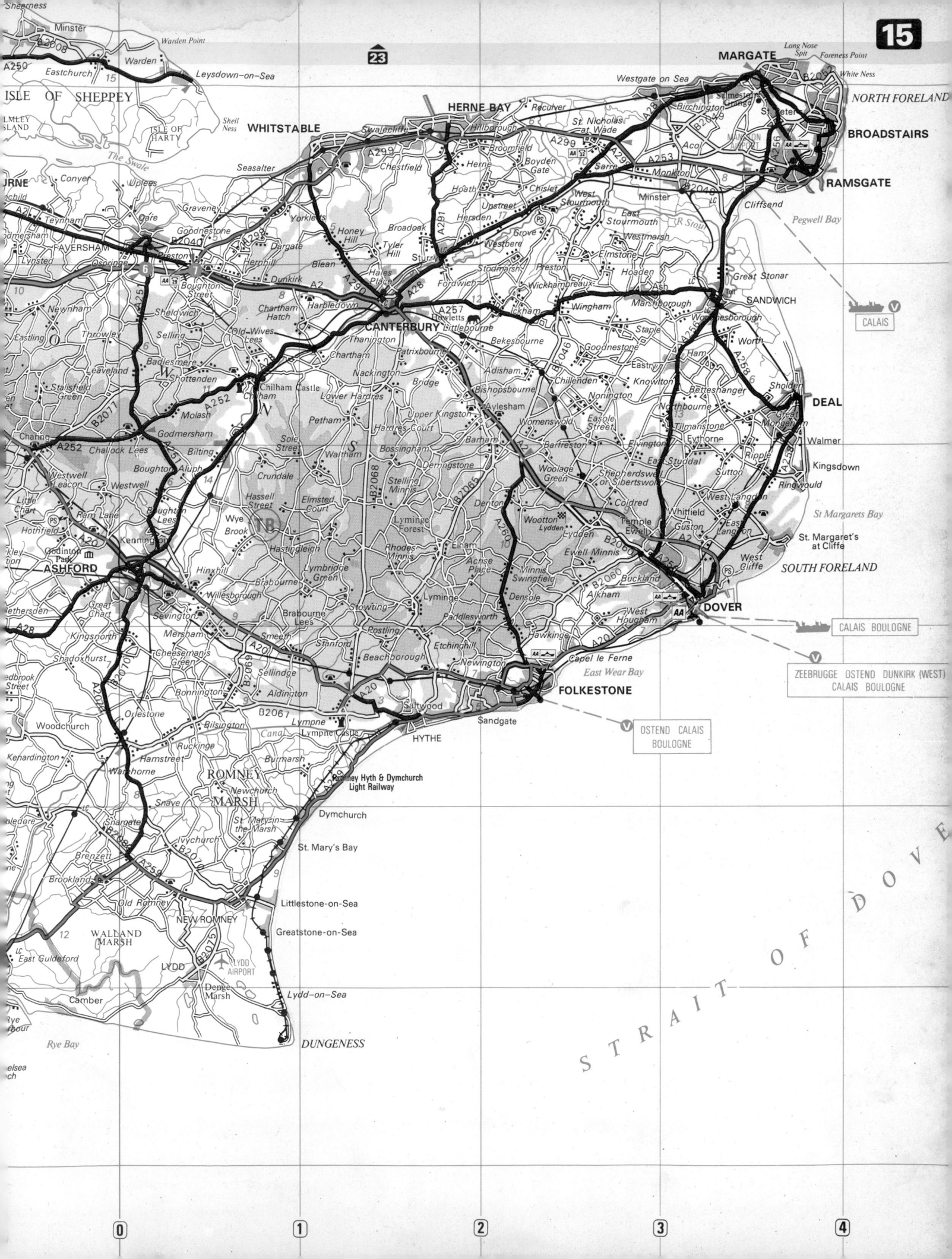

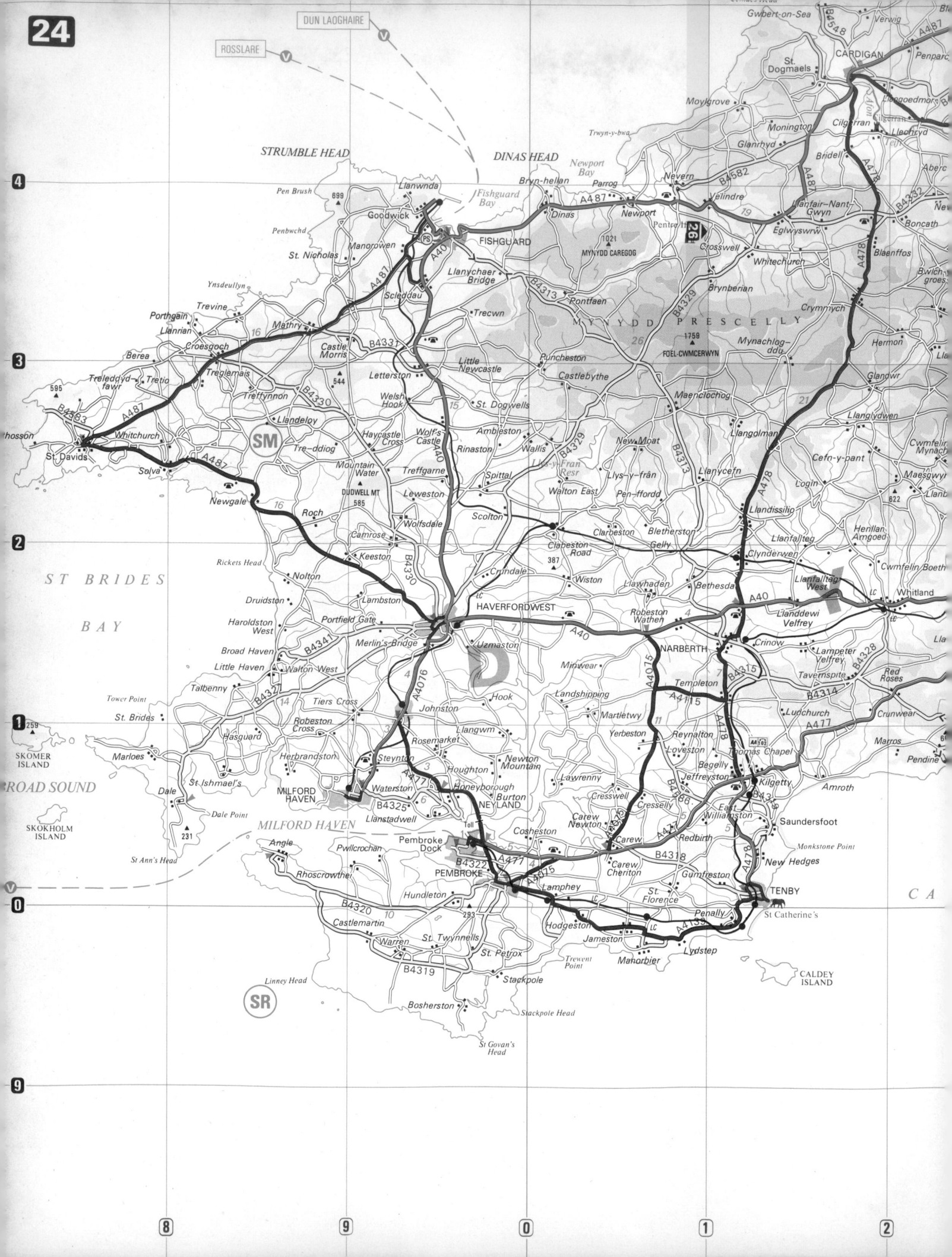

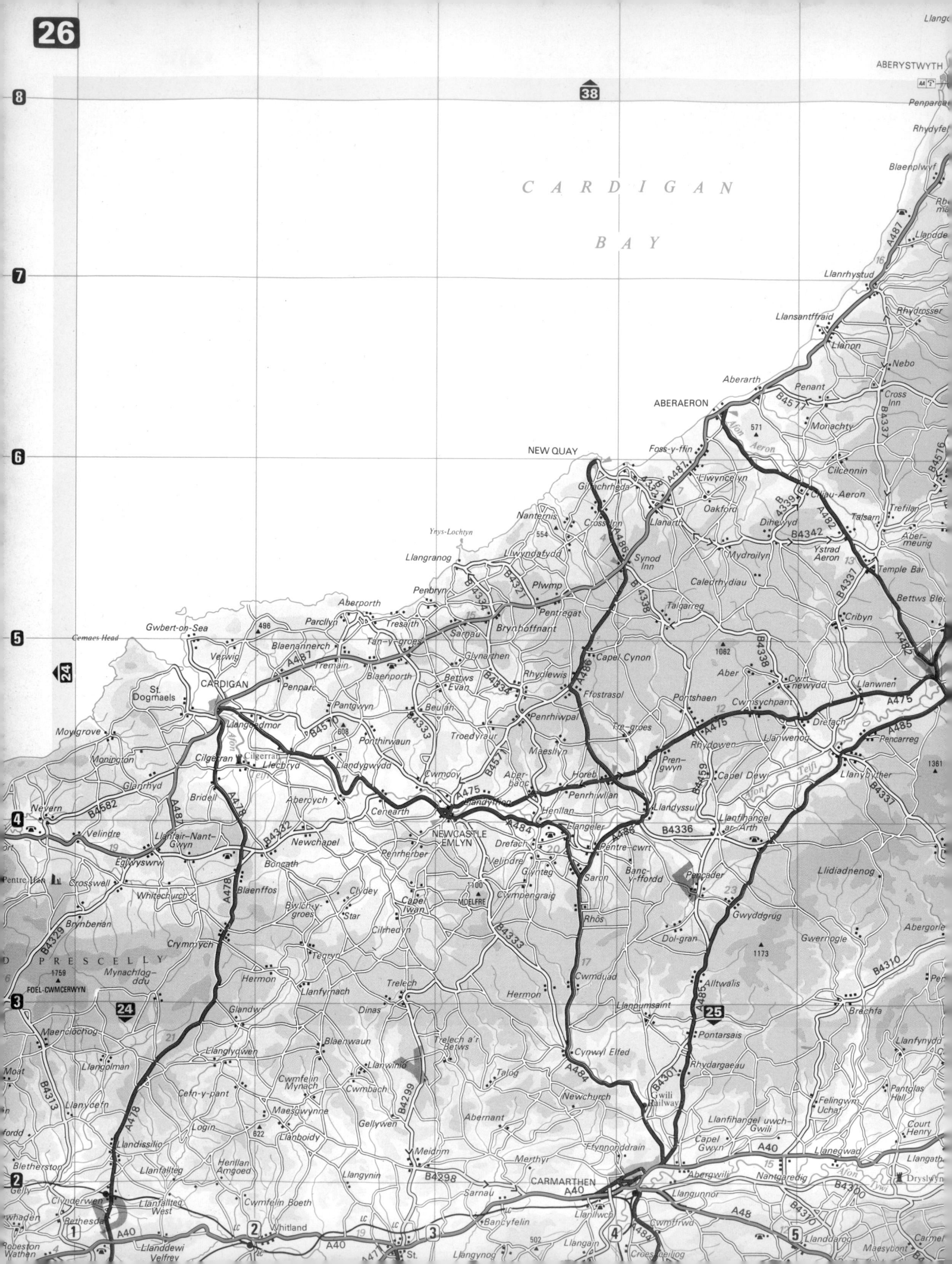

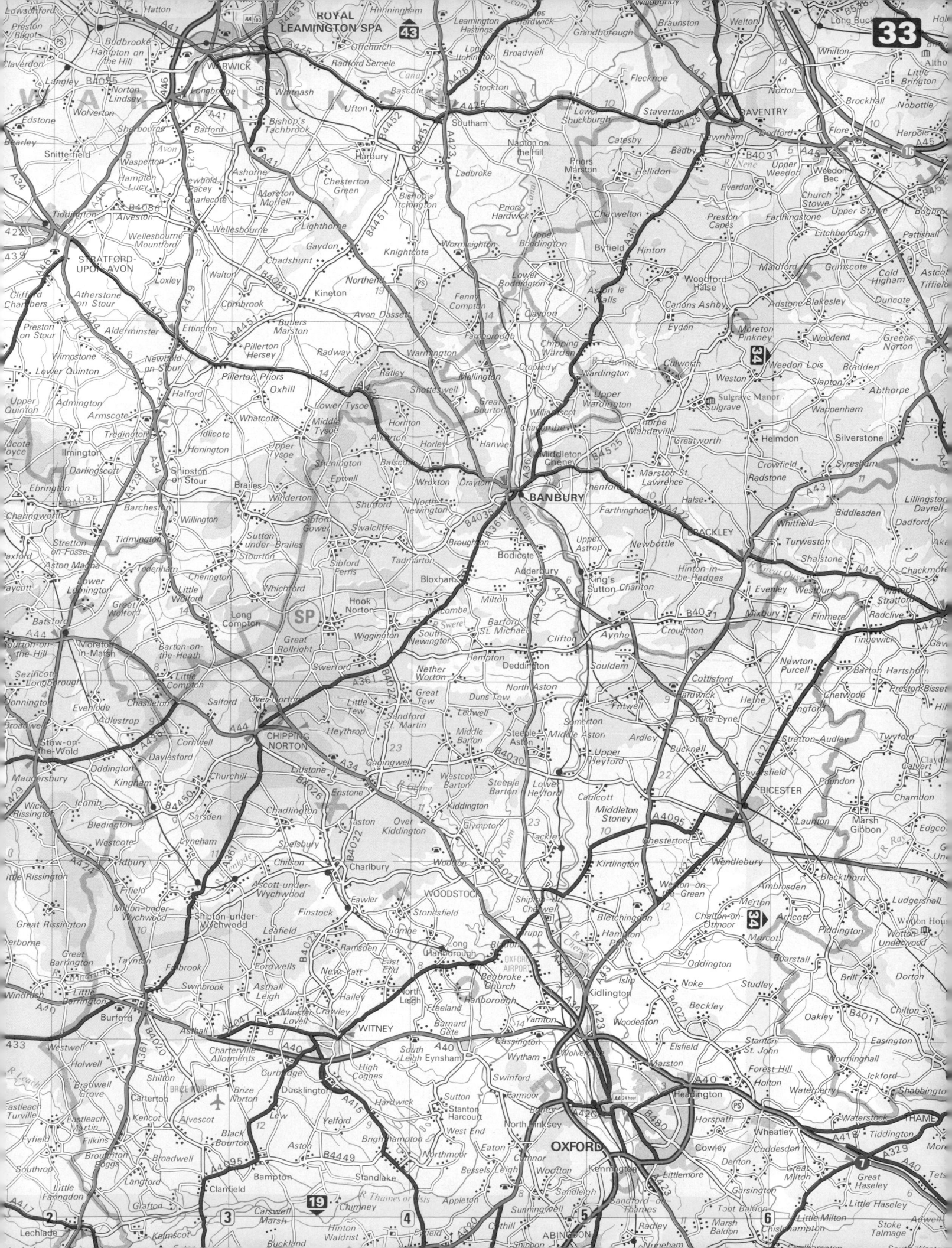

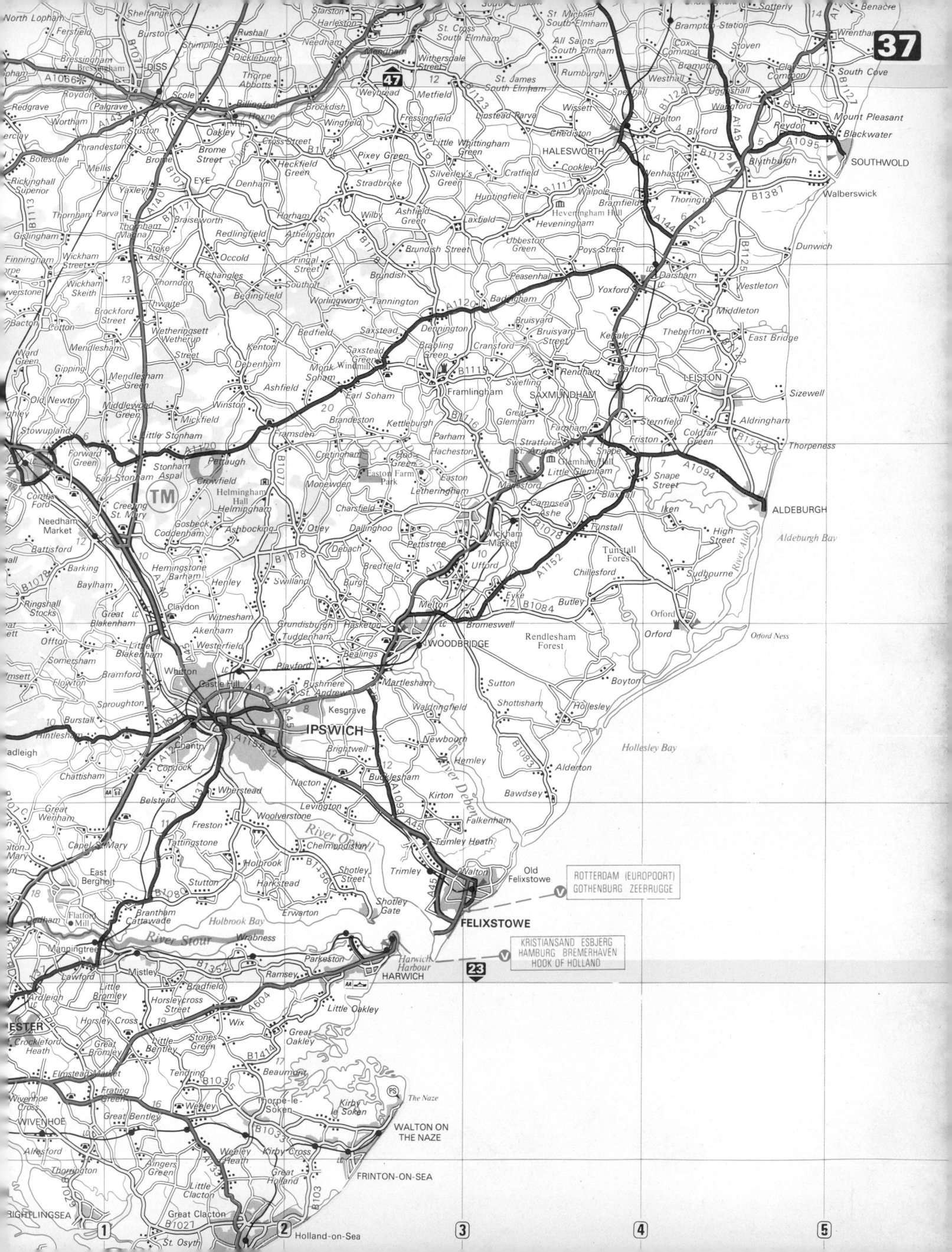

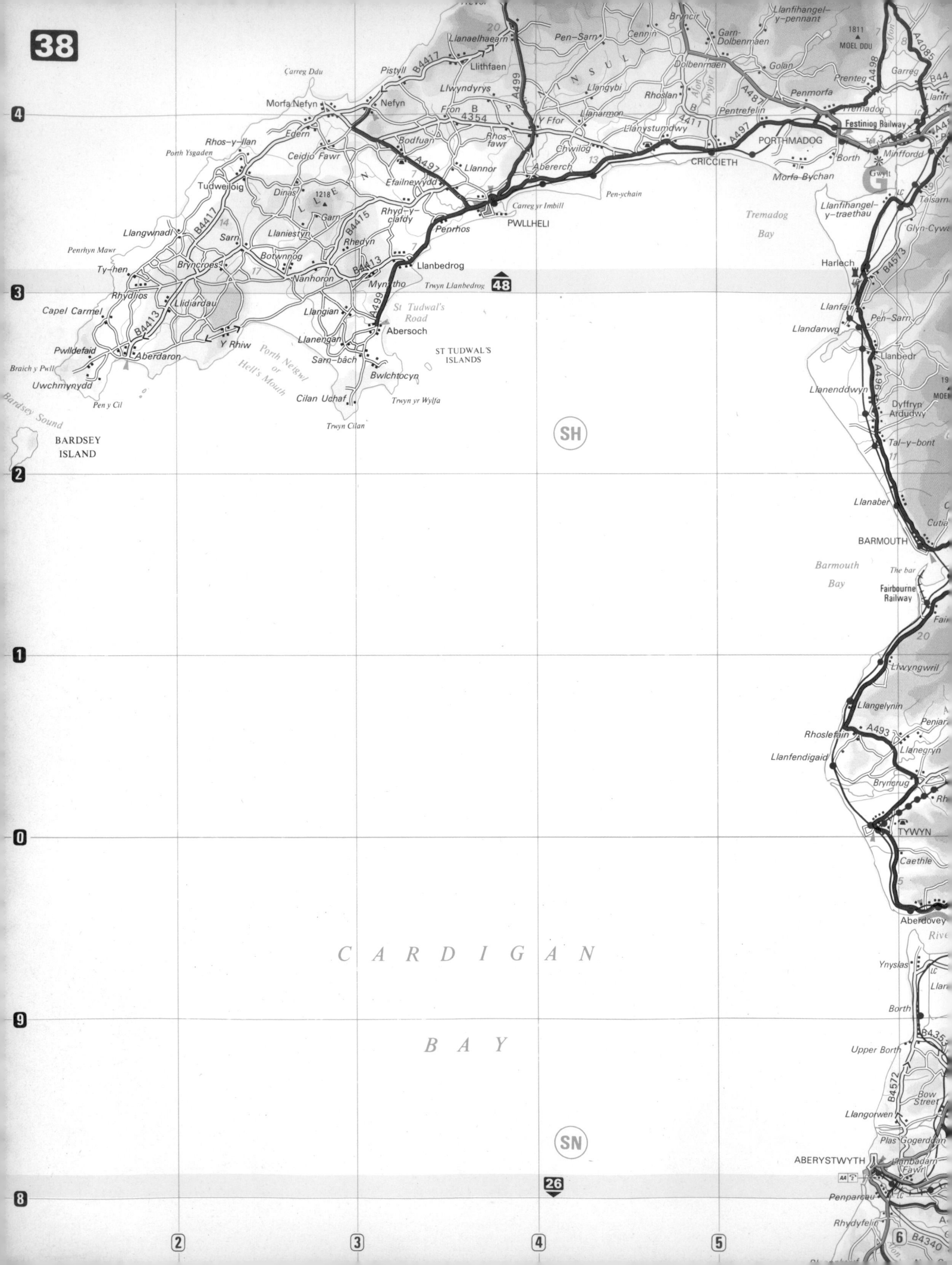

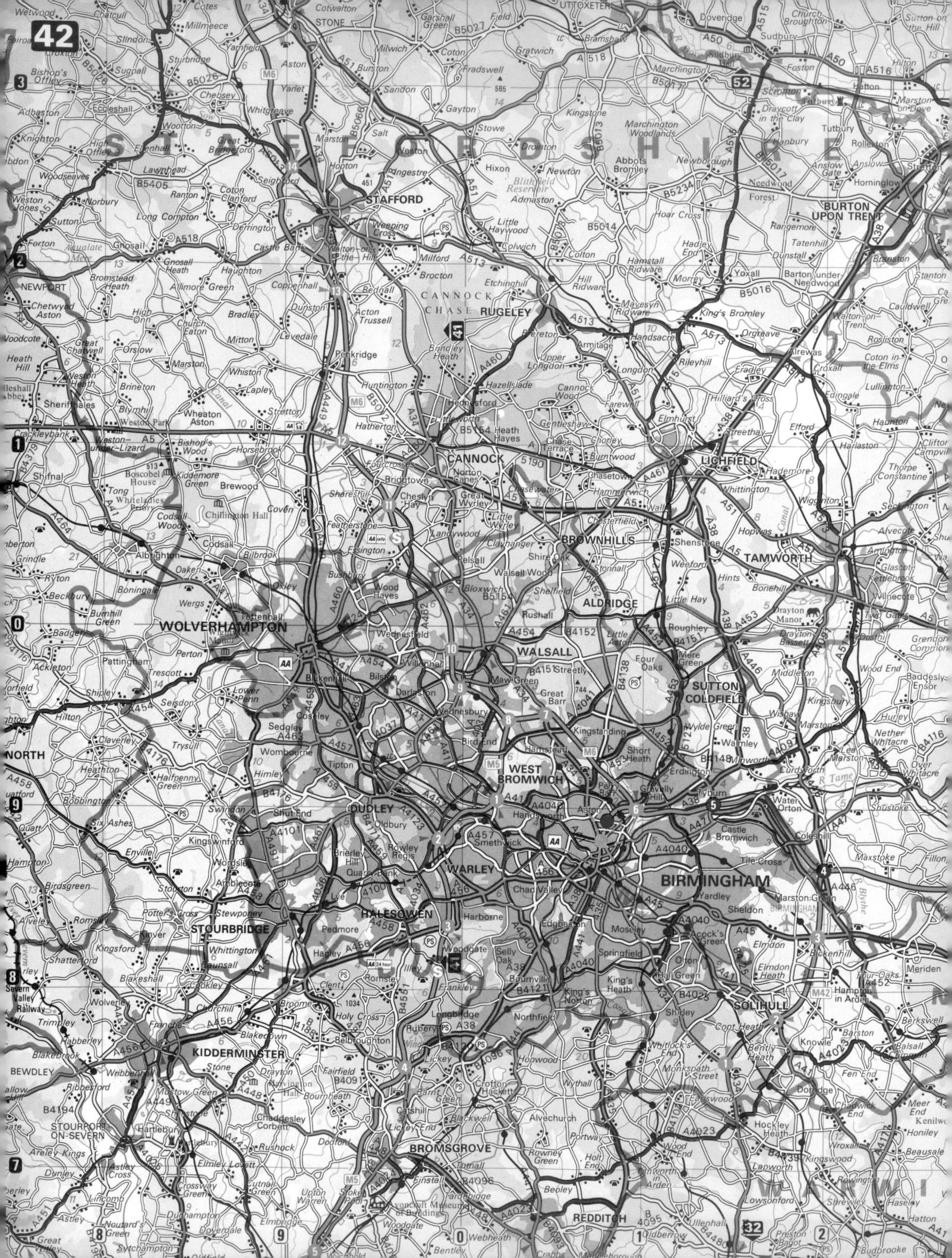

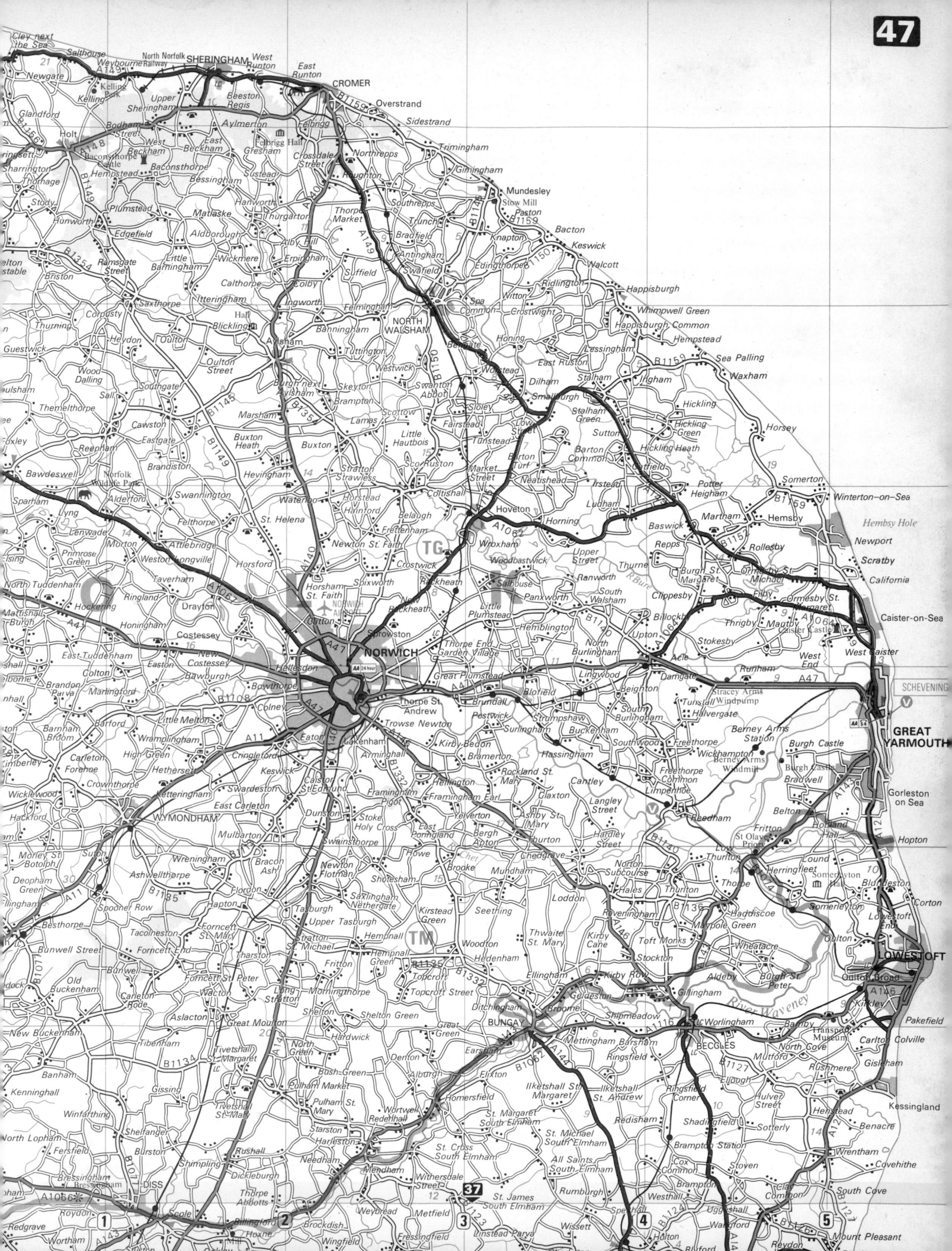

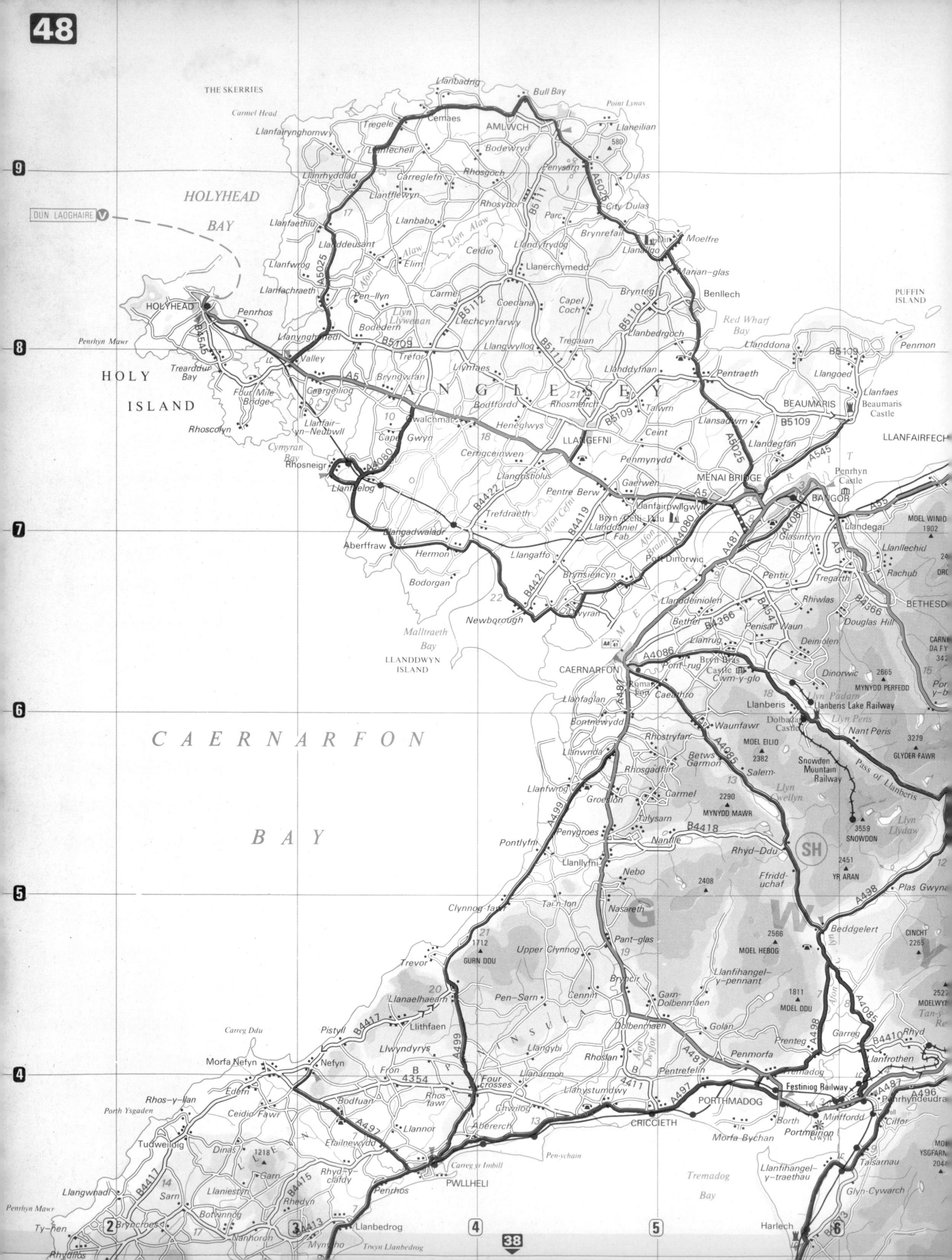

RIVER DEE

Point of Ayr

Great Ormes Head

Great Ormes Head

678

Toll

LLANDUDNO

Little Ormes Head

PRESTATYN

A548

Talacre

Gwespyr

Ffynnongroew

RHYL

Gronant

AA 118

A546

Penrhyn Bay

Rhos-on-Sea

B5119

Gwaenysgor

Meliden

Trelogan

Mostyn

Glan-y-don

CONWY

Penrhyn-side

A525

A547

Rhuddlan

Trelawnyd

Whitford

Downing

BAY

Llanrhos

Llandrillo-yn-Rhos

Towyn

A5151

Cwm

Dyserth

Gorsedd

Carmel

Deganwy

Llandudno Junction

Mochdre

Pensarn

Plas Llwyngwern

Bodrhyddan Hall

HOLYWELL

NMAENMAWR

CONWY

Llansantffraid Glan Conwy

Old Colwyn

Llanddulas

COLWYN BAY

A55

Pen-y-cefn

Dwygyfylchi

Brynymaen

Llaneilian-yn-Rhos

Llysfaen

ABERGELE

A548

St. George

A547

Pengwern

Bodelwyddan

12

Rhuallt

A55

Henryd

Fford-las

B5381

Dolwen

Betws-yn-Rhos

6 A55

St. Asaph

Groesffordd Marli

950

B5122

Caerwys

Babel

Brynfo

2000

TAL-Y-FAN

Ty-'n-y-groes

Dawn

Plas-yn-Cefn

Tremeirchion

Graig

Lixwm

Roewen

Sannan

Graig

Trofarth

MOELFRE UCHAF

1298

Llanfair Talhaiarn

Henllan

A541

Trefnant

16

Bodfari

Nannerch

Llanbedr-y-cennin

Cafn

Eglwysbach

Gell

17

Llannefydd

DENBIGH

Llangwyfan

Rhydym

3091

FOEL-FRAS

Tal-y-Bont

MWDW EITHIN

1271

Llangernyw

B5382

Llansannan

B5382

B5428

Llandyrnog

Rhes-y-cae

Dolgarrog

B5384

Tan-y-fron

Groes

Llanrhaeadr

Pentre

Llanynys

1818

MOEL FAMMAU

Tafarn-y-Gelyn

Llanferres

3485

CARNEDD LLYWELYN

Trefriw

Llanddoget

Pandy Tudur

A544

Bylchau

B5435

Nantglyn

Pant-pastynog

8

Rhewl

Llanbedr-Dyffryn-Clwyd

RUTHIN

A494

Llyn Cowlyd Resr

LLANRWST

Gwydyr Castle

Gwytherin

BRYN TRILLYN

1627

Cyffylliog

Bontuchel

Llanfwrog

1531

Capel Curig

A5

Glyn

Gwydyr Uchaf Chapel

Melin-y-coed

MOEL SEISIOG

1534

Mynydd Hiraethog

Brenig Reservoir

CLOCAENOG

Efenechtyd

Graig-fechan

A4086

Pont Cyfyng

PS 6

OAKLANDS

Nebo

23

FOREST

Clocaenog

875

Llanfair Dyffryn Clwyd

Pentre-celyn

6

Gelli Gynan

2861

CARNEDD MOEL-SIABOD

Pont-y-pant

BETWS-Y-COED

Capel Garmon

A543

SJ

Clawdd-newydd

Dolwyddelan

Bishop Morgan's Cottage

Capel Garmon

Hafod-Dinbych

Alwen Reservoir

B5105

14

PS

Derwen

A525

Dolwyddelan Castle

Penmachno

Glan Conwy

Pentrefoelas

Cefn-brith

Llanfihangel Glyn Myfyr

Llanelidan

16

Rhiwbryfdir

Glan Conwy

Rhyd-lydan

Melin-y-wig

A494

50

1083

Ysbyty Ifan

Glasfryn

Llyn Conwy

Derwen

Bettws Gwerfil Goch

Gwyddelwern

Bryneglwys

Glanaber Terrace

River Conwy

Cerrigydrudion

A5

Ty-nant

A5104

Llantysilio Mountain

BLEANAU FFESTINIOG

2168

B4407

A5

Maerdy

Druid

A494

Plas Isaf

Corwen

Carrog

B5437

Glyn Dyfrdwy

Llantysilio

ygrisiau

FFESTINIOG

20

Gellioedd

Llangwm

Glan-yr-afon

Rhe

A496

B4391

2259

ARENIG FACH

A4212

Ciltalgarth

2188

CARNEDD Y FILIAST

2095

FOEL GOCH

Wenallt

B4402

Llandderfel

2066

MOEL FFERNA

Glyn Dyfr

Maentwrog

PS

1823

GRAIG WEN

Llyn Celyn

Glan-yr-afon

Cynwyd

LLANGO

Gellilydan

2801

ARENIG FAWR

Tryweryn

Fron-goch

Sarnau

Cefn-ddwysarn

9

Crogen

Pandy

A470

A4212

Rhiwlas

B4401

Llandrillo

Berwyn

Tregeiriog

B4500

Trawsfynydd

2021

BALA

Llanfor

Pale

2265

FOEL WEN

Llanarmon Dyffryn Ceiriog

Bronaber

PS

Bala Lake Railway

Rhos-y-gwaliau

Tyn-y-ffridd

Llangadwaladr

Llangower

39

B4403

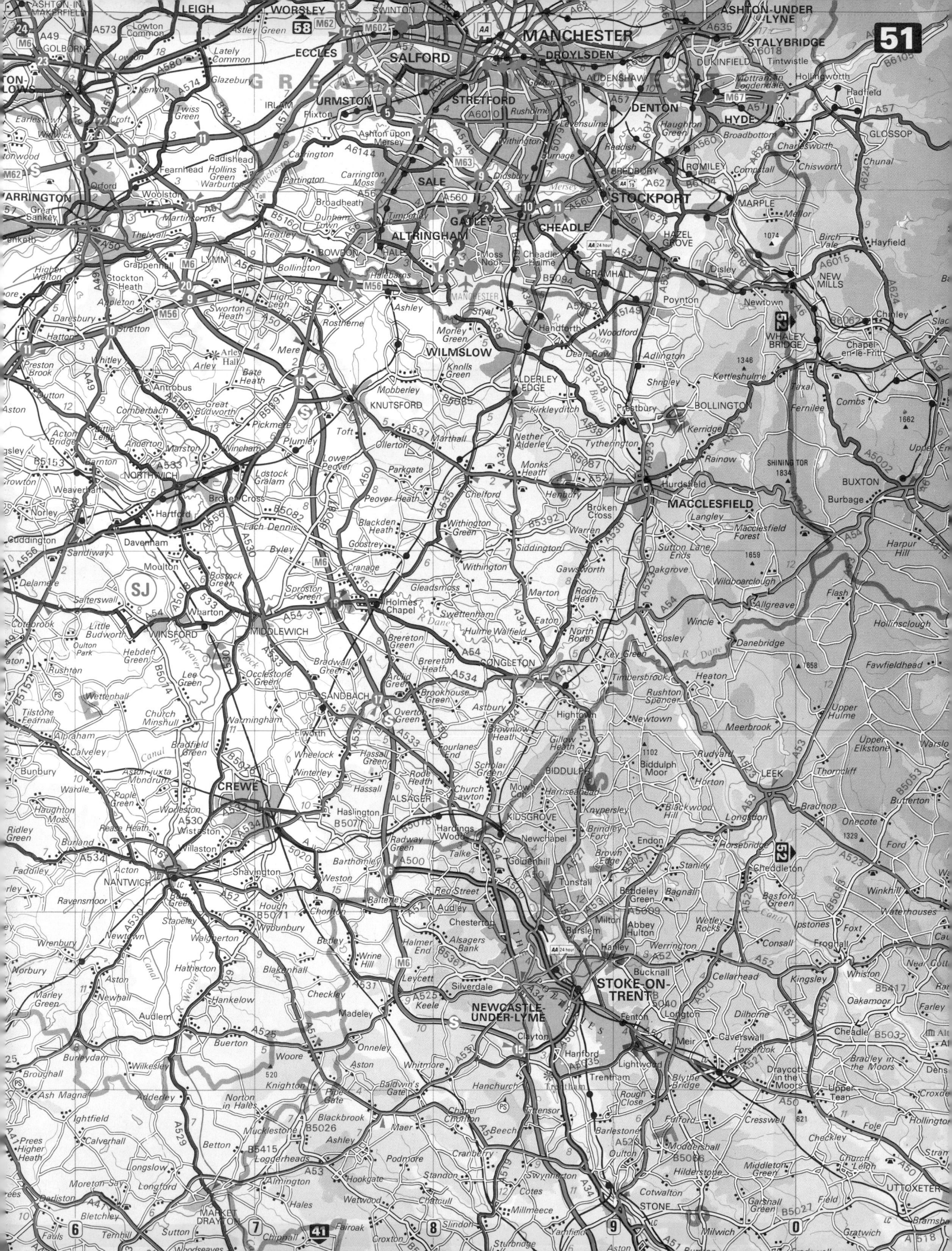

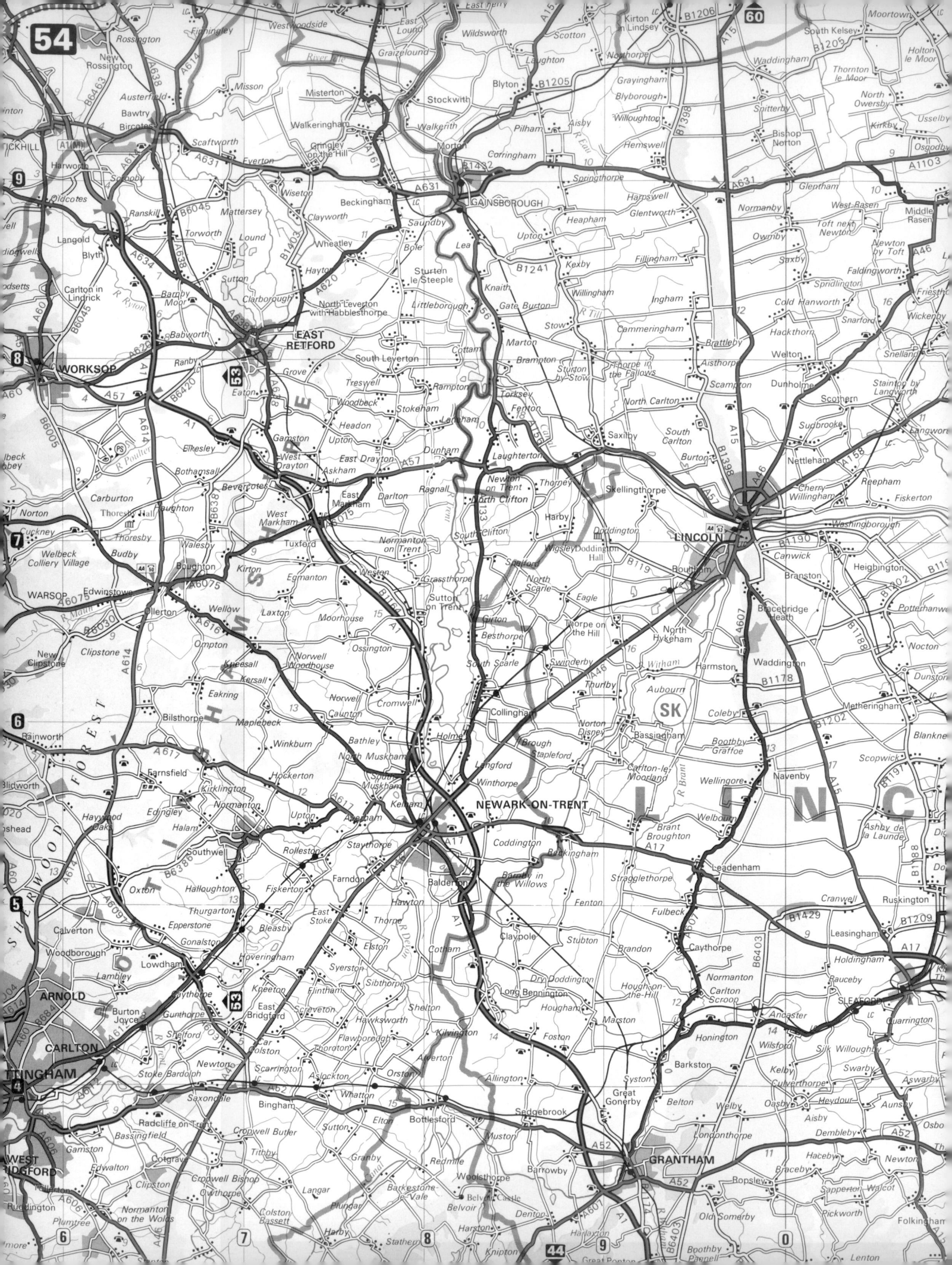

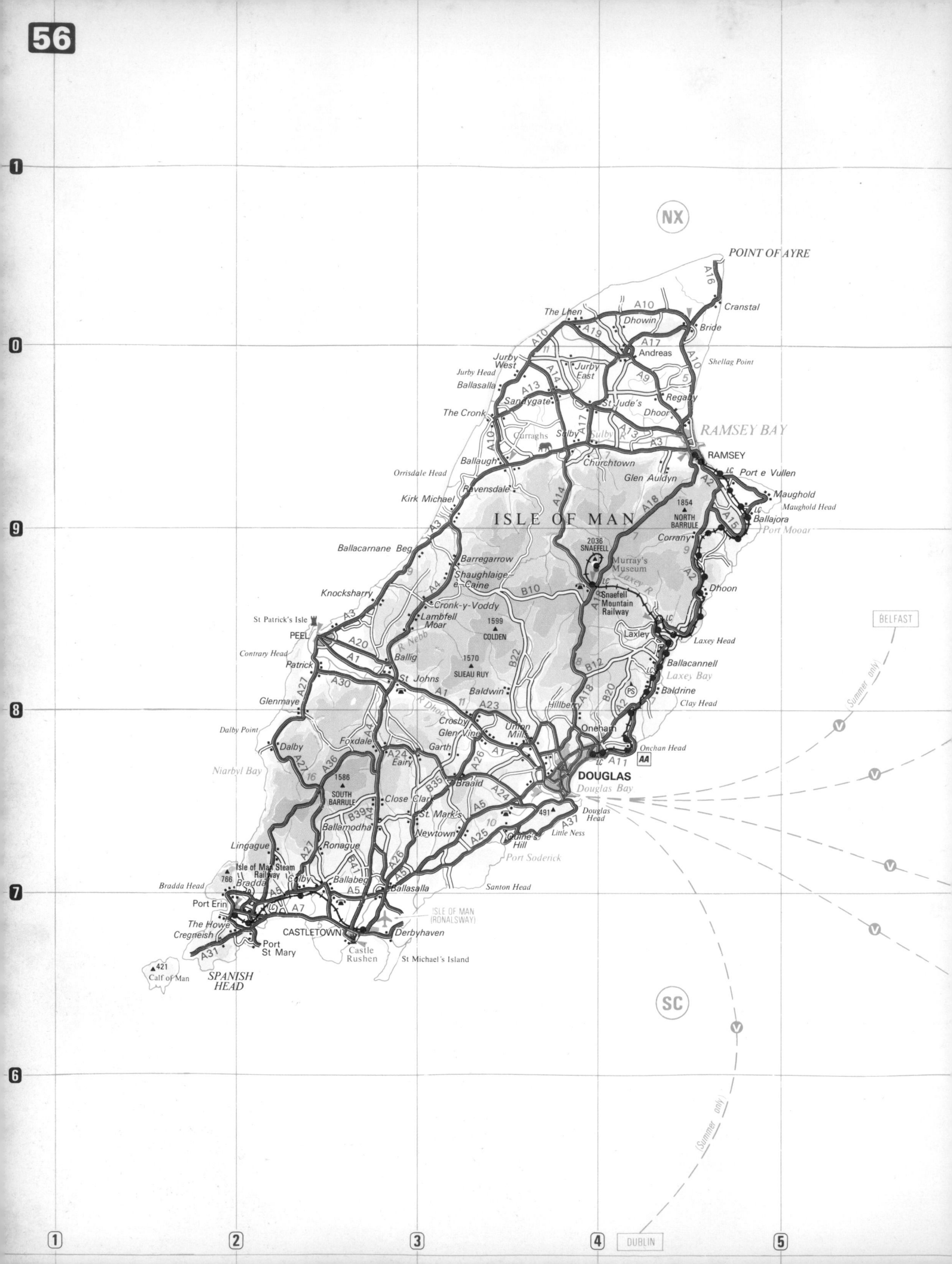

NX

POINT OF AYRE

A16

Cranstal

The Lhen
A10
Dhowin
Bride

A10
A19
A17
Andreas
A10

Jurby West
Jurby East
A9
Shellag Point

Jurby Head
A13
A14
5

Ballasalla
Sandygate
St Jude's
Regaby

The Cronk
A13
Dhoor

Curraghs
Sulby
Sulby R
A3
RAMSEY BAY

Ballaugh
Churchtown
A10
RAMSEY

Orrisdale Head
A14
Glen Auldyn
A2
Port e Vullen

Ravensdale
A18
LC
Maughold

Kirk Michael
1854
NORTH BARRULE
A15
Maughold Head

ISLE OF MAN
Ballajora
Port Mooar

2036 SNAEFELL
Corrany

Ballacarnane Beg
Murray's Museum
9

Barregarrow
Laxey R
A2

Shaughlaige-e-Caine
B10
Dhoon

Knocksharry
A4
Snaefell Mountain Railway

Cronk-y-Voddy
LC

St Patrick's Isle
Lambfell Moar
1599 COLDEN
Laxey

PEEL
A3
B22
Laxey Head

Contrary Head
A20
Ballig
1570 SLIEAU RUY
Ballacannell
Laxeys Bay

Patrick
A1
St Johns
B12
Baldrine

Glenmaye
A30
Baldwin
A18
B20
Clay Head

A27
A23
Hillberry
PS

Dalby Point
Crosby
Onchan

Dalby
Foxdale
Glen Vine
Union Mills
Onchan Head

Niarbyl Bay
A24
Garth
A26
A1
AA

16
Eairy
B35
A11

1586 SOUTH BARRULE
Braaid
A24
DOUGLAS
Douglas Bay

Close Clark
A5
Douglas Head

B39
A4
St Mark's
A37
491
Little Ness

Ballamodha
Newtown
A25
Quine's Hill
Port Soderick

Lingague
A27
Ronague
A26
Santon Head

Isle of Man Steam Railway
Colby
A41
766
Bradda
Ballabeg
Ballasalla

Bradda Head
A5
A5

Port Erin
A7
ISLE OF MAN (RONALDSWAY)

The Howe
CASTLETOWN
Derbyhaven

Cregneish
A31
Port St Mary
Castle Rushen
St Michael's Island

421 Calf of Man
SPANISH HEAD

SC

BELFAST

Summer only
V

V

V

V

Summer only

DUBLIN

1   2   3   4   5

1   0   9   8   7   6

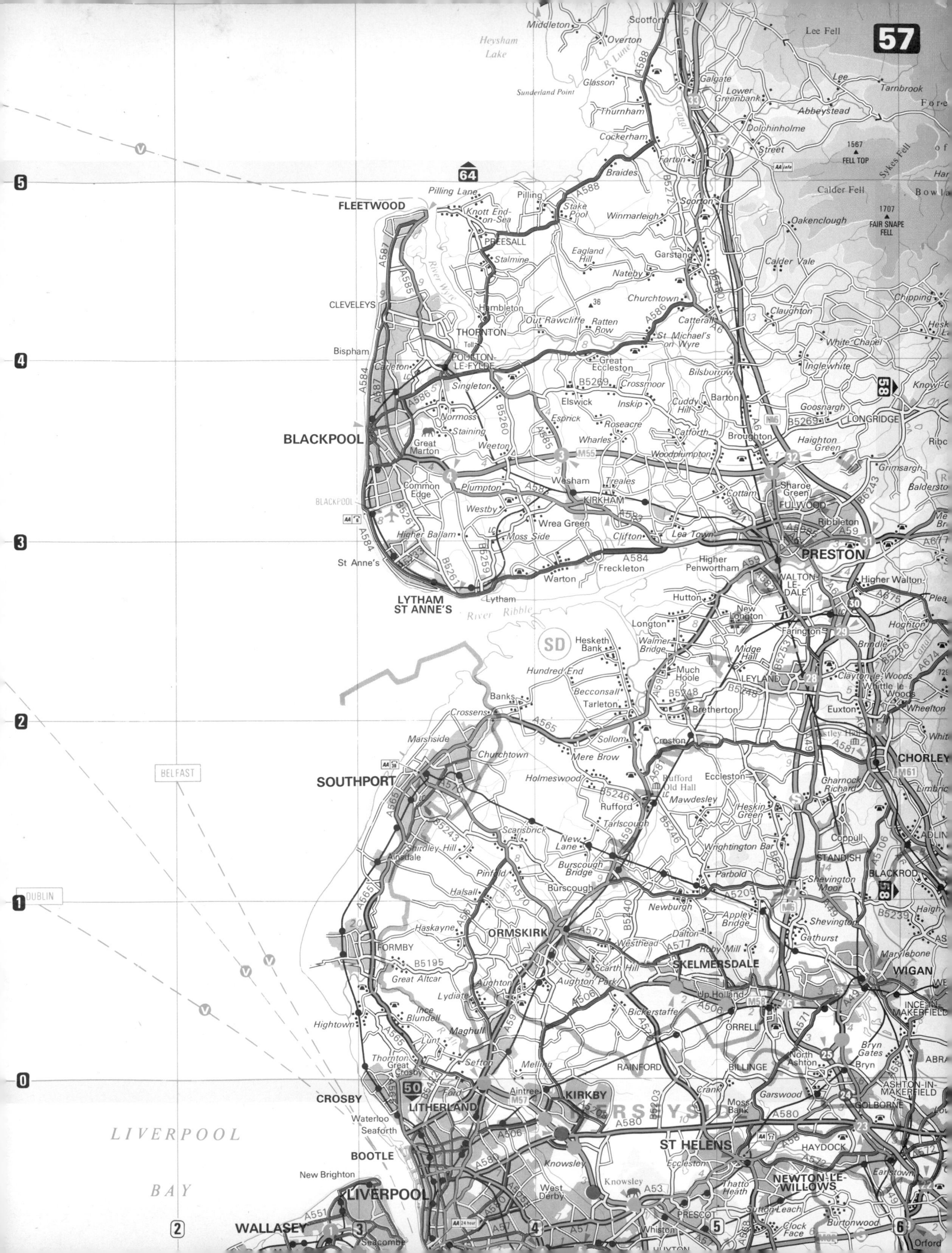

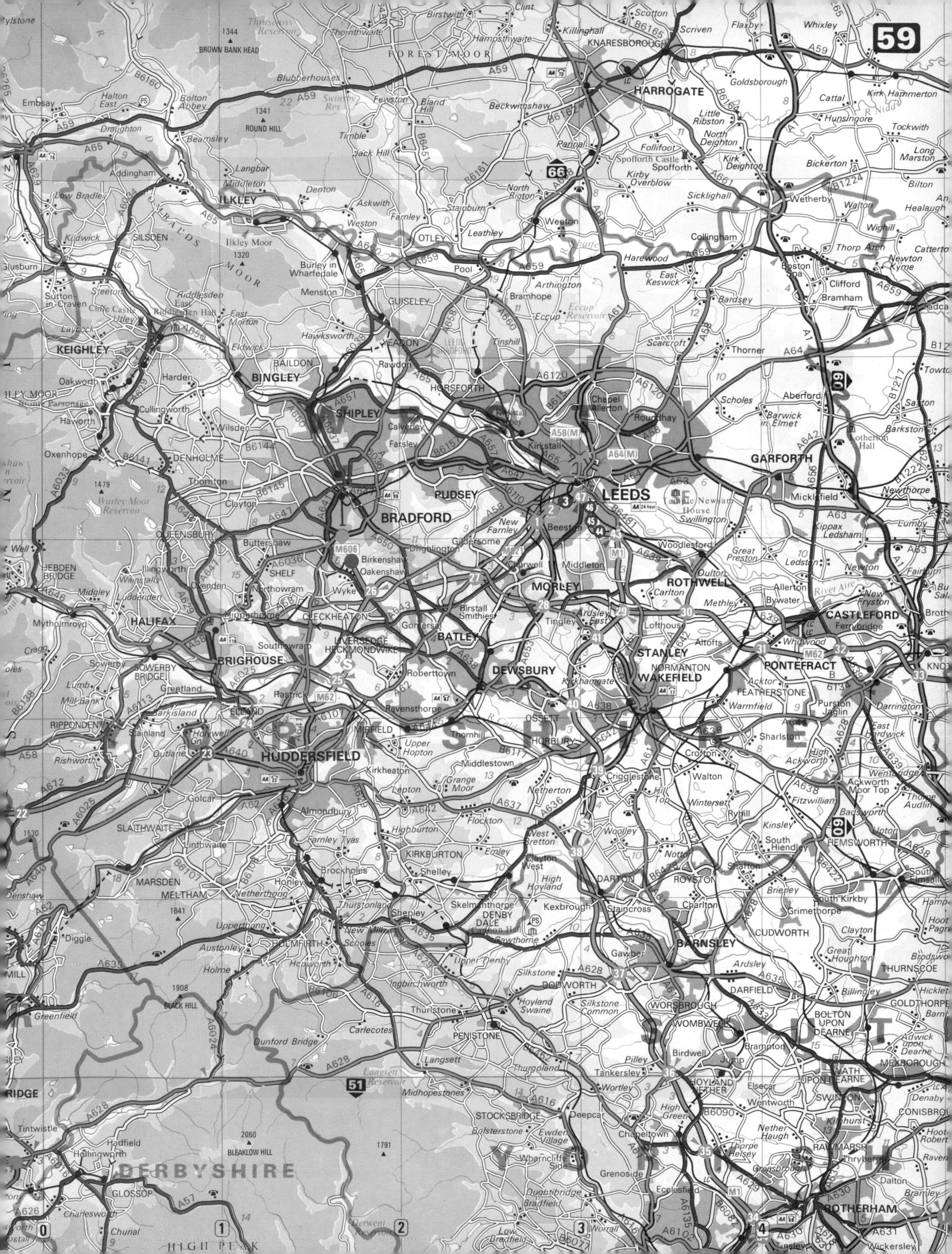

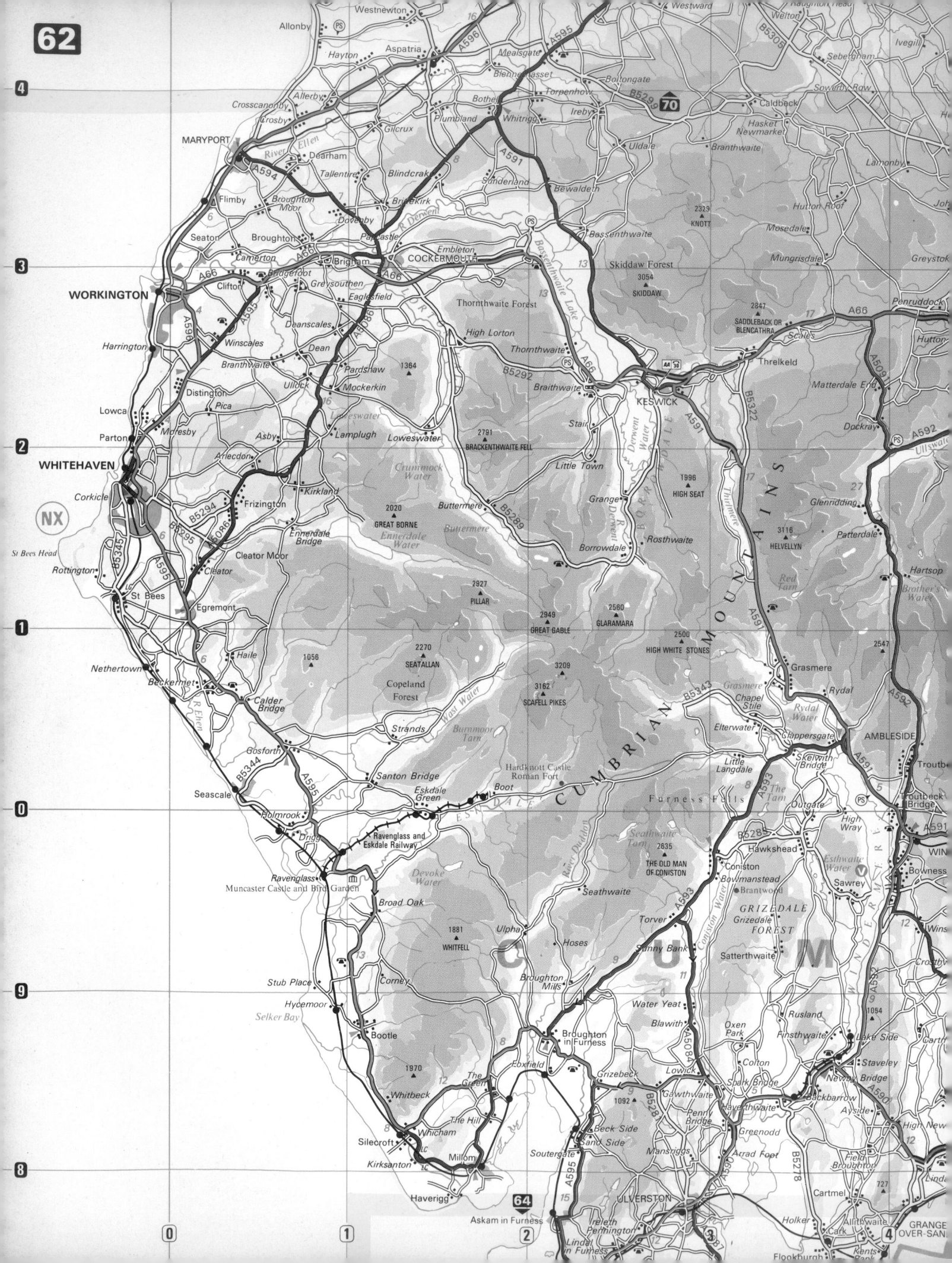

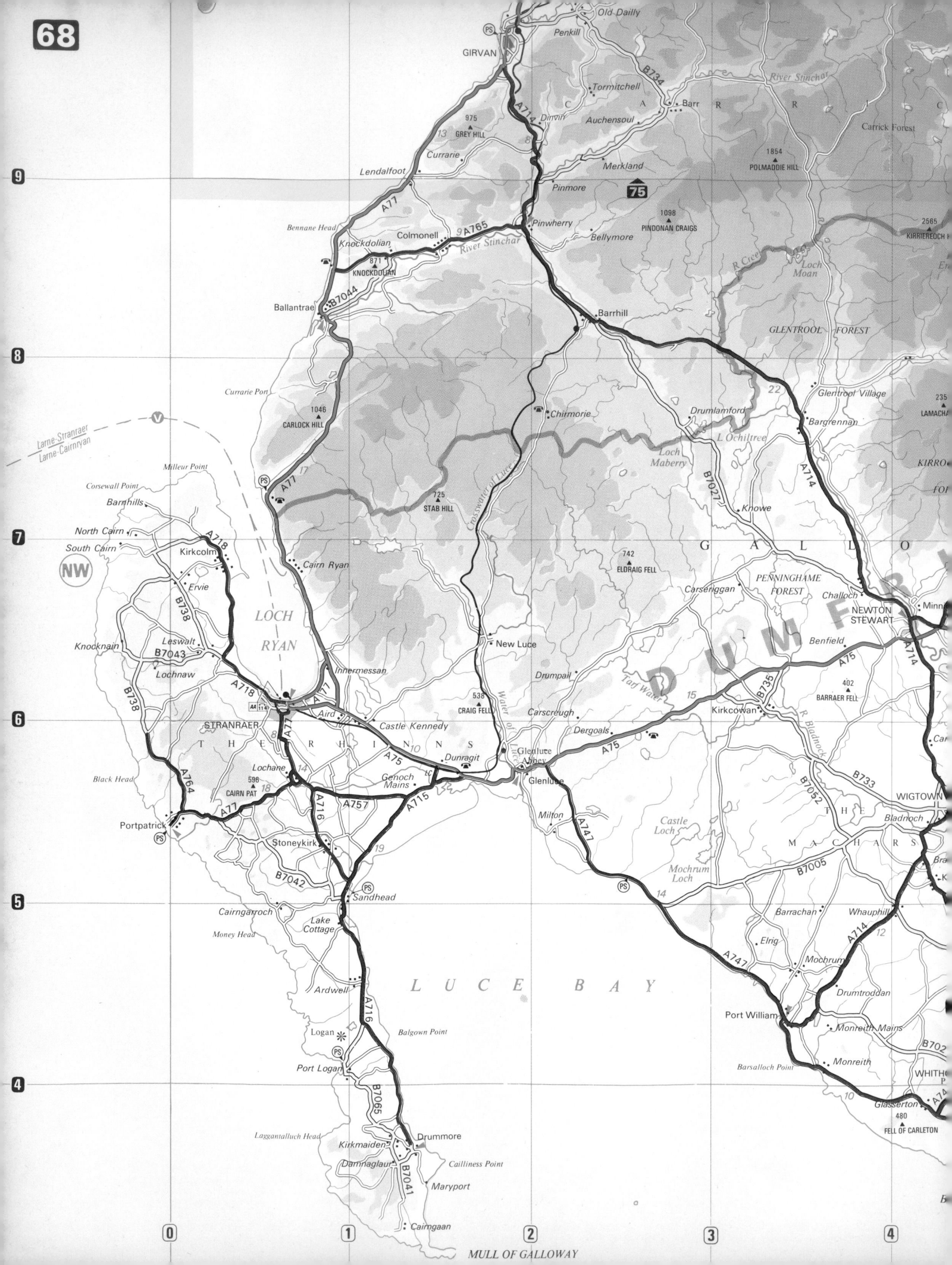

S E A

79

STAVANGER BERGEN
KRISTIANSAND OSLO
GOTHENBURG
ESBJERG

LDS

DERLAND

EAHAM

ale
don

Beacon Point

ton

Horden Point

NZ

Horden

LE

Blackhall

1281

esleden   PS

19   9

Sheraton   8
A119 Hart   A1088

A179

HARTLEPOOL

Elwick   *Hartlepool*
                            Bay
Dalton   AA
Piercy

7

A689   9   *Tees Bay*

Greatham

ston
    Newton   A178
    Bewley
    Cowpen Bewley   *Coatham*
Billingham   *The Flashes*
                    A1085   Redcar
9   Dormanstown   MARSKE-
Norton   AA Toll Markleatham   BY-THE-SEA
    5   Grangetown   A174   SALTBURN-BY-THE-SEA
    A66   Lazenby   New   BROTTON   Skinningrove
Tees   South   Wilton   Maske   LOFTUS   Boulby
                Bank   Upleatham   16   Staithes
MIDDLESBROUGH A1088   SKELTON   Port Mulgrave
    Acklam   Eston   *Guisborough Priory*   Easington Hinderwell
Thornaby A19 A172   Ormesby   GUISBOROUGH   Boosbeck   Lingdale   Roxby Runswick
on-Tees   Marton   A171   Liverton   Goldsborough
cliffe   Stainton   Nunthorpe   *Stanghow*   Ellerby   B1266   Lythe
    A19   Maltby   Newton under   Moorsholm   B1366   Mickleby   Sandsend
cliffe   Hilton   Roseberry   1078   A174   WHITBY
    66   Newby   Great   1051   21   A171   67 Dunsley   *Saltwick Bay*
        5   Tanton Ayton   6   7   8   Newholm Ruswarp
Seamer   Commondale

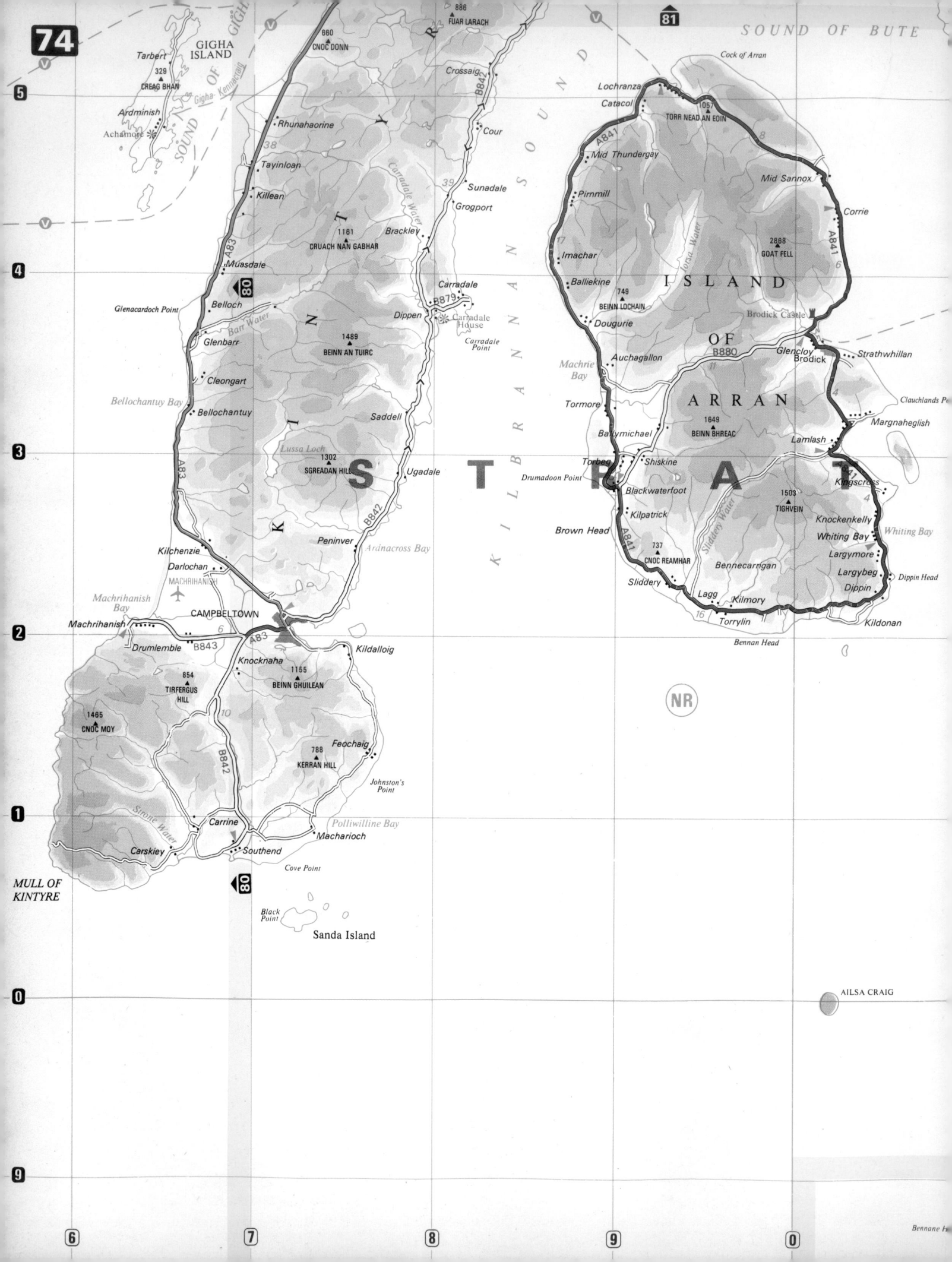

GIGHA ISLAND

SOUND OF BUTE

Tarbert
329
CREAG BHAN

Ardminish
Achamore

Cock of Arran

Lochranza
Catacol
TORR NEAD AN EOIN
1057

Rhunahaorine

CNOC DONN
660

886
FUAR LARACH

Crossaig

Cour

Mid Thundergay

Mid Sannox

Tayinloan

Killean

Sunadale

Grogport

Pirnmill

Corrie

GOAT FELL
2888

Brackley

I S L A N D

Imachar

1161
CRUACH NAN GABHAR

Muasdale

Belloch

Glenacardoch Point

Balliekine

BEINN LOCHAIN
749

Dougurie

Brodick Castle

Dippen

Carradale

B879

Carradale House

Carradale Point

Auchagallon

O F

Glencloy
Brodick

Strathwhillan

Glenbarr

1489
BEINN AN TUIRC

Machrie Bay

A R R A N

Cleongart

Tormore

1649
BEINN BHREAC

Clauchlands Pt

Bellochantuy Bay

Bellochantuy

Saddell

Ballymichael

Lamlash

Margnaheglish

Lussa Loch

Torbeg

Shiskine

1302
SGREADAN HILL

Drumadoon Point

Blackwaterfoot

Kingscross

Ugadale

Kilpatrick

1503
TIGHVEIN

Peninver

Brown Head

Knockenkelly

Kilchenzie

Ardnacross Bay

737
CNOC REAMHAR

Whiting Bay

Whiting Bay

Darlochan

MACHRIHANISH

Bennecarrigan

Largymore

Sliddery

Largybeg

Dippin Head

CAMPBELTOWN

Machrihanish Bay

Lagg

Kilmory

Dippin

Machrihanish

Kildalloig

Torrylin

Kildonan

Drumlemble

B843

Bennan Head

Knocknaha

854
TIRFERGUS HILL

1155
BEINN GHUILEAN

NR

1465
CNOC MOY

Feochaig

788
KERRAN HILL

Johnston's Point

AILSA CRAIG

Carrine

Macharioch

Polliwilline Bay

Carskiey

Southend

Cove Point

*MULL OF
KINTYRE*

Black Point

Sanda Island

Bennane H

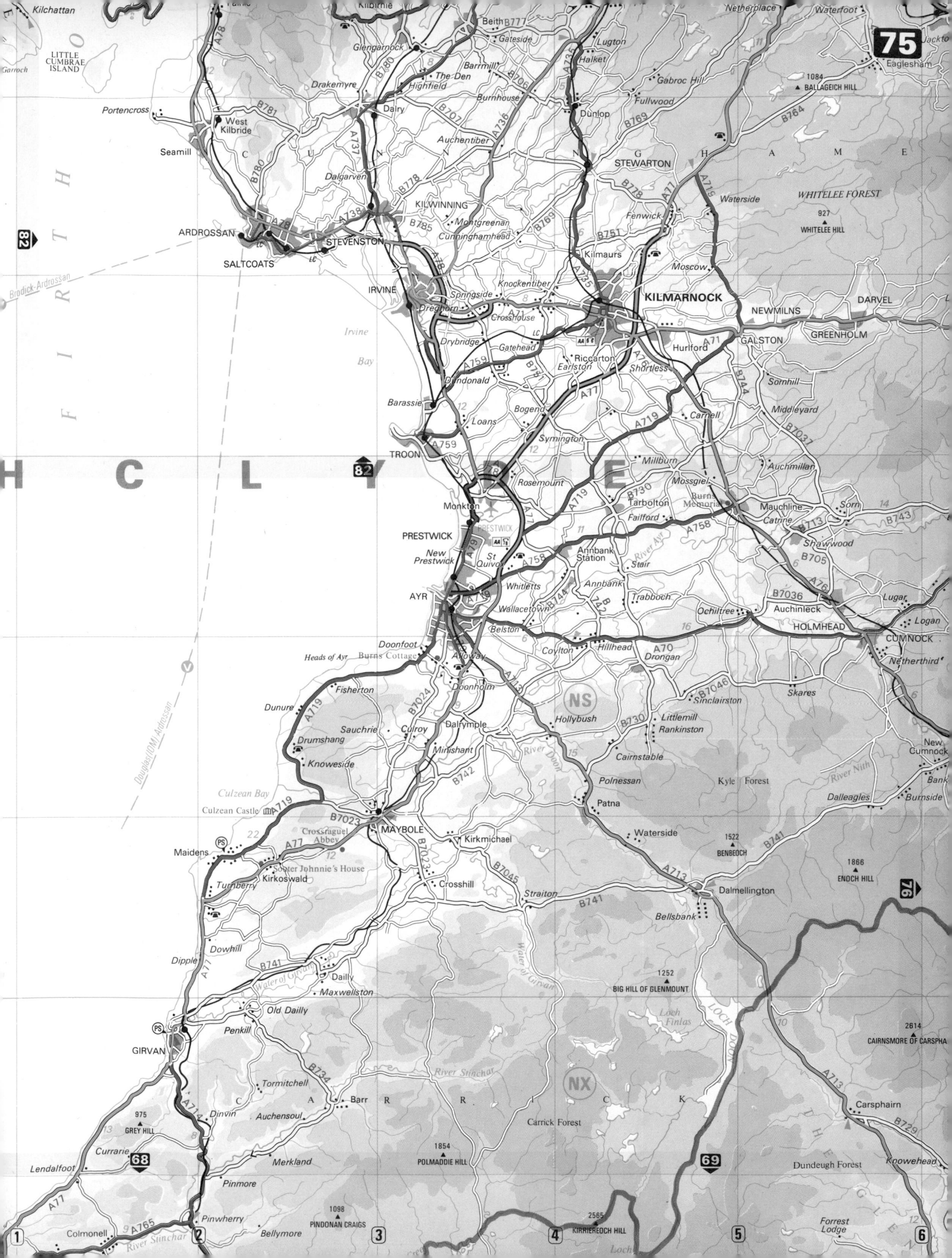

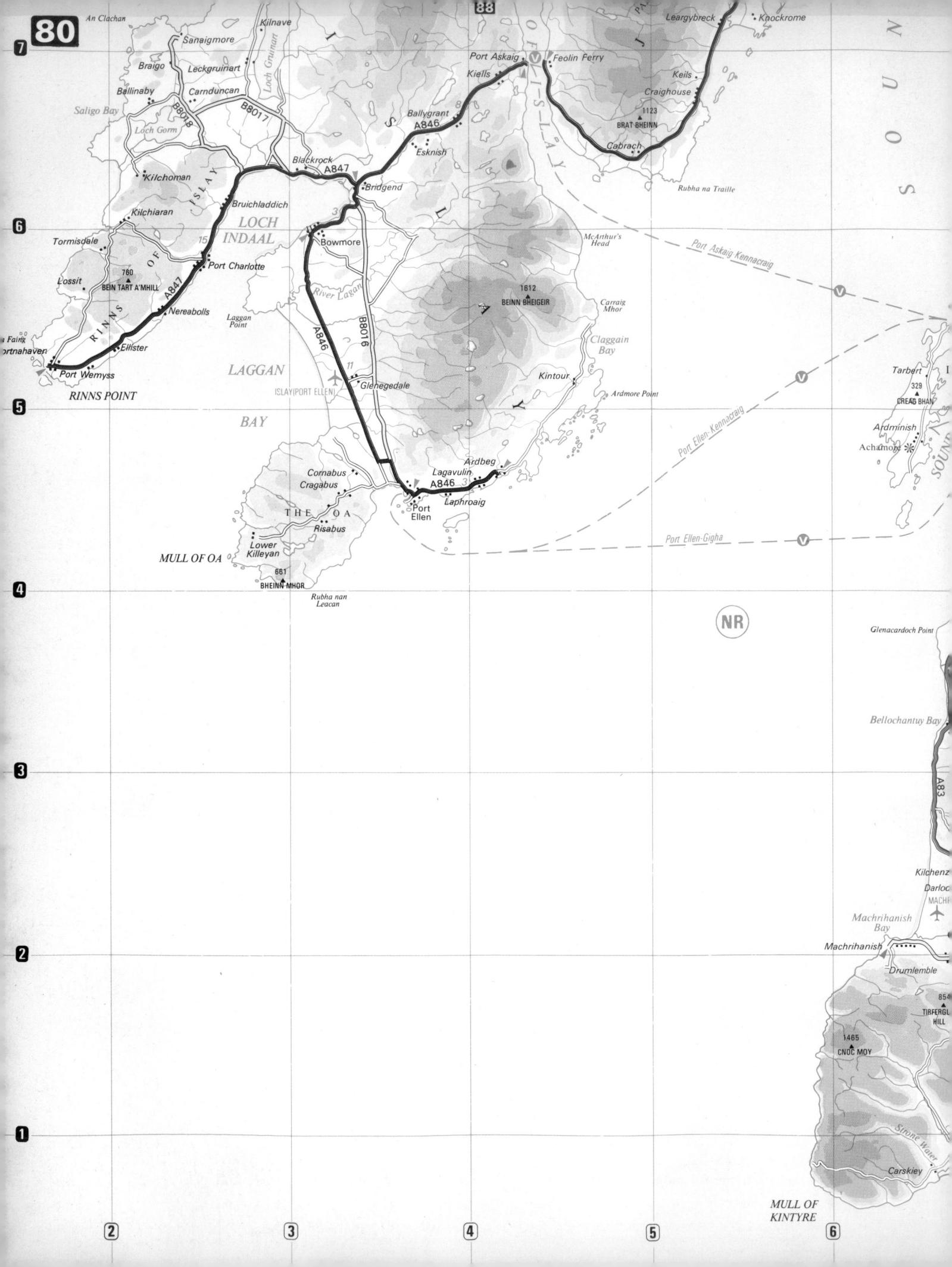

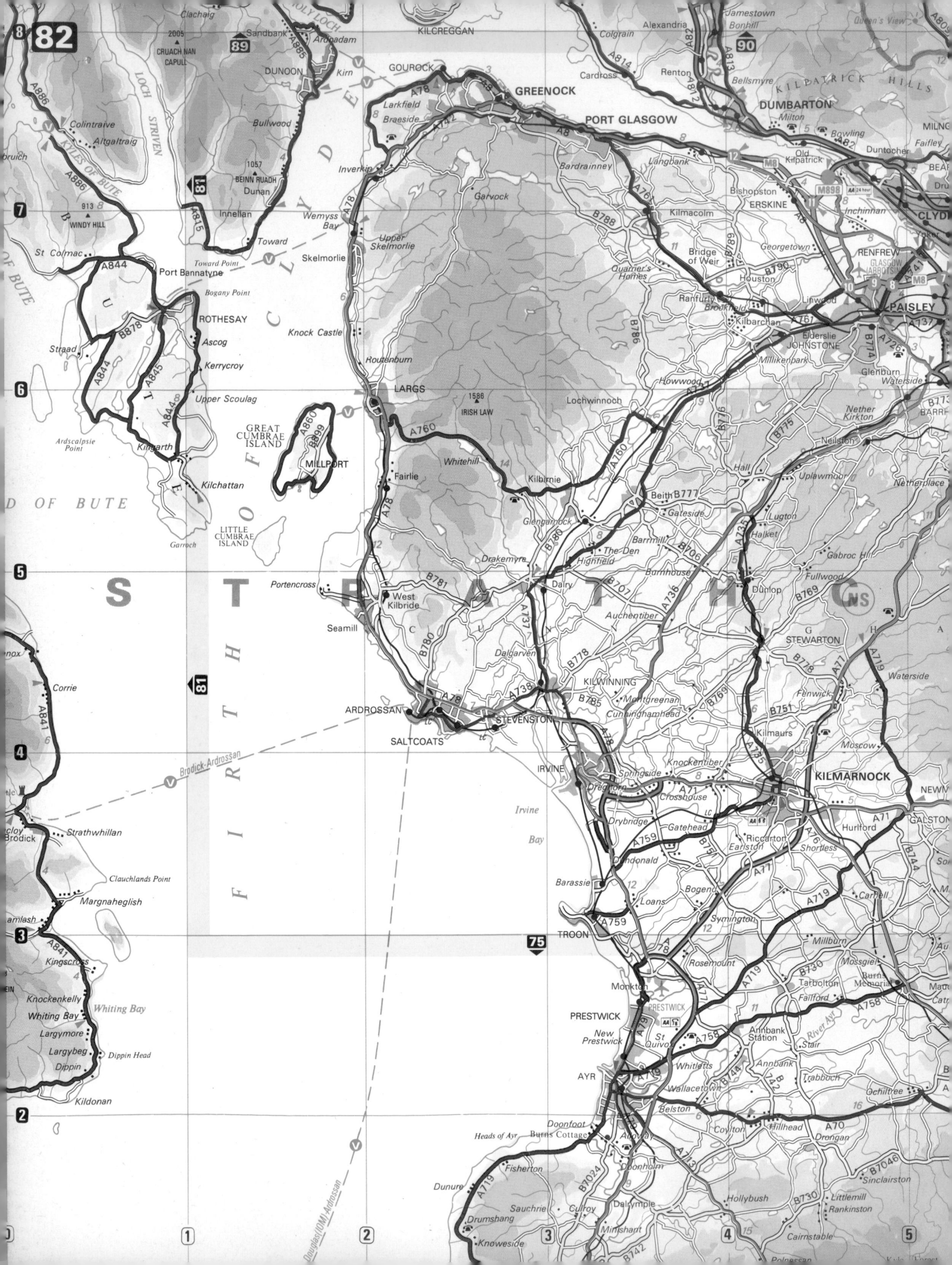

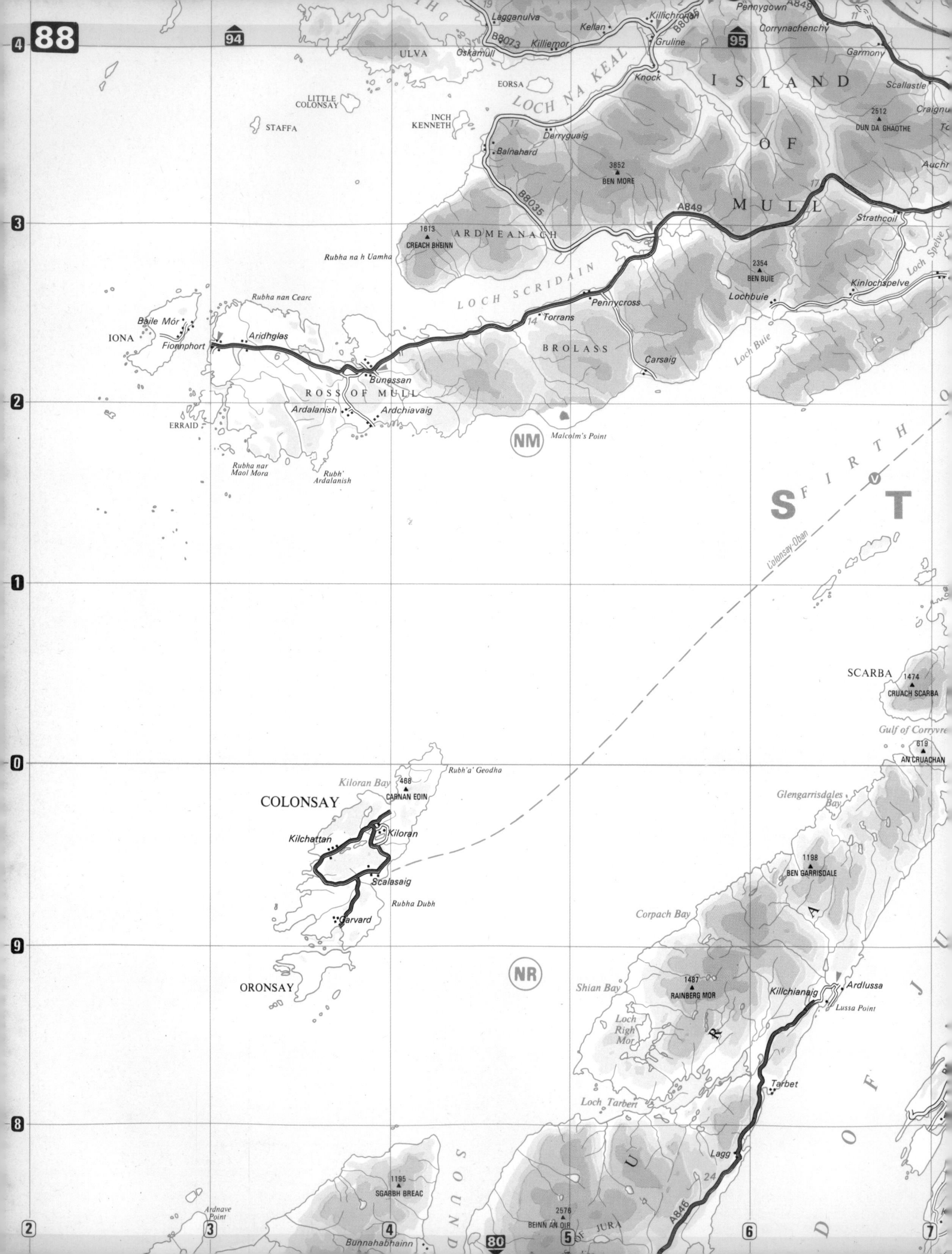

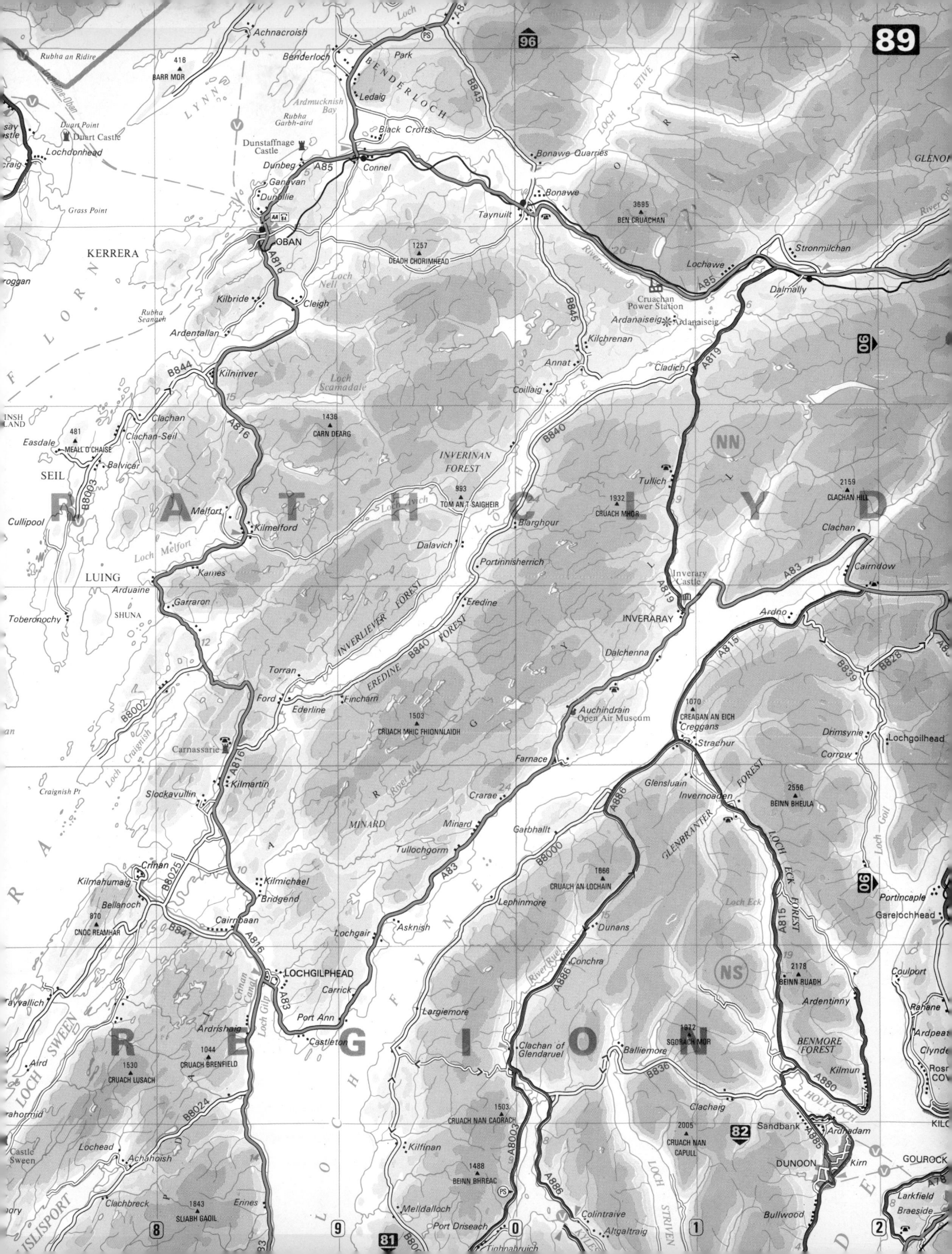

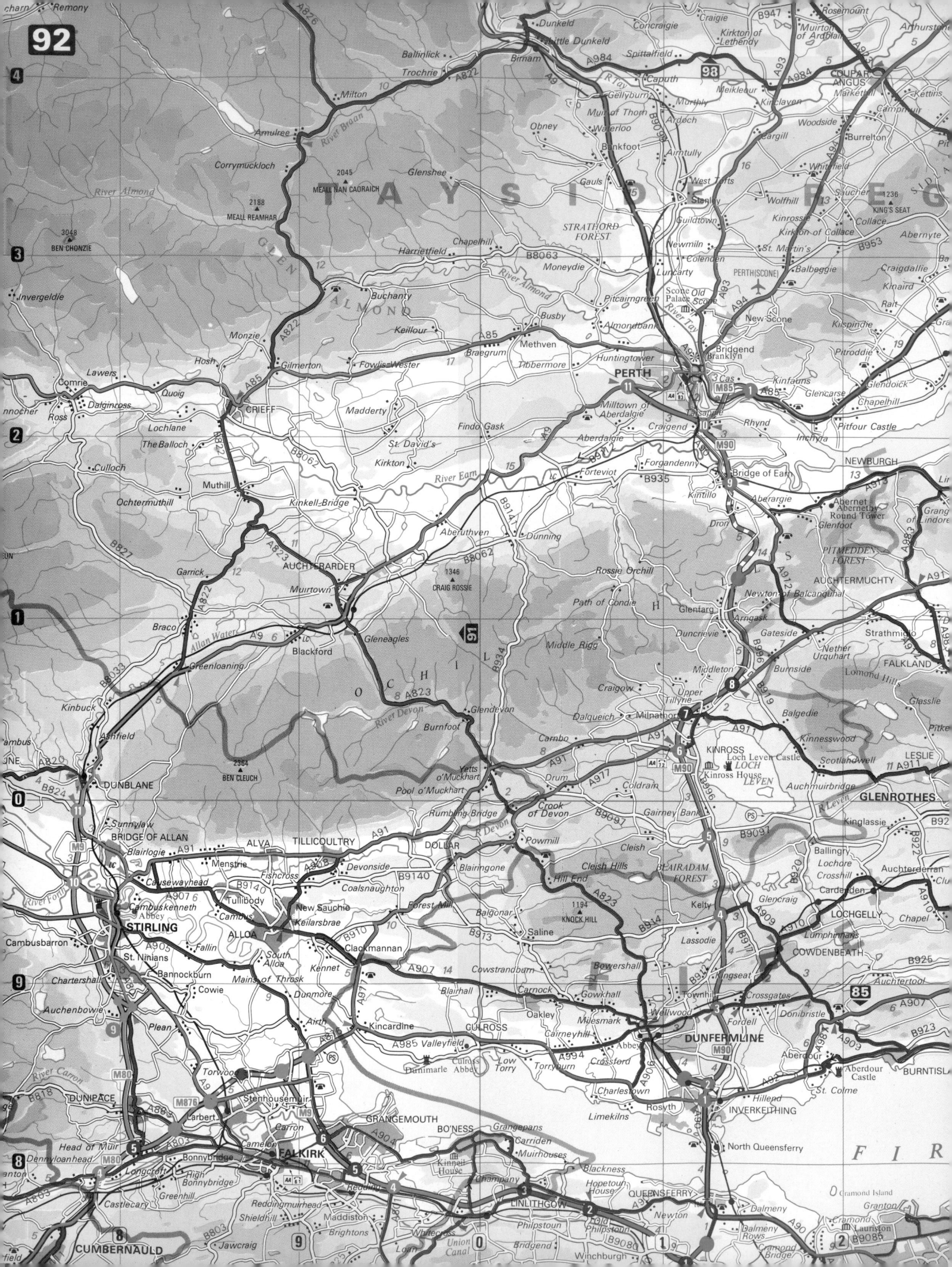

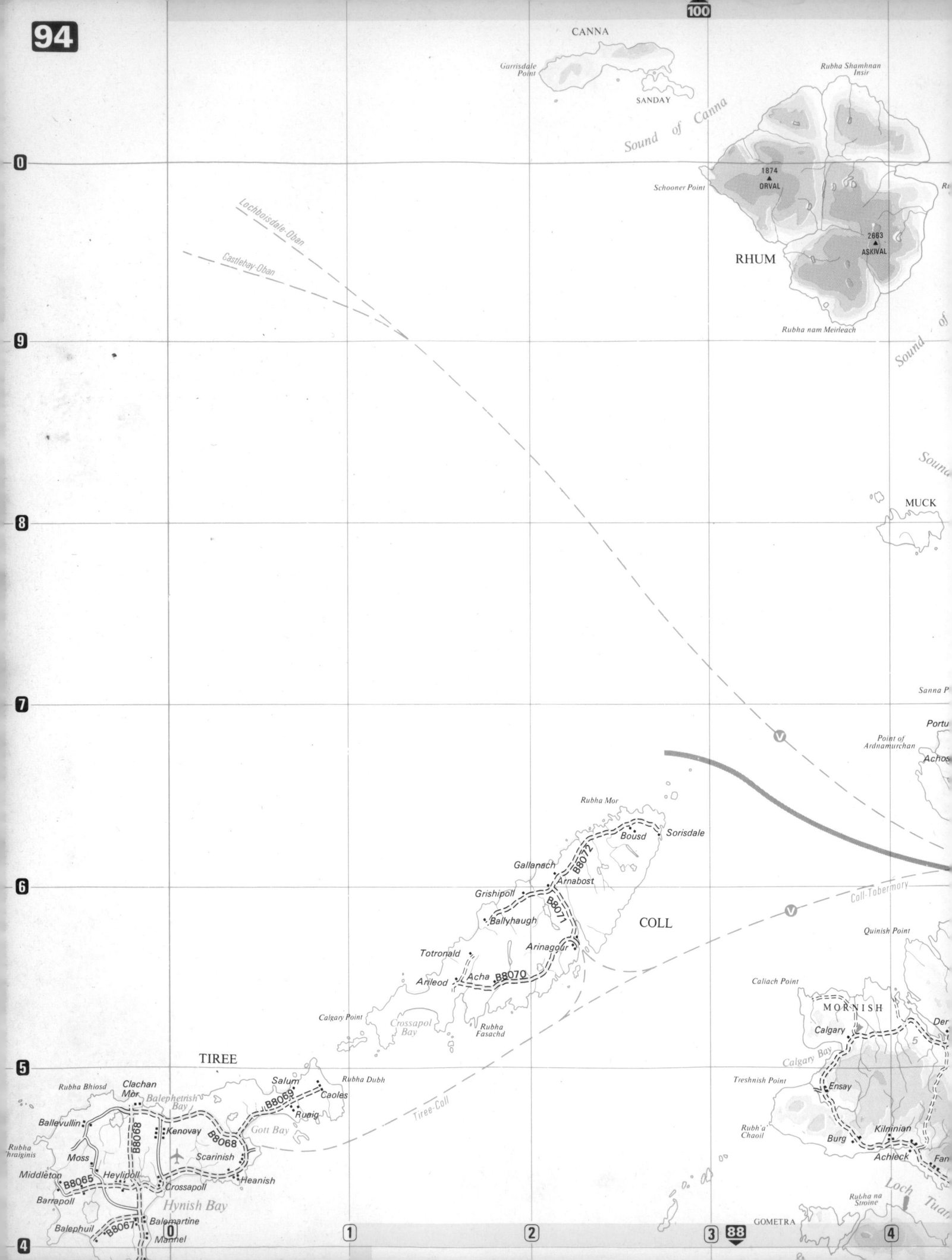

CANNA

*Garrisdale
Point*

SANDAY

Sound of Canna

100

*Rubha Shamhnan
Insir*

1874
▲
ORVAL

Schooner Point

2663
▲
ASKIVAL

RHUM

Rubha nam Meirleach

Sound of

MUCK

Lochboisdale-Oban

Castlebay-Oban

Sound

Sanna P

Portu

*Point of
Ardnamurchan*

Achos

Ⓥ

Rubha Mor

Bousd Sorisdale

B8072

Gallanach

Arnabost

Grishipoll

B8071

Ballyhaugh

COLL

Coll-Tobermory

Ⓥ

Quinish Point

Totronald

Arinagour

Caliach Point

Arileod Acha B8070

MORNISH

Der

Calgary

Calgary Point

*Crossapol
Bay*

*Rubha
Fasachd*

Calgary Bay

TIREE

Treshnish Point

Ensay

Rubha Bhiosd Clachan
Mòr

Salum

Rubha Dubh

*Balephetrish
Bay*

B8069 Caoles

*Rubh'a
Chaoil*

Kilninian

Ballevullin

Ruaig

Gott Bay

Burg

*Rubha
'hraiginis*

Kenovay

B8068

Moss

Scarinish

Achleck Fan

Middleton B8065 Heylipoll

Crossapoll

Heanish

*Rubha na
Smine*

Loch Tual

Barrapoll

Hynish Bay

Tiree-Coll

Balephuil B8067 Balemartine

GOMETRA

88
▼

Mannel

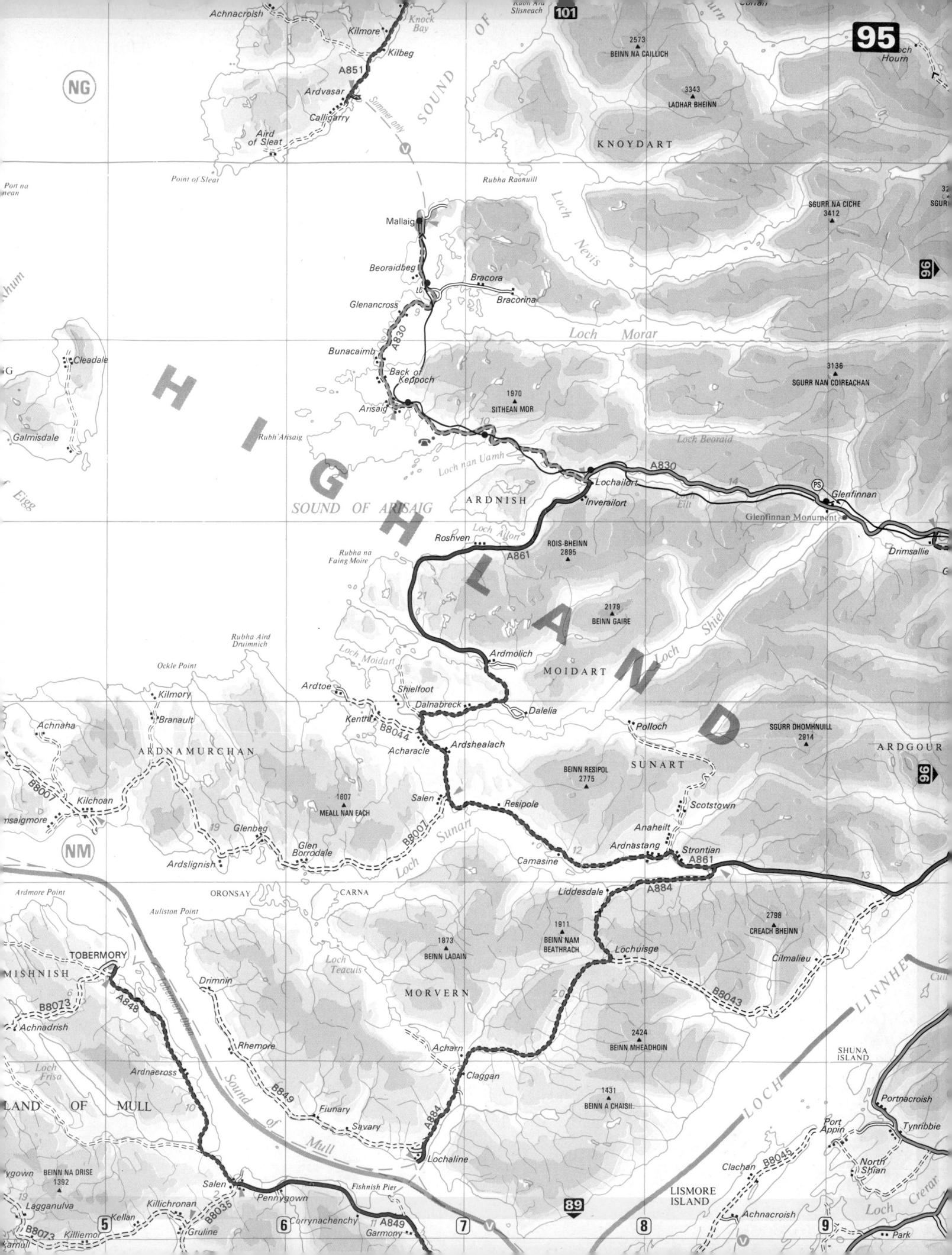

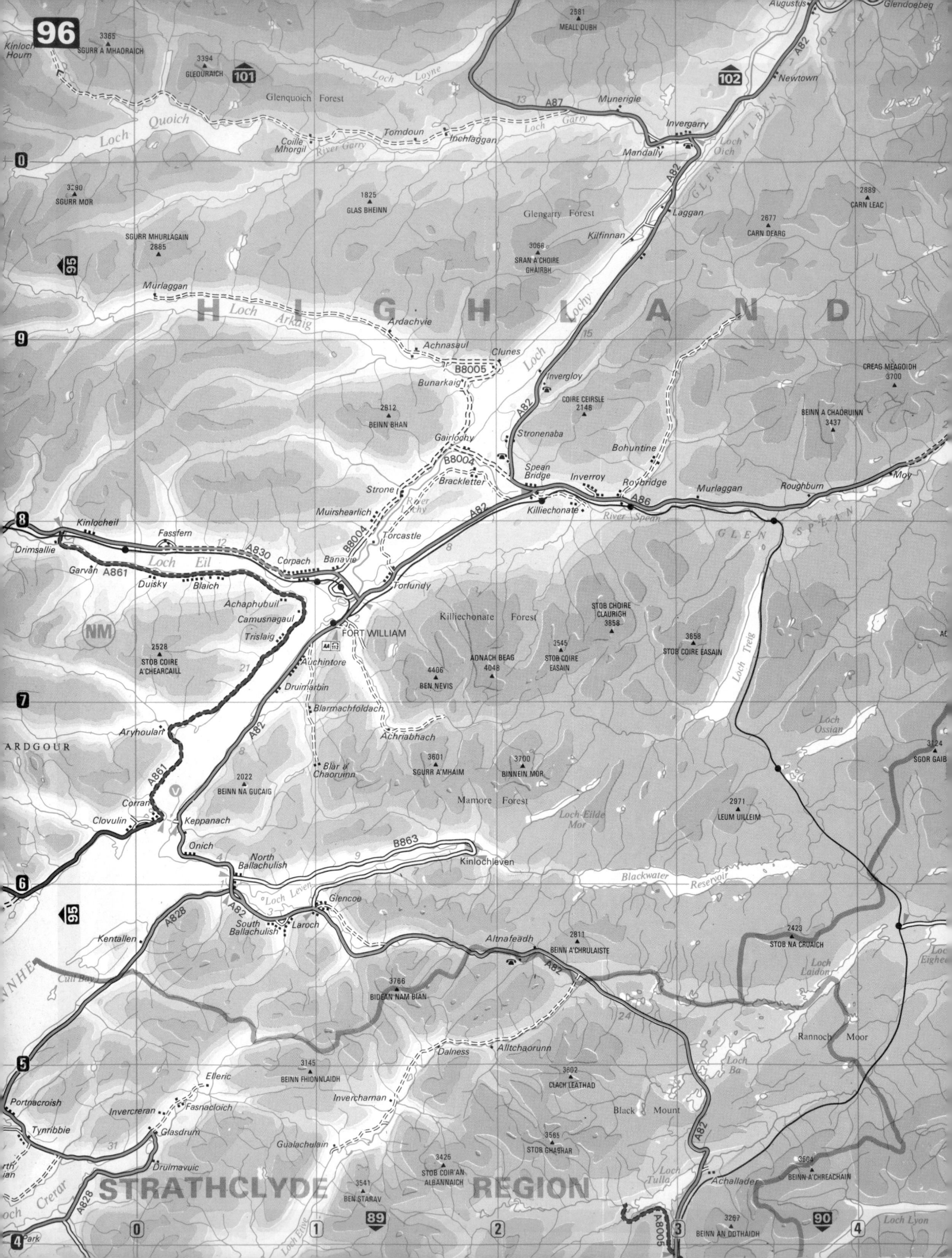

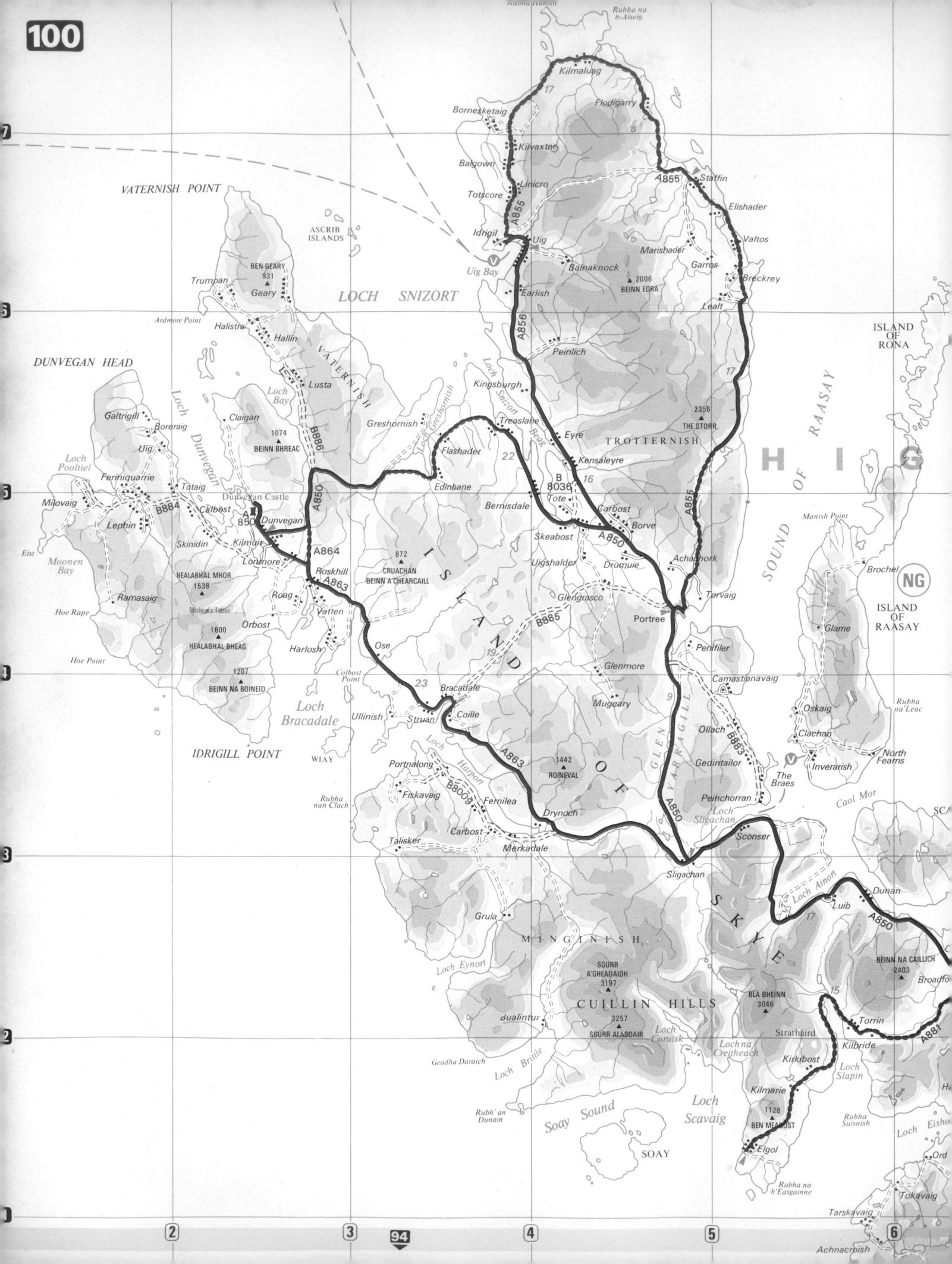

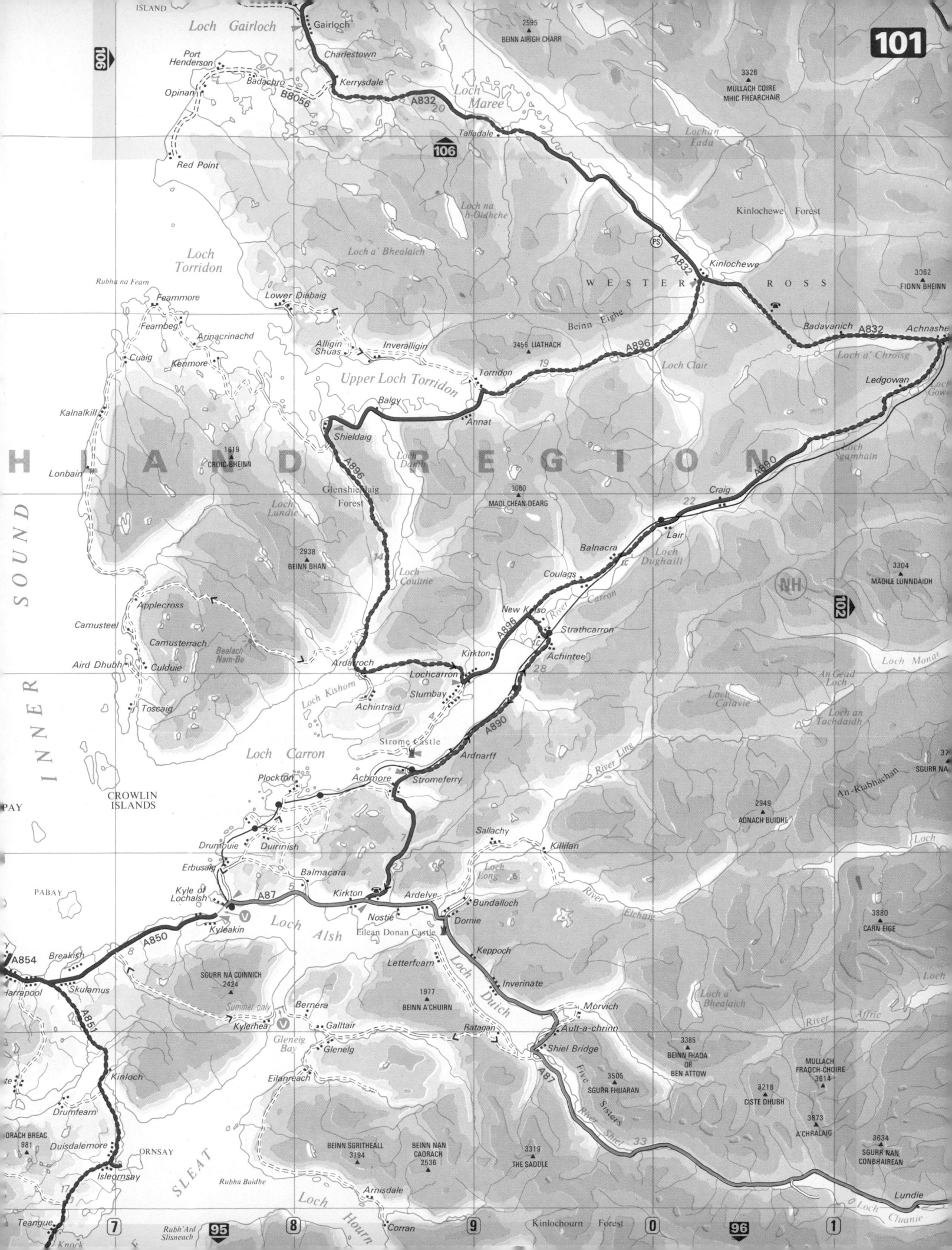

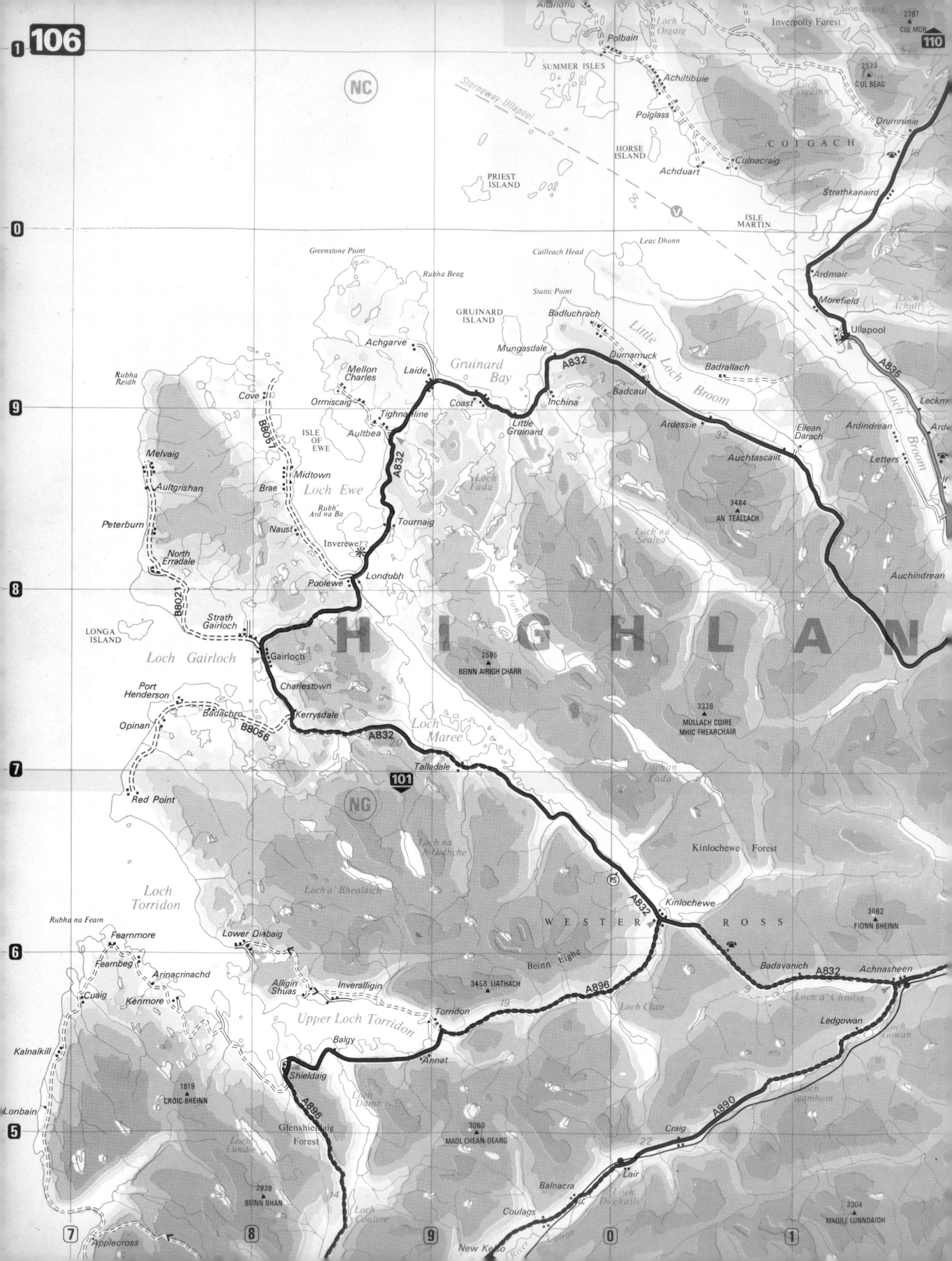

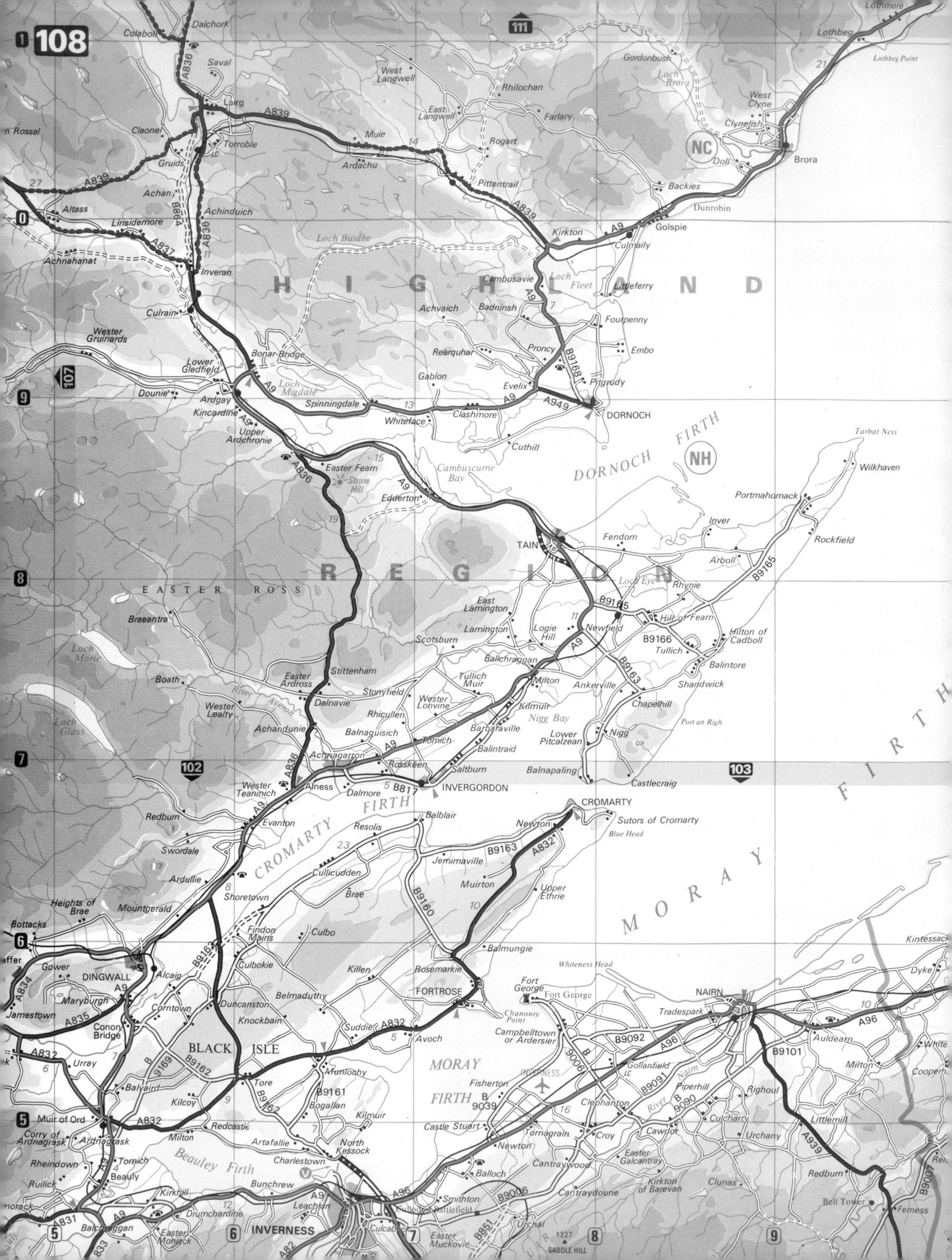

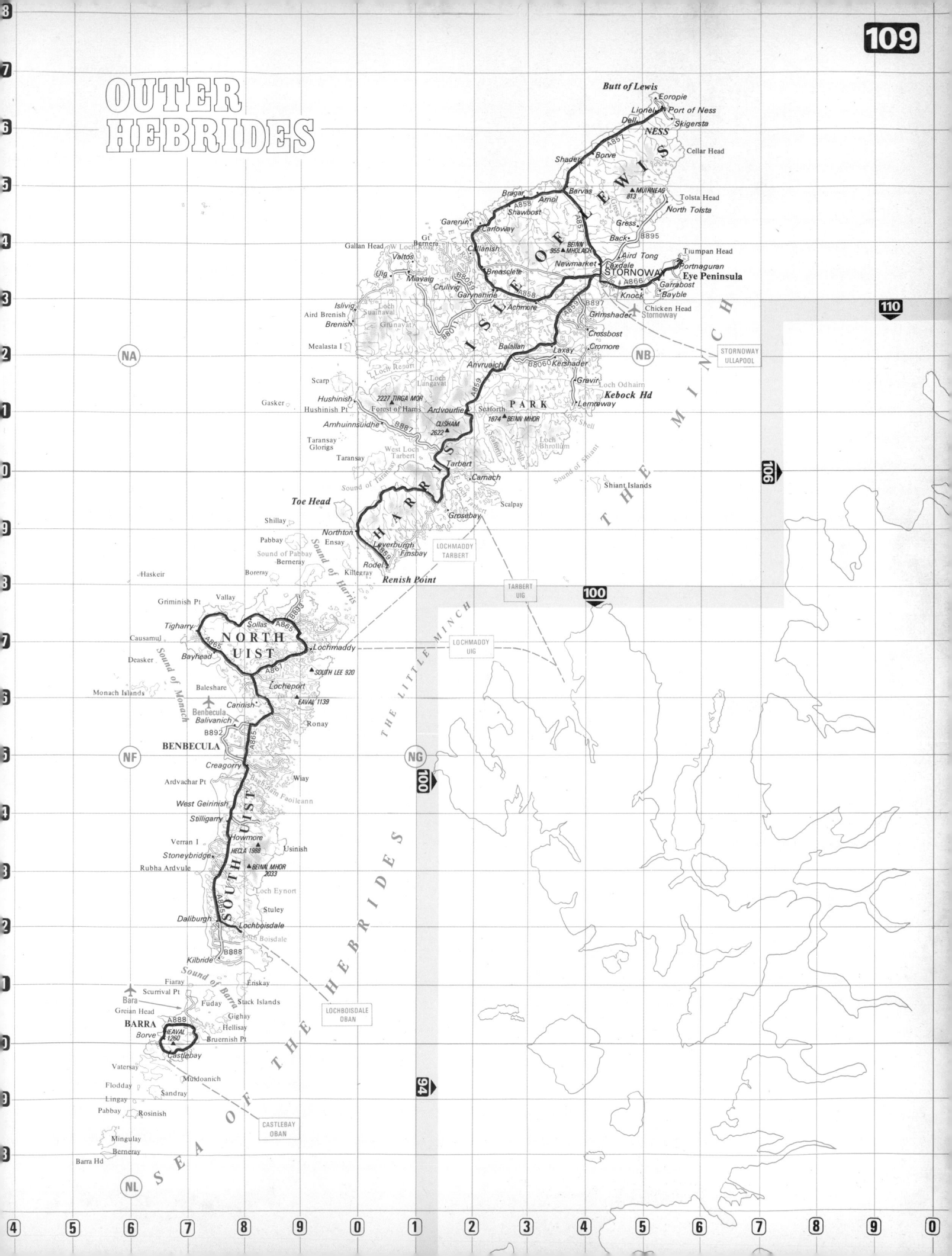

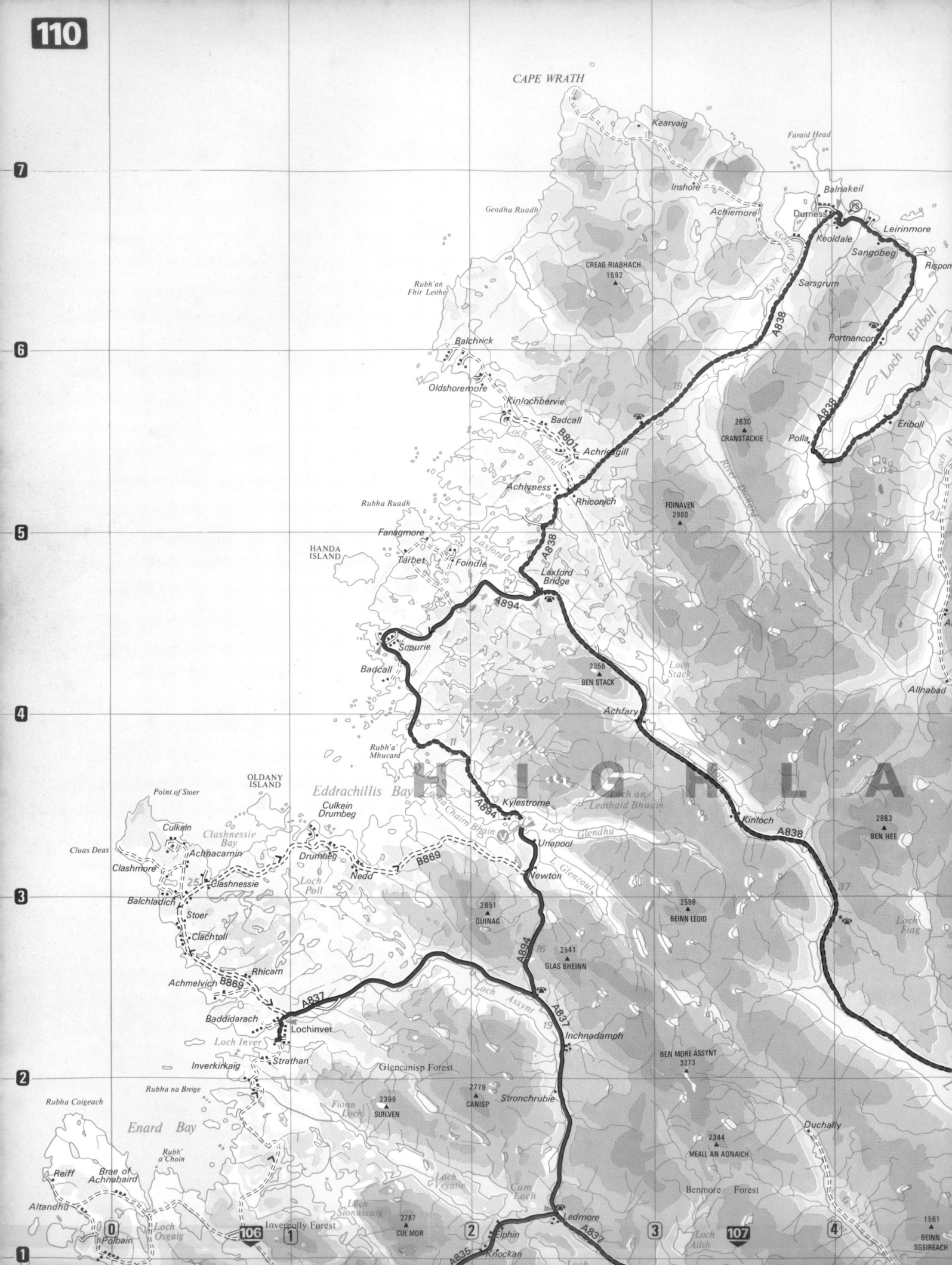

CAPE WRATH

Kearvaig

Faraid Head

Inshore

Balnakeil

Geodha Ruadh

Achiemore

Durness · PS

Leirinmore

Keoldale

Sangobeg

Rispon

CREAG RIABHACH
1592

Sarsgrum

Rubh'an
Fhir Leithe

A838

Portnancon

Loch
Eriboll

Balchrick

2630
CRANSTACKIE

Polla

Eriboll

19

Oldshoremore

Kinlochbervie

Badcall

B801

Achriesgill

Loch Inchard

Achlyness

Rubha Ruadh

Rhiconich

FOINAVEN
2980

Fanagmore

A838

HANDA
ISLAND

Tarbet

Foindle

Laxford
Bridge

A894

Loch Laxford

Scourie

Badcall

2356
BEN STACK

Loch
Stack

Achfary

Allnabad

Rubh'a'
Mhucard

11

HIGHLA

Loch More

Eddrachillis Bay

Loch a Chairn Bhain

A894

Kylestrome

Loch an
Ledhaid Bhuain

Kinloch

A838

2863
BEN HEE

OLDANY
ISLAND

Point of Stoer

Culkein
Drumbeg

Unapool

Loch Glendhu

Culkein

Clashnessie
Bay

Drumbeg

V

L. Glencoul

37

Cluas Deas

Achnacarnin

Newton

Clashmore

Drumbeg

B869

2651
QUINAG

2599
BEINN LEOID

Loch
Fiag

Clashnessie

Nedd

Balchladich

Loch
Poll

A894

16

2541
GLAS BHEINN

Stoer

Clachtoll

Rhicarn

19

Achmelvich B869

A837

Loch Assynt

A837

Baddidarach

Lochinver

Inchnadamph

Loch Inver

BEN MORE ASSYNT
3273

Inverkirkaig

Strathan

Glencanisp Forest

2779
CANISP

Stronchrubie

Duchally

Rubha na Breige

2399
SUILVEN

2344
MEALL AN AONAICH

Rubha Coigeach

Fionn
Loch

Enard Bay

Rubh'
a'Choin

Benmore Forest

Reiff

Brae of
Achnahaird

Loch
Sionascaig

1561
BEINN
SGEIREACH

Altandhu

Polbain

Loch
Osgaig

106

Inverpolly Forest

1

2787
CUL MOR

2

Elphin

A837

3

107

4

A835

Knockan

Cam
Loch

Ledmore

Loch
Ailsh

7

6

5

4

3

2

1

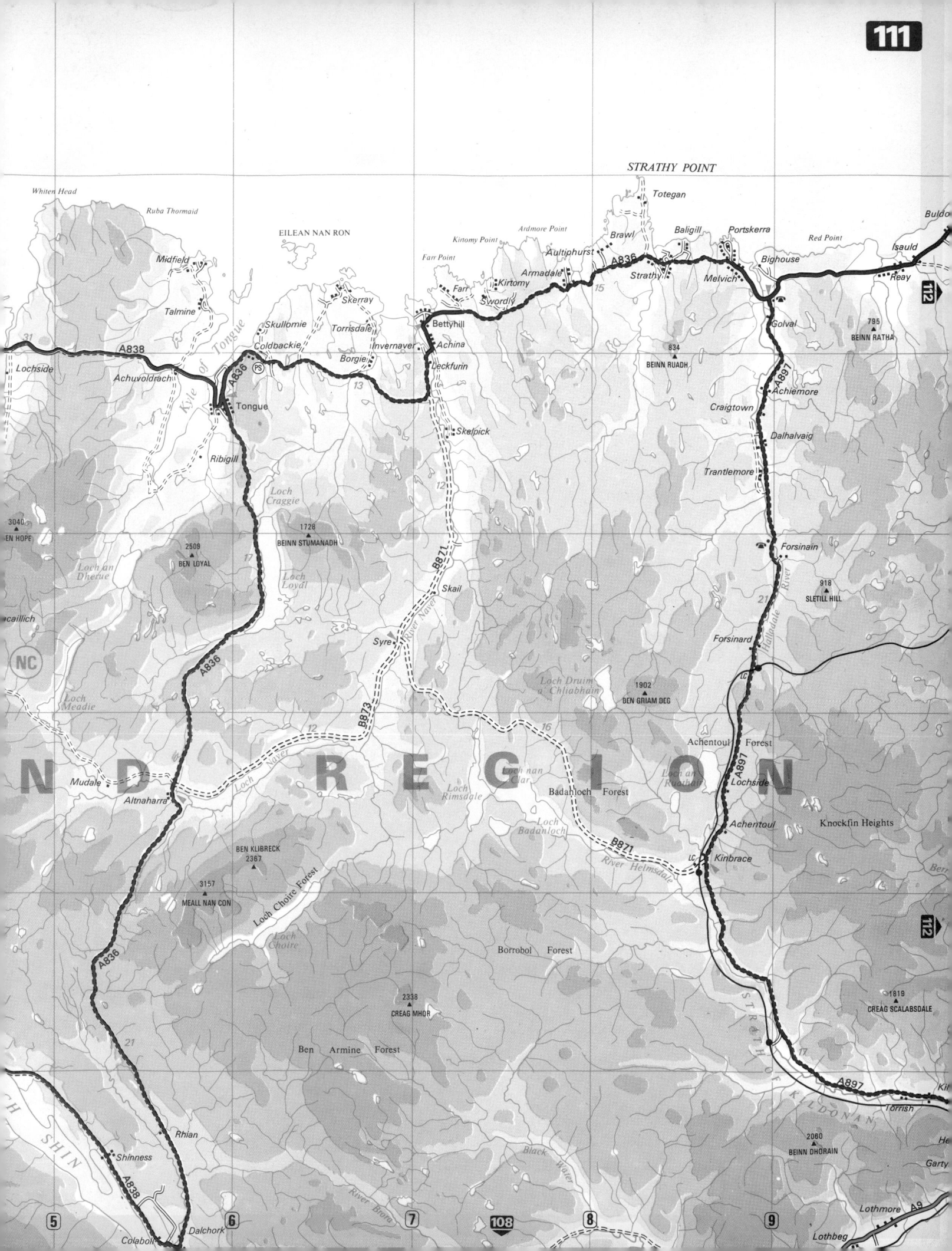

STRATHY POINT

Whiten Head
Ruba Thormaid

EILEAN NAN RON

Midfield
Talmine

A838

Lochside

Achuvoldrach
Kyle of Tongue
A836
PS
Tongue

Ribigill

Skerray
Skullomie
Coldbackie
Torrisdale
Borgie
Invernaver

Bettyhill
Achina
Leckfurin

Farr Point
Farr
Swordly
Kirtomy

Kirtomy Point
Ardmore Point
Aultiphurst
Armadale

Brawl
Baligill
Strathy

Totegan

Portskerra
Bighouse
Melvich

Red Point

Buldo

Isauld
Reay

112

795
BEINN RATHA

Golval

A897

Achiemore

Craigtown

Dalhalvaig

Trantlemore

834
BEINN RUADH

A836

15

13

12

Skelpick

B871

Loch
Craggie

1728
BEINN STUMANADH

3040
EN HOPE

Loch an
Dherue

2509
BEN LOYAL

17

Loch
Loyal

Skail

Syre
River Naver

918
SLETILL HILL

Forsinain

Forsinard
Halladale River

21

NC

Loch
Meadie

Loch Naver

B873

12

B873

16

Loch Druim
a' Chliabhain

1902
BEN GRIAM DEG

LC

 caillich

N D   R E G I O N

Mudale

Altnaharra

BEN KLIBRECK
2367

3157
MEALL NAN CON

Loch Choire Forest

Loch
Choire

Loch nan
Clar

Loch
Rimsdale

Loch
Badanloch

Badanloch Forest

Loch an
Ruathair

B871

River Helmsdale

Achentoul Forest

Lochside

Achentoul

A897

Kinbrace

Knockfin Heights

LC

112

Borrobol Forest

2338
CREAG MHOR

Ben   Armine   Forest

A836

21

1819
CREAG SCALABSDALE

STRATH OF KILDONAN

17

A897

Torrish

OCH SHIN

Rhian

Shinness

A838

2060
BEINN DHORAIN

Black
Water

River Brora

Colaboll
Dalchork

Lothmore

A9

Lothbeg

Garty

He

Ki

Berr

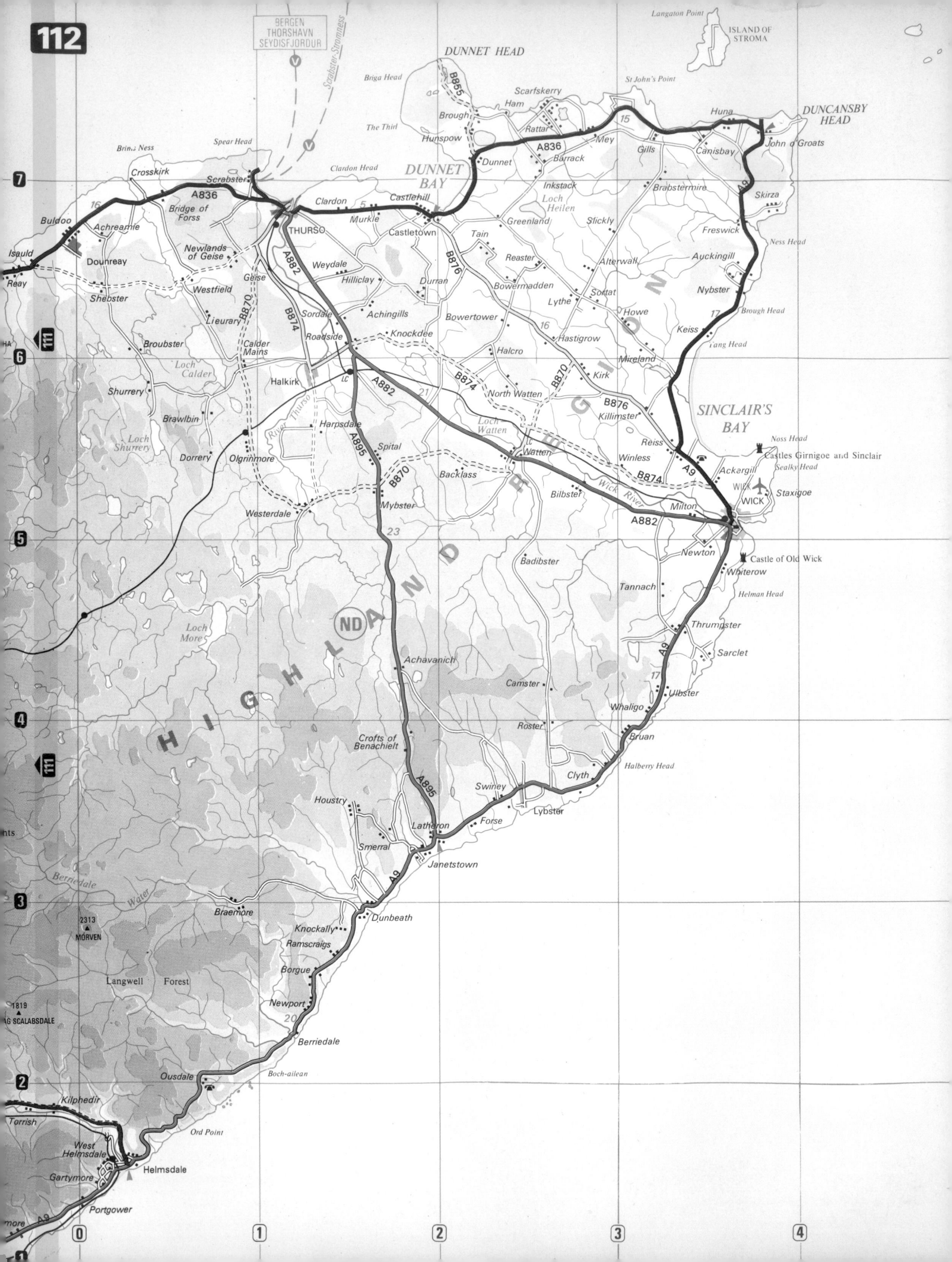

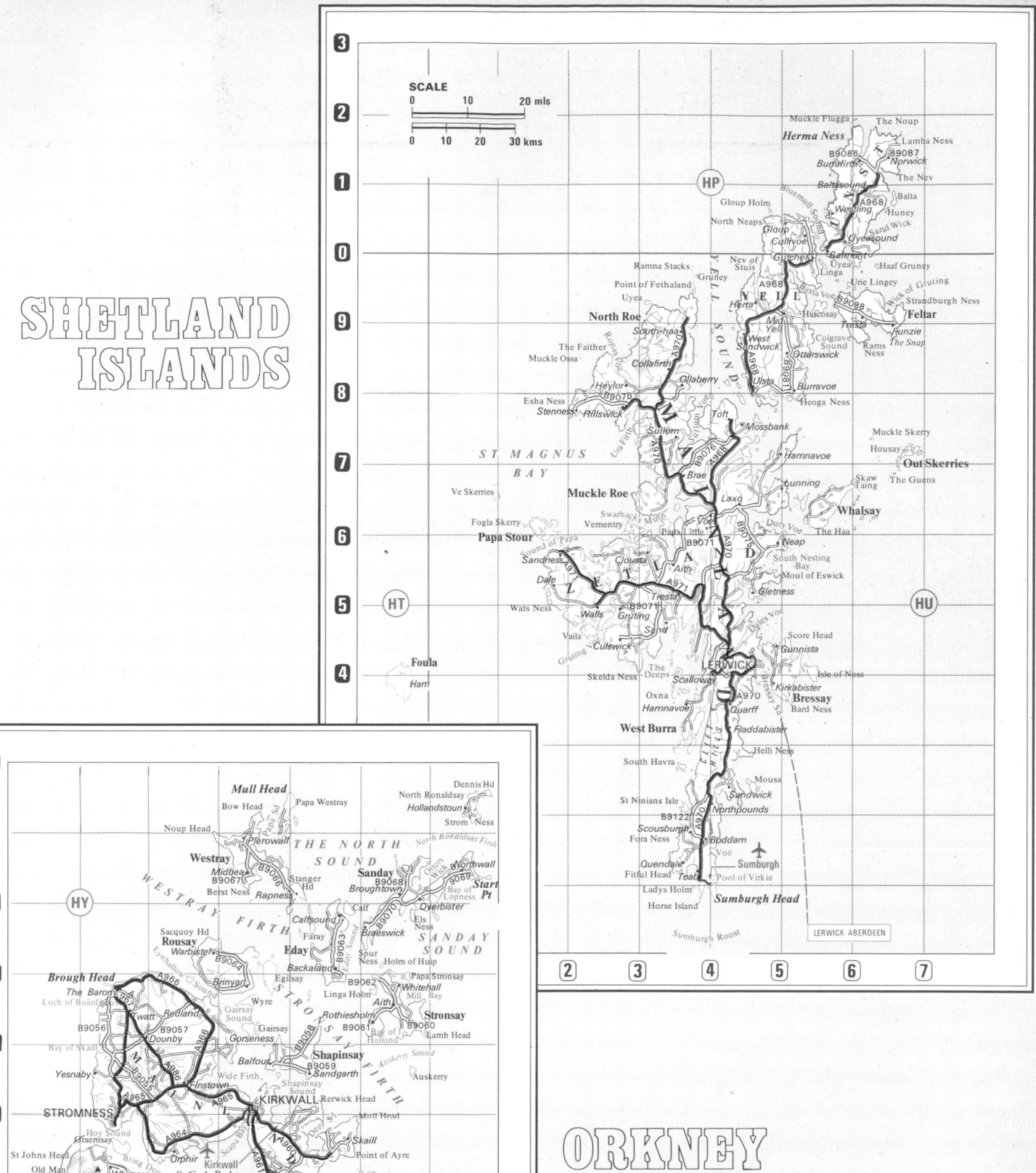

SHETLAND ISLANDS

ORKNEY ISLANDS

Motorway Maps

The maps on the following pages depict the principal motorways in Great Britain and are arranged in easy-to-follow strips. Enlarged details of many motorway junctions have been included to help the driver approach these without hesitation. The motorway guide opposite gives an overall picture of the system and enables the driver to plan extended use of motorways.

Legend

AA 15	AA road service centres. Breakdown and road service information. Normally 0900-1730 hrs.
AA	AA service centres. Breakdown/information service normal hours
AA info	AA motorway information service centres. Normally 0900-1730 hrs. Callers only
AA 24 hour	AA service centres 24 hour breakdown/information service
——3——	Motorway with junction number
▪▪▪▪▪▪▪	Motorway under construction
=======	Motorway projected
A3	Primary route
A35	Dual carriageway
A27	A road
B2147	B road
————	Unclassified road
– – – –	Road under construction
——6——	Junction with restricted access
——S——	Service area (open)
——S——	Service area (future)
✈	Airport
3	Mileage between junctions and service areas.

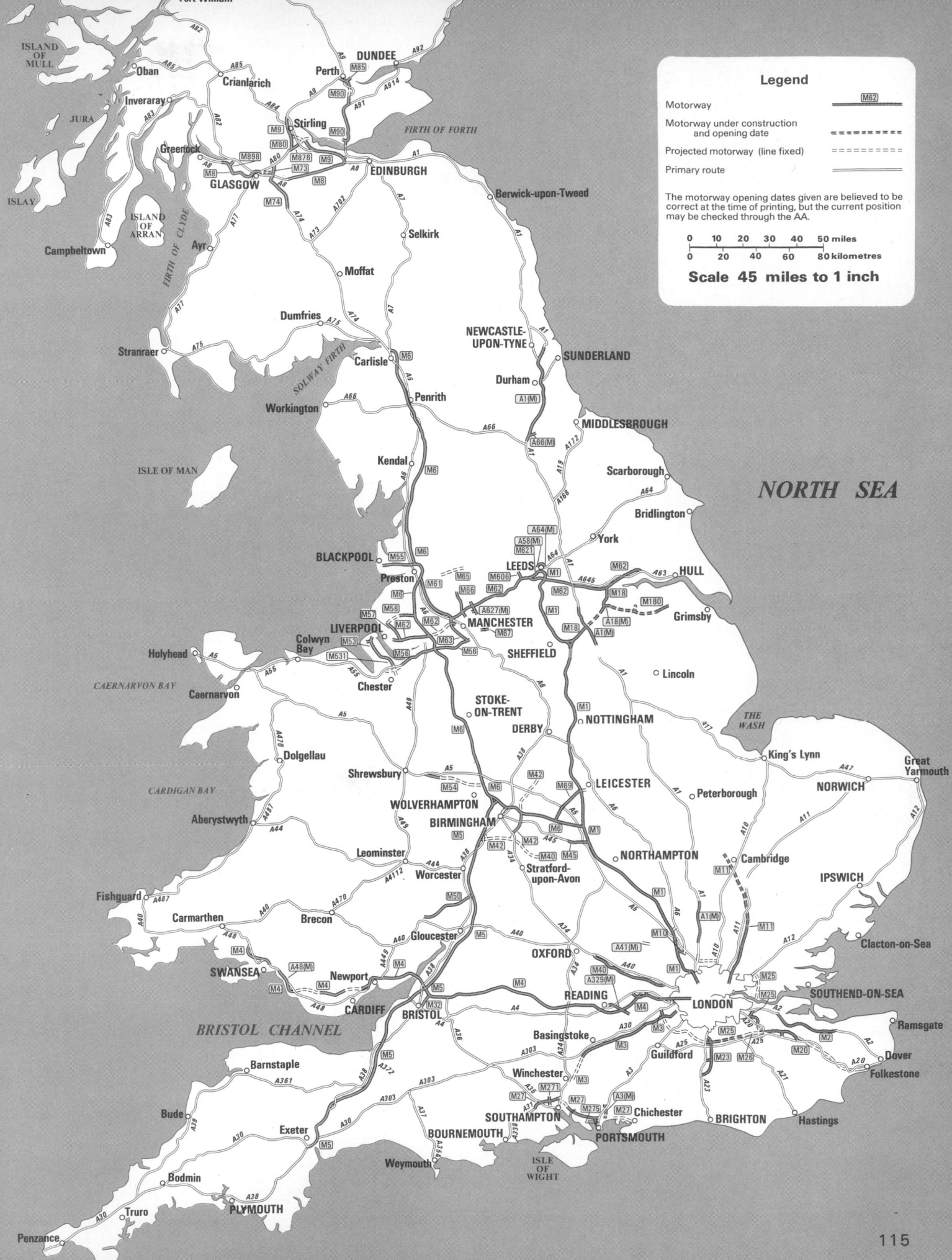

LONDON–MILTON KEYNES

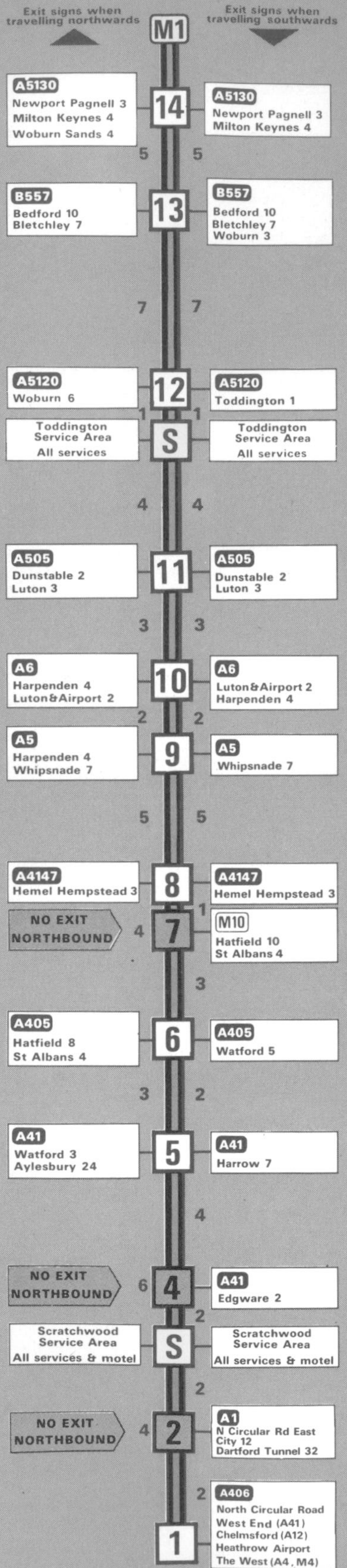

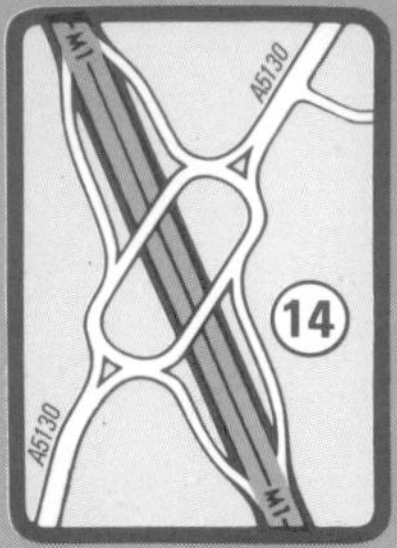

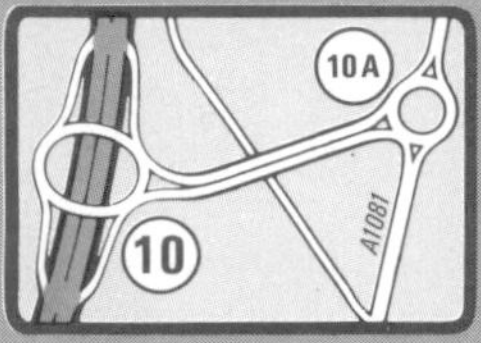

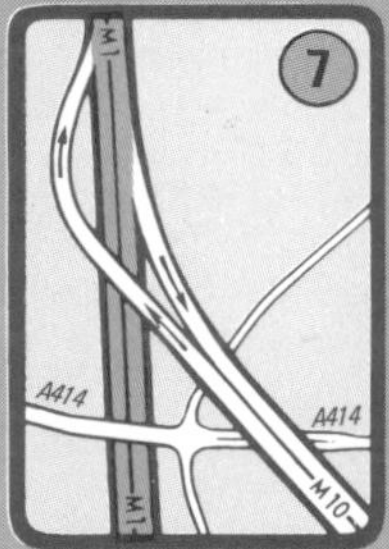

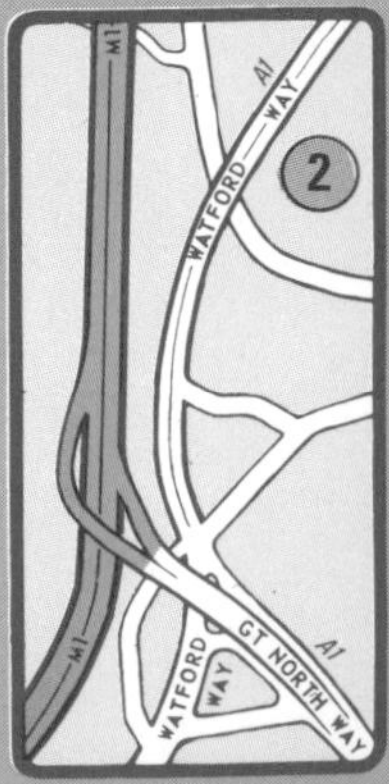

Exit signs when travelling northwards
Exit signs when travelling southwards
M1
A5130 Newport Pagnell 3 Milton Keynes 4 Woburn Sands 4
14
A5130 Newport Pagnell 3 Milton Keynes 4
5 5
B557 Bedford 10 Bletchley 7
13
B557 Bedford 10 Bletchley 7 Woburn 3
7 7
A5120 Woburn 6
12
A5120 Toddington 1
1 1
Toddington Service Area All services
S
Toddington Service Area All services
4 4
A505 Dunstable 2 Luton 3
11
A505 Dunstable 2 Luton 3
3 3
A6 Harpenden 4 Luton&Airport 2
10
A6 Luton&Airport 2 Harpenden 4
2 2
A5 Harpenden 4 Whipsnade 7
9
A5 Whipsnade 7
5 5
A4147 Hemel Hempstead 3
8
A4147 Hemel Hempstead 3
1
NO EXIT NORTHBOUND
4
7
M10 Hatfield 10 St Albans 4
3
A405 Hatfield 8 St Albans 4
6
A405 Watford 5
3 2
A41 Watford 3 Aylesbury 24
5
A41 Harrow 7
4
NO EXIT NORTHBOUND
6
4
A41 Edgware 2
2
Scratchwood Service Area All services & motel
S
Scratchwood Service Area All services & motel
2
NO EXIT NORTHBOUND
4
2
A1 N Circular Rd East City 12 Dartford Tunnel 32
2
A406 North Circular Road West End (A41) Chelmsford (A12) Heathrow Airport The West (A4, M4)
1

M1
A5130
14

10A
10
A1081

7
M1
A414
M10

M1
A1
WATFORD WAY
GT NORTH WAY
2

THE NORTH
MILTON KEYNES
BEDFORD
Bletchley
Woburn Sands
Aspley Guise
Woburn
Ampthill
Flitwick
LETCHWORTH
Leighton Buzzard
Toddington
TODDINGTON
Barton in the Clay
DUNSTABLE
LUTON
HITCHIN
Markyate
0 4miles
M1
HARPENDEN
Redbourn
HEMEL HEMPSTEAD
A1(M)
WELWYN GARDEN CITY
A1(M) STEVENAGE
King's Langley
M10
ST ALBANS
All purpose road to become M25
Hatfield
London Colney
WATFORD
Radlett
A1(M)
Potters Bar
BUSHEY
Borehamwood
Northwood
SCRATCHWOOD
Stanmore
Totteridge
Cockfosters
Harrow
Barnet
Finchley
Southgate
Wembley
Brent
Golders Green
Southall
LONDON
Islington
M4
A40(M)
M41
Marble Arch

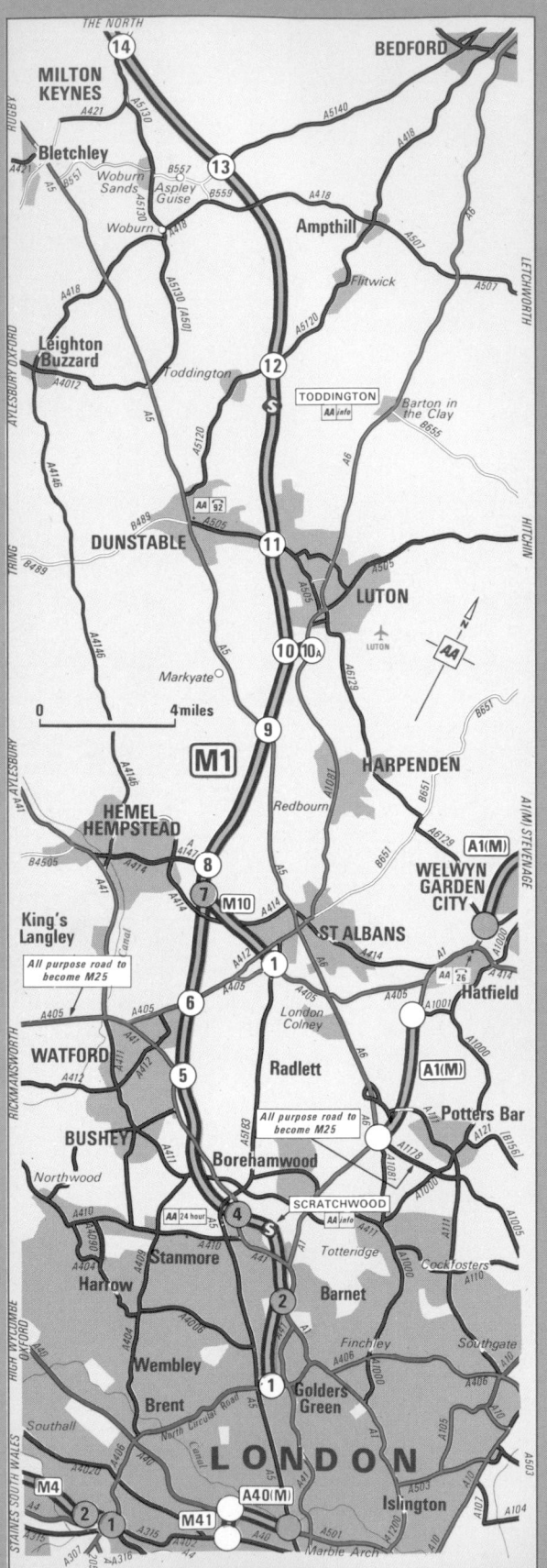

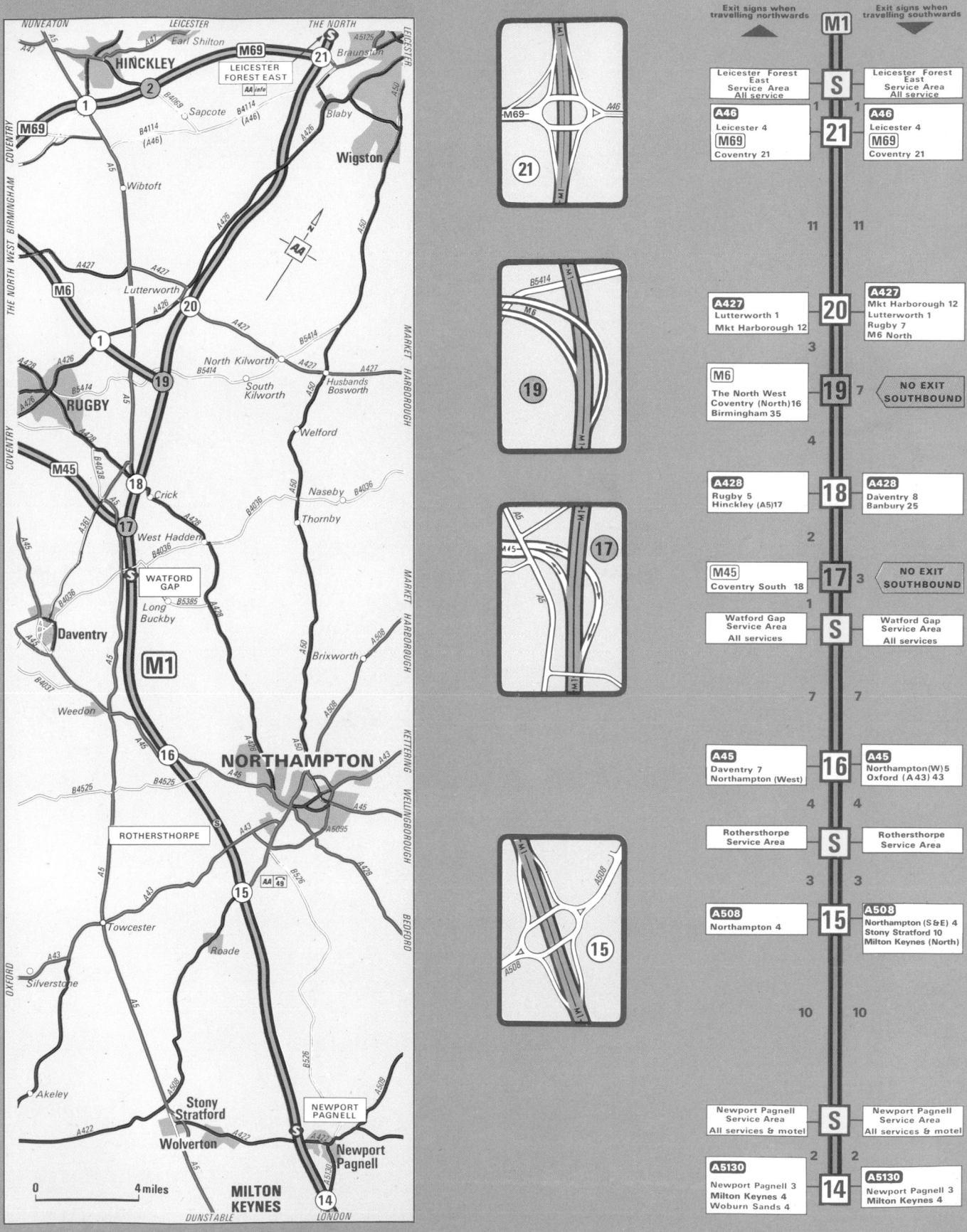

Exit signs when travelling northwards   Exit signs when travelling southwards

M1

21

Leicester Forest East Service Area All service   **S**   Leicester Forest East Service Area All service

1   1

A46 Leicester 4   **21**   A46 Leicester 4
M69 Coventry 21   M69 Coventry 21

11   11

19

A427 Lutterworth 1 Mkt Harborough 12   **20**   A427 Mkt Harborough 12 Lutterworth 1 Rugby 7 M6 North

M6 The North West Coventry (North) 16 Birmingham 35   **19**   7   NO EXIT SOUTHBOUND

4   4

17

A428 Rugby 5 Hinckley (A5) 17   **18**   A428 Daventry 8 Banbury 25

2   2

M45 Coventry South 18   **17**   3   NO EXIT SOUTHBOUND

1

Watford Gap Service Area All services   **S**   Watford Gap Service Area All services

7   7

A45 Daventry 7 Northampton (West)   **16**   A45 Northampton (W) 5 Oxford (A43) 43

4   4

Rothersthorpe Service Area   **S**   Rothersthorpe Service Area

3   3

15

A508 Northampton 4   **15**   A508 Northampton (S & E) 4 Stony Stratford 10 Milton Keynes (North)

10   10

Newport Pagnell Service Area All services & motel   **S**   Newport Pagnell Service Area All services & motel

2   2

A5130 Newport Pagnell 3 Milton Keynes 4 Woburn Sands 4   **14**   A5130 Newport Pagnell 3 Milton Keynes 4

LEICESTER–BOLSOVER

M1

29
| A617 | A617 |
| Chesterfield 5 | Mansfield 7 (Matlock)14 |

7   7

28
A38	A38
Mansfield 7	Derby West 17
Matlock 12	Matlock 12

3   3

27
A608	A608
Mansfield 8	Heanor 6
	Hucknall 4

6   6

26
A610	A610
Nottingham 5	Nottingham 5
Ilkeston 5	Ilkeston 5

2   2

S
| Trowell Service Area | Trowell Service Area |
| All services | All services |

4   4

25
A52	A52
Nottingham 8	Nottingham 8
Derby 8	Derby 8
Ilkeston 6	

5   5

24
A6	A6
East Midlands Airport 3	East Midlands Airport 3
Derby (South) 10	Loughborough 7
A648	
Nottingham (Sth) 10	

6   6

23
A512	A512
Loughborough 4	Loughborough 4
	Ashby 9

5   5

22
A50	A50
Ashby 9	Leicester 8
Burton-on-Trent 18	

7   7

S
| Leicester Forest East Service Area | Leicester Forest East Service Area |
| All services | All services |

1   1

21
A46	A46
Leicester 4	Leicester 4
M69	M69
Coventry 21	Coventry 21

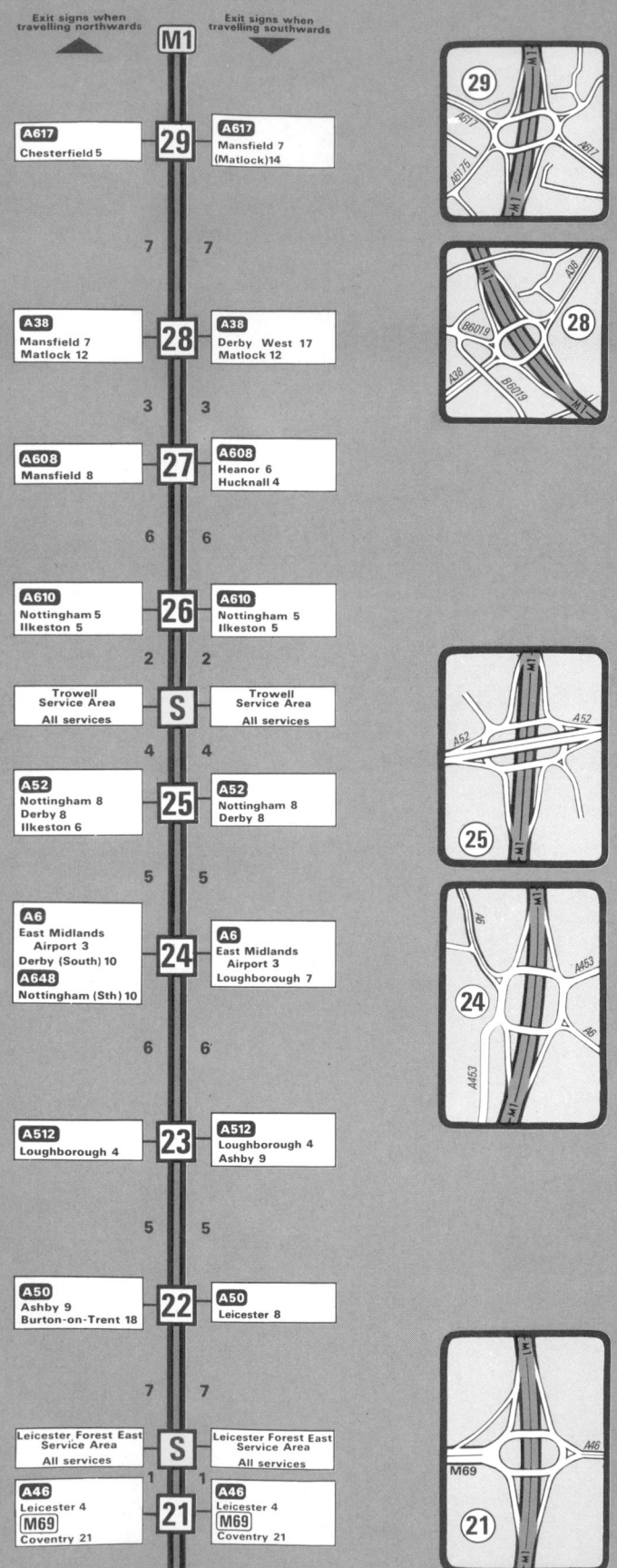

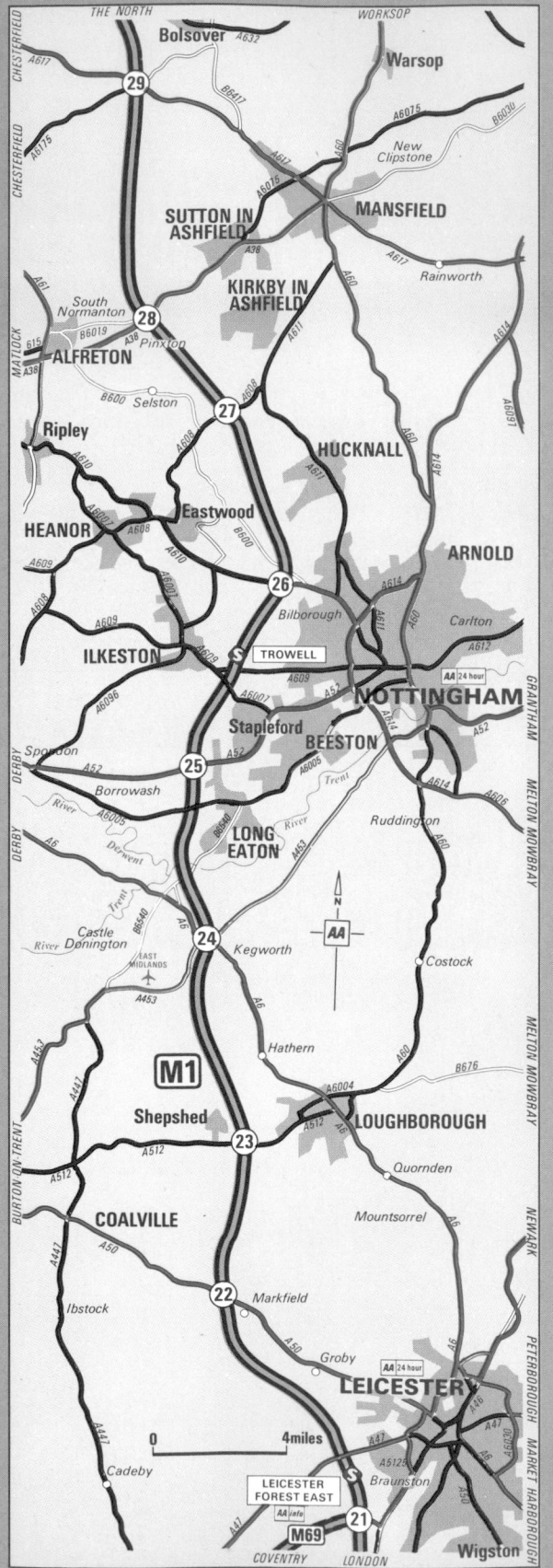

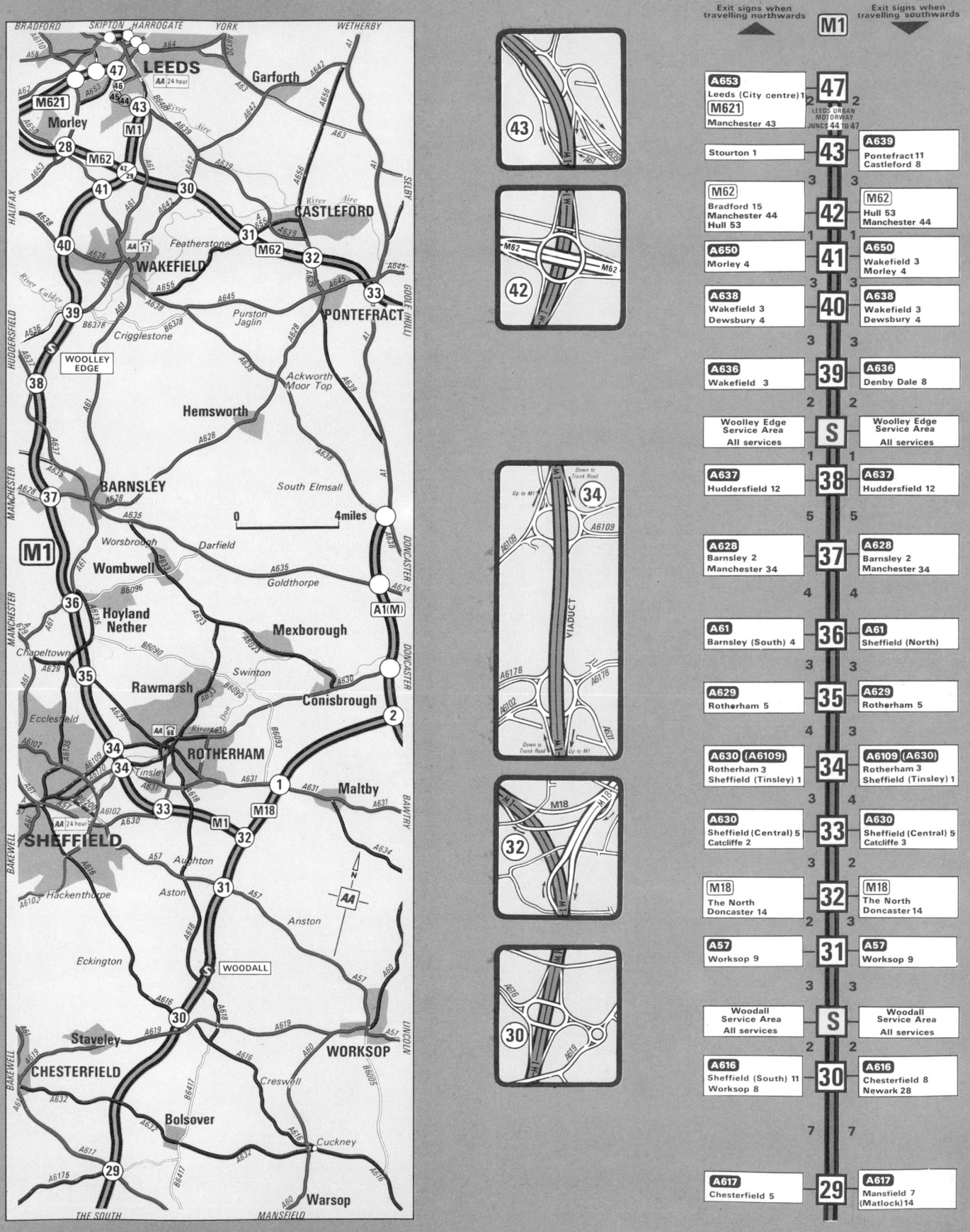

ROCHESTER–FAVERSHAM

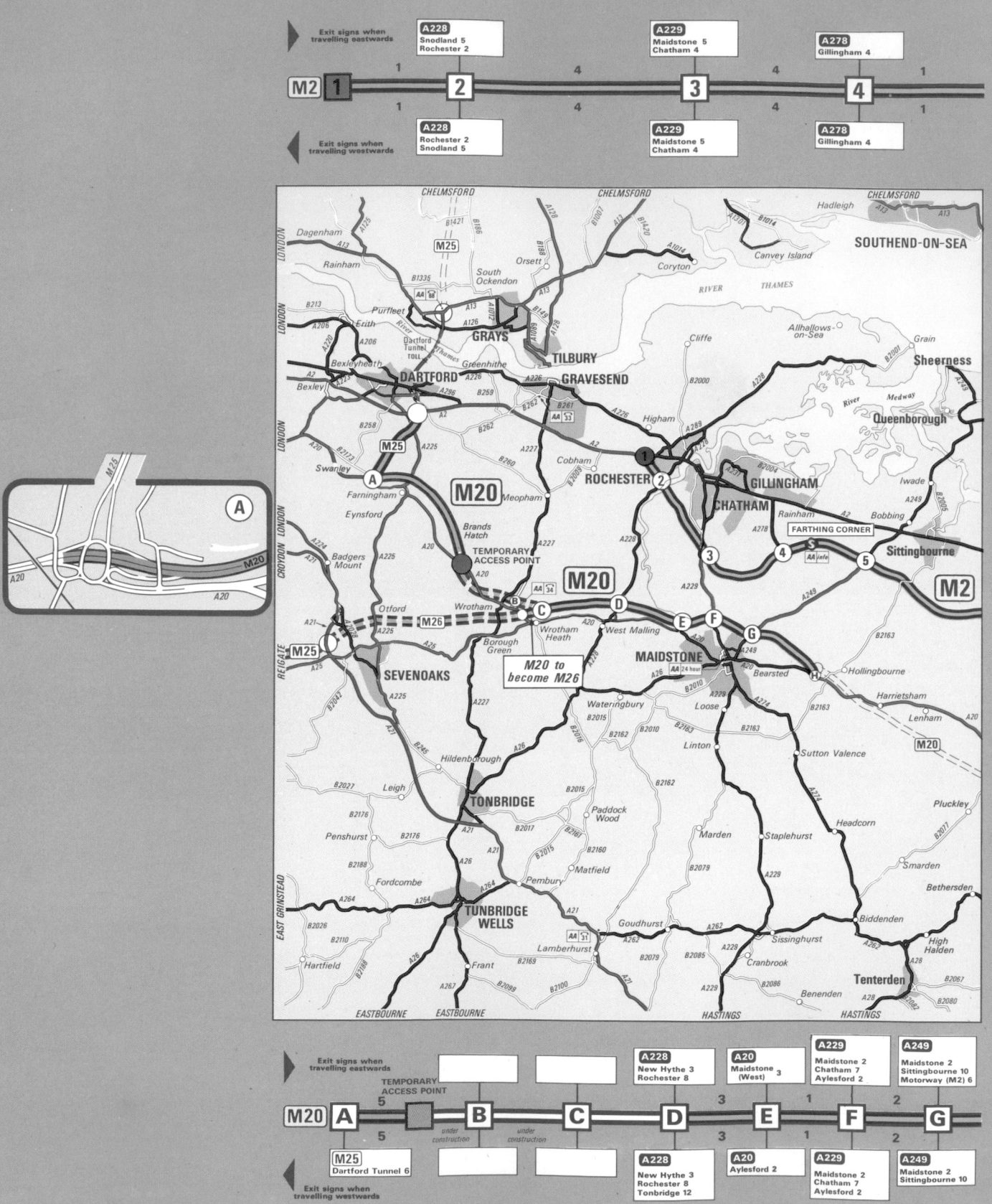

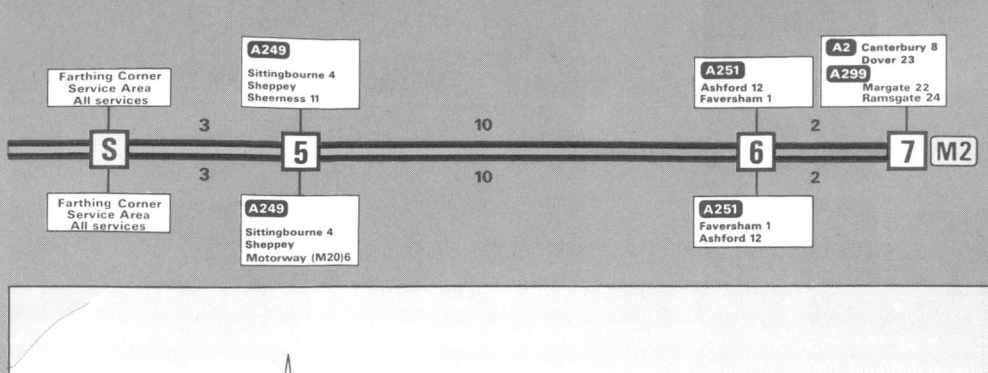

Farthing Corner Service Area All services		A249 Sittingbourne 4 Sheppey Sheerness 11		A251 Ashford 12 Faversham 1	A2 Canterbury 8 Dover 23 / A299 Margate 22 Ramsgate 24
S	3	5	10	6	2 7 M2

| Farthing Corner Service Area All services | 3 | A249 Sittingbourne 4 Sheppey Motorway (M20)6 | 10 | A251 Faversham 1 Ashford 12 | 2 |

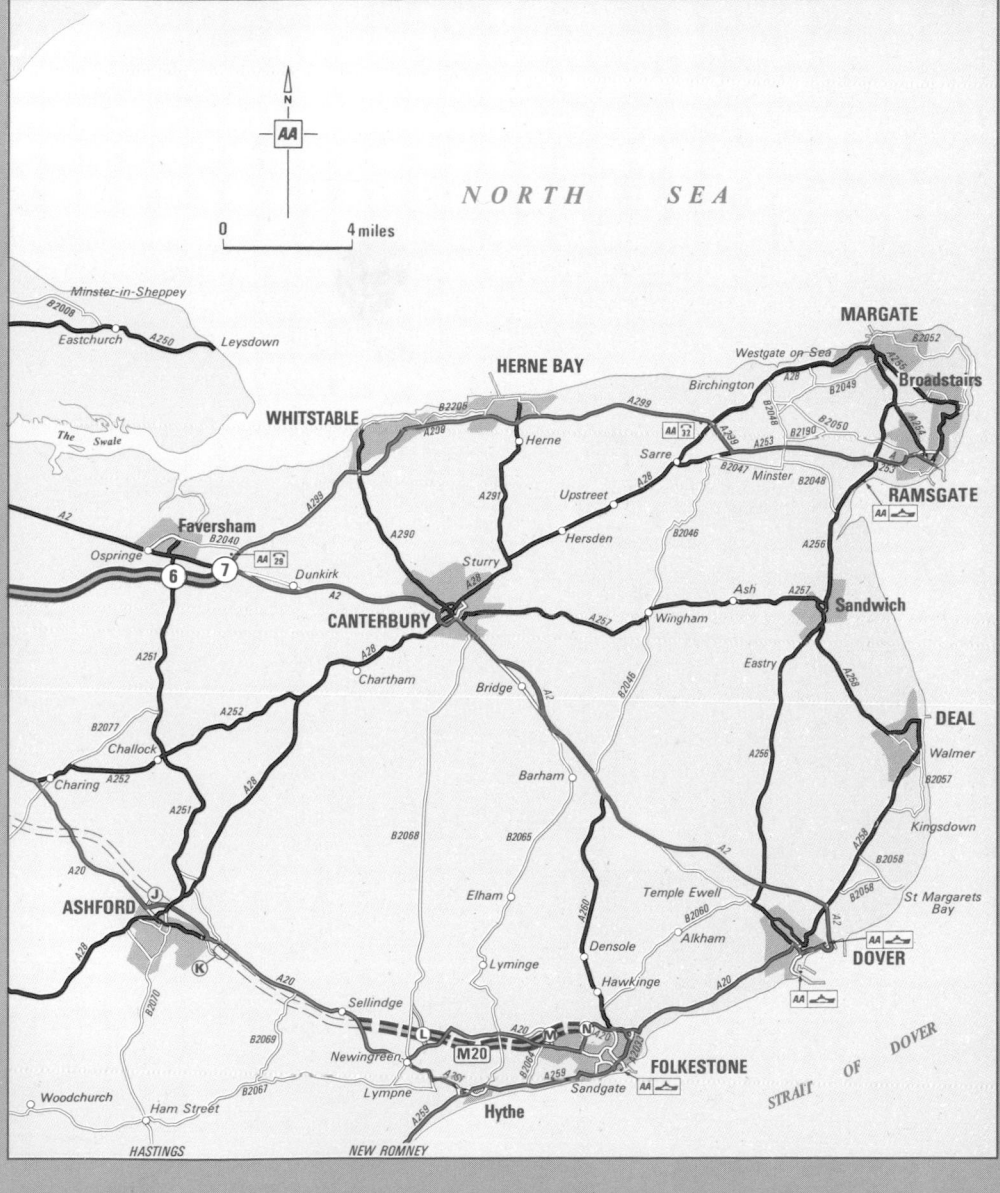

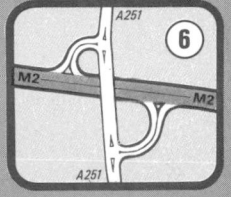

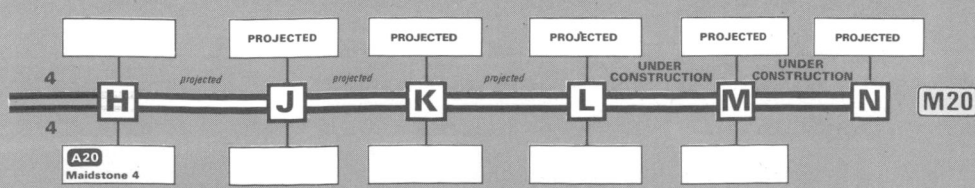

SOUTHAMPTON–BASINGSTOKE–LONDON

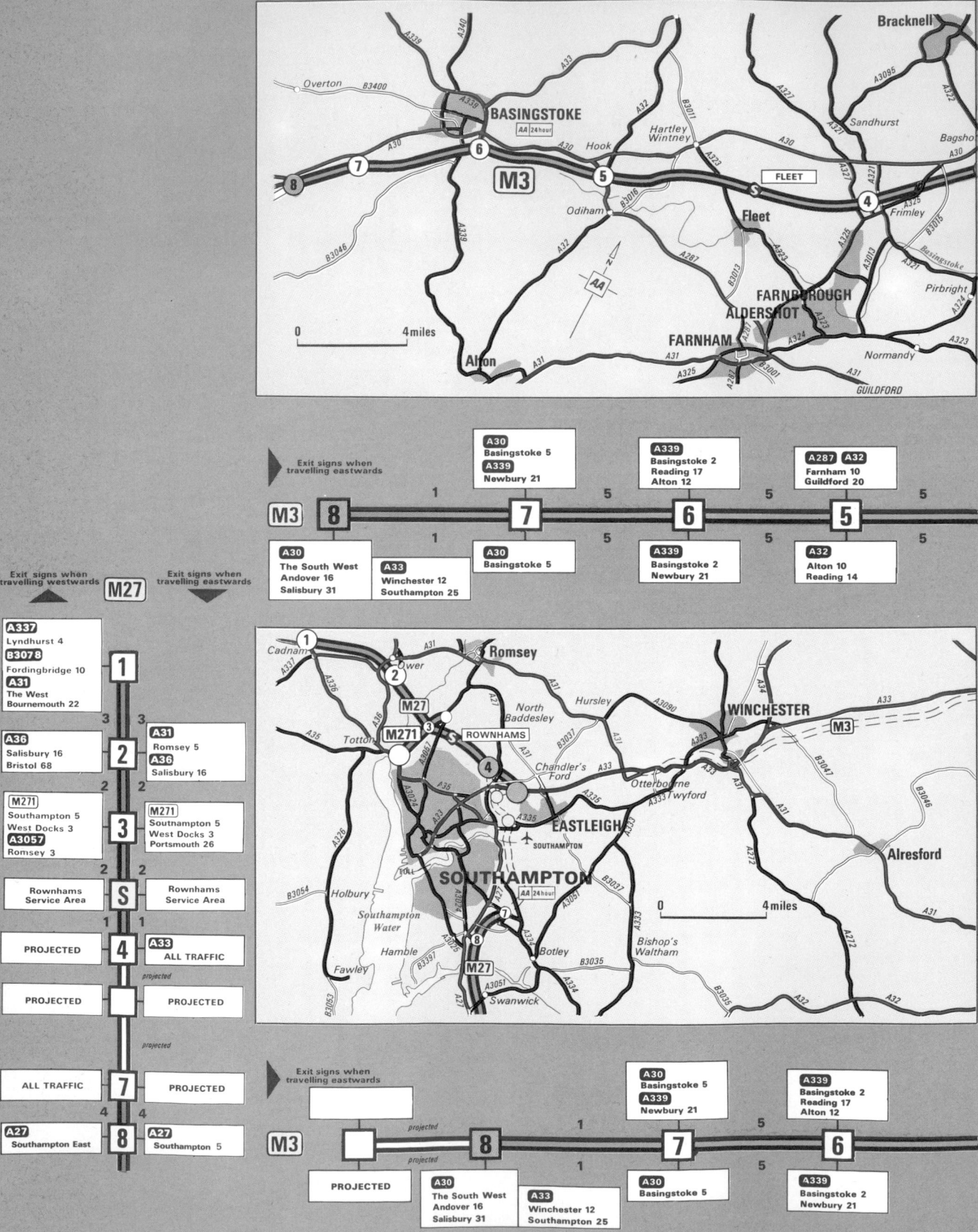

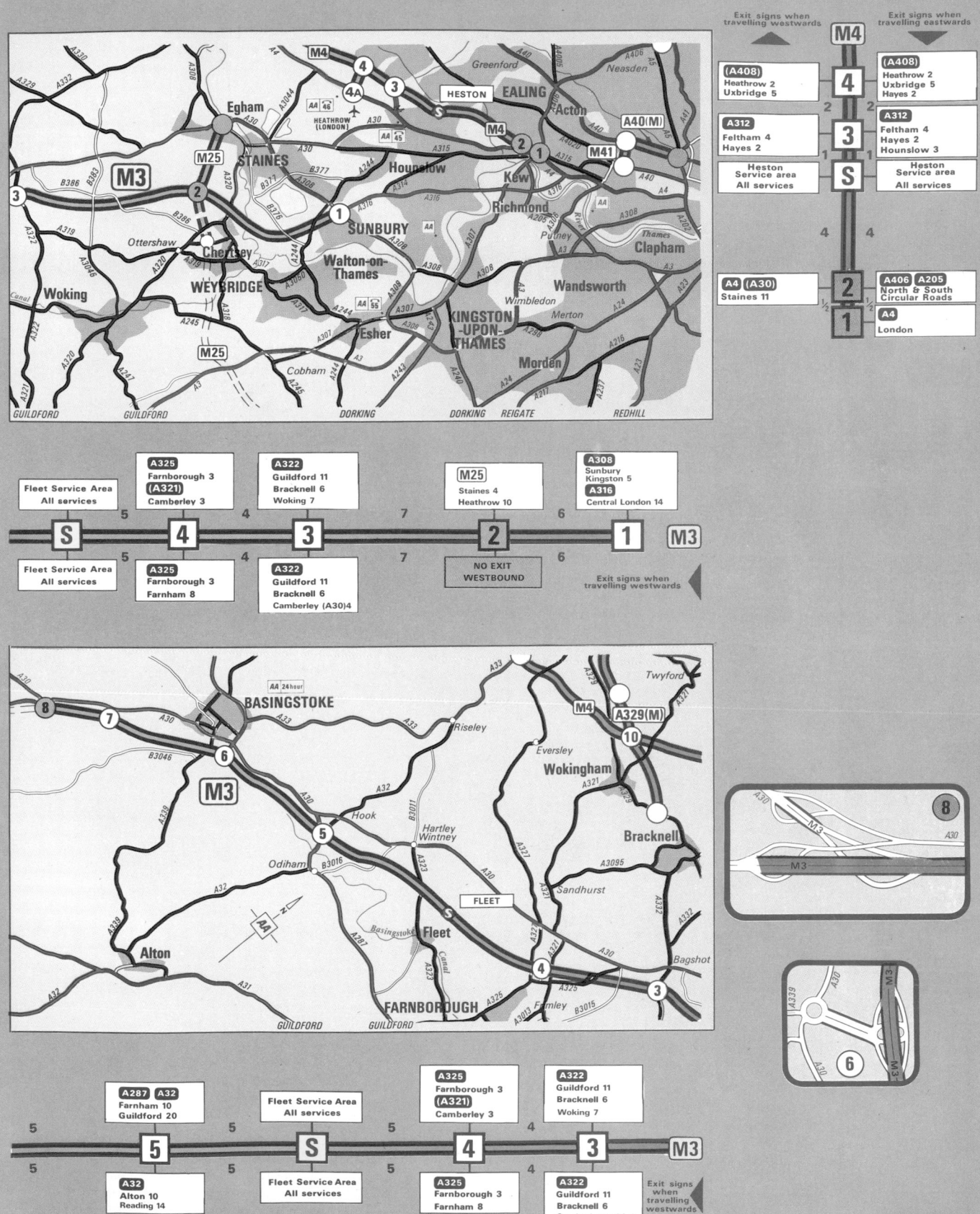

LONDON–READING

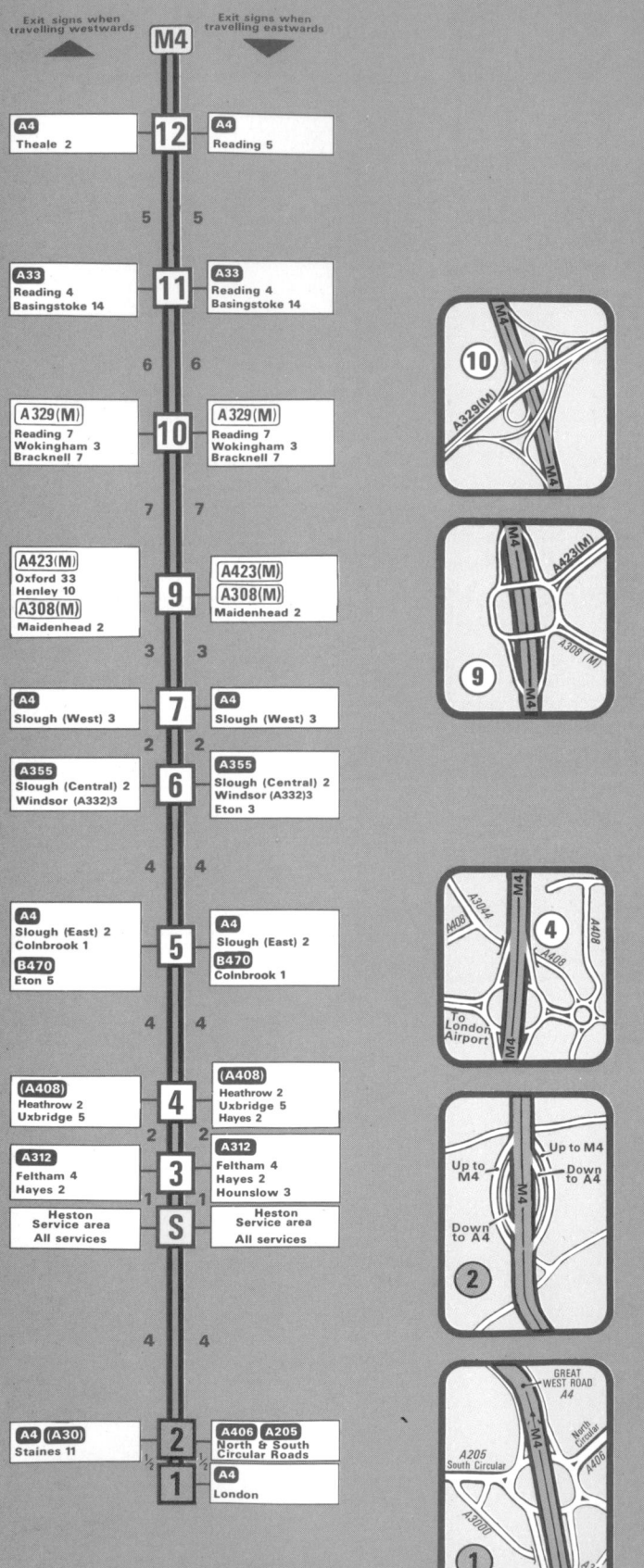

Exit signs when travelling westwards — Exit signs when travelling eastwards

M4

	12	
A4 Theale 2		**A4** Reading 5

5 — 5

| **A33** Reading 4 Basingstoke 14 | 11 | **A33** Reading 4 Basingstoke 14 |

6 — 6

| **A329(M)** Reading 7 Wokingham 3 Bracknell 7 | 10 | **A329(M)** Reading 7 Wokingham 3 Bracknell 7 |

7 — 7

| **A423(M)** Oxford 33 Henley 10 **A308(M)** Maidenhead 2 | 9 | **A423(M)** **A308(M)** Maidenhead 2 |

3 — 3

| **A4** Slough (West) 3 | 7 | **A4** Slough (West) 3 |

2 — 2

| **A355** Slough (Central) 2 Windsor (A332)3 | 6 | **A355** Slough (Central) 2 Windsor (A332)3 Eton 3 |

4 — 4

| **A4** Slough (East) 2 Colnbrook 1 **B470** Eton 5 | 5 | **A4** Slough (East) 2 **B470** Colnbrook 1 |

4 — 4

| **(A408)** Heathrow 2 Uxbridge 5 | 4 | **(A408)** Heathrow 2 Uxbridge 5 Hayes 2 |

2 — 2

| **A312** Feltham 4 Hayes 2 | 3 | **A312** Feltham 4 Hayes 2 Hounslow 3 |

1 — 1

| Heston Service area All services | **S** | Heston Service area All services |

4 — 4

| **A4 (A30)** Staines 11 | 2 | **A406 A205** North & South Circular Roads |

½ — ½

| | 1 | **A4** London |

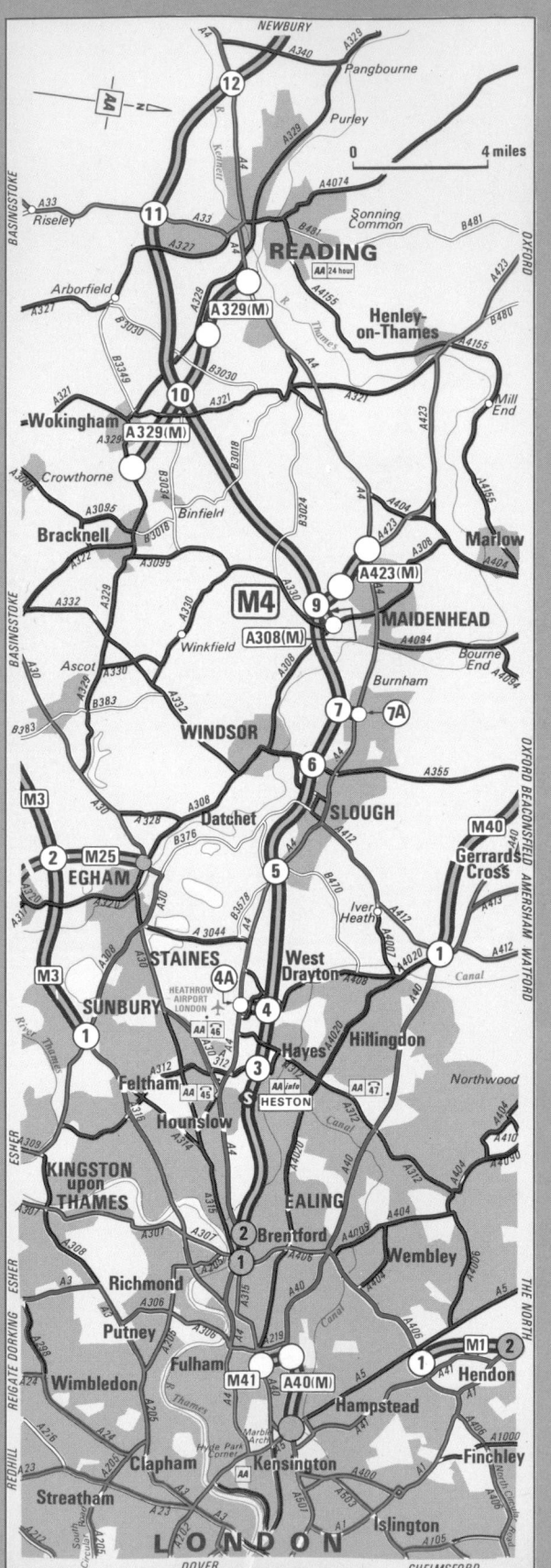

124

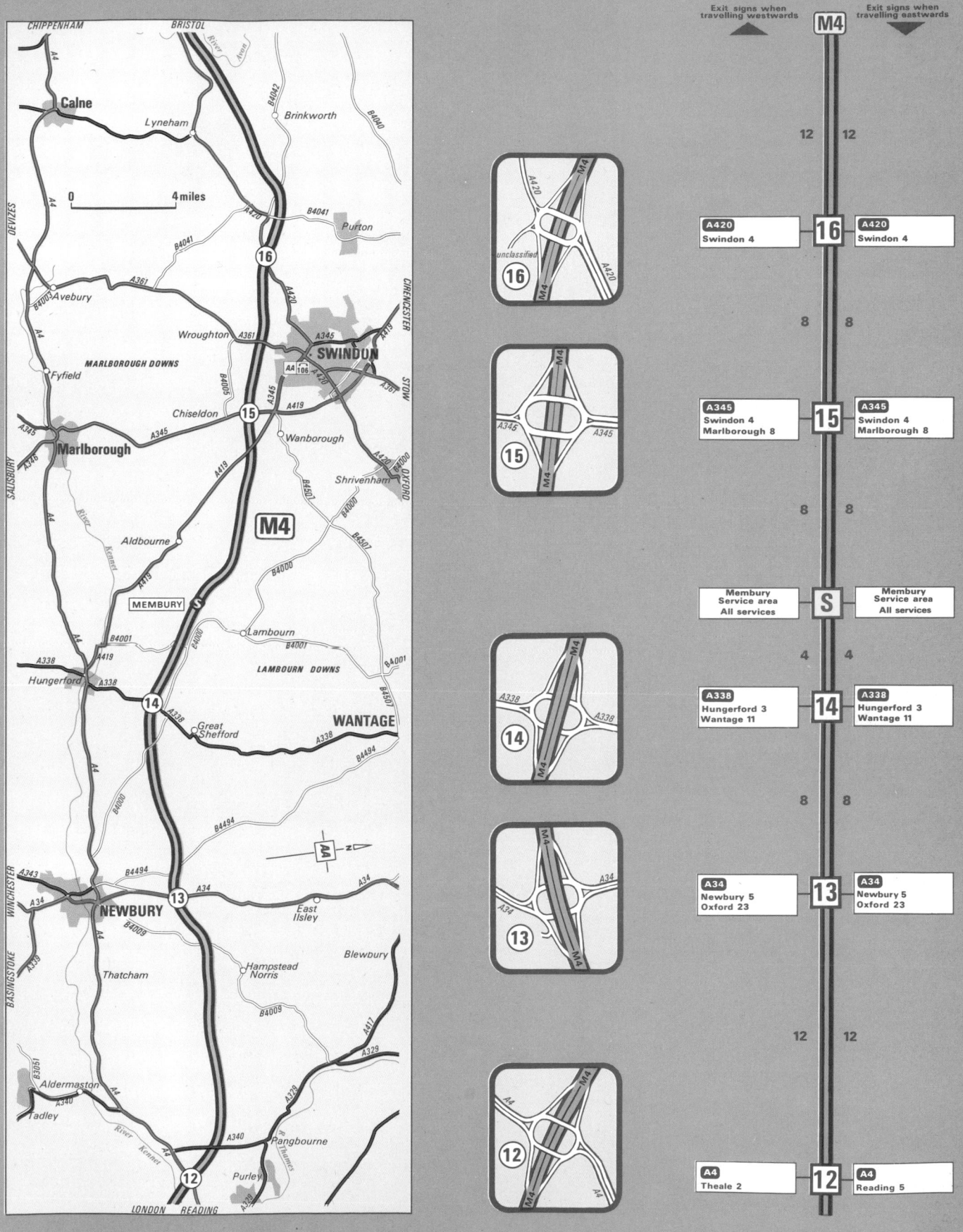

Exit signs when travelling westwards

Exit signs when travelling eastwards

M4

12   12

A420 Swindon 4   **16**   **A420** Swindon 4

8   8

A345 Swindon 4 Marlborough 8   **15**   **A345** Swindon 4 Marlborough 8

8   8

Membury Service area All services   **S**   Membury Service area All services

4   4

A338 Hungerford 3 Wantage 11   **14**   **A338** Hungerford 3 Wantage 11

8   8

A34 Newbury 5 Oxford 23   **13**   **A34** Newbury 5 Oxford 23

12   12

A4 Theale 2   **12**   **A4** Reading 5

CALNE–CASTLETON

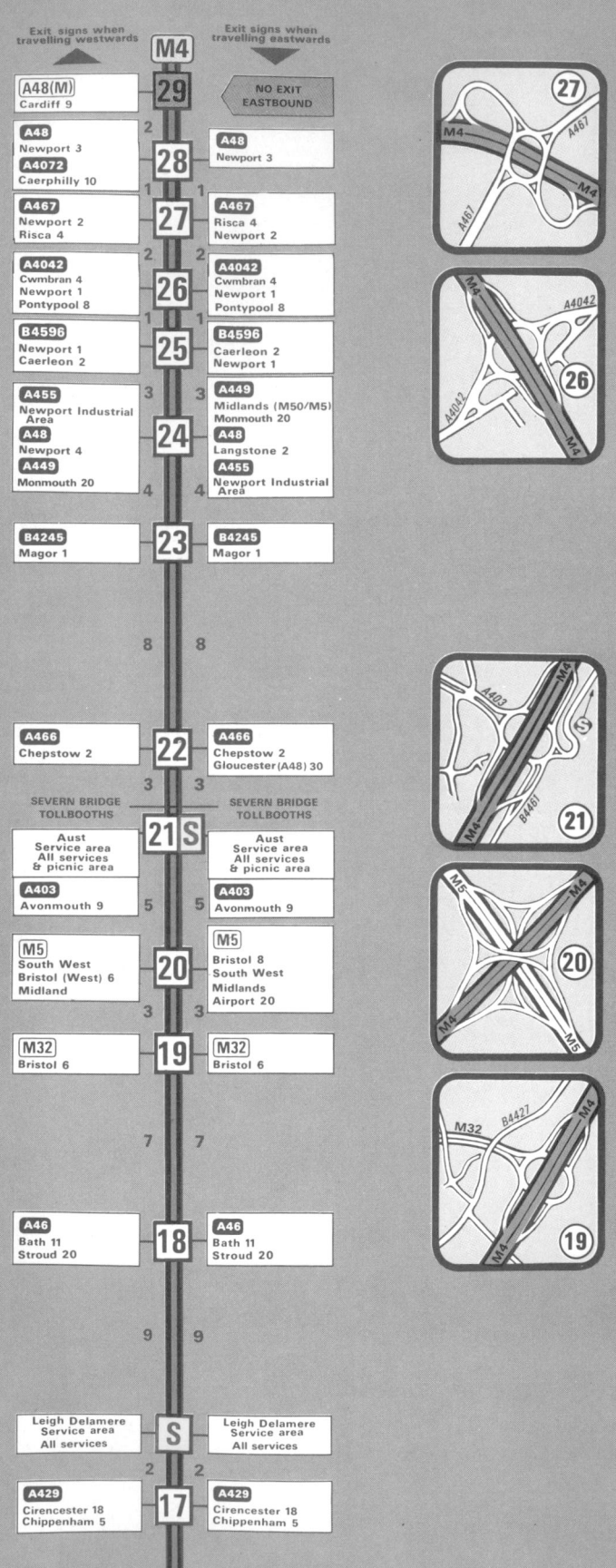

Exit signs when travelling westwards ▲ | **M4** | ▼ **Exit signs when travelling eastwards**

Westward	Exit	Eastward
A48(M) Cardiff 9	**29**	**NO EXIT EASTBOUND**
A48 Newport 3 / **A4072** Caerphilly 10	**28**	**A48** Newport 3
A467 Newport 2 / Risca 4	**27**	**A467** Risca 4 / Newport 2
A4042 Cwmbran 4 / Newport 1 / Pontypool 8	**26**	**A4042** Cwmbran 4 / Newport 1 / Pontypool 8
B4596 Newport 1 / Caerleon 2	**25**	**B4596** Caerleon 2 / Newport 1
A455 Newport Industrial Area / **A48** Newport 4 / **A449** Monmouth 20	**24**	**A449** Midlands (M50/M5) Monmouth 20 / **A48** Langstone 2 / **A455** Newport Industrial Area
B4245 Magor 1	**23**	**B4245** Magor 1
A466 Chepstow 2	**22**	**A466** Chepstow 2 / Gloucester (A48) 30
SEVERN BRIDGE TOLLBOOTHS	**21 S**	SEVERN BRIDGE TOLLBOOTHS
Aust Service area All services & picnic area		Aust Service area All services & picnic area
A403 Avonmouth 9		**A403** Avonmouth 9
M5 South West Bristol (West) 6 Midland	**20**	**M5** Bristol 8 South West Midlands Airport 20
M32 Bristol 6	**19**	**M32** Bristol 6
A46 Bath 11 Stroud 20	**18**	**A46** Bath 11 Stroud 20
Leigh Delamere Service area All services	**S**	Leigh Delamere Service area All services
A429 Cirencester 18 Chippenham 5	**17**	**A429** Cirencester 18 Chippenham 5

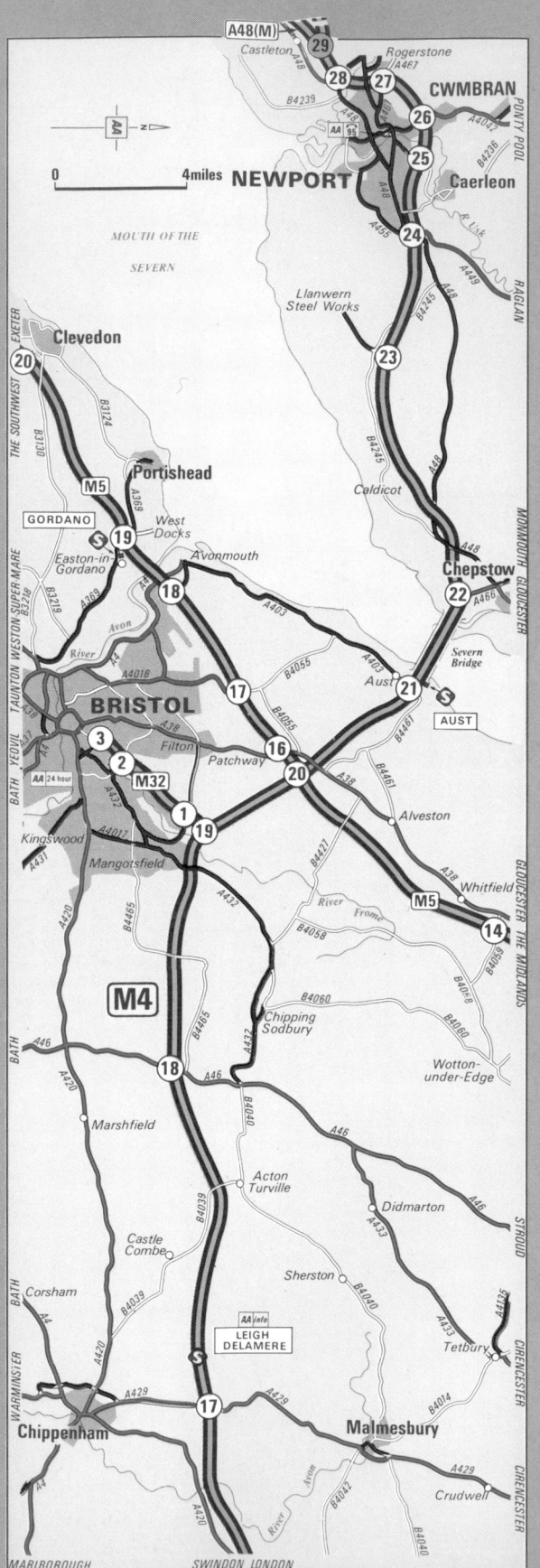

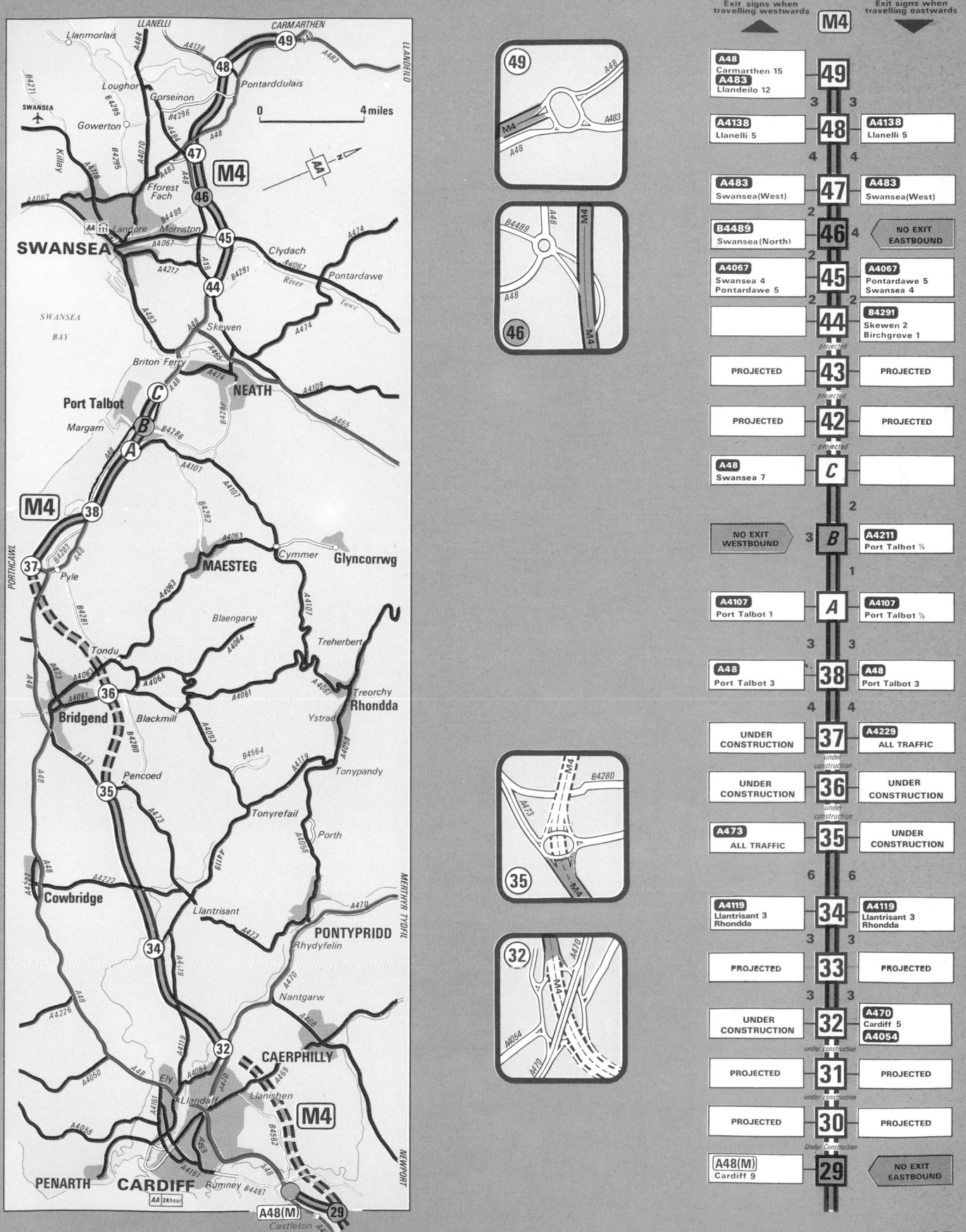

Exit signs when travelling westwards | **M4** | Exit signs when travelling eastwards

Westwards	Jct	Eastwards
A48 Carmarthen 15 / A483 Llandeilo 12	49	
A4138 Llanelli 5	48	A4138 Llanelli 5
A483 Swansea (West)	47	A483 Swansea (West)
B4489 Swansea (North)	46	NO EXIT EASTBOUND
A4067 Swansea 4 / Pontardawe 5	45	A4067 Pontardawe 5 / Swansea 4
	44	B4291 Skewen 2 / Birchgrove 1
PROJECTED	43	PROJECTED
PROJECTED	42	PROJECTED
A48 Swansea 7	C	
NO EXIT WESTBOUND	B	A4211 Port Talbot ½
A4107 Port Talbot 1	A	A4107 Port Talbot ½
A48 Port Talbot 3	38	A48 Port Talbot 3
UNDER CONSTRUCTION	37	A4229 ALL TRAFFIC
UNDER CONSTRUCTION	36	UNDER CONSTRUCTION
A473 ALL TRAFFIC	35	UNDER CONSTRUCTION
A4119 Llantrisant 3 / Rhondda	34	A4119 Llantrisant 3 / Rhondda
PROJECTED	33	PROJECTED
UNDER CONSTRUCTION	32	A470 Cardiff 5 / A4054
PROJECTED	31	PROJECTED
PROJECTED	30	PROJECTED
A48(M) Cardiff 9	29	NO EXIT EASTBOUND

127

BIRMINGHAM–TEWKESBURY

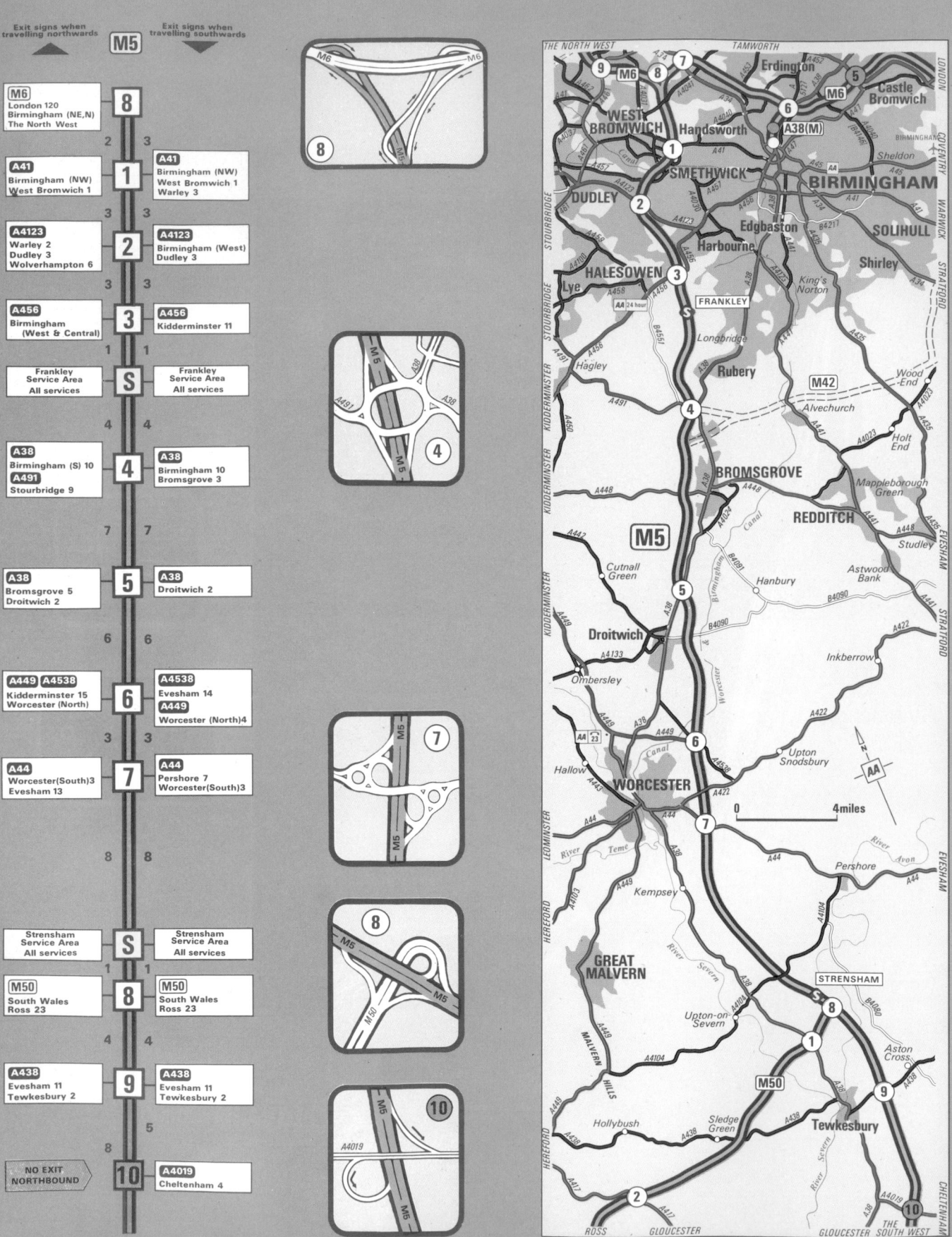

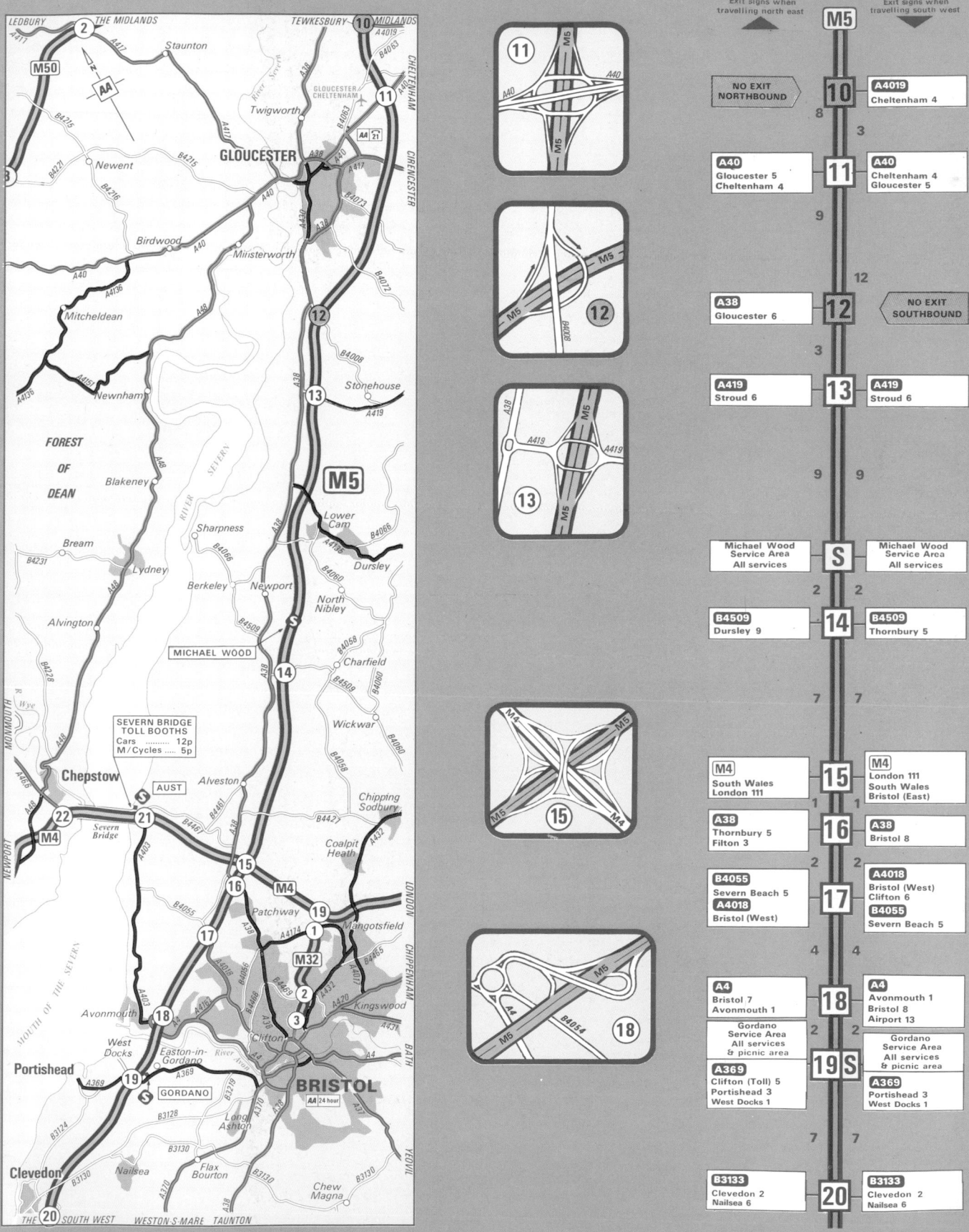

CLEVEDON–WATERLOO CROSS

Exit signs when travelling north east ▲

Exit signs when travelling south west ▼

M5

20
B3133	B3133
Clevedon 2	Clevedon 2
Nailsea 6	Nailsea 6

6   6

21
A370	A370
Weston-super-Mare 5	Weston-super-Mare 5
Bristol South 17	

7   7

P
| Brent Knoll (W) | Brent Knoll (E) |
| Rest Area | Rest Area |

3   3

22
A38	A38
Weston-super-Mare 9	Highbridge 2
Burnham-on-Sea 3	Burnham-on-Sea 3
Bristol (South) 24	
Airport 17	

5   5

23
A38	A38
Highbridge 5	Bridgwater 4
(A39)	(A39)
Glastonbury 14	Glastonbury 14

5   5

24
A38	(A39)
Bridgwater 2	Minehead 28
Minehead 28	

7   7

25
A358	A358
Taunton 2	Taunton 2
Yeovil 24	Yeovil 24

5   5

S
Taunton Deane	Taunton Deane
Service Area	Service Area
All services	All services

2   2

26
A38	A38
Wellington 2	Wellington 2
Taunton 6	

8   8

27
A373	A373
Tiverton 7	Tiverton 7
Wellington 8	

㉑ ㉒ ㉔

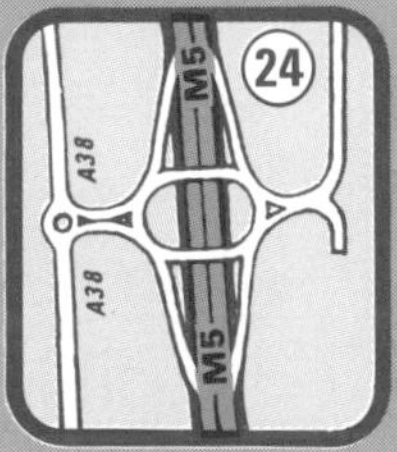

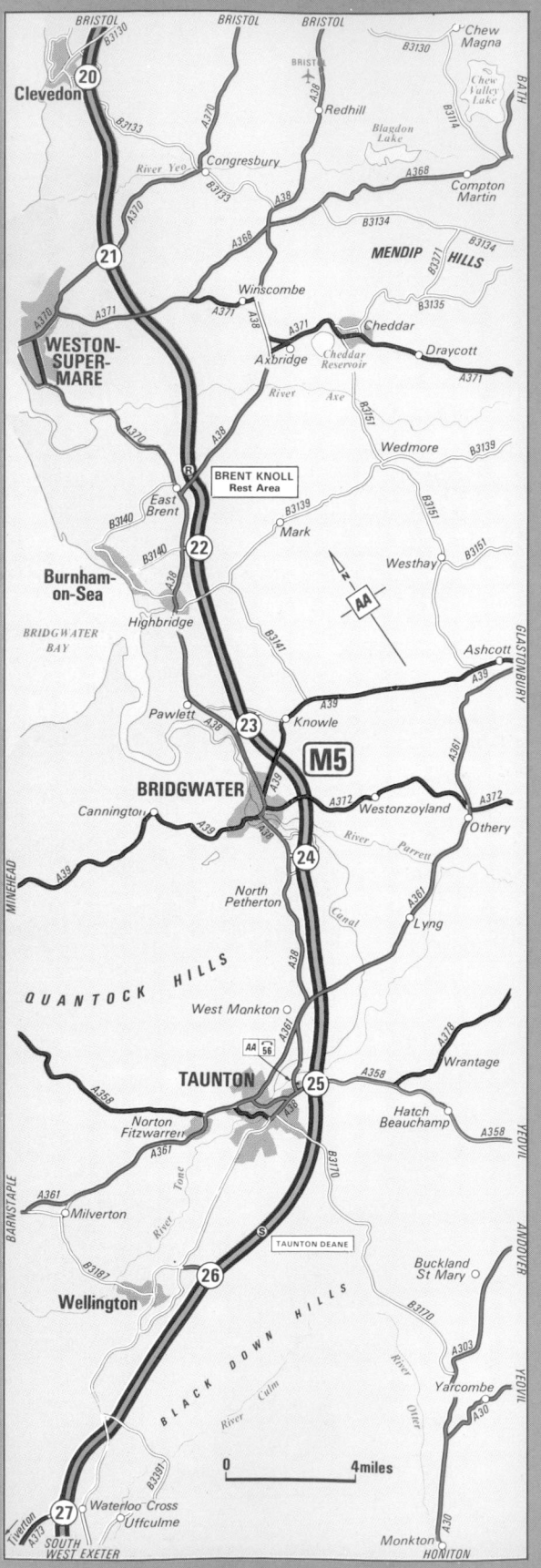

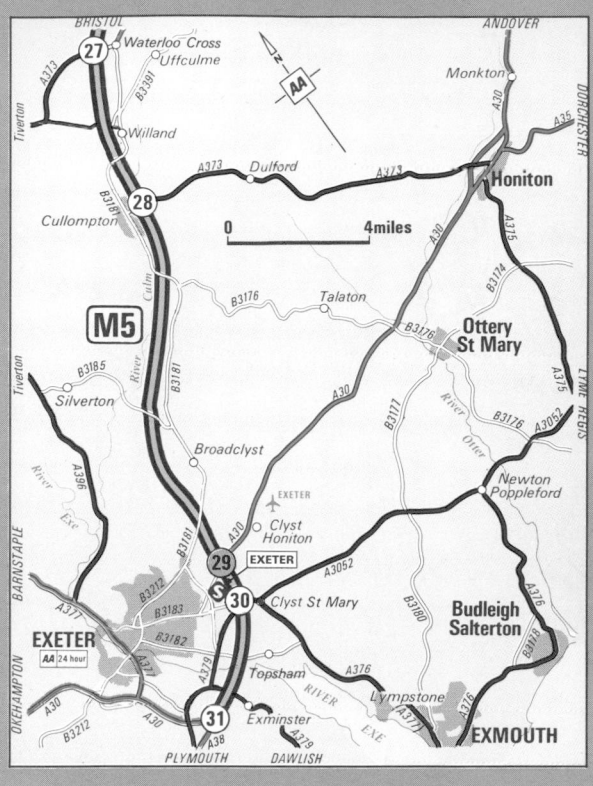

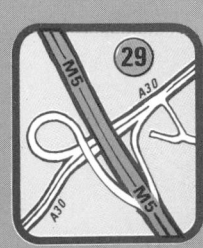

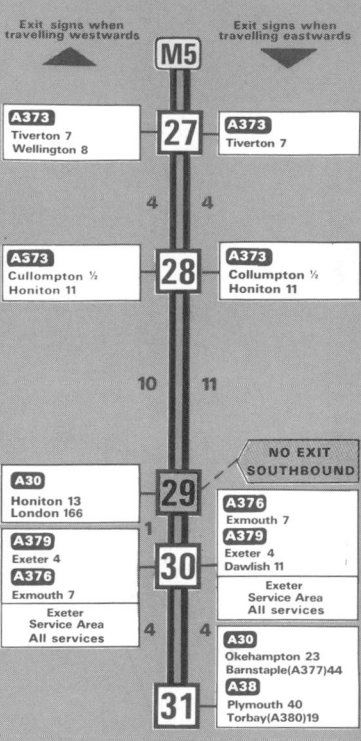

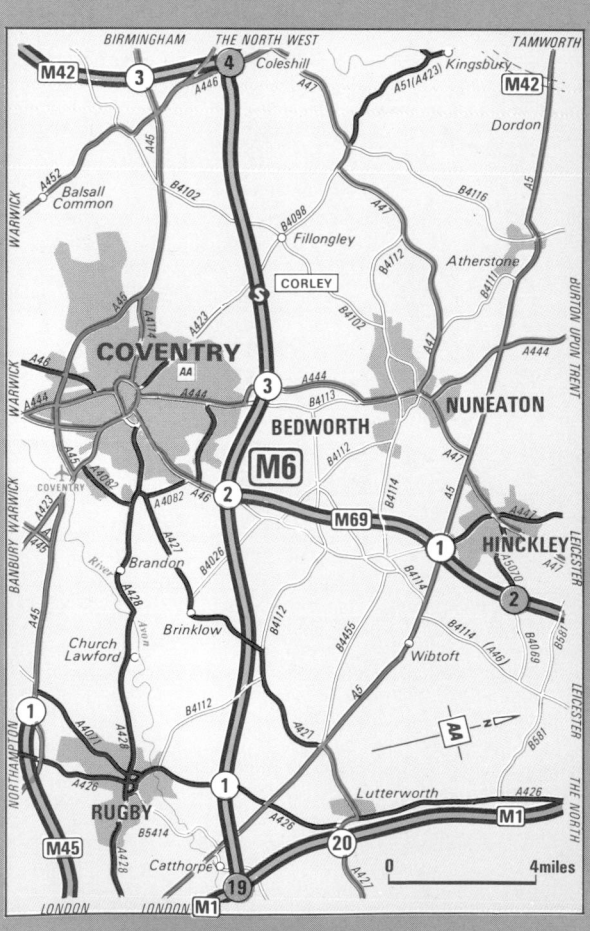

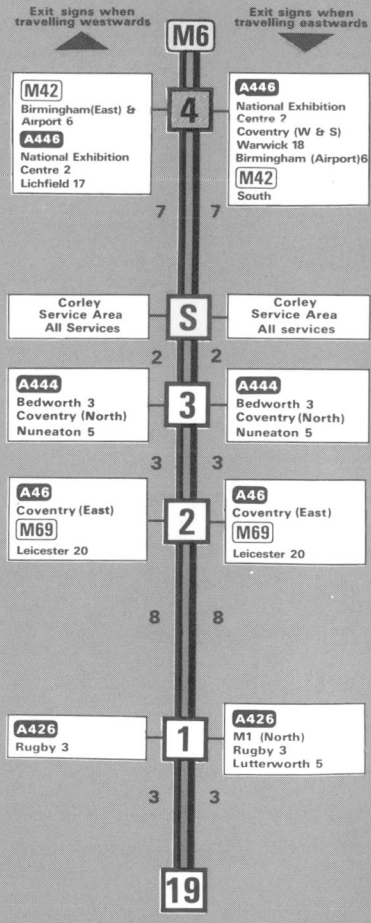

COLESHILL–STOKE

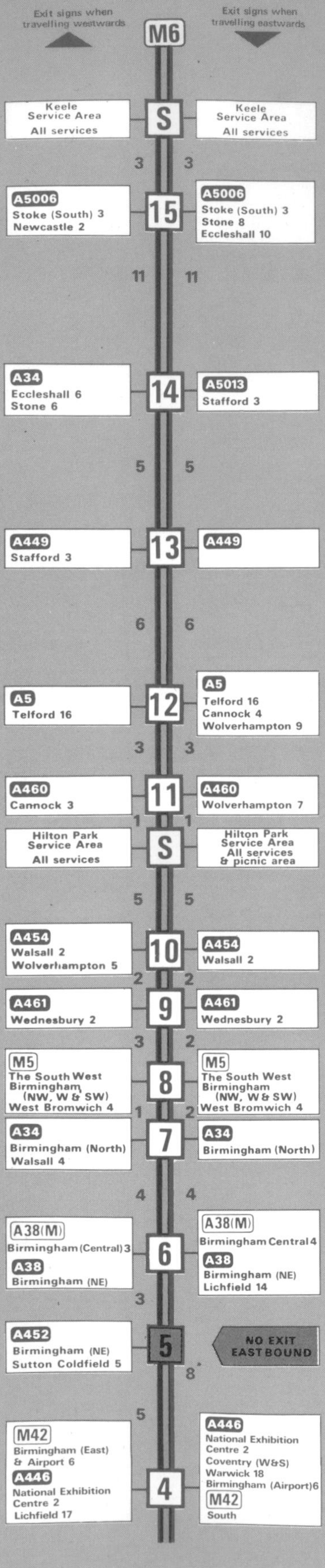

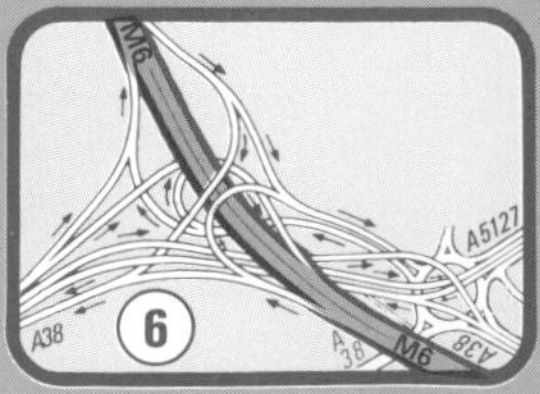

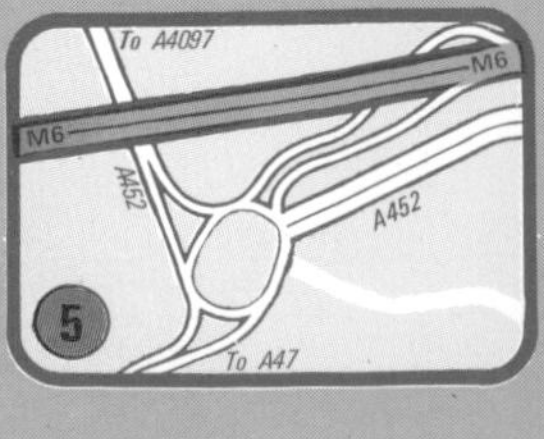

M6

Westbound	Jct	Eastbound
S Keele Service Area — All services	**S**	Keele Service Area — All services
3		3
A5006 Stoke (South) 3 — Newcastle 2	**15**	**A5006** Stoke (South) 3 — Stone 8 — Eccleshall 10
11		11
A34 Eccleshall 6 — Stone 6	**14**	**A5013** Stafford 3
5		5
A449 Stafford 3	**13**	**A449**
6		6
A5 Telford 16	**12**	**A5** Telford 16 — Cannock 4 — Wolverhampton 9
3		3
A460 Cannock 3	**11**	**A460** Wolverhampton 7
1		1
S Hilton Park Service Area — All services	**S**	Hilton Park Service Area — All services & picnic area
5		5
A454 Walsall 2 — Wolverhampton 5	**10**	**A454** Walsall 2
2		2
A461 Wednesbury 2	**9**	**A461** Wednesbury 2
3		2
M5 The South West Birmingham (NW, W & SW) — West Bromwich 4	**8**	**M5** The South West Birmingham (NW, W & SW) — West Bromwich 4
1		2
A34 Birmingham (North) — Walsall 4	**7**	**A34** Birmingham (North)
4		4
A38(M) Birmingham (Central) 3 — **A38** Birmingham (NE)	**6**	**A38(M)** Birmingham Central 4 — **A38** Birmingham (NE) — Lichfield 14
3		
A452 Birmingham (NE) — Sutton Coldfield 5	**5**	NO EXIT EAST BOUND
5		8
M42 Birmingham (East) & Airport 6 — **A446** National Exhibition Centre 2 — Lichfield 17	**4**	**A446** National Exhibition Centre 2 — Coventry (W&S) — Warwick 18 — Birmingham (Airport) 6 — **M42** South

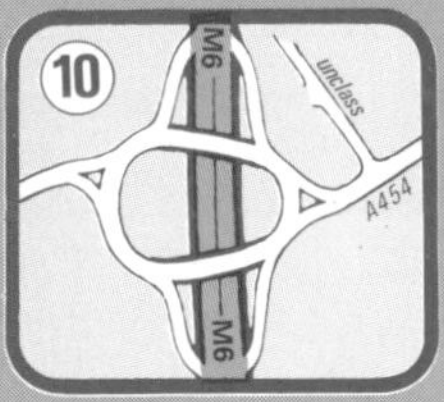

10 — M6 / A454 roundabout

6 — motorway interchange — A38 / A5127 / M6

5 — To A4097 / M6 / A452 / A47

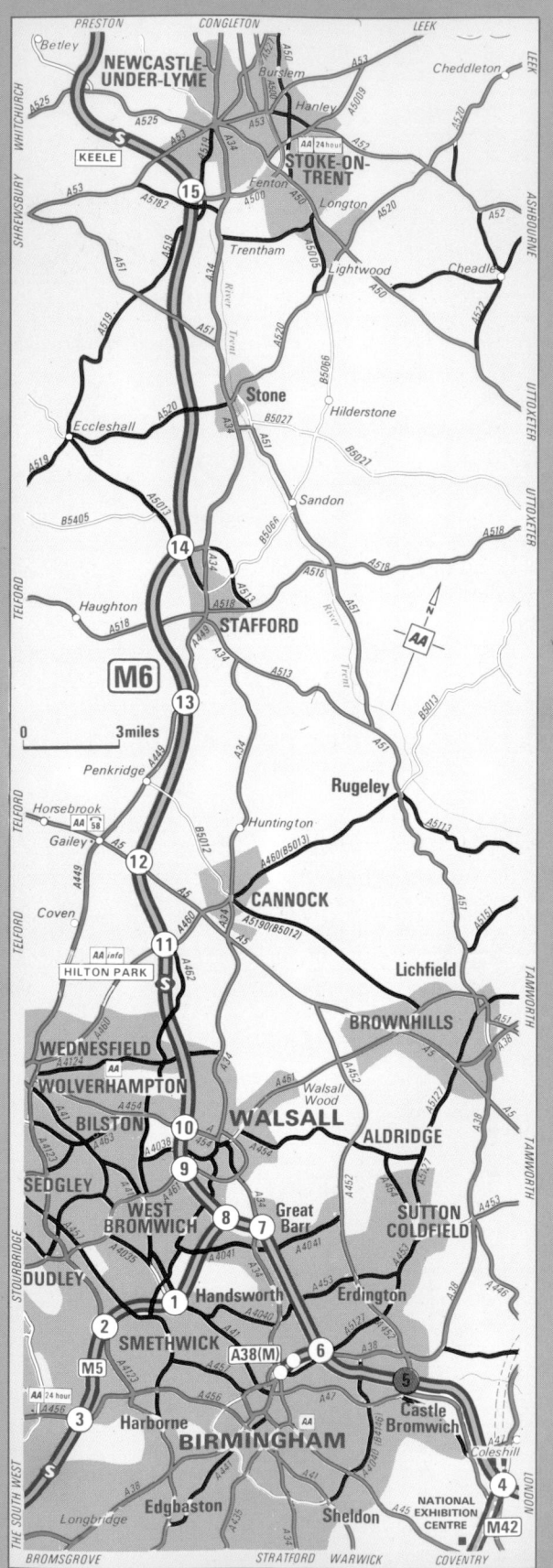

132

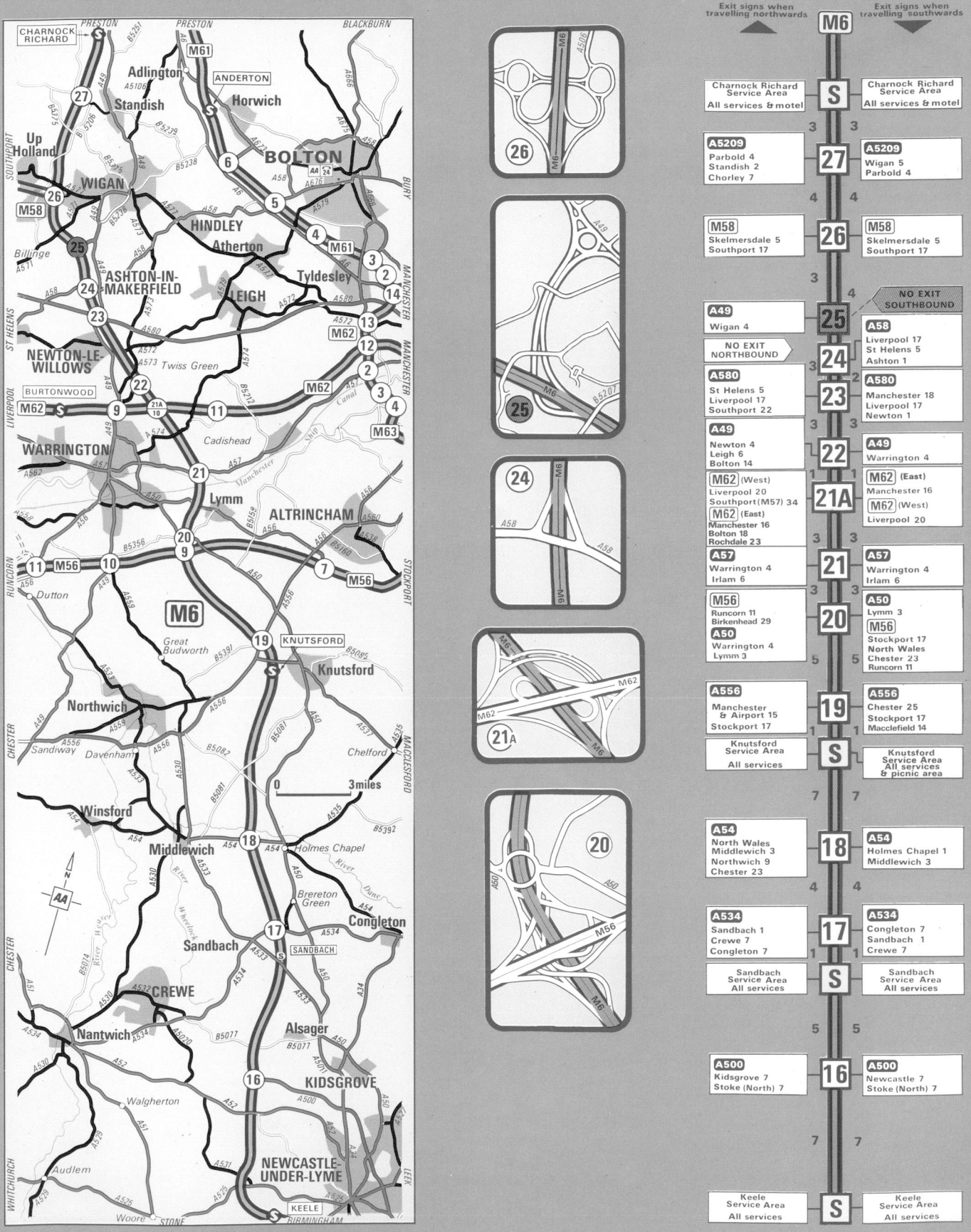

0   3 miles

Exit signs when travelling northwards ◄   **M6**   ▼ **Exit signs when travelling southwards**

Jct	Northbound	Southbound
S	Charnock Richard Service Area — All services & motel	Charnock Richard Service Area — All services & motel
27	A5209 Parbold 4, Standish 2, Chorley 7	A5209 Wigan 5, Parbold 4
26	M58 Skelmersdale 5, Southport 17	M58 Skelmersdale 5, Southport 17
25	A49 Wigan 4	NO EXIT SOUTHBOUND
24	NO EXIT NORTHBOUND	A58 Liverpool 17, St Helens 5, Ashton 1
23	A580 St Helens 5, Liverpool 17, Southport 22	A580 Manchester 18, Liverpool 17, Newton 1
22	A49 Newton 4, Leigh 6, Bolton 14	A49 Warrington 4
21A	M62 (West) Liverpool 20, Southport (M57) 34; M62 (East) Manchester 16, Bolton 18, Rochdale 23	M62 (East) Manchester 16; M62 (West) Liverpool 20
21	A57 Warrington 4, Irlam 6	A57 Warrington 4, Irlam 6
20	M56 Runcorn 11, Birkenhead 29; A50 Warrington 4, Lymm 3	A50 Lymm 3; M56 Stockport 17, North Wales, Chester 23, Runcorn 11
19	A556 Manchester & Airport 15, Stockport 17	A556 Chester 25, Stockport 17, Macclesfield 14
S	Knutsford Service Area — All services	Knutsford Service Area — All services & picnic area
18	A54 North Wales, Middlewich 3, Northwich 9, Chester 23	A54 Holmes Chapel 1, Middlewich 3
17	A534 Sandbach 1, Crewe 7, Congleton 7	A534 Congleton 7, Sandbach 1, Crewe 7
S	Sandbach Service Area — All services	Sandbach Service Area — All services
16	A500 Kidsgrove 7, Stoke (North) 7	A500 Newcastle 7, Stoke (North) 7
S	Keele Service Area — All services	Keele Service Area — All services

133

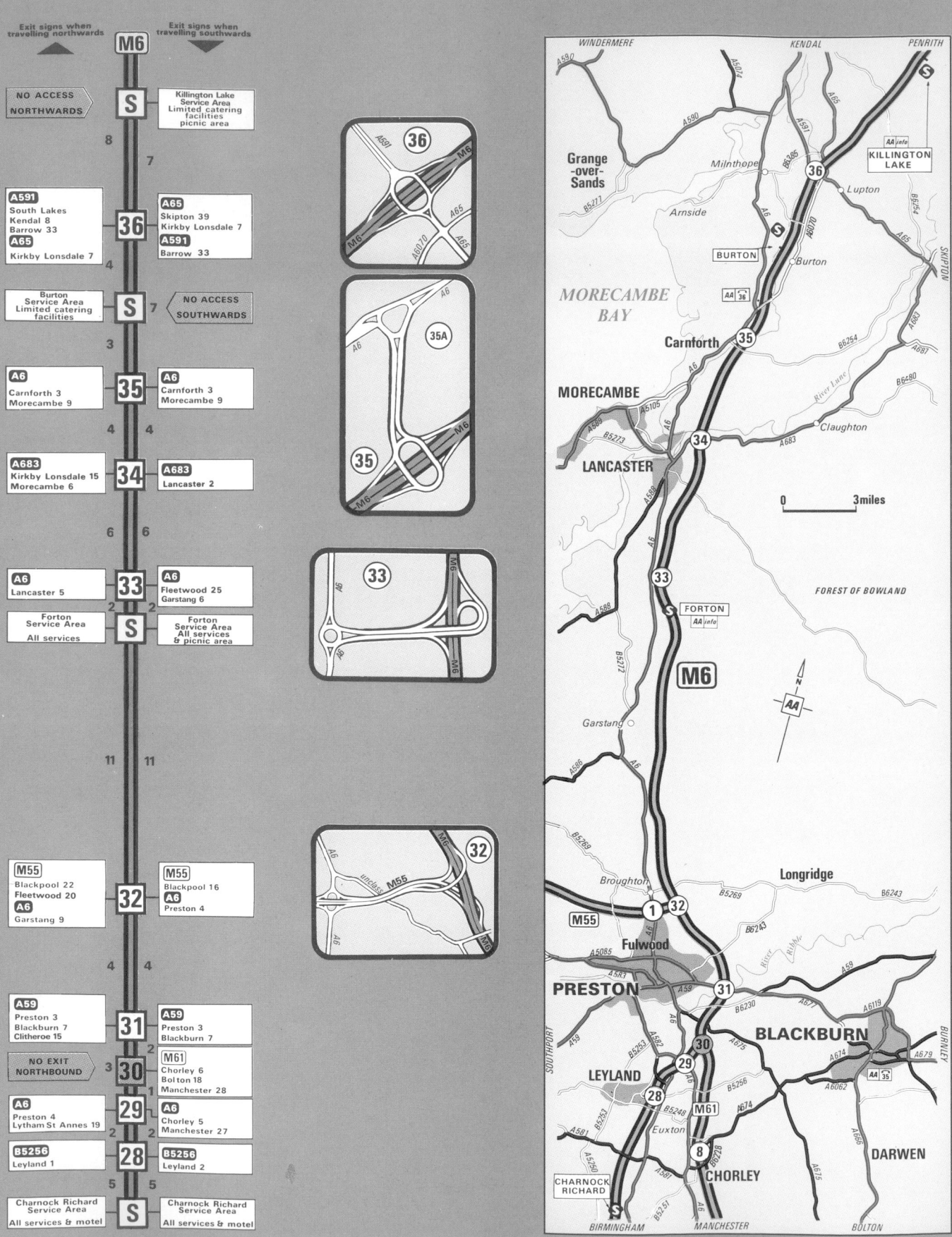

M6

S

NO ACCESS
NORTHWARDS

Killington Lake
Service Area
Limited catering
facilities
picnic area

8

7

36

A591
South Lakes
Kendal 8
Barrow 33
A65
Kirkby Lonsdale 7

A65
Skipton 39
Kirkby Lonsdale 7
A591
Barrow 33

4

S

Burton
Service Area
Limited catering
facilities

NO ACCESS
SOUTHWARDS

7

3

35

A6
Carnforth 3
Morecambe 9

A6
Carnforth 3
Morecambe 9

4

4

34

A683
Kirkby Lonsdale 15
Morecambe 6

A683
Lancaster 2

6

6

33

A6
Lancaster 5

A6
Fleetwood 25
Garstang 6

2

2

S

Forton
Service Area

All services

Forton
Service Area
All services
& picnic area

11

11

32

M55
Blackpool 22
Fleetwood 20
A6
Garstang 9

M55
Blackpool 16
A6
Preston 4

4

4

31

A59
Preston 3
Blackburn 7
Clitheroe 15

A59
Preston 3
Blackburn 7

2

2

30

NO EXIT
NORTHBOUND

M61
Chorley 6
Bolton 18
Manchester 28

3

1

29

A6
Preston 4
Lytham St Annes 19

A6
Chorley 5
Manchester 27

2

2

28

B5256
Leyland 1

B5256
Leyland 2

5

5

S

Charnock Richard
Service Area

All services & motel

Charnock Richard
Service Area

All services & motel

KENDAL–CARLISLE

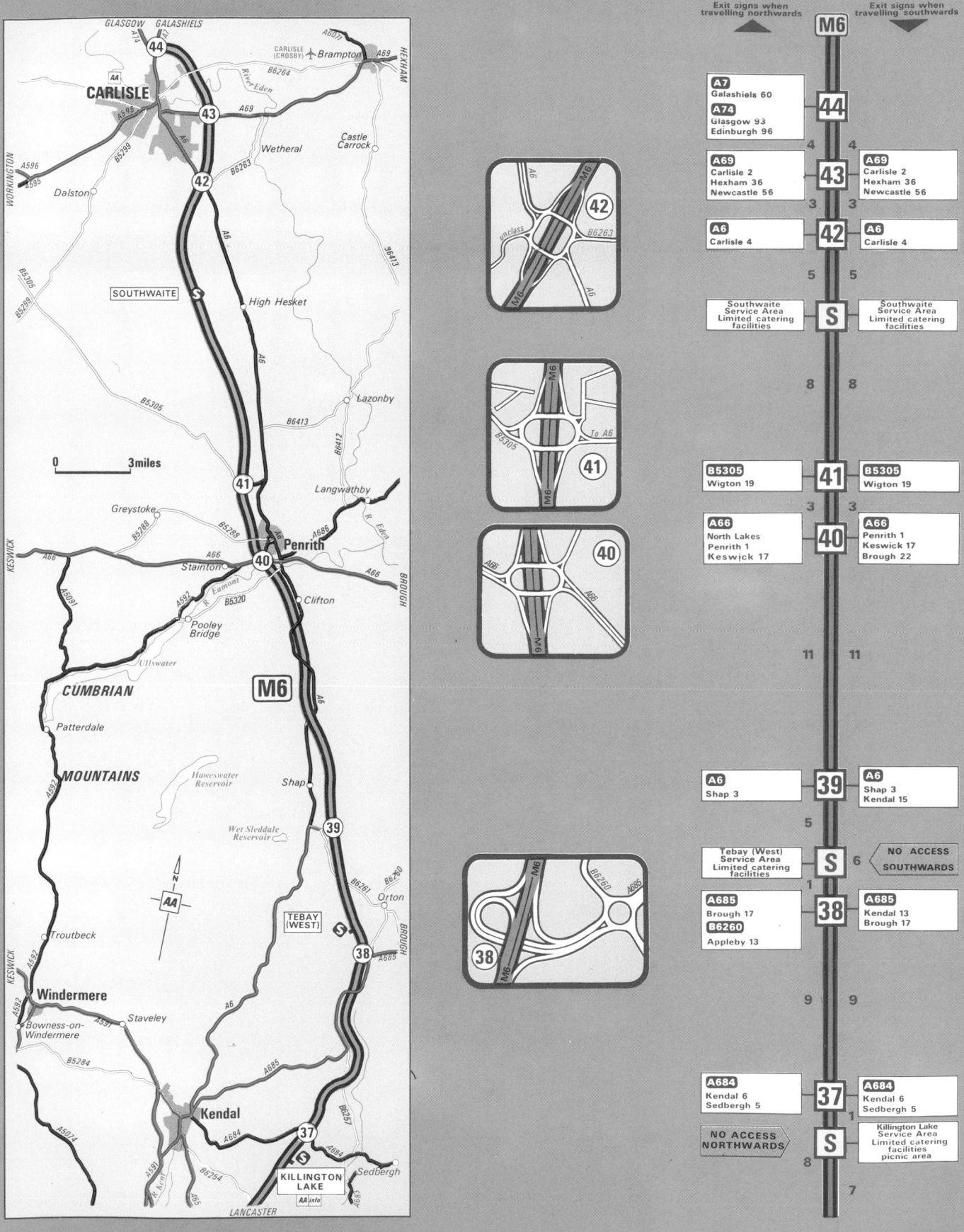

LONDON AREA

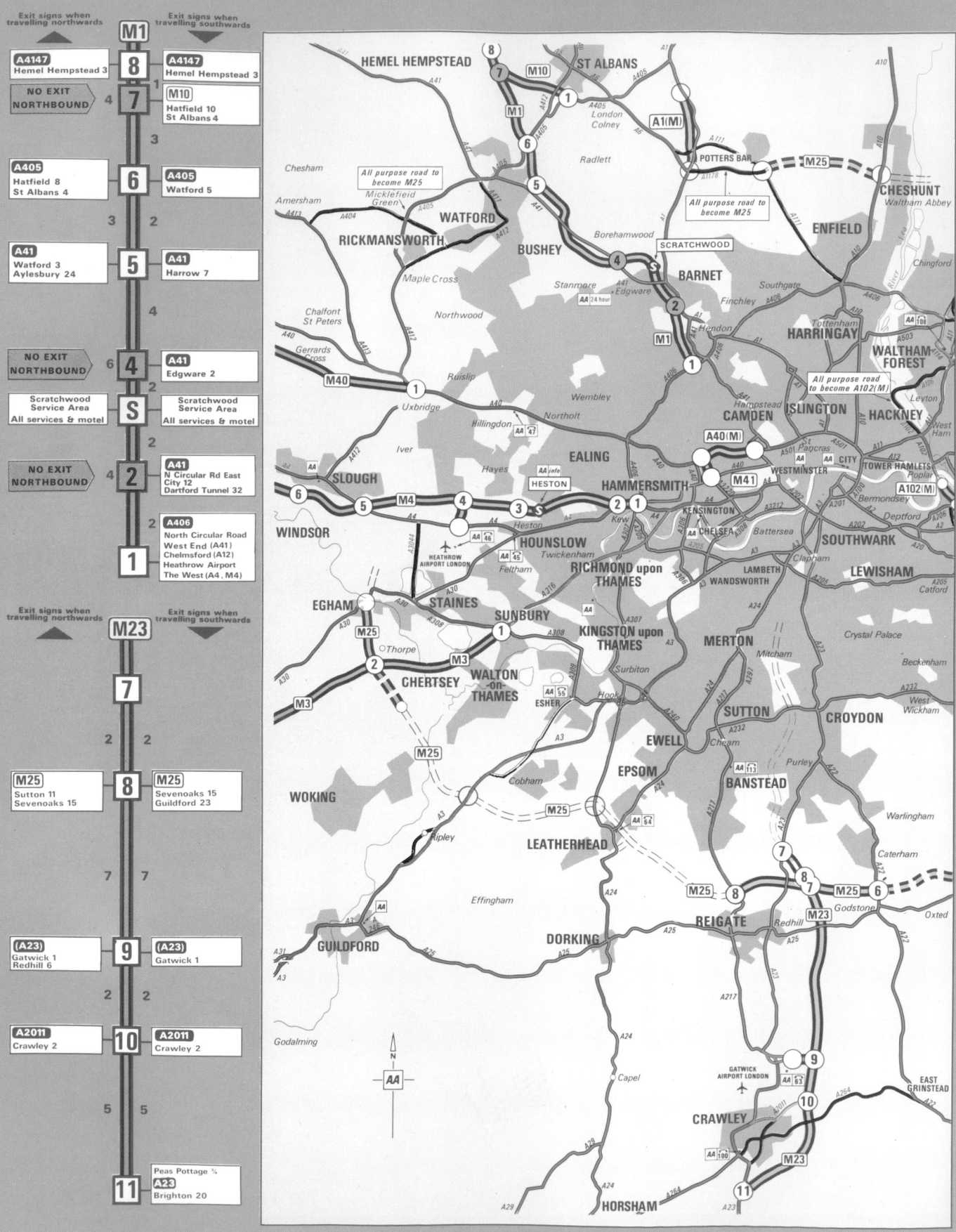

M1

Exit signs when travelling northwards | Exit signs when travelling southwards

8
A4147 Hemel Hempstead 3 | A4147 Hemel Hempstead 3

7
NO EXIT NORTHBOUND | M10 Hatfield 10 St Albans 4

6
A405 Hatfield 8 St Albans 4 | A405 Watford 5

5
A41 Watford 3 Aylesbury 24 | A41 Harrow 7

4
NO EXIT NORTHBOUND | A41 Edgware 2

S
Scratchwood Service Area All services & motel | Scratchwood Service Area All services & motel

2
NO EXIT NORTHBOUND | A41 N Circular Rd East City 12 Dartford Tunnel 32

1
| A406 North Circular Road West End (A41) Chelmsford (A12) Heathrow Airport The West (A4, M4)

M23

Exit signs when travelling northwards | Exit signs when travelling southwards

7

8
M25 Sutton 11 Sevenoaks 15 | M25 Sevenoaks 15 Guildford 23

9
(A23) Gatwick 1 Redhill 6 | (A23) Gatwick 1

10
A2011 Crawley 2 | A2011 Crawley 2

11
| Peas Pottage ¼ A23 Brighton 20

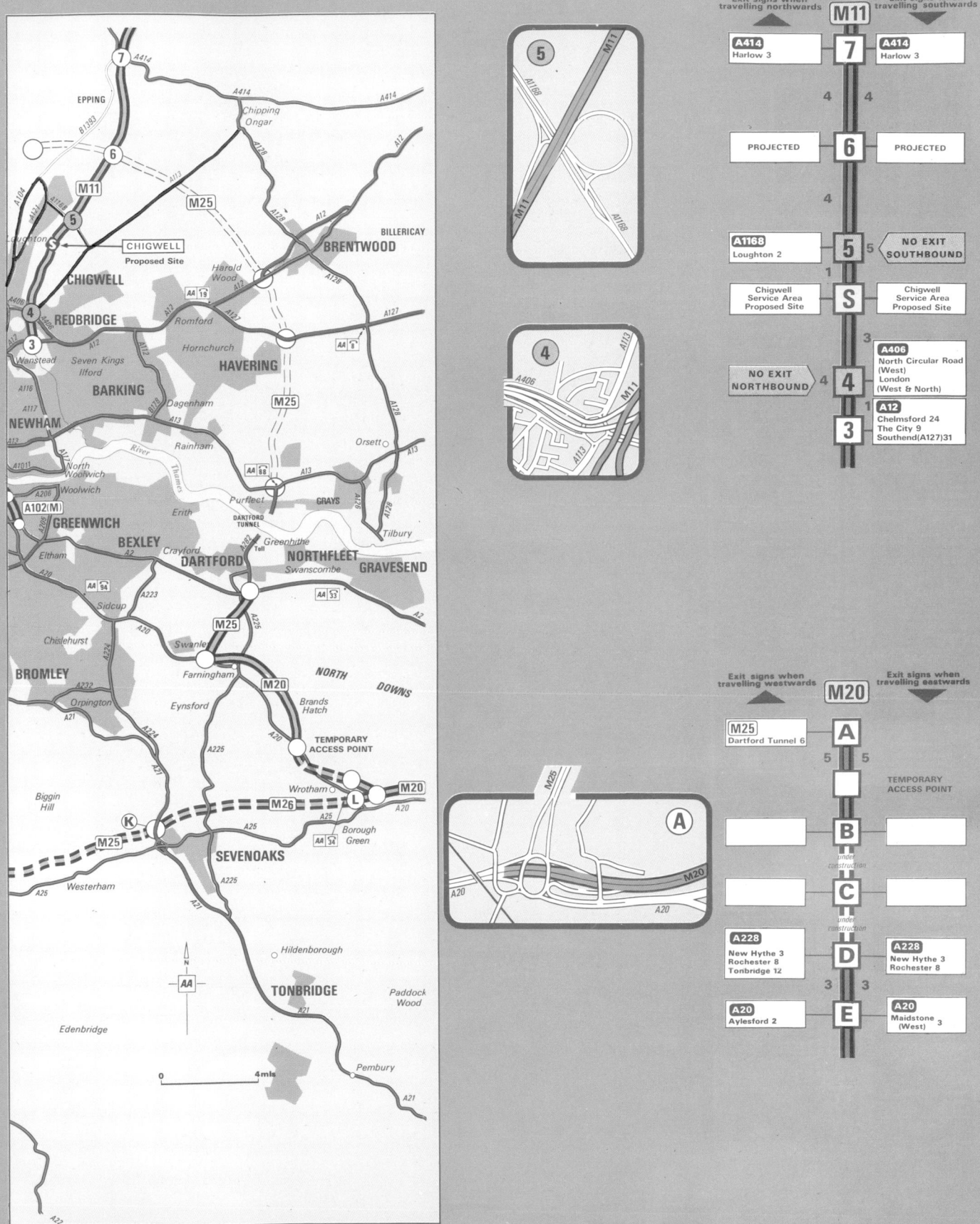

Exit signs when travelling northwards

Exit signs when travelling southwards

M11

| A414 Harlow 3 | **7** | A414 Harlow 3 |

4   4

| PROJECTED | **6** | PROJECTED |

4

| A1168 Loughton 2 | **5** | NO EXIT SOUTHBOUND |

1

| Chigwell Service Area Proposed Site | **S** | Chigwell Service Area Proposed Site |

3

| NO EXIT NORTHBOUND | **4** | A406 North Circular Road (West) London (West & North) |

1

| | **3** | A12 Chelmsford 24 The City 9 Southend(A127)31 |

Exit signs when travelling westwards

Exit signs when travelling eastwards

M20

| M25 Dartford Tunnel 6 | **A** | |

5   5

| | | TEMPORARY ACCESS POINT |

| | **B** | |

under construction

| | **C** | |

under construction

| A228 New Hythe 3 Rochester 8 Tonbridge 12 | **D** | A228 New Hythe 3 Rochester 8 |

3   3

| A20 Aylesford 2 | **E** | A20 Maidstone (West) 3 |

TEMPORARY ACCESS POINT

CADNAM–CHICHESTER

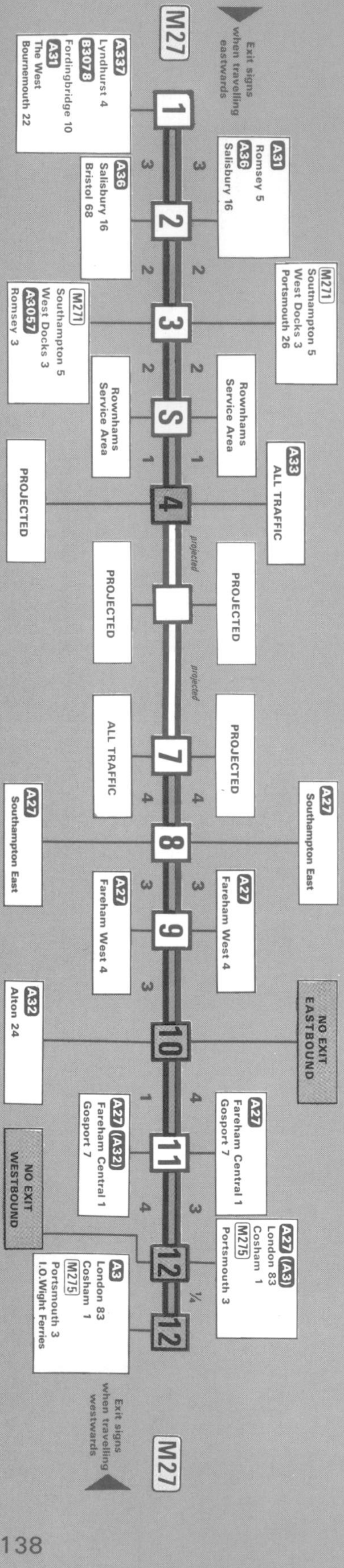

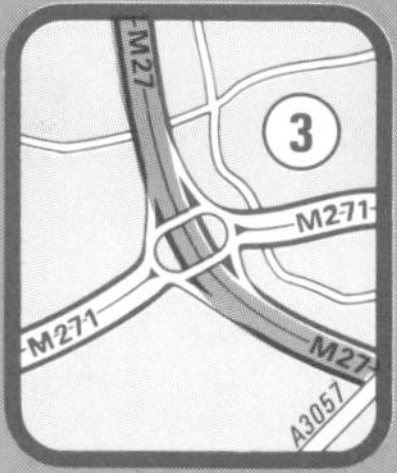

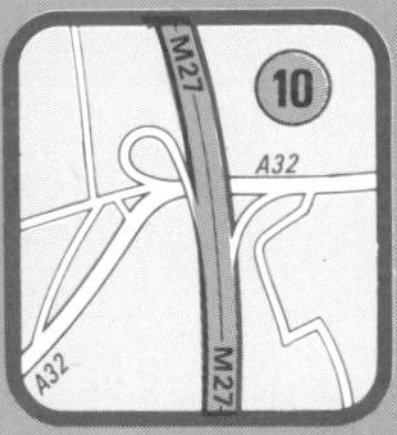

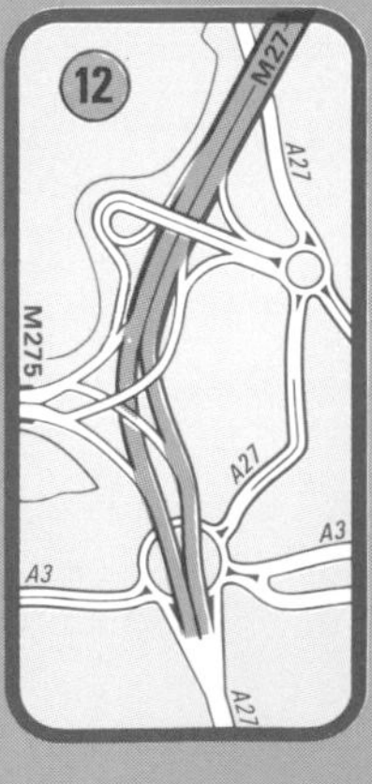

M27

▼ Exit signs when travelling eastwards

A337 Lyndhurst 4
B3078 Fordingbridge 10
A31 The West
Bournemouth 22

1

A31 Romsey 5
A36 Salisbury 16

A36 Salisbury 16
Bristol 68

2

3 | 2 | 2 | 3

M271 Southampton 5
West Docks 3
Portsmouth 26

M271 Southampton 5
West Docks 3
Romsey 3

3

2 | 2 | 2 | 2

Rownhams
Service Area

Rownhams
Service Area

S

1 | 1

PROJECTED

A33 ALL TRAFFIC

4

projected

PROJECTED

PROJECTED

PROJECTED

projected

ALL TRAFFIC

PROJECTED

7

4 | 4 | 4 | 4

A27 Southampton East

A27 Southampton East

8

3 | 3 | 3 | 3

A27 Fareham West 4

A27 Fareham West 4

9

3 | 3 | 3 | 3

A32 Alton 24

NO EXIT
EASTBOUND

10

A27 (A32) Fareham
Central 1
Gosport 7

1 | 4 | 4 | 3

A27 Fareham Central 1
Gosport 7

NO EXIT
WESTBOUND

11

4 | 3 | 3

A27 (A3) London 83
Cosham 1
M275 Portsmouth 3

A3 London 83
M275 Cosham 1
I.O.Wight Ferries

12

¼

12

▲ Exit signs when travelling westwards

M27

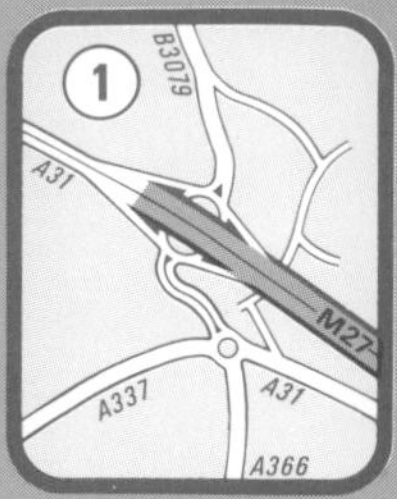

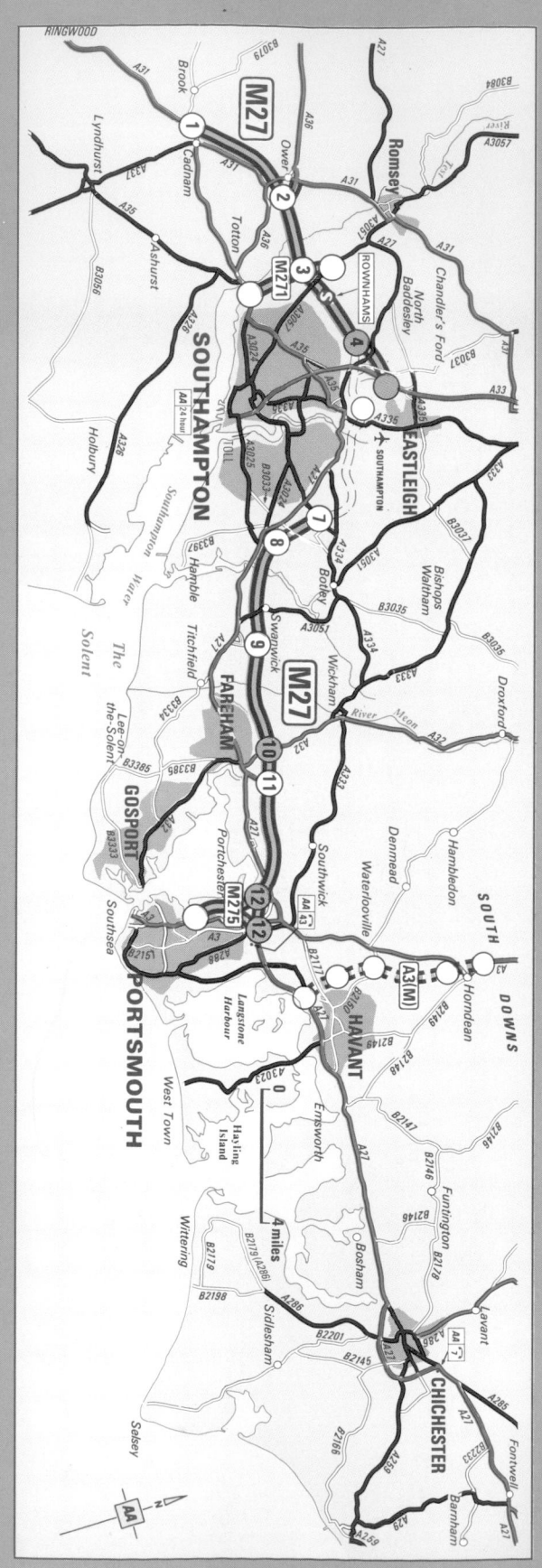

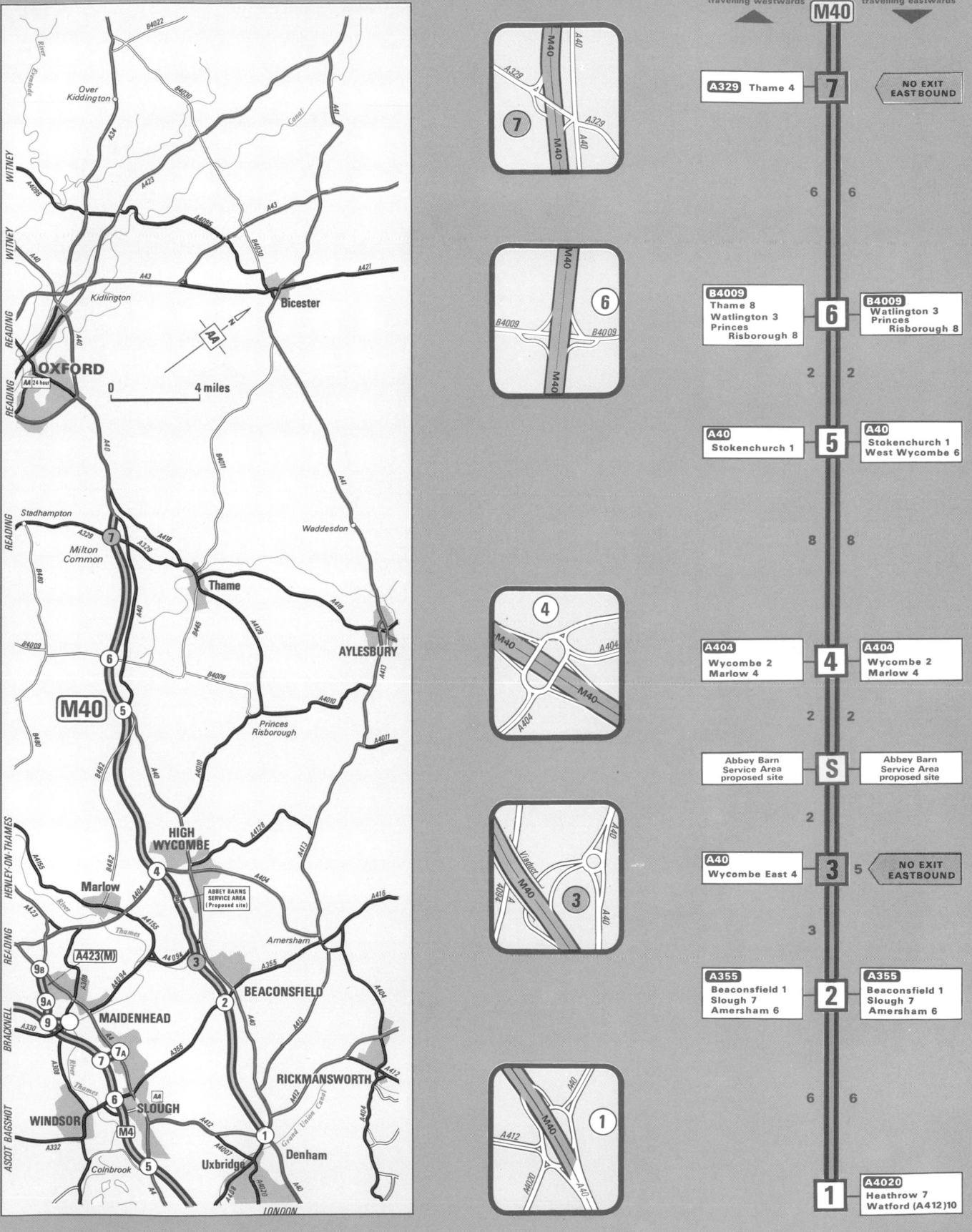

BROMSGROVE–COLESHILL

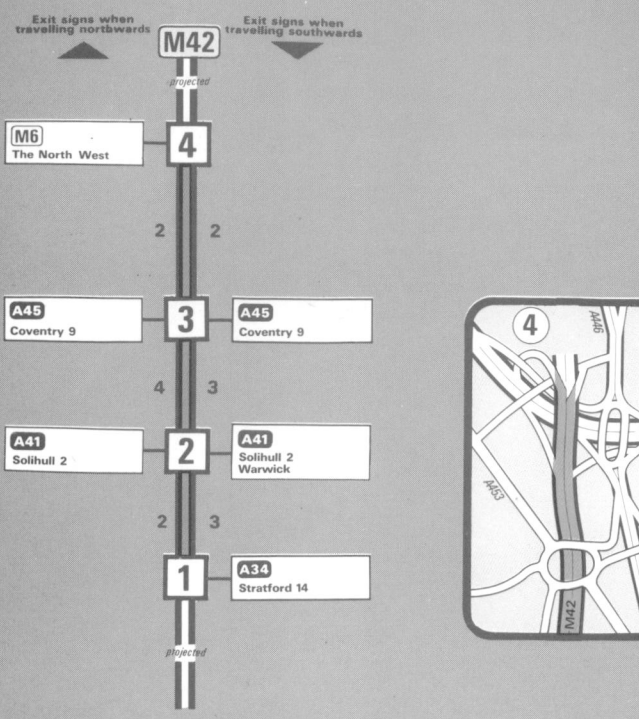

Exit signs when travelling northwards

Exit signs when travelling southwards

M42
projected

M6
The North West

4

2   2

A45
Coventry 9

A45
Coventry 9

3

4   3

A41
Solihull 2

A41
Solihull 2
Warwick

2

2   3

A34
Stratford 14

1

projected

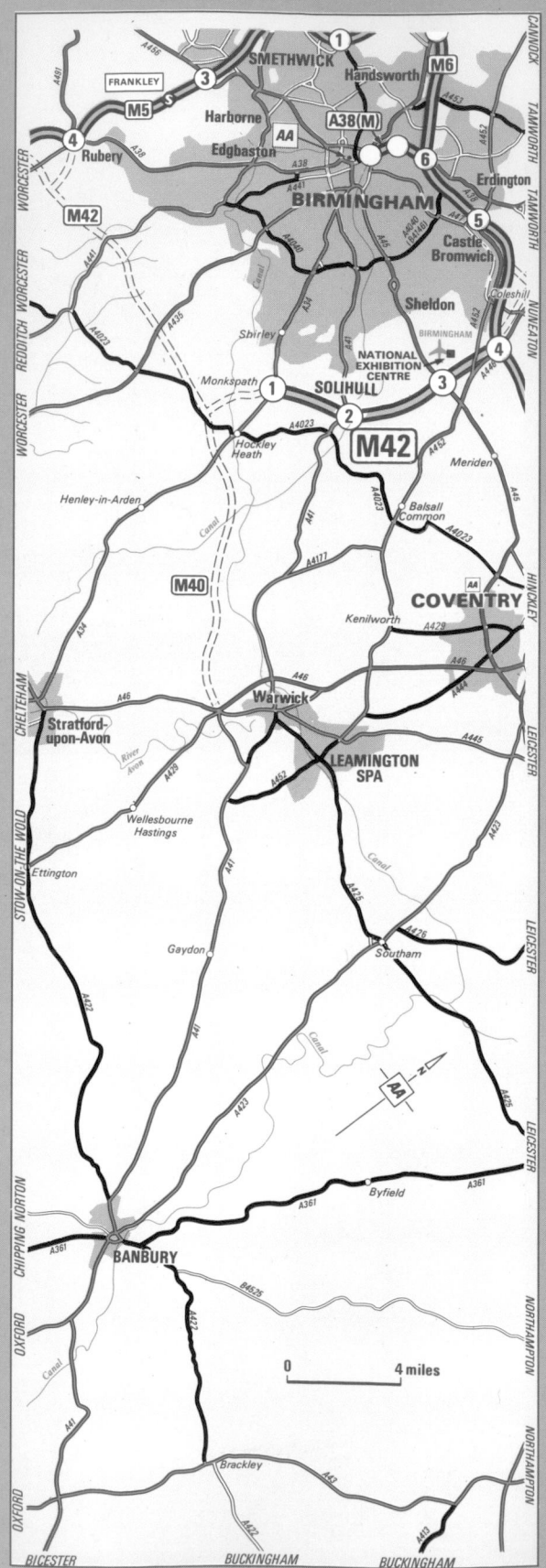

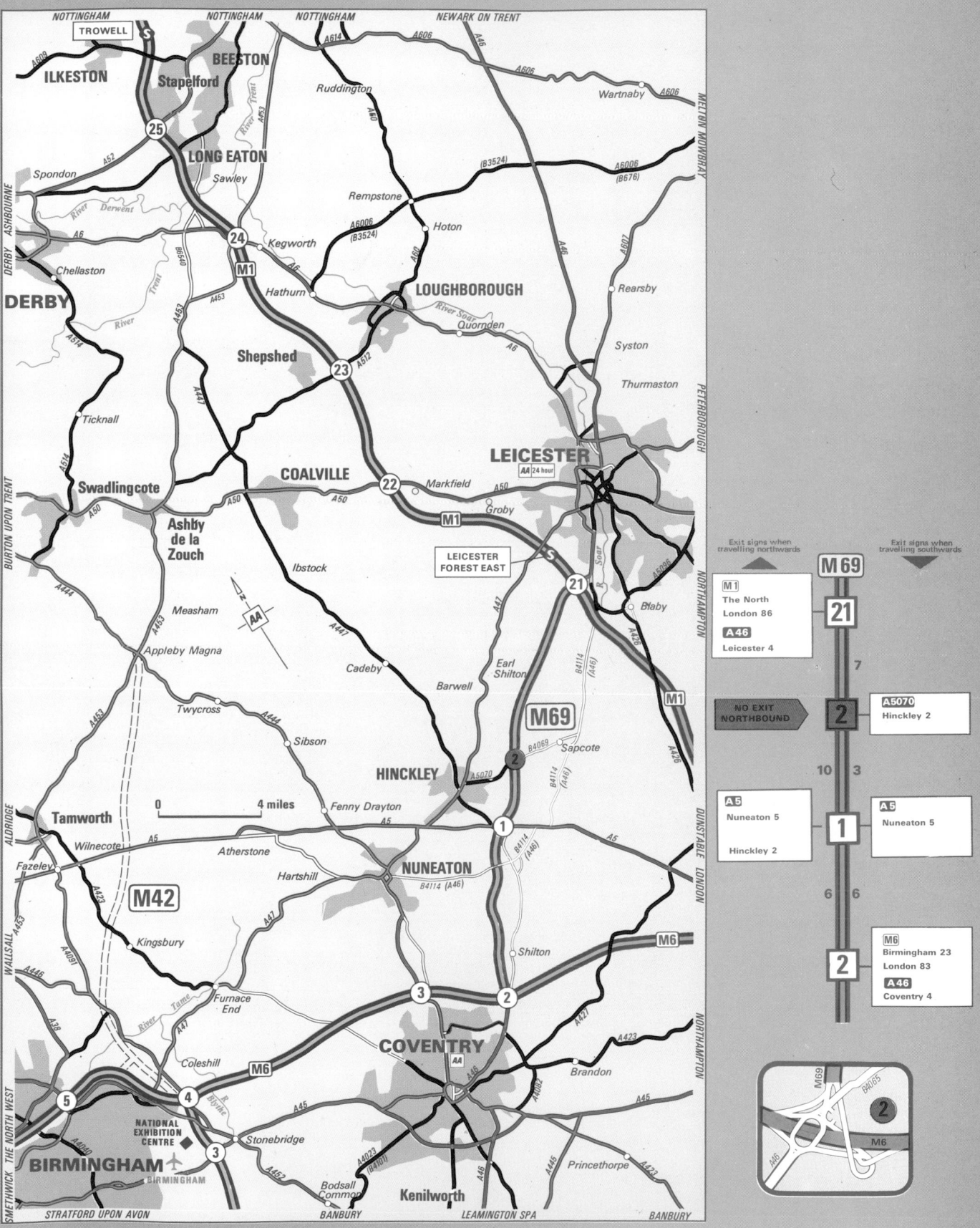

LIVERPOOL–HUDDERSFIELD

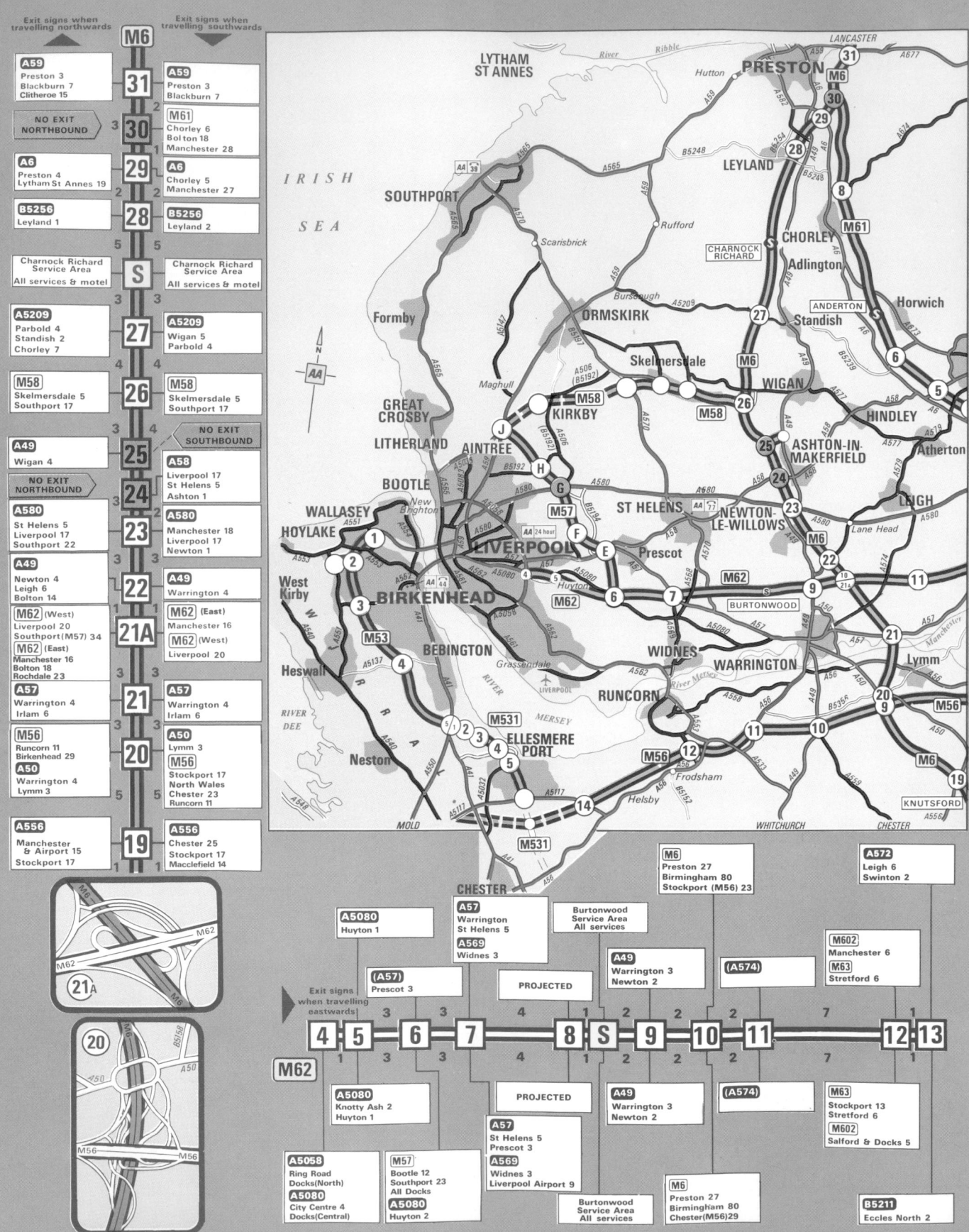

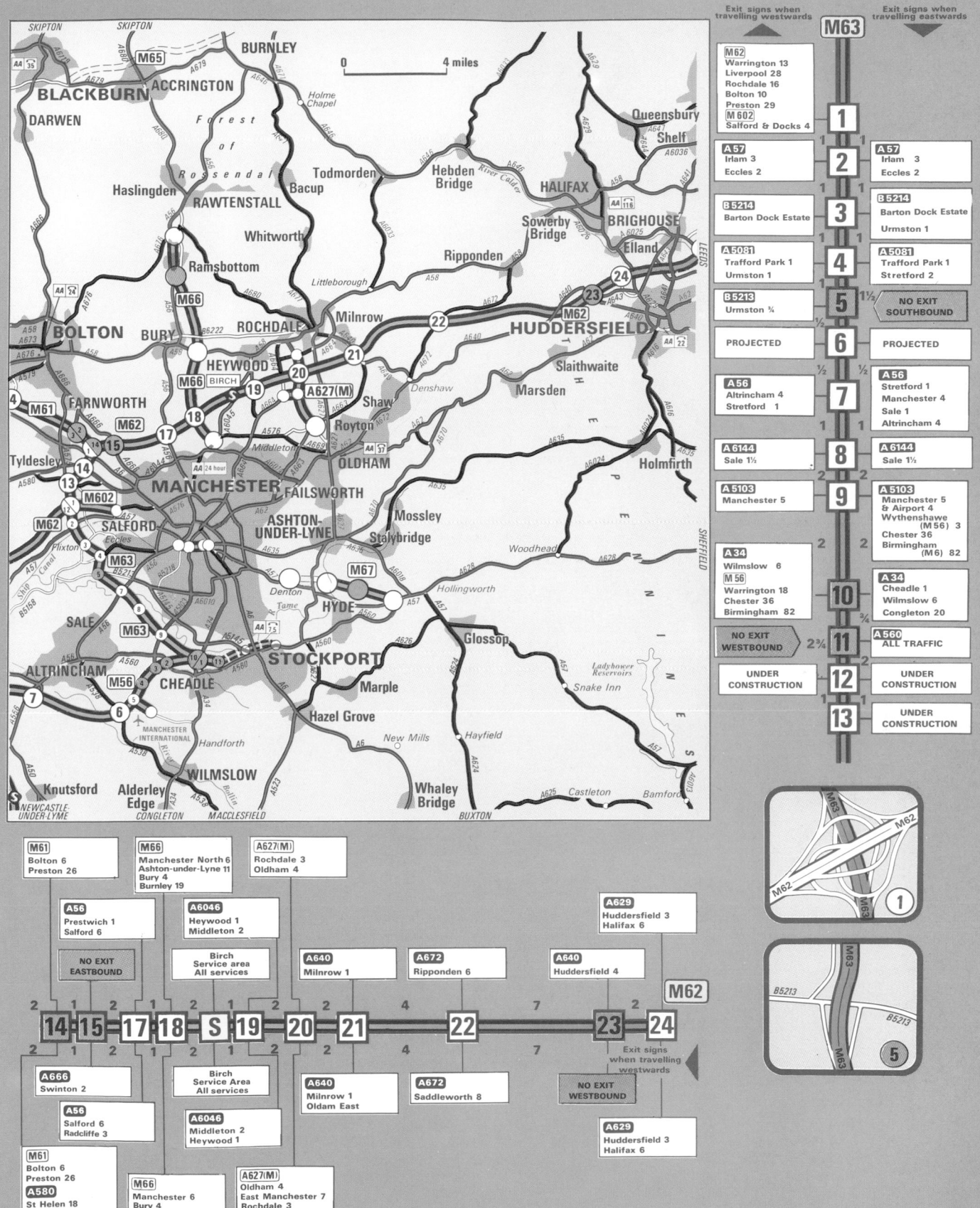

Map labels

SKIPTON SKIPTON BURNLEY
AA 35 M65 A679
BLACKBURN ACCRINGTON
DARWEN
Forest
of
Haslingden Rossendale Todmorden Hebden Bridge HALIFAX Queensbury Shelf
RAWTENSTALL Bacup Sowerby Bridge BRIGHOUSE
Whitworth Ripponden Elland
Ramsbottom AA 24 Littleborough Milnrow
M66 Denshaw Slaithwaite
BOLTON BURY ROCHDALE HUDDERSFIELD M62
FARNWORTH HEYWOOD Marsden
M66 BIRCH Shaw Holmfirth
M61 A627(M) Royton
M62 OLDHAM
Tyldesley Middleton
MANCHESTER FAILSWORTH Mossley
M602 ASHTON-UNDER-LYNE Stalybridge Woodhead
SALFORD Eccles M67 Hollingworth Glossop
M63 Denton Tame HYDE
SALE M63 Ladybower Reservoirs
ALTRINCHAM M56 Marple Snake Inn
CHEADLE Hazel Grove
MANCHESTER INTERNATIONAL New Mills Hayfield
WILMSLOW Handforth
Knutsford Alderley Edge Whaley Bridge Castleton Bamford
NEWCASTLE-UNDER-LYME CONGLETON MACCLESFIELD BUXTON

0 ——— 4 miles

M63 exit signs

Exit signs when travelling westwards / **M63** / **Exit signs when travelling eastwards**

#	Westwards	Eastwards
1	M62 Warrington 13 / Liverpool 28 / Rochdale 16 / Bolton 10 / Preston 29 / M602 Salford & Docks 4	
2	A57 Irlam 3 / Eccles 2	A57 Irlam 3 / Eccles 2
3	B5214 Barton Dock Estate	B5214 Barton Dock Estate / Urmston 1
4	A5081 Trafford Park 1 / Urmston 1	A5081 Trafford Park 1 / Stretford 2
5	B5213 Urmston ¾	NO EXIT SOUTHBOUND (1½)
6	PROJECTED	PROJECTED
7	A56 Altrincham 4 / Stretford 1	A56 Stretford 1 / Manchester 4 / Sale 1 / Altrincham 4
8	A6144 Sale 1½	A6144 Sale 1½
9	A5103 Manchester 5	A5103 Manchester 5 & Airport / Wythenshawe (M56) 3 / Chester 36 / Birmingham (M6) 82
10	A34 Wilmslow 6 / M56 Warrington 18 / Chester 36 / Birmingham 82	A34 Cheadle 1 / Wilmslow 6 / Congleton 20
11	NO EXIT WESTBOUND (2¾)	A560 ALL TRAFFIC
12	UNDER CONSTRUCTION	UNDER CONSTRUCTION
13		UNDER CONSTRUCTION

M62 strip (lower)

M61 Bolton 6 / Preston 26
M66 Manchester North 6 / Ashton-under-Lyne 11 / Bury 4 / Burnley 19
A627(M) Rochdale 3 / Oldham 4
A56 Prestwich 1 / Salford 6
A6046 Heywood 1 / Middleton 2
A629 Huddersfield 3 / Halifax 6
NO EXIT EASTBOUND
Birch Service area All services
A640 Milnrow 1
A672 Ripponden 6
A640 Huddersfield 4

14 – 15 – 17 – 18 – S – 19 – 20 – 21 – 22 – 23 – 24 M62

A666 Swinton 2
Birch Service Area All services
A640 Milnrow 1 / Oldam East
A672 Saddleworth 8
NO EXIT WESTBOUND
A56 Salford 6 / Radcliffe 3
A6046 Middleton 2 / Heywood 1
A629 Huddersfield 3 / Halifax 6
M61 Bolton 6 / Preston 26
A580 St Helen 18
M66 Manchester 6 / Bury 4
A627(M) Oldham 4 / East Manchester 7 / Rochdale 3

Exit signs when travelling westwards

M63/M62 (1)
B5213 / M63 (5)

HUDDERSFIELD–HULL

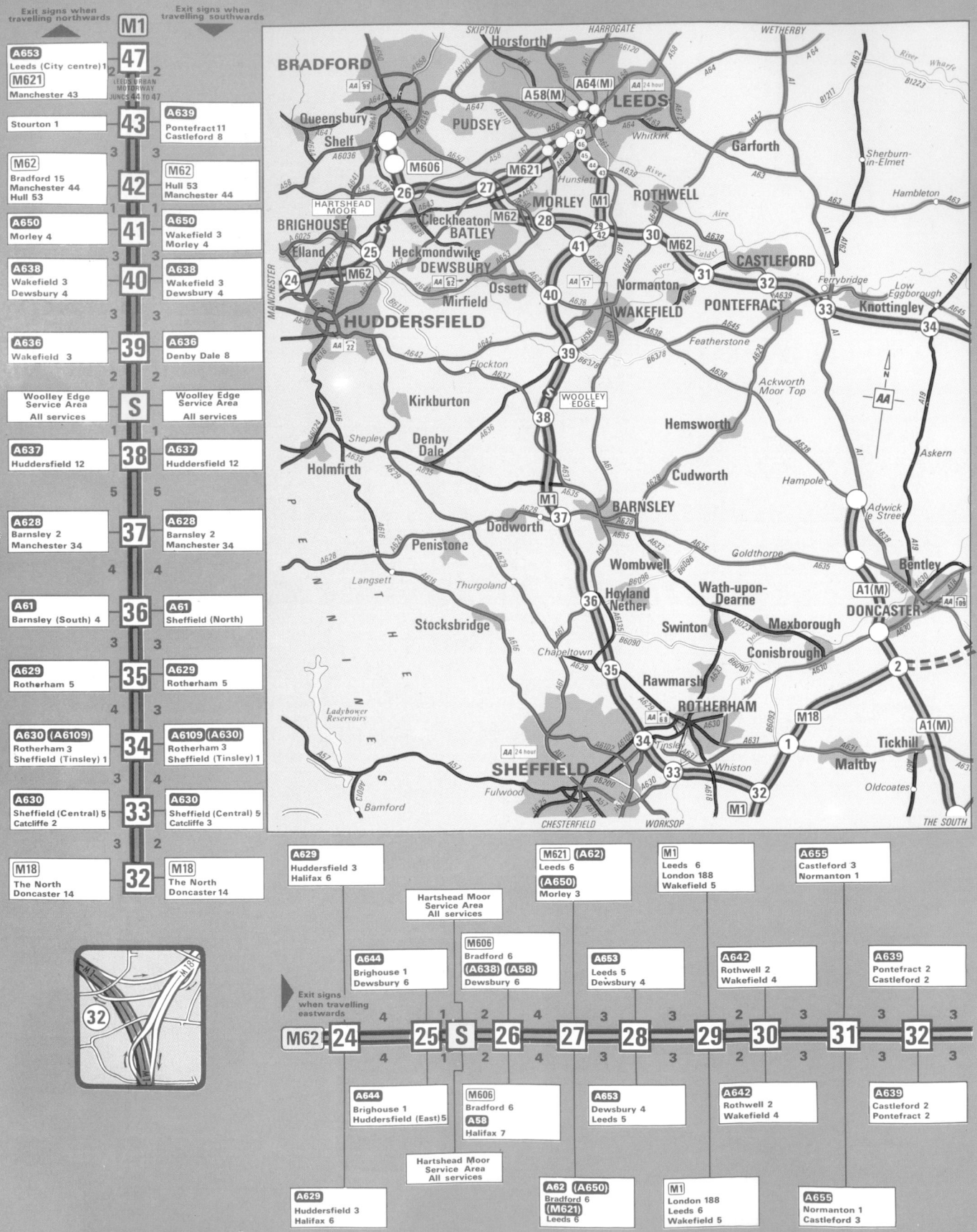

M1

Northbound	Jct	Southbound
A653 Leeds (City centre)1 **M621** Manchester 43	**47**	2
Stourton 1	**43**	**A639** Pontefract 11 Castleford 8
M62 Bradford 15 Manchester 44 Hull 53	**42**	**M62** Hull 53 Manchester 44
A650 Morley 4	**41**	**A650** Wakefield 3 Morley 4
A638 Wakefield 3 Dewsbury 4	**40**	**A638** Wakefield 3 Dewsbury 4
A636 Wakefield 3	**39**	**A636** Denby Dale 8
Woolley Edge Service Area All services	**S**	Woolley Edge Service Area All services
A637 Huddersfield 12	**38**	**A637** Huddersfield 12
A628 Barnsley 2 Manchester 34	**37**	**A628** Barnsley 2 Manchester 34
A61 Barnsley (South) 4	**36**	**A61** Sheffield (North)
A629 Rotherham 5	**35**	**A629** Rotherham 5
A630 (A6109) Rotherham 3 Sheffield (Tinsley) 1	**34**	**A6109** (A630) Rotherham 3 Sheffield (Tinsley) 1
A630 Sheffield (Central) 5 Catcliffe 2	**33**	**A630** Sheffield (Central) 5 Catcliffe 3
M18 The North Doncaster 14	**32**	**M18** The North Doncaster 14

LEEDS URBAN MOTORWAY JUNCS 44 to 47

M62

Eastbound	M62	24	25	S	26	27	28	29	30	31	32

Westbound signs:
- **A629** Huddersfield 3 Halifax 6
- **M621** (A62) Leeds 6 (A650) Morley 3
- **M1** Leeds 6 London 188 Wakefield 5
- **A655** Castleford 3 Normanton 1

- **A644** Brighouse 1 Dewsbury 6
- Hartshead Moor Service Area All services
- **M606** Bradford 6 (A638) (A58) Dewsbury 6
- **A653** Leeds 5 Dewsbury 4
- **A642** Rothwell 2 Wakefield 4
- **A639** Pontefract 2 Castleford 2

Eastbound signs:
- **A644** Brighouse 1 Huddersfield (East) 5
- **M606** Bradford 6 **A58** Halifax 7
- **A653** Dewsbury 4 Leeds 5
- **A642** Rothwell 2 Wakefield 4
- **A639** Castleford 2 Pontefract 2

- **A629** Huddersfield 3 Halifax 6
- Hartshead Moor Service Area All services
- **A62** (A650) Bradford 6 (M621) Leeds 6
- **M1** London 188 Leeds 6 Wakefield 5
- **A655** Normanton 1 Castleford 3

144

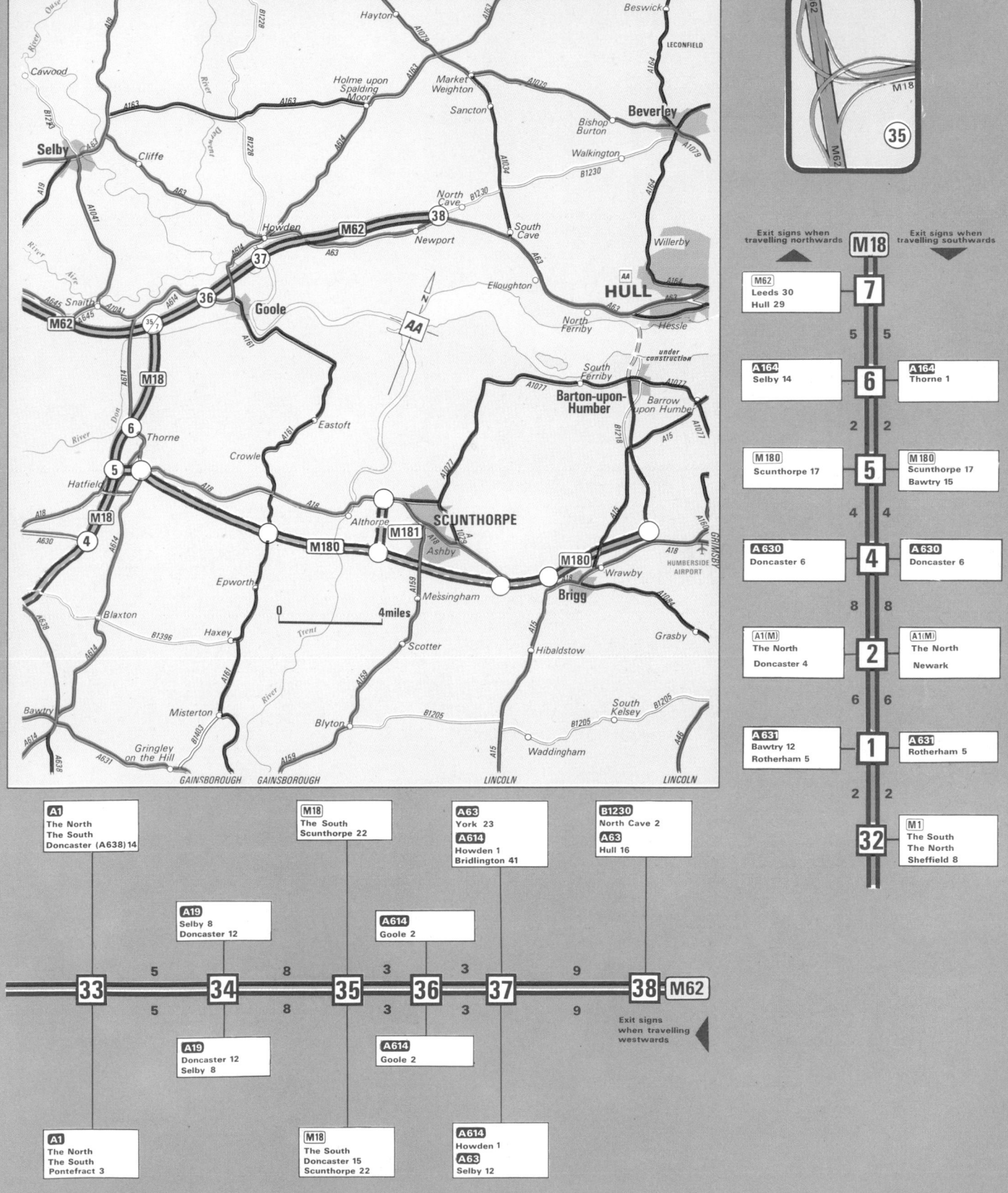

M18

M62 Leeds 30 Hull 29	**7**	
5		5
A164 Selby 14	**6**	A164 Thorne 1
2		2
M180 Scunthorpe 17	**5**	M180 Scunthorpe 17 Bawtry 15
4		4
A630 Doncaster 6	**4**	A630 Doncaster 6
8		8
A1(M) The North Doncaster 4	**2**	A1(M) The North Newark
6		6
A631 Bawtry 12 Rotherham 5	**1**	A631 Rotherham 5
2		2
	32	M1 The South The North Sheffield 8

M62

| A1 The North The South Doncaster (A638) 14 | | M18 The South Scunthorpe 22 | | A63 York 23 / A614 Howden 1 Bridlington 41 | | B1230 North Cave 2 / A63 Hull 16 |

| | A19 Selby 8 Doncaster 12 | | A614 Goole 2 | | |

| **33** | 5 | **34** | 8 | **35** | 3 | **36** | 3 | **37** | 9 | **38** M62 |
| | 5 | | 8 | | 3 | | 3 | | 9 | |

| | A19 Doncaster 12 Selby 8 | | A614 Goole 2 | | |

Exit signs when travelling westwards ◀

| A1 The North The South Pontefract 3 | | M18 The South Doncaster 15 Scunthorpe 22 | | A614 Howden 1 / A63 Selby 12 |

145

GLASGOW AREA

Exit signs when travelling westwards ▲
Exit signs when travelling eastwards ▼

M8

Westwards	Junction	Eastwards
A8 Greenock 8	**12**	
	4 4	
M898 Erskine Bridge 1	**11**	**M898** Erskine Bridge 1
	3 3	
A726 Paisley 2 Linwood 2	**10**	**A726** Paisley 2 Linwood 2
	1 1	
Glasgow Airport ½	**9**	Glasgow Airport ½
A741 Paisley 1 Renfrew 1	**8**	**A741** Paisley 1 Renfrew 1
	2 2	
A754 Renfrew 1 Hillington 1	**7**	**A754** Renfrew 1 Hillington 1
	1 1	
A739 Clyde Tunnel 1	**N**	**A739** Clyde Tunnel 1
	1 1	
(A736) Irvine 24	**M**	**(A77)** Kilmarnock 20 Govan ½
	½	
B768 Govan 1 Kilmarnock 20	**L**	NO EXIT EASTBOUND
	½ 2	
PROJECTED	**K**	NO EXIT EASTBOUND
NO EXIT WESTBOUND 1	**J**	**(A8)**
Rutherglen 3 Kilmarnock 21	**H**	NO EXIT EASTBOUND 1
Anderston ½ Partick 2	**G**	**A814** Clydebank ½
	1 1	
A82 Dumbarton 15 Kelvinside 2	**F**	**A82** Dumbarton 15
	½	
A81 Aberfoyle 22 Cowcaddens ½	**E**	NO EXIT EASTBOUND 1
	½	
A8 City Centre (S)1 **A803** Kirkintilloch 7	**D**	**A803** Kirkintilloch 7 Townhead ½
	1	
NO EXIT WESTBOUND 2	**C**	Fruit Market 1
	1	
Fruit Market 1 Dennistoun 1	**B**	Carlisle 94 Edinburgh 45
	A	**A80** Stirling 26

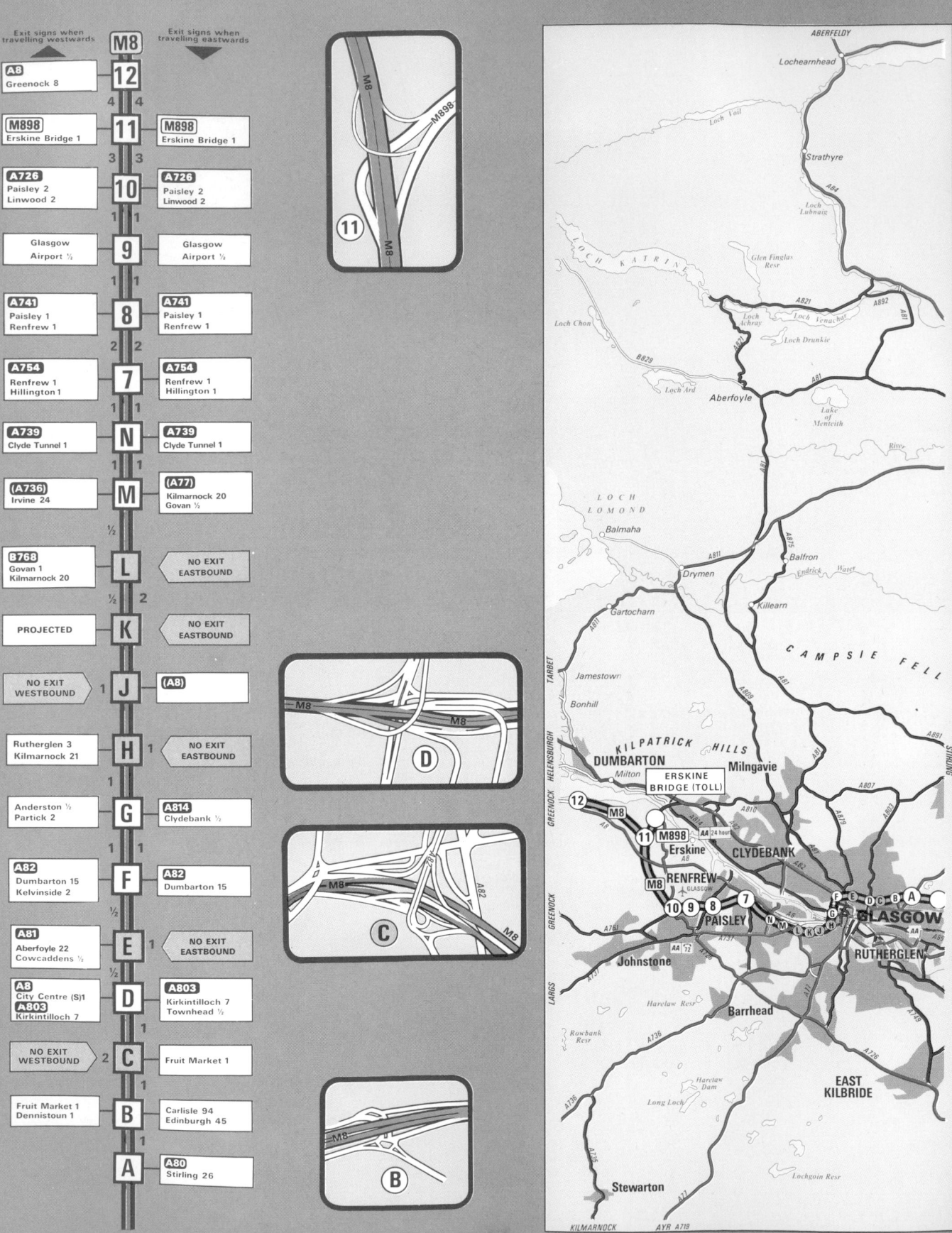

146

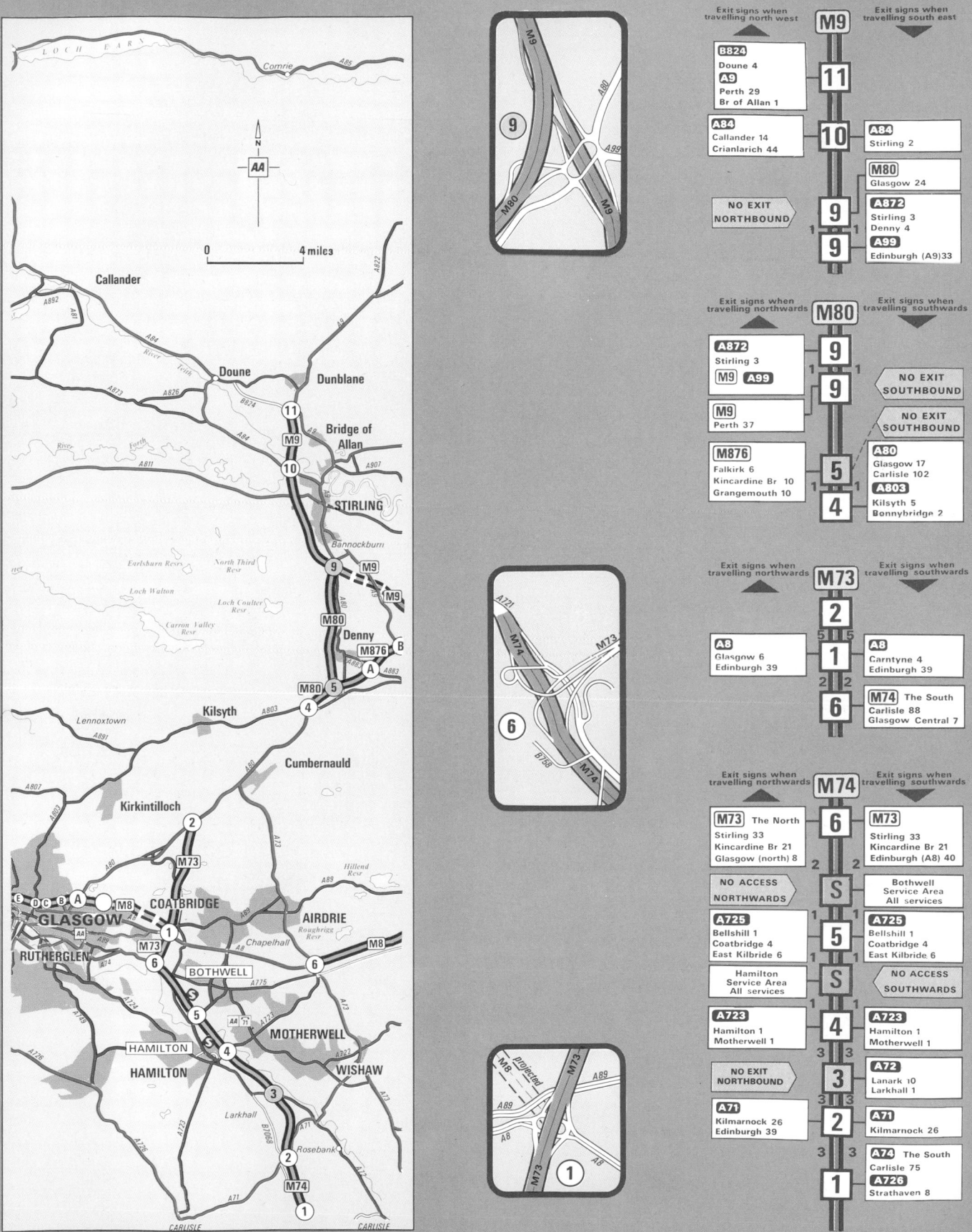

Map labels

LOCH EARN
Comrie
A85
A822

Callander
A84
A81
A892

Doune
River Teith
A873
A826
B824

Dunblane
Bridge of Allan
A9
A84
A907

STIRLING
Bannockburn
A811
River Forth

9 M9
M9
North Third Resr
Earlsburn Resr
Loch Walton
Loch Coulter Resr
Carron Valley Resr

M80
Denny
M876 B
A883
A

M80 5
4 Kilsyth A803
Lennoxtown A891

Cumbernauld
A807
A803
A80
A73

Kirkintilloch
2 M73
Hillend Resr
A89

E D C B A M8 COATBRIDGE
GLASGOW Roughrigg Resr
AIRDRIE
A89 M8
RUTHERGLEN 1
M73 A8 Chapelhall
6 BOTHWELL 6
A724 A775 A73
5 MOTHERWELL
AA 71
HAMILTON 4
HAMILTON WISHAW
A723 A722
A776
3
Larkhall
B7068
A71
2 Rosebank
A71
M74
1
CARLISLE CARLISLE

0 ___ 4 miles

N
AA

M9 signs

Exit signs when travelling north west | Exit signs when travelling south east

M9

11
B824 Doune 4
A9 Perth 29 Br of Allan 1

10
A84 Callander 14 Crianlarich 44 | A84 Stirling 2

NO EXIT NORTHBOUND | **9** | M80 Glasgow 24
A872 Stirling 3 Denny 4

9 | A99 Edinburgh (A9)33

M80 signs

Exit signs when travelling northwards | M80 | Exit signs when travelling southwards

9
A872 Stirling 3

9
M9 A99 | NO EXIT SOUTHBOUND

M9 Perth 37 | NO EXIT SOUTHBOUND

5
M876 Falkirk 6 Kincardine Br 10 Grangemouth 10 | A80 Glasgow 17 Carlisle 102

4 | A803 Kilsyth 5 Bonnybridge 2

M73 signs

Exit signs when travelling northwards | M73 | Exit signs when travelling southwards

2

1
A8 Glasgow 6 Edinburgh 39 | A8 Carntyne 4 Edinburgh 39

6 | M74 The South Carlisle 88 Glasgow Central 7

M74 signs

Exit signs when travelling northwards | M74 | Exit signs when travelling southwards

6
M73 The North Stirling 33 Kincardine Br 21 Glasgow (north) 8 | M73 Stirling 33 Kincardine Br 21 Edinburgh (A8) 40

NO ACCESS NORTHWARDS | **S** | Bothwell Service Area All services

5
A725 Bellshill 1 Coatbridge 4 East Kilbride 6 | A725 Bellshill 1 Coatbridge 4 East Kilbride 6

Hamilton Service Area All services | **S** | NO ACCESS SOUTHWARDS

4
A723 Hamilton 1 Motherwell 1 | A723 Hamilton 1 Motherwell 1

NO EXIT NORTHWARDS | **3** | A72 Lanark 10 Larkhall 1

2
A71 Kilmarnock 26 Edinburgh 39 | A71 Kilmarnock 26

1 | A74 The South Carlisle 75
A726 Strathaven 8

147

EDINBURGH AREA

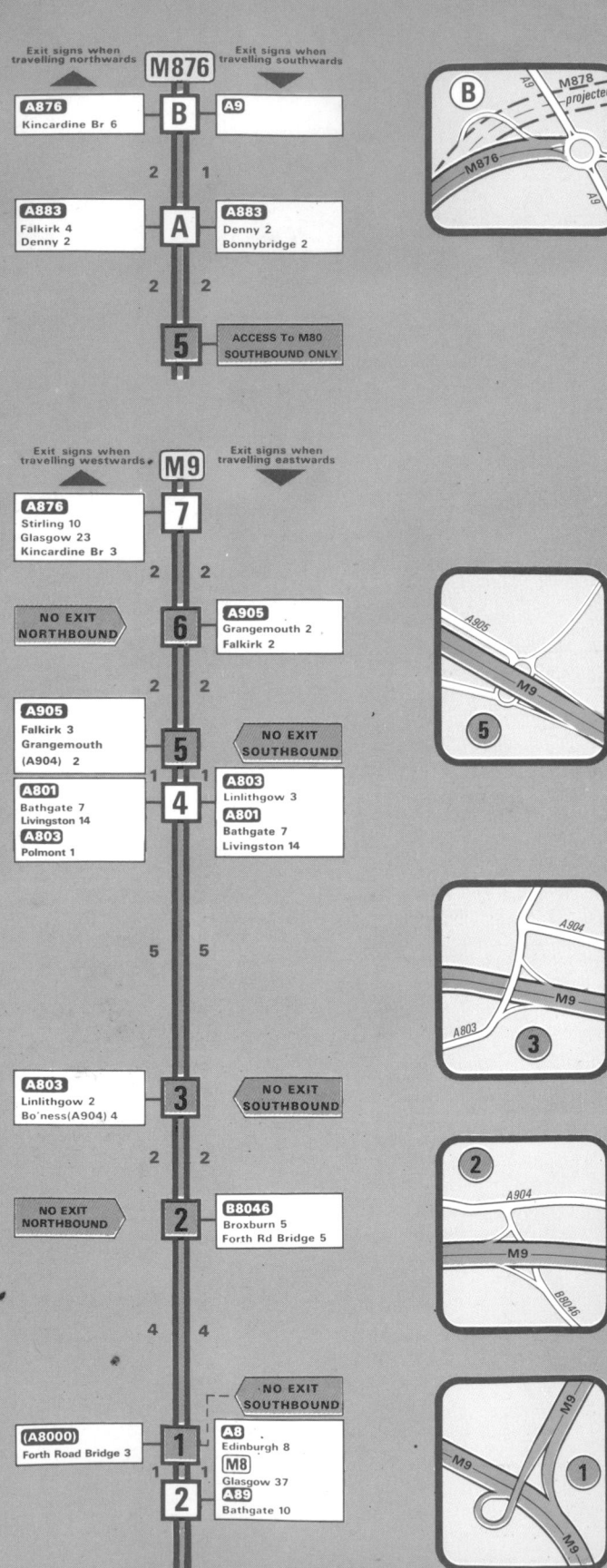

A876
Kincardine Br 6 — **B** — **A9**

2   1

A883
Falkirk 4
Denny 2 — **A** — **A883**
Denny 2
Bonnybridge 2

2   2

5 — ACCESS To M80
SOUTHBOUND ONLY

Exit signs when travelling westwards ◄ **M9** Exit signs when travelling eastwards ▼

A876
Stirling 10
Glasgow 23
Kincardine Br 3 — **7**

2   2

NO EXIT
NORTHBOUND — **6** — **A905**
Grangemouth 2
Falkirk 2

2   2

A905
Falkirk 3
Grangemouth
(A904) 2 — **5** — NO EXIT
SOUTHBOUND

1   1

A801
Bathgate 7
Livingston 14
A803
Polmont 1 — **4** — **A803**
Linlithgow 3
A801
Bathgate 7
Livingston 14

5   5

A803
Linlithgow 2
Bo'ness (A904) 4 — **3** — NO EXIT
SOUTHBOUND

2   2

NO EXIT
NORTHBOUND — **2** — **B8046**
Broxburn 5
Forth Rd Bridge 5

4   4

NO EXIT
SOUTHBOUND

(A8000)
Forth Road Bridge 3 — **1** — **A8**
Edinburgh 8
M8
Glasgow 37
2 — **A89**
Bathgate 10

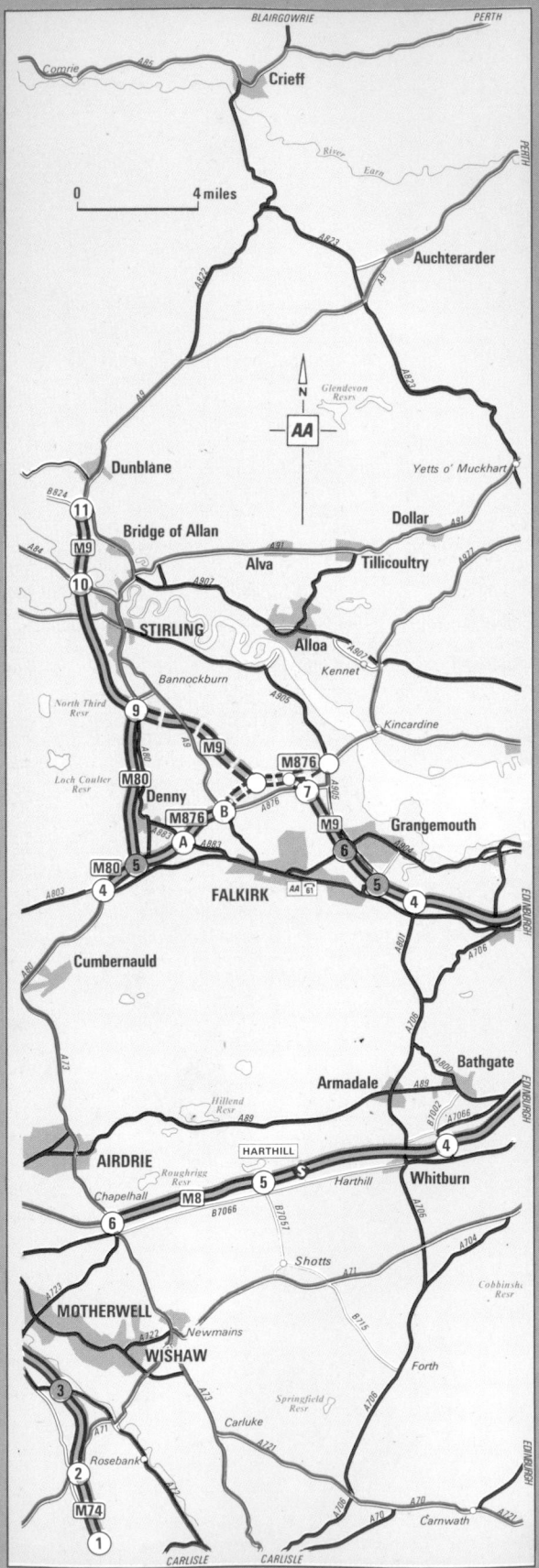

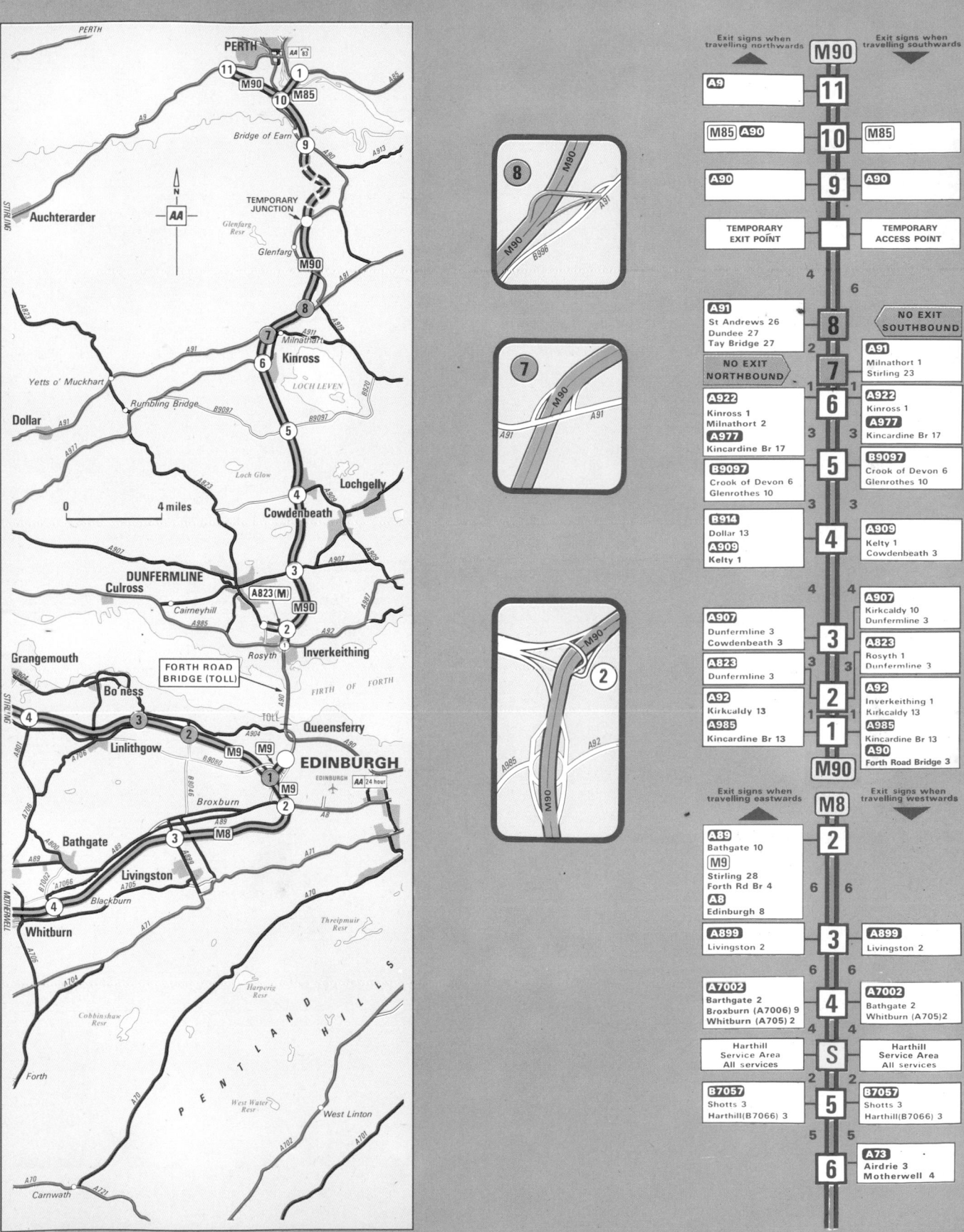

HATFIELD–BALDOCK

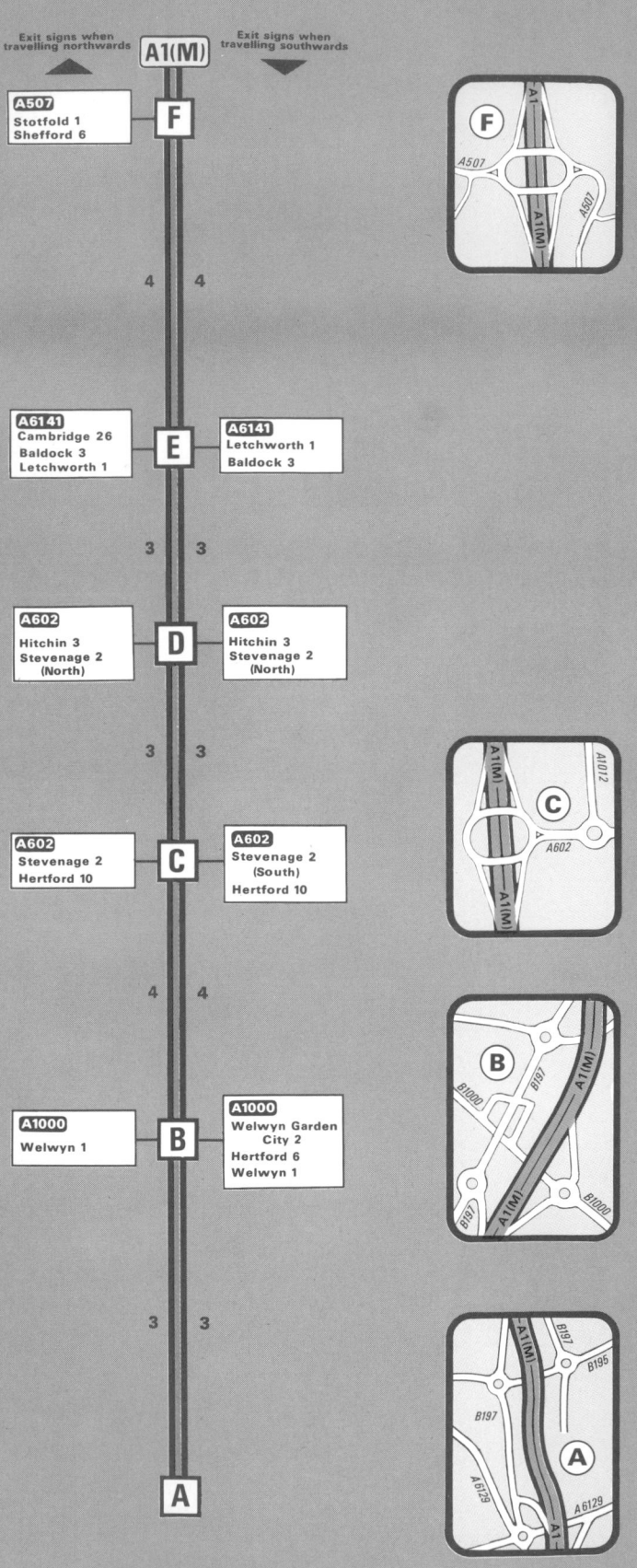

Exit signs when travelling northwards

Exit signs when travelling southwards

A1(M)

A507
Stotfold 1
Shefford 6

F

A6141
Cambridge 26
Baldock 3
Letchworth 1

A6141
Letchworth 1
Baldock 3

E

4 | 4

3 | 3

A602
Hitchin 3
Stevenage 2
(North)

A602
Hitchin 3
Stevenage 2
(North)

D

3 | 3

A602
Stevenage 2
Hertford 10

A602
Stevenage 2
(South)
Hertford 10

C

4 | 4

A1000
Welwyn 1

A1000
Welwyn Garden
City 2
Hertford 6
Welwyn 1

B

3 | 3

A

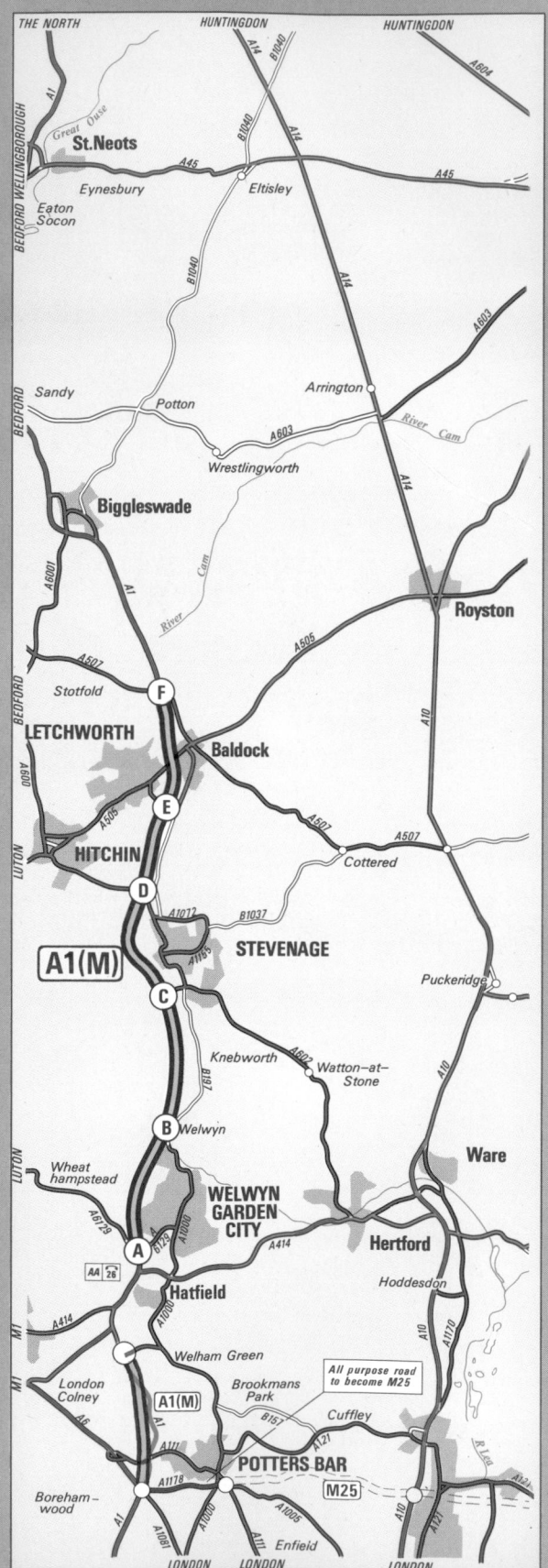

LONDON–CAMBRIDGE

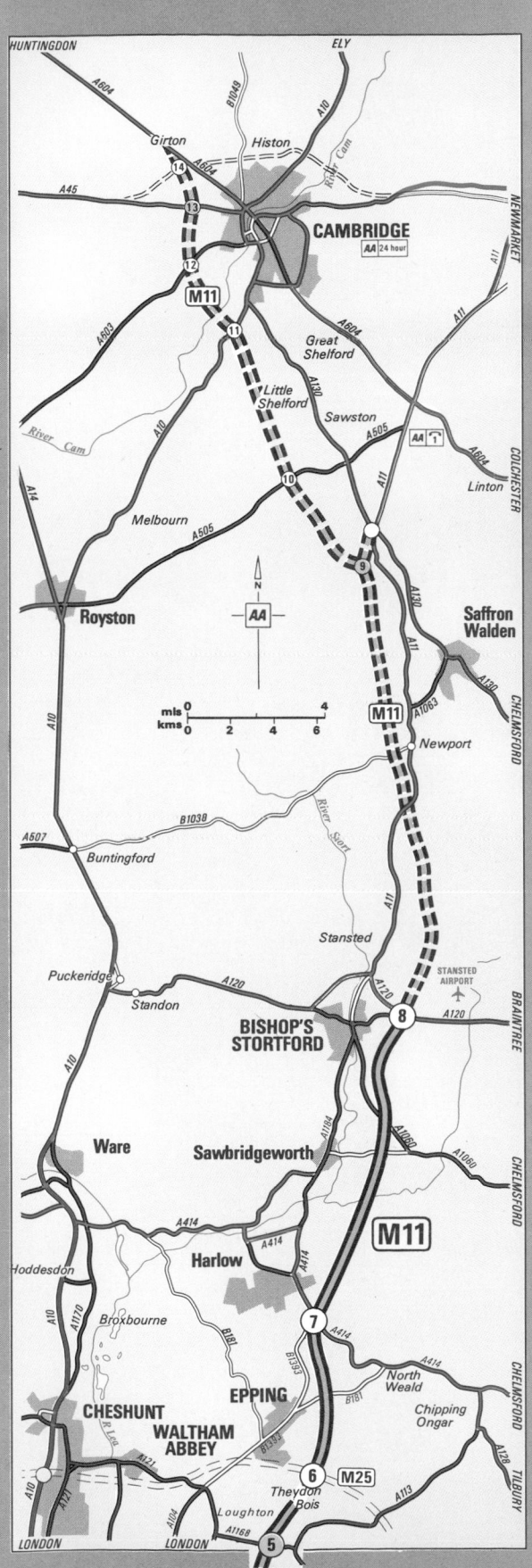

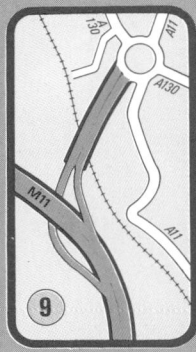

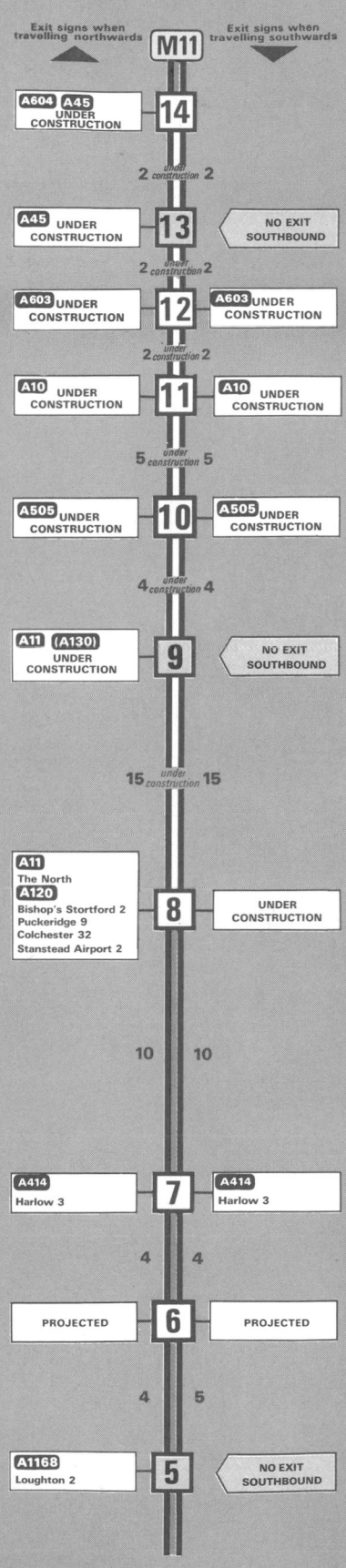

SCOTCH CORNER—TYNESIDE

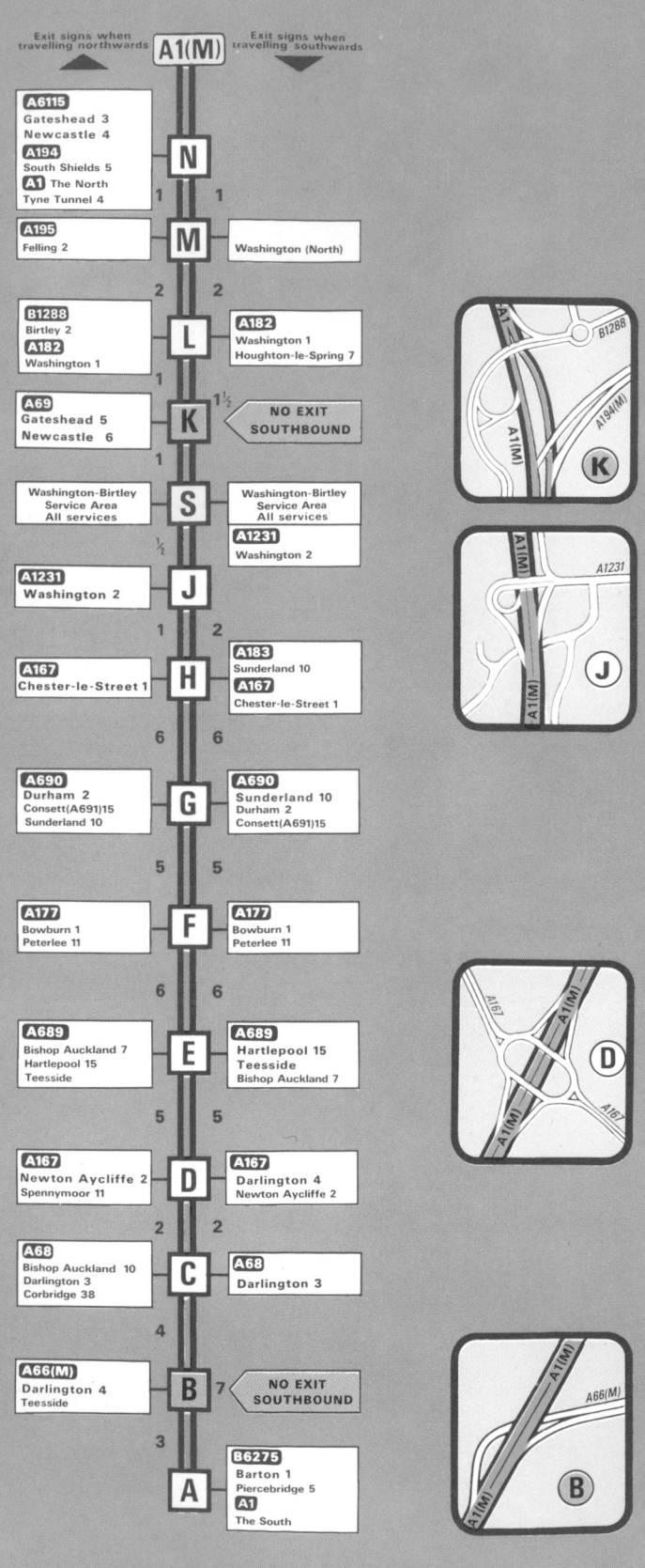

Exit signs when travelling northwards

Exit signs when travelling southwards

A1(M)

N
- **A6115** Gateshead 3 / Newcastle 4
- **A194** South Shields 5
- **A1** The North / Tyne Tunnel 4

1 | 1

M
- **A195** Felling 2
- Washington (North)

2 | 2

L
- **B1288** Birtley 2
- **A182** Washington 1
- **A182** Washington 1 / Houghton-le-Spring 7

1 | 1½

K
- **A69** Gateshead 5 / Newcastle 6
- NO EXIT SOUTHBOUND

1 |

S
- Washington-Birtley Service Area All services
- Washington-Birtley Service Area All services
- **A1231** Washington 2

½ | ½

J
- **A1231** Washington 2

| 2

H
- **A167** Chester-le-Street 1
- **A183** Sunderland 10
- **A167** Chester-le-Street 1

6 | 6

G
- **A690** Durham 2 / Consett (A691) 15 / Sunderland 10
- **A690** Sunderland 10 / Durham 2 / Consett (A691) 15

5 | 5

F
- **A177** Bowburn 1 / Peterlee 11
- **A177** Bowburn 1 / Peterlee 11

6 | 6

E
- **A689** Bishop Auckland 7 / Hartlepool 15 / Teesside
- **A689** Hartlepool 15 / Teesside / Bishop Auckland 7

5 | 5

D
- **A167** Newton Aycliffe 2 / Spennymoor 11
- **A167** Darlington 4 / Newton Aycliffe 2

2 | 2

C
- **A68** Bishop Auckland 10 / Darlington 3 / Corbridge 38
- **A68** Darlington 3

4 |

B
- **A66(M)** Darlington 4 / Teesside
- NO EXIT SOUTHBOUND 7

3 |

A
- **B6275** Barton 1 / Piercebridge 5
- **A1** The South

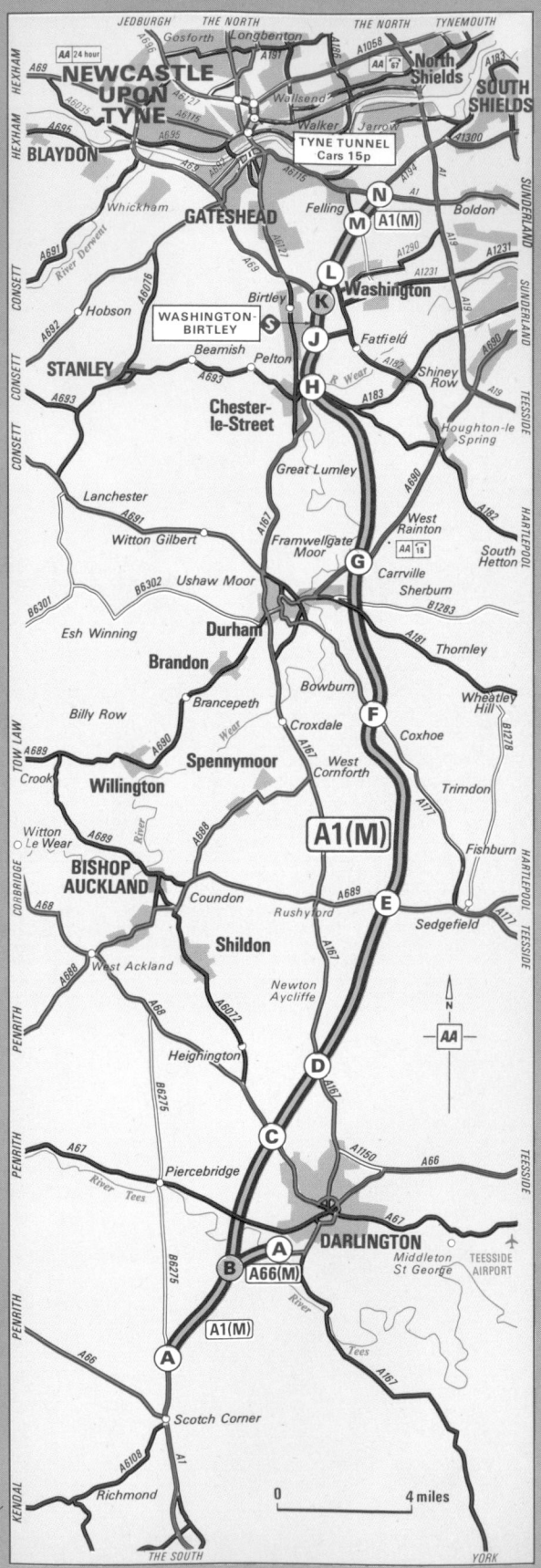

TYNE TUNNEL Cars 15p

A1(M)

0 — 4 miles

Key to Town Plans

Figures in red denote page numbers

Recommended route	▅▅▅▅
Other roads	
Restricted roads (access only/buses only)	
Traffic roundabout	
Official car park (open air)	P
Multi-storey car park	G
Parking available on payment (open air)	P
Parking zone	
One-way street	←
Pedestrians only	
Convenience	C
Convenience with facilities for the disabled	C &
Tourist information centre	i

Inverness 169
Aberdeen 154
Dundee 164
Perth 180
Glasgow 167
Edinburgh 165
Ayr 155
Stranraer 183
Newcastle-upon-Tyne 178
Sunderland 187
Carlisle 161
Stockton-on-Tees 186
Middlesbrough 174
Kendal 171
Scarborough 183
York 191
Blackpool 157
Bradford 155
Leeds 171
Hull 170
Liverpool 173
Manchester 175
Grimsby 168
Holyhead 169
Sheffield 184
Chester 161
Lincoln 171
Hanley 186
Stoke-on-Trent 186
Nottingham 179
Derby 163
Leicester 172
Norwich 177
Great Yarmouth 166
Wolverhampton 191
Aberystwyth 154
Birmingham 156
Coventry 162
Northampton 177
Cambridge 160
Stratford-upon-Avon 187
Ipswich 170
Luton 172
Harwich 168
Gloucester 162
Oxford 179
Chelmsford 161
Swansea 188
Swindon 188
District 192–193
Central 195–204
Southend-on-Sea 184
Cardiff 160
Reading 182
LONDON
Margate 174
Bristol 158
Bath 155
Medway Towns 176
Maidstone 172
Ramsgate 182
Barnstaple 154
Guildford 168
Dover 163
Salisbury 183
Winchester 189
Folkestone 166
Taunton 189
Southampton 185
Chichester 162
Brighton 157
Hastings 169
Exeter 164
Poole 159
Portsmouth 181
Bournemouth 159
Weymouth 187
Plymouth 180
Paignton 190
Torquay 190
Brixham 190
Penzance 180

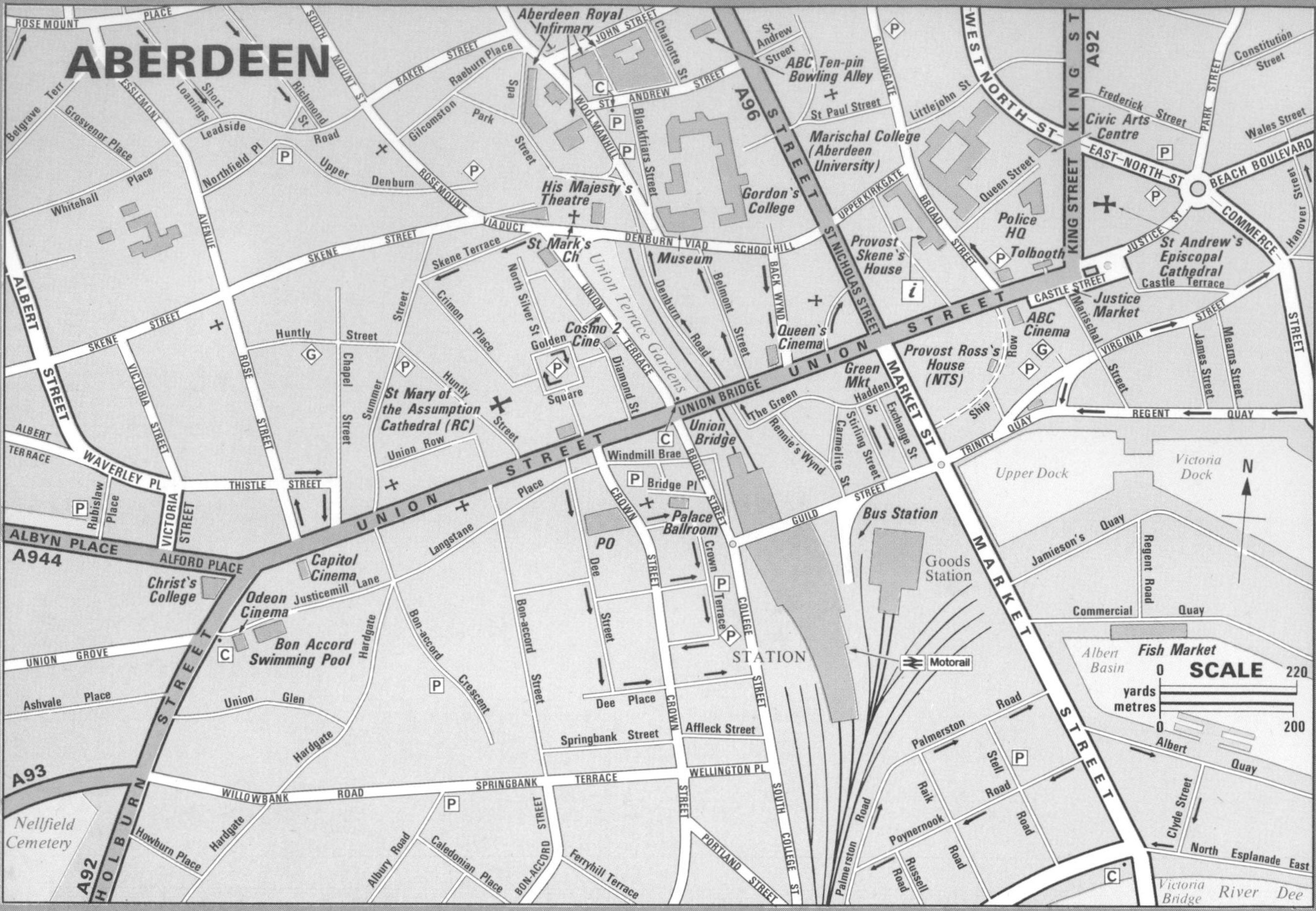

ABERDEEN

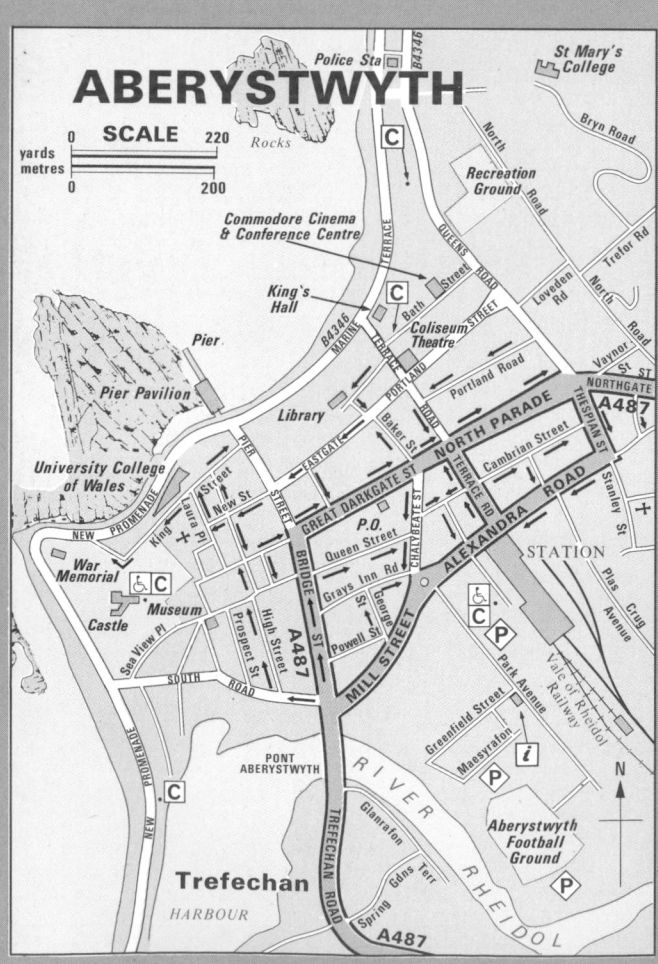

ABERYSTWYTH

BARNSTAPLE

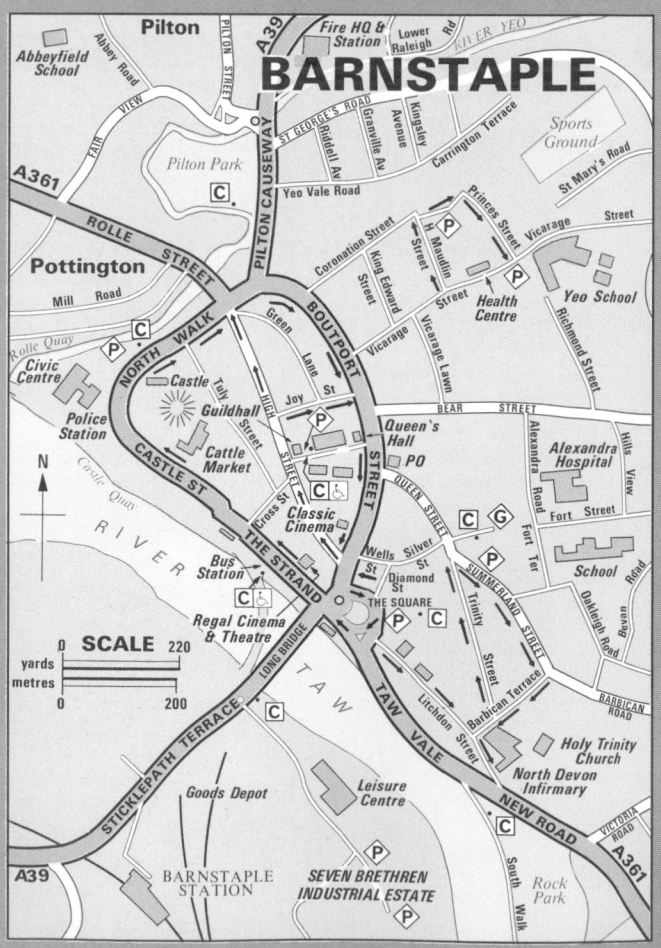

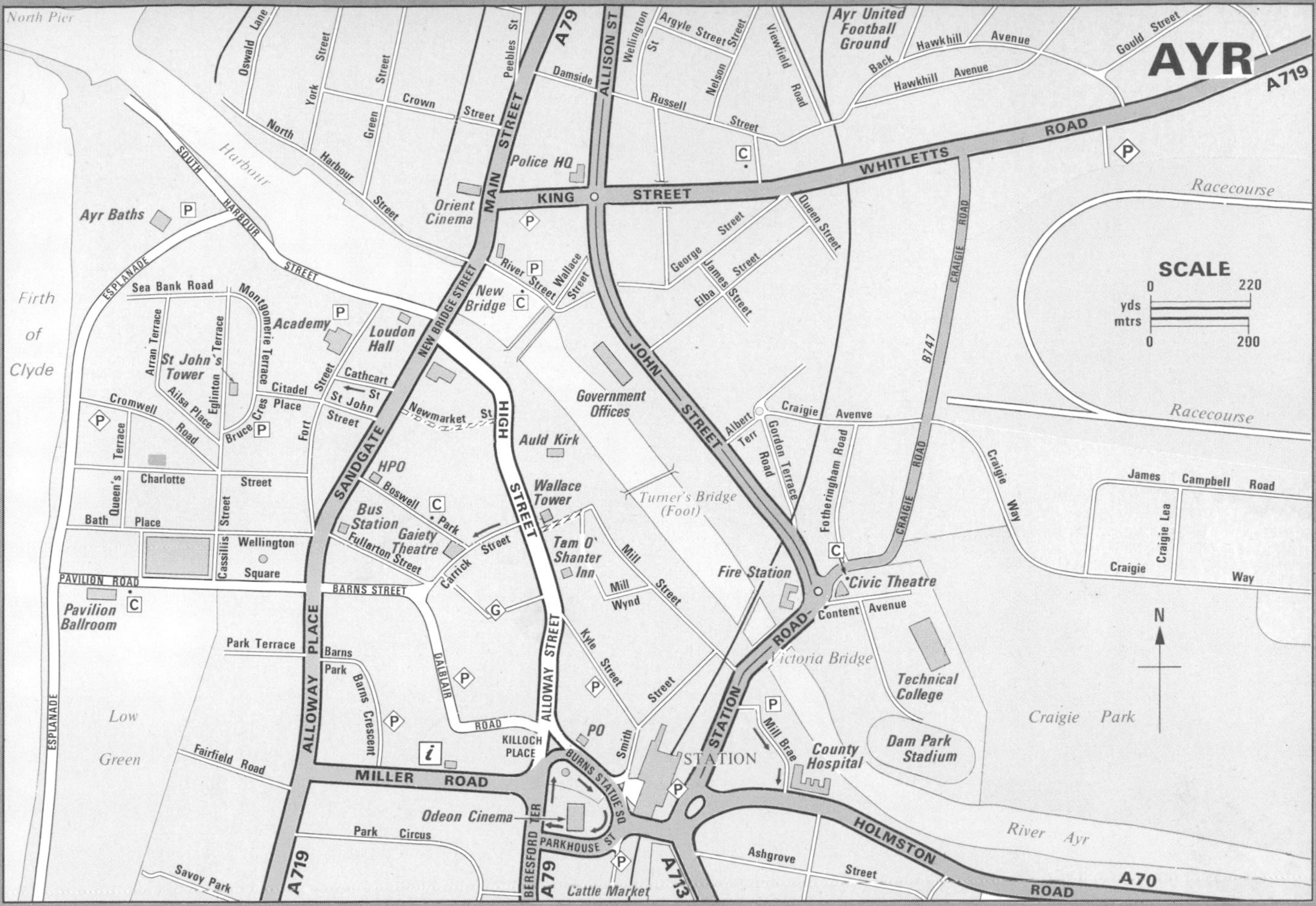

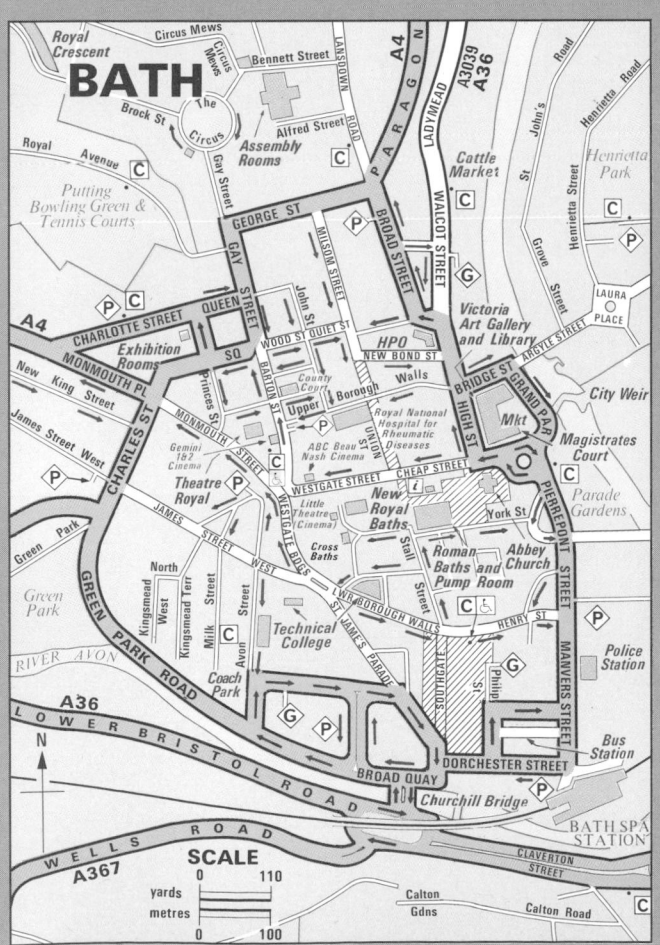

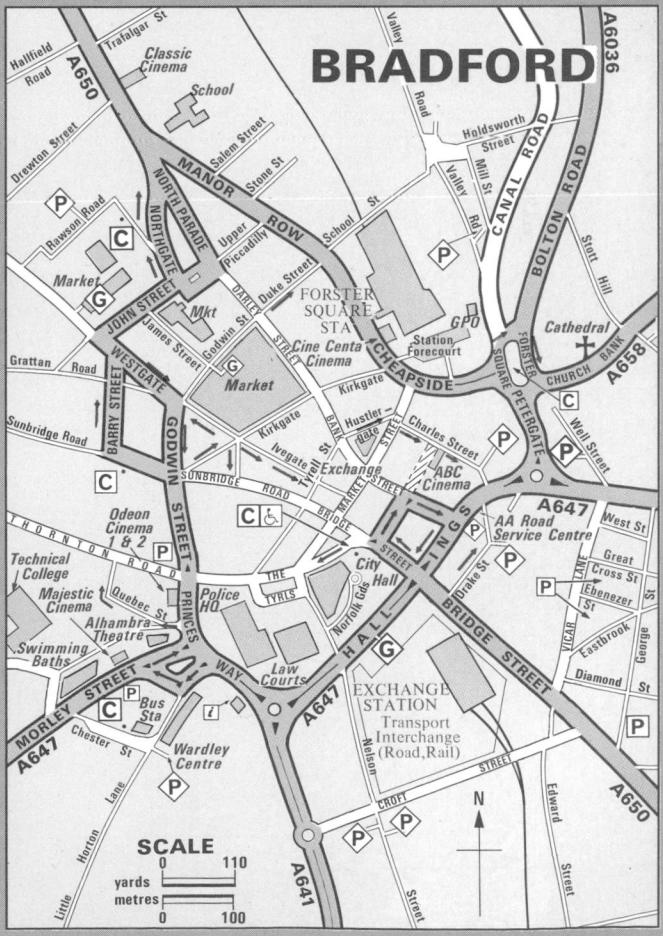

BIRMINGHAM

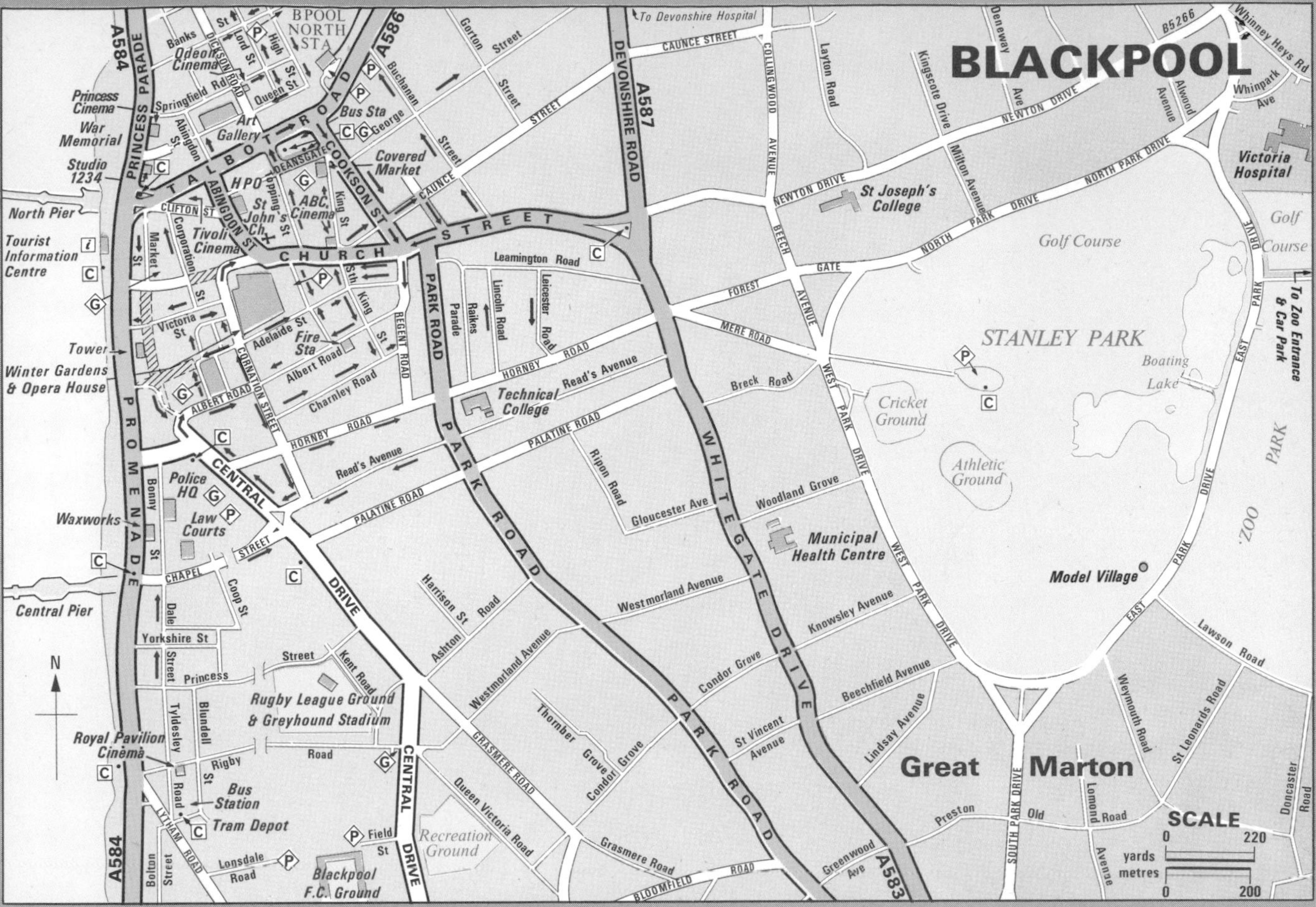

BLACKPOOL

Whinney Heys Rd
B5266
Newton Drive
Kingscote Drive
Deeneway
Whinpark Ave
Victoria Hospital
Golf Course
NORTH PARK DRIVE
St Joseph's College
Golf Course
To Zoo Entrance & Car Park
GATE
FOREST DRIVE
MERE ROAD
STANLEY PARK
Boating Lake
Cricket Ground
Athletic Ground
Breck Road
Woodland Grove
Model Village
Municipal Health Centre
Knowsley Avenue
Gloucester Ave
Beechfield Avenue
Lindsay Avenue
Condor Grove
St Vincent Avenue
Great Marton
Preston Old Lomond Road
St Leonards Road
Doncaster Road
Weymouth Road
Greenwood Ave
A583

To Devonshire Hospital
CAUNCE STREET
GARTON STREET
COLLINGWOOD
DEVONSHIRE ROAD
A587
WHITEGATE DRIVE
PARK ROAD
Leamington Road
Lincoln Road
Leicester Road
Read's Avenue
Hornby Road
Technical College
Palatine Road
Ripon Road
Westmorland Avenue
Harrison St
Ashton Road
Westmorland Avenue
Thornber Grove
Condali Grove
Grasmere Road
Queen Victoria Road
Recreation Ground
Blackpool F.C. Ground
Longdale Road
Bolton St
Lytham Road
A584
CENTRAL DRIVE
Rugby League Ground & Greyhound Stadium
Royal Pavilion Cinema
Bus Station
Tram Depot
Central Pier
Waxworks
Law Courts
Police HQ
CHAPEL
Yorkshire St
Blundell
Tyldesley
Princess
Rigby
Dale
Coop St
Bonny St
CENTRAL STREET
PROMENADE
Winter Gardens & Opera House
Tower
North Pier
Tourist Information Centre
Princess Cinema
War Memorial
Studio 1234
A584
TALBOT ROAD
A586
B'POOL NORTH STA
Banks
Odeon Cinema
Springfield Rd
Abingdon St
Buchanan St
Queens
George St
Bus Sta
Art Gallery
Covered Market
Deansgate
HPO
St John's Ch
ABC Cinema
King St
Tivoli Cinema
Corporation St
CHURCH STREET
Market St
Adelaide St
Fire Sta
Albert Road
Charnley Road
HORNBY ROAD
REGENT ROAD
Read's Avenue
PALATINE ROAD

SCALE
yards 0 220
metres 0 200
N

BRIGHTON

DYKE ROAD
A2010
Highdown Road
Addison Road
Julian Road
Osmond Road
Nizells Av
St Anns Well Gardens
New Sussex Hospital
York Road
Victoria Road
Norfolk Terr
B2122
Montpelier Place
Montpelier Road
Montpelier Terrace
Classic Cinema
Hampton St
Spring St
B2066
WESTERN ROAD
Embassy Cinema
Western St
Montpelier St
Bedford Place
Oriental Pl
Little Preston St
Sillwood St
Sillwood Road
Regency Square
Cannon Place
Castle Street
Russell Sq
Regency Road
AA Service Centre
Stone Street
Access only Mon-Sat 09.00-18.00
Russell Road
A259
KINGS ROAD
West Pier
Summer Months Only
Brighton Centre
Kingswest Centre & Odeon Film Centre
Doll's Museum
ABC Cinema
Waxworks

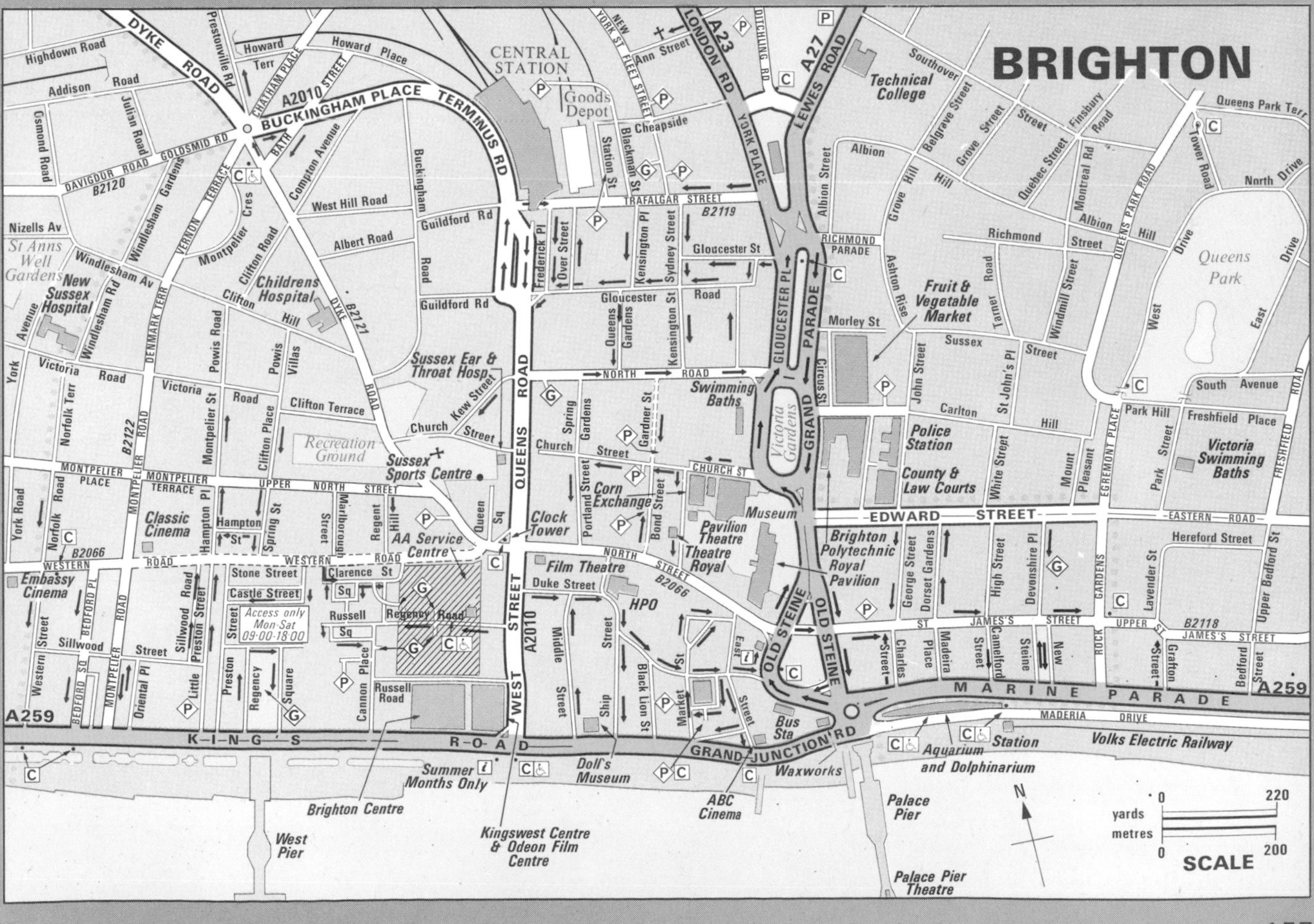

Howard St
Prestonville Rd
Chatham Place
BUCKINGHAM PLACE
TERMINUS RD
Howard Place
Vernon Terrace
Windlesham Gardens
Windlesham Rd
Compton Avenue
West Hill Road
Buckingham Road
Guildford Rd
Frederick Pl
Over Street
Clifton Road
Denmark Terr
Montpelier Cres
Montpelier Villas
Clifton Terrace
Powis Road
Powis Villas
Clifton Place
Clifton Hill
Childrens Hospital
B2121
B2120
Davigdor Road
Goldsmid Rd
Campden Avenue
Guildford Rd
Sussex Ear & Throat Hosp
Kew Street
Church Street
Recreation Ground
UPPER NORTH STREET
Marlborough St
Regent St
Queens Road
WEST STREET
A2010
Sussex Sports Centre
Spring Gardens
Gardner St
Gloucester Road
Kensington Gardens
Kensington St
Sydney Street
Trafalgar Street
B2119
Gloucester St
Queens Gardens
North Road
Portland Street
Bond Street
Corn Exchange
Clock Tower
Film Theatre
Duke Street
HPO
B2066
Ship St
Black Lion St
Middle St
Market St
GRAND JUNCTION RD
Bus Sta
Station St
Blackman St
Cheapside
Station St
CENTRAL STATION
Goods Depot
Ann Street
New St
York St
Fleet St
LONDON RD
A23
A27
York Place
GLOUCESTER PL
GRAND PARADE
Victoria Gardens
Pavilion Theatre Theatre Royal
Museum
Brighton Polytechnic Royal Pavilion
OLD STEINE
Swimming Baths
CHURCH STREET
EDWARD STREET
New Road
Aquarium and Dolphinarium
Station
Volks Electric Railway
Palace Pier
Palace Pier Theatre
MARINE PARADE
A259
DITCHLING RD
LEWES ROAD
Technical College
Southover
Grove Hill
Belgrove Street
Albion Hill
Albion Street
Quebec Street
Montreal Rd
North Drive
Richmond Parade
Ashton Rise
Richmond Street
Fruit & Vegetable Market
Morley St
Sussex Street
Carlton Hill
John Street
St John's Pl
Police Station
County & Law Courts
George Street
Dorset Gardens
St James's Street
High Street
Mount Pleasant
White Street
Devonshire Pl
Egremont Place
Park Hill
Freshfield Place
Victoria Swimming Baths
Lavender St
Hereford Street
Upper Bedford St
B2118
Clifton St
Bedford St
James's St
Finsbury Road
Queens Park Terr
Tower Road
Queens Park
West Drive
East Drive
Windmill Street
Tarnet Road
South Avenue
EASTERN ROAD
Freshfield Road
QUEENS PARK ROAD

SCALE
yards 0 220
metres 0 200
N

157

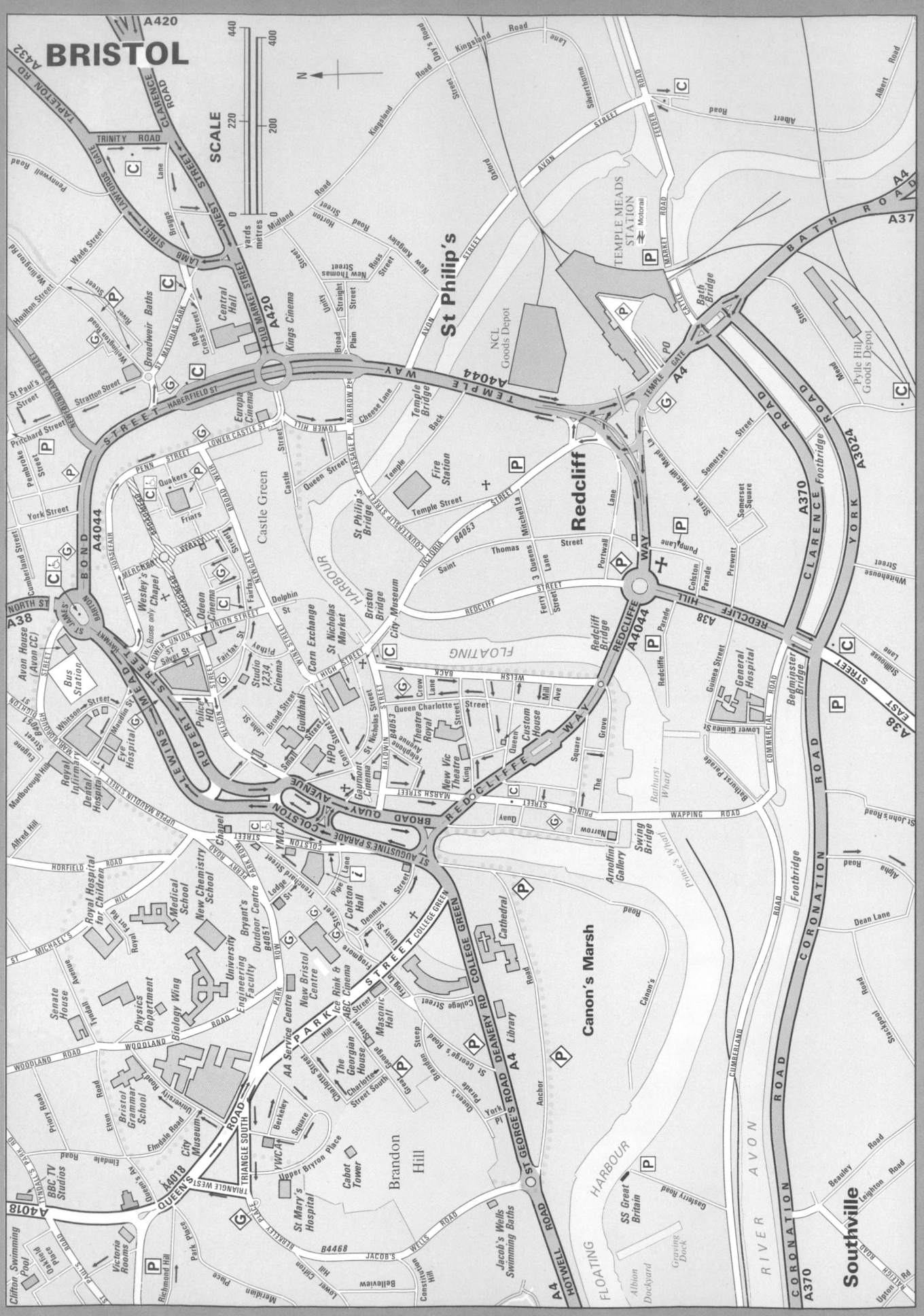

BRISTOL

A420

A4432 TAPLETON RD

CLARENCE ROAD

TRINITY ROAD

SCALE

Pennywell Road
Houlton Street
St Paul's Street
Pritchard Street
Pembroke
York Street
Cumberland Street

Wade Street
Braggs
Lane
Broadweir Baths
Red Cross Lane
Stratton Street

Central Hall
Kings Cinema
Europa Cinema

LAWFORDS GATE
LAMB STREET
WEST STREET
OLD MARKET STREET
A420

Horton Street
Midland
New Thomas Street
Straight Street
Union Street
Broad
Plain
Back

St Philip's

Kingsland Road
Day's Road
Silverthorne

TEMPLE MEADS STATION
Motorail
Market Road
NCL Goods Depot

AVON STREET
FEEDER ROAD

Albert Road
BATH ROAD A4
A37

Oxford Street

BOND STREET
A4044

PENN STREET
Fairfax
Haberfield St
LOWER CASTLE ST
TOWER HILL
NARROW PL
Cheese Lane

Quakers
Friars
THE HORSEFAIR
MERCHANT STREET

Castle Green
Castle Street
Dolphin St

HARBOUR
Queen Street
Bristol Bridge
City Museum

TEMPLE WAY A4044
Temple Bridge
St Philip's Bridge
COUNTERSLIP STREET
VICTORIA
B4053
Temple Street
Saint Thomas Street
Fire Station

REDCLIFF
Somerset Street
Somerset Square

Redcliff Mead La
Street Redcliff Footbridge

Pyle Hill Goods Depot

NORTH ST
A38
Avon House (Avon CC)
ST JAMES BARTON

Bus Station
Eugene Street
Whitson Street
Marlborough Street

Wesley's Chapel
Odeon
Corn Exchange
Bristol Market
High Street

THE TRAMWAY
BARTON
UPPER UNION STREET
UNION STREET
Silver St
Pithay
Fairfax
St Nicholas
PENN STREET

Studio 1,2,3,4 Cinema
Guildhall
Police HQ
Small St
John St
Broad Street
PO

Crow Lane
Back
WELSH BACK
Queen Charlotte Street
Theatre Royal
New Vic Theatre
Custom House
King Street
Queen Square
The Grove

Mitchell La
Thomas
3 Queens
Parade
Portwall Lane
Colston Parade
Ferry Street

REDCLIFF WAY
Redcliff Bridge
REDCLIFFE HILL A38
A4044
Redcliffe
Parade

General Hospital
Guinea Street
Lower Guinea St

YORK ROAD A3024
CLARENCE ROAD A370
Whitehouse Street

BEDMINSTER BRIDGE
A38 EAST STREET
Stillhouse Lane

Royal Infirmary
Eye Hospital
Dental Hospital
Royal
Fort Rd

Maudlin Street
UPPER MAUDLIN STREET
MARLBOROUGH ST

New Chemistry School
Medical School
Bryant's Outdoor Centre
B4051

Marsh Street
Telephone Avenue
Baldwin Street
Gaumont Cinema

BROAD QUAY
COLSTON AVENUE
COLSTON STREET
ST AUGUSTINE'S PARADE
RUPERT STREET
LEWINS MEAD

Marsh
Street
Prince
Street
Quay
Narrow Quay
Arnolfini Gallery

Bathurst Wharf
The Grove
WAPPING ROAD
Swing Bridge
Prince's Wharf

St John's Road
Alpha Road

HORFIELD ROAD
Alfred Hill
Royal Hospital for Children
St Michael's Hill

University Engineering Faculty
Woodland Road

Tankard's Close
Park Row
Frog Lane
Denmark St
Colston Hall
Pipe Lane
i

YMCA
Lodge St
Trenchard Street

College Street
COLLEGE GREEN
Cathedral
Library
Canon's
Canon's Marsh

FLOATING HARBOUR

Alpha Road
Dean Lane

Senate House
Tyndall
Physics Department
Biology Wing
WOODLAND ROAD

University Road
PARK ROW
PARK STREET

AA Service Centre
New Bristol Centre
Ice Rink & ABC Cinema
Hill Street
Masonic Hall
Charlotte Street
The Georgian House
Charlotte Street South

Great George Street
Brandon Hill
Steep Street
Brandon Steep
St George's Road
Queen's Parade
Anchor Road

Deanery Rd
A4 College Street

Cumberland Road

Stackpool Road
Leighton Road
Beauley Road

BBC TV Studios
Elmdale Road
Tyndall's Park
Queen's Rd
A4018

QUEEN'S ROAD
TRIANGLE SOUTH
TRIANGLE WEST

Bristol Grammar School
City Museum
Berkeley Square
YWCA
Upper Byron Place

St Mary's Hospital
B4468
JACOB'S WELLS ROAD
Constitution Hill
Lower Clifton Hill

Brandon Hill
Cabot Tower

Jacob's Wells Baths
Jacob's Wells Swimming Baths
SS Great Britain
Graving Dock
Albion Dockyard

HOTWELL ROAD A4
ST GEORGE'S ROAD

FLOATING HARBOUR

RIVER AVON
CORONATION ROAD A370

Southville

Coronation Road
Gasferry Road

Clifton Swimming Pool
Victoria Rooms
Richmond Hill
Meridian Place
Park Place
Belleview

A4018

158

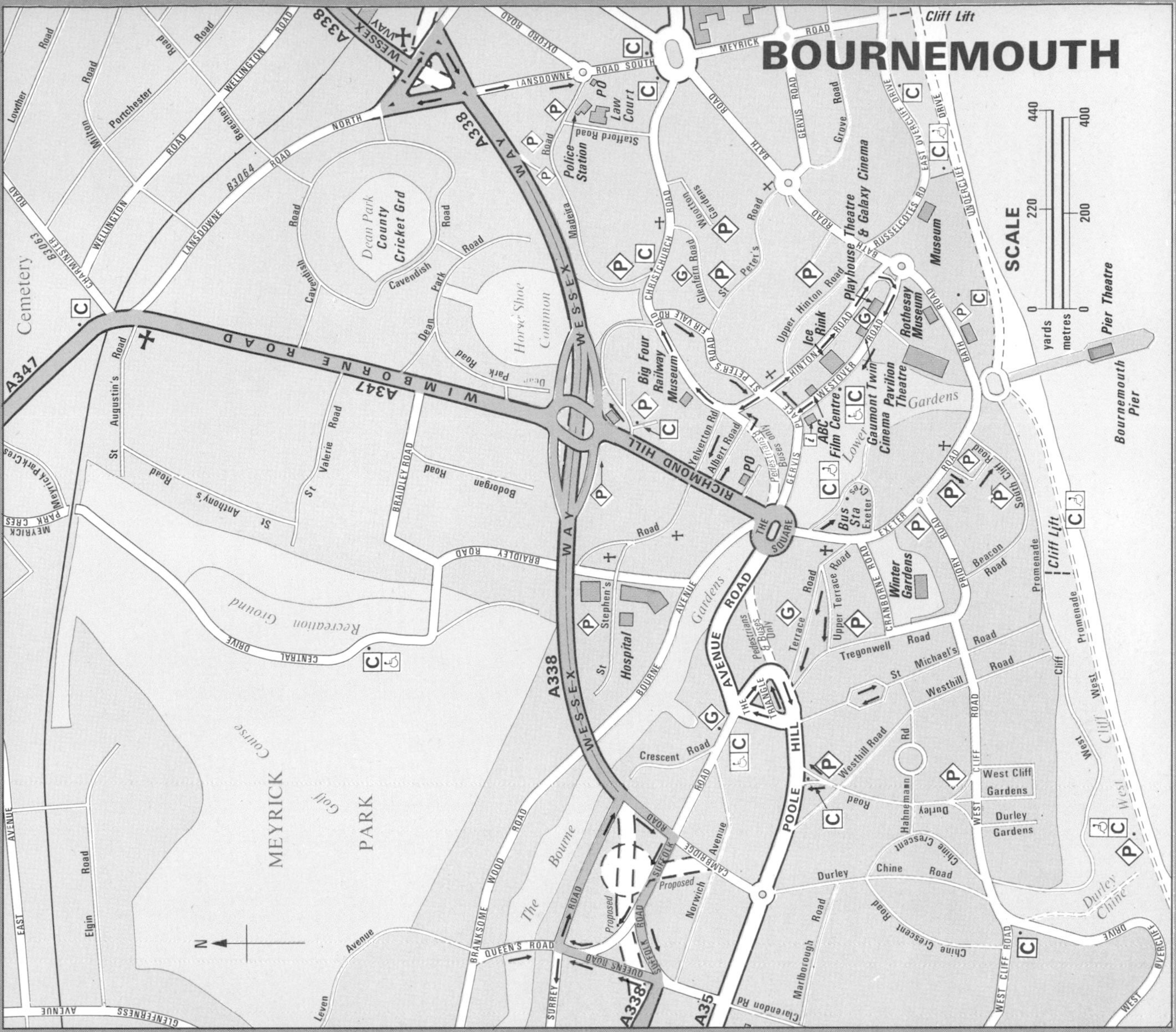

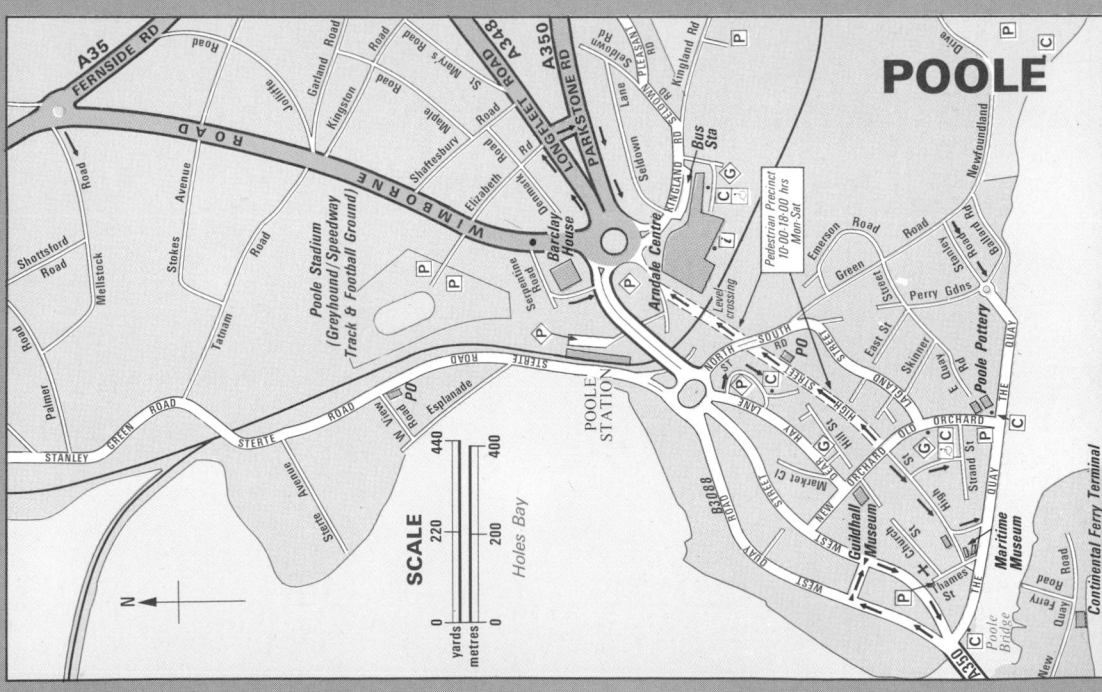

BOURNEMOUTH

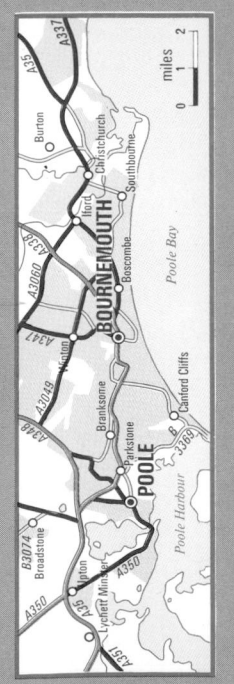

POOLE

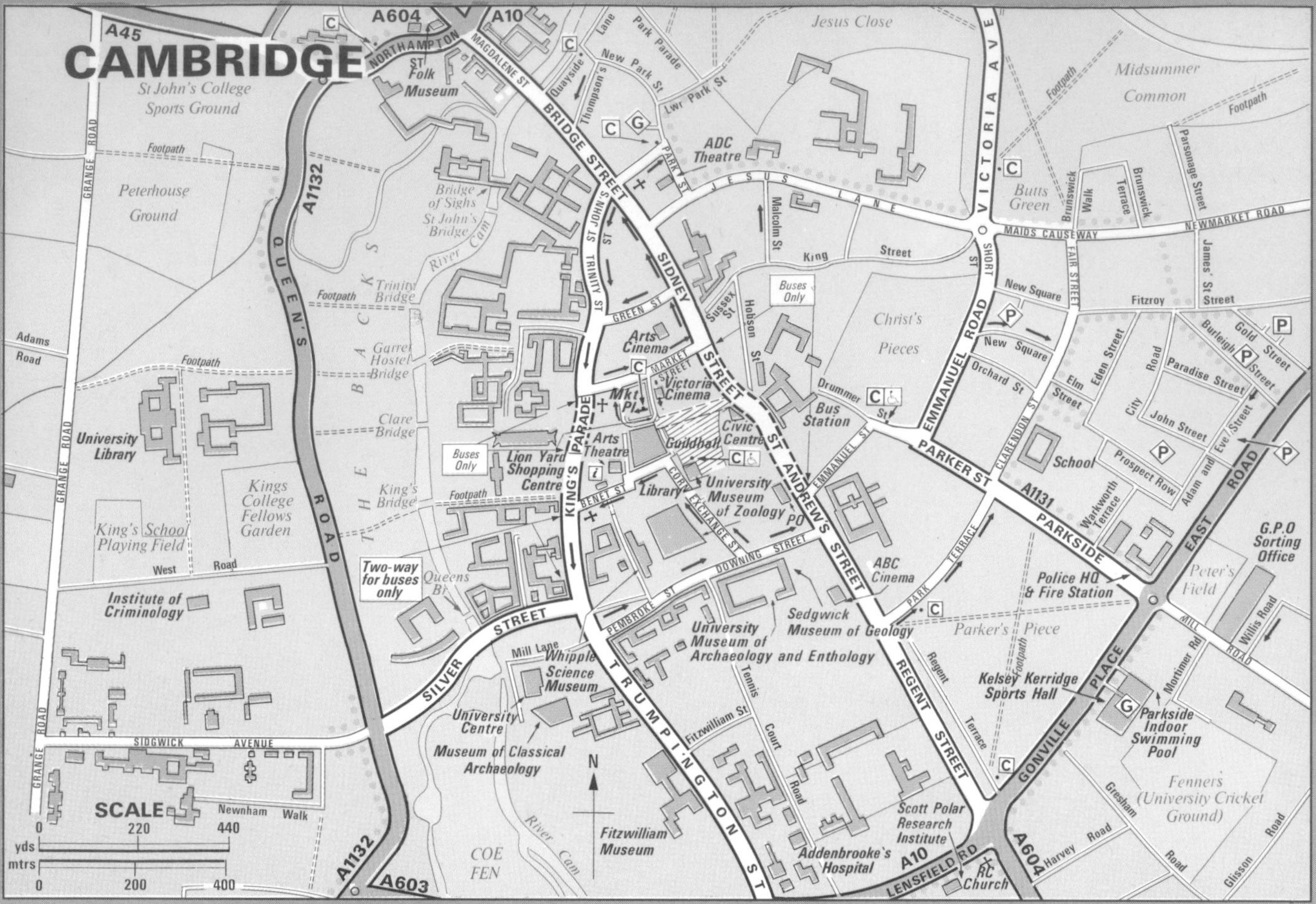

CAMBRIDGE

A45 · A604 · A10 · A1132 · NORTHAMPTON · St Folk Museum · MAGDALENE ST · Quayside · New Park St · Park Parade · Jesus Close · VICTORIA AVE · Midsummer Common · Footpath · Passage Street

St John's College Sports Ground · Peterhouse Ground · Bridge of Sighs · St John's Bridge · River Cam · BRIDGE STREET · Thompson's Lane · Lwr Park St · ADC Theatre · Butts Green · Brunswick · Walk · NEWMARKET ROAD

Adams Road · Footpath · Trinity Bridge · Garret Hostel Bridge · Clare Bridge · TRINITY ST · GREEN ST · SIDNEY STREET · Malcolm St · King · Street · MAIDS CAUSEWAY · FAIR ST · James's Street · Fitzroy · Street

University Library · King's School Playing Field · Kings College Fellows Garden · Institute of Criminology · King's Bridge · Footpath · Queens Br · West Road · THE BACKS · QUEENS ROAD · GRANGE ROAD · Arts Cinema · Mkt Pl · Victoria Cinema · Hobson St · Sussex St · Christ's Pieces · New Square · New Square · EMMANUEL ROAD · Orchard St · Drummer St · Bus Station · PARKER ST · Elm · Eden Street · City · Road · Paradise Street · Gold · Street · Burleigh Street · John Street · Prospect Row · Adam and Eve Street · EAST · ROAD

Two-way for buses only · Buses Only · Lion Yard Shopping Centre · Arts Theatre · Guildhall · Civic Centre · Library · University Museum of Zoology · University PO · EXCHANGE ST · ABC Cinema · PARK TERRACE · Wordsworth Terrace · School · ST ANDREW'S STREET · EMMANUEL · A1131 · PARKSIDE · Police HQ & Fire Station · G.P.O Sorting Office · Peter's Field · Willis Road

SCALE · yds · 220 · 440 · mtrs · 0 · 200 · 400 · Newnham Walk · SIDGWICK AVENUE · GRANGE ROAD · SILVER STREET · Mill Lane · Whipple Science Museum · University Centre · Museum of Classical Archaeology · TRUMPINGTON ST · PEMBROKE ST · DOWNING STREET · University Museum of Archaeology and Enthology · Sedgwick Museum of Geology · Tennis · Court · Fitzwilliam St · Parker's Piece · Kelsey Kerridge Sports Hall · REGENT STREET · Regent Terrace · GONVILLE PLACE · Parkside Indoor Swimming Pool · Fenners (University Cricket Ground) · Gresham Road · Glisson Road

N · Fitzwilliam Museum · River Cam · COE FEN · A1132 · A603 · Scott Polar Research Institute · Addenbrooke's Hospital · A10 · LENSFIELD RD · RC Church · A604 · Harvey Road · Mortimer Rd · Tenison Terrace

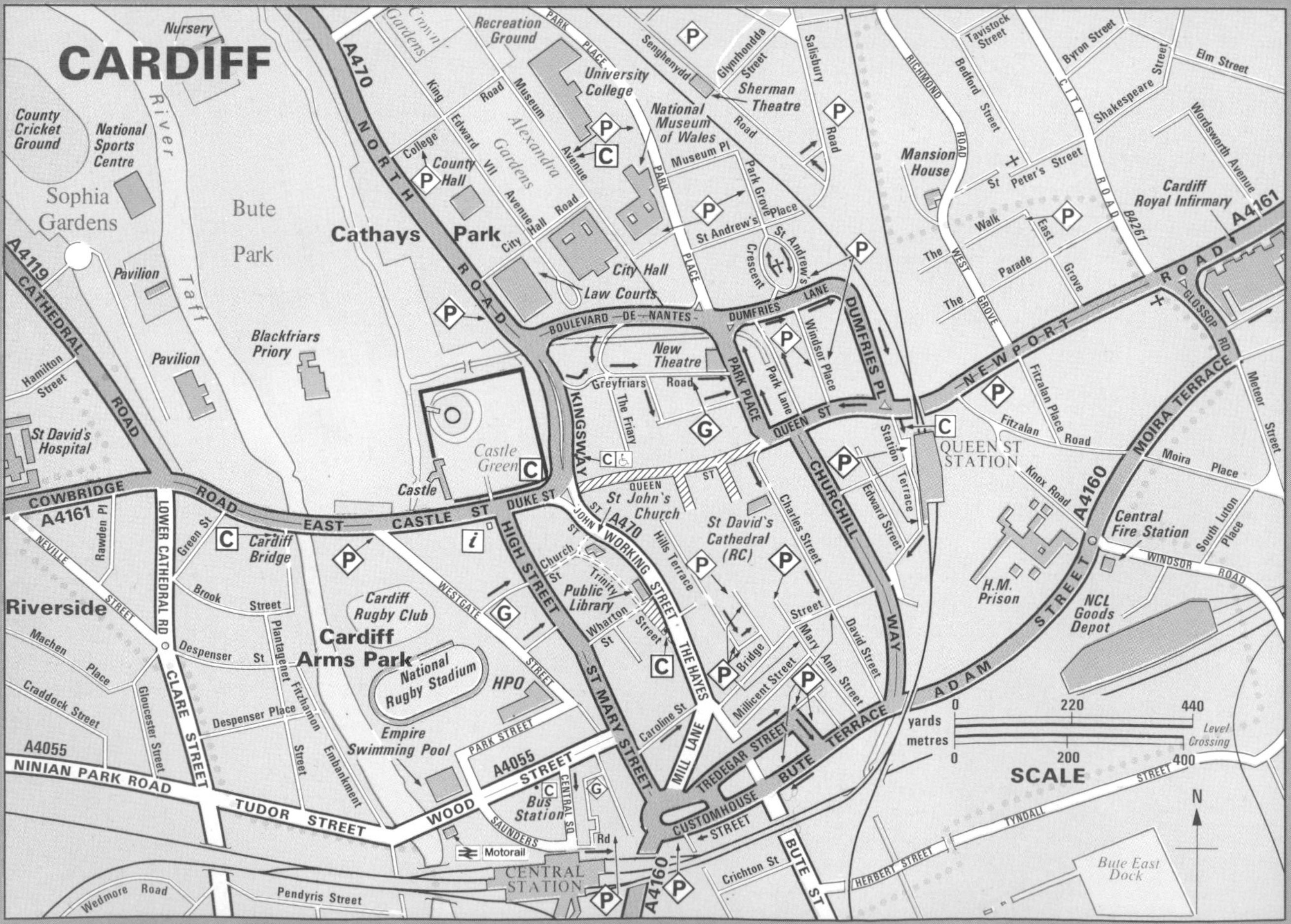

CARDIFF

Nursery · CROWN GARDENS · Recreation Ground · PARK PLACE · Senghenydd Rd · Glynrhondda St · Salisbury · Road · Tavistock Street · Byron Street · Elm Street

County Cricket Ground · National Sports Centre · River Taff · A470 · NORTH ROAD · King Edward VII Avenue · Museum Avenue · University College · National Museum of Wales · Museum Pl · Sherman Theatre · RICHMOND ROAD · Shakespeare Street · Wordsworth Avenue · CITY ROAD

Sophia Gardens · Pavilion · Bute Park · College Road · County Hall · Alexandra Gardens · Avenue Road · City Hall Road · Park · Park Grove · Park Place · Mansion House · St Peter's Street · St Peter's · The · Walk · Cardiff Royal Infirmary · A4161

A4119 · CATHEDRAL ROAD · Blackfriars Priory · Cathays Park · City Hall · Law Courts · BOULEVARD-DE-NANTES · St Andrew's Place · St Andrew's Crescent · DUMFRIES LANE · DUMFRIES PL · The Parade · The Grove · NEWPORT ROAD · A4261 · Glossop Rd · MOIRA TERRACE · A4160 · Meteor St

Hamilton Street · Pavilion · St David's Hospital · COWBRIDGE ROAD · A4161 · Rawden Pl · Green St · LOWER CATHEDRAL RD · Cardiff Bridge · EAST · CASTLE ST · Castle · Castle Green · KINGSWAY · New Theatre · Greyfriars Road · The Friary · PARK LANE · Windsor Place · DUMFRIES LANE · Fitzalan Place · Fitzalan Road · Moira Place

Riverside · NEVILLE ST · Brook Street · Despenser St · Craddock Street · Gloucester Street · Despenser Place · Cardiff Arms Park · Cardiff Rugby Club · National Rugby Stadium · HPO · Empire Swimming Pool · HIGH STREET · WESTGATE STREET · Church St · Trinity St · Wharton St · St John's Church · Queen St · QUEEN ST STATION · CHURCHILL WAY · Charles Street · Edward Street · David Street · St David's Cathedral (RC) · Mary Ann Street · Station Terrace · H.M. Prison · WINDSOR ROAD · South Luton Place · Central Fire Station · NCL Goods Depot

A4055 · NINIAN PARK ROAD · CLARE STREET · Machen Place · Despenser Street · Park Street · A4055 · WOOD STREET · ST MARY STREET · Caroline St · Mill Lane · THE HAYES · Hills Terrace · JOHN · WORKING STREET · Bridge St · Millicent Street · Bute Terrace · Tredegar Street · BUTE TERRACE · ADAM STREET · Knox Road

TUDOR STREET · Embankment · Central Rd · Bus Station · CUSTOMHOUSE STREET · Crichton St · BUTE ST · Herbert Street · TYNDALL STREET · Bute East Dock

Wedmore Road · Pendyris Street · Motorail · CENTRAL STATION · A4160 · Saunders Road · SCALE · yards · 220 · 440 · metres · 0 · 200 · 400 · Level Crossing · N

160

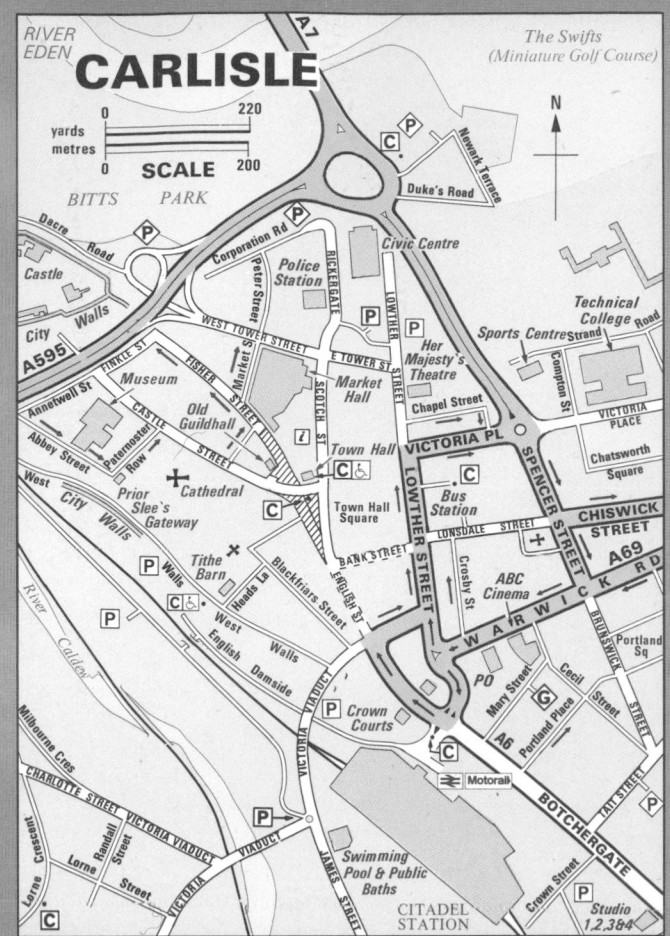

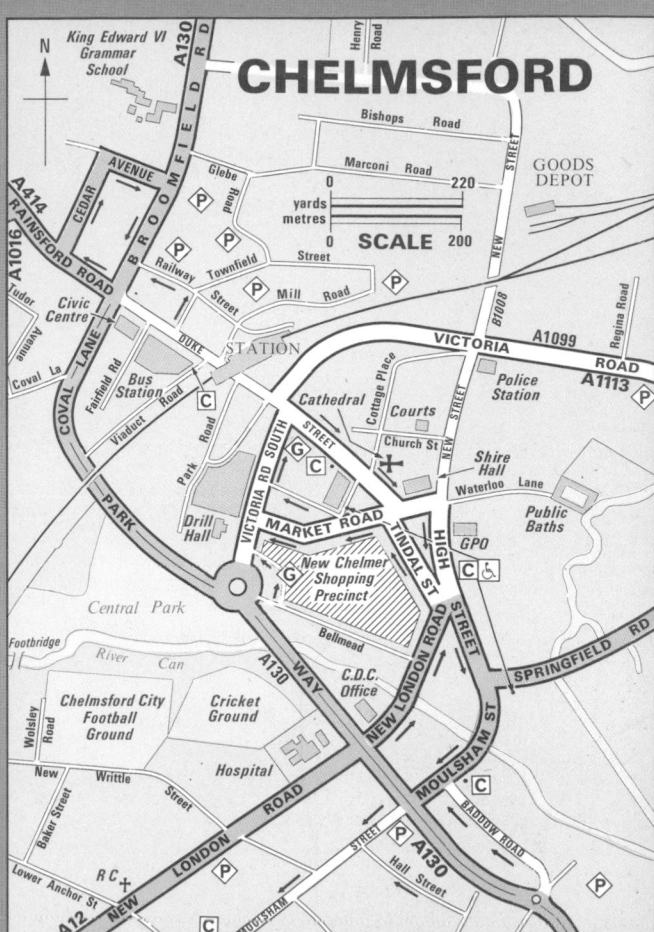

CARLISLE

RIVER EDEN

The Swifts
(Miniature Golf Course)

SCALE
yards 0 — 220
metres 0 — 200

BITTS PARK

A7

N

Dacre Road
Castle Walls
City Walls
A595
Annetwell St
Abbey Street
West City Walls
River Caldew
Milbourne Cres
Charlotte Street
Lorne Crescent
Randall Street
Lorne Street
VICTORIA VIADUCT
VICTORIA VIADUCT
JAMES STREET

Corporation Rd
Peter Street
RICKERGATE
Civic Centre
Police Station
Duke's Road
Newark Terrace
WEST TOWER STREET
E TOWER ST
Her Majesty's Theatre
Sports Centre
Compton St
Strand
Technical College
Road
Museum
TINKLE ST
FISHER ST
CASTLE STREET
SCOTCH ST
LOWTHER
Market Hall
Chapel Street
VICTORIA PLACE
VICTORIA PLACE
Chatsworth Square
Paternoster Row
Old Guildhall
Prior Slee's Gateway
Cathedral
Town Hall
Town Hall Square
LOWTHER STREET
SPENCER STREET
Bus Station
LONSDALE STREET
Crosby St
CHISWICK STREET
A69
Tithe Barn
Heads
Blackfriars Street
BANK STREET
Walls
West English Walls
Damside
ABC Cinema
WARWICK RD
BRUNSWICK STREET
Portland Sq
PO
Mary Street
Cecil Street
Portland Place
Portland Street
A6
Crown Courts
Swimming Pool & Public Baths
Motorail
Crown Street
CITADEL STATION
BOTCHERGATE
Studio 1,2,3&4

CHELMSFORD

N

King Edward VI Grammar School
A130
Henry Road
GOODS DEPOT
A1016
A414
RAINSFORD ROAD
Bishops Road
Marconi Road
NEW STREET
CEDAR AVENUE
BROOMFIELD
Glebe Rd
Railway Street
Townfield
Mill Road
Regina Road
Tudor Avenue
Coval Lane
Civic Centre
Fairfield Rd
Bus Station
DUKE STREET
STATION
VICTORIA
A1099
ROAD
A1113
Park Road
Cathedral
Cottage Place
Courts
Police Station
Church St
Shire Hall
COVAL LANE
Viaduct
VICTORIA RD SOUTH
HIGH STREET
Waterloo Lane
GPO
Public Baths
Drill Hall
MARKET ROAD
TINDAL ST
New Chelmer Shopping Precinct
Bellmead
Central Park
Footbridge
River Can
A130
NEW LONDON ROAD
C.D.C. Office
SPRINGFIELD RD
Wolsley Road
Chelmsford City Football Ground
Cricket Ground
Hospital
MOULSHAM ST
BADDOW ROAD
New Street
Writtle
Baker Street
Lower Anchor St
RC
A12
NEW LONDON ROAD
MOULSHAM
Hall Street
A130

SCALE
yards 0 — 220
metres 0 — 200

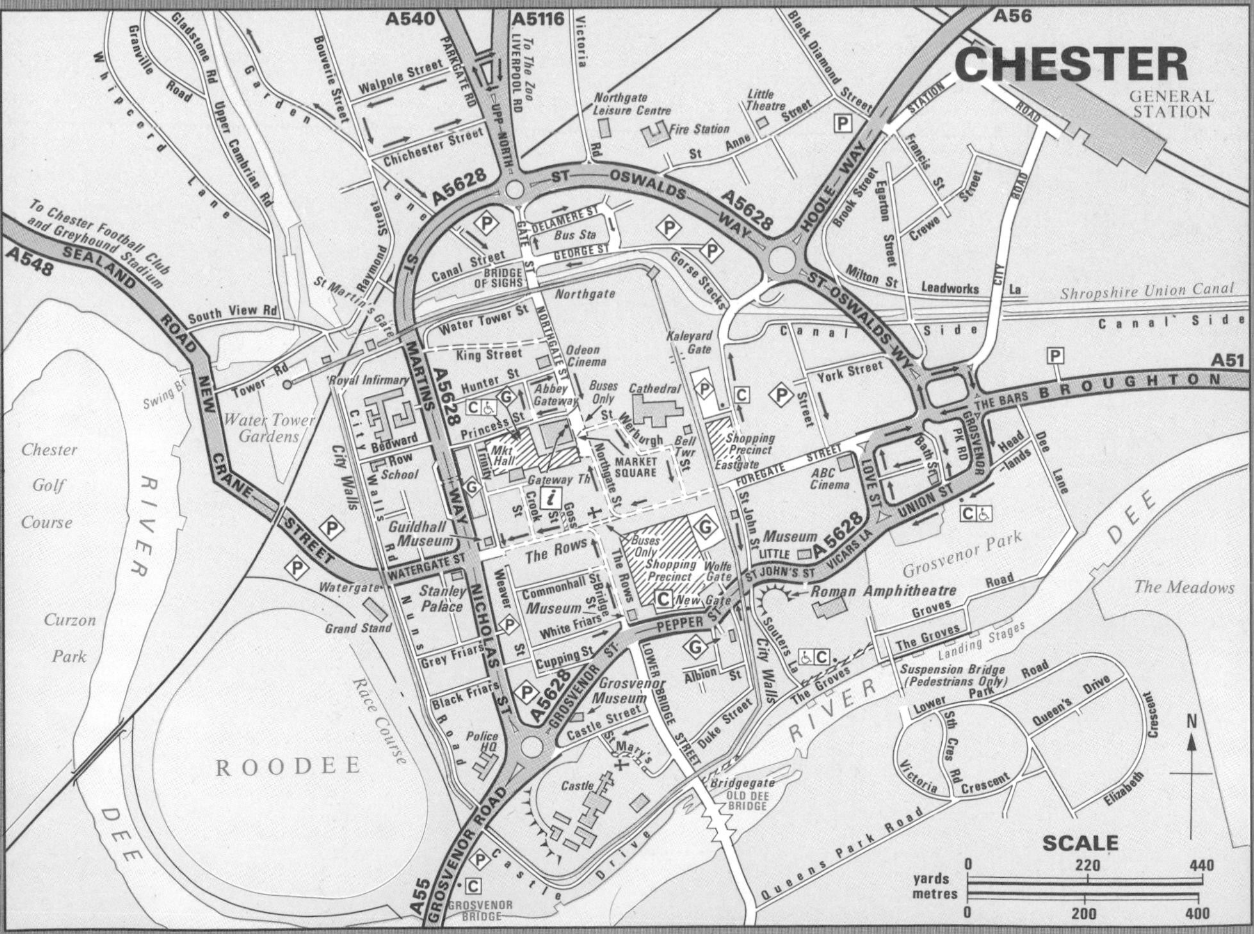

CHESTER

GENERAL STATION

A540
A5116
A56
Victoria
Granville Road
Gladstone Rd
Bouverie Street
Walpole Street
PARKGATE RD
To The Zoo
LIVERPOOL RD
UPP. NORTH
Northgate Leisure Centre
Little Theatre
St Anne
Fire Station
STATION
HOOLE WAY
ROAD
Black Diamond Street
Whipcord Lane
Upper Cambrian Rd
Chichester Street
A5628
ST OSWALDS WAY
A5628
Francis St
Egerton St
Brook Street
Crewe St
A548
SEALAND ROAD
To Chester Football Club and Greyhound Stadium
Garden Lane
Pemberton Road
St Martins
South View Rd
St Martins Gate
DELAMERE ST
Bus Sta
GEORGE ST
Canal Street
BRIDGE OF SIGHS
Northgate
Gorse Stacks
ST OSWALDS WY
Milton St
Leadworks La
CITY ROAD
Shropshire Union Canal
Canal Side
Swing Br
Tower Rd
Royal Infirmary
Water Tower St
King Street
Odeon Cinema
Kaleyard Gate
Canal
York Street
THE BARS
BROUGHTON
A51
Water Tower Gardens
Abbey Gateway
Cathedral
Buses Only
Northgate St
St Werburgh
Bell Twr
Grosvenor Park
Chester Golf Course
RIVER DEE
NEW CRANE STREET
CITY WALLS
Bedward Row
Kings School
Princes Av
Mkt Hall
Goss St
MARKET SQUARE
Shopping Precinct Eastgate
FOREGATE STREET
ABC Cinema
LOVE ST
UNION ST
GROSVENOR PK RD
Bath St
Dee Lane
Headlands
A5628
Guildhall Museum
WATERGATE ST
NICHOLAS ST
WEAVER ST
The Rows
Gateway Th
Crook St
Buses Only Shopping Precinct
Commonhall St
White Friars
Wolfe Gate
Museum LITTLE
Roman Amphitheatre
St John St
St John's St
VICARS LA
New Gate
Grosvenor Park
The Meadows
Watergate
Stanley Palace
GROSVENOR STREET
Grand Stand
Grey Friars
Cupping St
Black Friars
PEPPER STREET
LOWER BRIDGE STREET
Duke Street
City Walls
The Groves
Landing Stages
The Groves
Suspension Bridge (Pedestrians Only)
Lower Park Road
Queen's Drive
Crescent
Curzon Park
Race Course
ROODEE
A5628
Grosvenor Museum
Police HQ
Castle
St Mary's
Bridgegate
Old Dee Bridge
Albion St
RIVER DEE
Sth Cres Rd
Victoria Crescent
Elizabeth
Queens Park Road
A55
GROSVENOR ROAD
GROSVENOR BRIDGE
Castle Drive

N

SCALE
yards 0 — 220 — 440
metres 0 — 200 — 400

161.

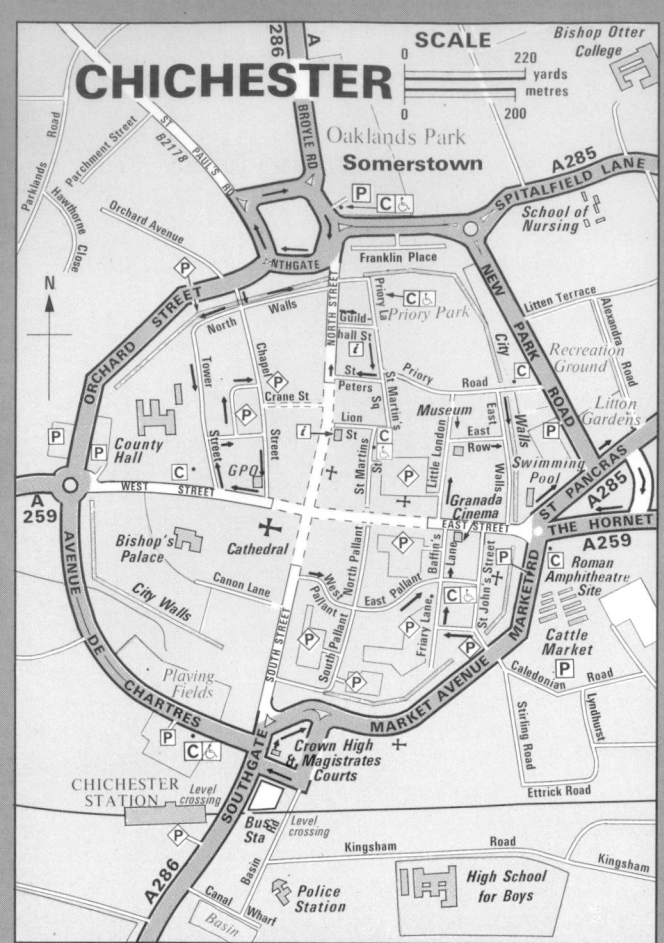

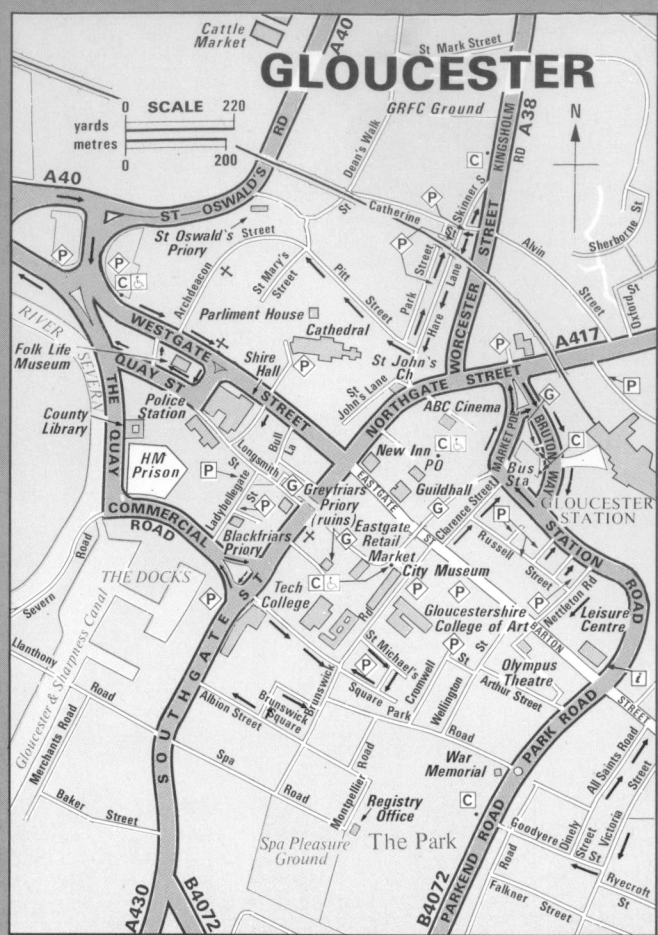

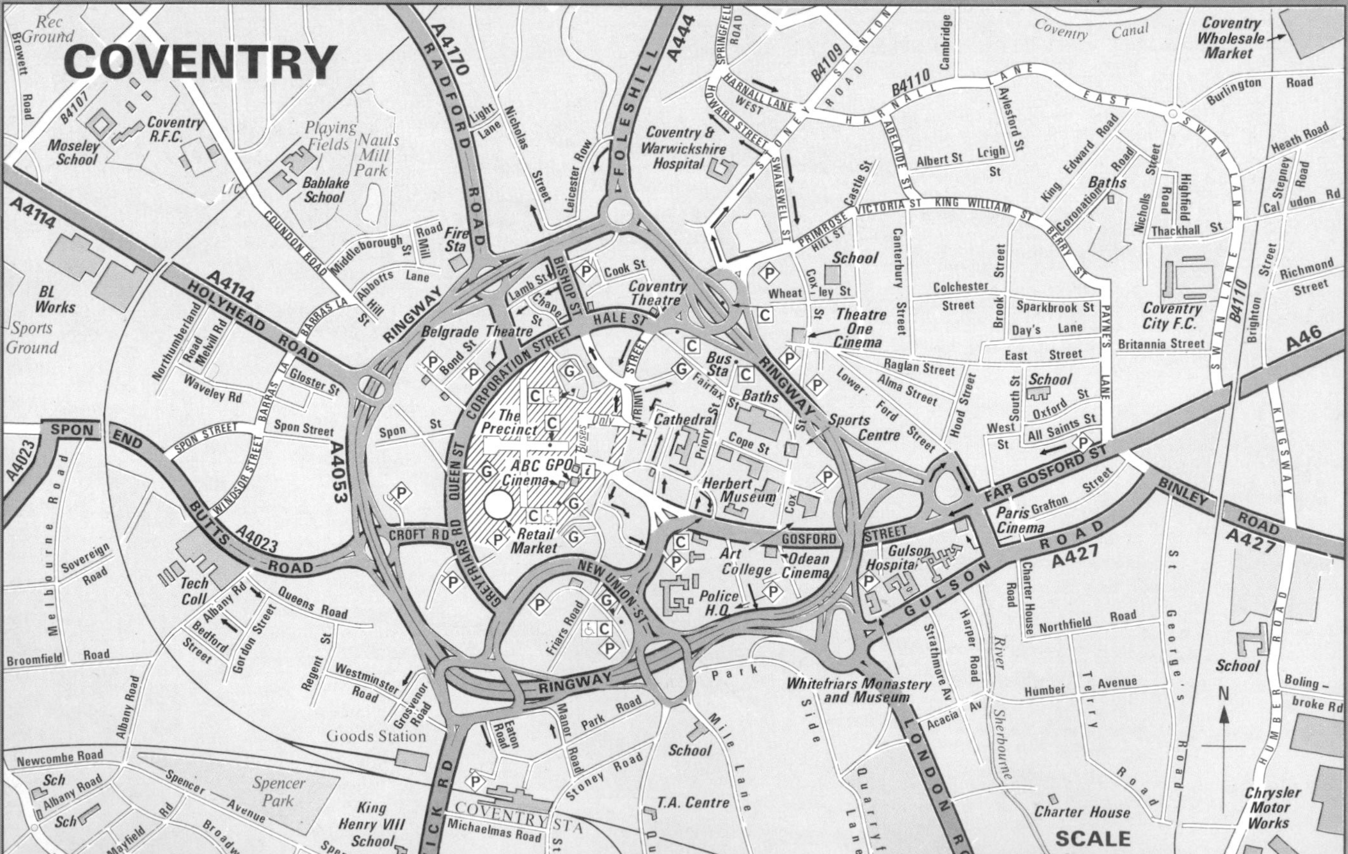

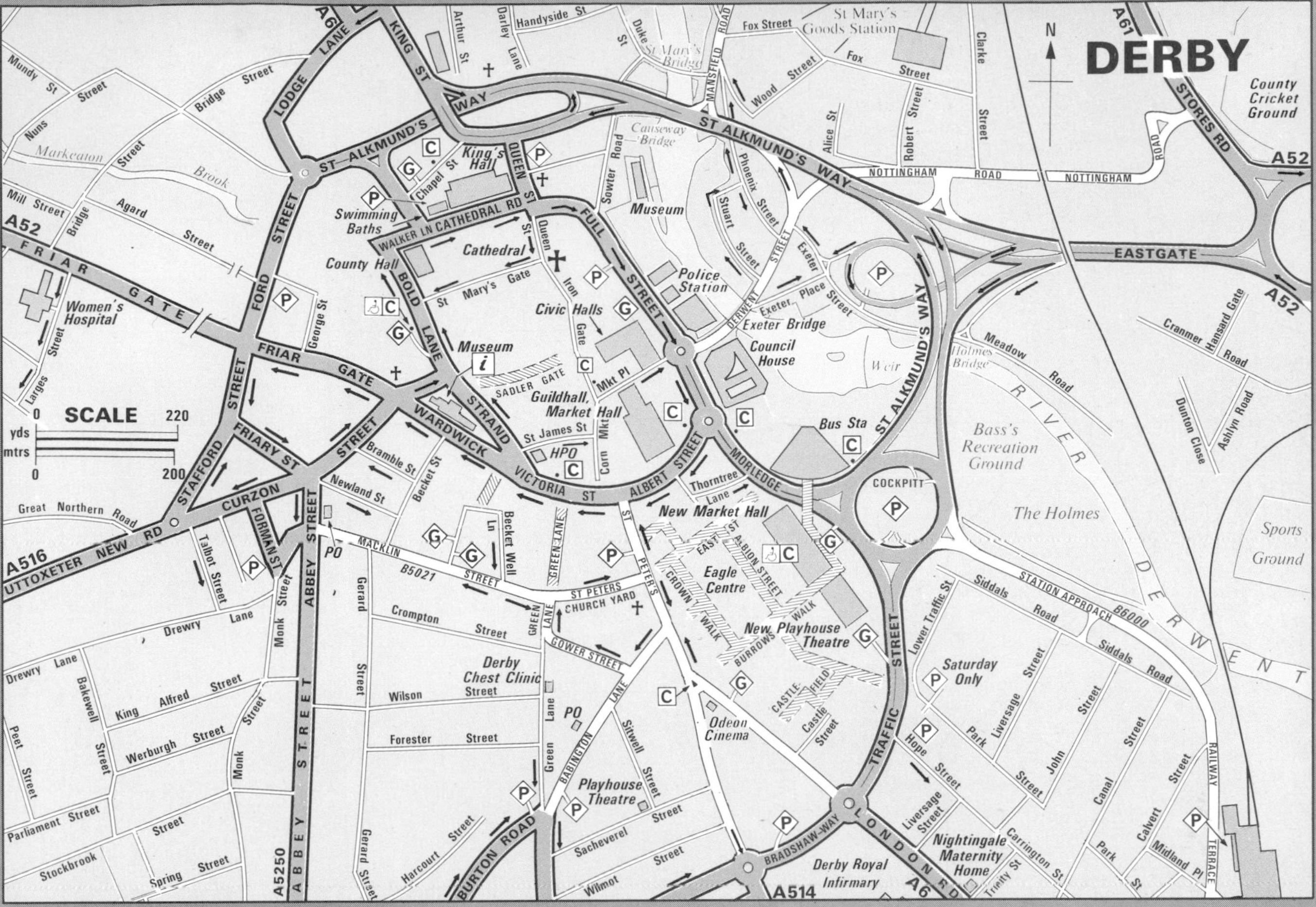
DERBY
N
County Cricket Ground
SCALE
0
220
yds
mtrs
0
200
A6
A61
A52
A516
A5250
A514
B5021
B6000
LODGE LANE
KING ST
ST ALKMUND'S WAY
ST ALKMUND'S
QUEEN ST
FORD STREET
FRIAR GATE
FRIARY ST
STAFFORD STREET
CURZON ST
UTTOXETER NEW RD
ABBEY STREET
FORMAN ST
WARDWICK
STRAND
VICTORIA ST
ALBERT STREET
MORLEDGE
FULL STREET
BOLD LANE
CATHEDRAL RD
WALKER LN
SADLER GATE
COCKPITT
TRAFFIC STREET
LONDON RD
BRADSHAW WAY
BURTON ROAD
NOTTINGHAM ROAD
EASTGATE
STORES RD
Handyside St
Arthur St
Darley Lane
Duke St
St Mary's Bridge
St Mary's Goods Station
Fox Street
Mansfield Road
Clarke Street
Mundy St
Bridge Street
Nuns Street
Markeaton Brook
Street
Mill Street
Agard Street
King's Hall
Chapel St
Swimming Baths
Sowter Road
Causeway Bridge
Museum
Phoenix Street
Stuart Street
Alice St
Robert Street
Wood Street
Cathedral
County Hall
St Mary's Gate
Iron Gate
Police Station
Civic Halls
Exeter Place
Exeter Street
Exeter Bridge
Council House
Derwent St
Women's Hospital
George St
Larges Street
Museum
Guildhall, Market Hall
Mkt Pl
Corn Mkt
St James St
HPO
Bus Sta
Weir
Holmes Bridge
Meadow Road
Cranmer Road
Hansard Gate
Bass's Recreation Ground
Denton Close
Ashlyn Road
RIVER DERWENT
The Holmes
Sports Ground
Great Northern Road
Newland St
Bramble St
Becket St
Becket Well Ln
Green Lane
Thorntree Lane
New Market Hall
East St
Albion St
Eagle Centre
MACKLIN STREET
PO
Talbot Street
Monk Street
Gerard Street
Crompton Street
ST PETERS CHURCH YARD
St Peter's St
Crown Walk
New Playhouse Theatre
Burrows Walk
Siddals Road
Station Approach
Lower Traffic St
Drewry Lane
Bakewell Street
King Alfred Street
Wilson Street
Derby Chest Clinic
GOWER STREET
Castle Field
Castle Street
Saturday Only
Liversage Street
Park Street
John Street
Odeon Cinema
Peet Street
Werburgh Street
Forester Street
PO
Sitwell Street
Babington Lane
Hope Street
Canal Street
Parliament Street
Street
Playhouse Theatre
Sacheverel Street
Liversage Street
Nightingale Maternity Home
Carrington St
Calvert Street
Railway Terrace
Stockbrook Street
Spring Street
Harcourt Street
Wilmot Street
Derby Royal Infirmary
Trinity St
Midland Pl
Park St

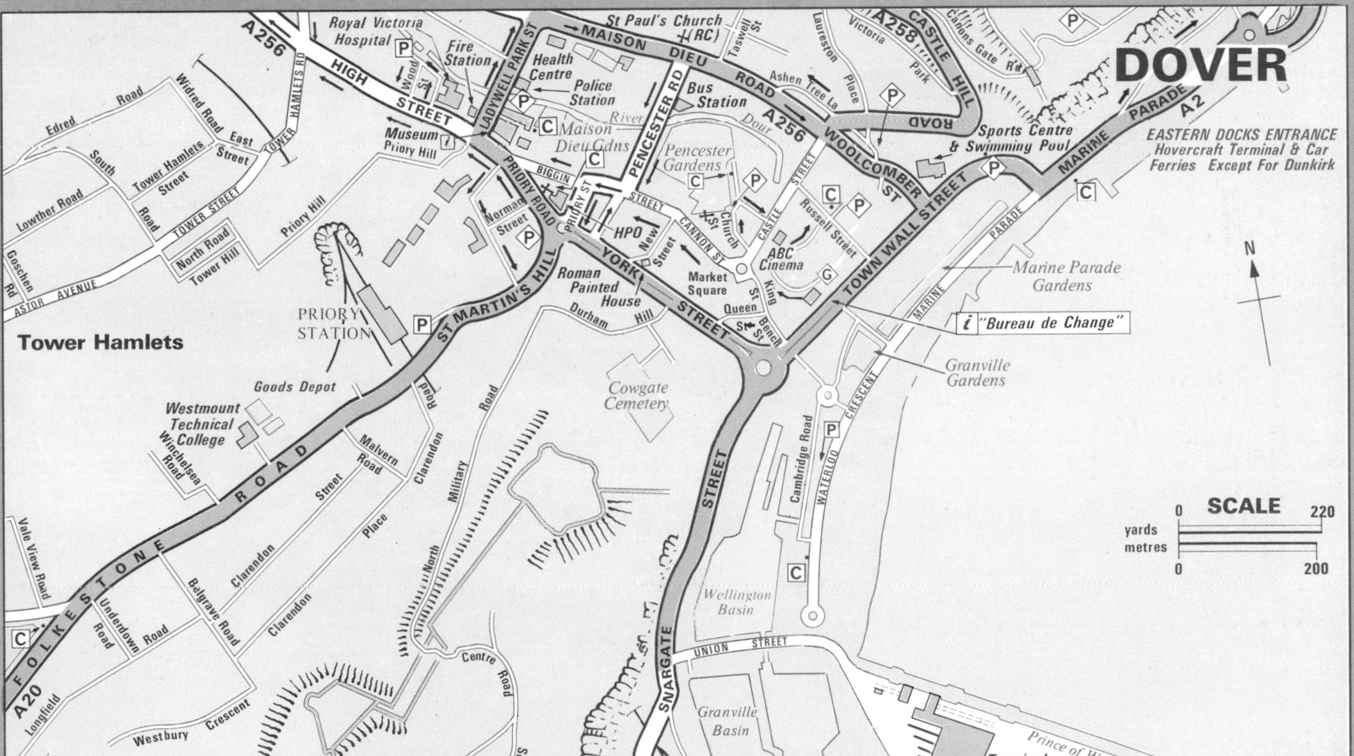
DOVER
A256
A258
A2
A20
Royal Victoria Hospital
MAISON DIEU ROAD
St Paul's Church (RC)
Taswell St
Laureston Place
Victoria Park
CASTLE HILL ROAD
Canons Gate Rd
HIGH STREET
Wood St
Fire Station
LADYWELL PARK ST
Health Centre
Police Station
Maison Dieu Gdns
River Dour
Bus Station
Ashen Tree La
WOOLCOMBER ST
Sports Centre & Swimming Pool
MARINE PARADE
EASTERN DOCKS ENTRANCE
Hovercraft Terminal & Car Ferries Except For Dunkirk
Edred Road
Widred Road
East Street
Tower Hamlets Street
TOWER HAMLETS RD
South Road
Museum
Priory Hill
PENCESTER RD
Pencester Gardens
BIGGIN
PRIORY ST
PRIORY ROAD
Lowther Road
TOWER STREET
Priory Hill
North Road
Tower Hill
Norman Street
HPO
New Street
CANNON ST
Church St
CASTLE STREET
Russell Street
ABC Cinema
TOWN WALL STREET
Marine Parade Gardens
N
Goschen Rd
ASTOR AVENUE
PRIORY STATION
ST MARTIN'S HILL
Roman Painted House
YORK STREET
Market Square
King St
Queen St
Bench St
Durham Hill
"Bureau de Change"
Granville Gardens
Tower Hamlets
Goods Depot
Cowgate Cemetery
Westmount Technical College
Winchelsea Road
Malvern Road
Clarendon Street
Military Road
Cambridge Road
WATERLOO CRESCENT
STREET
SCALE
0
220
yards
metres
0
200
FOLKESTONE ROAD
Vale View Road
Clarendon Place
North Military Road
Belgrave Road
Clarendon Road
Wellington Basin
Underdown Road
Longfield
Westbury Crescent
Centre Road
UNION STREET
SNARGATE
Granville Basin
Prince of Wales Pier
Terminal Building
South Road
Hardwicke Road
Western Heights
European Vehicle Recovery
Elizabeth Road
Tidal Basin
Seaspeed Hovercraft Terminal
Military Road
Limekiln Street
North Pier
South Pier
WESTERN DOCKS
Citadel Heights
Citadel Road
LORD WARDEN SQUARE
THE VIADUCT
INNER HARBOUR
Citadel HM Borstal

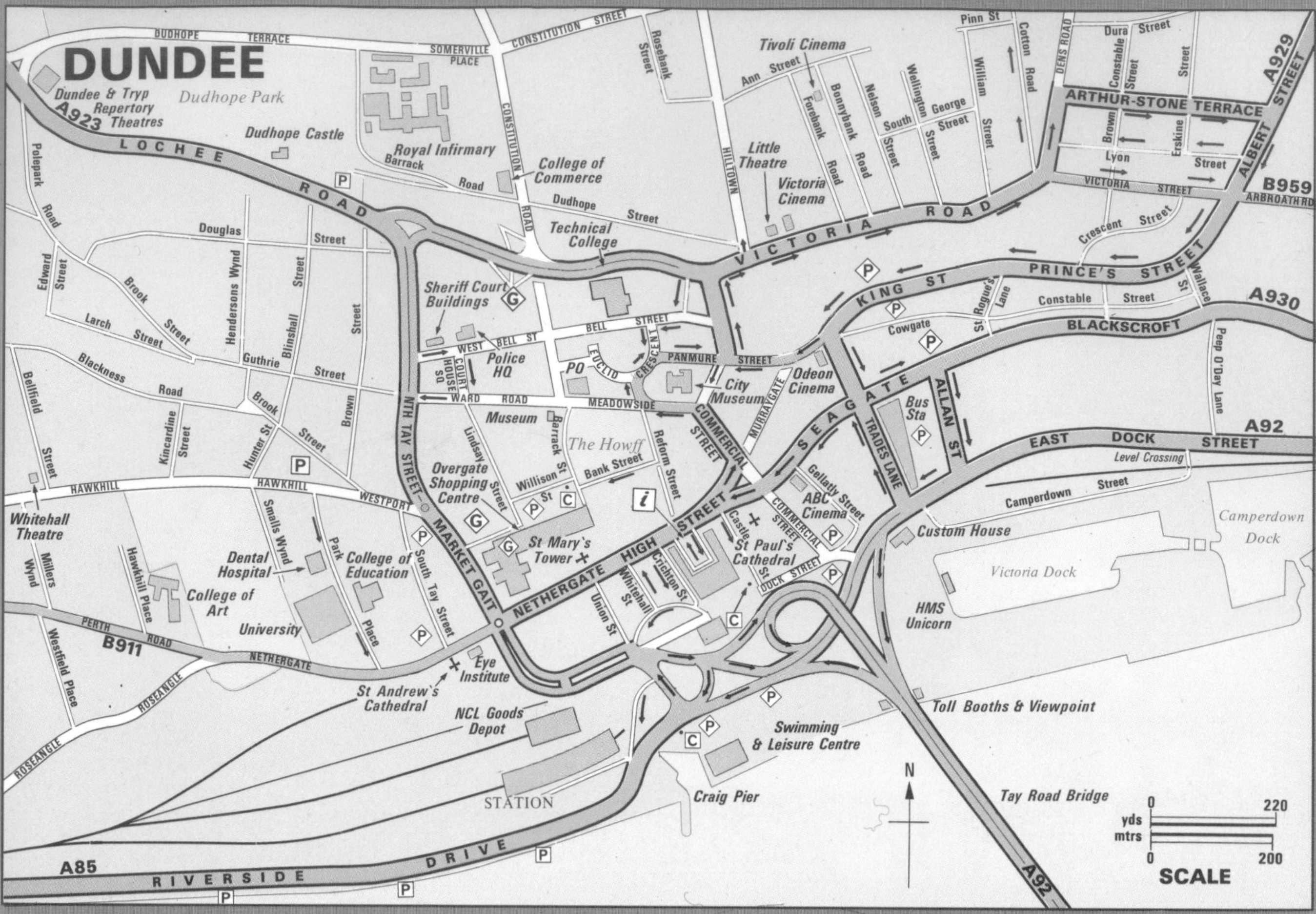

DUNDEE

Dundee & Tryp Repertory Theatres · Dudhope Park · Dudhope Castle · Royal Infirmary · College of Commerce · Tivoli Cinema · Little Theatre · Victoria Cinema · ARTHUR-STONE TERRACE · Technical College · Sheriff Court Buildings · Police HQ · City Museum · Odeon Cinema · Bus Sta · Museum · The Howff · Overgate Shopping Centre · St Mary's Tower · ABC Cinema · St Paul's Cathedral · Custom House · Camperdown Dock · Dental Hospital · College of Education · College of Art · University · Victoria Dock · HMS Unicorn · Whitehall Theatre · St Andrew's Cathedral · Eye Institute · NCL Goods Depot · Toll Booths & Viewpoint · Swimming & Leisure Centre · STATION · Craig Pier · Tay Road Bridge · Level Crossing

LOCHEE ROAD · VICTORIA ROAD · KING ST · PRINCE'S STREET · BLACKSCROFT · NETHERGATE · HIGH STREET · SEAGATE · EAST DOCK STREET · MARKET GAIT · HAWKHILL · PERTH ROAD · RIVERSIDE DRIVE

A923 · A929 · B959 · A930 · A92 · B911 · A85

N

SCALE
0 — 220 yds
0 — 200 mtrs

EXETER

NCL Goods Depot · ST DAVID'S STATION · Exeter Tech College · Fire Station · Bury Meadow · HM Prison · Barracks · St James' Park Halt · Exeter City FC · Odeon Cinema · Belmont Pleasure Ground · CENTRAL STA · Northernhay Gdns · Castle & Crown Court · ABC Cinema · City Wall · College of Art · Coach & Bus Sta · Clifton Hill Athletic Ground & Ski Slope · City Museum · City Library · Underground Passages · Civic Centre · City Police HQ & Court House · Royal Devon & Exeter Hospital (Heavitree) · Guildhall · Princesshay Pedestrians Only · Barnfield Th · Swimming Baths · Friernhay · Cathedral · Cathedral Close · Royal Devon & Exeter Hospital (Southernhay) · St Lukes College · Market · St George's Halls · Royal Devon & Exeter Hospital (Wonford) · Maritime Museum · W of Eng Eye Infirmary · Bull Meadow · Exeter School · St Thomas Pleasure Ground · ST THOMAS STATION · Exe Vale Hospital

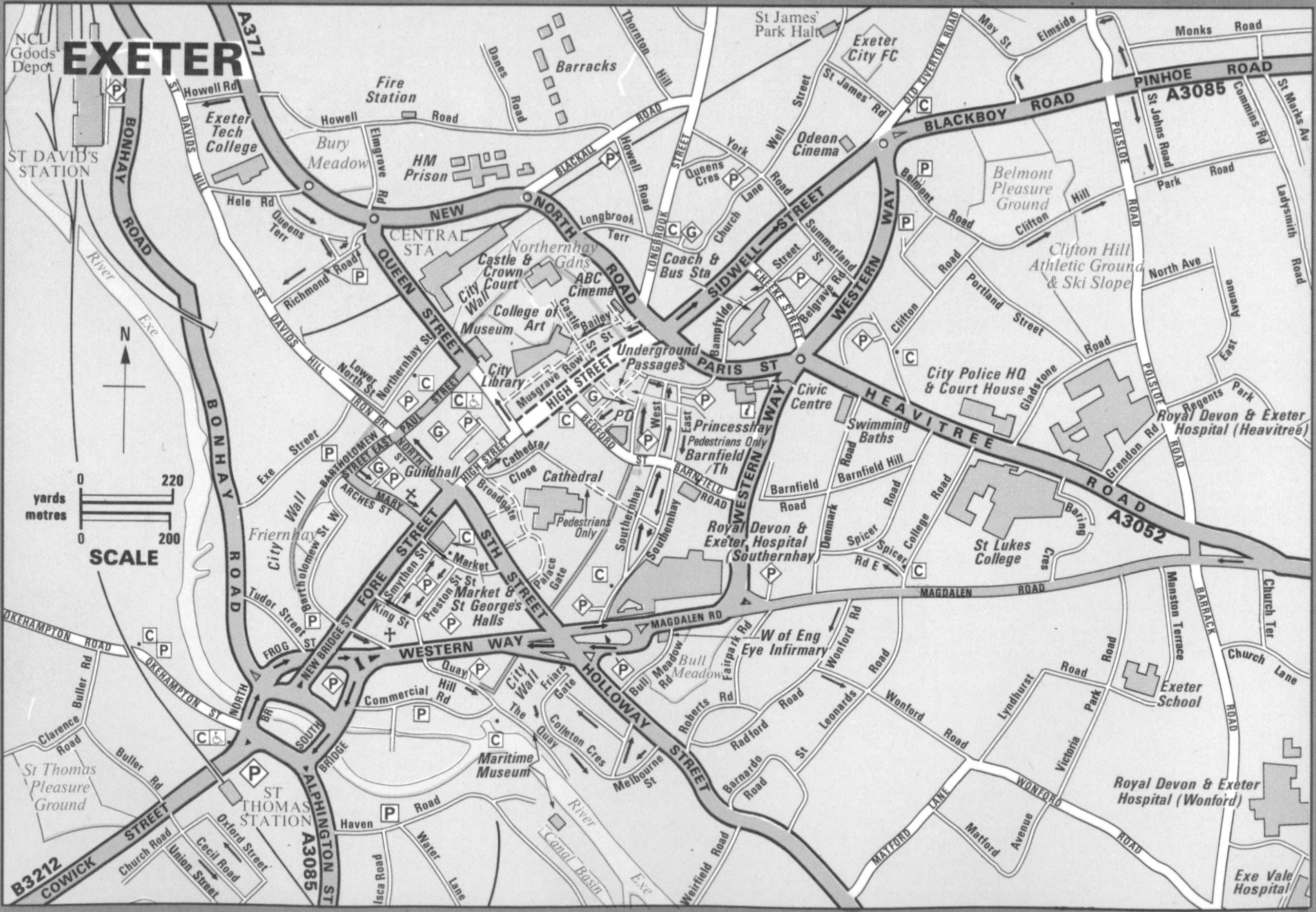

BONHAY ROAD · QUEEN STREET · NEW NORTH ROAD · BLACKBOY ROAD · PINHOE ROAD · SIDWELL STREET · WESTERN WAY · HEAVITREE ROAD · PARIS ST · ST DAVID'S HILL · FORE STREET · STH STREET · HIGH STREET · HOLLOWAY STREET · WESTERN WAY · OKEHAMPTON ROAD · COWICK STREET · ALPHINGTON ST · MAGDALEN ROAD

A377 · A3085 · A3052 · B3212 · A3085

River Exe · Canal Basin

N

SCALE
0 — 220 yards
0 — 200 metres

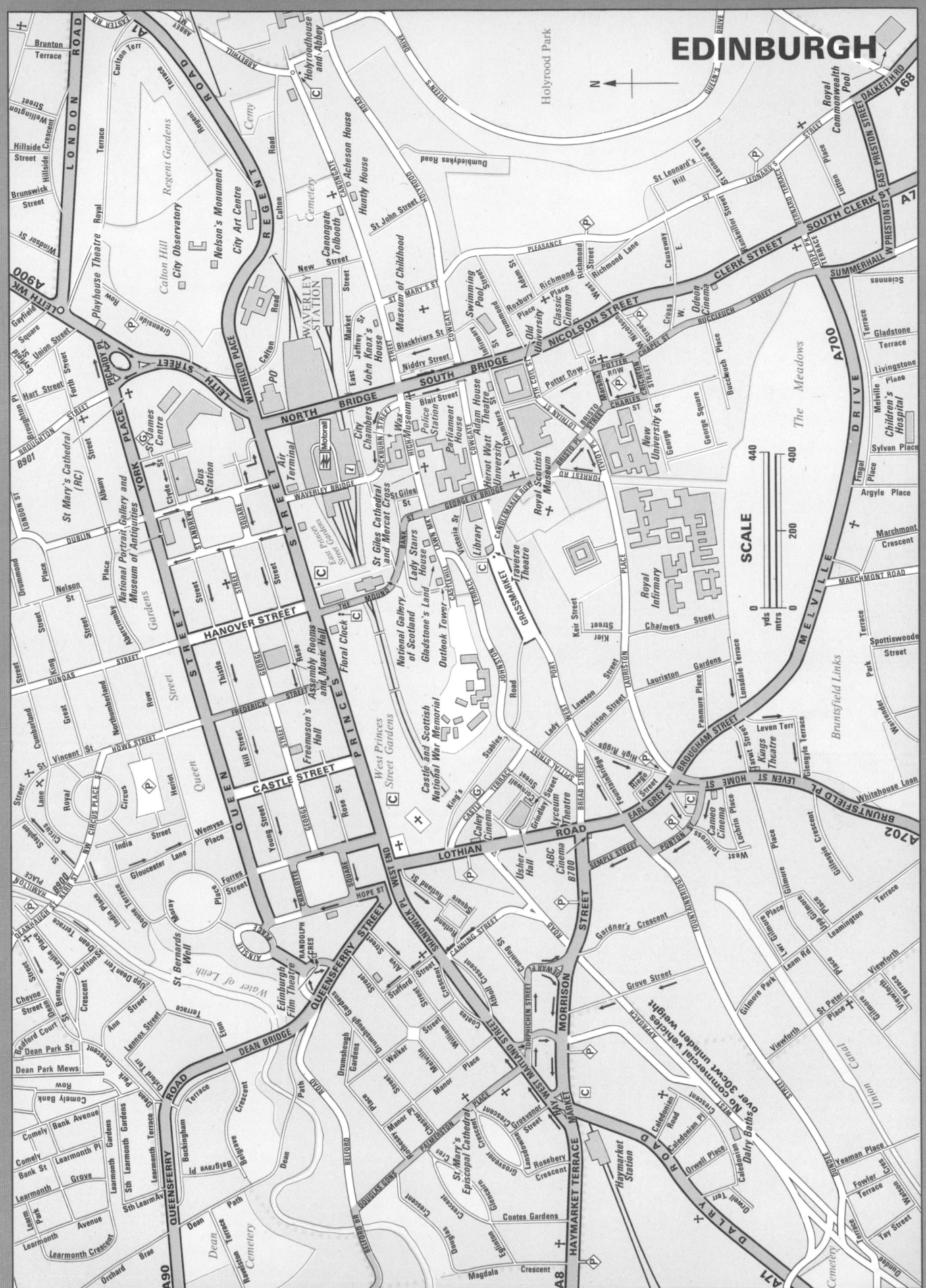

EDINBURGH

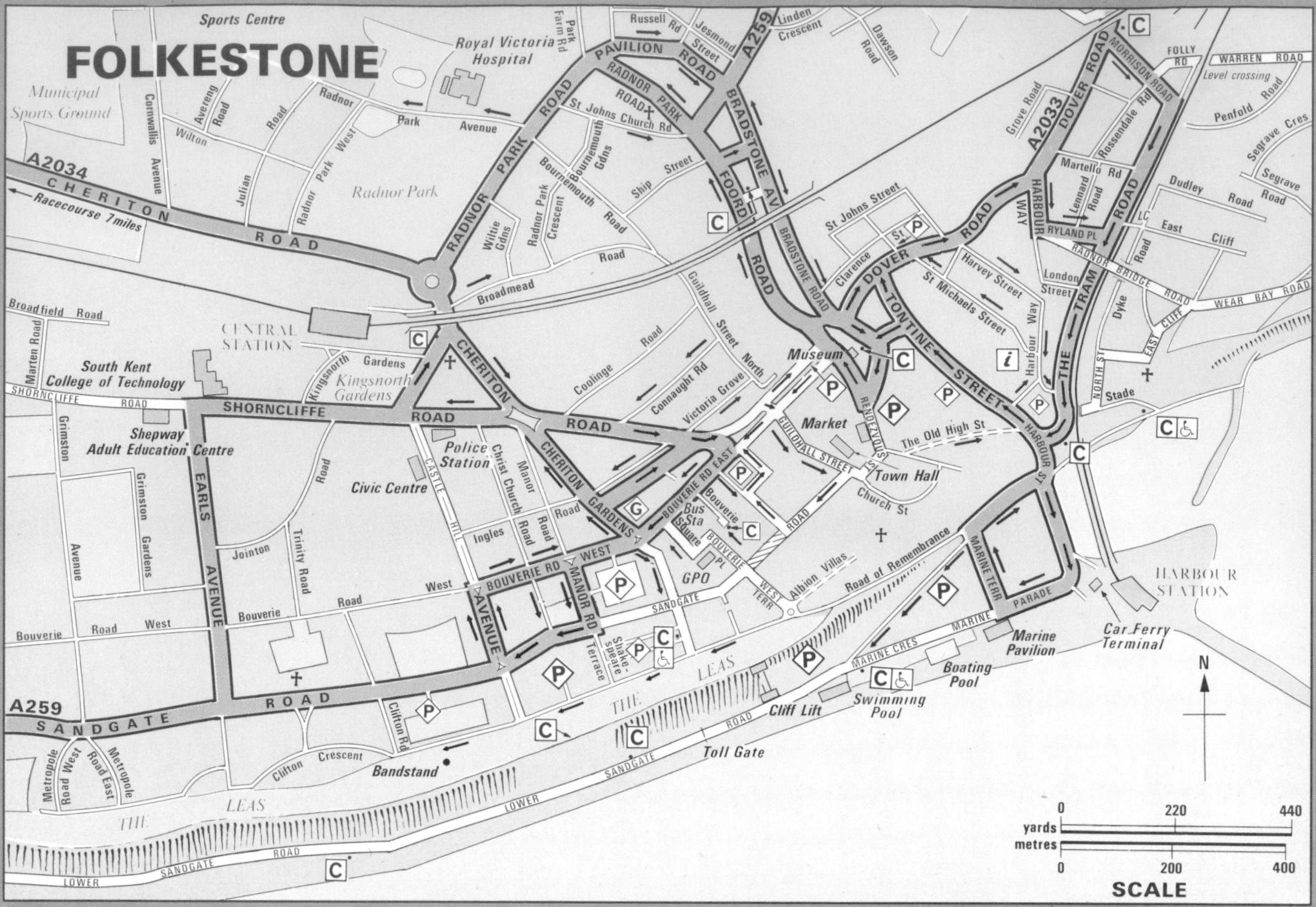

FOLKESTONE

Sports Centre
Royal Victoria Hospital
Municipal Sports Ground
RADNOR PARK ROAD
PAVILION ROAD
BRADSTONE AV
A259
Linden Crescent
Russell Rd
Jesmond Street
Dawson Road
FOLLY RD
WARREN ROAD
Level crossing
A2034
CHERITON ROAD
Racecourse 7miles
Radnor Park
St Johns Church Rd
Grove Road
A2033 DOVER ROAD
MORRISON ROAD
Penfold Road
Segrave Cres
Segrave Road
Radnor Park West
Cornwallis
Averenq Road
Wilton
Julian Road
Park Avenue
Radnor Avenue
Bournemouth Road
Ship Street
FOORD RD
Martello Rd
Rossendale Rd
Dudley Road
East Cliff
WEAR BAY ROAD
Broadfield Road
Broadmead
Radnor Park Crescent
Guildhall Street
St Johns Street
HARBOUR WAY
Lonnard Road
Harvey Street
RYLAND PL
LC
THE TRAM ROAD
RADNOR BRIDGE ROAD
EAST CLIFF
Broadfield Road
CENTRAL STATION
Kingsnorth Gardens
Coolinge Road
Connaught Rd
Victoria Grove
St Michaels Street
London Street
NORTH ST
Stade
South Kent College of Technology
SHORNCLIFFE ROAD
Kingsnorth Gardens
SHORNCLIFFE ROAD
CHERITON ROAD
Museum
DOVER STREET
Clarence
TONTINE STREET
HARBOUR ST
Shepway Adult Education Centre
Police Station
Christ Church
Manor Road
Market
The Old High St
Town Hall
Church St
HARBOUR STATION
Civic Centre
EARLS AVENUE
Ingles Road
BOUVERIE RD EAST
Bus Sta Square
Bouverie
Church St
Road of Remembrance
Car Ferry Terminal
Grimston Gardens
Trinity Road
BOUVERIE RD WEST
MANOR RD
GPO
WEST TERR
Albion Villas
MARINE TERR
PARADE
Marine Pavilion
Grimston Avenue
Jointon Road
West Road
Sandgate Road
MARINE CRES
Boating Pool
Bouverie Road West
Clifton Road
Sandgate Road
Swimming Pool
Cliff Lift
Marine Pavilion
A259 SANDGATE ROAD
THE LEAS
Toll Gate
Metropole Road West
Metropole Road East
Clifton Crescent
Bandstand
SANDGATE ROAD
THE LEAS
LOWER SANDGATE ROAD

N

SCALE
yards 0 220 440
metres 0 200 400

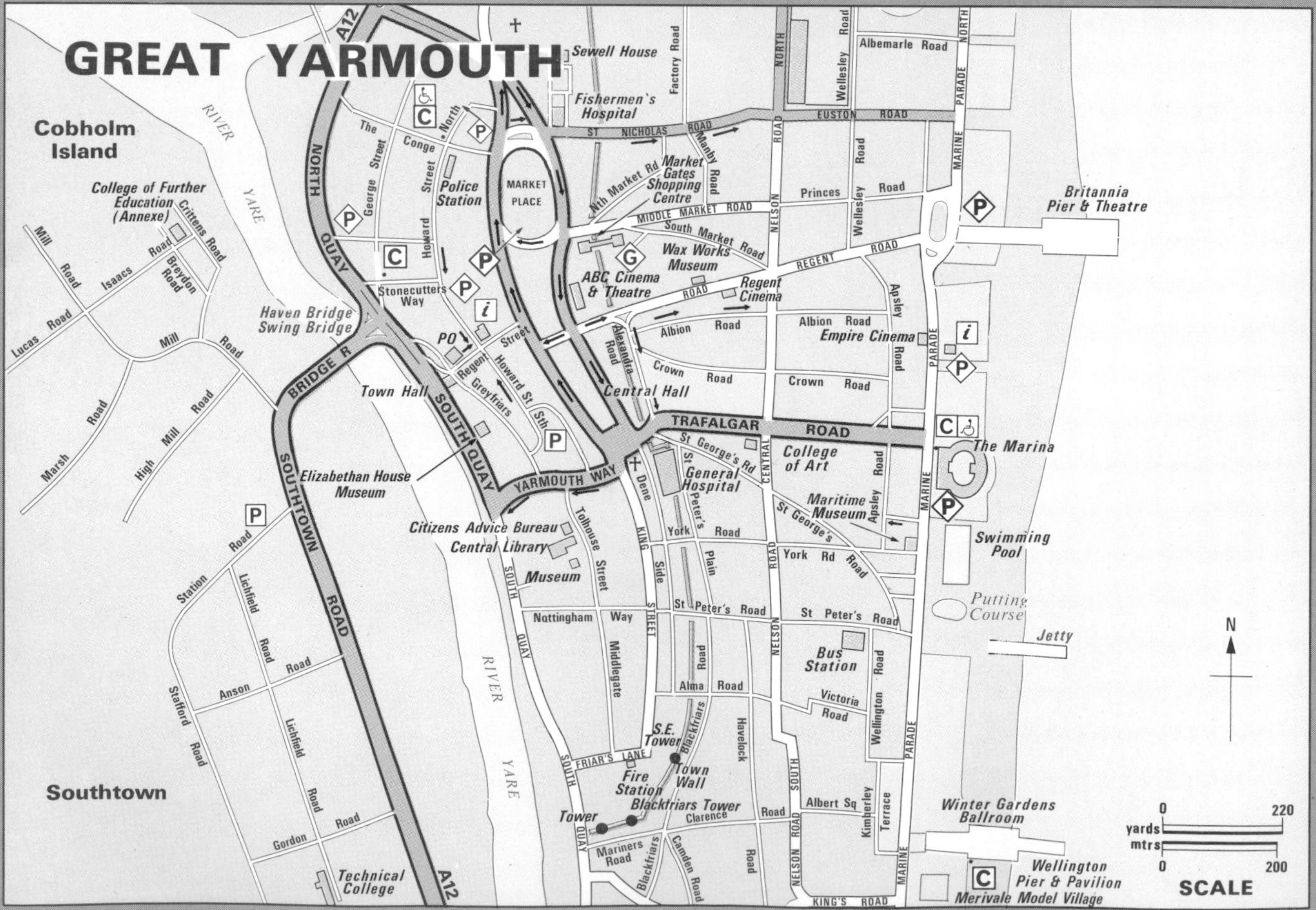

GREAT YARMOUTH

A12
Sewell House
Factory Road
Albemarle Road
NORTH
Cobholm Island
RIVER YARE
Fishermen's Hospital
Wellesley Road
MARINE PARADE
College of Further Education (Annexe)
NORTH QUAY
The Conge
George Street
ST NICHOLAS ROAD
Manby Rd
EUSTON ROAD
Britannia Pier & Theatre
Mill Road
Isaacs Road
Critten's Road
Breydon Road
Howard Street
Police Station
MARKET PLACE
Nth Market Rd
Market Gates Shopping Centre
Princes Road
Wellesley Road
Apsley Road
Lucas Road
Mill Road
Stonecutters Way
Haven Bridge Swing Bridge
HAVEN BRIDGE R
SOUTH QUAY
Regent Street
PO
Greyfriars
Howard St Sth
South Market Road
MIDDLE MARKET ROAD
Wax Works Museum
ABC Cinema & Theatre
Regent Cinema
REGENT ROAD
Albion Road
Empire Cinema
Albion Road
Marsh Road
High Mill Road
Town Hall
Elizabethan House Museum
YARMOUTH WAY
St George's Rd
Dene Side
Alexandra Road
Crown Road
Crown Road
The Marina
Station Road
Lichfield Road
SOUTHTOWN ROAD
Citizens Advice Bureau
Central Library
Museum
King Street
St Peter's Road
TRAFALGAR ROAD
General Hospital
College of Art
NELSON ROAD
St George's Road
Maritime Museum
Swimming Pool
Anson Road
Stafford Road
Lichfield Road
Nottingham Way
Middlegate
York Road
St Peter's Plain
York Rd
St Peter's Road
Putting Course
Gordon Road
SOUTH QUAY
FRIAR'S LANE
S.E. Tower
Town Wall
Alma Road
Bus Station
Victoria Road
Wellington Road
Jetty
Southtown
Fire Station
Blackfriars Tower
Blackfriars Road
Albert Sq
Kimberley Terrace
Winter Gardens Ballroom
Tower
Mariners Road
Camden Road
Clarence Road
NELSON ROAD SOUTH
KING'S ROAD
MARINE PARADE
Technical College
A12
Wellington Pier & Pavilion
Merivale Model Village

N

SCALE
yards 0 220
mtrs 0 200

166

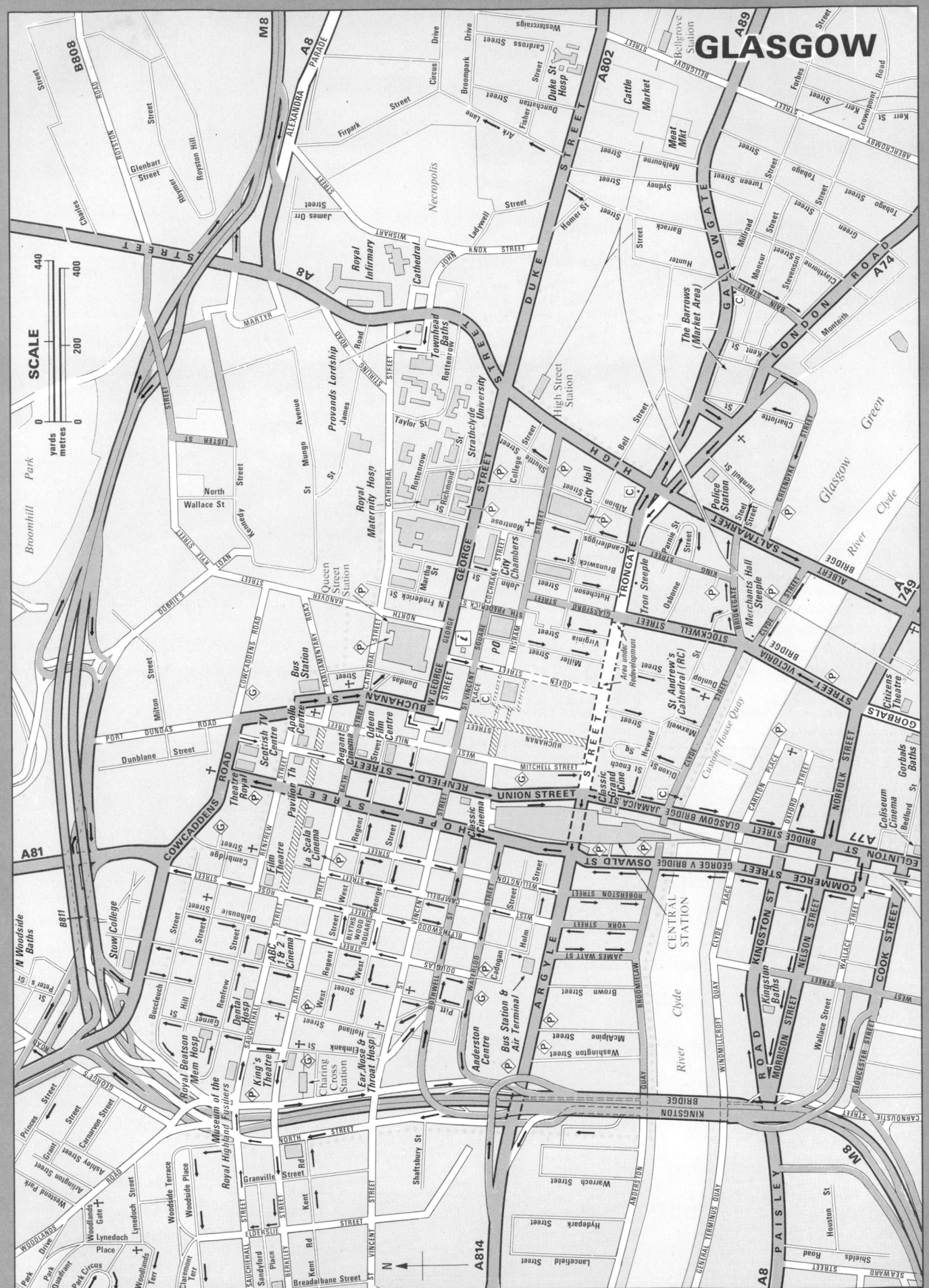

GLASGOW

167

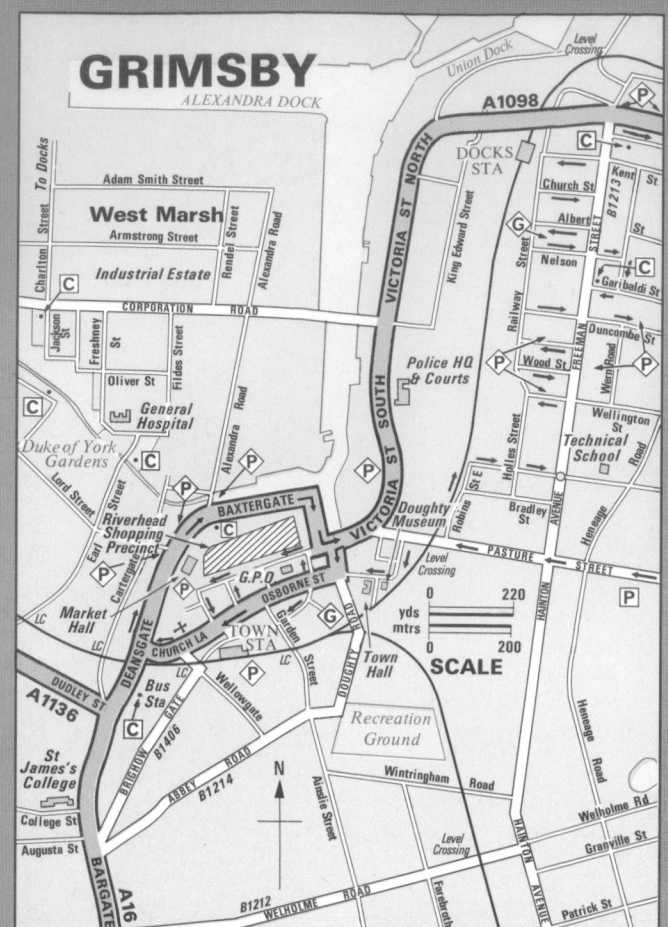

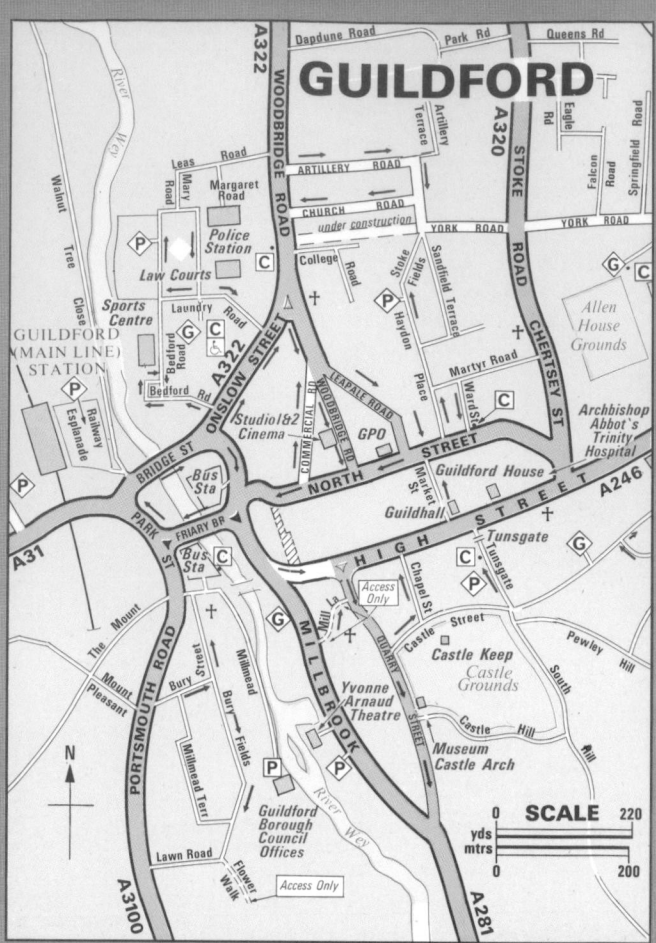

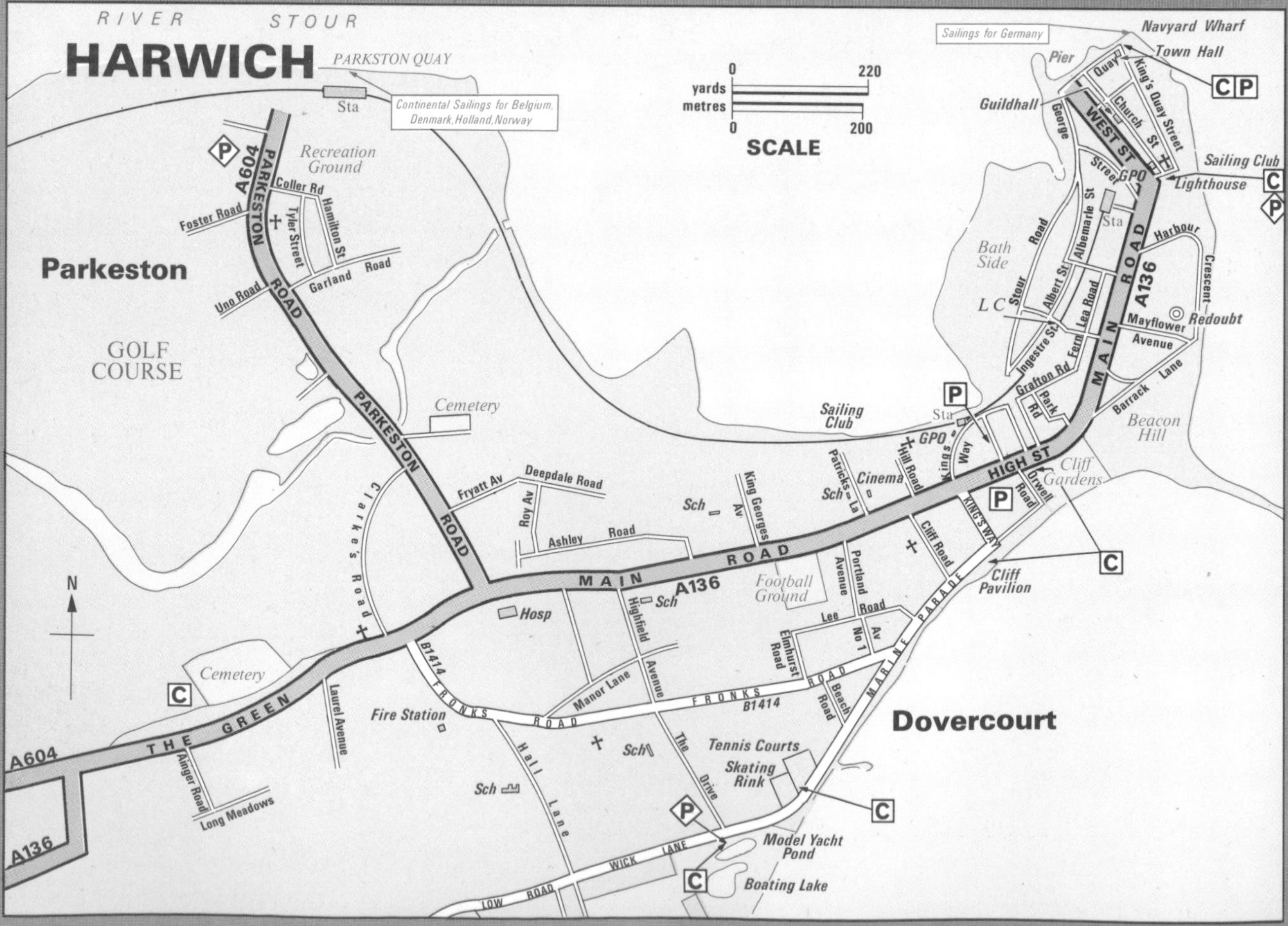

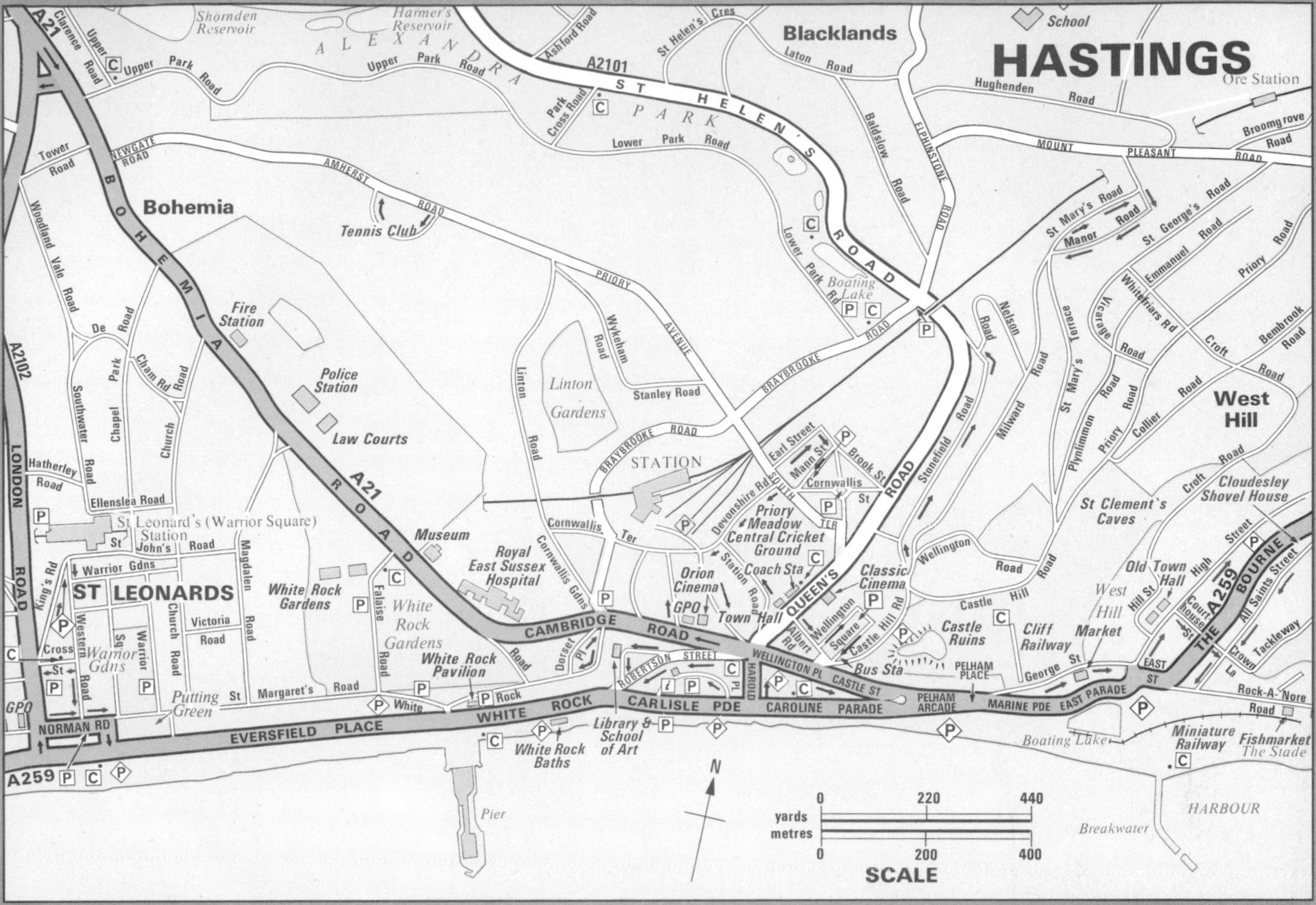

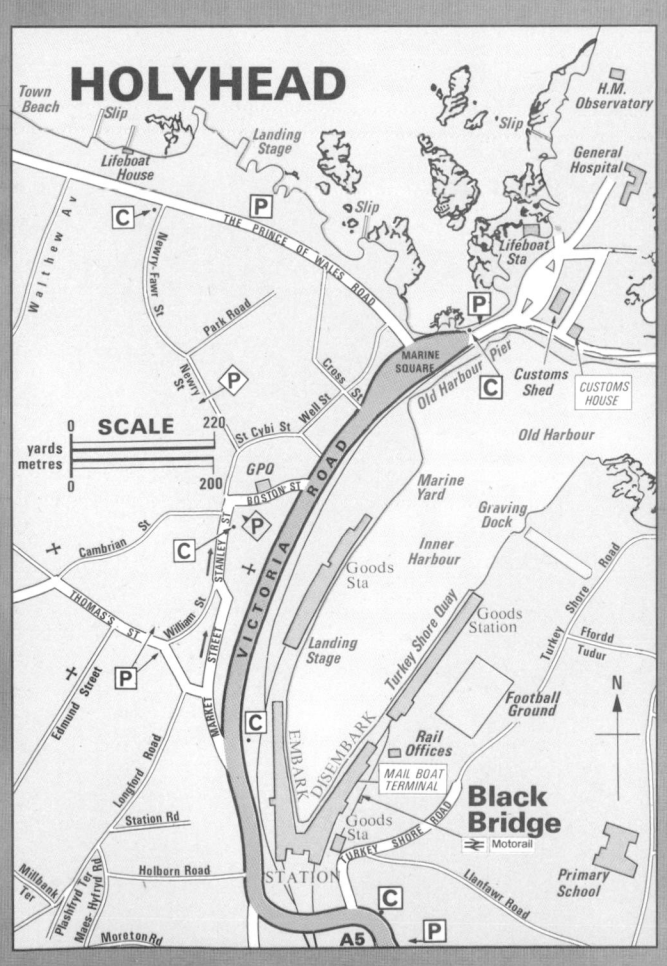

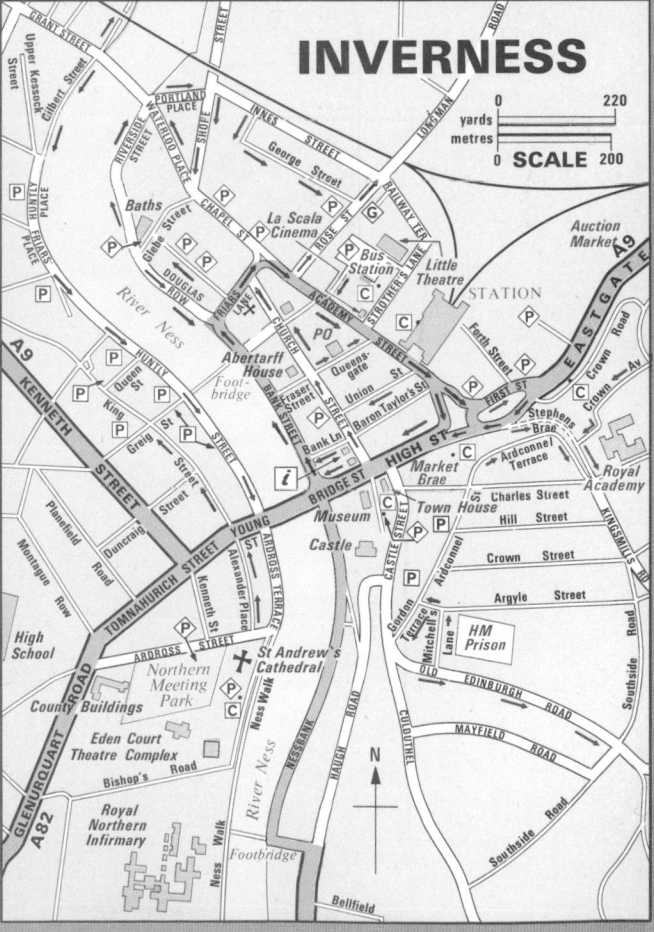

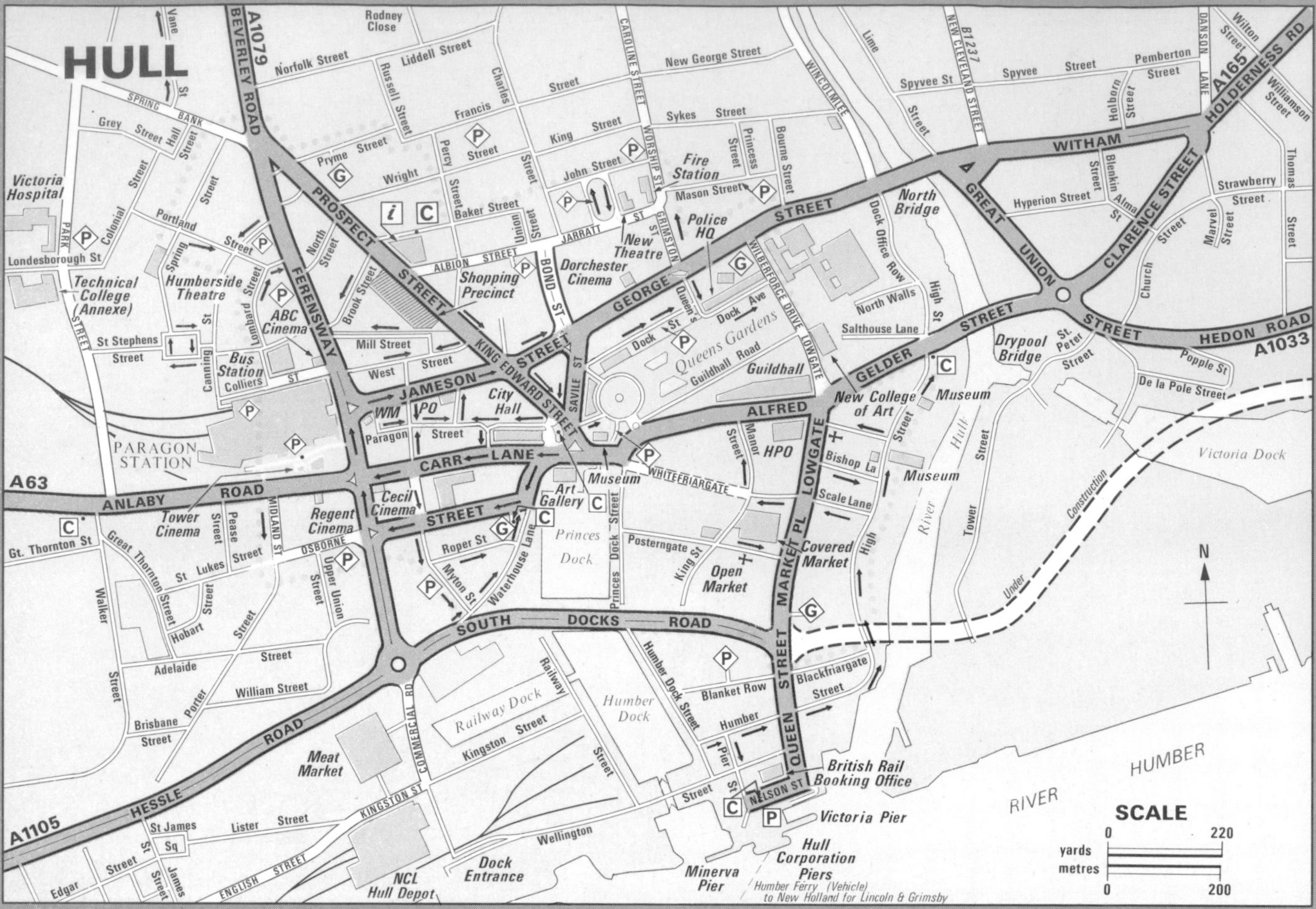

HULL

Victoria Hospital
Technical College (Annexe)
Londesborough St
St Stephens Street
Humberside Theatre
ABC Cinema
Bus Station
PARAGON STATION

BEVERLEY ROAD
A1079
PROSPECT STREET
FERENSWAY
JAMESON
Paragon
WM PO
City Hall
CARR LANE
Cecil Cinema
Regent Cinema
Tower Cinema
Gt. Thornton St
Great Thornton Street
St Lukes Street
Upper Union Street
Walker Street
Hobart Street
Adelaide Street
Brisbane Street
William Street
Porter Street

ANLABY ROAD
A63
HESSLE ROAD
A1105
MIDLAND ST
COMMERCIAL RD
KINGSTON ST
ENGLISH STREET

Spring Bank
Grey Street
Portland Street
Canning Street
Mill Street
West Street

Norfolk Street
Rodney Close
Liddell Street
Russell Street
Charles Street
Francis Street
Pryme Street
Wright Street
Baker Street
King Street
Percy Street
Jarratt Street
ALBION STREET
Brook Street
BOND ST

New George Street
Sykes Street
John Street
Caroline Street
WORSHIP STREET
Princess Street
Bourne Street
Mason Street
Fire Station
New Theatre
Dorchester Cinema
Shopping Precinct
KING EDWARD STREET
Savile St
Queen St
GEORGE STREET
Police HQ
Guildhall
Queens Gardens
Guildhall

WINCOMLEE
Spyvee St
Spyvee Street
Pemberton Street
Lime Street
NEW CLEVELAND STREET
B1237

WITHAM
GREAT UNION STREET
CLARENCE STREET
A165
HOLDERNESS RD
Wilton Street
Hodgson
Alma St
Marvel Street
Strawberry Street
Thomas Street

North Bridge
Dock Office Row
North Walls
High Street
Salthouse Lane
GELDER STREET
Drypool Bridge
St Peter St
HEDON ROAD
A1033
Popple St
De la Pole Street

New College of Art
Museum
LOWGATE
MARKET PL
ALFRED
HPO
WHITEFRIARGATE
Museum
Scale Lane
Bishop La
Art Gallery
Museum
Princes Dock
Posterngate
King St
Open Market
Covered Market
River Hull
Tower Street
Under Construction
Victoria Dock

SOUTH DOCKS ROAD
Blackfriargate
Blanket Row
Humber Street
British Rail Booking Office
Victoria Pier
NELSON STREET
Minerva Pier
Hull Corporation Piers
Humber Ferry (Vehicle) to New Holland for Lincoln & Grimsby

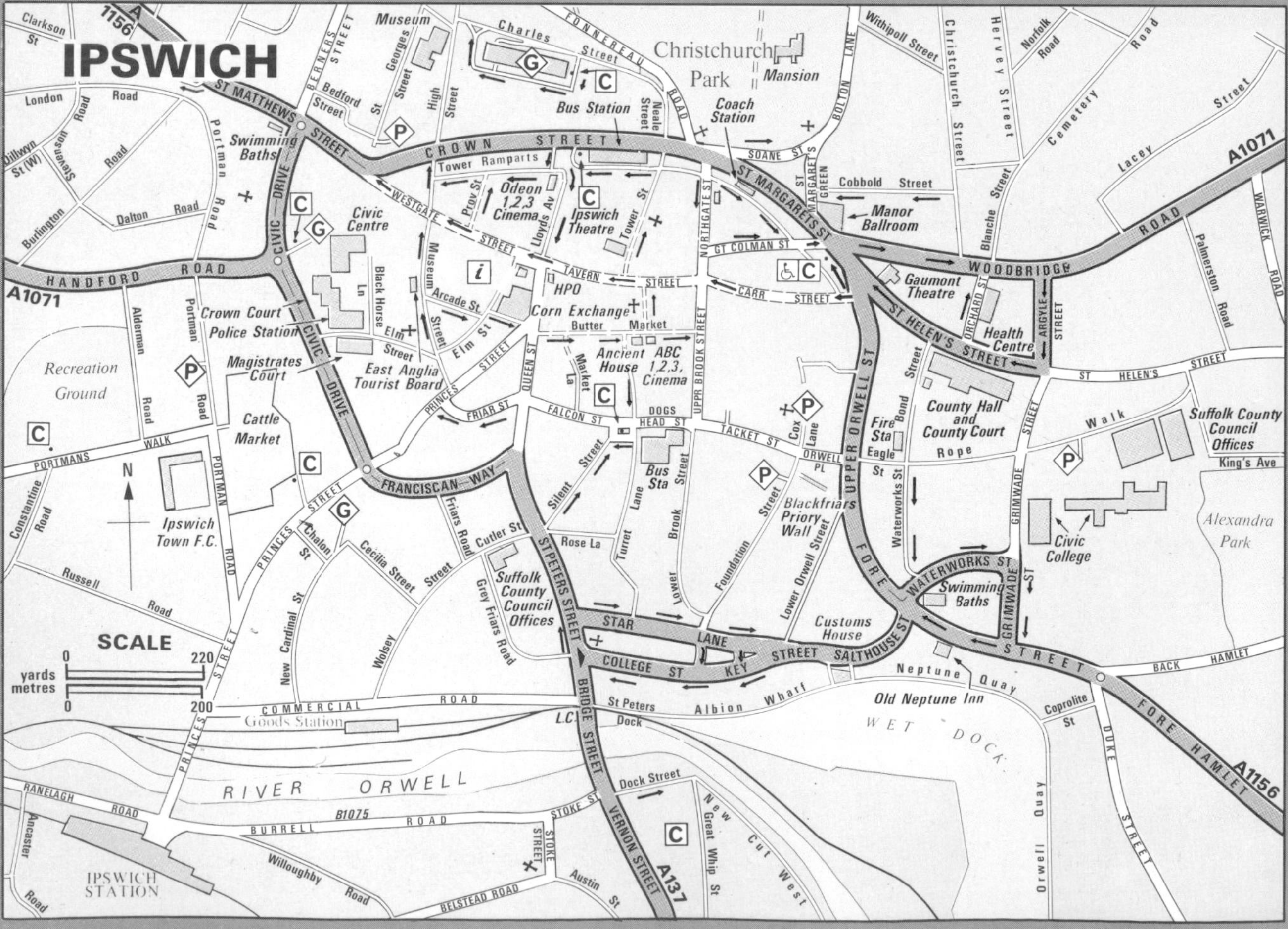

Railway Dock
Humber Dock
Kingston Street
Wellington Street
St James Sq
Lister Street
Edgar Street
NCL Hull Depot
Dock Entrance

QUEEN STREET
Pier St

RIVER HUMBER

N

SCALE
yards 0 — 220
metres 0 — 200

IPSWICH

Clarkson St
London Road
Dillwyn St (W)
Stevens Road
Burlington Road
Dalton Road
HANDFORD ROAD
A1071
Constantine Road
Russell Road

Museum
BERNERS STREET
Bedford Street
Georges Street
ST MATTHEWS STREET
Portman Road
Swimming Baths
CIVIC DRIVE
Civic Centre
WESTGATE STREET
Prov St
Museum Street
Black Horse Ln
Elm Street
Crown Court Police Station
Magistrates Court
Cattle Market
PORTMAN WALK
PORTMANS
Recreation Ground
PORTMAN ROAD
N
Ipswich Town F.C.
PRINCES STREET
New Cardinal Street
Chalon Street
Cecilia Street
FRANCISCAN WAY
Friars Street
Cutler St
Rose La
Suffolk County Council Offices
ST PETERS STREET
BRIDGE STREET
Wolsey St
Ranelagh Road
Tanaster Road
IPSWICH STATION

Charles Street
TONNEREAU STREET
Christchurch Park
Mansion
Neale Street
Bus Station
Coach Station
CROWN STREET
Tower Ramparts
Odeon 1,2,3 Cinema
Lloyds Av
Ipswich Theatre
Tower St
Tavern Street
HPO
Arcade St
Corn Exchange
Butter Market
Ancient House ABC 1,2,3 Cinema
Queen Street
FALCON STREET
Friar St
Silent Street
Turret Lane
DOGS HEAD ST
TACKET STREET
Cox Lane
Brook Street
Foundation Street
East Anglia Tourist Board
NORTHGATE ST
GT COLMAN ST

Withipoll Street
Christchurch Street
Hervey Street
Norfolk Road
BOLTON LANE
ST MARGARETS ST
St Margaret's Green
Cobbold Street
Manor Ballroom
ST HELEN'S STREET
Gaumont Theatre
Health Centre
Orchard Street
Fire Sta
Eagle St
Rope
UPPER ORWELL STREET
Waterworks St
Blackfriars Priory Wall
Customs House
WATERWORKS ST
Swimming Baths
Lower Orwell Street
Star Lane
KEY STREET
SALTHOUSE ST
FORE STREET
Neptune Quay
Old Neptune Inn
COLLEGE ST
St Peters Dock
Albion Wharf
WET DOCK

WOODBRIDGE ROAD
A1071
Lacey Street
Cemetery Road
ORWELL PL
County Hall and County Court
Civic College
GRIMWADE STREET
ST HELEN'S Walk
Suffolk County Council Offices
King's Ave
Alexandra Park
FORE HAMLET
A1156
Coprolite St
Duke Street
Orwell Quay
New Cut West

A1156
A1071
A137
Austin St
Stoke Street
VERNON STREET
LC
COMMERCIAL ROAD
Goods Station
RIVER ORWELL
BURRELL ROAD
B1075 ROAD
Willoughby Road
BELSTEAD ROAD

SCALE
yards 0 — 220
metres 0 — 200
N

170

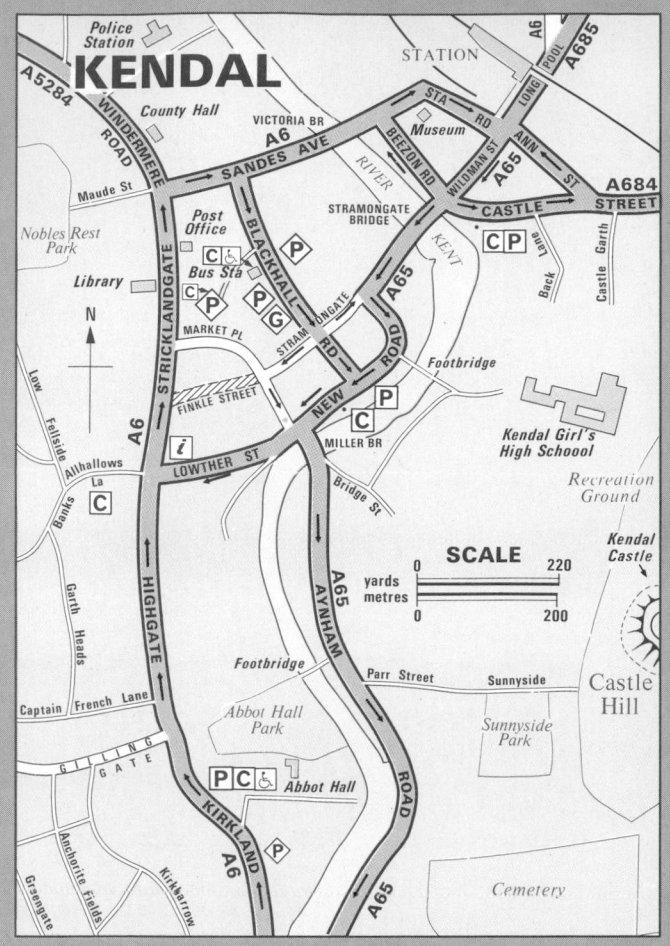

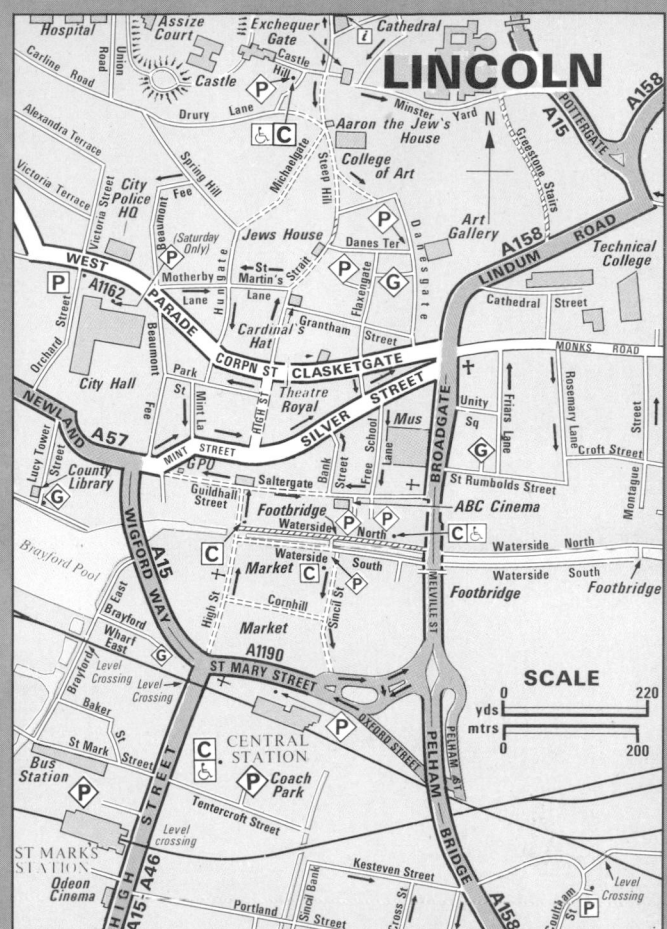

KENDAL

A5284
A6
Police Station
STATION
County Hall
A6
VICTORIA BR
Museum
A685
A6
LONG POOL
SANDES AVE
WINDERMERE ROAD
BEEZON RD
WILDMAN ST
ST ANN ST
A65
CASTLE STREET
A684
Maude St
STRAMONGATE BRIDGE
RIVER KENT
Castle Garth
Nobles Rest Park
Post Office
C P
Back Lane
C P
BLACKHALL
Library
Bus Sta
P G
STRICKLANDGATE
P G
Market Pl
A65 ROAD
Footbridge
N
FINKLE STREET
Castle Hill
Low
Fellside
NEW ST
C
Kendal Girl's High School
Allhallows La
i
LOWTHER ST
MILLER BR
Banks
Bridge St
Recreation Ground
C
HIGHGATE
A6
AYNHAM
Kendal Castle
Garth Heads
Footbridge
Parr Street
Sunnyside
Captain French Lane
SCALE
yards 220
metres 200
Abbot Hall Park
Sunnyside Park
Castle Hill
GILLING GATE
KIRKLAND
P C
Kirkbarrow
Abbot Hall
Cemetery
Anchorite Fields
Greengate
A6
A65 ROAD

LINCOLN

Hospital
Carline Road
Union Road
Assize Court
Exchequer Gate
Cathedral
A158
Castle
i
Alexandra Terrace
Castle Hill
Drury Lane
Minster Yard
Greestone Stairs
POTTERGATE
A15
Aaron the Jew's House
N
Victoria Terrace
City Police HQ
Spring Hill
College of Art
LINDUM ROAD
Art Gallery
A158
Technical College
WEST
A1162
Motherby
(Saturday Only)
Jews House
Danes Ter
P
G
Cathedral Street
MONKS ROAD
Orchard St
Beaumont Fee
Cardinal's Hat
Grantham Street
Unity Sq
Friars Lane
Rosemary Lane
Croft Street
City Hall
PARADE
CORPN ST
CLASKETGATE
SILVER STREET
BROADGATE
Theatre Royal
St Rumbolds Street
Montague St
NEWLAND
A57
MINT STREET
HIGH STREET
Free School Lane
Mus
G
Lucy Tower
County Library
GPO
Saltergate
ABC Cinema
WIGFORD WAY
Guildhall Street
Footbridge
C
North
C
Waterside North
A15
Waterside Market
C
Waterside South
Brayford Pool
East
Cornhill
Footbridge
Brayford Wharf East
Market
A1190
High St
Sincil St
MELVILLE ST
ST MARY STREET
Level Crossing
Level Crossing
SCALE
yds 220
mtrs 200
St Mark
Baker
P
OXFORD STREET
PELHAM ST
CENTRAL STATION
C
Bus Station
Coach Park
ST MARKS STATION
Tentercroft Street
Level crossing
Kesteven Street
Sincil Bank
A158
Odeon Cinema
Portland
Portland Street
Cross St
P
Level Crossing
HIGH STREET A15/A46
PELHAM BRIDGE

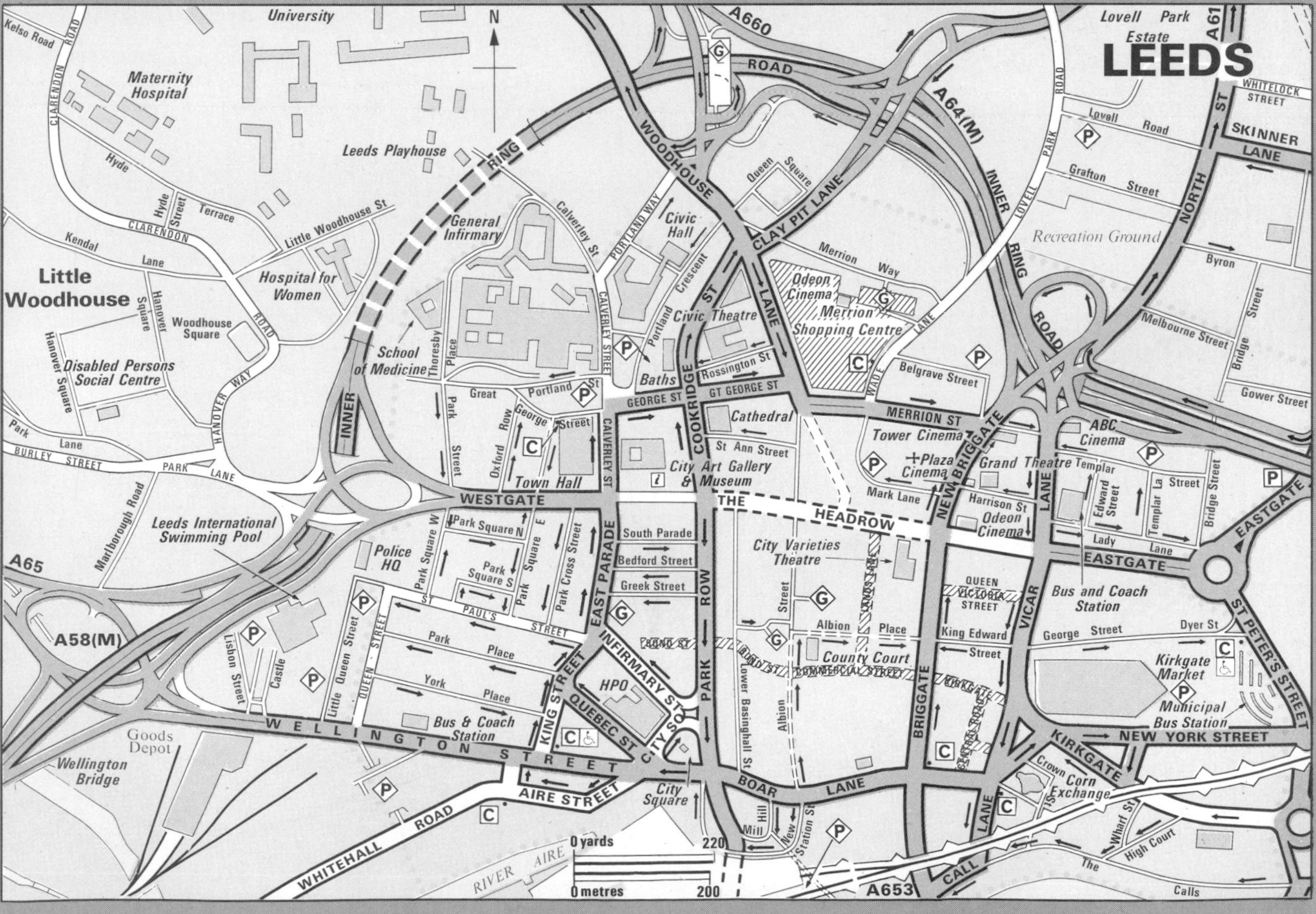

LEEDS

Kelso Road
University
N
A660 ROAD
Lovell Park Estate
A61
Maternity Hospital
CLARENDON ROAD
WOODHOUSE LANE
A64(M)
Lovell Road
WHITELOCK STREET
SKINNER LANE
Leeds Playhouse
RING
Queen Square
INNER
Grafton Street
Hyde Street
Little Woodhouse St
General Infirmary
Calverley St
PORTLAND WAY
CLAY PIT LANE
Recreation Ground
Byron
Little Woodhouse
CLARENDON
Civic Hall
Merrion Way
NORTH ST
Kendal Lane
Hospital for Women
Portland Crescent
Civic Theatre
Odeon Cinema
G
Melbourne Street
Woodhouse Square
School of Medicine
Thoresby Place
Baths
Rossington St
Merrion Shopping Centre
C
Belgrave Street
Bridge Street
Disabled Persons Social Centre
HANOVER WAY
INNER
Great George Street
Portland Street
GT GEORGE ST
MERRION ST
ABC Cinema
Gower Street
Park Lane
BURLEY LANE
PARK LANE
Oxford Row
George St
Cathedral
Tower Cinema
NEW BRIGGATE
P
Templar Street
Town Hall
C
St Ann Street
Plaza Cinema
Grand Theatre
Templar La
A65
WESTGATE
City Art Gallery & Museum
i
Odeon Cinema
Edward Street
Leeds International Swimming Pool
Park Square N
South Parade
THE HEADROW
Mark Lane
Harrison St
Lady Lane
EASTGATE
Police HQ
Park Square W
Bedford Street
City Varieties Theatre
VICAR LANE
ST PETER'S STREET
A58(M)
Park Square S
Greek Street
G
Albion Place
QUEEN VICTORIA STREET
Bus and Coach Station
P
EAST PARADE
ST PAUL'S STREET
PARK ROW
G
County Court
King Edward Street
George Street
Dyer St
Castle
Little Queen Street
York Place
HPO
INFIRMARY ST
Lower Basinghall St
Albion
BRIGGATE
Kirkgate Market
C
Goods Depot
KING STREET
QUEBEC ST
CITY SQ
COMMERCIAL ST
Municipal Bus Station
Wellington Bridge
Bus & Coach Station
C
KIRKGATE
NEW YORK STREET
WELLINGTON STREET
AIRE STREET
City Square
BOAR LANE
Crown Corn Exchange
WHITEHALL ROAD
C
0 yards 220
CALL LANE
High Court
RIVER AIRE
0 metres 200
A653
The Calls

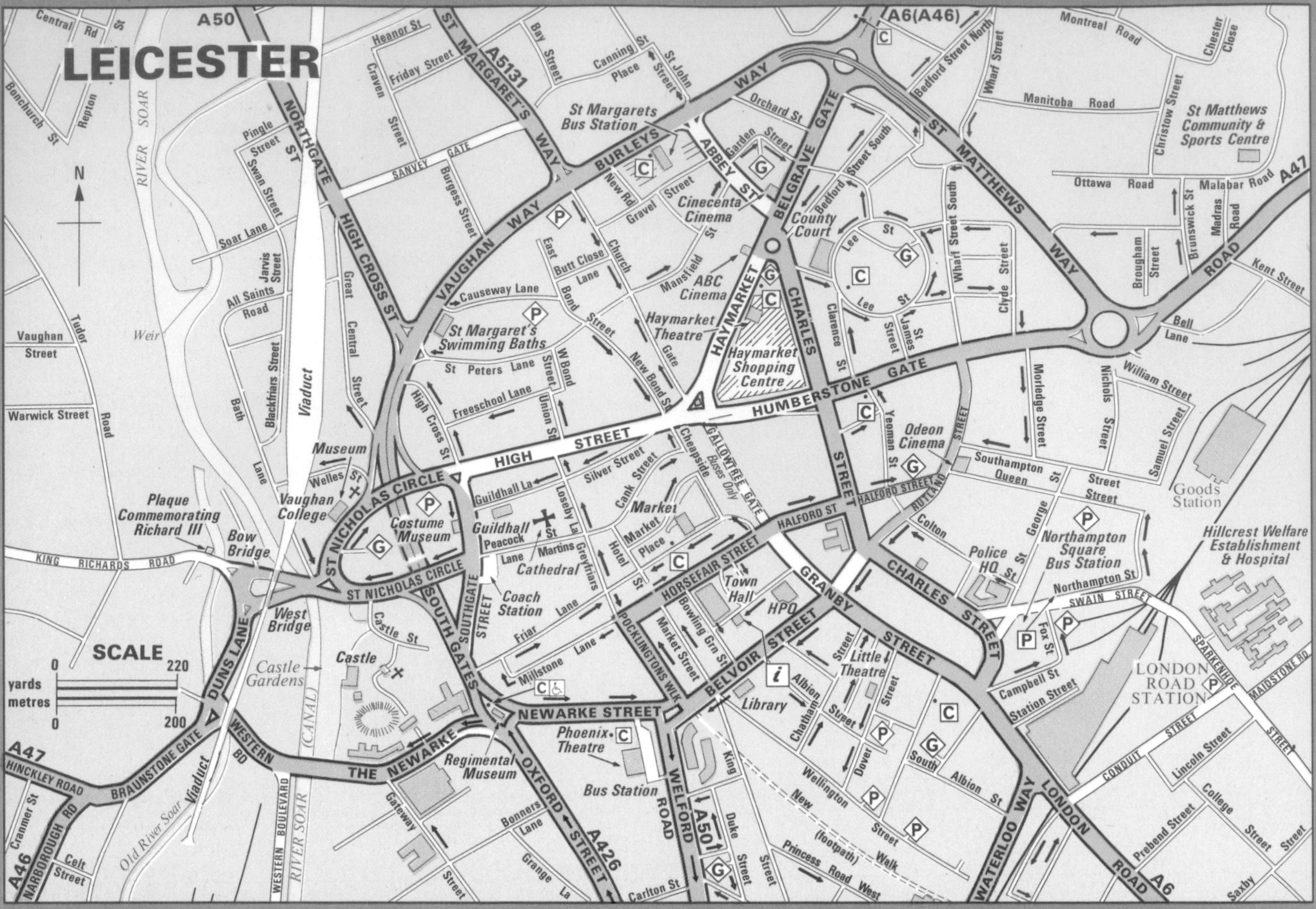

LEICESTER

LUTON

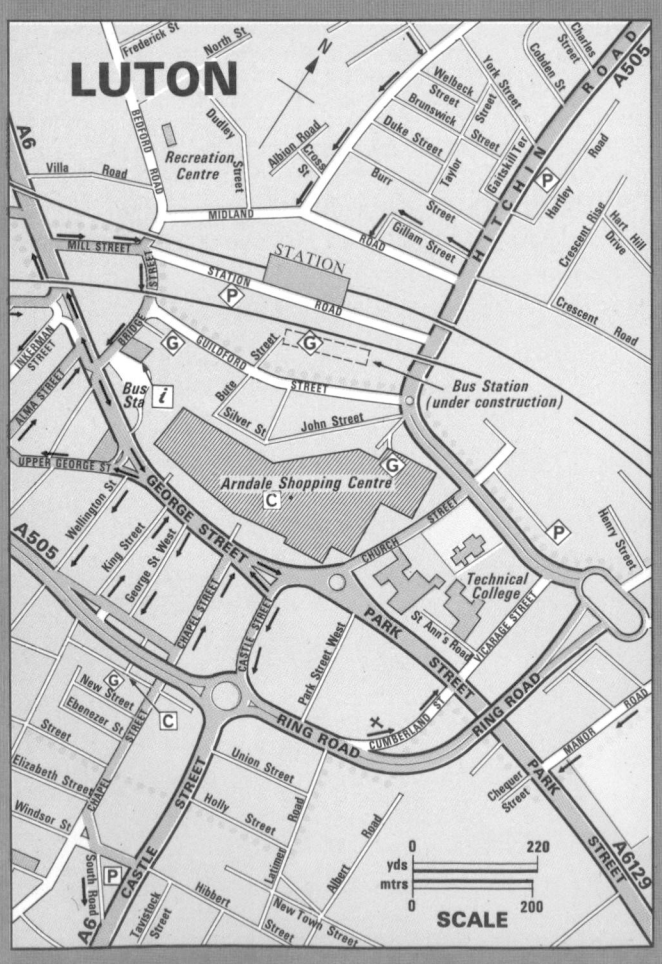

MAIDSTONE

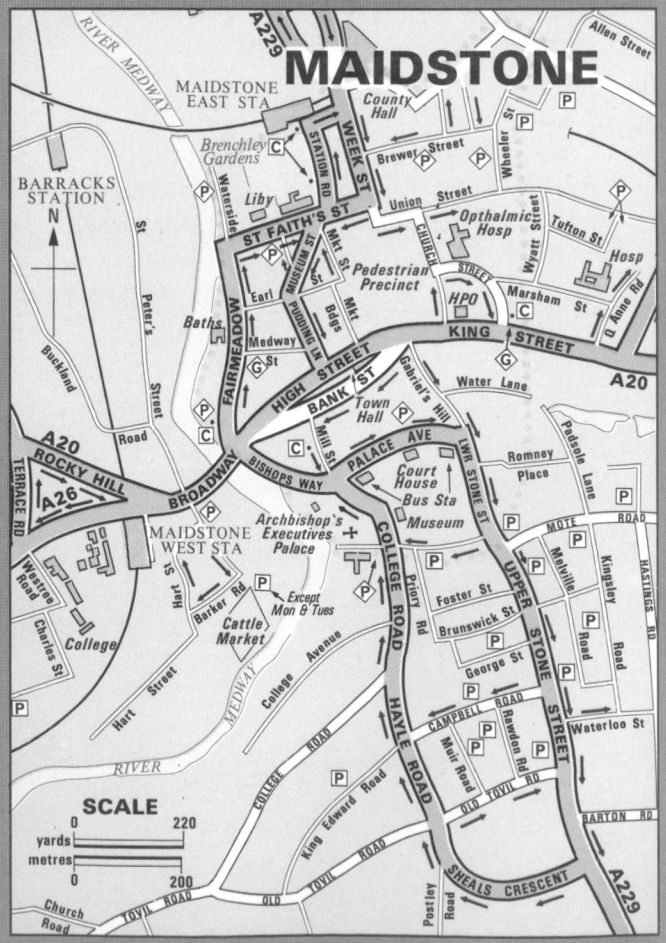

LIVERPOOL

MARGATE

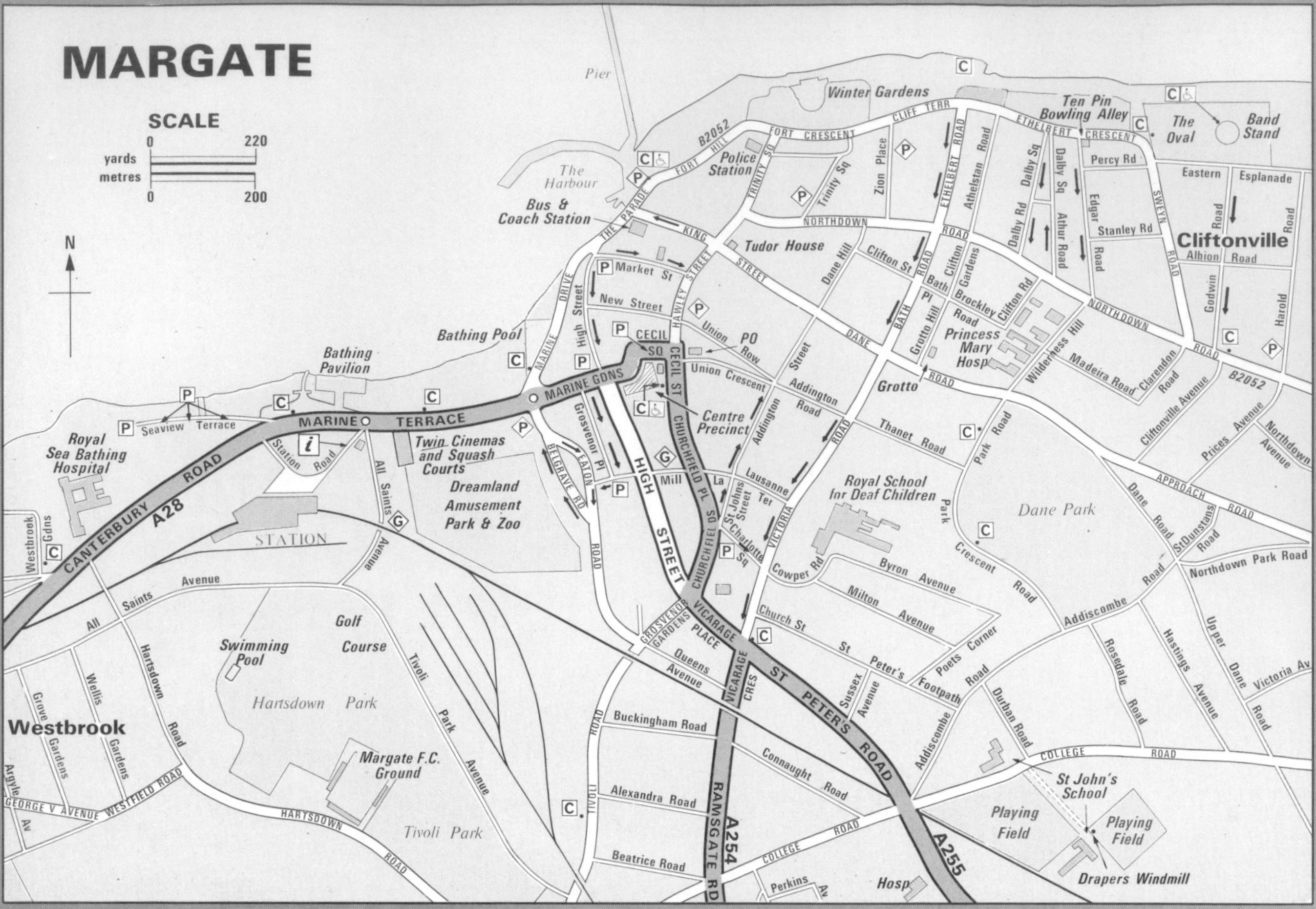
MARGATE
SCALE
yards
metres
0
220
0
200
N
Pier
The Harbour
Winter Gardens
Ten Pin Bowling Alley
The Oval
Band Stand
Police Station
Bus & Coach Station
Tudor House
Cliftonville
Bathing Pool
Bathing Pavilion
Royal Sea Bathing Hospital
Twin Cinemas and Squash Courts
Dreamland Amusement Park & Zoo
Centre Precinct
PO
Princess Mary Hosp
Grotto
Royal School for Deaf Children
Dane Park
STATION
Golf Course
Swimming Pool
Hartsdown Park
Westbrook
Margate F.C. Ground
Tivoli Park
St John's School
Playing Field
Playing Field
Drapers Windmill
Hosp
FORT CRESCENT
CLIFF TERR
ETHELBERT CRESCENT
FORT HILL
B2052
THE PARADE
KING STREET
NORTHDOWN ROAD
MARINE TERRACE
MARINE GDNS
CECIL SQ
CECIL ST
HIGH STREET
CHURCHFIELD PL
VICARAGE PLACE
VICARAGE CRES
ST PETER'S ROAD
RAMSGATE RD
A254
A255
A28
CANTERBURY ROAD
COLLEGE ROAD
HARTSDOWN ROAD
WESTFIELD ROAD
GEORGE V AVENUE
Seaview Terrace
Station Road
All Saints Avenue
Trinity Sq
Zion Place
Ethelbert Road
Athelstan Road
Dalby Sq
Dalby Rd
Arthur Road
Percy Rd
Edgar Road
Stanley Rd
Eastern Esplanade
Sweyn Road
Norfolk Road
Albion Road
Godwin Road
Harold Road
Dane Hill
Clifton St
Bath Pl
Clifton Gardens
Brockley Road
Clifton Rd
Grotto Hill
Wilderness Hill
Madeira Road
Clarendon Road
Cliftonville Avenue
Prices Avenue
Northdown Avenue
Market St
New Street
Hawley Street
Union Row
Union Crescent
Addington Street
Addington Road
Thanet Road
Park Road
Park Crescent Road
Dane Road
St Dunstans Road
Approach Road
Northdown Park Road
Marine Drive
Grosvenor Pl
Belgrave Rd
Eaton Rd
Mill La
St Johns Street
Lausanne Ter
Victoria Road
St Charlotte Sq
Cowper Rd
Byron Avenue
Milton Avenue
Church St
St Peter's Footpath
Poets Corner
Addiscombe Road
Rosedale Road
Hastings Avenue
Upper Dane Road
Victoria Av
Grosvenor Gardens
Queens Avenue
Buckingham Road
Alexandra Road
Beatrice Road
Tivoli Road
Tivoli Park Avenue
Connaught Road
Sussex Avenue
Durban Road
Perkins Av
Westbrook Gdns
Hartsdown Road
Grove Gardens
Wellis Gardens
Argyle Av

MIDDLESBROUGH

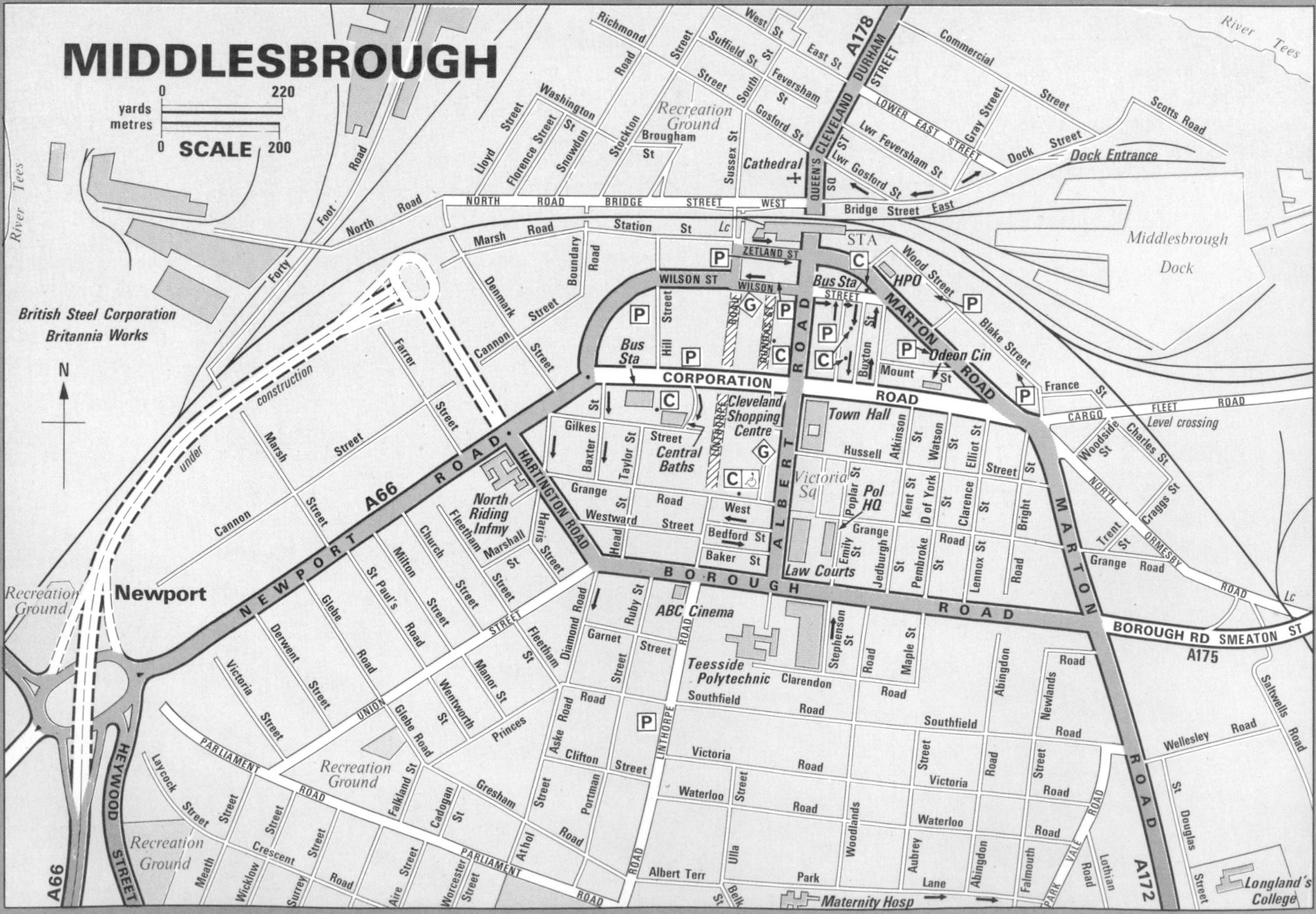
MIDDLESBROUGH
yards
metres
0
220
0
200
SCALE
N
River Tees
Middlesbrough Dock
Dock Entrance
British Steel Corporation Britannia Works
Cathedral
Recreation Ground
STA
Bus Sta
HPO
Odeon Cin
Cleveland Shopping Centre
Town Hall
Central Baths
Victoria Sq
Pol HQ
Law Courts
North Riding Infmy
ABC Cinema
Teesside Polytechnic
Newport
Recreation Ground
Recreation Ground
Recreation Ground
Maternity Hosp
Longland's College
under construction
Level crossing
A178
A66
A172
A175
NORTH ROAD
BRIDGE STREET WEST
Bridge Street East
Station St
Marsh Road
ZETLAND ST
WILSON ST
CORPORATION ROAD
ALBERT ROAD
MARTON ROAD
BOROUGH ROAD
BOROUGH RD
SMEATON ST
NEWPORT ROAD
HARTINGTON ROAD
HEYWOOD STREET
PARLIAMENT ROAD
UNION STREET
QUEEN'S SQ
CLEVELAND STREET
DURHAM STREET
LINTHORPE ROAD
CARGO FLEET ROAD
NORTH ORMESBY ROAD
Richmond Road
West St
Suffield St
East St
Feversham St
Commercial Street
Scotts Road
Washington St
Lloyd Street
Florence Street
Snowdon St
Stockton Street
Brougham St
South St
Gosford St
LOWER EAST STREET
Lwr Feversham St
Lwr Gosford St
Grey Street
Dock Street
Sussex St
Forty Foot Road
Denmark Street
Boundary Road
Cannon Street
Farrer Street
Marsh Street
Cannon Street
Hill Street
Wood Street
Blake Street
France St
Woodside St
Charles St
Craggs St
Trent St
Grange Road
Bus Sta
Gilkes St
Baxter St
Taylor St
Grange Road
Westward Street
Head St
West St
Bedford St
Baker St
Mount St
Burton St
Atkinson St
Watson St
Elliot St
Russell St
Poplar St
Emily St
Grange Road
Kent St
D of York St
Clarence St
Jedburgh St
Pembroke St
Lennox St
Bright St
Road
Marshall St
Fleetham St
Harris Street
Church Street
Milton Street
St Paul's Road
Glebe Road
Derwent Street
Victoria Street
Wentworth St
Manor St
Fleetham St
Diamond Road
Ruby St
Garnet Street
Princes Road
Glebe Road
Gresham Road
Aske Road
Clifton Street
Portman Street
Southfield Road
Clarendon Road
Stephenson St
Maple St
Abingdon Road
Newlands Road
Victoria Road
Waterloo Road
Southfield Road
Victoria Road
Waterloo Road
Woodlands Road
Ulla St
Park Lane
Aubrey St
Abingdon Road
Falmouth St
Park Vale Road
Lothian Road
Albert Terr
Belk St
Wellesley Road
Saltwells Road
St Douglas Street
Laycock Street
Crescent Road
Meath Street
Wicklow Street
Surrey Street
Aire Street
Worcester Street
Athol Street
Cadogan St
Falkland St
Lc

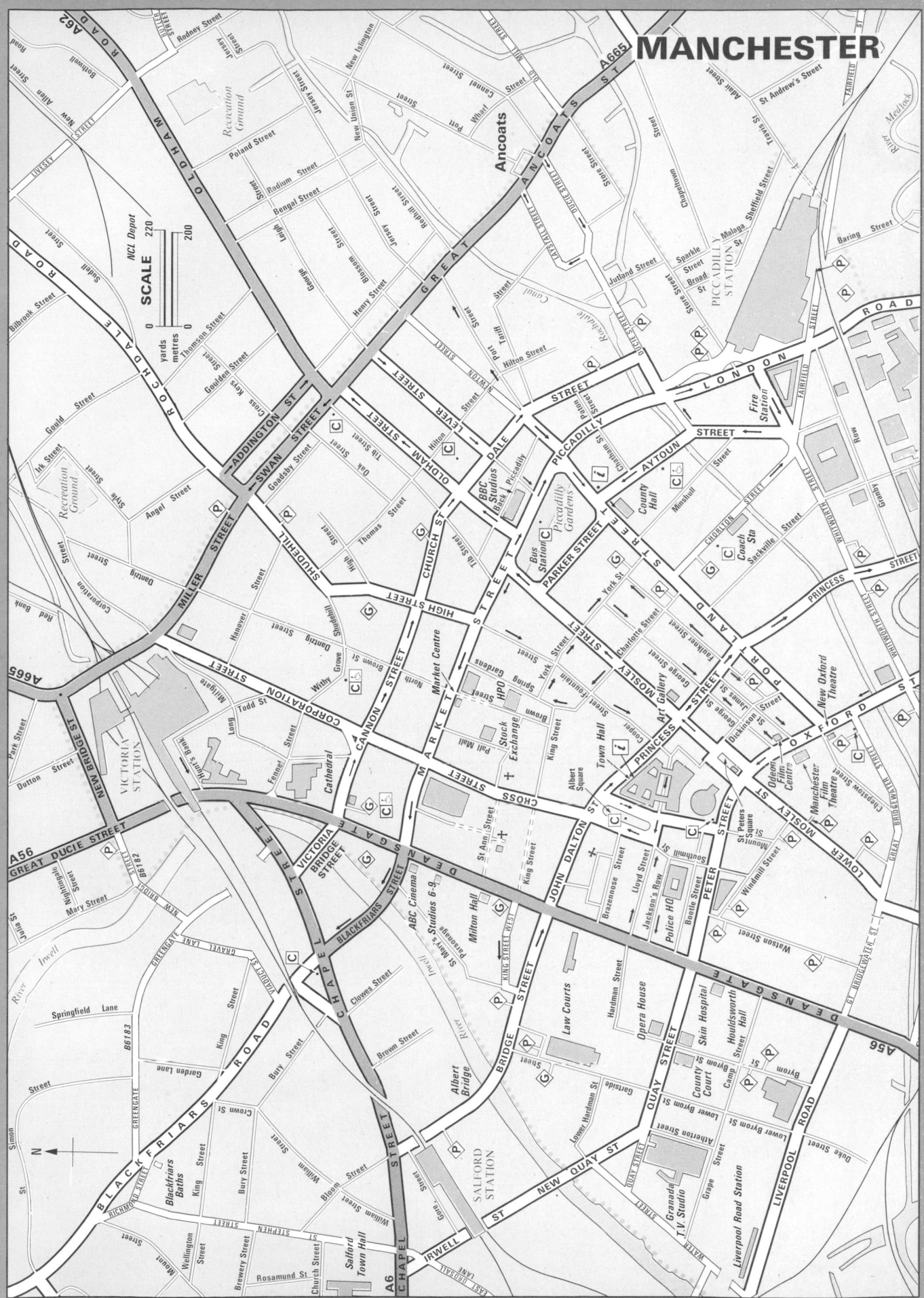

MANCHESTER

SCALE

Ancoats

175

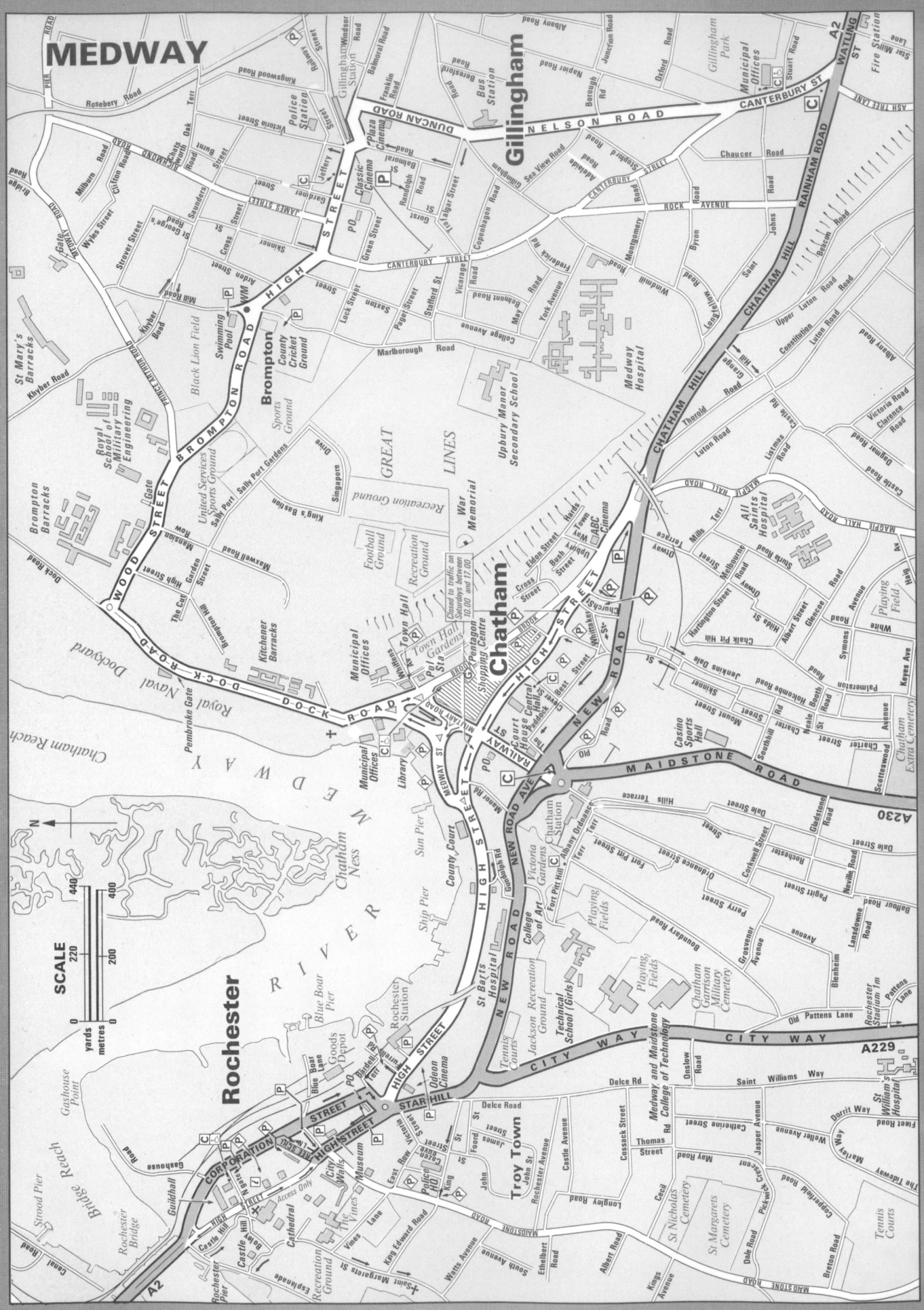

MEDWAY

Gillingham

Brompton

Chatham

Rochester

Troy Town

SCALE

N

yards
metres

Closed to traffic on Saturdays between 10.00 and 17.00

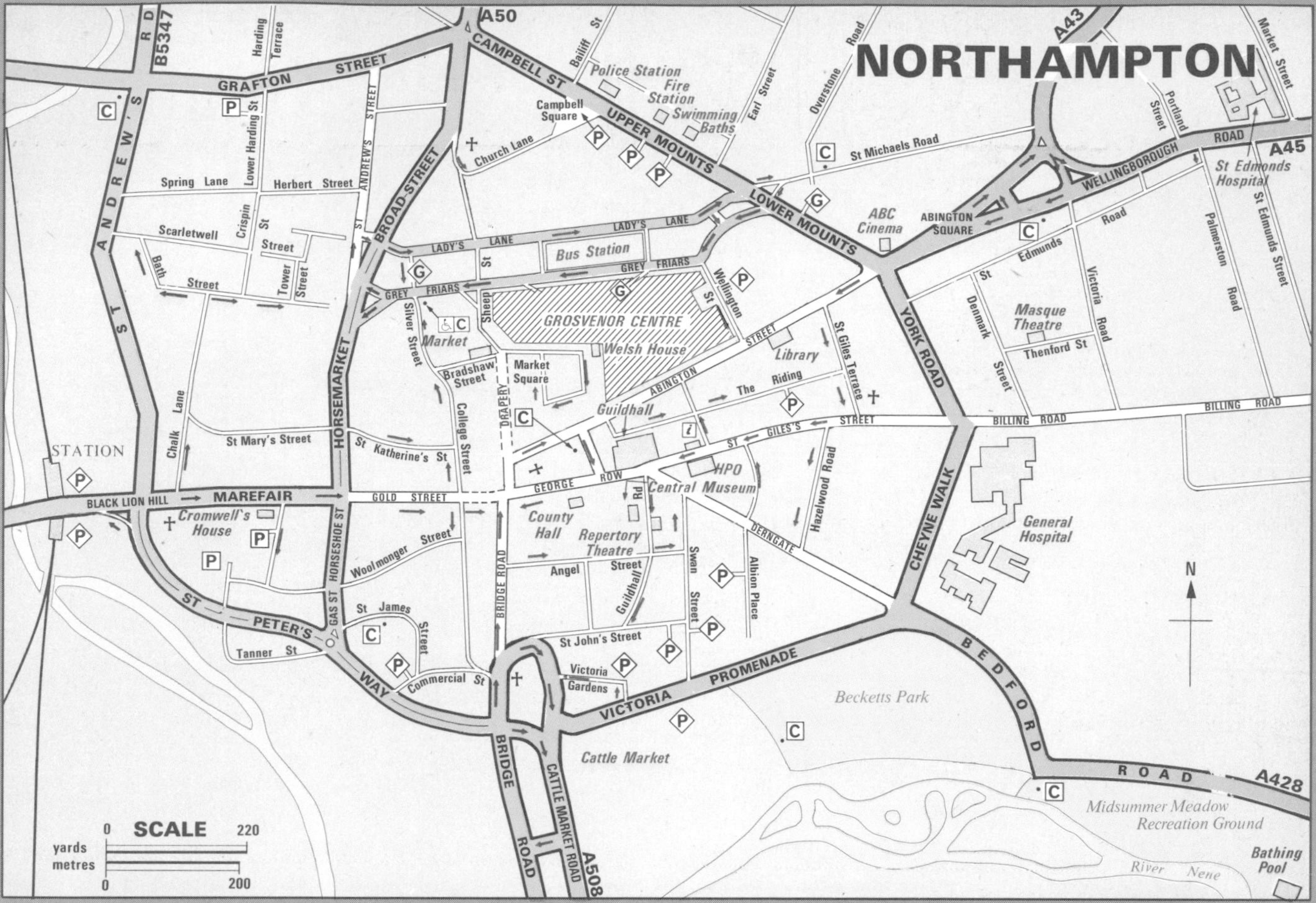

NORTHAMPTON

B5347 · A50 · A43 · A45 · A428 · A508

Harding Terrace · Lower Harding St · Herbert Street · Spring Lane · Scarletwell Street · Crispin Street · Bath Street · Chalk Lane · Tower Street · Silver Street · Bradshaw Street · St Mary's Street · St Katherine's St · College Street · Market Square · Black Lion Hill · MAREFAIR · Cromwell's House · Gold Street · Woolmonger Street · St James Street · Tanner St · Commercial St · Victoria Gardens · Cattle Market

GRAFTON STREET · CAMPBELL ST · Campbell Square · Police Station · Fire Station · Swimming Baths · St Michaels Road · Overstone Road · BROAD STREET · UPPER MOUNTS · Church Lane · LADY'S LANE · Bus Station · GREY FRIARS · Sheep St · GROSVENOR CENTRE · Welsh House · Market · Guildhall · Library · The Riding · St Giles Terrace · St GILES'S STREET · HPO · Central Museum · George Row · County Hall · Repertory Theatre · Angel St · Guildhall Road · St John's Street · Swan Street · Albion Place · Victoria PROMENADE · Beckett's Park · Cattle Market

LOWER MOUNTS · ABC Cinema · Abington Square · St Edmonds Hospital · WELLINGBOROUGH ROAD · St Edmunds Street · Edmunds St · Denmark St · Masque Theatre · Thenford St · Victoria Road · Palmerston Road · BILLING ROAD · YORK ROAD · Wellington Street · Abington Street · Hazelwood Road · Derngate · CHEYNE WALK · General Hospital · BEDFORD ROAD · Midsummer Meadow Recreation Ground · River Nene · Bathing Pool

ST ANDREW'S RD · ST ANDREWS STREET · HORSEMARKET · GAS ST · HORSESHOE ST · BRIDGE ROAD · ST PETER'S WAY · BRIDGE · CATTLE MARKET ROAD

STATION

N

SCALE
yards 0 — 220
metres 0 — 200

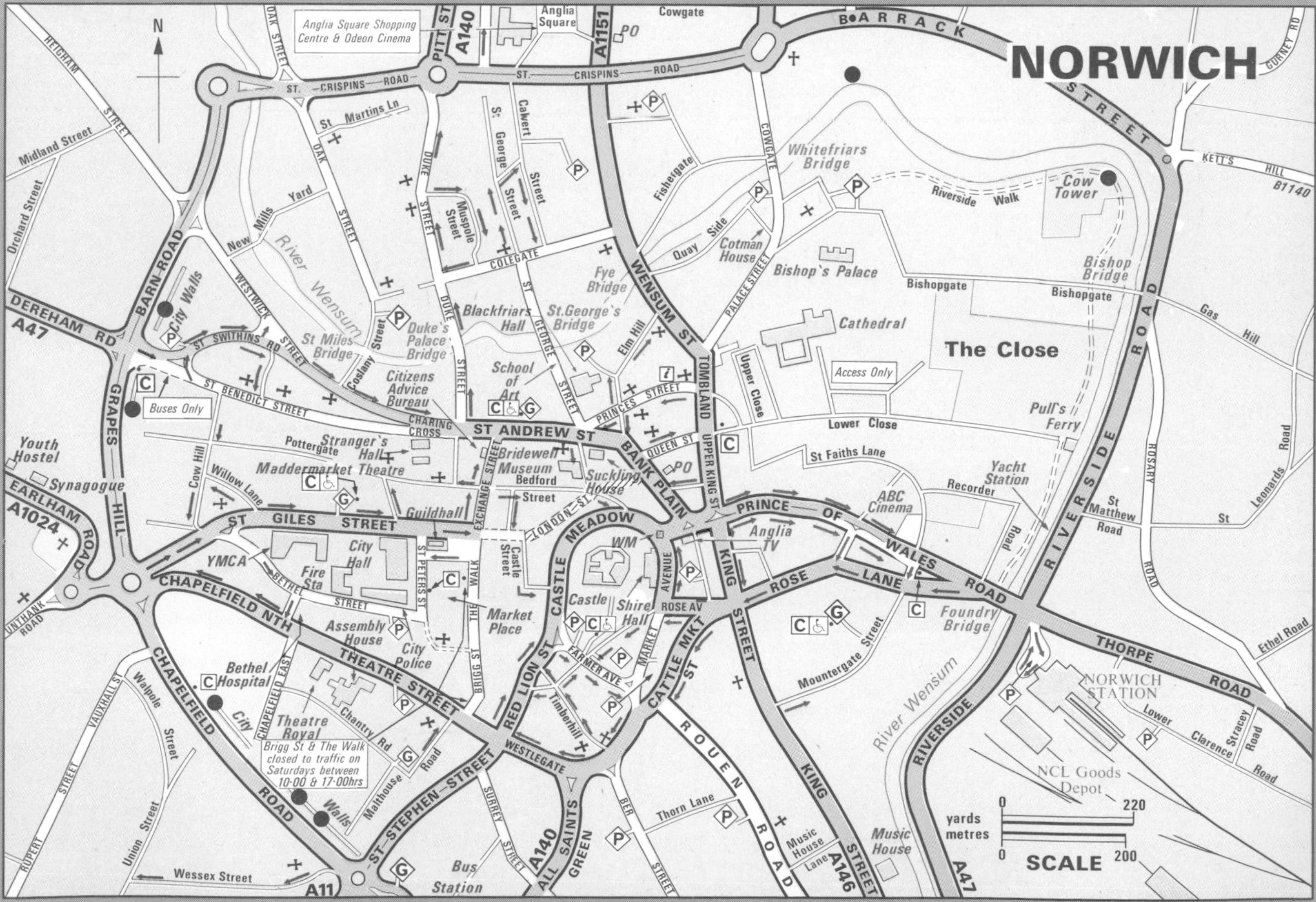

NORWICH

A140 · A1151 · A151 · A47 · A1024 · A11 · A146 · A43 · B1140 · A1024

Anglia Square Shopping Centre & Odeon Cinema · Anglia Square · Cowgate · BARRACK STREET · KETT'S HILL · ST CRISPINS ROAD · PITT ST · OAK STREET · St Martins Ln · St Martins Yard · Midland Street · Heigham Street · Orchard Street · New Mills Yard · River Wensum · Duke Street · Calvert Street · St George's Street · Magpole Street · COLEGATE · Fye Bridge · Quay Side · Whitefriars Bridge · Riverside Walk · Cow Tower · Cotman House · Bishop's Palace · Bishop Bridge · Bishopgate · Gas Hill

DEREHAM RD · BARN ROAD · WESTWICK ST · St Swithins Rd · St Miles Bridge · Coslany St · Duke's Palace Bridge · Blackfriars Hall · St George's Bridge · St Benedict Street · Citizens Advice Bureau · CHARING CROSS · Elm Hill · School of Art · Princes Street · TOMBLAND · WENSUM ST · PALACE STREET · Cathedral · The Close · Upper Close · Access Only · Lower Close · Pull's Ferry · ROSARY ROAD

GRAPES HILL · Youth Hostel · Synagogue · Cow Hill · Willow Lane · Pottergate · Stranger's Hall · Maddermarket Theatre · Bedford Street · Bridewell Museum · Suckling House · ST ANDREW ST · BANK PLAIN · Queen St · PO · UPPER KING ST · St Faiths Lane · Recorder Road · Yacht Station · ABC Cinema · Anglia TV · RIVERSIDE ROAD · St Matthew Road · St Leonards Road

EARLHAM ROAD · UNTHANK ROAD · ST GILES STREET · YMCA · City Hall · Fire Sta · St Peters St · Guildhall · EXCHANGE STREET · CASTLE MEADOW · Castle Street · Castle · Shire Hall · Rose Av · PRINCE OF WALES ROAD · WALES · ROSE LANE · KING STREET · Foundry Bridge · THORPE ROAD · NORWICH STATION · Lower Clarence Road · Ethel Road

CHAPELFIELD NTH · THEATRE STREET · Assembly House · City Police · Market Place · RED LION STREET · Brigg St & The Walk closed to traffic on Saturdays between 10·00 & 17·00hrs · CHAPELFIELD ROAD · Bethel Hospital · Theatre Royal · Chantry Rd · Chapelfield East · Walls · ST STEPHEN'S STREET · Surrey St · Farmers Ave · Timberhill · Ber St · WESTLEGATE · CATTLE MKT STREET · Rouen ROAD · Music House Lane · Music House · Thorn Lane · Mountergate Street · Mountergate · River Wensum · RIVERSIDE · NCL Goods Depot

VAUXHALL ST · Walpole St · Rupert St · Union Street · Wessex Street · Bus Station · ALL SAINTS GREEN · Queens Road

N

SCALE
yards 0 — 220
metres 0 — 200

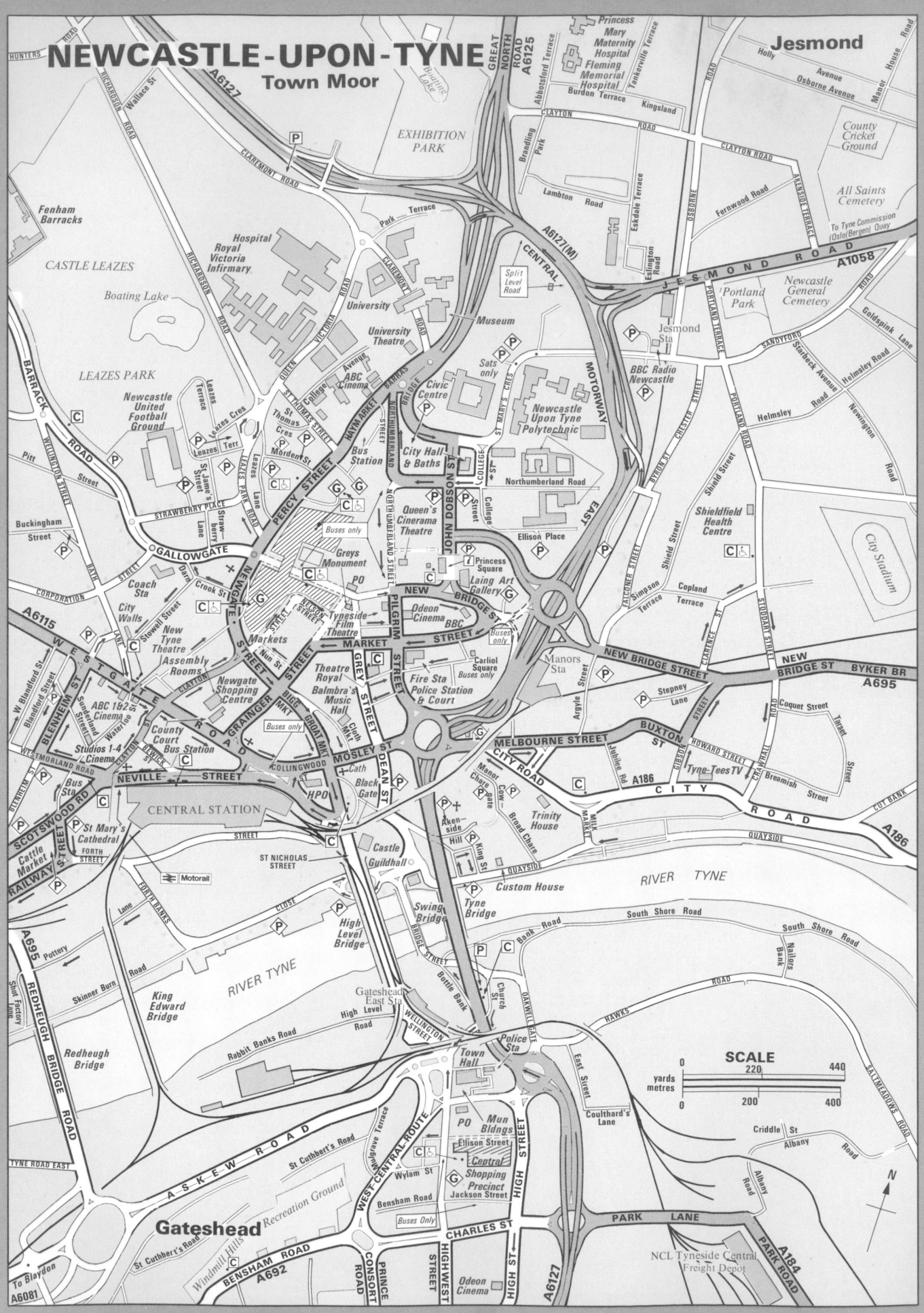

NEWCASTLE-UPON-TYNE
Town Moor

Jesmond

Gateshead

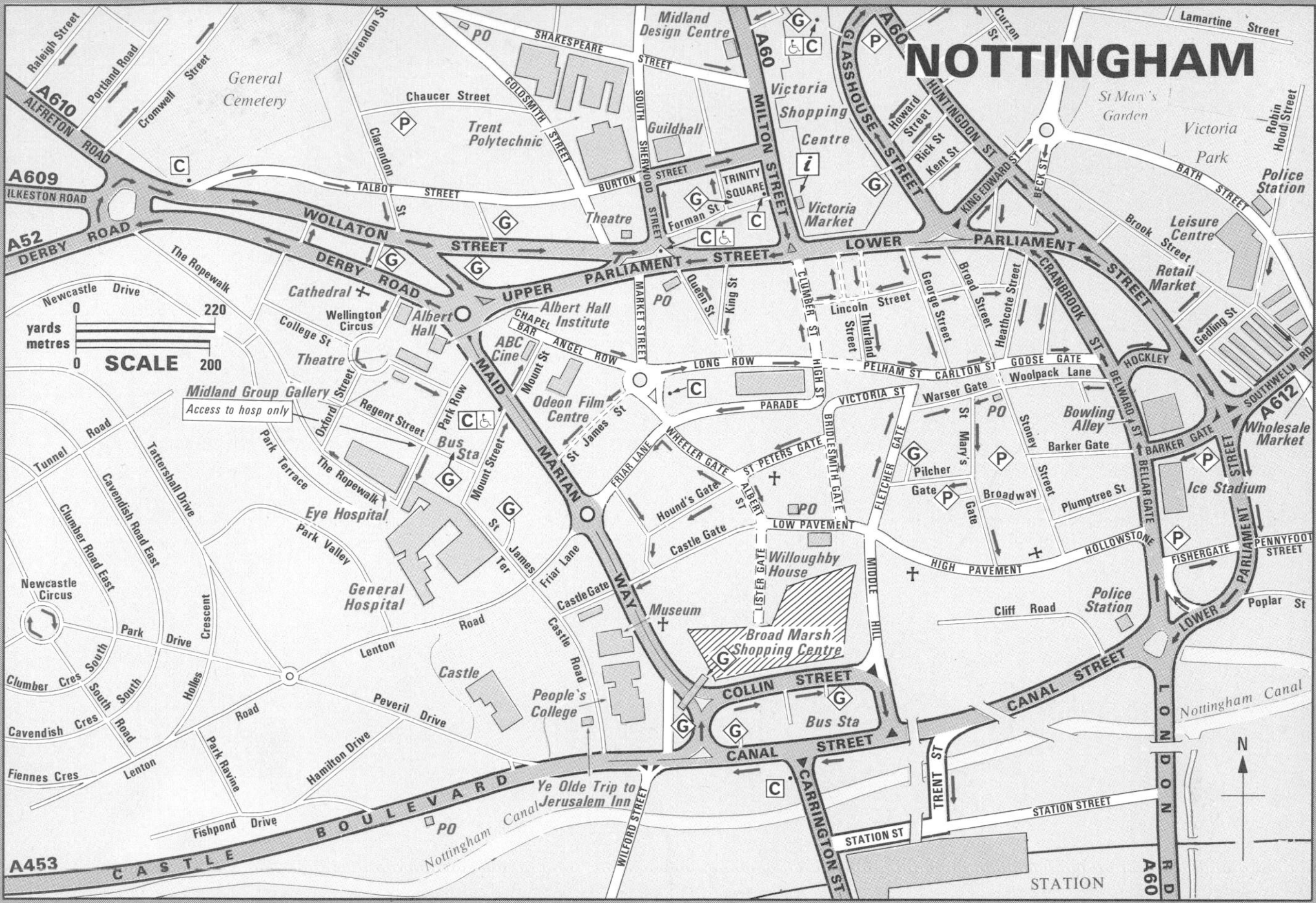

NOTTINGHAM

Raleigh Street · Portland Road · Cromwell Street · A610 · ALFRETON ROAD · A609 · ILKESTON ROAD · A52 · DERBY ROAD · A453

General Cemetery · Clarendon St · Chaucer Street · SHAKESPEARE STREET · GOLDSMITH STREET · Trent Polytechnic · SOUTH SHERWOOD STREET · BURTON STREET · Guildhall · PO · Midland Design Centre · A60 · GLASSHOUSE STREET · HUNTINGDON STREET · Curzon St · Lamartine Street · St Mary's Garden · Victoria Park · Robin Hood Street · Bath Street · Police Station

Talbot St · WOLLATON STREET · DERBY ROAD · Theatre · Forman St · TRINITY SQUARE · Victoria Shopping Centre · Victoria Market · Howard Street · Rick St · Kent St · KING EDWARD ST · BECK ST · Leisure Centre · Brook Street · Retail Market · Gedling St

Cathedral · Wellington Circus · College St · Albert Hall · Theatre · Chapel Bar · UPPER PARLIAMENT STREET · Albert Hall Institute · Angel Row · ABC Cine · Market Street · PO · Queen St · LOWER PARLIAMENT STREET · CLUMBER ST · Lincoln Street · George Street · Broad Street · Heathcote Street · CRANBROOK STREET · HOCKLEY · A612 · SOUTHWELL RD · Wholesale Market

SCALE · Newcastle Drive · The Ropewalk · yards · metres · 220 · 200 · Midland Group Gallery · Access to hosp only · Oxford Street · Regent Street · Park Row · Mount St · LONG ROW · PARADE · PELHAM ST · CARLTON ST · GOOSE GATE · Warser Gate · Woolpack Lane · BELWARD ST · Bowling Alley · Barker Gate · BARKER GATE · BELLAR GATE · Ice Stadium

Tunnel Road · Tattershall Drive · Cavendish Road East · Clumber Road East · Newcastle Circus · Park Drive · Crescent · Clumber Cres South · South Road · Cavendish Cres South · Fiennes Cres · Lenton · Park Ravine · Hamilton Drive · Peveril Drive · Fishpond Drive · CASTLE BOULEVARD

Eye Hospital · Park Valley · General Hospital · People's College · MAID MARIAN WAY · Castle Road · Castle · Friar Lane · Mount St · Park Terrace · The Ropewalk · Bus Sta · St James St · Castle Gate · Museum · Castle · WHEELER GATE · ST PETERS GATE · FRIAR LANE · Hound's Gate · Castle Gate · Low Pavement · Willoughby House · Broad Marsh Shopping Centre · BRIDLESMITH GATE · FLETCHER GATE · St Mary's St · St Mary's Gate · Pilcher Gate · Stoney St · Broadway · Plumptree St · HOLLOWSTONE · HIGH PAVEMENT · Cliff Road · Police Station · FISHERGATE · Poplar St · PENNYFOOT STREET · A612

COLLIN STREET · Bus Sta · CANAL STREET · Ye Olde Trip to Jerusalem Inn · WILFORD STREET · PO · Nottingham Canal · CARRINGTON ST · TRENT ST · STATION STREET · STATION ST · STATION · CANAL STREET · LONDON RD · Nottingham Canal · A60

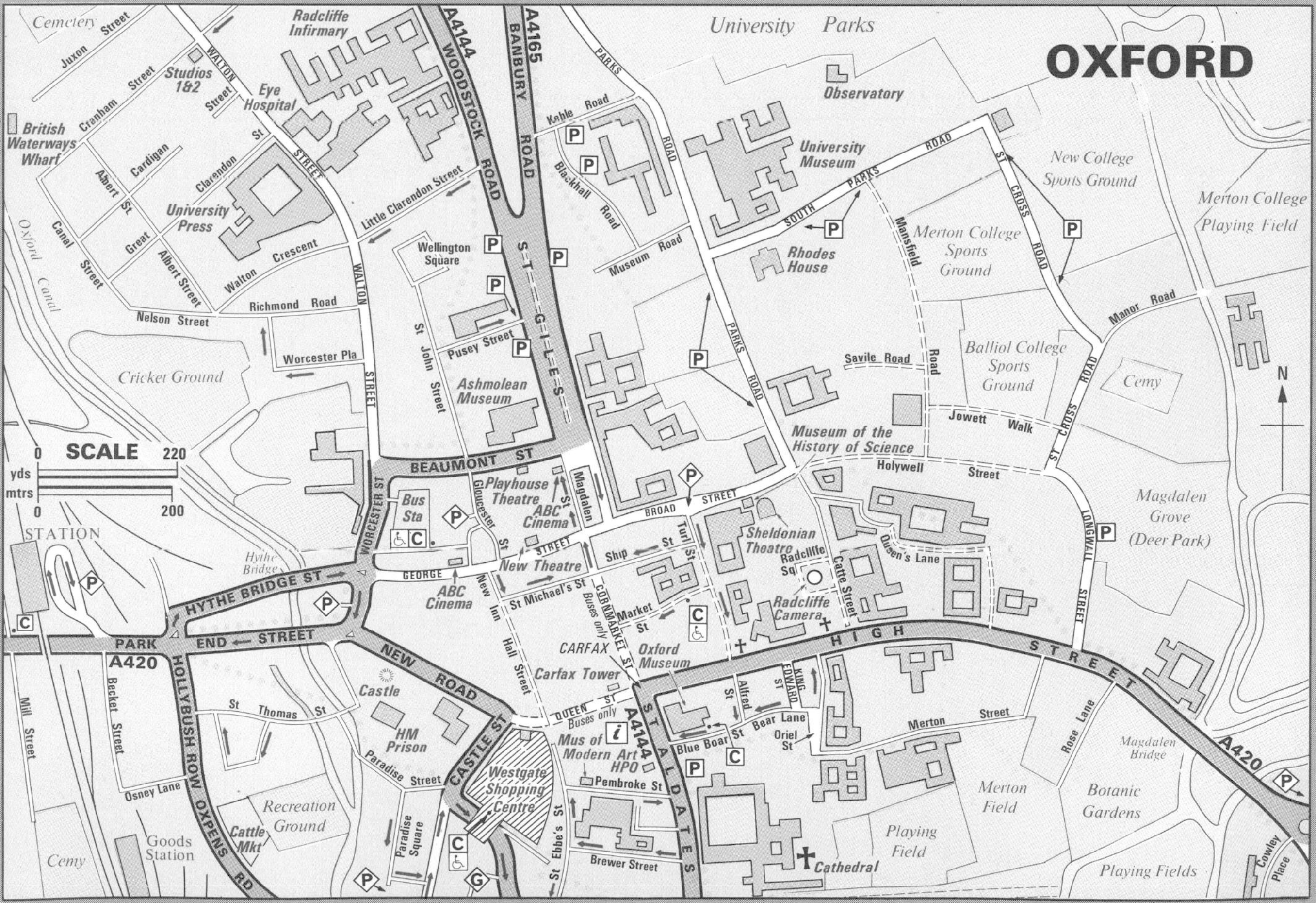

N

OXFORD

Cemetery Street · Juxon Street · WALTON STREET · Radcliffe Infirmary · A4144 · WOODSTOCK ROAD · A4165 · BANBURY ROAD · PARKS ROAD · University Parks · Observatory · New College Sports Ground · Merton College Playing Field

British Waterways Wharf · Studios 1 & 2 · Eye Hospital · Cranham St · Cardigan St · Albert St · Great Clarendon Street · University Press · Albert Street · Nelson Street · Richmond Road · Little Clarendon Street · Wellington Square · Worcester Pla · Pusey Street · St John Street · Walton Crescent · Keble Road · Blackhall Road · Museum Road · University Museum · Rhodes House · SOUTH PARKS ROAD · Mansfield Road · Merton College Sports Ground · CROSS ROAD · New College Sports Ground · MANOR ROAD · Cemy

Oxford Canal · Canal Street · Cricket Ground · STATION · Hythe Bridge · Worcester St · Bus Sta · Beaumont St · Playhouse Theatre · ABC Cinema · Gloucester Street · New Theatre · Ashmolean Museum · ST GILES · Magdalen Street · BROAD STREET · Museum of the History of Science · Savile Road · Jowett Walk · HOLYWELL STREET · Balliol College Sports Ground · LONGWALL STREET · Magdalen Grove (Deer Park) · A420

SCALE · yds · mtrs · 220 · 200 · HYTHE BRIDGE ST · George St · ABC Cinema · New Inn Hall St · St Michael's St · Ship St · CORNMARKET · Market · Sheldonian Theatre · Radcliffe Sq · Radcliffe Camera · Catte Street · Queen's Lane · HIGH STREET · A420

PARK END STREET · A420 · NEW ROAD · HOLLYBUSH ROW · OXPENS RD · Castle St · Hall St · CARFAX · Carfax Tower · Oxford Museum · QUEEN STREET · Buses only · St Ebbe's St · Westgate Shopping Centre · ST ALDATES · Mus of Modern Art · HPO · Blue Boar St · Bear Lane · King Edward St · Alfred St · Oriel St · Merton Street · Rose Lane · Botanic Gardens · Magdalen Bridge · Cowley Place

Mill St · St Thomas St · Becket Street · HM Prison · Paradise Street · Osney Lane · Cattle Mkt · Goods Station · Brewer Street · Pembroke St · Cathedral · Merton Field · Playing Field · Playing Fields · Recreation Ground · Cemy

N

179

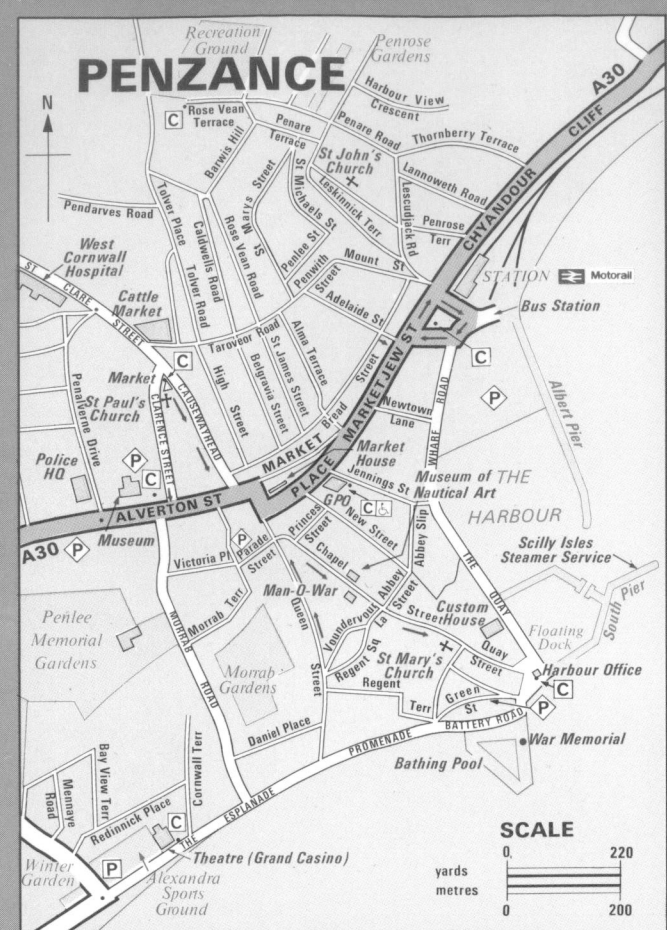

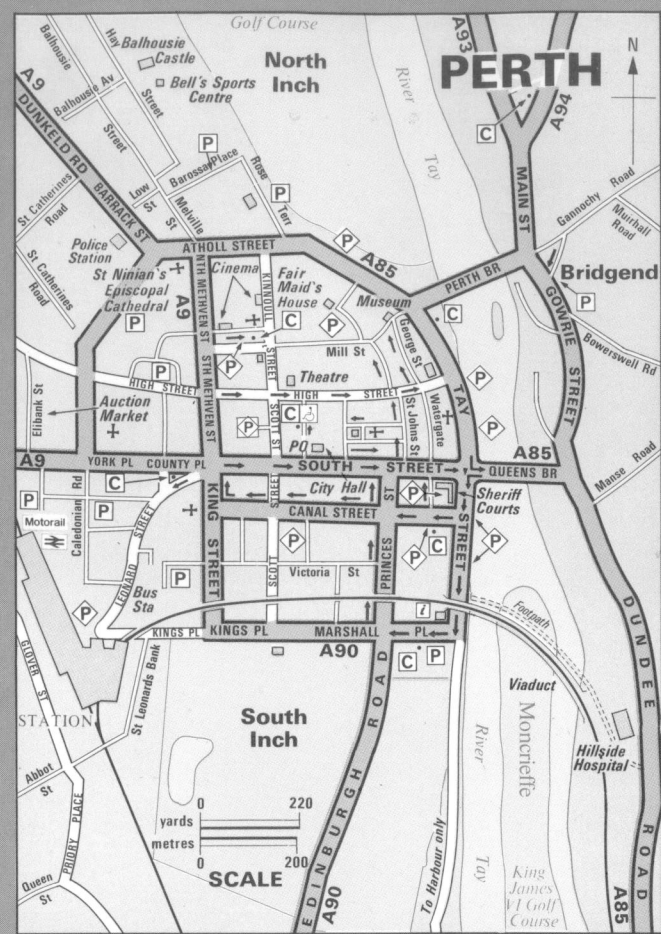

PENZANCE

PERTH

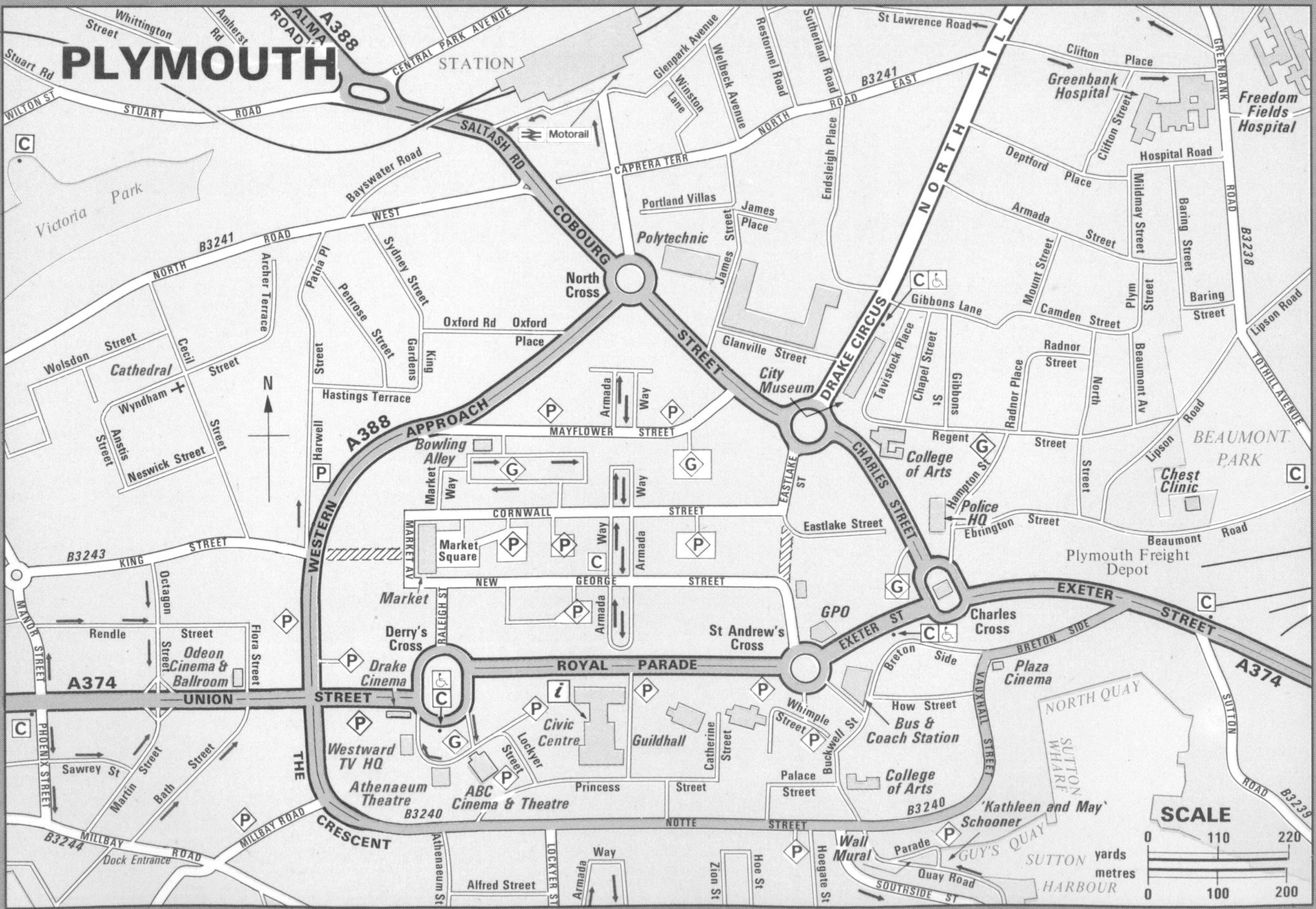

PLYMOUTH

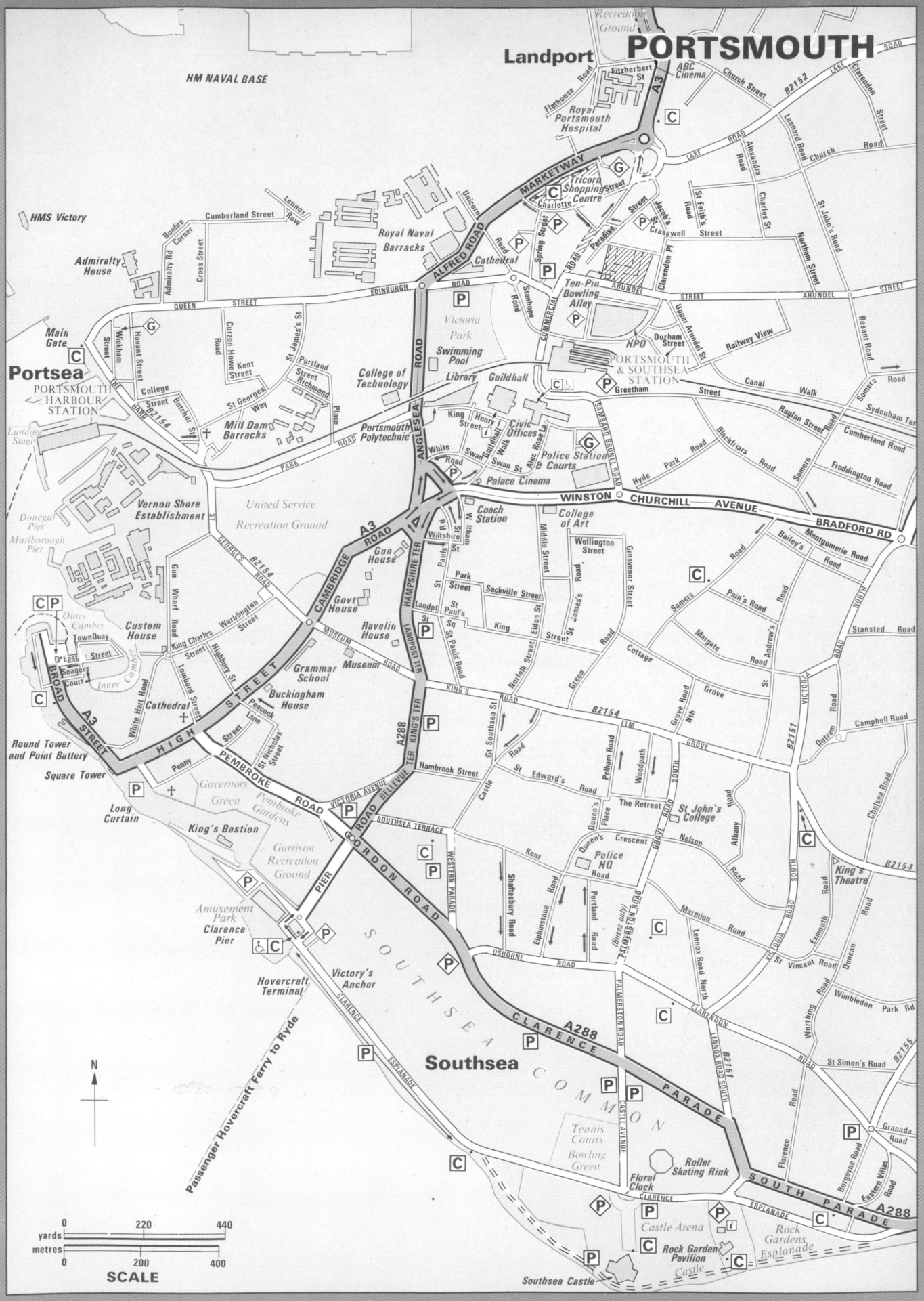

PORTSMOUTH

Landport

HM NAVAL BASE

HMS Victory

Admiralty House

Portsea

Main Gate

PORTSMOUTH HARBOUR STATION

Landing Stage

Donegal Pier
Marlborough Pier

Vernon Shore Establishment

United Service Recreation Ground

Custom House
Town Quay
Outer Camber
East Seagers Court
Inner Camber

Round Tower and Point Battery

Square Tower

Long Curtain

King's Bastion

Amusement Park
Clarence Pier

Hovercraft Terminal

Victory's Anchor

Southsea

Royal Naval Barracks

Cumberland Street
Lennox Row
Bonfire Corner
Admiralty Rd
Cross Street

Queen Street
Curzon Howe Road
St James's St
Kent Street
Portland Street
Richmond Place

Mill Dam Barracks
St Georges Way

Edinburgh Road

Alfred Road

Victoria Park

Swimming Pool

Library

College of Technology

Portsmouth Polytechnic

College Street
Butcher St
Havant Street
Wickham Street

Park Road

George's Road
Gun Wharf Road
Warblington Street
King Charles Street
Highbury Street
Lombard Street

Cambridge Road
A3 Road

Gun House

Govt House

Ravelin House

Museum Road

Museum

Grammar School
Buckingham House

Cathedral
White Hart Road
St Nicholas Street
Peacock Lane

Penny

Pembroke Road

Governors Green

Pembroke Gardens

Garrison Recreation Ground

Gordon Road

Pier Road

Victoria Avenue

Western Parade

Bellevue Ter
King's Ter
A288

Hampshire Ter

Landport Ter

Wiltshire St
St Pauls Rd
Park Street
Landpt St
St Paul's Sq
St Pauls Road
King Street

Hambrook Street
Castle

Cathedral

Marketway

Tricorn Shopping Centre

Charlotte Street
Paradise Street
Jacob's Street
Crasswell Street

Spring Street

Unicorn Road
Stanhope Road
Commercial Road
Arundel Street

Ten-Pin Bowling Alley

HPO

Durham Street
Upper Arundel St

PORTSMOUTH & SOUTHSEA STATION

Greetham Street

Guildhall

Civic Offices

King Street
Henry I Walk
White Road
Swan Street
Swan Walk
Alec Rose La

Police Station & Courts

Palace Cinema

Coach Station

College of Art

Wellington Street
Grosvenor Street
Middle Street
Sackville Street
King Street
Norfolk Street
Eldon St
James's Street
Green Road

King's Road

Gt Southsea St
Elm Grove
Pelham Road
Castle Road

WINSTON CHURCHILL AVENUE

BRADFORD RD

Somers Road

Bailey's Road
Montgomerie Road
Pain's Road
St Andrew's Road
Margate Road
Cottage Grove

Woodpath
GROVE ROAD SOUTH

St Edward's Road

Shaftesbury Road
Elphinstone Road
Osborne Road

The Retreat
St John's College

Queen's Place
Queen's Crescent
Nelson Road
Albany Road
Kent Road

Police HQ
Portland Road

SOUTHSEA COMMON

CLARENCE PARADE

A288

Tennis Courts
Bowling Green

Floral Clock

Roller Skating Rink

Castle Avenue

Castle Arena

Rock Garden Pavilion

Southsea Castle

Rock Gardens Esplanade

SOUTH PARADE
A288

ABC Cinema
Fitzherbert St
Flathouse Road

Royal Portsmouth Hospital

Church Street
B2152
Clarendon Road
St John's Road

St Faith's Road
Charles St
Northam Street
Alexandria Road
Leonard Road
Church Road

Arundel Street
Railway View
Besant Road

Canal Walk
Somer's Road
Sydenham Ter

Raglan Street
Cumberland Road
Blackfriars Road
Froddington Road

Hyde Park Road

Victoria Road

Somers Road
Grove Road
Nth
Stansted Road
Campbell Road

B2151

Chelsea Road

Clarendon Road
King's Theatre
B2154

Victoria Road South

St Vincent Road
Marmion Road
Lennox Road North
Duncan Road
Ermouth Road
Worthing Road
Wimbledon Park Rd
St Simon's Road
B2155

Granada Road
Florence Road
Burgoyne Road
Easter Villas
Palmerston Road
Clarendon Road
Lennox Road South

Esplanade

N

SCALE

yards	0 — 220 — 440	
metres	0 — 200 — 400	

Passenger Hovercraft ferry to Ryde

181

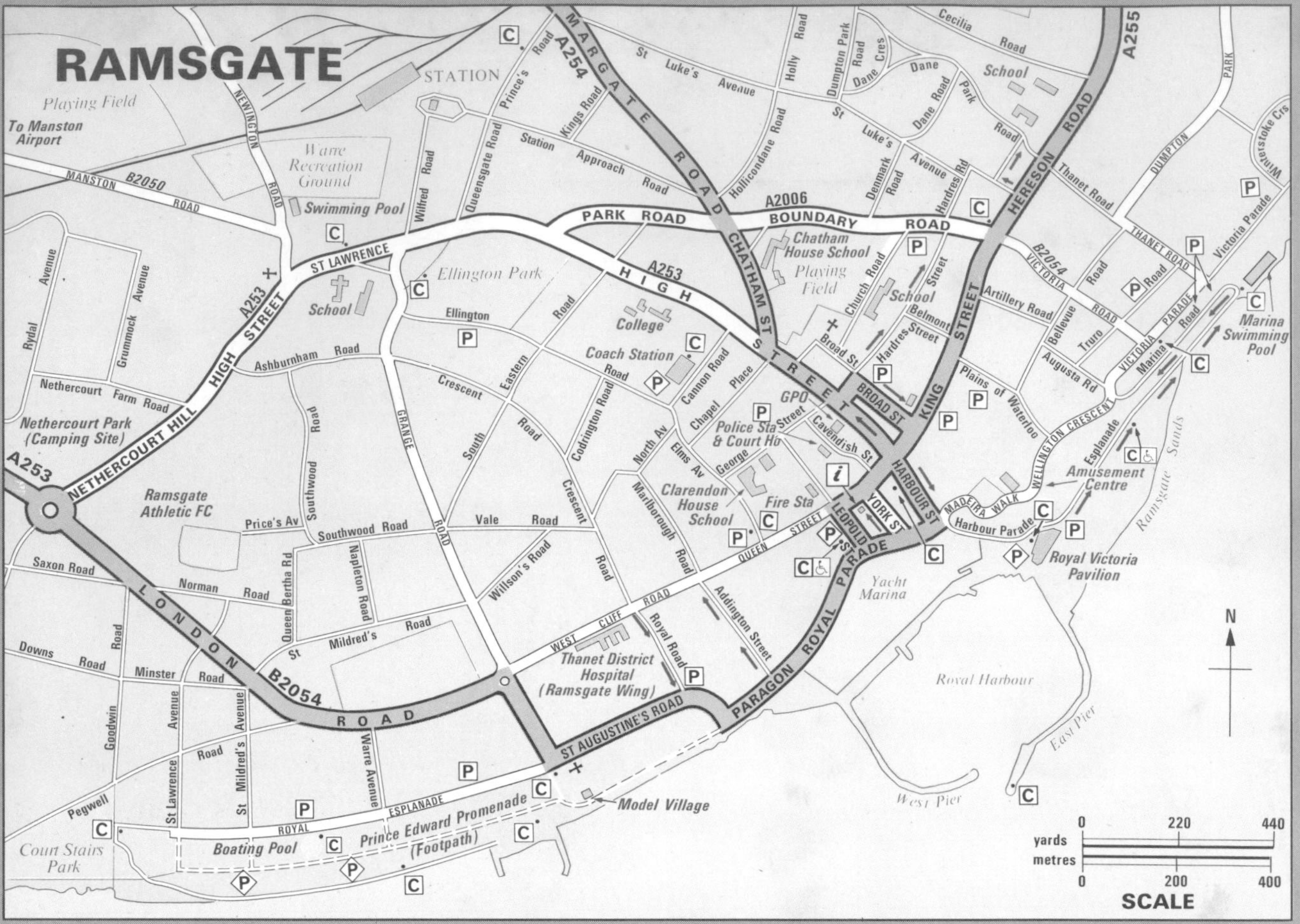
RAMSGATE
STATION
Playing Field
To Manston Airport
Warre Recreation Ground
Swimming Pool
MANSTON B2050 ROAD
NEWINGTON ROAD
Prince's Road
Kings Road
A254
MARGATE ROAD
St Luke's Avenue
Holly Road
Dumpton Park Road
Dane Cres
Dane Road
Dane Park
Cecilia Road
School
A255
HERESON ROAD
Queensgate Road
Wilfred Road
Station Approach Road
Hollicondane Road
Denmark Road
St Luke's Avenue
Hardres Rd
Thanet Road
DUMPTON PARK
Winstanley Cres
PARK ROAD
A2006 BOUNDARY ROAD
ST LAWRENCE
HIGH STREET
A253
Ellington Park
Ellington
School
Chatham House School
Playing Field
CHATHAM ST
Church Road
School
Belmont Street
Hardres Street
Broad St
BROAD ST
KING STREET
Artillery Road
B2054 VICTORIA ROAD
THANET ROAD
Victoria Parade
Marina Swimming Pool
College
Coach Station
Cannon Road
Chapel Place
GPO
Cavendish St
Police Sta & Court Ho
Plains of Waterloo
Bellevue
Truro Road
Augusta Rd
VICTORIA PARADE
Marina Road
WELLINGTON CRESCENT
Esplanade
Amusement Centre
Ramsgate Sands
Rydal Avenue
Grummock Avenue
Ashburnham Road
Nethercourt Farm Road
Nethercourt Park (Camping Site)
NETHERCOURT HILL
A253
Ramsgate Athletic FC
Crescent
GRANGE ROAD
South Eastern Road
Codrington Road
North Av
Elms Av
George Street
Clarendon House School
Fire Sta
i
HARBOUR ST
YORK ST
LEOPOLD ST
MADEIRA WALK
Harbour Parade
Royal Victoria Pavilion
Southwood Road
Price's Av
Southwood Road
Vale Road
Crescent Road
Marlborough Road
QUEEN STREET
ROYAL PARADE
Yacht Marina
Saxon Road
Norman Road
Queen Bertha Rd
Napleton Road
Willson's Road
CLIFF ROAD
WEST
Addington Street
St Mildred's Road
Royal Road
Downs Road
Minster Road
Thanet District Hospital (Ramsgate Wing)
PARAGON
Royal Harbour
LONDON
B2054 ROAD
ST AUGUSTINE'S ROAD
East Pier
Goodwin Road
St Lawrence Avenue
St Mildred's Avenue
Warre Avenue
Model Village
West Pier
Pegwell
ROYAL ESPLANADE
Court Stairs Park
Boating Pool
Prince Edward Promenade (Footpath)
N
yards
metres
0
220
440
0
200
400
SCALE

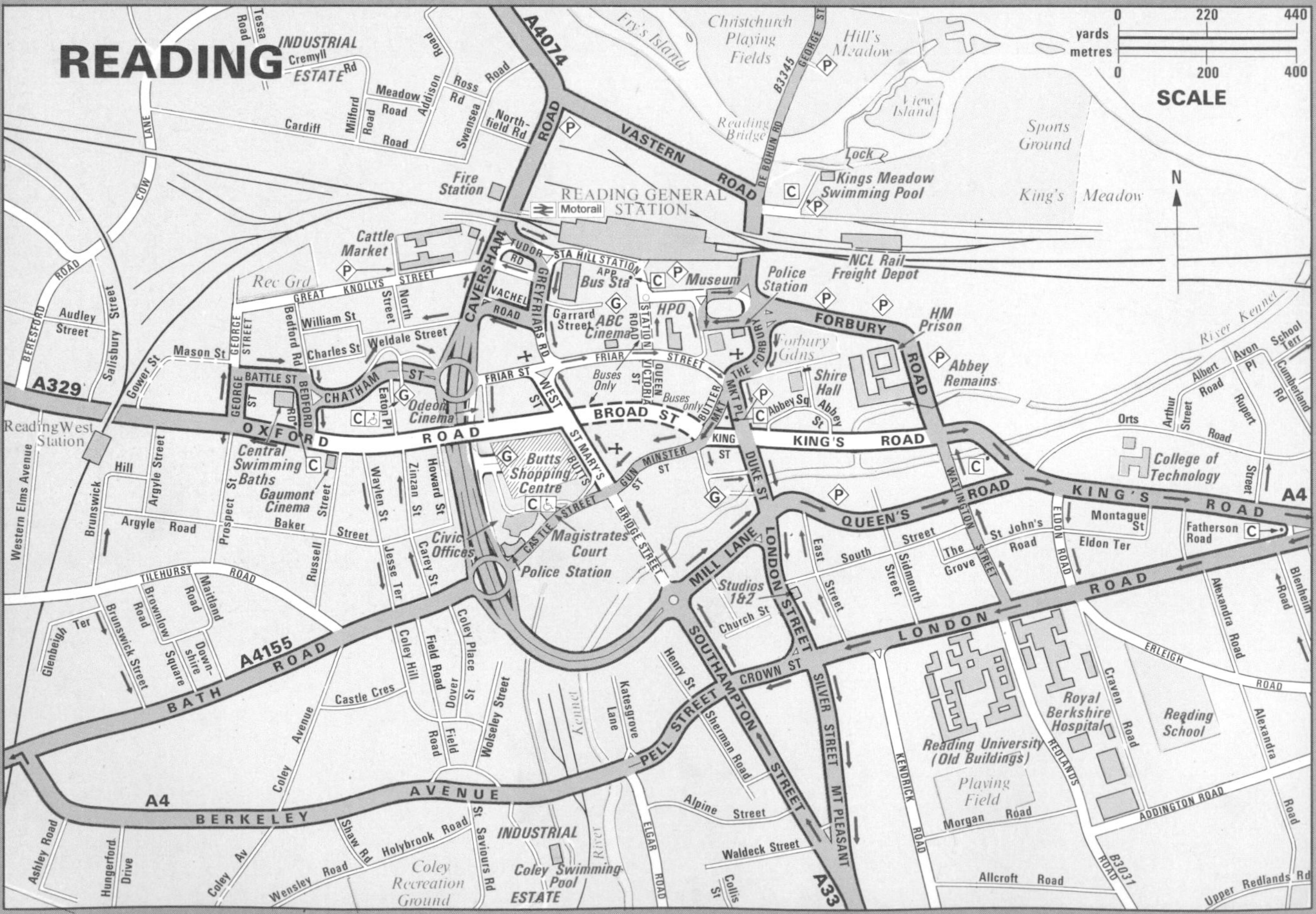
READING
INDUSTRIAL ESTATE
Tessa Road
Cremyll Rd
Meadow Road
Milford Road
Addison Road
Ross Rd
Swansea Road
North-field Rd
Cardiff Road
A4074
ROAD
VASTERN ROAD
Fry's Island
Christchurch Playing Fields
Hill's Meadow
GEORGE ST
B3345
Reading Bridge
View Island
DE BOHUN RD
Lock
Kings Meadow Swimming Pool
Sports Ground
King's Meadow
yards
metres
0
220
440
0
200
400
SCALE
N
COW LANE
Fire Station
READING GENERAL STATION
Motorail
Cattle Market
TUDOR RD
STA HILL STATION APP
Bus Sta
Museum
NCL Rail Freight Depot
Police Station
Rec Grd
GREAT KNOLLYS STREET
VACHEL ROAD
CAVERSHAM
GREYFRIARS RD
Garrard Street
ABC Cinema
STATION ROAD
HPO
FORBURY ROAD
HM Prison
BERESFORD ROAD
Audley Street
Salisbury Street
GEORGE STREET
William St
North Street
Weldale Street
Charles St
Bedford Rd
Mason St
Forbury Gdns
ASHBY
River Kennet
School Terr
Avon Pl
Albert Road
Cumberland Rd
Rupert
Abbey Remains
FRIAR STREET
QUEEN VICTORIA ST
BATTLE ST
BEDFORD
CHATHAM ST
FRIAR ST
WEST ST
Buses Only
BROAD ST
BUTTER MKT
THE FORBURY
MKT PL
Shire Hall
Abbey Sq
Abbey St
A329
Gower St
Eaton Pl
Odeon Cinema
Reading West Station
OXFORD ROAD
KING
KING'S ROAD
Orts Road
Arthur Street
Street
Western Elms Avenue
Hill
Argyle Street
Central Swimming Baths
Gaumont Cinema
Waylen St
Zinzan St
Howard St
Butts Shopping Centre
ST MARY'S BUTTS
GUN STREET
MINSTER ST
ST
DUKE ST
WALLINGFORD STREET
College of Technology
A4
KING'S ROAD
Brunswick Street
Argyle Road
Prospect St
Baker Street
Russell Street
Jesse Ter
Carey St
Civic Offices
CASTLE STREET
Magistrates' Court
Police Station
BRIDGE STREET
QUEEN'S ROAD
East
South Street
Sidmouth Street
St John's Road
The Grove
ELDON ROAD
Montague St
Eldon Ter
Fatherson Road
Blenheim Road
TILEHURST ROAD
Brownlow Road
Maitland Road
Glenbeigh Ter
Brunswick Street
Downshire Square
Coley Place
Coley Hill
Field Road
Dover St
MILL LANE
Studios 1&2
Church St
LONDON STREET
LONDON ROAD
Alexandra Road
ERLEIGH ROAD
A4155
BATH ROAD
Castle Cres
Wolseley Street
Henry St
SOUTHAMPTON STREET
CROWN ST
SILVER STREET
Royal Berkshire Hospital
Craven Road
Reading School
Alexandra Road
Coley Avenue
Field Road
Kennet
Katesgrove Lane
PELL STREET
Sherman Road
Reading University (Old Buildings)
REDLANDS ROAD
A4
AVENUE
BERKELEY
Alpine Street
MT PLEASANT
KENDRICK ROAD
Playing Field
Morgan Road
ADDINGTON ROAD
Ashley Road
Hungerford Drive
Coley Av
Shaw Rd
Holybrook Road
St Saviours Rd
INDUSTRIAL
River
ELGAR ROAD
Waldeck Street
B3031
A33
Wensley Road
Coley Recreation Ground
Coley Swimming Pool
ESTATE
Collis St
Allcroft Road
Upper Redlands Road

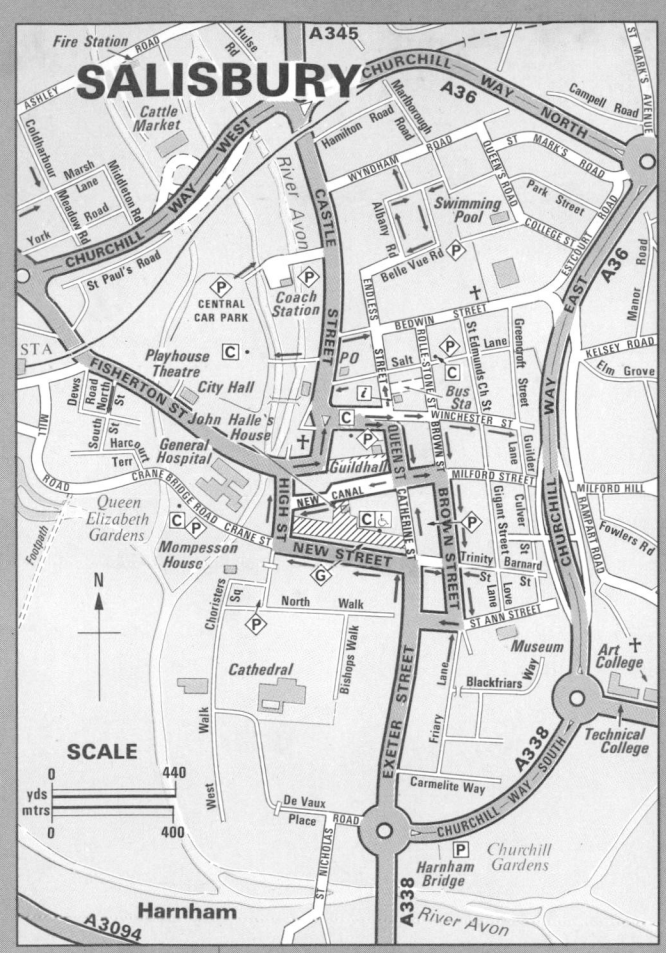

SALISBURY

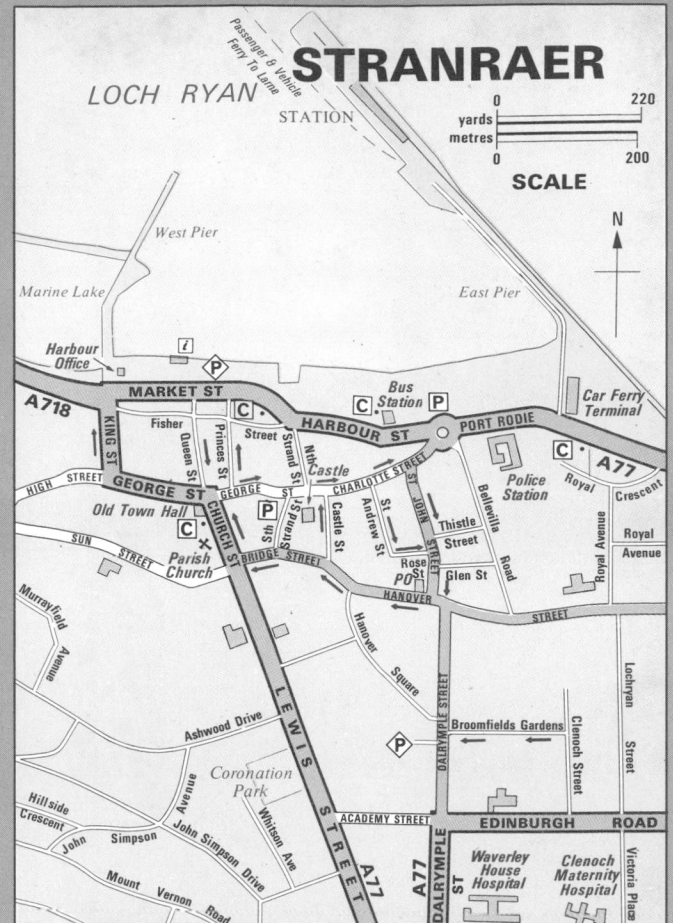

STRANRAER

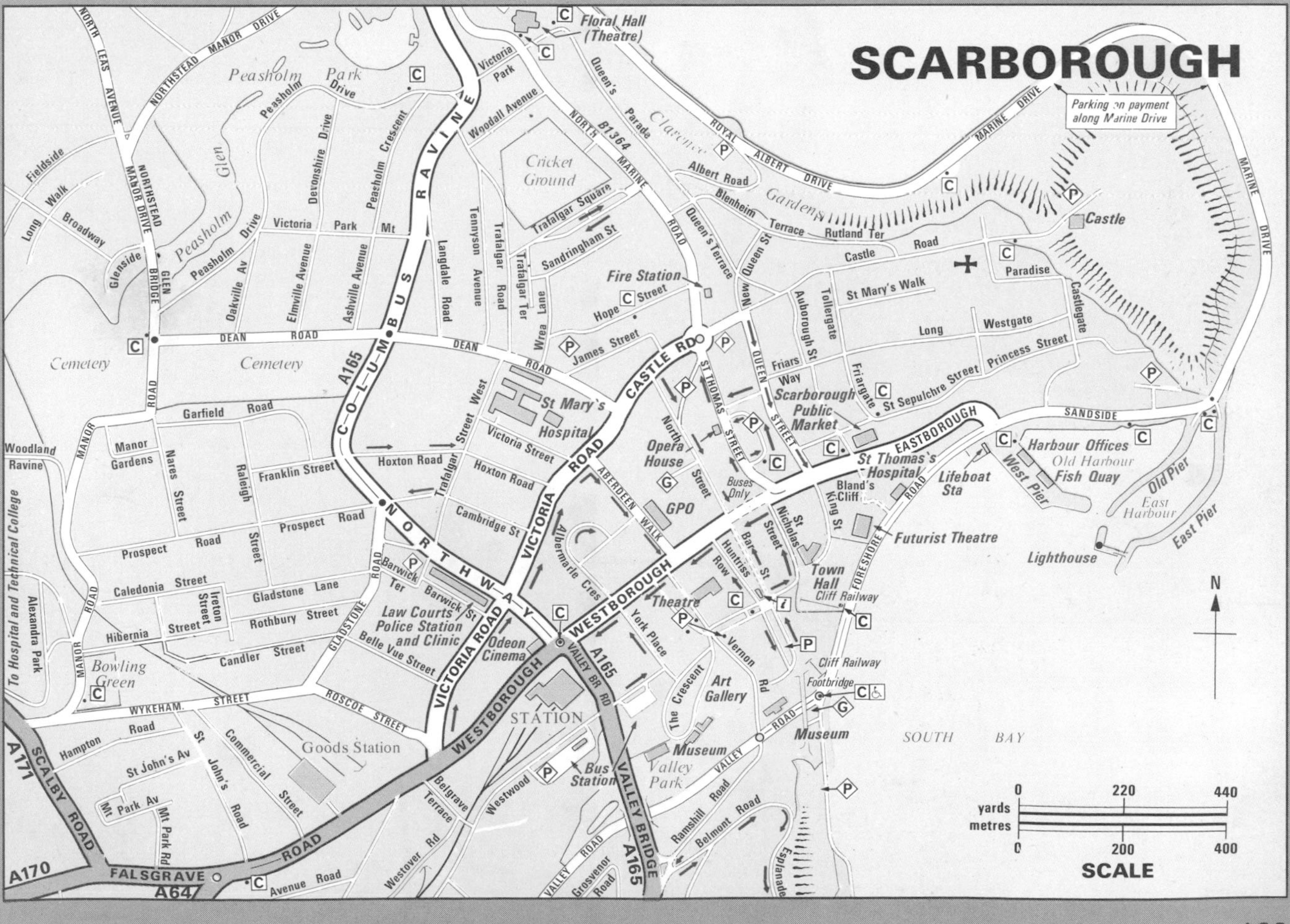

SCARBOROUGH

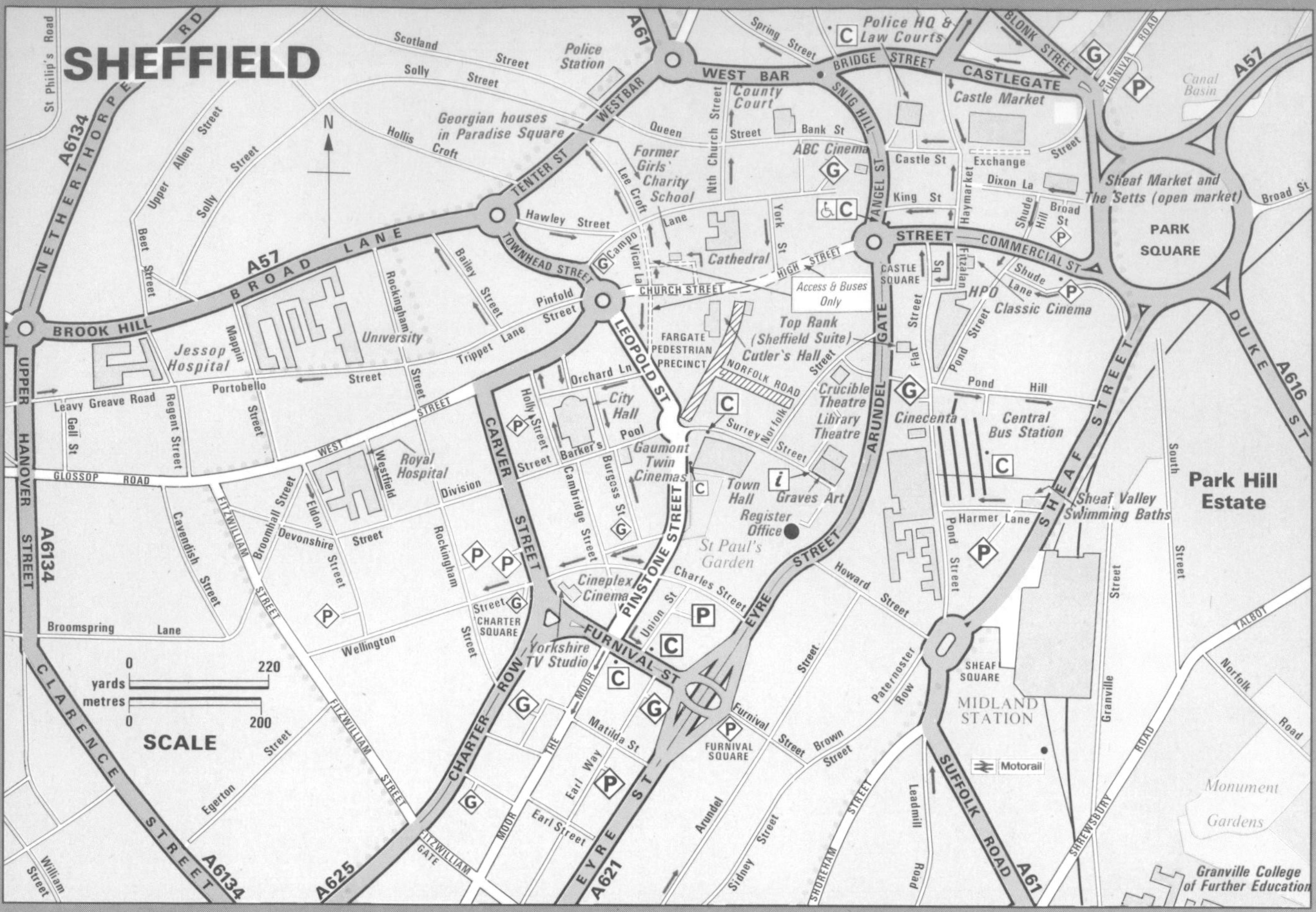

SHEFFIELD

St Philip's Road · RD · A6134 · NETHERTHORPE · A57 · BROAD LANE

Scotland Street · Solly Street · Hollis Croft · Upper Allen Street · Beet Street · Bailey Street · Rockingham Street

Police Station · Georgian houses in Paradise Square · Former Girls' Charity School · Campo Lane · Vicar Lane

WEST BAR · WESTBAR · TENTER ST · Hawley Street · Townhead Street · Pinfold Street · Trippet Lane · Orchard Lane

Queen Street · Church Street · Nth Church Street · York St · Bank St · High Street

Police Station · Spring Street · Police HQ & Law Courts · BRIDGE STREET · SNIG HILL · CASTLEGATE · BLONK STREET · Canal Basin · A57

County Court · Castle Market · Castle St · Exchange · Dixon La · King St · Sheaf Market and The Setts (open market) · Broad St

ABC Cinema · Cathedral · CASTLE SQUARE · HPO · Shude Hill · Classic Cinema · PARK SQUARE

Access & Buses Only · Fargate Pedestrian Precinct · Top Rank (Sheffield Suite) · Cutler's Hall · NORFOLK ROAD · Crucible Theatre · Library Theatre · Cinecenta · Central Bus Station

BROOK HILL · A57 · University · Jessop Hospital · Mappin Street · Portobello · Leavy Greave Road · Regent Street

UPPER HANOVER STREET · A6134 · GLOSSOP ROAD · Cavendish Street · Broomhall Street · WEST · Westfield · Royal Hospital · Division Street · CARVER STREET · City Hall · Barker's Pool · LEOPOLD ST

Devonshire Street · Eldon Street · Rockingham Street · Cambridge Street · Burgess Street · Surrey Street · Norfolk Street

Broomspring Lane · Wellington Street · CHARTER ROW · FITZWILLIAM STREET · PINSTONE STREET · Charles Street · Union Street · Eyre Street · Howard Street · Harmer Lane

Gaumont Twin Cinemas · Town Hall · Graves Art · Register Office · St Paul's Garden · Central Bus Station · Sheaf Valley Swimming Baths · Park Hill Estate

CLARENCE STREET · A6134 · Egerton Street · William Street · A625 · A621 · FITZWILLIAM GATE · THE MOOR · EYRE ST · Matilda St · FURNIVAL ST · Earl Way · Earl Street · Furnival Square · Furnival Street · Brown Street

Cineplex Cinema · CHARTER SQUARE · Yorkshire TV Studio · Sidney Street · Shoreham Street · Paternoster Row · SHEAF SQUARE

SHEAF STREET · MIDLAND STATION · Motorail · SUFFOLK ROAD · A61 · Leadmill · Granville Street · DUKE ST · A616 · TALBOT STREET · Norfolk Road

South Street · Park Hill Estate · Monument Gardens · Granville College of Further Education · SHREWSBURY ROAD

SCALE · 0 220 yards · 0 200 metres

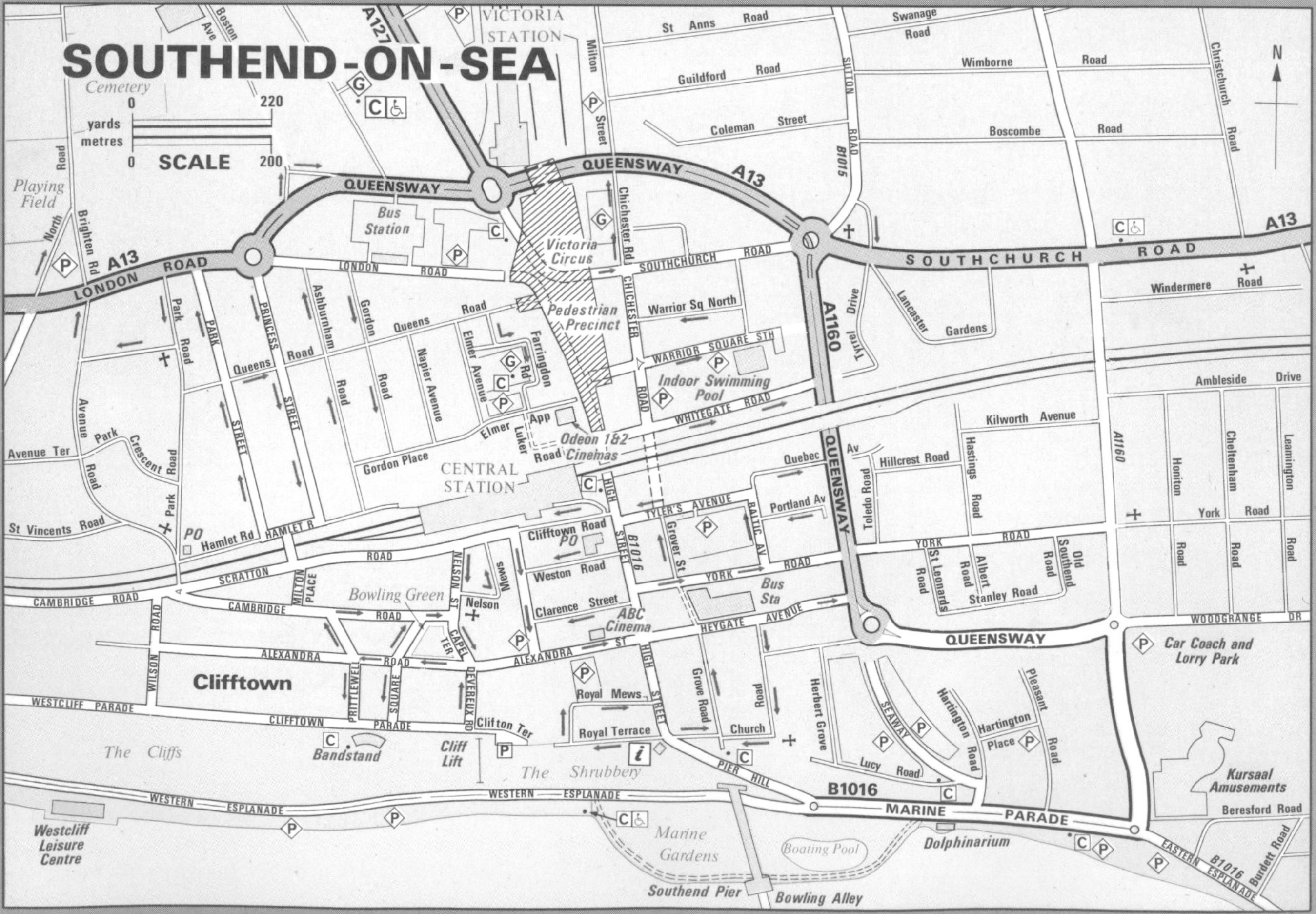

SOUTHEND-ON-SEA

Boston Ave · A127 · VICTORIA STATION · St Anns Road · Swanage Road · Wimborne Road · Christchurch Road

Cemetery · Milton Street · Guildford Road · Coleman Street · Boscombe Road · SUTTON · B1015

Playing Field · QUEENSWAY · A13 · Bus Station · Victoria Circus · Chichester Rd · SOUTHCHURCH ROAD · SOUTHCHURCH ROAD · A13

Brighton Road · North Road · LONDON ROAD · A13 · Park Road · Princess Street · Ashburnham Road · Gordon Road · Queens Road · Napier Avenue · Elmer Avenue · Ferrington Rd · Pedestrian Precinct · Warrior Sq North · WARRIOR SQUARE STH · A1160 · Tyrel Drive · Lancaster Gardens · Windermere Road

Avenue Road · Park Crescent · Avenue Ter · Gordon Place · Queens Road · Indoor Swimming Pool · WHITEGATE ROAD · Quebec Av · Kilworth Avenue · Ambleside Drive

St Vincents Road · Central Station · Elmer Lane · App · Odeon 1 & 2 Cinemas · Hillcrest Road · Hastings Road · Honiton Road · Cheltenham Road · Leamington Road

PO · Hamlet Rd · Clifftown Road · PO · Weston Road · York Road · Portland Av · York Street · QUEENSWAY · Quebec Av · Toledo Road · York Road · Albert Road · St Leonards Road · Old Southend Road

CAMBRIDGE ROAD · SCRATTON ROAD · MILTON PLACE · Bowling Green · Nelson Street · Clarence Street · Bus Sta · HEYGATE AVENUE · Kilworth Avenue · WOODGRANGE DR

Clifftown · WESTCLIFF PARADE · ALEXANDRA ROAD · NELSON STREET · CAPEL TER · ALEXANDRA STREET · ABC Cinema · PRITTLEWELL SQUARE · BEVERLEY RD · CLIFFTOWN PARADE · Royal Mews · Clifton Ter · Royal Terrace · Grove Road · Herbert Grove · Church Road · Hartington Place · Hartington Road · Pleasant Road · Car Coach and Lorry Park · Beresford Road

The Cliffs · Bandstand · Cliff Lift · The Shrubbery · Pier Hill · B1016 · MARINE PARADE · Lucy Road · Kursaal Amusements

Westcliff Leisure Centre · WESTERN ESPLANADE · WESTERN ESPLANADE · Marine Gardens · Boating Pool · Southend Pier · Bowling Alley · Dolphinarium · EASTERN ESPLANADE · B1016 · Burdett Road

SCALE · 0 220 yards · 0 200 metres

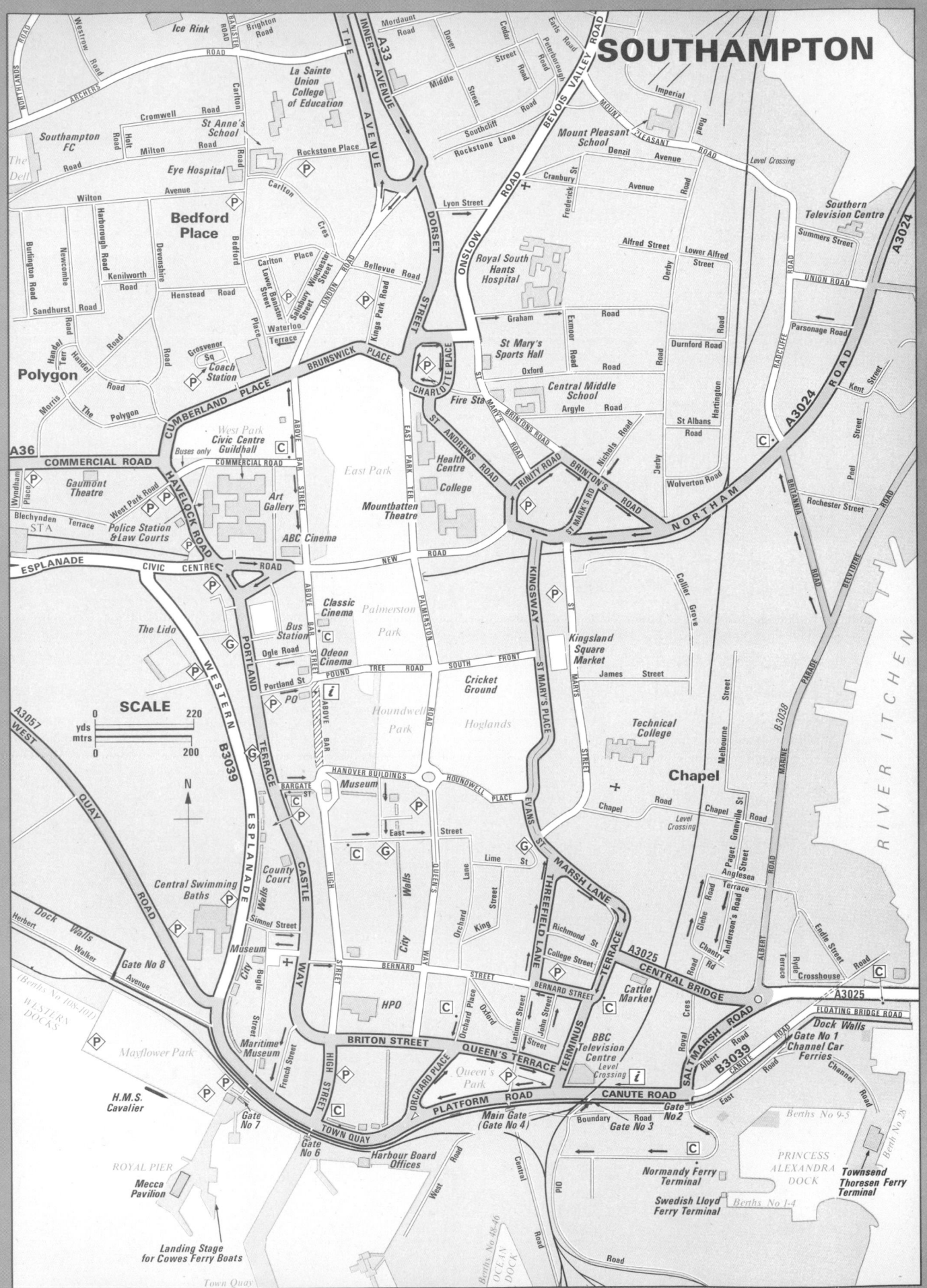

SOUTHAMPTON

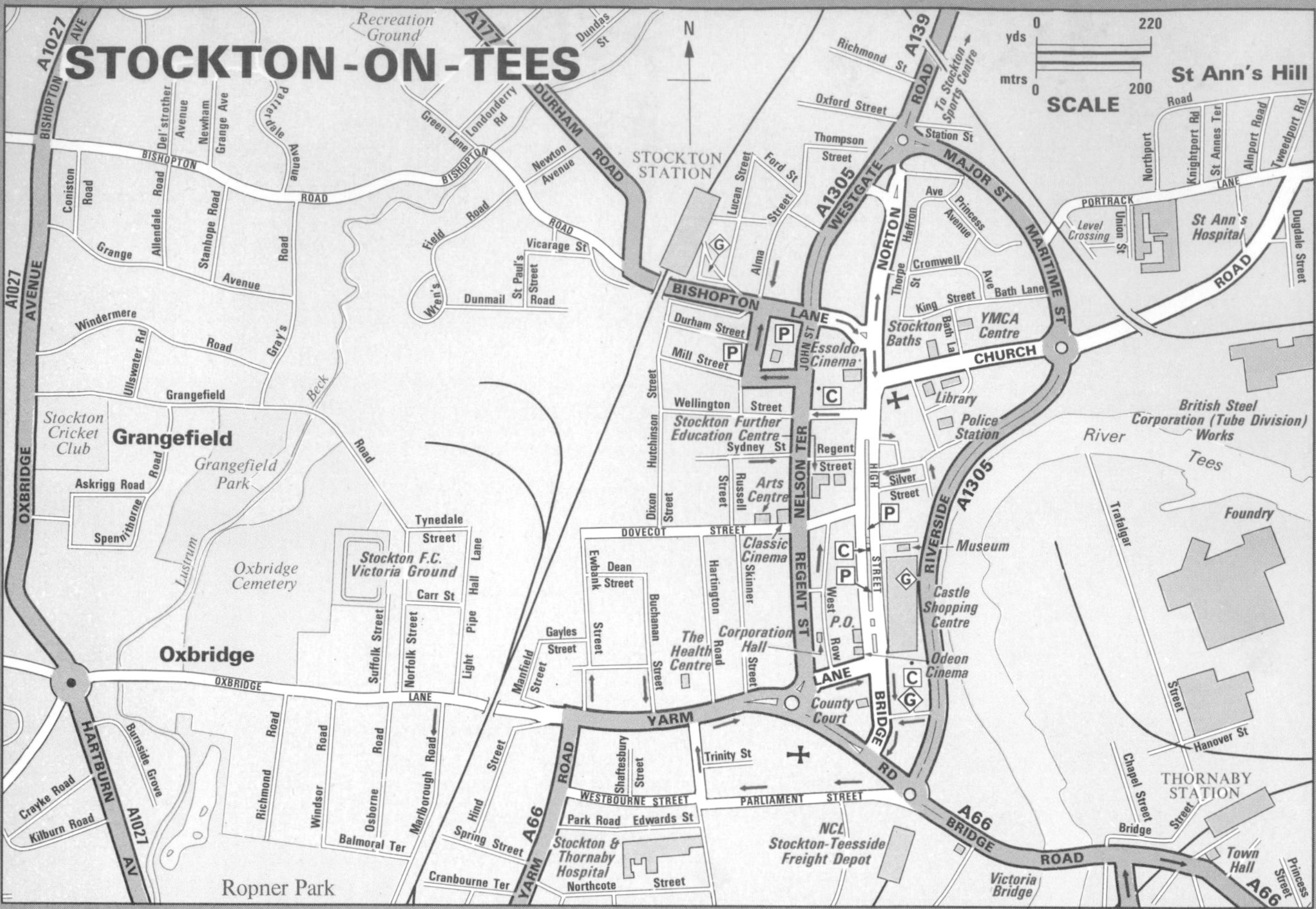

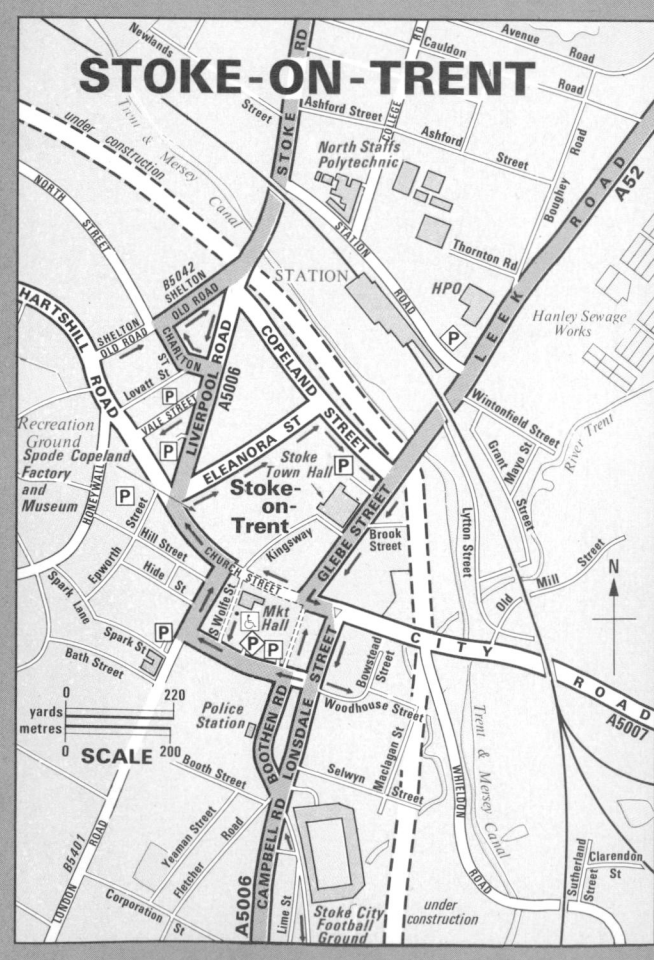
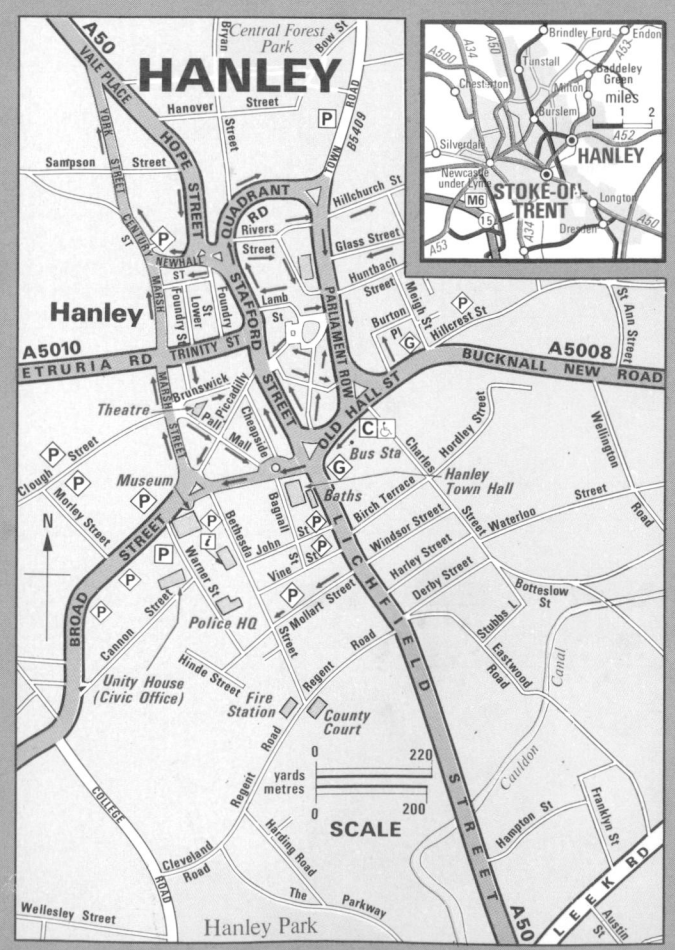

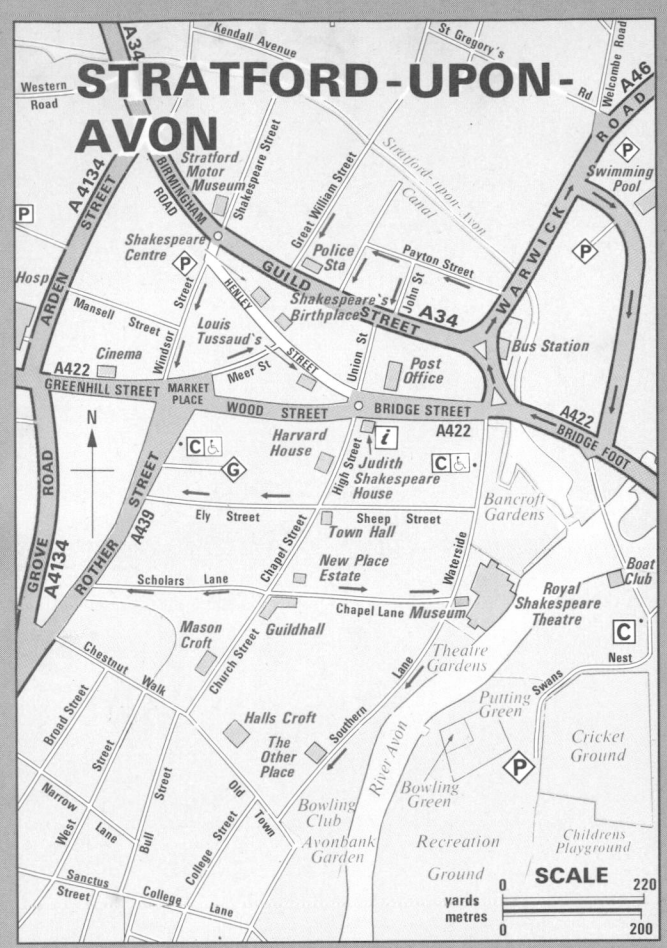

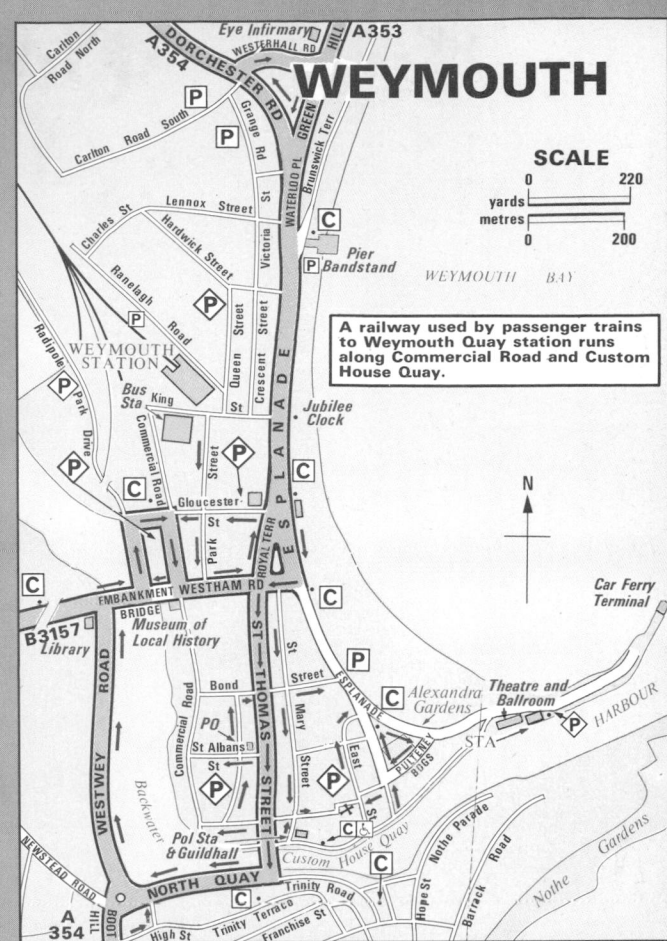

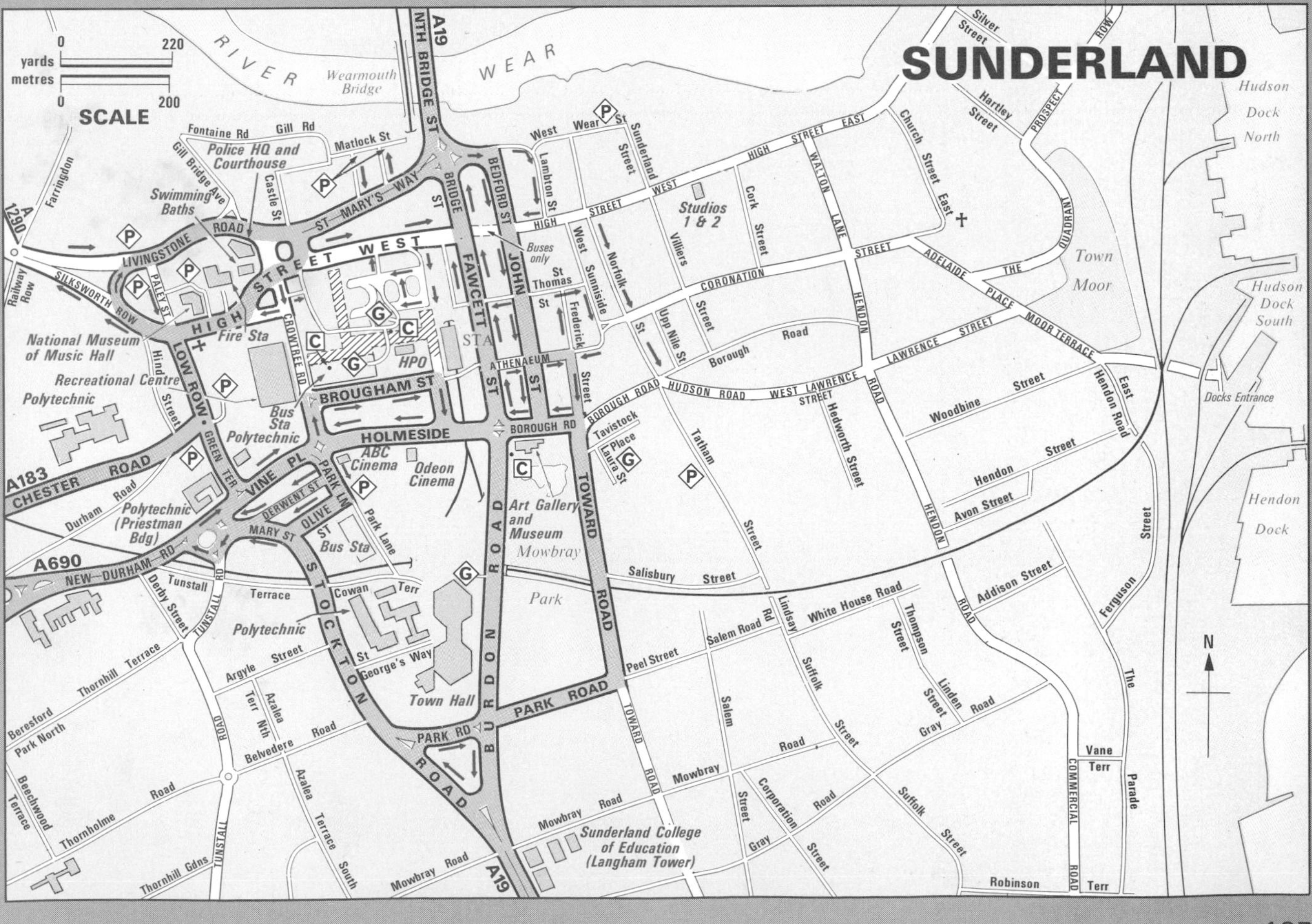

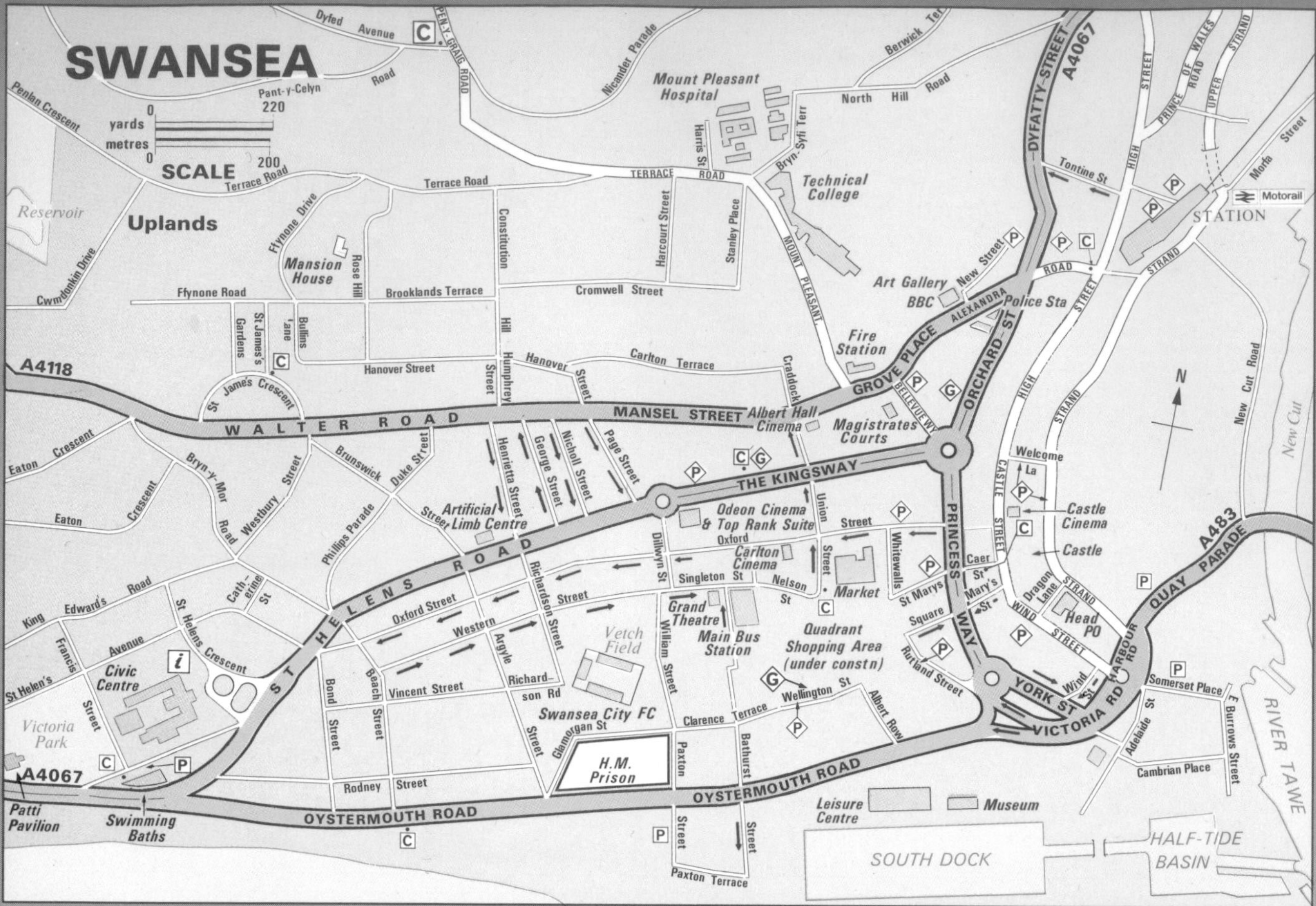

SWANSEA

SCALE
yards 0 ... 220
metres 0 ... 200

Uplands

Reservoir

Dyfed Avenue
Pant-y-Celyn
Penlan Crescent
Cwmdonkin Drive
Terrace Road
Terrace Road
Terrace Road
Constitution
Mansion House
Ffynone Drive
Rose Hill
Brooklands Terrace
Cromwell Street
Harcourt Street
Stanley Place
Mount Pleasant Hospital
Harris St
Nicander Parade
North Hill
Bryn-Syfi Terr
Berwick Terr
Technical College
TERRACE
MOUNT PLEASANT

Ffynone Road
St James's Gardens
Ballins Lane
Hanover Street
Humphrey Street
Hanover Street
Carlton Terrace
Craddock St
GROVE PLACE
ORCHARD ST
BELLEVUE WAY
Art Gallery
BBC
New Street
Fire Station
Police Sta
DYFATTY STREET
A4067
Tontine St
Motorail
STATION
HIGH STREET
PRINCE OF WALES ROAD
UPPER STRAND
Morfa Street
STRAND

A4118
WALTER ROAD
St James's Crescent
Eaton Crescent
Bryn-y-Mor
Eaton
Crescent
Brunswick
Duke Street
MANSEL STREET
Albert Hall Cinema
Magistrates Courts
THE KINGSWAY
ALEXANDRA RD
NEW CUT ROAD
New Cut

Westbury Street
Phillips Parade
Artificial Limb Centre
Henrietta Street
George Street
Nichol Street
Page Street
Dillwyn St
Odeon Cinema & Top Rank Suite
Oxford
Carlton Cinema
Union Street
Welcome La
Castle Cinema
Castle
CASTLE STREET
N

King Edward's Road
St Catherine St
St Helen's Crescent
Oxford Street
Western
Argyle
Richardson Street
Singleton St
Nelson St
Whitewalls
St Marys
Caer St
St Mary's St
WIND STREET
STRAND
PRINCESS WAY
Dragon Lane

Francis Street
Civic Centre
i
Victoria Park
Vetch Field
William Street
Bond Street
Beach Street
Vincent Street
Richard son St
Grand Theatre
Main Bus Station
Market
Square
Burland Street
Head PO
Somerset Place

A4067
Swimming Baths
Patti Pavilion
Swansea City FC
Rodney Street
Glamorgan St
Clarence Terrace
Paxton Street
Wellington St
Bathurst St
Albert Row
Quadrant Shopping Area (under const'n)
York St
VICTORIA RD
HARBOUR RD
QUAY PARADE
A483
Cambrian Place
Adelaide St
Burrows Street
RIVER TAWE

H.M. Prison
OYSTERMOUTH ROAD
Paxton Terrace
Leisure Centre
Museum
SOUTH DOCK
HALF-TIDE BASIN

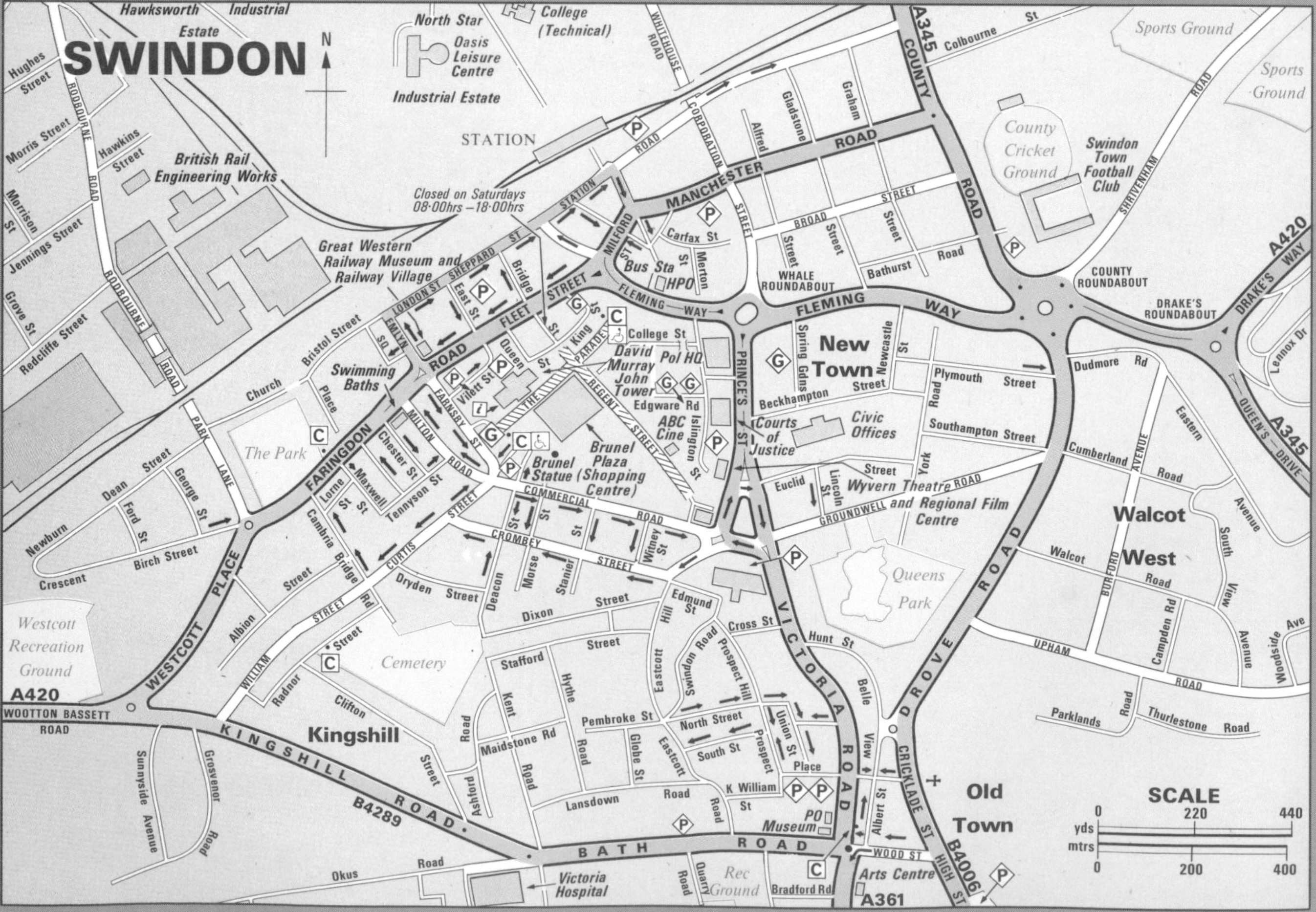

SWINDON

N

Hawksworth Industrial Estate
North Star
Oasis Leisure Centre
Industrial Estate
College (Technical)
WHITEHOUSE ROAD
A345
COUNTY ROAD
Colbourne St
Sports Ground
Sports Ground

Hughes Street
Morris Street
Morrison St
Jennings Street
Grove St
Redcliffe Street
BIRDWOURE ROAD
RODBOURNE ROAD
Hawkins Street
British Rail Engineering Works
STATION
Closed on Saturdays 08-00hrs–18-00hrs
Great Western Railway Museum and Railway Village
STATION ROAD
CORPORATION ST
MANCHESTER ROAD
Graham St
Gladstone St
Alfred St
Broad Street
Merton Street
Bathurst Street
County Cricket Ground
Swindon Town Football Club
SHRIVENHAM ROAD

London St
Bristol Street
Church Place
Swimming Baths
The Park
SHEPPARD ST
EAST ST
FLEET STREET
Bus Sta
HPO
FLEMING WAY
WHALE WHABOUT
Broad Street
New Town
Newcastle St
Spring Gdns
Plymouth Street
County Roundabout
DRAKE'S ROUNDABOUT
A420
DRAKE'S WAY
Lennox Dr

Dean Street
George St
Newburn Crescent
Birch Street
PARK LANE
WESTCOTT PLACE
Chester St
Maxwell St
FARINGDON ROAD
MILTON ROAD
Vilett St
i
King St
College St
Pol HQ
Islington St
Edgware Rd
ABC Cine
Brunel Statue
Brunel Plaza (Shopping Centre)
PRINCE'S ST
Beckhampton
Courts of Justice
Civic Offices
Southampton Street
Euclid Street
Wyvern Theatre and Regional Film Centre
GROUNDWELL ROAD
VICTORIA ROAD
GROVE ROAD
Rape
York Street
Dudmore Rd
Cumberland Road
Eastern Avenue
Walcot West

Westcott Recreation Ground
A420
WOOTTON BASSETT ROAD
Albion St
William Street
Radnor Street
Cambria Bridge Rd
CURTIS STREET
Tennyson St
Lorne St
Dryden Street
COMMERCIAL ROAD
CROMBEY STREET
Moose St
Stanley St
Witney St
Dixon Street
Cemetery
Deacon St
Stafford Street
Kent Road
Hythe Road
Cross St
Hunt St
Prospect Hill
Lincoln Street
Edmund St
Prospect Place
Queens Park
Walcot Road
UPHAM ROAD
Camden Rd
Parklands Road
South Avenue
Wood side Ave
Thurlestone Road

Kingshill
KINGSHILL ROAD
B4289
Grosvenor Road
Sunnyside Avenue
Clifton Street
Maidstone Rd
Pembroke St
North Street
South St
BELLE VIEW ROAD
CRICKLADE ST
Old Town
B4006
SCALE
yds 0 ... 220 ... 440
mtrs 0 ... 200 ... 400

Okus Road
BATH ROAD
Victoria Hospital
Lansdown
Globe St
Eastcott
K William St
PO
Museum
WOOD ST
HIGH ST
Arts Centre
A361
Rec Ground
Bradford Rd

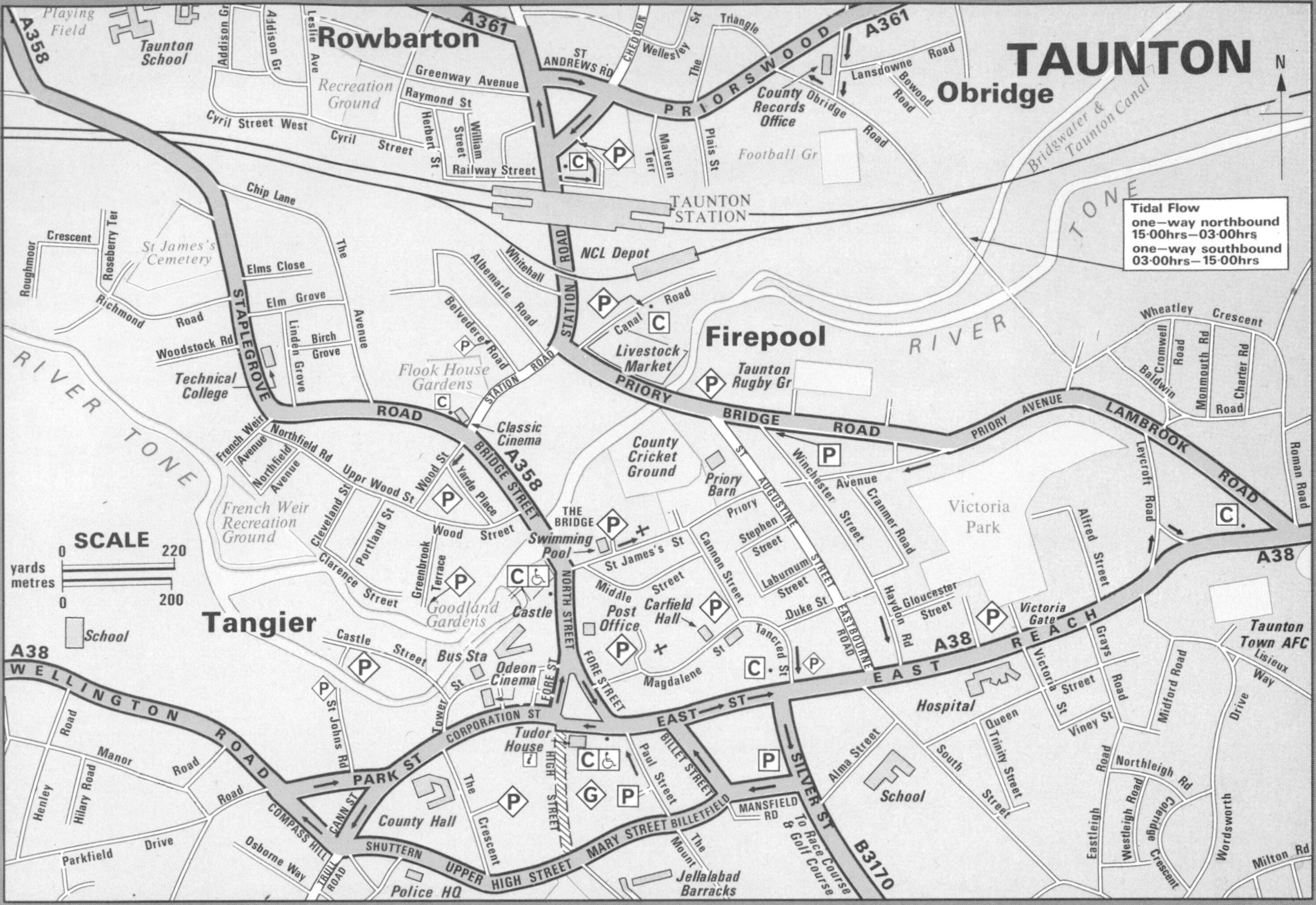

TAUNTON

Rowbarton

Obridge

N

Taunton School
Playing Field
A358
A361
A361
Addison Gr · Addison Gr · Leslie Ave
Recreation Ground
Greenway Avenue
Raymond St · William Street
Cyril Street West · Cyril Street · Herbert St · Railway Street
Chip Lane
St James's Cemetery
Roseberry Ter · Crescent
Roughmoor
Richmond Road · Elms Close · Elm Grove
Woodstock Rd · Linden Grove · Birch Grove
The Avenue
Technical College
STAPLEGROVE
Belvedere Road
Albemarle Road
Whitehall
ROAD
Flook House Gardens
Northfield Rd · Northfield Avenue
French Weir Avenue
Uppr Wood St · Wood St · Wood Street
Yarde Place
Cleveland Street
Portland St
Clarence Street
Greenbrook Terrace
Goodland Gardens
French Weir Recreation Ground
BRIDGE STREET
A358
THE BRIDGE
Swimming Pool
Castle
Castle Street
Bus Sta
Odeon Cinema
FORE STREET
North Street
Classic Cinema
ROAD
STATION ROAD
NCL Depot
Canal Road
Livestock Market
Taunton Rugby Gr
PRIORY BRIDGE ROAD
County Cricket Ground
Priory Barn
St James's St
Cannon Street
Middle Street
Post Office
Carfield Hall
Magdalene St
Duke St
Tancred St
Priory
St Stephen Street
AUGUSTINE STREET
Labumnul Street
Haydon Rd
Gloucester St
Winchester Avenue
Cranmer Road
EASTBOURNE ROAD
County Records Office
Obridge Road
Football Gr
Plais St
Malvern Terr
Lansdowne Road
Bewood Road
RIVER TONE
BRIDGWATER & TAUNTON CANAL
PRIORSWOOD ROAD
St Andrews Rd
Welles · The Triangle
Creedon Rd
Wheatley Crescent
Cromwell Road
Charter Rd
Baldwin St
Monmouth Rd
Roman Road
LAMBROOK ROAD
PRIORY AVENUE
Leycroft Road
Alfred Street
Victoria Park
Victoria Gate
Grays Rd
A38
Taunton Town AFC
Lisieux Way
Northleigh Rd
Cottage Rd
Westleigh Road
Eastleigh
Crescent
Wordsworth Rd
Milton Rd

TAUNTON STATION

Firepool

Tangier

SCALE
yards 0 — 220
metres 0 — 200
School

WELLINGTON ROAD
A38
Henley Rd · Manor Road · Hilary Road
Parkfield Drive
Osborne Way
COMPASS HILL
CANN ST
BULL ST
PARK ST
St Johns Rd
County Hall
The Crescent
SHUTTERN
UPPER HIGH STREET
MARY STREET
BILLETFIELD
Tudor House
HIGH STREET
Paul Street
EAST ST
SILVER ST
Police HQ
Mansfield Rd
Jellalabad Barracks
The Mount
To Race Course & Golf Course
Hospital
Alma Street
South Street
Queen Street
Trinity St
Viney St
Victoria St
Midford Rd
School
B3170

RIVER TONE

Tidal Flow
one—way northbound
15·00hrs—03·00hrs
one—way southbound
03·00hrs—15·00hrs

WINCHESTER

N

Fulflood

A272
STOCKBRIDGE ROAD
Cheriton Close
Cheriton Road
Hatherley Road
Fairfield Road
Cranworth Road
Westgate School
Fordington Road
Western Road
Fordington Avenue
Byron Avenue
Milverton Road
Greenhill Road
Playing Field
Playing Field
STOCKBRIDGE ROAD
B3420
ANDOVER RD
WORTHY LANE
STATION
SUSSEX ST
Newburgh Street
ST PAUL'S HILL
CLIFTON TERRACE
NEWBURGH STREET
Tower Street
St Paul's Hospital
ORAM'S ARBOUR
Clifton
West End Terrace
ROMSEY ROAD
HM Prison & Remand Centre
County Police HQ
A3090
Royal Hampshire County Hospital
West Hill
West Hill
Royal Green Jackets Regimental Museum
Royal Hampshire Regimental Museum
St James Lane
West Hill Cemetery
Winchester Barracks
King Alfred's College
Sleepers Hill
Winchester City Football Ground
Christchurch Road
Beaufort Road
Sparkford Rd
Airlie Rd
Sleepers Hill Road
Compton Road
St Michael's Road
St Swithun St
Canon Street
Kingsgate
Romans
Kingsgate Park
A3333
ST CROSS RD
SOUTHGATE STREET
Symonds St
Thomas Street
Staple Gardens
JEWRY STREET
Library
Cinema
Cross St
County Offices
St Peter St
St George's Street
Law Court Castle
Old Guildhall
The Square
City Museum
City Offices
Cathedral
Guildhall
The Close
Abbey House
Winchester College Street
St Mary's College
College Walk
St Swithun St
Canon Street
Coach Station
Market
Playing Field
Swan Lane
CITY ROAD
NORTH WALLS
Saxon Road
Monks Road
A3090
HYDE STREET
King Alfred Pl
Hyde Close
Hyde Abbey
Gordon Road
Hyde Abbey Road
Park Avenue
North Walls Recreation Ground
Recreation Centre
School
School of Art
Police Station
Fire Station
UNION ST
Upper Brook Street
Middle Brook Street
Lower Brook Street
Parchment Street
Tanner St
Market Lane
FRIARSGATE
EASTGATE ST
Bus Sta
THE BROADWAY
BRIDGE STREET
A272
Colebrook Street
Abbey House
Wolvesey Castle
Winchester College
Hyde
River Itchen
EASTON LANE
Wales Street
BEGGAR'S LANE
Beggar's Lane
St John's St
MAGDALEN HILL
B3404
Blue Ball Hill
Water Lane
To Victoria Hospital
CHESIL STREET
St Giles's Hill
The Soke
Ebden Rd
Moss Road
Frimstone Road
Imber Road
Northbrook Av
Stratton Road
QUARRY ROAD
PETERSFIELD ROAD
B3046
Canute Road
St Catherine's Road
Portal Road
Vale Road
Dell Road
Wharf Hill
Bar End

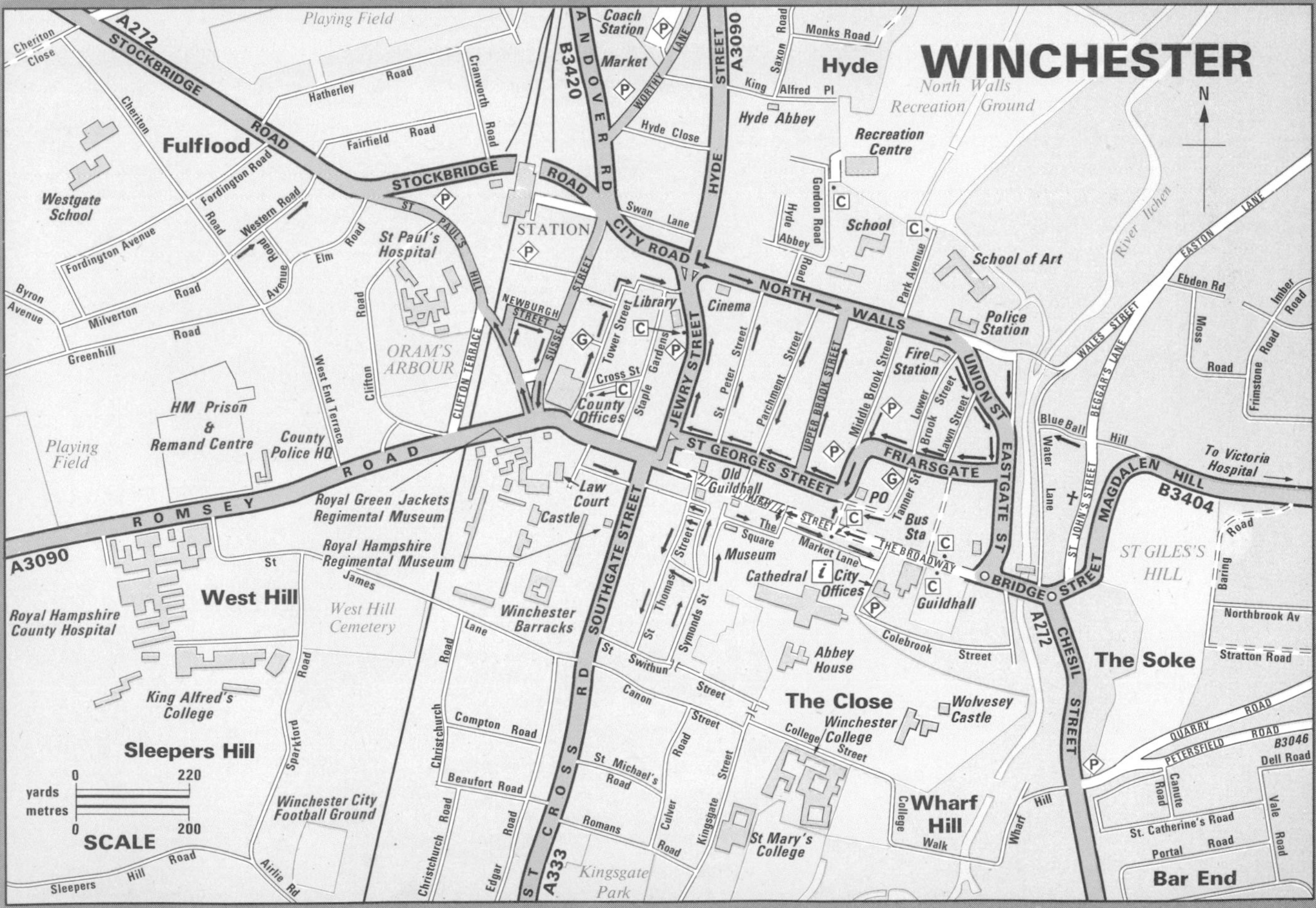

SCALE
yards 0 — 220
metres 0 — 200

189

TORQUAY

St Vincents St
St Michaels Road
Barton Road
Torquay Grammar School (Boys)
A379
Lymington Road
Bus & Coach Station
Recreation Ground
Ash Hill Road
Ash Hill Road
St Marychurch Road
Princes Road
Princes Road East
Warberry Copse
Higher Warberry Road
Ellacombe
Rosehill Childrens Hospital
Middle Warberry Road
Lower Warberry Road
Warberry Road

To Torbay Hospital
A380
NEWTON ROAD
Teignmouth Road
Technical College
Upton Road
Ten Pin Bowl
Law Courts
Castle Road
ABC Cinema
Market Hall
Market Street
Castle Circus
Stentiford
Upper
Hunsdon Road
Hillseoon

Torre Station
Tor Park Road
EAST STREET
5TH ST
Vansittart Road
UNION ST
Police Station
St Efrides Road
Church Road
TOR HILL ROAD
ABBEY ROAD
Colony Cinema
Odeon Cinema
HPO
Braddons Hill Road West
Coach Station
The Terrace
TORWOOD STREET

BELGRAVE RD
LUCIUS STREET
Croft Road
St Lukes
St Lukes Road
Warren Road
St Lukes Road North
Warren Road
FLEET STREET
VAUGHAN PARADE

Playground
Sherwell Hill
Sherwell Park
Sherwell Lane
Old Mill Road
FALKLAND ROAD
Mill Lane
Chestnut Avenue
BELGRAVE ROAD
Lawn Tennis Club
Sheddon Hill
Pimlico
St Lukes Road South
Warren Road
Royal Terrace Gardens
Vaughan Rd
CARY PDE
STRAND
INNER HARBOUR
VICTORIA PARADE
Hill Road East
P

Goshen Rd
Walnut Rd
Tor Valley Park
AVENUE ROAD
Tennis Courts
Torre Abbey
Abbey Gardens
TORBAY ROAD
SCALE
yards 0 220
0 200 metres
Princess Gdns
Princess Theatre
Pavilion Theatre
OUTER HARBOUR
Aquarium
Beacon Quay
Beacon Cove
BEACON HILL
Royal Torbay Yacht Club

Rathmore Road
RATHMORE ROAD
Walnut Rd
Rec Gnd
Putting Green
The King's Gardens
Torquay Athletic RFC & Torquay Cricket Club
TORQUAY STATION
A379
Tune Tor Abbey Sands
Harbreck Rock
PRINCESS PIER
HALDON PIER
"Coral Island" Leisure Complex

Inset (Torbay area)
Newton Abbot
A380
Maidencombe
Babbacombe Bay
A381
Kingskerswell
Babbacombe
Cockington
TORQUAY
PAIGNTON
Tor Bay
Collaton St Mary
Goodrington
Galmpton
Berry Head
Churston Ferrers
B3205
BRIXHAM
Dartmouth
Kingswear
A379
Stoke Fleming
miles 0 1 2

BRIXHAM

Lakes Road
North Boundary Road
Fishcombe Rd
Fishcombe Point
Fishcombe Cove
Battery Gardens
Brixham Cricket Club
LANE
Marine Research Station

Lichfield Dr
Gollands
Pillar Avenue
NORTHFIELDS
The Close
NORTH FURZEHAM ROAD
QUEENS ROAD
OUTER
Lindthorpe Way
NORTHFIELDS LA SOUTH
Cumbers Drive
Furzeham Park
Cumbers Estate
Nelson Road
Furzeham Road
Oxen Cove
HARBOUR

NEW ROAD
A3022
Brookdale Park
Langley Avenue
Hillside Avenue
Cudhill Road
Parkham Road
Glenmore Rd
Theatre
Bone Cavern
BONE
South Furzeham Road
Higher Furzeham Road
LR MANOR ROAD
STATION HILL
Library
Museum
Golden Hind
Inner Harbour
New Pier
Brixham Yacht Club

MIDDLE STREET
FORE STREET
Bus Sta
KING STREET
Elkins Hill
Garlics
Heath
Windmill Hill Rd
Rea Hill
Berry Head Road
RANSCOMBE ROAD
Wall Park

Fire and Ambulance Station
BOLTON STREET
Mount Pleasant Road
Windmill Hill
Windmill Road
Rea Road
Heath Pk
DREW STREET
DOCTORS ROAD
Knick Knack Lane
Brixham Cottage Hospital
Police Station
Astley Park
Castor Road
Sellick Avenue
Penn
Barn Lane
Century Road
Higher Ranscombe Road
Wall Park Close
B3205

PAIGNTON

A379
SEAWAY RD
Marine Dve
Barcombe Heights
Barcombe Road
Cecil Road
Rowcroft Road
WITS RD
Rutland Road
Paris Rd
OLD TORQUAY ROAD
Langs Road
Preston
Esplanade
Preston Sands
B3201

Winsu Avenue
Southfield Road
Laura Grove
Barcombe Avenue
UPPER MANOR ROAD
MANOR ROAD
Oldway Mansion and Grounds
Oldway Gardens
Kings Road
Upper Morin Road
Colin Rd
SCALE
yards 0 220
0 200 metres

Higher Polsham Rd
Lower Polsham Road
Polsham Road
TORQUAY ROAD
A379
Police Station
Courtland Road
Steartfield Road
B3201
Esplanade closed to traffic during the summer
Paignton Pier
Esplanade

Kirkham House
Victoria Park
Bishop's Palace Tower
Torbay Cinema
Beach Rd
Garfield Road
Kernou Rd
Festival Hall
B3201
Adelphi Rd

Monastery Road
Palace Avenue Theatre
Winner Hill Road
Palace Avenue
Church St
Tower Rd
Victoria St
Dendy Rd
GERSTON RD
Coverdale Rd
Palace Place
Fire Sta
Regent Cinema
New Street
STATION
Queen's Park
Torbay and Dartmouth Railway
Adelphi Ln
DARTMOUTH ROAD
HYDE ROAD
TORQUAY ROAD
TOTNES ROAD
A385
Primley Park
Clifton Road
Conway Road
Fisher Road
ELMSLEIGH ROAD
A379
Belle Vue Road
Cleveland Road
St Andrew's Road
Keysfield Road
Cliff Road
Roundham

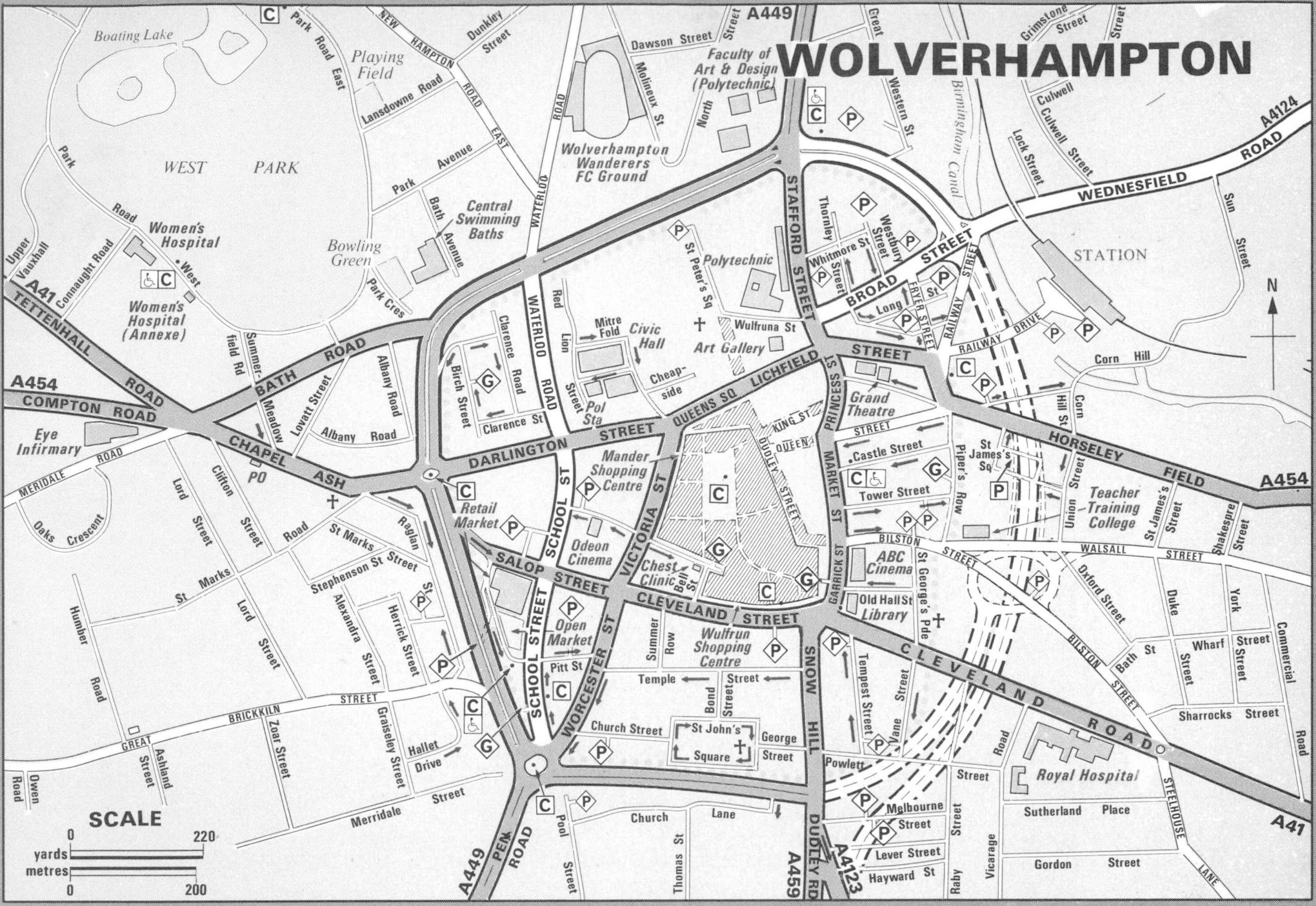

Boating Lake

WEST PARK

Playing Field

Park Road East
New Hampton Road East
Dunkley Street
Dawson Street
Faculty of Art & Design (Polytechnic)
A449

Women's Hospital

Lansdowne Road
Molineux St
North
Western St
Stafford Street
Grimstone Street
Culwell Street
A4124
Lock Street
Culwell St
WEDNESFIELD ROAD
Sun Street
Birmingham Canal

Park Road
Park Avenue
Park Cres
Bath Avenue
Central Swimming Baths
Wolverhampton Wanderers FC Ground
Polytechnic
Thornley St
Whitmore St
Washburn Street
Broad Street
Long Street
Railway Drive
Corn Hill
STATION

N

Upper Vauxhall
A41
TETTENHALL ROAD
Connaught Road
Summerfield Rd
Meadow
Waterloo Road
BATH ROAD
Albany Road
Clarence Street
Lovatt Street
Birch Street
Red Lion Street
Mitre Fold
St Peter's Sq
Civic Hall
Wulfruna St
Art Gallery
Cheapside
BROAD STREET
Piper's Row
St James's
Corn St
Hill St
HORSELEY FIELD
A454

Women's Hospital (Annexe)

A454
COMPTON ROAD
CHAPEL ASH
DARLINGTON STREET
SCHOOL STREET
VICTORIA STREET
QUEENS SQ
LICHFIELD STREET
Grand Theatre
Castle Street
Tower Street
Teacher Training College
Shakespeare St
Duke St
York St

Eye Infirmary
MERIDALE ROAD
Clifton Street
St Marks Road
Raglan Street
St Marks Street
Pol Sta
Mander Shopping Centre
KING ST
QUEEN ST
DUDLEY STREET
PRINCESS ST
MARKET ST
KING ST
BILSTON STREET
ABC Cinema
St George's Pde
Oxford Street
Walsall Street
BILSTON STREET
Bath St
Wharf Street
Commercial Road

Oaks Crescent
Humber Road
Lord Street
St Street
Alexandra Street
Stephenson St
Herrick Street
SALOP STREET
Odeon Cinema
Chest Clinic
Bell St
CLEVELAND STREET
Open Market
Summer Row
Wulfrun Shopping Centre
Temple Street
Bond Street
Old Hall St
Library
GARRICK ST
Tempest Street
Vane Street
CLEVELAND ROAD
Street
Street
Royal Hospital
Sutherland Place
Sharrocks Street
Gordon Street
STEECHOUSE LANE
A41

Owen Road
Ashland St
Zaar Street
BRICKKILN STREET
Graiseley Street
GREAT STREET
Hallet Drive
WORCESTER ST
Pitt St
Church Street
St John's Square
George Street
SNOW HILL
Powlett Street
Street
Melbourne Street
Lever Street
Hayward St
Raby Street
Vicarage Road

SCALE
yards 0 — 220
metres 0 — 200

A449 PENN ROAD
Pool Street
Merridale Street
Thomas St
Church Lane
A4123 DUDLEY RD
A4459

A19 BOOTHAM
B1363 GILLYGATE
Bootham Row
Deanery Gardens
City Walls
LORD MAYOR'S WALK
Monkgate Health Centre
MONKGATE
A1036
County Hospital

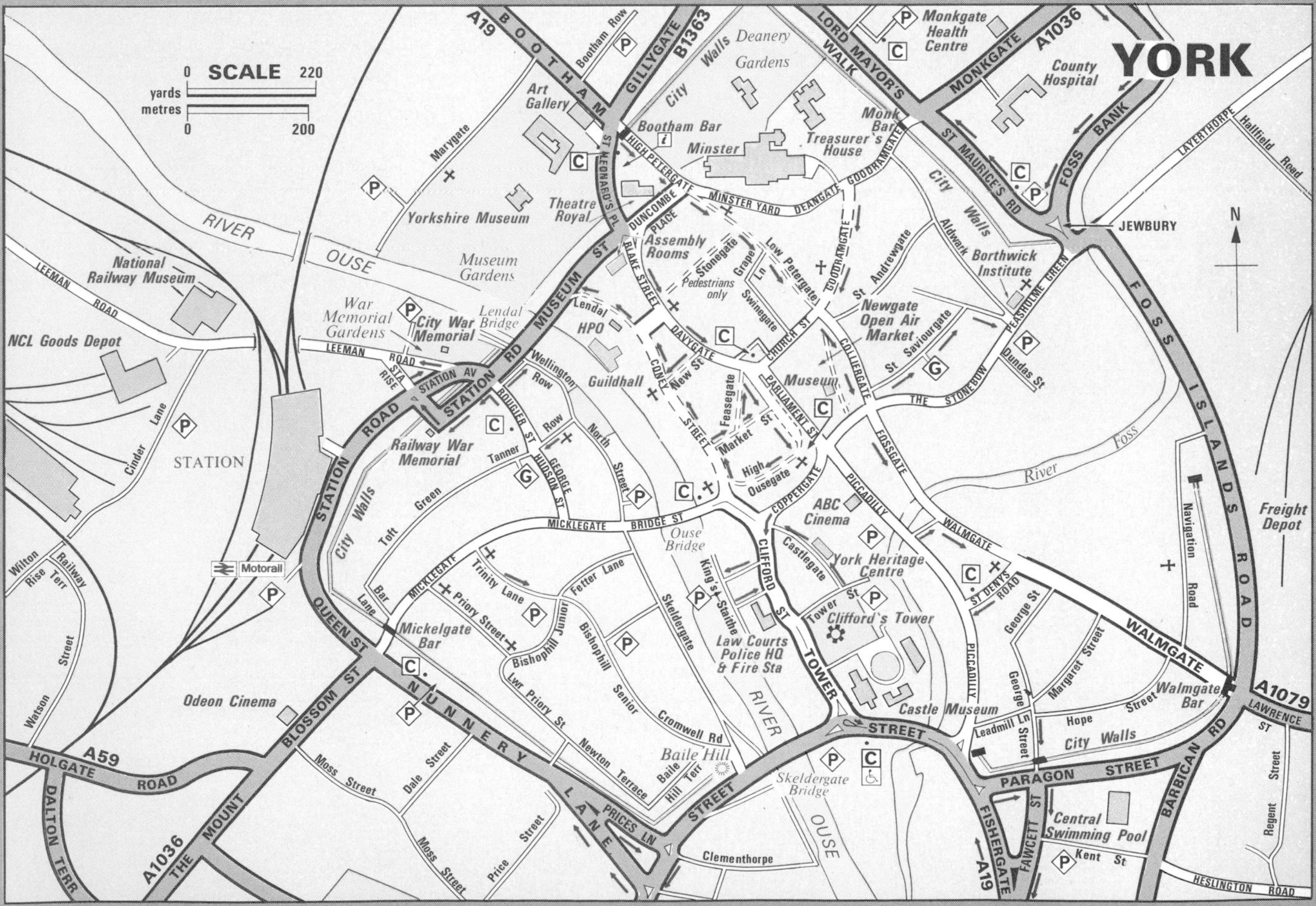

SCALE
yards 0 — 220
metres 0 — 200

Marygate
Art Gallery
Yorkshire Museum
Bootham Bar
Minster
Monk Bar
ST MAURICE'S RD
FOSS BANK
LAYERTHORPE
Haxby Road

RIVER OUSE
Museum Gardens
Theatre Royal
HIGH PETERGATE
Treasurer's House
City Walls
St Andrewgate
Aldwark
Borthwick Institute
JEWBURY
N

National Railway Museum
LEEMAN ROAD
War Memorial Gardens
City War Memorial
Lendal Bridge
MUSEUM ST
Assembly Rooms
ST LEONARD'S PL
DUNCOMBE PLACE
BLAKE STREET
Stonegate
MINSTER YARD
DEANGATE
GOODRAMGATE
Low Petergate
Pedestrians only
Swinegate
Grape Lane
Newgate Open Air Market
EASTGATE GREEN
River Foss
FOSS ISLANDS ROAD

NCL Goods Depot
LEEMAN ROAD
HPO
Wellington Row
STATION RD
Guildhall
DAVYGATE
CHURCH ST
Museum
PARLIAMENT ST
COLLIERGATE
THE STONEBOW
Dundas St
Freight Depot

Cinder Lane
STATION
STATION AV
Tanner Row
Station Rise
Railway War Memorial
George St
North St
Feasegate
New St
Market
High Ousegate
FOSSGATE
PICCADILLY
WALMGATE
Navigation Road

Wilton Rise
Railway Terr
QUEEN ST
City Walls
Toft Green
MICKLEGATE
BRIDGE ST
Ouse Bridge
Coppergate
ABC Cinema
Castlegate
York Heritage Centre
ST DENYS
ROAD
George St
WALMGATE
Margaret Street

Watson Street
Motorail
MICKLEGATE
Trinity Lane
Priory Street
Fetter Lane
King's Staithe
Clifford St
Clifford's Tower
Piccadilly
Walmgate Bar
A1079
LAWRENCE ST

Odeon Cinema
BLOSSOM ST
Bar Lane
Mickelgate Bar
Bishophill Junior
Bishophill Senior
Skeldergate
Law Courts Police HQ & Fire Sta
Castle Museum
Leadmill Ln
Hope Street
George Street
Regent Street

HOLGATE ROAD
A59
DALTON TERR
THE MOUNT
A1036
NUNNERY LANE
PRICES LN
Moss Street
Dale Street
Price Street
Newton Terrace
Cromwell Rd
Baile Hill
Baile Terr
Hill Terr
SKELDERGATE
Skeldergate Bridge
RIVER OUSE
PARAGON STREET
BARBICAN RD
Central Swimming Pool
FAWCETT ST
FISHERGATE
A19
Kent St
HESLINGTON ROAD
Clementhorpe

London District

Key to Inner London Maps

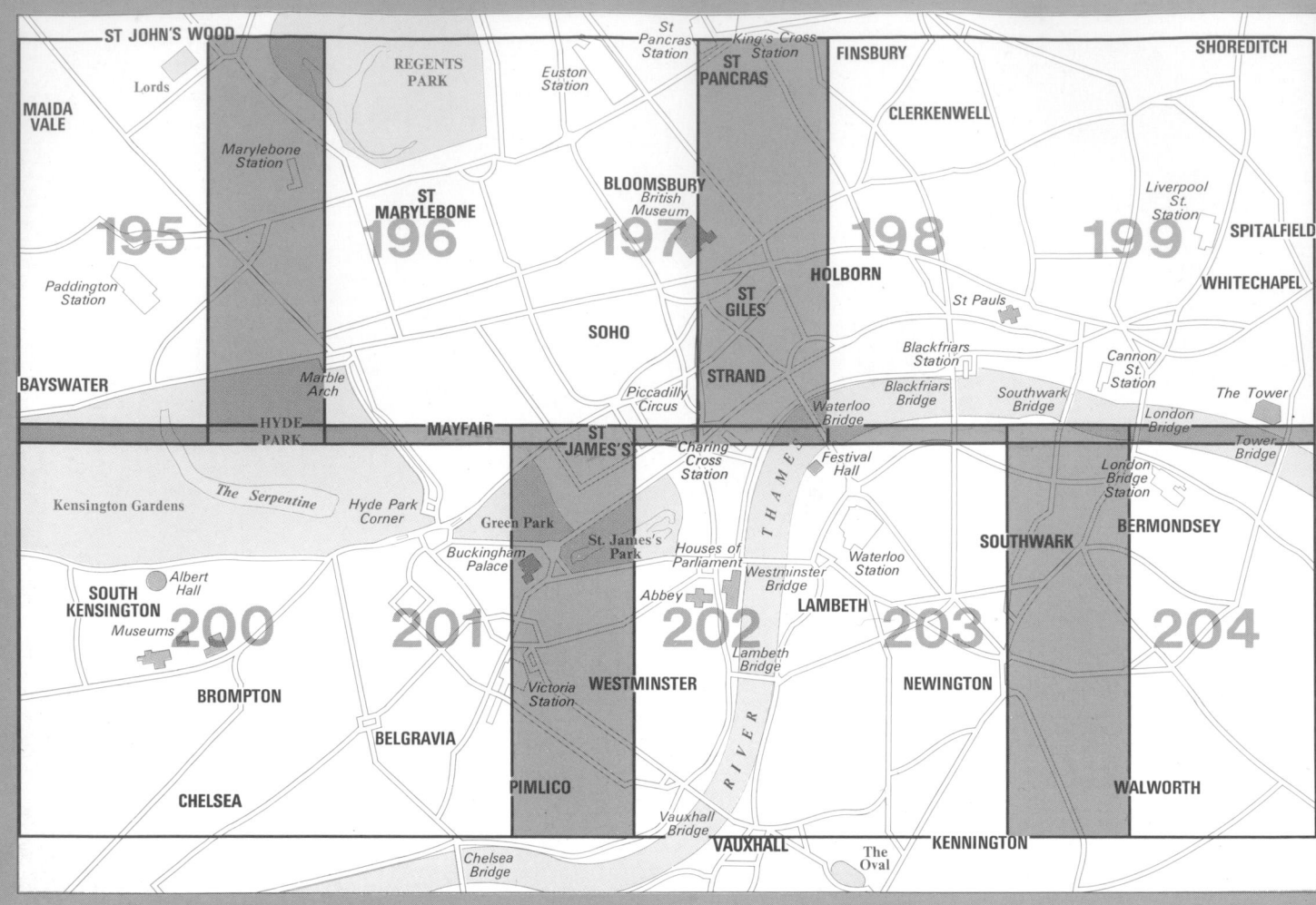

Legend

Motorway		Hospital	Ⓗ	
One-way street		Post office	Ⓟ.Ⓞ	
No vehicular access		Church or religious centre	+	
Traffic roundabout		Water feature	*Thames*	
Banned turn		Park or open space		
Parking	Ⓟ	Place of interest	*Museum*	
Garage parking	Ⓖ	A.A. Service centre	**AA**	
British Rail Station	Euston Station	District name	**STRAND**	
London Transport Station	Holborn ⊖	Overlap extent and number of continuing page	198	
Police station	POL			

Scale: seven inches to one mile

KENSINGTON GARDENS

The Long Water

195

HYDE

Round Pond

Budge's Walk

Lancaster Walk

Physical Energy

Serpentine Bridge

Serpentine

The Serpentine

Boat House

Pier

Restaurant & Cafe

Lido

Serpentine Gallery

Kensington Palace

The Dial Walk

Palace Avenue

The Broad Walk

The Flower Walk

Albert Mem

ROTTEN ROW

NEW RIDE

THE CARRIAGE

Royal Garden Hotel

KENSINGTON ROAD

Knightsbridge Barracks

Bowater House

KNIGHTS

Kensington Palace Hotel

Palace Gate

Queen's Gate

KENSINGTON GORE

Alexandra Gate

KENSINGTON ROAD

Princes Gate

PRINCE OF WALES GATE

Knightsbri

De Vere Hotel

Hyde Park Gate

Portland Hotel

Royal Albert Hall

Royal School of Needlework

ENNISMORE

RUTLAND GATE

RUTLAND GDNS

TREVOR

Raphael St

PO

Knightsbridge Fire Station

Prince of Wales Hotel

Jay Mews

Montpelier

TREVOR SQUARE

Basil St

Capital Hotel

Albert Place

Kensington Gate

Queen's Gate Mews

PRINCE CONSORT ROAD

ENNISMORE GDNS

ENNISMORE MEWS

Montpelier PL

Trevor Sq

Cro Co

Douro Place

Canning Place

Queen's Gate Terrace

Royal College of Music

PRINCE'S GARDENS

MONTPELIER SQUARE

HANS ROAD

Basil St

St Alban's Grove

Victoria Grove

Queen's Gate Mews

Gore Street

Imperial College

PRINCE'S GARDENS

ENNISMORE GARDENS

Montpelier PL

BROMPTON PL

Beaufort Gardens

Christ Church

Cottesmore Gdns

Launceston Place

Petersham Place

Embassy House Hotel

GARDENS MEWS ENNISMORE ST

EXHIBITION ROAD

CHEVAL PLACE

BROMPTON

Stanford

Eldon Road

ELVASTON PLACE

Queen's Gate

Science Museum

City & Guilds College

Brompton Oratory

BROMPTON SQUARE

EGERTON

YEOMANS ROW

OVINGTON SQUARE

Kynance Mews

Persham Mews

Queen's Gate Gdns

Geological Museum

Victoria and Albert Museum

BEAUCHAMP PLACE

WALTON

Cornwall Gardens

Queens Gate Gdns

Queen's Gate Pl

British Museum of Natural History

THURLOE PLACE

EGERTON GDNS

FIRST STREET

HASKER STREET

MILNER STREET

LENNOX GARDENS

West London Air Terminal

Emperor's Gate

GRENVILLE PL

Southwell Gdns

Queen's Gate Mews

Queens Gate Gdns

Baden-Powell House

CROMWELL ROAD

CROMWELL GDNS

Rembrandt Hotel

EGERTON TERR

OVINGTON SQUARE

LENNOX GDNS MEWS

LENNOX GARDENS

Buckingham Hotel

Hosp

Milton Court Hotel

Tudor Court Hotel

THURLOE

THURLOE PLACE

Alexander Pl

DONNE PLACE

RAWLINGS STREET

HALSEY STREET

MOORE STREET

CROMWELL ROAD

Penta Hotel

ASHBURN GDNS

ASHBURN MEWS

Gloucester Road

STANHOPE GARDENS

Stanhope Ct Hotel

Queensberry Place

CROMWELL MEWS

THURLOE SQUARE

Thurloe Square

South Terrace

DRAYCOTT AVENUE

DENVER STREET

ROSEMOOR STREET

CADOGAN

Bailey's Hotel

STANHOPE MEWS E

QUEEN'S GATE

South Kensington

PO

PELHAM STREET

Gloucester Hotel

COURTFIELD GARDENS

HARRINGTON GARDENS

STANHOPE GARDENS

HARRINGTON ROAD

REECE MEWS

BUTE STREET

Eden Hotel

COLBECK MEWS

CLAREVILLE ST

CLARVILLE GROVE

MANSON PLACE

ONSLOW GARDENS

PELHAM CRESCENT

LUCAN PLACE

SLOANE AVENUE

IXWORTH PLACE

POL

PO

COLLINGHAM GARDENS

SOUTH KENSINGTON

Onslow Court Hotel

SUMNER PLACE

ONSLOW SQUARE

SYDNEY PL

WHITEHEAD'S

CRANLEY PLACE

ONSLOW SQUARE

WETHERBY

BINA GARDENS

JOHN MEWS

BRECHIN PLACE

CLAREVILLE STREET

BROMPTON ROAD

ONSLOW GARDENS

SUMNER PLACE

PELHAM PLACE

BURY WALK

POND PLACE

STEWARTS GROVE

SYDNEY STREET

CALE

PO

Paris Pullman

DRAYTON GARDENS

ROLAND GARDENS

ROLAND WAY

CRANLEY MEWS

EVELYN GARDENS

SELWOOD PLACE

NEVILLE TERRACE

FOULIS TERR

Brompton Hosp

Royal Marsden Hosp

ST LUKES STREET

ASTELL STREET

GODFREY STREET

CALE STREET

JUBILEE PLACE

MARKHAM SQUARE

CALE STREET

WELLINGTON SQUARE

SMITH STREET

BOLTON GARDENS

BROMPTON

THISTLE GROVE

EVELYN GDNS

Women's Hosp

SOUTH PARADE

NEVILLE STREET

CHELSEA SQUARE

OLD CHURCH STREET

DOVEHOUSE STREET

BRITTEN STREET

MARKHAM STREET

BURNSALL STREET

RADNOR WALK

TEDWORTH

THE BOLTONS

CRESSWELL PLACE

PRIORY WALK

HARLEY GARDENS

ROLAND GARDENS

CHELSEA

Odeon

REDCLIFFE SQUARE

THE LITTLE BOLTONS

GILSTON ROAD

ELM PLACE

ELM PARK GARDENS

ELM PARK ROAD

Chelsea Fire Station

PO

Chelsea Town Hall

REDCLIFFE

HARCOURT TERRACE

TREGUNTER ROAD

ABC Cinema

THE FULHAM ROAD

CARLYLE SQ

MANRESA ROAD

OAKLEY GARDENS

SHAWFIELD STREET

FLOOD

SMITH TERRACE

REDCLIFFE MEWS

CARLYLE SQ

KING'S ROAD

The London Street Index

All the streets shown on the Inner London maps are listed alphabetically in this index. To find a street on the maps use the reference figures given with each street. The relevant page number is shown in italics. The two numbers in the second set of figures are the National Grid reference numbers (the National Grid is explained on page XIII), and the two letters indicate in which quarter of the grid square the street is located. (*ie* north-west, north-east, south-west, or south-east).

Buckingham Palace stands at the head of The Mall.

HMS President can be seen from the Embankment above Blackfriars Bridge.

Gilbert Rd SE11 203 18NW
Gilbert St W1 196 81SW
Gillingham St SW1 201 98NW
Gilston Rd SW10 200 68SW
Giltspur St EC1 198 11SE
Gladstone St SE1 203 19SE
Glasshouse St W1 197 90NW
Glasshouse Walk SE11 202 08SE
Gledhow Gdns SW5 200 68NW
Glentworth St NW1 196 72SE
Gloucester Pl W1/NW1 196 72SE
Gloucester Rd SW7 200 69SW
Gloucester Sq W2 195 71SW
Gloucester St SW1 201 98SW
Gloucester Ter W2 195 61SW
Gloucester Way EC1 198 12NW
Godfrey St SW3 200 78SW
Goding St SE11 202 08SW
Godliman St EC4 199 21SW
Golden Ln EC1 199 22NW
Golden Sq W1 197 90NW
Goodge St W1 197 91NW
Gordon Sq WC1 197 92NW
Gordon St WC1 197 92SE
Gore St SW7 200 69SW
Gosfield St W1 197 91NW
Goswell Rd EC1 198 12NE
Gough St WC1 198 02SE
Goulston St E1 199 31SW
Gower Pl WC1 197 92SE
Gower St WC1 197 92NW
Gracechurch St EC3 199 20NE
Grafton Pl NW1 197 92NE
Grafton St W1 197 80NE
Grafton Way W1/WC1 197 92SW
Graham Ter SW1 201 88NW
Grange, The SE1 204 39SE
Grange Ct WC2 198 01SE
Grange Rd SE1 204 39SW
Grange Walk SE1 204 39SW
Granville Sq WC1 198 02NE
Grape St WC2 197 01SW
Gravel Ln E1 199 31SE
Gray St SE1 203 19NW
Gray's Inn Rd WC1 198 02NE
Gt Castle St W1 197 81SE
Gt Central St NW1 196 71NW
Gt College St SW1 202 09SW
Gt Cumberland Pl W1 196 71SE
Gt Dover St SE1 200 29SE
Gt Eastern St EC2 199 32SW
Gt George St SW1 202 99NE
Gt Guildford St SE1 203 20SW
Gt James St WC1 198 01NE
Gt Marlborough St W1 197 91SW
Gt Ormond St WC1 198 02SE
Gt Percy St WC1 198 02NE
Gt Peter St SW1 202 99SE

St. Pauls Cathedral, seen from Ludgate Hill.

Gt Portland St W1 197 81NE
Gt Pulteney St W1 197 90NW
Gt Queen St WC2 197 01SW
Gt Russell St WC1 197 01NW
Gt Scotland Yard SW1 202 00SW
Gt Smith St SW1 202 99SE
Gt Suffolk St SE1 203 10SE
Gt Sutton St EC1 198 12SE
Gt Titchfield St W1 197 91NW
Gt Tower St EC3 199 30NW
Gt Winchester St EC2 199 21SE
Gt Windmill St W1 197 90NE
Greek St W1 197 91SE
Greencoat Pl SW1 202 98NW
Green St W1 196 80NW
Grendon St NW8 195 72SW
Grenville Pl SW7 200 69SW
Grenville St WC1 197 02SW
Gresham St EC2 199 21SW
Gresse St W1 197 91SE
Greville St EC1 198 11NW
Greycoat Pl SW1 202 99SE
Greycoat St SW1 202 99SE
Grey Eagle St E1 199 32SE
Grosvenor Cres SW1 201 89NW
Grosvenor Gdns SW1 201 89SE
Grosvenor Hill W1 196 80NE
Grosvenor Pl SW1 201 89NE
Grosvenor Rd SW1 202 97NW
Grosvenor Sq W1 196 80NW
Grosvenor St W1 196 80NE
Grove End Rd NW8 195 62NW
Guildhouse St SW1 201 98NW
Guilford St WC1 197 02SW
Gundulf St SE11 203 18NW
Gutter Ln EC2 199 21SW
Guy St SE1 204 29NE

H

Haberdasher St N1 199 22NE
Hackney Rd E2 199 32NE
Half Moon St W1 201 80SE
Halkin St SW1 201 89NW
Hall Pl W2 195 61NE
Hall Rd NW8 195 62NW
Hall St EC1 198 12NE
Hallam St W1 196 81NE
Halsey St SW3 200 78NE
Hamilton Gdns NW8 195 62NW
Hamilton Pl W1 201 80SW
Hamilton Ter NW8 195 62NW
Hampstead Rd NW1 197 92NW
Hampton St SE1/17 203 28NW
Hanbury St E1 199 31NE
Handel St WC1 197 02SW
Hankey Pl SE1 204 29NE

Hanover Sq W1 196 81SE
Hanover St W1 197 81SE
Hanover Ter NW1 196 72NE
Hans Cres SW1 200 79SE
Hans Pl SW1 201 79SE
Hans Rd SW3 200 79SE
Hanson St W1 197 91NW
Hanway St W1 197 91SE
Harcourt St W1 196 71NW
Harcourt Ter SW10 200 58SE
Hardwick St EC1 198 12NW
Harewood Av NW1 196 72SW
Harley Gdns SW10 200 68SW
Harley St W1 196 81NE
Harmsworth St SE17 203 18SE
Harper Rd SE1 203 29SW
Harpur St WC1 198 01NE
Harriet Walk SW1 201 79NE
Harrington Gdns SW7 200 68NW
Harrington Rd SW7 200 68NE
Harrington St NW1 197 92NW
Harrison St WC1 197 02NW
Harrow Pl E1 199 31SW
Harrow Rd W2/W9 195 61NW
Harrowby St W1 196 71SW
Hasker St SW3 200 78NW
Hassard St E2 199 32NE
Hastings St WC1 197 02NW
Hatfields SE1 203 10SW
Hatton Gdns EC1 198 11NW
Hatton St NW8 195 62SE
Hatton Wall EC1 198 11NW
Hayes Pl NW1 196 72SW
Hay Hill W1 196 80NE
Hayles St SE11 203 18NE
Haymarket SW1 197 90NE
Hay's La SE1 204 30NE
Hays Mews W1 201 80NE
Headfort Pl SW1 201 89NW
Hearn St EC2 199 32SW
Heathcote St WC1 198 02SE
Helmet Row EC1 199 22SW
Henrietta Pl W1 196 81NE
Henrietta St WC2 197 00NW
Henshaw St SE17 204 28NE
Herbal Hill EC1 198 12SW
Herbrand St WC1 197 02SW
Hercules Rd SE1 203 19SW
Hereford Sq SW7 200 68NW
Hermit St EC1 198 12NE
Herrick St SW1 202 98NE
Hertford St W1 201 80SE
Hethpool St W2 195 62SE
Heygate St SE17 203 28NW
Hide Pl SW1 202 98NE
High Holborn WC1 197 01SW
Hill St W1 201 80SW
Hinde St W1 196 81SW
Hobart Pl SW1 201 89SE
Holbein Pl SW1 201 88NW
Holborn EC1 198 11NW
Holborn Circus EC1 198 11NW
Holborn Viaduct EC1 198 11NW
Holles St W1 196 81SE
Holyoak Rd SE11 203 18NE
Holywell Ln EC2 199 32SW
Homer St W1 196 71NW
Hopton St SE1 203 10SE
Horseferry Rd SW1 202 99SE
Horseguards Av SW1 202 00SW
Hosier Ln EC1 198 11NE
Houghton St WC2 198 01SE
Houndsditch EC3 199 31SW
Howick Pl SW1 202 99SW
Howland St W1 197 91NW
Howley Pl W2 195 61NW
Hoxton Sq N1 199 32NW
Hoxton St N1 199 32NW
Hudson's Pl SW1 201 88NE
Hugh St SW1 201 88NE
Hunter St WC1 197 02SW
Huntley St WC1 197 92SW
Hyde Pk Cre W2 195 71SW
Hyde Pk Gdns W2 195 60NE
Hyde Pk Gdns Mews W2 195 60NE
Hyde Pk Gt SW7 199 69NW
Hyde Pk Sq W2 195 71SW
Hyde Pk St W2 195 71SW

I

Iliffe St SE17 203 18SE
Inner Circle NW1 196 82NW
Inverness Ter W2 195 51SE
Inville Rd SE17 204 28SE
Ironmonger Ln EC2 199 21SE
Ironmonger Row EC1 199 22NW
Irving St WC2 197 90NE
Ives St SW3 200 78NW

Ivor Pl NW1 196 72SE
Ixworth Pl SW3 200 78NW

J

James St W1 196 81SW
James St WC2 197 00NW
Jay Mews SW7 200 69NW
Jermyn St SW1 202 90SW
Jewry St EC3 199 31SE
Jockey's Fields WC1 198 01NE
John St WC1 197 02SE
John Adam St WC2 197 00NW
John Carpenter St EC4 198 10NE
John Islip St SW1 202 98SE
John Princes St W1 197 81SE
John's Mews WC1 198 02SE
Joiner St SE1 204 20SE
Jonathan St SE11 202 08SE
Jubilee Pl SW3 200 78SW
Judd St WC1 197 02NW
Juxon St SE11 203 08NE

K

Kean St WC2 198 01SE
Keeley St WC2 198 01SE
Kemble St WC2 198 01SE
Kempsford Rd SE11 203 18NE
Kempshead Rd SE5 204 38SW
Kendal St W2 195 71SW
Kennings Way SE11 203 18SW
Kennington Ln SE11 203 08SE
Kennington Pk Rd SE11 203 18SE
Kennington Rd SE1/11 203 19SW
Kensington Ct W8 200 59NE
Kensington Ct Pl W8 200 59SE
Kensington Gt W8 200 69SW
Kensington Gore SW7 200 69SW
Kensington Rd W8/SW7 200 59NE
Kenton St WC1 197 02SW
Keyworth St SE1 203 19SE
Keyse Rd SE1 204 39SE
King and Queen St SE17 204 28NE
King Charles St SW1 202 09NW
King Edward Wa SE1 203 19SW
King James St SE1 203 19NE
King William St EC4 199 20NE
Kinglake St SE17 204 38SW
Kingly St W1 197 90NW
King's Bench St SE1 203 19NE
King's Cross Rd WC1 198 02NE
King's Mews WC1 198 02SE
King's Rd SW1/SW3 201 67NE
Kingsland Rd E2 199 32NW
Kingsway WC2 198 01SE
Kinnerton St SW1 201 89NW
Kipling St SE1 204 29NE
Kirby St EC1 198 11NW
Knightsbridge SW1/SW7 200 79NE
Knox St W1 196 71NE
Kynance Mews SW7 200 59SE

L

Lackington St EC2 199 21NE
Lamb St E1 199 31NE
Lambeth Br SW1 202 08NW
Lambeth High St SE1 202 08NE
Lambeth Palace Rd SE1 202 09SW
Lambeth Rd SE1 203 09SE
Lambeth Walk SE11 203 08NE
Lamb's Conduit St WC1 198 02SE
Lamb's Passage EC1 199 22SE
Lanark Rd W9 195 62NW
Lancaster Gt W2 195 60NW
Lancaster Mews W2 195 60NW
Lancaster Pl WC2 198 00NE
Lancaster St SE1 203 19NE
Lancaster Ter W2 195 60NE
Lancelot Pl SW7 200 79NE
Lancing St NW1 197 92NE
Langham Pl W1 196 81NE
Langham St W1 197 81NE
Lansdowne Ter WC1 197 02SW
Lant St SE1 203 29NW
Larcom St SE17 203 28NW
Lauderdale Rd W9 195 52NE
Launceston Pl W8 200 69SW
Lavington St SE1 203 10SE
Law St SE1 204 29SE
Laystall St EC1 198 12SW
Leadenhall St EC3 199 31SW
Leather Ln EC1 198 11NW

Leathermarket St SE1 204 39NW
Lees Pl W1 196 80NW
Leicester Pl WC2 197 90NE
Leicester Sq WC2 197 90NE
Leicester St WC2 197 90NE
Leigh St WC1 197 02NW
Leinster Gdns W2 195 60NW
Leinster Ter W2 195 60NW
Lennox Gdns SW1 200 79SE
Lennox Gdns Mews SW1 200 78NE
Leonard St EC2 199 22SE
Leroy St SE1 204 39SW
Lever St EC1 199 12NE
Lexington St W1 197 90NW
Leyden St E1 199 31NE
Library St SE1 203 19NE
Lilestone St NW8 195 72SW
Lime St EC3 199 31SW
Lincoln's Inn Fields WC2 198 01SE
Linhope St NW1 196 72SE
Lisle St W1 197 90NE
Lisson Gv NW1/8 195 62SE
Lisson St NW1 195 71NW
Little Boltons, The SW10 200 68SW
Little Britain EC1 198 11NE
Little Portland St W1 197 91SW
Little Russell St WC1 197 01NW
Liverpool Grove SE17 204 28SE
Liverpool St EC2 199 31NW
Lloyd Baker St WC1 198 12NW
Lloyd's Av EC3 199 31SW
Lloyd Sq WC1 198 12NW
Lloyd St WC1 198 12NW
Lloyd's Row EC1 198 12NE
Lodge Rd NW8 195 62NE
Loman St SE1 203 19NE
Lombard St EC3 199 21SE
London Bridge EC4 199 20NE
London Br SE1 204 20SE
London Rd SE1 203 19SE
London St W2 195 61SE
London Wall EC1/2 199 21NW
Long Acre WC2 197 00NW
Long Ln EC1 199 11NE
Long Ln SE1 204 29NE
Long St E2 199 32NE
Longford St NW1 196 82SE
Longmoore St SW1 201 98NW
Longville Rd SE11 203 18NE
Lothbury EC2 199 21SE
Loughborough St SE11 203 08SE
Love Lane EC2 199 21SW
Lower Belgrave St SW1 201 89SE
Lower Grosvenor Pl SW1 201 89SE
Lower James St W1 197 90NW
Lower John St W1 197 90NW
Lower Marsh SE1 203 19NW
Lower Sloane St SW1 201 88NW
Lower Thames St EC3 199 20NE
Lowndes Pl SW1 201 89SW
Lowndes Sq SW1 201 79NE
Lowndes St SW1 201 89SW
Lucan Pl SW3 201 78NW
Ludgate Circus EC4 198 11SE
Ludgate Hill EC4 198 11SE
Luke St EC2 199 32SW
Lupus St SW1 201 88SE
Luton St NW8 195 62SE
Luxborough St W1 196 81NW
Lyall St SW1 201 89SW
Lynton Rd SE1 204 38SW
Lyons Pl NW8 195 62SE
Lytham St SE17 204 28SE

M

Mabledon Pl WC1 197 92NE
Macclesfield Rd EC1 199 22NW
Macklin St WC2 197 01SW
Mackworth St NW1 197 92NW
Maddox St W1 197 80NE
Madron St SE17 204 38SW
Magdalen St SE1 204 30SW
Maida Av W2 195 61NW
Maida Vale W9 195 62NW
Maiden Ln WC2 197 00NW
Malet St WC1 197 91NE
Mall, The SW1 202 90SE
Mallow St EC1 199 22SE
Maltby St SE1 204 39SE
Manchester Sq W1 196 81SW
Manchester St W1 196 81NW
Manciple St SE1 204 29NE
Mandeville Pl W1 196 81SW
Manor Pl SE17 203 28SW
Manresa Rd SW3 200 78SW
Mansell St E1 199 31SE

London Street Index

The Church of St. Mary le Strand.

Principal Airports

Aberdeen	Aberdeen (6 m) (0224) 2331, 574281, 722331
Alderney	St Agnes (048 182) 2886, 2889, 2711
Barra	Island Foreshore, Barra (889 3181) 041
Belfast (Aldergrove)	Belfast (16 m) (0232) 29271
Bembridge	Sandown (098 387) 2511, (098 384) 2646
Benbecula	Benbecula, South Uist (0870) 2051
Biggin Hill	Biggin Hill (09594) 72277
Birmingham (Elmdon)	Birmingham (5½ m) (021) 743 4272, 779 2537
Blackpool (Squires Gate)	Blackpool (2½ m) (0253) 43061
Bournemouth (Hurn)	Bournemouth (5 m); Christchurch (3 m) (02015) 6311, 72445
Bristol (Lulsgate)	Bristol (7 m) (027587) 4441
Cambridge	Cambridge (1½ m) (0223) 61133
Carlisle (Crosby)	Carlisle (6 m) (022873) 641
Compton Abbas	Shaftesbury (3 m) Fontmell Magna 767
Coventry	Coventry (3 m) (0203) 301717, 301792
East Midlands	Derby (7 m) (0332) 810621
Edinburgh	Edinburgh (5 m) (031) 334 2351
Elstree	Watford, Herts (2½ m) (01-953) 3502, 4411
Exeter	Exeter (4½ m) (0392) 67433
Fairoaks	Woking, Surrey (099 05) 7300, 7700
Glamorgan (Rhoose)	Cardiff (10 m) (0446) 710296
Glasgow (Abbotsinch)	Glasgow (6 m) (041) 887 1111
Glenforsa (Mull)	Salen, Isle of Mull, Aros 377
Gloucester/Cheltenham (Staverton)	Gloucester (4 m); Cheltenham (4 m) (0452) 713351, 712285
Guernsey	St Peter Port (2½ m) (0481) 37766
Hawarden	Chester (4 m) (0244) 24646
Humberside	Grimsby (10 m); Scunthorpe (15 m) (065 28) 456
Inverness (Dalcross)	Inverness (7 m) (0463) 32471
Ipswich	Ipswich (2 m) (0473) 70111
Islay (Port Ellen)	Port Ellen, Islay, Port Ellen 2361
Jersey States Airport	St Helier (0534) 22271, 41272
Kirkwall	Kirkwall, Orkney (3 m) (031) 443 8971, (0856) 2421
Lashenden (Headcorn)	Headcorn, Kent (2 m) (0622) 890226, 890671
Leavesden	Watford, Herts (2 m) (09273) 74000
Leeds/Bradford (Yeardon)	Leeds (8 m); Bradford (6 m) (0532) 503431
Liverpool	Liverpool (5½ m) (051) 427 4101
London (Gatwick)	Redhill, Surrey (5 m) (0293) 28822
London (Heathrow)	Central London (12 m) (01-759) 4321
London (Westland Heliport)	London SW11 (01-228) 0181
Luton	Luton (1½ m) (0582) 36061
Lydd	Ashford, Kent (18 m); Folkestone (18 m); Hastings (15 m) (0679) 20401
Manchester International Airport	Manchester (8 m) (061) 437 5233

Heathrow Airport

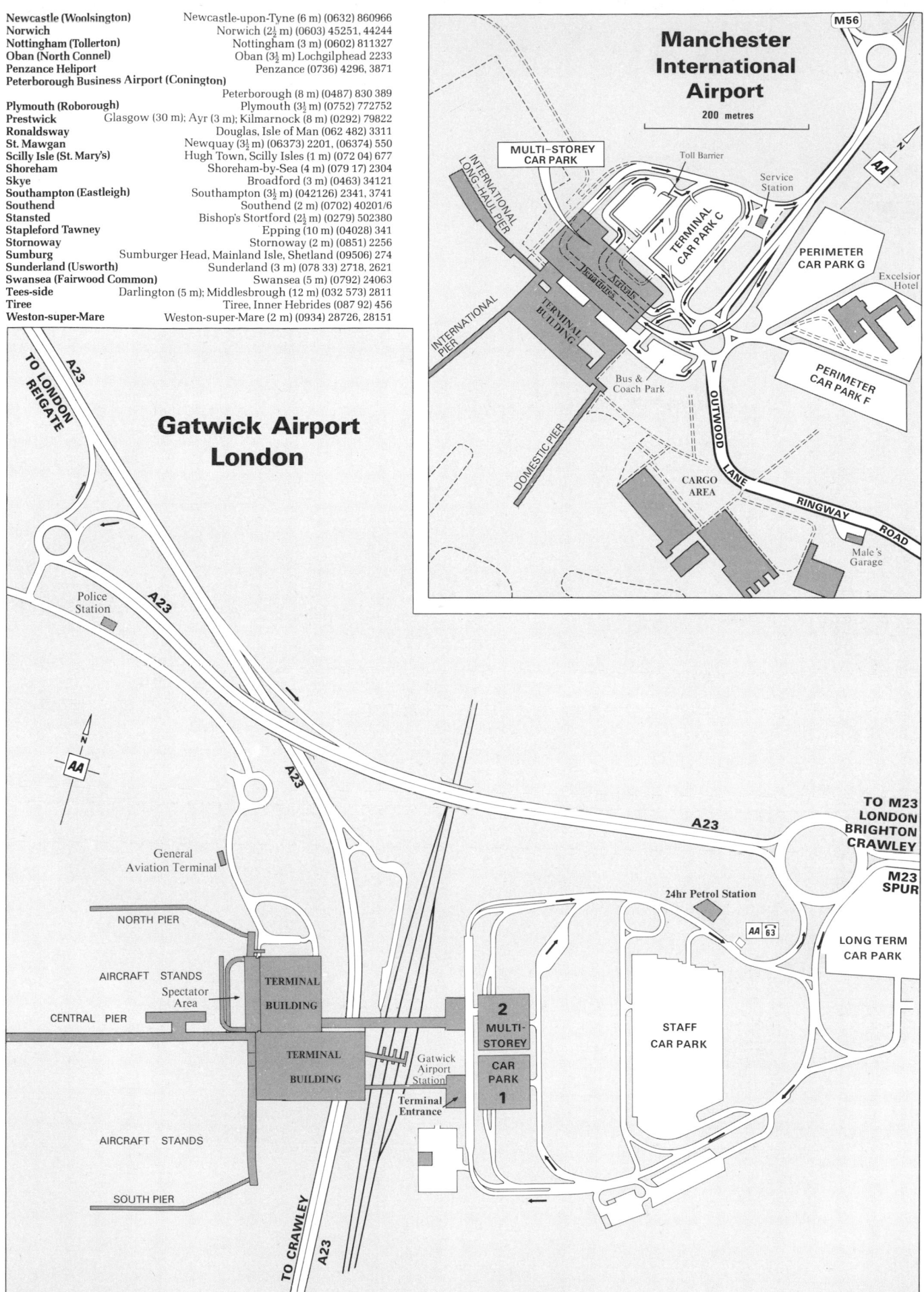

Manchester International Airport

200 metres

Gatwick Airport London

Index to Atlas

The towns and villages shown on the main maps of this atlas are listed alphabetically in the index. To find a place in the atlas, use the reference numbers given with each placename. The relevant page number is given with the National Grid reference number, so that the place can be quickly and accurately pinpointed. The National Grid system is explained on page XIII.

Altarnun Auchmithie

Altarnun	4	SX 2281
Altassmore	108	NC 5000
Alterwall	112	ND 2865
Altgaltraig	89	NS 0473
Altham	58	SD 7632
Althorne	23	TQ 9098
Althorpe	60	SE 8309
Altnaharra	110	NC 5635
Altofts	59	SE 3723
Alton (Derby.)	53	SK 3664
Alton (Hants.)	12	SU 7139
Alton (Staffs.)	52	SK 0742
Alton Pancras	9	ST 6902
Alton Priors	18	SU 1062
Altrincham	51	SJ 7687
Alva	91	NS 8897
Alvanley	50	SJ 4973
Alvaston	53	SK 3933
Alvechurch	42	SP 0272
Alvecote	42	SK 2404
Alvediston	10	ST 9723
Alveley	41	SO 7584
Alverdiscott	6	SS 5225
Alverstoke	11	SZ 5998
Alverstone	11	SZ 5785
Alverton	54	SK 7942
Alves	103	NJ 1362
Alvescot	33	SP 2704
Alveston (Avon)	29	ST 6388
Alveston (Warw.)	33	SP 2256
Alvie	103	NH 8609
Alvingham	55	TF 3691
Alvington	29	SO 6000
Alwalton	45	TL 1395
Alwinton	78	NT 9206
Alyth	98	NO 2448
Ambergate	53	SK 3451
Amber Hill	55	TF 2346
Amberley (Glos.)	32	SO 8401
Amberley (W. Susx.)	12	TQ 0313
Amble	79	NU 2604
Amblecote	41	SO 8885
Ambleside	62	NY 3704
Ambleston	24	SN 0026
Ambrosden	34	SP 6019
Amcotts	60	SE 8514
Amersham	20	SU 9597
Amesbury	18	SU 1541
Amington	42	SK 2304
Amisfield Town	70	NY 0082
Amlwch	48	SH 4392
Ammanford	25	SN 6212
Amotherby	67	SE 7473
Ampfield	11	SU 3923
Ampleforth	66	SE 5878
Ampney Crucis	32	SP 0602
Ampney St. Mary	32	SP 0802
Ampney St. Peter	32	SP 0701
Amport	19	SU 2944
Ampthill	35	TL 0337
Ampton	36	TL 8671
Amroth	24	SN 1607
Amulree	91	NN 8936
Anaheilt	95	NM 8162
Ancaster	54	SK 9843
Anchor	40	SO 1785
Ancroft	87	NT 9945
Ancrum	78	NT 6224
Ancton	12	SU 9800
Anderby	55	TF 5275
Anderson	10	SY 8797
Anderton	51	SJ 6475
Andover	19	SU 3645
Andover Down	19	SU 3946
Andoversford	32	SP 0219
Andreas	56	SC 4199
Angersleigh	8	ST 1918
Angle	24	SM 8603
Angmering	12	TQ 0704
Angram	60	SE 5148
Ankerville	108	NH 8174
Anlaby	61	TA 0328
Anmer	46	TF 7429
Annan	70	NY 1966
Annat (Highld.)	101	NG 8954
Annat (Strath.)	89	NN 0322
Annathill	84	NS 7270
Anna Valley	19	SU 3444
Annbank	75	NS 4022
Annesley Woodhouse	53	SK 4953
Annfield Plain	72	NZ 1551
Annochie	105	NJ 9342
Annscroft	40	SJ 4407
Ansley	43	SP 2991
Anslow	42	SK 2125
Anslow Gate	42	SK 2024
Anstey (Herts.)	35	TL 4032
Anstey (Leic.)	43	SK 5408
Anston	53	SK 5184
Anstruther	93	NO 5603
Ansty (Warw.)	43	SP 3983
Ansty (Wilts.)	10	ST 9526
Ansty (W Susx.)	13	TQ 2923
Anthill Common	11	SU 6412
Anthorn	70	NY 1958
Antingham	47	TG 2533
Antony	4	SX 3954
Antrobus	51	SJ 6479
Anwick	55	TF 1150
Anwoth	69	NX 5856
Apethorpe	44	TL 0295
Apley	55	TF 1075
Apperknowle	53	SK 3878
Apperley	32	SO 8628
Appleby (Cumbr.)	63	NY 6820
Appleby (Humbs.)	61	SE 9414
Appleby Magna	43	SK 3110
Appleby Parva	43	SK 3109
Appleby Street	35	TL 3304
Applecross	101	NG 7144
Appledore (Devon.)	6	SS 4630
Appledore (Devon.)	8	ST 0614
Appledore (Kent)	15	TQ 9529
Appleford	19	SU 5293
Appleshaw	19	SU 3048
Appleton (Ches.)	51	SJ 6484
Appleton (Oxon.)	33	SP 4401
Appleton-le-Moors	66	SE 7387
Appleton-le-Street	66	SE 7373
Appleton Roebuck	60	SE 5542
Appleton Wiske	66	NZ 3904
Appletreehall	78	NT 5117
Appletreewick	65	SE 0560
Appley	8	ST 0721
Appley Bridge	57	SD 5209
Apse Heath	11	SZ 5682
Apsley End	35	TL 1232
Apuldram	12	SU 8403
Arbirlot	93	NO 6040
Arboll	108	NH 8881
Arborfield	20	SU 7567
Arborfield Cross	20	SU 7666
Arborfield Garrison	20	SU 7665
Arbroath	93	NO 6340
Arbuthnott	99	NO 8074
Archiestown	103	NJ 2344
Arclid Green	51	SJ 7962
Ardacha	108	NC 6703
Ardachvie	96	NN 1490
Ardanaiseig	89	NN 0824
Ardarroch	101	NG 8339
Ardbeg	80	NR 4146
Ardcharnich	106	NH 1789
Ardchiavaig	88	NM 3818
Ardchyle	90	NN 5229
Arddleen	40	SJ 2516
Ardeley	35	TL 3127
Ardelve	101	NG 8727
Arden	90	NS 3684
Ardens Grafton	32	SP 1154
Ardentinny	89	NS 1887
Ardeonaig	91	NN 6635
Ardersier or Campbelltown	103	NH 7854
Ardessie	106	NH 0589
Ardgay	108	NH 5990
Ardindrean	106	NH 1588
Ardingly	13	TQ 3429
Ardington	19	SU 4388
Ardlair	104	NJ 5528
Ardleigh	23	TM 0529
Ardler	98	NO 2641
Ardley	33	SP 5427
Ardlui	90	NN 3115
Ardmair	106	NH 1198
Ardmay	90	NN 2802
Ardminish	80	NR 6448
Ardmolich	95	NM 7171
Ardnadam	82	NS 1580
Ardnagrask	102	NH 5149
Ardnarff	101	NG 8935
Ardnastang	95	NM 8061
Ardo	105	NJ 8538
Ardoch	92	NO 0937
Ardoyne	104	NJ 6527
Ardpatrick	81	NR 7560
Ardpeaton	90	NS 2185
Ardrishaig	89	NR 8585
Ardroil	63	NB 0432
Ardrossan	82	NS 2342
Ardshealach	95	NM 6967
Ardsley	59	SE 3805
Ardsley East	59	SE 3024
Ardslignish	95	NM 5661
Ardtalnaig	91	NN 7039
Ardullie	102	NH 5963
Ardvasar	95	NG 6303
Ardvorlich	90	NN 6322
Ardwell	68	NX 1045
Areley Kings	41	SO 8070
Argoed Mill	30	SN 9962
Aridhglas	88	NM 3123
Arinacrinachd	101	NG 7458
Arinagour	94	NM 2257
Arisaig	95	NM 6586
Arivruach	109	NB 2417
Arkendale	66	SE 3860
Arkesden	35	TL 4834
Arkholme	64	SD 5871
Arkley	21	TQ 2296
Arksey	60	SE 5706
Arkwright Town	53	SK 4270
Arlecdon	62	NY 0419
Arlesey	35	TL 1935
Arleston	41	SJ 6410
Arley (Ches.)	51	SJ 6780
Arley (Warw.)	43	SP 2890
Arlingham	32	SO 7010
Arlington (Devon)	6	SS 6140
Arlington (E Susx)	13	TQ 5407
Arlington (Glos.)	32	SP 1006
Armadale (Highld.)	111	NC 7864
Armadale (Lothian)	84	NS 9368
Armathwaite	71	NY 5046
Arminghall	47	TG 2504
Armitage	42	SK 0816
Armscote	33	SP 2444
Armthorpe	60	SE 6105
Arnabost	94	NM 2159
Arncliffe	65	SD 9371
Arncliffe Cote	65	SD 9470
Arncott	34	SP 6117
Arncroach	93	NO 5105
Arnesby	43	SP 6192
Arngask	92	NO 1310
Arnisdale	101	NG 8410
Arniston Engine	85	NT 3462
Arnol	109	NB 3148
Arnold	53	SK 5745
Arnprior	90	NS 6194
Arnside	63	SD 4578
Arrad Foot	62	SD 3080
Arram	61	TA 0344
Arrathorne	65	SE 2093
Arreton	11	SZ 5386
Arrington	35	TL 3250
Arrochar	90	NN 2904
Arrow	32	SP 0856
Artafallie	102	NH 6249
Arthington	59	SE 2644
Arthingworth	44	SP 7581
Arthog	39	SH 6414
Arthrath	105	NJ 9636
Artrochie	105	NK 0032
Arundel	12	TQ 0107
Aryhoulan	96	NN 0168
Asby	62	NY 0620
Ascog	82	NS 1063
Ascot	20	SU 9168
Ascott-under-Wychwood	33	SP 2918
Asenby	66	SE 3975
Asfordby	44	SK 7018
Asfordby Hill	44	SK 7219
Asgarby (Lincs.)	55	TF 1145
Asgarby (Lincs.)	55	TF 3366
Ash (Kent)	21	TQ 5964
Ash (Kent)	15	TR 2958
Ash (Somer.)	9	ST 4720
Ashampstead	19	SU 5676
Ashbocking	37	TM 1654
Ashbourne	52	SK 1846
Ashbrittle	8	ST 0521
Ash Bullayne	7	SS 7704
Ashburton	5	SX 7569
Ashbury (Devon.)	6	SX 5097
Ashbury (Oxon.)	18	SU 2685
Ashby	60	SE 9008
Ashby by Partney	55	TF 4266
Ashby cum Fenby	61	TA 2500
Ashby de la Launde	54	TF 0455
Ashby-de-la-Zouch	43	SK 3516
Ashby Folville	44	SK 7012
Ashby Magna	43	SP 5690
Ashby Parva	43	SP 5288
Ashby St. Ledgers	43	SP 5768
Ashby St. Mary	47	TG 3202
Ashchurch	32	SO 9233
Ashcombe	8	SX 9179
Ashcott	17	ST 4336
Ashdon	36	TL 5842
Asheldham	23	TL 9701
Ashen	36	TL 7442
Ashendon	34	SP 7014
Ashfield (Central)	91	NN 7803
Ashfield (Suff.)	37	TM 2062
Ashfield Green	37	TM 2673
Ashford (Derby.)	52	SK 1969
Ashford (Devon.)	6	SS 5335
Ashford (Kent)	15	TR 0142
Ashford (Surrey)	20	TQ 0671
Ashford Bowdler	40	SO 5170
Ashford Carbonel	40	SO 5270
Ashford Hill	19	SU 5562
Ashgill	84	NS 7849
Ashill (Devon.)	8	ST 0811
Ashill (Norf.)	46	TF 8804
Ashill (Somer.)	8	ST 3217
Ashingdon	22	TQ 8693
Ashington (Northum.)	79	NZ 2687
Ashington (W Susx)	12	TQ 1315
Ashkirk	77	NT 4722
Ashleworth	32	SO 8125
Ashley (Cambs.)	36	TL 6961
Ashley (Devon.)	7	SS 6411
Ashley (Glos.)	18	ST 9394
Ashley (Hants.)	11	SU 3831
Ashley (Northants.)	44	SP 7991
Ashley (Staffs.)	51	SJ 7536
Ashley Green	34	SP 9705
Ashley Heath	10	SU 1105
Ash Magna	51	SJ 5739
Ashmansworth	19	SU 4156
Ashmansworthy	6	SS 3317
Ash Mill	7	SS 7823
Ashmore	10	ST 9117
Ashorne	33	SP 3057
Ashover	53	SK 3463
Ashow	44	SP 3170
Ashperton	31	SO 6441
Ashprington	5	SX 8157
Ash Priors	16	ST 1429
Ashreigney	6	SS 6213
Ashtead	21	TQ 1858
Ash Thomas	8	ST 0010
Ashton (Ches.)	50	SJ 5069
Ashton (Corn.)	2	SW 6028
Ashton (Devon.)	5	SX 8584
Ashton (Here. and Worc.)	30	SO 5164
Ashton (Northants.)	34	SP 7649
Ashton (Northants.)	45	TL 0588
Ashton Common	18	ST 8958
Ashton-in-Makerfield	57	SJ 5799
Ashton Keynes	18	SU 0494
Ashton under Hill	32	SO 9938
Ashton-under-Lyne	51	SJ 9399
Ashton upon Mersey	51	SJ 7792
Ashurst (Hants.)	11	SU 3310
Ashurst (Kent)	13	TQ 5038
Ashurst (W Susx)	12	TQ 1716
Ashurstwood	13	TQ 4236
Ashwater	4	SX 3895
Ashwell (Herts.)	35	TL 2639
Ashwell (Leic.)	44	SK 8613
Ashwellthorpe	47	TM 1397
Ashwick	17	ST 6447
Ashwicken	46	TF 7018
Askam in Furness	64	SD 2177
Askern	60	SE 5613
Askerswell	9	SY 5292
Askett	34	SP 8105
Askham (Cumbr.)	63	NY 5123
Askham (Notts.)	54	SK 7374
Askham Bryan	60	SE 5548
Askham Richard	60	SE 5347
Askrigg	65	SD 9491
Askwith	59	SE 1648
Aslackby	45	TF 0830
Aslacton	47	TM 1591
Aslockton	54	SK 7440
Aspatria	70	NY 1442
Aspenden	35	TL 3528
Aspley Guise	34	SP 9436
Aspley Heath	34	SP 9334
Aspull	58	SD 6108
Asselby	60	SE 7127
Assington	36	TL 9338
Astbury	51	SJ 8461
Astcote	34	SP 6753
Asterley	40	SJ 3707
Asterton	40	SO 3991
Asthall	33	SP 2811
Asthall Leigh	33	SP 3012
Astley (Here. and Worc.)	41	SO 7867
Astley (Salop)	40	SJ 5218
Astley (Warw.)	43	SP 3189
Astley Abbots	41	SO 7096
Astley Cross	41	SO 8069
Astley Green	51	SJ 7099
Aston (Berks.)	20	SU 7884
Aston (Ches.)	51	SJ 5578
Aston (Ches.)	51	SJ 6046
Aston (Derby.)	52	SK 1883
Aston (Here. and Worc.)	40	SO 4571
Aston (Herts.)	35	TL 2722
Aston (Oxon.)	33	SP 3302
Aston (Salop)	40	SJ 5228
Aston (Salop)	41	SJ 6109
Aston (Staffs.)	41	SJ 7540
Aston (Staffs.)	41	SJ 9131
Aston (S Yorks.)	53	SK 4685
Aston (W Mids)	42	SP 0789
Aston Abbotts	34	SP 8420
Aston Blank (Cold Aston)	32	SP 1219
Aston Botterell	41	SO 6284
Aston Cantlow	32	SP 1359
Aston Clinton	34	SP 8812
Aston Crews	29	SO 6723
Aston End	35	TL 2724
Aston Eyre	41	SO 6594
Aston Flamville	43	SP 4692
Aston Ingham	29	SO 6823
Aston juxta Mondrum	51	SJ 6556
Aston le Walls	33	SP 4950
Aston Magna	33	SP 1935
Aston on Clun	40	SO 3981
Aston-on-Trent	43	SK 4129
Aston Rogers	40	SJ 3406
Aston Rowant	20	SU 7299
Aston Sandford	34	SP 7507
Aston Somerville	32	SP 0438
Aston Subedge	32	SP 1341
Aston Tirrold	19	SU 5586
Aston Upthorpe	19	SU 5586
Astwick	35	TL 2138
Astwood	34	SP 9547
Astwood Bank	32	SP 0362
Aswarby (Lincs.)	54	TF 0639
Aswardby (Lincs.)	54	TF 3770
Atcham	40	SJ 5408
Athelington	37	TM 2170
Athelney	17	ST 3428
Athelstaneford	86	NT 5377
Atherington	6	SS 5923
Atherstone	43	SP 3097
Atherstone on Stour	33	SP 2050
Atherton	58	SD 6703
Atlow	53	SK 2248
Attenborough	53	SK 5134
Attleborough (Norf.)	47	TM 0495
Attleborough (Warw.)	43	SP 3790
Attlebridge	47	TG 1216
Atwick	67	TA 1850
Atworth	18	ST 8565
Aubourn	54	SK 9262
Auchagallon	81	NR 8934
Aucharnie	104	NJ 6341
Auchattie	99	NO 6994
Auchenblae	99	NO 7278
Auchenbowie	84	NS 7988
Auchencairn	59	NX 7951
Auchencarroch	90	NS 4182
Auchencrow	87	NT 8560
Auchendinny	85	NT 2561
Auchengray	85	NS 9953
Auchenhalrig	104	NJ 3661
Auchenheath	84	NS 8043
Auchentiber	82	NS 3647
Auchgourish	103	NH 9315
Auchindrain	89	NN 0303
Auchindrean	106	NH 1980
Auchininna	105	NJ 6446
Auchinleck (Strath.)	75	NS 5422
Auchinloch	84	NS 6670
Auchintore	96	NN 0972
Auchleuchries	105	NK 0136
Auchleven	104	NJ 6224
Auchlochan	84	NS 8037
Auchlyne	90	NN 5129
Auchmillan	75	NS 5129
Auchmithie	99	NO 6744

Auchmuirbridge Bashley

Auchmuirbridge	92	NO 2101
Auchnacree	98	NO 4663
Auchnagatt	105	NJ 9341
Auchronie	98	NO 4480
Auchterarder	91	NN 9312
Auchterderran	92	NT 2195
Auchterhouse	93	NO 3337
Auchtermuchty	92	NO 2311
Auchterneed	102	NH 4959
Auchtertool	92	NT 2190
Auchtoo	90	NN 5620
Auckingill	112	ND 3764
Auckley	60	SE 6501
Audenshaw	51	SJ 9196
Audlem	51	SJ 6543
Audley	51	SJ 7950
Aughton (Humbs.)	60	SE 7038
Aughton (Lancs.)	57	SD 3804
Aughton (Lancs.)	64	SD 5467
Aughton (S Yorks.)	53	SK 4586
Aughton Park	57	SD 4106
Auldearn	103	NH 9155
Aulden	30	SO 4654
Auldhame	86	NT 5984
Auldhouse	84	NS 6250
Ault-a-chrinn	101	NG 9420
Aultbea	106	NG 8789
Aultgrishan	106	NG 7485
Aultiphurst	111	NC 8065
Aultmore (Grampn.)	104	NJ 4053
Aultnagoire	102	NH 5423
Aulton	104	NJ 6028
Aundorach	103	NH 9716
Aunsby	54	TF 0438
Auquhorthies	105	NJ 8329
Aust	29	ST 5789
Austerfield	53	SK 6594
Austonley	59	SE 1207
Austrey	43	SK 2906
Austwick	65	SD 7668
Authorpe	55	TF 3980
Authorpe Row	55	TF 5373
Avebury	18	SU 0969
Aveley	21	TQ 5680
Avening	18	ST 8797
Averham	54	SK 7654
Aveton Gifford	5	SX 6947
Avielochan	103	NH 9016
Aviemore	103	NH 8912
Avington	19	SU 3767
Avoch	103	NH 6955
Avon	9	SZ 1498
Avonbridge	84	NS 9072
Avon Dassett	33	SP 4150
Avonmouth	29	ST 5177
Avonwick	5	SX 7158
Awbridge	11	SU 3323
Awkley	29	ST 5885
Awliscombe	8	ST 1301
Awre	32	SO 7008
Awsworth	53	SK 4843
Axbridge	17	ST 4254
Axford (Hants.)	19	SU 6043
Axford (Wilts.)	18	SU 2369
Axminster	8	SY 2998
Axmouth	8	SY 2591
Aylburton	29	SO 6101
Ayle	71	NY 7149
Aylesbeare	8	SY 0391
Aylesbury	34	SP 8213
Aylesby	61	TA 2007
Aylesford	14	TQ 7359
Aylesham	15	TR 2352
Aylestone	43	SK 5701
Aylmerton	47	TG 1839
Aylsham	47	TG 1926
Aylton	31	SO 6537
Aymestrey	30	SO 4265
Aynho	33	SP 5133
Ayot St. Lawrence	35	TL 1916
Ayot St. Peter	35	TL 2115
Ayr	75	NS 3321
Aysgarth	65	SE 0088
Ayside	62	SD 3983
Ayston	44	SK 8601
Aythorpe Roding	22	TL 5815
Ayton (Berwick.)	87	NT 9260
Ayton (N Yorks.)	67	SE 9884
Azerley	66	SE 2574
B		
Babbinswood	40	SJ 3329
Babcary	17	ST 5628
Babel	27	SN 8235
Babell	50	SJ 1574
Babraham	35	TL 5150
Babworth	53	SK 6880
Back	109	NB 4840
Backaland	113	HY 5630
Backbarrow	62	SD 3584
Backford	50	SJ 3971
Backies	108	NC 8302
Backmuir of New Gilston	93	NO 4308
Back of Keppoch	95	NM 6587
Backwell	29	ST 4868
Backworth	79	NZ 2972
Bacon End	22	TL 6018
Baconsthorpe	47	TG 1237
Bacton (Here. and Worc.)	30	SO 3732
Bacton (Norf.)	47	TG 3434
Bacton (Suff.)	37	TM 0466
Bacup	58	SD 8622
Badachro	106	NG 7873
Badbury	18	SU 1980
Badby	33	SP 5559
Badcall (Highld.)	110	NC 1541
Badcall (Highld.)	110	NC 2355
Badcaul	106	NH 0191
Baddeley Green	51	SJ 9250
Baddesley Ensor	42	SP 2798
Baddidarach	110	NC 0923
Badenscoth	105	NJ 7038
Badenyon	104	NJ 3419
Badger	41	SO 7699
Badgers Mount	21	TQ 5061
Badgeworth (Glos.)	32	SO 9019
Badgworth (Somer.)	17	ST 3952
Badingham	37	TM 3067
Badlesmere	15	TR 0154
Badluarach	106	NG 9994
Badminton	18	ST 8082
Badrallach	106	NH 0691
Badsey	32	SP 0743
Badsworth	60	SE 4614
Badwell Ash	36	TL 9969
Bagby	66	SE 4680
Bagendon	32	SP 0006
Bagillt	50	SJ 2175
Baginton	43	SP 3474
Baglan	24	SS 7493
Bagley	40	SJ 4027
Bagnall	51	SJ 9250
Bagshot (Surrey)	20	SU 9163
Bagshot (Wilts.)	19	SU 3165
Bagthorpe (Norf.)	46	TF 7932
Bagthorpe (Notts.)	53	SK 4751
Bagworth	43	SK 4408
Bagwy Llydiart	29	SO 4427
Baildon	59	SE 1539
Bailebeag	102	NH 5018
Baile Mor	88	NM 2824
Baillieston	84	NS 6764
Bainbridge	66	SD 9390
Bainton (Cambs.)	45	TF 0906
Bainton (Humbs.)	67	SE 9652
Bairnkine	78	NT 6515
Baker's End	35	TL 3917
Baker Street	22	TQ 6381
Bakewell	53	SK 2168
Bala	49	SH 9236
Balallan	109	NB 2720
Balbeg	102	NH 4924
Balbeggie	92	NO 1629
Balbithan	105	NJ 7917
Balblair	103	NH 7066
Balchladich	110	NC 0330
Balchraggan	102	NH 5343
Balchrick	110	NC 1960
Balcombe	13	TQ 3130
Balcurvie	93	NO 3400
Baldersby	66	SE 3578
Balderstone	58	SD 6332
Balderton	54	SK 8151
Baldhu	2	SW 7743
Baldinnie	93	NO 4311
Baldock	35	TL 2434
Baldrine	56	SC 4281
Baldwin	57	SC 3581
Baldwinholme	70	NY 3351
Baldwin's Gate	51	SJ 7939
Bale	46	TG 0136
Balemartine	94	NL 9841
Balephuil	94	NL 9640
Balerno	85	NT 1666
Balfield	99	NO 5468
Balfour	113	HY 4716
Balfron	84	NS 5488
Balgaveny	105	NJ 6640
Balgavies	99	NO 5351
Balgedie	92	NO 1603
Balgove	105	NJ 8133
Balgowan	97	NN 6394
Balgown	100	NG 3868
Balgray	93	NO 4138
Balgrochan	84	NS 6278
Balhalgardy	105	NJ 7623
Balhary	98	NO 2646
Baligill	111	NC 8566
Balintore (Highld.)	108	NH 8675
Balintore (Tays.)	98	NO 2859
Balintraid	108	NH 7370
Balivanich	109	NF 7755
Balkeerie	98	NO 3244
Balkholme	60	SE 7828
Ball	40	SJ 3026
Ballabeg	56	SC 2470
Ballacannell	56	SC 4382
Ballacarnane Beg	56	SC 3088
Ballajora	56	SC 4790
Ballamodha	56	SC 2773
Ballantrae	68	NX 0882
Ballantrushal	109	NB 3853
Ballasalla (I. of M.)	56	SC 2870
Ballasalla (I. of M.)	56	SC 3497
Ballater	98	NO 3695
Ballaugh	56	SC 3493
Ballchraggan	108	NH 7775
Ballechin	97	NN 9353
Ballencrieff	86	NT 4878
Ballevullin	94	NL 9546
Ball Hill	19	SU 4263
Balliekine	81	NR 8739
Balliemore (Strath.)	89	NM 8228
Ballig	56	SC 2882
Ballinaby	80	NR 2267
Ballindean	93	NO 2529
Ballinger Common	34	SP 9103
Ballingham	31	SO 5731
Ballingry	92	NT 1797
Ballinluig	98	NN 9852
Ballintuim	98	NO 1054
Balloch (Highld.)	103	NH 7346
Balloch (Strath.)	90	NS 3981
Balloch (Tays.)	91	NN 8419
Balloch (Tays.)	98	NO 3557
Ballochan	99	NO 5290
Balls Cross	12	SU 9826
Ballygown	94	NM 4343
Ballygrant	80	NR 3966
Ballymichael	81	NR 9231
Balmacara	101	NG 8028
Balmaclellan	69	NX 6578
Balmacneil	98	NN 9850
Balmae	69	NX 6845
Balmaha	90	NS 4290
Balmalcolm	93	NO 3108
Balmedie	105	NJ 9617
Balmerino	93	NO 3524
Balmerlawn	11	SU 3003
Balmore	84	NS 6073
Balmullo	93	NO 4220
Balmungie	103	NH 7359
Balnacra	101	NG 9746
Balnafoich	103	NH 6835
Balnaguard	97	NN 9451
Balnaguisich	108	NH 6771
Balnahard	88	NM 4534
Balnakeil	110	NC 3968
Balnaknock	100	NG 4162
Balnapaling	103	NH 7969
Balquhidder	90	NN 5320
Balsall Common	42	SP 2377
Balscote	33	SP 3841
Balsham	36	TL 5850
Baltasound (Unst)	113	HP 6208
Balterley	51	SJ 7550
Balthangie	105	NJ 8351
Baltonsborough	17	ST 5434
Balvaird	102	NH 5452
Balvicar	89	NM 7616
Bamburgh	87	NU 1834
Bamford	53	SK 2083
Bampton (Cumbr.)	63	NY 5118
Bampton (Devon.)	8	SS 9522
Bampton (Oxon.)	33	SP 3103
Banavie	96	NN 1177
Banbury	33	SP 4540
Banchory	99	NO 6995
Banchory Devenick	99	NJ 9101
Bancyfelin	25	SN 3218
Banc-y-ffordd	26	SN 4037
Banff	105	NJ 6863
Bangor	48	SH 5872
Bangor-is-y-coed	50	SJ 3945
Banham	47	TM 0688
Bank	11	SU 2807
Bankend (Dumf. and Galwy.)	70	NY 0268
Bankend (Strath.)	84	NS 8033
Bankfoot	92	NO 0635
Bankglen	76	NS 5912
Bankhead (Grampn.)	104	NJ 6608
Bankhead (Grampn.)	105	NJ 8910
Bank Newton	65	SD 9152
Banks (Cumbr.)	71	NY 5664
Banks (Lancs.)	57	SD 3820
Bankshill	70	NY 1981
Bank Street	31	SO 6362
Banningham	47	TG 2129
Bannister Green	22	TL 6920
Bannockburn	91	NS 8190
Banstead	21	TQ 2559
Bantham	5	SX 6643
Banton	84	NS 7479
Banwell	17	ST 3959
Bapchild	15	TQ 9363
Barassie	82	NS 3232
Barbaraville	108	NH 7471
Barber Booth	52	SK 1184
Barbon	63	SD 6282
Barbrook	7	SS 7147
Barby	43	SP 5470
Barcheston	33	SP 2639
Barcombe	13	TQ 4214
Barcombe Cross	13	TQ 4216
Barden	65	SE 1493
Bardfield Saling	22	TL 6826
Bardney	55	TF 1169
Bardon Mill	71	NY 7764
Bardowie	84	NS 5873
Bardrainney	82	NS 3372
Bardsea	64	SD 3074
Bardsey	59	SE 3643
Bardsley	58	SD 9201
Bardwell	36	TL 9473
Barewood	30	SO 3856
Barford (Norf.)	47	TG 1007
Barford (Warw.)	33	SP 2660
Barford St. Martin	10	SU 0531
Barford St. Michael	33	SP 4332
Barfreston	15	TR 2650
Bargoed	28	SO 1500
Bargrennan	68	NX 3476
Barham (Cambs.)	45	TL 1375
Barham (Kent)	15	TR 2050
Barham (Suff.)	37	TM 1451
Barholm	45	TF 0811
Barkby	43	SK 6309
Barkestone-le-Vale	54	SK 7734
Barkham	20	SU 7866
Barking (Gtr London)	21	TQ 4785
Barking (Suff.)	37	TM 0653
Barkingside	21	TQ 4489
Barkisland	59	SE 0419
Barkston (Lincs.)	54	SK 9241
Barkston (N Yorks.)	60	SE 4936
Barkway	35	TL 3835
Barkwith	55	TF 1681
Barlaston	51	SJ 8938
Barlavington	12	SU 9716
Barlborough	53	SK 4777
Barlby	60	SE 6334
Barlestone	43	SK 4205
Barley (Herts.)	35	TL 4038
Barley (Lancs.)	58	SD 8240
Barleythorpe	44	SK 8409
Barling	23	TQ 9289
Barlow (Derby.)	53	SK 3474
Barlow (N Yorks.)	60	SE 6428
Barlow (Tyne and Wear)	72	NZ 1560
Barmby Moor	60	SE 7748
Barmby on the Marsh	60	SE 6828
Barmer	46	TF 8133
Barmouth	38	SH 6115
Barmpton	72	NZ 3118
Barmston	67	TA 1659
Barnack	45	TF 0705
Barnacle	43	SP 3884
Barnard Castle	72	NZ 0516
Barnard Gate	33	SP 4010
Barnardiston	36	TL 7148
Barnburgh	60	SE 4803
Barnby	47	TM 4789
Barnby Dun	60	SE 6109
Barnby in the Willows	54	SK 8552
Barnby Moor	53	SK 6684
Barnes	21	TQ 2276
Barnet	21	TQ 2494
Barnetby le Wold	61	TA 0509
Barney	46	TF 9932
Barnham (Suff.)	36	TL 8779
Barnham (W Susx)	12	SU 9604
Barnham Broom	47	TG 0807
Barnhead	99	NO 6657
Barnhill	103	NJ 1457
Barnhills	68	NW 9871
Barningham (Durham)	65	NZ 0810
Barningham (Suff.)	36	TL 9676
Barnoldby le Beck	61	TA 2303
Barnoldswick	58	SD 8746
Barns Green	12	TQ 1227
Barnsley (Glos.)	32	SP 0705
Barnsley (S Yorks.)	59	SE 3406
Barnstaple	6	SS 5533
Barnston (Essex)	22	TL 6519
Barnston (Mers.)	50	SJ 2783
Barnt Green	41	SP 0073
Barnton	51	SJ 6374
Barnwell	45	TL 0485
Barnwood	32	SO 8518
Barr	75	NX 2794
Barrachan	68	NX 3649
Barrack	105	NJ 8942
Barrapoll	94	NL 9542
Barras	99	NO 8580
Barrasford	78	NY 9273
Barregarrow	57	SC 3288
Barrhead	82	NS 5058
Barrhill (Strath.)	68	NX 2382
Barrington (Cambs.)	35	TL 3949
Barrington (Somer.)	9	ST 3918
Barripper	2	SW 6338
Barrmill	82	NS 3651
Barrow (Lancs.)	58	SD 7338
Barrow (Leic.)	44	SK 8815
Barrow (Salop)	41	SJ 6500
Barrow (Somer.)	17	ST 7231
Barrow (Suff.)	36	TL 7663
Barrowby	54	SK 8736
Barrowden	44	SK 9400
Barrowford	58	SD 8538
Barrow Gurney	29	ST 5267
Barrow-in-Furness	64	SD 1969
Barrow Street	10	ST 8330
Barrow upon Humber	61	TA 0721
Barrow upon Soar	43	SK 5717
Barrow upon Trent	43	SK 3528
Barry (Angus)	93	NO 5334
Barry (S Glam.)	28	ST 1168
Barry Island	28	ST 1166
Barsby	43	SK 6911
Barsham	47	TM 3989
Barston	42	SP 2078
Bartestree	31	SO 5641
Barthol Chapel	105	NJ 8134
Barthomley	51	SJ 7652
Bartley	11	SU 3012
Bartlow	36	TL 5845
Barton (Cambs.)	35	TL 4055
Barton (Ches.)	50	SJ 4454
Barton (Devon.)	5	SX 9067
Barton (Glos.)	32	SP 0925
Barton (Lancs.)	57	SD 5136
Barton (N Yorks.)	66	NZ 2208
Barton (Warw.)	32	SP 1051
Barton Bendish	46	TF 7105
Barton Common	47	TG 3522
Barton Hartshorn	34	SP 6431
Barton in Fabis	53	SK 5232
Barton in the Beans	43	SK 3906
Barton in the Clay	35	TL 0831
Barton-le-Street	66	SE 7274
Barton-le-Willows	66	SE 7163
Barton Mills	36	TL 7273
Barton on Sea	11	SZ 2493
Barton-on-the-Heath	33	SP 2532
Barton St. David	17	ST 5431
Barton Seagrave	44	SP 8877
Barton Stacey	19	SU 4340
Barton Turf	47	TG 3421
Barton-under-Needwood	42	SK 1818
Barton-Upon-Humber	61	TA 0222
Barvas	109	NB 3649
Barway	45	TL 5475
Barwell	43	SP 4496
Barwick	9	ST 5513
Barwick in Elmet	59	SE 3937
Baschurch	40	SJ 4222
Bascote	33	SP 4063
Basford Green	51	SJ 9951
Bashall Eaves	58	SD 6943
Bashley	11	SZ 2496

Bishop Auckland Bowden Hill

Bishop Auckland	72	NZ 2029
Bishopbriggs	84	NS 6070
Bishop Burton	61	SE 9839
Bishop Middleham	72	NZ 3231
Bishop Monkton	66	SE 3266
Bishop Norton	54	SK 9892
Bishopsbourne	15	TR 1852
Bishops Cannings	18	SU 0364
Bishop's Castle	40	SO 3288
Bishop's Caundle	9	ST 6912
Bishop's Cleeve	32	SO 9527
Bishop's Frome	31	SO 6648
Bishop's Itchington	33	SP 3857
Bishops Lydeard	18	ST 1629
Bishop's Nympton	7	SS 7523
Bishop's Offley	41	SJ 7729
Bishop's Stortford	22	TL 4821
Bishop's Sutton	11	SU 6031
Bishop's Tachbrook	33	SP 3161
Bishop's Tawton	6	SS 5630
Bishopsteignton	8	SX 9173
Bishopstoke	11	SU 4619
Bishopston	25	SS 5889
Bishopstone (Bucks.)	34	SP 8010
Bishopstone (E Susx)	13	TQ 4701
Bishopstone (Here. and Worc.)	30	SO 4143
Bishopstone (Wilts.)	10	SU 0625
Bishopstone (Wilts.)	18	SU 2483
Bishop Sutton	17	ST 5859
Bishop's Waltham	11	SU 5517
Bishopswood (Somer.)	8	ST 2512
Bishop's Wood (Staffs.)	41	SJ 8309
Bishopsworth	29	ST 5768
Bishop Thornton	66	SE 2663
Bishopthorpe	60	SE 5947
Bishopton (Durham)	72	NZ 3621
Bishopton (Strath.)	82	NS 4371
Bishop Wilton	67	SE 7955
Bishton	29	ST 3887
Bisley (Glos.)	32	SO 9005
Bisley (Surrey)	20	SU 9559
Bispham	57	SD 3139
Bissoe	2	SW 7741
Bisterne Close	11	SU 2202
Bitchfield	44	SK 9828
Bittadon	6	SS 5441
Bittaford	5	SX 6557
Bittering	46	TF 9317
Bitterley	40	SO 5577
Bitterne	11	SU 4513
Bitteswell	43	SP 5385
Bitton	29	ST 6769
Bix	20	SU 7285
Blaby	43	SP 5697
Blackacre	77	NY 0490
Blackadder	87	NT 8452
Blackawton	5	SX 8050
Blackborough	8	ST 0909
Blackborough End	46	TF 6614
Black Bourton	33	SP 2804
Blackboys	13	TQ 5220
Blackbrook	51	SJ 7639
Blackburn (Grampn.)	105	NJ 8212
Blackburn (Lancs.)	58	SD 6827
Blackburn (Lothian)	85	NS 9865
Black Callerton	72	NZ 1769
Black Crofts	89	NM 9234
Blackden Heath	51	SJ 7871
Black Dog (Devon.)	7	SS 8009
Blackdog (Grampn.)	105	NJ 9514
Blackfield	11	SU 4402
Blackford (Cumbr.)	70	NY 3962
Blackford (Somer.)	17	ST 4147
Blackford (Somer.)	17	ST 6526
Blackford (Tays.)	91	NN 8908
Blackfordby	43	SK 3318
Blackgang	11	SZ 4876
Blackhall Colliery	73	NZ 4539
Blackhaugh	86	NT 4238
Blackheath (Essex)	23	TM 0021
Blackheath (Surrey)	20	TQ 0346
Blackhill (Grampn.)	105	NK 0843
Blackland	18	SU 0168
Blackley	58	SD 8503
Blacklunans	98	NO 1560
Blackmill	28	SS 9386
Blackmoor	12	SU 7833
Blackmoor Gate	7	SS 6443
Blackmore	22	TL 6001
Blackmore End	36	TL 7430
Blackness	85	NT 0579
Blacknest	12	SU 7941
Black Notley	22	TL 7620
Blacko	58	SD 8541
Blackpill	25	SS 6290
Blackpool	57	SD 3035
Blackpool Gate	71	NY 5377
Blackridge	84	NS 8967
Blackrock (Gwent)	28	SO 2112
Blackrock (Islay)	80	NR 3063
Blackrod	58	SD 6110
Blackshaw	70	NY 0465
Blacksmith's Corner	36	TM 0131
Blackstone	13	TQ 2416
Blackthorn	34	SP 6219
Blackthorpe	36	TL 9063
Blacktoft	60	SE 8424
Blacktop	105	NJ 8604
Black Torrington	6	SS 4605
Blackwater (Corn.)	2	SW 7346
Blackwater (Hants.)	20	SU 8559
Blackwater (I. of W.)	11	SZ 5086
Blackwater (Suff.)	37	TM 5077
Blackwaterfoot	81	NR 8928
Blackwell (Derby.)	52	SK 1272
Blackwell (Here. and Worc.)	41	SO 9972
Blackwood (Gwent)	28	ST 1797
Blackwood (Strath.)	84	NS 7943
Blackwood Hill	51	SJ 9255
Blacon	50	SJ 3767
Bladnoch	68	NX 4254
Bladon	33	SP 4414
Blaenannerch	26	SN 2449
Blaenau Ffestiniog	49	SH 7045
Blaenavon	29	SO 2509
Blaenawey	29	SO 2919
Blaengarw	28	SS 9092
Blaengwrach	28	SN 8605
Blaengwynfi	28	SS 8996
Blaenplwyf	26	SN 5775
Blaenporth	26	SN 2648
Blaenrhondda	28	SS 9299
Blaenwaun	25	SN 2327
Blagdon	5	SX 8561
Blagdon Hill	8	ST 2118
Blaich	96	NN 0476
Blaina	28	SO 2008
Blair Atholl	97	NN 8765
Blair Drummond	91	NS 7398
Blairgowrie	98	NO 1745
Blairhall	85	NT 0089
Blairingone	91	NS 9896
Blairlogie	91	NS 8396
Blairskaith	84	NS 5975
Blaisdon	32	SO 7016
Blakebrook	41	SO 8077
Blakedown	41	SO 8778
Blakelaw	87	NT 7730
Blakemere	30	SO 3641
Blakeney (Glos.)	29	SO 6707
Blakeney (Norf.)	46	TG 0243
Blakenhall (Ches.)	51	SJ 7247
Blakenhall (W Mids)	41	SO 9297
Blakeshall	41	SO 8381
Blakesley	34	SP 6250
Blanchland	72	NY 9650
Blandford Forum	10	ST 8806
Blandford St. Mary	10	ST 8805
Bland Hill	65	SE 2053
Blanefield	84	NS 5579
Blankney	54	TF 0660
Blarghour	89	NM 9913
Blarmachfoldach	96	NN 0969
Blashford	10	SU 1406
Blaston	44	SP 8095
Blatherwycke	44	SP 9795
Blawith	62	SD 2888
Blaxhall	37	TM 3657
Blaxton	60	SE 6600
Blaydon	72	NZ 1863
Bleadon	17	ST 3456
Blean	15	TR 1260
Bleasby	54	SK 7049
Blebocraigs	93	NO 4214
Bleddfa	40	SO 2068
Bledington	33	SP 2422
Bledlow	34	SP 7802
Bledlow Ridge	20	SU 7898
Blegbie	86	NT 4861
Blencarn	63	NY 6331
Blencogo	70	NY 1947
Blencow	63	NY 4532
Blendworth	12	SU 7113
Blennerhasset	70	NY 1741
Bletchingdon	33	SP 5017
Bletchingley	21	TQ 3250
Bletchley (Bucks.)	34	SP 8733
Bletchley (Salop)	51	SJ 6233
Bletherston	24	SN 0721
Bletsoe	34	TL 0258
Blewbury	19	SU 5385
Blickling	47	TG 1728
Blidworth	53	SK 5855
Blindcrake	62	NY 1434
Blindley Heath	21	TQ 3645
Blisland	4	SX 0973
Blissford	10	SU 1713
Bliss Gate	41	SO 7472
Blisworth	34	SP 7253
Blockley	32	SP 1634
Blofield	47	TG 3309
Blo Norton	36	TM 0179
Blore	52	SK 1349
Bloxham	33	SP 4235
Bloxwich	42	SJ 9902
Bloxworth	10	SY 8894
Blubberhouses	65	SE 1655
Blue Anchor	16	ST 0343
Blue Bell Hill	14	TQ 7462
Blundeston	47	TM 5197
Blunham	35	TL 1551
Blunsdon St. Andrew	18	SU 1389
Bluntisham	45	TL 3674
Blyborough	54	SK 9394
Blyford	37	TM 4276
Blymhill	41	SJ 8112
Blyth (Northum.)	79	NZ 3181
Blyth (Notts.)	53	SK 6287
Blyth Bridge	85	NT 1345
Blythburgh	37	TM 4575
Blythe Bridge	51	SJ 9541
Blyton	54	SK 8594
Boarhills	93	NO 5614
Boarhunt	11	SU 6008
Boarshead	13	TQ 5332
Boarstall	34	SP 6214
Boasley Cross	5	SX 5093
Boath	108	NH 5773
Boat of Garten	103	NH 9419
Bobbing	14	TQ 8865
Bobbington	41	SO 8090
Bobbingworth	22	TL 5305
Bocaddon	4	SX 1758
Bocking	22	TL 7623
Bocking Churchstreet	22	TL 7525
Boconnoc	4	SX 1460
Boddam (Grampn.)	105	NK 1342
Boddam (Shetld.)	113	HU 3915
Boddington	32	SO 8925
Bodedern	48	SH 3380
Bodelwyddan	49	SJ 0075
Bodenham (Here. and Worc.)	31	SO 5251
Bodenham (Wilts.)	10	SU 1626
Bodewryd	48	SH 3990
Bodfari	49	SJ 0970
Bodffordd	48	SH 4276
Bodfuan	48	SH 3237
Bodham Street	47	TG 1240
Bodiam	14	TQ 7826
Bodicote	33	SP 4537
Bodieve	4	SW 9973
Bodle Street Green	13	TQ 6514
Bodmin	4	SX 0767
Bodney	46	TL 8398
Bodorgan	48	SH 3867
Bogbrae	105	NK 0335
Bogend	82	NS 3932
Bogmoor	104	NJ 3562
Bogniebrae	104	NJ 5945
Bognor Regis	12	SZ 9399
Bograxie	105	NJ 7119
Bogside	84	NS 8353
Bog, The	40	SO 3597
Bogton	105	NJ 6751
Bogue	69	NX 6481
Bohortha	3	SW 8632
Bohuntine	96	NN 2882
Bojewyan	2	SW 3934
Bolam	72	NZ 1922
Bold Heath	50	SJ 5389
Boldon	72	NZ 3661
Boldon Colliery	72	NZ 3462
Boldre	11	SZ 3198
Boldron	72	NZ 0314
Bole	54	SK 7987
Bolehill	53	SK 2955
Boleside	86	NT 4933
Bolham Water	8	ST 1612
Bolingey	2	SW 7653
Bollington (Ches.)	51	SJ 7286
Bollington (Ches.)	51	SJ 9377
Bolney	13	TQ 2622
Bolnhurst	35	TL 0859
Bolshan	99	NO 6252
Bolsover	53	SK 4770
Bolsterstone	53	SK 2696
Bolstone	31	SO 5532
Boltby	66	SE 4886
Bolton (Cumbr.)	63	NY 6323
Bolton (Gtr Mches.)	58	SD 7108
Bolton (Humbs.)	67	SE 7752
Bolton (Lothian)	86	NT 5070
Bolton (Northum.)	79	NU 1013
Bolton Abbey	65	SE 0754
Bolton by Bowland	58	SD 7849
Boltonfellend	71	NY 4768
Boltongate	70	NY 2340
Bolton le Sands	64	SD 4867
Bolton-on-Swale	66	SE 2599
Bolton Percy	60	SE 5341
Bolton Upon Dearne	59	SE 4502
Bolventor	4	SX 1876
Bomere Heath	40	SJ 4719
Bonar-Bridge	108	NH 6191
Bonawe	89	NN 0133
Bonby	61	TA 0015
Boncath	26	SN 2038
Bonchester Bridge	78	NT 5811
Bondleigh	7	SS 6504
Bonehill	42	SK 1902
Bo'Ness	85	NS 9981
Bonhill	90	NS 3979
Boningale	41	SJ 8102
Bonjedward	78	NT 6523
Bonkle	84	NS 8356
Bonnington (Kent)	15	TR 0536
Bonnington (Lothian)	85	NT 1269
Bonnington Smiddy	93	NO 5739
Bonnybank	93	NO 3503
Bonnybridge	84	NS 8280
Bonnykelly	105	NJ 8553
Bonnyrigg	85	NT 3065
Bonnyton (Tays.)	93	NO 3338
Bonnyton (Tays.)	99	NO 6655
Bonsall	53	SK 2758
Bont	29	SO 3819
Bontddu	39	SH 6618
Bont-dolgadfan	39	SH 8800
Bontgoch Elerch	39	SN 6886
Bontnewydd (Gwyn.)	48	SH 4859
Bont Newydd (Gwyn.)	39	SH 7720
Bontuchel	49	SJ 0857
Bonvilston	28	ST 0674
Booker	20	SU 8491
Booley	41	SJ 5725
Boosbeck	73	NZ 6516
Boot	62	NY 1700
Boothby Graffoe	54	SK 9859
Boothby Pagnell	54	SK 9730
Boothstown	58	SD 7200
Bootle (Cumbr.)	62	SD 1088
Bootle (Mers.)	50	SJ 3394
Boquhan	90	NS 5387
Boraston	41	SO 6170
Borden	14	TQ 8863
Bordley	65	SD 9465
Boreham (Essex)	22	TL 7509
Boreham (Wilts.)	18	ST 8944
Boreham Street	13	TQ 6611
Borehamwood	21	TQ 1996
Boreland (Dumf. and Galwy.)	77	NY 1790
Boreraig	100	NG 1853
Borgie	111	NC 6759
Borgue (Dumf. and Galwy.)	69	NX 6248
Borgue (Highld.)	112	ND 1325
Borley	36	TL 8442
Bornesketaig	100	NG 3771
Borness	69	NX 6145
Boroughbridge	66	SE 3966
Borough Green	21	TQ 6057
Borras Head	50	SJ 3653
Borrowash	53	SK 4134
Borrowby	66	SE 4289
Borrowdale (Cumbr.)	62	NY 2514
Borth	38	SN 6089
Borthwickbrae	77	NT 4113
Borthwickshiels	77	NT 4315
Borve (Barra)	109	NF 6501
Borve (Island of Skye)	100	NG 4448
Borwick	64	SD 5273
Bosavern	2	SW 3730
Bosbury	31	SO 6943
Boscastle	4	SX 0990
Boscombe (Dorset)	10	SZ 1191
Boscombe (Wilts.)	11	SU 2038
Boscoppa	4	SX 0353
Bosham	12	SU 8004
Bosherston	24	SR 9694
Boskednan	2	SW 4434
Bosley	51	SJ 9165
Bossall	66	SE 7160
Bossiney	4	SX 0688
Bossingham	15	TR 1549
Bostock Green	51	SJ 6769
Boston	55	TF 3244
Boston Spa	59	SE 4245
Botallack	2	SW 3632
Botcheston	43	SK 4804
Botesdale	37	TM 0475
Bothal	79	NZ 2386
Bothamsall	53	SK 6773
Bothel	62	NY 1838
Bothenhampton	9	SY 4791
Bothwell	84	NS 7058
Botley (Bucks.)	34	SP 9802
Botley (Hants.)	11	SU 5112
Botley (Oxon.)	33	SP 4806
Botolphs	12	TQ 1909
Bottacks	102	NH 4860
Bottesford (Humbs.)	60	SE 9107
Bottesford (Leic.)	54	SK 8038
Bottisham	36	TL 5460
Bottomcraig	93	NO 3724
Bottoms	58	SD 9321
Botusfleming	4	SX 4061
Botwnnog	48	SH 2631
Boughrood	30	SO 1239
Boughspring	29	ST 5597
Boughton (Norf.)	46	TF 7002
Boughton (Northants.)	44	SP 7565
Boughton (Notts.)	53	SK 6768
Boughton Aluph	15	TR 0348
Boughton Green	14	TQ 7651
Boughton Lees	15	TR 0247
Boughton Malherbe	14	TQ 8849
Boughton Street	15	TR 0559
Boulby	73	NZ 7519
Bouldon	40	SO 5485
Boulmer	79	NU 2614
Boultham	54	SK 9568
Bourn	35	TL 3256
Bourne	45	TF 0920
Bournebridge	21	TQ 5194
Bourne End (Beds.)	34	SP 9644
Bourne End (Bucks.)	20	SU 8987
Bourne End (Herts.)	34	TL 0206
Bournemouth	10	SZ 0991
Bournes Green	32	SO 9104
Bournheath	41	SO 9474
Bournmoor	72	NZ 3051
Bournville	42	SP 0480
Bourton (Avon)	17	ST 3864
Bourton (Dorset)	17	ST 7630
Bourton (Oxon.)	18	SU 2387
Bourton (Salop)	41	SO 5996
Bourton on Dunsmore	43	SP 4370
Bourton-on-the-Hill	32	SP 1732
Bourton-on-the-Water	32	SP 1620
Bousd	94	NM 2563
Boveney	20	SU 9377
Boverton	28	SS 9868
Bovey Tracey	5	SX 8178
Bovingdon	35	TL 0103
Bovington Camp	10	SY 8389
Bow (Devon.)	7	SS 7201
Bowbank	63	NY 9423
Bow Brickhill	34	SP 9034
Bowburn	72	NZ 3038
Bowcombe	11	SZ 4786
Bowd	8	SY 1190
Bowden (Borders)	86	NT 5530
Bowden (Devon.)	5	SX 8448
Bowden Hill	18	ST 9367

Bowdon Brockworth

Place	Page	Grid ref.
Bowdon	51	SJ 7586
Bowerchalke	10	SU 0122
Bowermadden	112	ND 2364
Bowers Gifford	22	TQ 7588
Bowershall	92	NT 0991
Bowertower	112	ND 2362
Bowes	72	NY 9913
Bowhill	77	NT 4227
Bowley	31	SO 5352
Bowlhead Green	12	SU 9138
Bowling	82	NS 4473
Bowling Bank	50	SJ 3948
Bowling Green	32	SO 8151
Bowmanstead	62	SD 3096
Bowmore	80	NR 3159
Bowness-on-Solway	70	NY 2262
Bowness-on-Windermere	62	SD 4097
Bow of Fife	93	NO 3112
Bowsden	87	NT 9941
Bow Street	38	SN 6284
Bowthorpe	47	TG 1709
Box (Glos.)	32	SO 8600
Box (Wilts.)	18	ST 8268
Boxbush	32	SO 7412
Boxford (Berks.)	19	SU 4271
Boxford (Suff.)	36	TL 9640
Boxgrove	12	SU 9007
Boxley	14	TQ 7759
Boxted (Suff.)	32	TL 8250
Boxworth	35	TL 3464
Boyden Gate	15	TR 2264
Boylestone	52	SK 1835
Boyndie	104	NJ 6463
Boyndie Bay	104	NJ 6765
Boyndlie	105	NJ 9162
Boynton	67	TA 1368
Boysack	99	NO 6249
Boyton (Corn.)	4	SX 3192
Boyton (Suff.)	37	TM 3747
Boyton (Wilts.)	10	ST 9539
Bozeat	34	SP 9059
Braaid	56	SC 3176
Brabling Green	37	TM 2964
Brabourne	15	TR 1041
Brabourne Lees	15	TR 0840
Brabstermire	112	ND 3169
Bracadale	100	NG 3538
Braceborough	45	TF 0713
Bracebridge Heath	54	SK 9767
Braceby	54	TF 0135
Bracewell	58	SD 8648
Brackenfield	53	SK 3759
Brackletter	96	NN 1882
Brackley (Northants.)	33	SP 5837
Brackley (Strath.)	81	NR 7941
Bracknell	20	SU 8769
Braco	91	NN 8309
Bracobrae	104	NJ 5053
Bracon Ash	47	TM 1899
Bracora	95	NM 7192
Bracorina	95	NM 7292
Bradbourne	53	SK 2052
Bradbury	72	NZ 3128
Bradda	56	SC 1970
Bradden	34	SP 6448
Braddock	4	SX 1662
Bradenham	20	SU 8297
Bradenstoke	18	SU 0079
Bradfield (Berks.)	19	SU 6072
Bradfield (Essex)	23	TM 1430
Bradfield (Norf.)	47	TG 2633
Bradfield (S Yorks.)	53	SK 2692
Bradfield Combust	36	TL 8957
Bradfield Green	51	SJ 6859
Bradfield St. Clare	36	TL 9057
Bradfield St. George	36	TL 9059
Bradford (Devon.)	6	SS 4207
Bradford (Northum.)	87	NU 1532
Bradford (W Yorks.)	59	SE 1633
Bradford Abbas	9	ST 5814
Bradford Leigh	18	ST 8362
Bradford on Avon	18	ST 8260
Bradford-on-Tone	8	ST 1722
Bradford Peverell	9	SY 6592
Brading	11	SZ 6087
Bradley (Derby.)	53	SK 2145
Bradley (Hants.)	19	SU 6341
Bradley (Here. and Worc.)	32	SO 9860
Bradley (Humbs.)	61	TA 2406
Bradley (N Yorks.)	65	SE 0380
Bradley (Staffs.)	41	SJ 8717
Bradley Green	32	SO 9861
Bradley in the Moors	52	SK 0541
Bradmore	53	SK 5831
Bradninch	8	SS 9903
Bradnop	52	SK 0155
Bradpole	9	SY 4794
Bradshaw	58	SD 7312
Bradstone	4	SX 3880
Bradwell (Bucks.)	34	SP 8339
Bradwell (Derby.)	52	SK 1781
Bradwell (Essex)	22	TL 8023
Bradwell (Norf.)	47	TG 5003
Bradwell Green	51	SJ 7563
Bradwell Grove	33	SP 2308
Bradwell-on-Sea	23	TM 0006
Bradwell Waterside	23	TL 9907
Bradworthy	6	SS 3213
Brae (Highld.)	106	NG 8185
Brae (Highld.)	103	NH 6662
Brae (Shetld.)	113	HU 3567
Braedownie	98	NO 2875
Braefield	102	NH 4130
Braegrum	92	NO 0024
Braehead (Strath.)	84	NS 8134
Braehead (Strath.)	84	NS 9550
Braehead (Tays.)	99	NO 6852
Braehead (Wigtown.)	68	NX 4252
Braemore	112	ND 0630
Brae of Achnahaird	110	NB 9913
Braeside	82	NS 2375
Braeswick	113	HY 6037
Brafferton (Durham)	72	NZ 2921
Brafferton (N Yorks.)	66	SE 4370
Brafield-on-the-Green	34	SP 8158
Bragar	109	NB 2847
Bragbury End	35	TL 2621
Braidwood	84	NS 8448
Braigo	80	NR 2369
Brailes	33	SP 3139
Brailsford	53	SK 2541
Braintree	22	TL 7622
Braiseworth	37	TM 1371
Braishfield	11	SU 3725
Braithwaite	62	NY 2323
Braithwell	53	SK 5394
Bramber	12	TQ 1810
Bramcote	53	SK 5037
Bramdean	11	SU 6127
Bramerton	47	TG 2904
Bramfield (Herts.)	35	TL 2915
Bramfield (Suff.)	37	TM 4073
Bramford	37	TM 1246
Bramhall	51	SJ 8984
Bramham	59	SE 4242
Bramhope	59	SE 2443
Bramley (Hants.)	19	SU 6358
Bramley (Surrey)	12	TQ 0044
Bramley (S Yorks.)	53	SK 4892
Brampford Speke	8	SX 9298
Brampton (Cambs.)	45	TL 2170
Brampton (Cumbr.)	71	NY 5361
Brampton (Cumbr.)	63	NY 6723
Brampton (Lincs.)	54	SK 8479
Brampton (Norf.)	47	TG 2224
Brampton (Suff.)	47	TM 4381
Brampton (S Yorks.)	59	SE 4101
Brampton Abbotts	29	SO 6026
Brampton Ash	44	SP 7887
Brampton Bryan	40	SO 3672
Bramshall	52	SK 0633
Bramshaw	11	SU 2615
Bramshill	20	SU 7461
Bramshott	12	SU 8432
Branault	95	NM 5369
Brancaster	46	TF 7743
Brancepeth	72	NZ 2238
Branchill	103	NJ 0852
Branderburgh	104	NJ 2371
Brandesburton	61	TA 1147
Brandeston	37	TM 2460
Brandiston	47	TG 1321
Brandon (Durham)	72	NZ 2439
Brandon (Lincs.)	54	SK 9048
Brandon (Northum.)	79	NU 0417
Brandon (Suff.)	46	TL 7886
Brandon (Warw.)	43	SP 4076
Brandon Bank	46	TL 6289
Brandon Creek	46	TL 6091
Brandon Parva	47	TG 0708
Brandsby	66	SE 5872
Brands Hatch	21	TQ 5764
Brane	2	SW 4028
Bran End	22	TL 6525
Branscombe	8	SY 1988
Bransford	32	SO 7952
Bransgore	10	SZ 1897
Branston (Leic.)	44	SK 8029
Branston (Lincs.)	54	TF 0167
Branston (Staffs.)	42	SK 2221
Branstone	11	SZ 5583
Brant Broughton	54	SK 9154
Brantham	37	TM 1034
Branthwaite	62	NY 0525
Brantingham	61	SE 9429
Branton	79	NU 0416
Branxholme	77	NT 4611
Branxton	87	NT 8937
Brassington	53	SK 2354
Brasted	21	TQ 4755
Brasted Chart	21	TQ 4653
Bratoft	55	TF 4765
Brattleby	54	SK 9480
Bratton	18	ST 9152
Bratton Clovelly	5	SX 4691
Bratton Fleming	7	SS 6437
Bratton Seymour	17	ST 6729
Braughing	35	TL 3925
Braunston (Leic.)	44	SK 8306
Braunston (Northants.)	43	SP 5366
Braunstone	43	SK 5502
Braunton	6	SS 4836
Brawby	67	SE 7378
Brawl	111	NC 8066
Brawlbin	112	ND 0757
Bray	20	SU 9079
Braybrooke	44	SP 7684
Brayford	7	SS 6834
Bray Shop	4	SX 3374
Brayton	60	SE 6030
Brazacott	4	SX 2691
Breachwood Green	35	TL 1522
Breaclete	109	NB 1536
Breadsall	53	SK 3639
Breadstone	32	SO 7000
Breage	2	SW 6128
Breakish	101	NG 6723
Bream	29	SO 6005
Breamore	10	SU 1517
Brean	17	ST 2955
Brearton	66	SE 3260
Breasclete	109	NB 2135
Breaston	53	SK 4533
Brechfa	25	SN 5230
Brechin	99	NO 5960
Breckles	46	TL 9594
Breckrey	100	NG 5061
Brecon	28	SO 0428
Bredbury	51	SJ 9292
Brede	14	TQ 8218
Bredenbury	31	SO 6056
Bredfield	37	TM 2653
Bredgar	14	TQ 8860
Bredhurst	14	TQ 7962
Bredon	32	SO 9236
Bredon's Norton	32	SO 9339
Bredwardine	30	SO 3344
Breedon on the Hill	43	SK 4022
Breich	85	NS 9560
Breighton	60	SE 7033
Breinton	30	SO 4739
Bremhill	18	ST 9873
Brenchley	14	TQ 6741
Brendon	7	SS 7648
Brenish	109	NA 9926
Brent	21	TQ 2084
Brent Eleigh	36	TL 9447
Brentford	21	TQ 1778
Brent Knoll	17	ST 3350
Brent Pelham	35	TL 4330
Brentwood	22	TQ 5993
Brenzett	15	TR 0027
Brereton	42	SK 0516
Brereton Green	51	SJ 7764
Brereton Heath	51	SJ 8064
Bressingham	47	TM 0780
Bretby	43	SK 2923
Bretford	43	SP 4277
Bretforton	32	SP 0943
Bretherton	57	SD 4720
Brettenham (Norf.)	46	TL 9383
Brettenham (Suff.)	36	TL 9653
Bretton	50	SJ 3563
Brewham	17	ST 7136
Brewood	41	SJ 8808
Briantspuddle	10	SY 8193
Bricket Wood	35	TL 1301
Bricklehampton	32	SO 9842
Bride	56	NX 4501
Bridekirk	62	NY 1133
Bridell	26	SN 1742
Bridestowe	5	SX 5189
Brideswell	104	NJ 5739
Bridford	5	SX 8186
Bridge	15	TR 1854
Bridge End (Lincs.)	55	TF 1436
Bridgefoot	62	NY 0529
Bridge Green	35	TL 4636
Bridgemary	11	SU 5702
Bridgend (Dumf. and Galwy.)	77	NT 0708
Bridgend (Dumf. and Galwy.)	86	NT 5235
Bridgend (Fife.)	93	NO 3911
Bridgend (Grampn.)	104	NJ 3731
Bridgend (Islay)	80	NR 3362
Bridgend (Lothian)	85	NT 0475
Bridgend (Mid Glam.)	28	SS 9079
Bridgend (Strath.)	89	NR 8592
Bridgend (Strath.)	84	NS 6970
Bridgend (Tays.)	92	NO 1224
Bridgend (Tays.)	99	NO 5368
Bridgend of Lintrathen	98	NO 2854
Bridge of Alford	104	NJ 5617
Bridge of Allan	91	NS 7897
Bridge of Avon	104	NJ 1835
Bridge of Cally	98	NO 1351
Bridge of Canny	99	NO 6597
Bridge of Dee	69	NX 7360
Bridge of Don	105	NJ 9409
Bridge of Dye	99	NO 6585
Bridge of Earn	92	NO 1318
Bridge of Feugh	99	NO 7094
Bridge of Gairn	98	NO 3597
Bridge of Gaur	97	NN 5056
Bridge of Muchalls	99	NO 8991
Bridge of Orchy	90	NN 2939
Bridge of Weir	82	NS 3865
Bridgerule	6	SS 2803
Bridges	40	SO 3996
Bridge Sollers	30	SO 4142
Bridge Street	36	TL 8749
Bridgetown	16	SS 9233
Bridge Trafford	50	SJ 4471
Bridgeyate	29	ST 6873
Bridgham	46	TL 9686
Bridgnorth	41	SO 7193
Bridgtown	41	SJ 9808
Bridgwater	17	ST 3037
Bridlington	67	TA 1766
Bridport	9	SY 4692
Bridstow	29	SO 5824
Brierfield	58	SD 8436
Brierley (Glos.)	29	SO 6215
Brierley (Here. and Worc.)	30	SO 4956
Brierley (S Yorks.)	59	SE 4011
Brierley Hill	41	SO 9187
Brigg	61	TA 0007
Brigham (Cumbr.)	62	NY 0830
Brigham (Humbs.)	67	TA 0753
Brighouse	59	SE 1423
Brighstone	11	SZ 4282
Brightgate	53	SK 2659
Brighthampton	33	SP 3803
Brightling	13	TQ 6821
Brightlingsea	23	TM 0816
Brighton (Corn.)	3	SW 9054
Brighton (E Susx)	13	TQ 3105
Brightons	84	NS 9277
Brightwalton	19	SU 4278
Brightwell (Oxon.)	19	SU 5790
Brightwell (Suff.)	37	TM 2543
Brightwell Baldwin	19	SU 6594
Brignall	72	NZ 0712
Brig o'Turk	90	NN 5306
Brigsley	61	TA 2501
Brigsteer	63	SD 4889
Brigstock	44	SP 9485
Brill	34	SP 6513
Brilley	30	SO 2549
Brimfield	40	SO 5267
Brimington	53	SK 4073
Brimpsfield	32	SO 9312
Brimpton	19	SU 5564
Brind	60	SE 7430
Brindle	57	SD 5924
Brindley Ford	51	SJ 8754
Brindley Heath	41	SJ 9914
Brineton	41	SJ 8013
Bringhurst	44	SP 8492
Brington	45	TL 0875
Brinningham	46	TG 0334
Brinkhill	55	TF 3773
Brinkley	36	TL 6254
Brinklow	43	SP 4379
Brinkworth	18	SU 0184
Brinscall	58	SD 6321
Brinsley	53	SK 4548
Brinsop	30	SO 4344
Brinsworth	53	SK 4190
Brinton	46	TG 0335
Brinyan	113	HY 4327
Brisley	46	TF 9421
Brislington	29	ST 6170
Bristol	29	ST 5872
Briston	47	TG 0632
Britannia	58	SD 8821
Britford	10	SU 1528
British Legion Village	14	TQ 7257
Briton Ferry	28	SS 7394
Britwell Salome	19	SU 6792
Brixham	5	SX 9255
Brixton	5	SX 5452
Brixton Deverill	10	ST 8638
Brixworth	44	SP 7470
Brize Norton	33	SP 2907
Broad Blunsdon	18	SU 1490
Broadbottom	51	SJ 9993
Broadbridge	12	SU 8105
Broadbridge Heath	12	TQ 1431
Broad Campden	32	SP 1537
Broad Chalke	10	SU 0325
Broadclyst	8	SX 9897
Broadford	100	NG 6423
Broad Green	32	SO 7656
Broadhaugh	77	NT 4509
Broad Haven	24	SM 8613
Broadheath (Gtr Mches.)	51	SJ 7689
Broadheath (Here. and Worc.)	31	SO 6665
Broadheath (Here. and Worc.)	32	SO 8156
Broadhembury	8	ST 1004
Broadhempston	5	SX 8066
Broad Hill (Cambs.)	36	TL 5976
Broad Hinton	18	SU 1076
Broad Laying	19	SU 4362
Broadley (Grampn.)	104	NJ 4161
Broadley (Gtr Mches.)	58	SD 8716
Broadley Common	35	TL 4207
Broad Marston	32	SP 1346
Broadmayne	9	SY 7286
Broadmeadows	86	NT 4130
Broadmere	19	SU 6247
Broad Oak (Cumbr.)	62	SD 1194
Broadoak (Dorset)	9	SY 4496
Broadoak (E Susx)	13	TQ 6022
Broad Oak (E Susx)	14	TQ 8320
Broad Oak (Here. and Worc.)	29	SO 4721
Broadoak (Kent)	15	TR 1661
Broadrashes	104	NJ 4354
Broadstairs	15	TR 3967
Broadstone (Dorset)	10	SZ 0095
Broadstone (Salop)	40	SO 5389
Broad Street	14	TQ 8356
Broad Town	18	SU 0977
Broadwas	32	SO 7555
Broadwater	12	TQ 1504
Broadway (Here. and Worc.)	32	SP 0937
Broadway (Somer.)	8	ST 3215
Broadwell (Glos.)	33	SP 2027
Broadwell (Oxon.)	33	SP 2503
Broadwell (Warw.)	33	SP 4565
Broadwell Lane End	29	SO 5811
Broadwey	9	SY 6683
Broadwindsor	9	ST 4302
Broadwood-Kelly	6	SS 6105
Broadwoodwidger	4	SX 4089
Brockbridge	11	SU 6018
Brockdam	79	NU 1624
Brockdish	37	TM 2179
Brockenhurst	11	SU 2902
Brocketsbrae	84	NS 8239
Brockford Street	37	TM 1166
Brockhall	34	SP 6362
Brockham	21	TQ 2049
Brockhampton	31	SO 5932
Brockholes	59	SE 1411
Brocklesby	61	TA 1311
Brockley	29	ST 4666
Brockley Green	36	TL 8254
Brockton (Salop)	40	SJ 3104
Brockton (Salop)	41	SJ 7103
Brockton (Salop)	40	SO 3285
Brockton (Salop)	41	SO 5793
Brockweir	29	SO 5301
Brockworth	32	SO 8916

Brocton Butterwick

Brocton	41	SJ 9619
Brodick	81	NS 0136
Brodsworth	60	SE 5007
Brogborough	34	SP 9638
Brokenborough	18	ST 9189
Broken Cross (Ches.)	51	SJ 6872
Broken Cross (Ches.)	51	SJ 8973
Bromborough	50	SJ 3582
Brome	37	TM 1376
Brome Street	37	TM 1576
Bromeswell	37	TM 3050
Bromfield (Cumbr.)	70	NY 1746
Bromfield (Salop)	40	SO 4876
Bromham (Beds.)	34	TL 0051
Bromham (Wilts.)	18	ST 9665
Bromley (Gtr London)	21	TQ 4069
Bromley Common	21	TQ 4266
Brompton (Kent)	14	TQ 7668
Brompton (N Yorks.)	66	SE 3796
Brompton (N Yorks.)	67	SE 9482
Brompton-on-Swale	65	SE 2199
Brompton Ralph	16	ST 0832
Brompton Regis	16	SS 9531
Bromsash	29	SO 6424
Bromsgrove	41	SO 9570
Bromstead Heath	41	SJ 7917
Bromyard	31	SO 6554
Bromyard Downs	31	SO 6655
Bronaber	49	SH 7131
Bronant	27	SN 6467
Bronington	50	SJ 4839
Bronllys	30	SO 1435
Bronygarth	50	SJ 2636
Brook (Hants.)	11	SU 2713
Brook (Hants.)	11	SU 3428
Brook (I. of W.)	11	SZ 3983
Brook (Kent)	15	TR 0644
Brook (Surrey)	12	SU 9338
Brooke (Leic.)	44	SK 8405
Brooke (Norf.)	47	TM 2999
Brookfield	82	NS 4164
Brookhouse	64	SD 5464
Brookhouse Green	51	SJ 8061
Brookland	15	TQ 9825
Brookmans Park	35	TL 2404
Brooks	40	SO 1499
Brook Street	21	TQ 5792
Brookthorpe	32	SO 8312
Brookwood	20	SU 9557
Broom (Beds.)	35	TL 1743
Broom (Warw.)	32	SP 0953
Broome (Here. and Worc.)	41	SO 9078
Broome (Norf.)	47	TM 3591
Broome (Salop)	40	SO 3981
Broomer's Corner	12	TQ 1221
Broomfield (Essex)	22	TL 7009
Broomfield (Kent)	14	TQ 8452
Broomfield (Kent)	15	TR 2066
Broomfield (Somer.)	16	ST 2231
Broomfleet	60	SE 8727
Broom Hill (Dorset)	10	SU 0302
Broomhill (Northum.)	79	NU 2400
Brora	108	NC 9003
Broseley	41	SJ 6701
Brothertoft	55	TF 2746
Brotherton	60	SE 4825
Brotton	73	NZ 6819
Broubster	112	ND 0360
Brough (Cumbr.)	63	NY 7914
Brough (Derby.)	52	SK 1882
Brough (Highld.)	112	ND 2273
Brough (Humbs.)	61	SE 9326
Brough (Notts.)	54	SK 8358
Broughall	51	SJ 5641
Brough Sowerby	63	NY 7912
Broughton (Borders)	85	NT 1136
Broughton (Bucks.)	34	SP 8940
Broughton (Cambs.)	45	TL 2878
Broughton (Clwyd)	50	SJ 3363
Broughton (Cumbr.)	62	NY 0731
Broughton (Gtr Mches.)	58	SD 8201
Broughton (Hants.)	11	SU 3132
Broughton (Humbs.)	61	SE 9508
Broughton (Lancs.)	57	SD 5234
Broughton (Mid Glam.)	28	SS 9271
Broughton (Northants.)	44	SP 8375
Broughton (N Yorks.)	65	SD 9451
Broughton (N Yorks.)	67	SE 7673
Broughton (Oxon.)	33	SP 4238
Broughton Astley	43	SP 5292
Broughton Gifford	18	ST 8763
Broughton Hackett	32	SO 9254
Broughton in Furness	62	SD 2087
Broughton Mills	62	SD 2290
Broughton Moor	62	NY 0533
Broughton Poggs	33	SP 2303
Broughtown	113	HY 6540
Broughty Ferry	93	NO 4630
Brown Candover	11	SU 5839
Brown Edge	51	SJ 9053
Brownhill (Grampn.)	105	NJ 8640
Brownhills (W Mids)	42	SK 0405
Brownlow Heath	51	SJ 8360
Brownmuir	99	NO 7477
Brownston	5	SX 6952
Broxbourne	35	TL 3707
Broxburn (Lothian)	85	NT 0872
Broxburn (Lothian)	86	NT 6977
Broxted	22	TL 5727
Broxwood	30	SO 3654
Bruan	112	ND 3039
Brue	109	NB 3349
Bruera	50	SJ 4360
Bruichladdich	80	NR 2661
Bruisyard	37	TM 3266
Bruisyard Street	37	TM 3365
Brund	52	SK 1061
Brundall	47	TG 3208
Brundish	37	TM 2669
Brundish Street	37	TM 2671
Bruntingthorpe	43	SP 6090
Brunton (Fife.)	93	NO 3220
Brunton (Northum.)	79	NU 2024
Brushford	16	SS 9225
Brushford Barton	7	SS 6707
Bruton	17	ST 6834
Bryanston	10	ST 8706
Brydekirk	70	NY 1870
Brymbo	50	SJ 2953
Bryn (Gtr Mches.)	57	SD 5600
Bryn (Salop)	40	SO 2985
Bryn (W Glam.)	28	SS 8192
Brynamman	25	SN 7114
Brynberian	26	SN 1035
Bryncae	28	SS 9983
Bryncethin	28	SS 9184
Bryncir	48	SH 4641
Bryn-coch	25	SS 7499
Bryncroes	48	SH 2231
Bryncrug	38	SH 6003
Bryneglwys	50	SJ 1447
Brynford	50	SJ 1774
Bryn Gates	57	SD 5901
Bryngwran	48	SH 3477
Bryngwyn (Gwent)	29	SO 3909
Bryngwyn (Powys)	30	SO 1849
Bryn-henllan	24	SN 0139
Brynhoffnant	26	SN 3351
Brynmawr	28	SO 1911
Brynmenyn	28	SS 9084
Brynna	28	SS 9883
Brynrefail	48	SH 4786
Brynsadler	28	ST 0380
Brynsiencyn	48	SH 4867
Brynteg	48	SH 4982
Bryn-y-maen (Clwyd)	49	SH 8376
Bualintur	100	NG 4020
Bubbenhall	43	SP 3672
Bubwith	60	SE 7136
Buccleuch	77	NT 3214
Buchanty	91	NN 9328
Buchlyvie	90	NS 5793
Buckabank	70	NY 3749
Buckden (Cambs.)	45	TL 1967
Buckden (N Yorks.)	65	SD 9477
Buckenham	47	TG 3505
Buckerell	8	ST 1200
Buckfast	5	SX 7367
Buckfastleigh	5	SX 7466
Buckhaven	93	NT 3598
Buckholm	86	NT 4838
Buckhorn Weston	17	ST 7524
Buckhurst Hill	21	TQ 4193
Buckie	104	NJ 4265
Buckingham	34	SP 6933
Buckland (Bucks.)	34	SP 8812
Buckland (Devon.)	5	SX 6743
Buckland (Glos.)	32	SP 0836
Buckland (Herts.)	35	TL 3533
Buckland (Kent)	15	TR 2942
Buckland (Oxon.)	19	SU 3497
Buckland (Surrey)	21	TQ 2250
Buckland Brewer	6	SS 4120
Buckland Common	34	SP 9306
Buckland Dinham	18	ST 7550
Buckland Filleigh	6	SS 4609
Buckland in the Moor	5	SX 7273
Buckland Monachorum	5	SX 4868
Buckland Newton	9	ST 6905
Buckland St. Mary	8	ST 2713
Buckland-Tout-Saints	5	SX 7546
Bucklebury	19	SU 5570
Bucklerheads	93	NO 4636
Bucklers Hard	11	SZ 4099
Bucklesham	37	TM 2442
Buckley	50	SJ 2764
Buckminster	44	SK 8722
Bucknall (Lincs.)	55	TF 1668
Bucknall (Staffs.)	51	SJ 9147
Bucknell (Oxon.)	33	SP 5525
Bucknell (Salop)	40	SO 3574
Bucksburn	105	NJ 8909
Buck's Cross	6	SS 3422
Bucks Green	12	TQ 0732
Bucks Hill	35	TL 0500
Bucks Horn Oak	12	SU 8142
Buck's Mills	6	SS 3523
Buckton (Here. and Worc.)	40	SO 3873
Buckton (Northum.)	87	NU 0838
Buckworth	55	TL 1476
Budbrooke	33	SP 2565
Budby	53	SK 6169
Bude	6	SS 2006
Budlake	8	SS 9700
Budle	87	NU 1534
Budleigh Salterton	8	SY 0682
Budock Water	2	SW 7832
Buerton	51	SJ 6843
Bugbrooke	34	SP 6757
Bugle	4	SX 0158
Bugthorpe	67	SE 7757
Builth Road	30	SO 0253
Builth Wells	30	SO 0351
Bulby	45	TF 0526
Buldoo	112	NC 9967
Bulford	18	SU 1643
Bulkeley	50	SJ 5254
Bulkington (Warw.)	43	SP 3986
Bulkington (Wilts.)	18	ST 9458
Bulkworthy	6	SS 3914
Bulley	32	SO 7519
Bullwood	82	NS 1674
Bulmer (Essex)	36	TL 8440
Bulmer (N Yorks.)	66	SE 6967
Bulmer Tye	36	TL 8438
Bulphan	22	TQ 6385
Bulverhythe	14	TQ 7809
Bulwell	53	SK 5345
Bulwick	44	SP 9694
Bumble's Green	35	TL 4005
Bunacaimb	95	NM 6588
Bunbury	51	SJ 5658
Bunchrew	102	NH 6145
Buncton	12	TQ 1413
Bundalloch	101	NG 8927
Bunessan	88	NM 3821
Bungay	47	TM 3389
Bunnahabhainn	88	NR 4173
Bunny	43	SK 5829
Buntingford	35	TL 3629
Bunwell	47	TM 1293
Bunwell Street	47	TM 1194
Burbage (Derby.)	52	SK 0472
Burbage (Leic.)	43	SP 4492
Burbage (Wilts.)	18	SU 2261
Burcombe (Wilts.)	10	SU 0630
Burcot	19	SU 5595
Bures	36	TL 9034
Burford	33	SP 2512
Burgess Hill	13	TQ 3118
Burgh (Suff.)	37	TM 2251
Burgh by Sands	70	NY 3259
Burgh Castle	47	TG 4805
Burghclere	19	SU 4660
Burghead	103	NJ 1168
Burghfield	19	SU 6668
Burghfield Common	19	SU 6466
Burghfield Hill	19	SU 6567
Burgh Heath	21	TQ 2458
Burghill	30	SO 4744
Burgh Le Marsh	55	TF 5065
Burgh Muir	105	NJ 7622
Burgh next Aylsham	47	TG 2125
Burgh on Bain	55	TF 2186
Burgh St. Margaret	47	TG 4413
Burgh St. Peter	47	TM 4693
Burghwallis	60	SE 5312
Burham	14	TQ 7262
Buriton	12	SU 7319
Burland	51	SJ 6153
Burlawn	4	SW 9970
Burleigh	20	SU 9069
Burlescombe	8	ST 0716
Burleston	9	SY 7794
Burley (Hants.)	11	SU 2103
Burley (Leic.)	44	SK 8810
Burleydam	51	SJ 6042
Burley in Wharfedale	59	SE 1646
Burley Street	11	SU 2004
Burlingjobb	30	SO 2558
Burlton	40	SJ 4526
Burmarsh	15	TR 1032
Burmington	33	SP 2637
Burn	60	SE 5928
Burnage	51	SJ 8692
Burnaston	53	SK 2832
Burnby	60	SE 8346
Burneside	63	SD 5095
Burneston	66	SE 3084
Burnett	17	ST 6665
Burnfoot (Borders)	77	NT 4113
Burnfoot (Borders)	78	NT 5116
Burnfoot (Tays.)	91	NN 9804
Burnham (Berks. Bucks.)	20	SU 9382
Burnham (Humbs.)	61	TA 0517
Burnham Beeches	20	SU 9585
Burnham Deepdale	46	TF 8044
Burnham Green	35	TL 2616
Burnham Market	46	TF 8342
Burnham Norton	46	TF 8243
Burnham-on-Crouch	23	TQ 9496
Burnham-on-Sea	17	ST 3049
Burnham Overy	46	TF 8442
Burnham Thorpe	46	TF 8541
Burnhaven	105	NK 1244
Burnhead	76	NX 8595
Burnhervie	105	NJ 7319
Burnhill Green	41	SJ 7800
Burnhope	72	NZ 1948
Burnhouse	82	NS 3850
Burniston	67	TA 0193
Burnley	58	SD 8332
Burnmouth	87	NT 9560
Burnopfield	72	NZ 1756
Burnside (Fife.)	92	NO 1607
Burnside (Lothian)	85	NT 0971
Burnside (Tays.)	99	NO 5050
Burnside of Duntrune	93	NO 4434
Burntisland	85	NT 2385
Burntwood	42	SK 0609
Burnt Yates	66	SE 2461
Burpham (Surrey)	20	TQ 0151
Burpham (W. Susx.)	12	TQ 0408
Burradon (Northum.)	79	NT 9806
Burradon (Tyne and Wear)	79	NZ 2772
Burra Firth (Unst.)	113	HP 6113
Burravoe (Shetld.)	113	HU 3666
Burravoe (Yell.)	113	HU 5280
Burrelton	92	NO 1936
Burridge	11	SU 5110
Burrill	66	SE 2387
Burringham	60	SE 8309
Burrington (Avon)	17	ST 4759
Burrington (Devon.)	6	SS 6316
Burrington (Here. and Worc.)	40	SO 4472
Burrough Green	36	TL 6355
Burrough on the Hill	44	SK 7510
Burrow Bridge	17	ST 3530
Burrowhill	20	SU 9763
Burry Port	25	SN 4400
Burscough	57	SD 4310
Burscough Bridge	57	SD 4411
Bursea	60	SE 8033
Burshill	61	TA 0948
Bursledon	11	SU 4809
Burslem	51	SJ 8749
Burstall	37	TM 0944
Burstock	9	ST 4202
Burston (Norf.)	47	TM 1383
Burston (Staffs.)	41	SJ 9330
Burstow	13	TQ 3141
Burstwick	61	TA 2228
Burtersett	65	SD 8989
Burton (Ches.)	50	SJ 3174
Burton (Ches.)	50	SJ 5063
Burton (Cumbr.)	64	SD 5276
Burton (Dorset)	10	SZ 1794
Burton (Dyfed)	24	SM 9805
Burton (Lincs.)	54	SK 9574
Burton (Northum.)	87	NU 1732
Burton (Somer.)	16	ST 1944
Burton (Wilts.)	18	ST 8179
Burton Agnes	67	TA 1063
Burton Bradstock	9	SY 4889
Burton Coggles	44	SK 9725
Burton Fleming	67	TA 0872
Burton Green (Clwyd)	50	SJ 3458
Burton Green (Warw.)	43	SP 2675
Burton Hastings	43	SP 4189
Burton in Lonsdale	64	SD 6572
Burton Joyce	53	SK 6443
Burton Latimer	44	SP 9074
Burton Lazars	44	SK 7716
Burton Leonard	66	SE 3263
Burton on the Wolds	43	SK 5821
Burton Overy	43	SP 6798
Burton Pedwardine	55	TF 1142
Burton Pidsea	61	TA 2431
Burton Salmon	60	SE 4827
Burton upon Stather	60	SE 8617
Burton upon Trent	42	SK 2423
Burtonwood	51	SJ 5692
Burwardsley	50	SJ 5156
Burwarton	41	SO 6185
Burwash	13	TQ 6724
Burwash Common	13	TQ 6423
Burwell (Cambs.)	36	TL 5866
Burwell (Lincs.)	55	TF 3579
Burwick (Shetld.)	113	HU 3940
Burwick (South Ronaldsay)	113	ND 4384
Bury (Cambs.)	45	TL 2883
Bury (Gtr. Mches.)	58	SD 8010
Bury (Somer.)	16	SS 9427
Bury (W. Susx.)	12	TQ 0113
Bury Green	35	TL 4521
Bury St. Edmunds	36	TL 8564
Burythorpe	67	SE 7964
Busbridge	12	SU 9842
Busby (Strath.)	84	NS 5856
Busby (Tays.)	92	NO 0327
Buscot	18	SU 2297
Bushbury	41	SJ 9202
Bushey	20	TQ 1395
Bushey Heath	21	TQ 1594
Bush Green	47	TM 2187
Bushley	32	SO 8734
Bushton	18	SU 0677
Butcher's Pasture	22	TL 6024
Butcombe	17	ST 5161
Butleigh	17	ST 5233
Butleigh Wootton	17	ST 5034
Butlers Marston	33	SP 3150
Butley	37	TM 3651
Butsfield	72	NZ 1044
Buttercrambe	66	SE 7358
Butterknowle	72	NZ 1025
Butterleigh	8	SS 9708
Buttermere (Cumbr.)	62	NY 1717
Buttermere (Wilts.)	19	SU 3361
Buttershaw	59	SE 1329
Butterstone	98	NO 0646
Butterton	52	SK 0756
Butterwick (Humbs.)	60	SE 8305
Butterwick (Lincs.)	55	TF 3845
Butterwick (N. Yorks.)	66	SE 7377
Butterwick (N. Yorks.)	67	SE 9971

Butt Green Cawthorne

Butt Green	51	SJ 6651
Buttington	40	SJ 2408
Buttock's Booth	34	SP 7864
Buttonoak	41	SO 7578
Buxhall	36	TM 0057
Buxted	13	TQ 4923
Buxton (Derby.)	52	SK 0673
Buxton (Norf.)	47	TG 2222
Buxton Heath	47	TG 1821
Bwlch	28	SO 1422
Bwlchgwyn	50	SJ 2653
Bwlchllan	27	SN 5758
Bwlchtocyn	38	SH 3126
Bwlch-y-cibau	40	SJ 1717
Bwlch-y-ffridd	39	SO 0695
Bwlch-y-groes (Dyfed)	26	SN 2436
Bwlch-y-sarnau	27	SO 0274
Byers Green	72	NZ 2234
Byfield	33	SP 5153
Byfleet	20	TQ 0461
Byford	30	SO 3943
Bygrave	35	TL 2636
Byker	72	NZ 2763
Bylchau	49	SH 9762
Byley	51	SJ 7269
Bythorn	55	TL 0575
Byton	30	SO 3664
Byworth	12	SU 9921

C

Cabourne	61	TA 1301
Cabrach (Grampn.)	104	NJ 3826
Cadbury	8	SS 9105
Cadder	84	NS 6172
Caddington	35	TL 0619
Caddonfoot	86	NT 4534
Cadeby (Leic.)	43	SK 4202
Cadeby (S Yorks.)	60	SE 5100
Cadeleigh	8	SS 9107
Cade Street	13	TQ 6021
Cadgwith	2	SW 7214
Cadham	93	NO 2701
Cadishead	51	SJ 7091
Cadle	25	SS 6297
Cadley	18	SU 2066
Cadmore End	20	SU 7892
Cadnam	11	SU 2913
Cadney	61	TA 0103
Cadole	50	SJ 2062
Caeathro	48	SH 5061
Caehopkin	28	SN 8212
Caeo	27	SN 6739
Caerau (Mid Glam.)	28	SS 8594
Caerau (S Glam.)	28	ST 1375
Caerdeon	39	SH 6418
Caergeiliog	48	SH 3178
Caergwrle	50	SJ 3057
Caerleon	29	ST 3390
Caernarfon	48	SH 4862
Caerphilly	28	ST 1587
Caersws	39	SO 0392
Caerwent	29	ST 4790
Caerwys	50	SJ 1272
Caethle	38	SN 6099
Cairnbaan	89	NR 8390
Cairnbrogie	105	NJ 8527
Cairncross	87	NT 8963
Cairndow	89	NN 1810
Cairneyhill	85	NT 0486
Cairngaan	68	NX 1232
Cairngarroch (Dumf. and Galwy.)	68	NX 0649
Cairnhill (Grampn.)	105	NJ 6732
Cairnie	104	NJ 4945
Cairnorrie	105	NJ 8640
Cairnryan	68	NX 0668
Caister-on-Sea	47	TG 5212
Caistor	61	TA 1101
Caistor St. Edmund	47	TG 2303
Caistron	79	NT 9901
Calbost	100	NB 4117
Calbourne	11	SZ 4286
Calcot	19	SU 6672
Caldbeck	62	NY 3239
Caldbergh	66	SE 0984
Caldecote (Cambs.)	45	TL 1488
Caldecote (Cambs.)	35	TL 3456
Caldecote (Herts.)	35	TL 2338
Caldecott (Leic.)	44	SP 8693
Caldecott (Northants.)	44	SP 9968
Calderbank	84	NS 7662
Calder Bridge	62	NY 0405
Calderbrook	58	SD 9418
Caldercruix	84	NS 8167
Calder Mains	112	ND 0959
Caldermill	84	NS 6641
Calder Vale	57	SD 5345
Caldicot	29	ST 4888
Caldwell	72	NZ 1613
Caldy	50	SJ 2285
Caledrhydiau	26	SN 4753
Calgary	94	NM 3751
Califer	103	NJ 0857
California (Central)	84	NS 9076
California (Norf.)	47	TG 5114
Calke	43	SK 3722
Callaly	79	NU 0509
Callander	91	NN 6208
Callanish	109	NB 2133
Callestick	2	SW 7750
Calligarry	95	NG 6203
Callington	4	SX 3669
Callow	30	SO 4934
Callow End	32	SO 8349
Callow Hill (Here. and Worc.)	41	SO 7473
Callow Hill (Wilts.)	18	SU 0385
Callows Grave	31	SO 5966
Calmore	11	SU 3314
Calmsden	32	SP 0408
Calne	18	ST 9971
Calow	53	SK 4071
Calshot	11	SU 4701
Calstock	4	SX 4368
Calthorpe	47	TG 1831
Calthwaite	71	NY 4640
Calton (N Yorks.)	65	SD 9059
Calton (Staffs.)	52	SK 1050
Calveley	51	SJ 5958
Calver	53	SK 2374
Calverhall	51	SJ 6037
Calver Hill	30	SO 3748
Calverleigh	8	SS 9214
Calverley	59	SE 2036
Calvert	34	SP 6824
Calverton (Bucks.)	34	SP 7938
Calverton (Notts.)	53	SK 6149
Calvine	97	NN 8066
Cam	18	ST 7599
Camastianavaig	100	NG 5039
Camber	15	TQ 9619
Camberley	20	SU 8760
Camberwell	21	TQ 3376
Camblesforth	60	SE 6425
Cambo	79	NZ 0285
Cambois	79	NZ 3083
Camborne	2	SW 6440
Cambridge	35	TL 4658
Cambus	91	NS 8593
Cambusbarron	91	NS 7792
Cambuskenneth	91	NS 8094
Cambuslang	84	NS 6459
Camden	21	TQ 2784
Camelford	4	SX 1083
Camelon	84	NS 8680
Camelsdale	12	SU 8932
Camerory	103	NJ 0231
Camerton (Avon)	17	ST 6857
Camerton (Cumbr.)	62	NY 0330
Camghouran	97	NN 5556
Cammachmore	99	NO 9295
Cammeringham	54	SK 9482
Campbelltown or Ardersier	103	NH 7854
Campbeltown	81	NR 7120
Campmuir	92	NO 2137
Campsall	60	SE 5313
Campsea Ashe	37	TM 3356
Camp, The	32	SO 9308
Campton	35	TL 1238
Camrose	24	SM 9220
Camserney	97	NN 8149
Camusteel	101	NG 7042
Camusterrach	101	NG 7141
Camusvrachan	97	NN 6248
Canada	11	SU 2817
Candlesby	55	TF 4567
Cane End	19	SU 6779
Canewdon	23	TQ 8994
Canford Bottom	10	SU 0300
Canford Cliffs	10	SZ 0689
Canisbay	112	ND 3472
Cann Common	10	ST 8920
Cannich	102	NH 3331
Cannington	17	ST 2539
Cannock	41	SJ 9710
Cannock Wood	42	SK 0412
Canonbie	70	NY 3976
Canon Bridge	30	SO 4341
Canon Frome	31	SO 6543
Canon Pyon	30	SO 4549
Canons Ashby	33	SP 5750
Canonstown	2	SW 5335
Canterbury	15	TR 1557
Cantley (Norf.)	47	TG 3704
Cantley (S Yorks.)	60	SE 6202
Cantlop	40	SJ 5205
Canton	28	ST 1577
Cantraydoune	103	NH 7946
Cantraywood	103	NH 7748
Cantsfield	65	SD 6172
Canwick	54	SK 9869
Canworthy Water	4	SX 2291
Caoles	94	NM 0848
Capel	12	TQ 1740
Capel Bangor	39	SN 6580
Capel Betws Lleucu	27	SN 6058
Capel Carmel	38	SH 1628
Capel Coch	48	SH 4582
Capel Curig	49	SH 7258
Capel Cynon	26	SN 3849
Capel Dewi	26	SN 4542
Capel Garmon	49	SH 8155
Capel Gywn (Dyfed)	25	SN 4622
Capel Gwyn (Gwyn.)	48	SH 3575
Capel Gwynfe	25	SN 7222
Capel Hendre	25	SN 5911
Capel Isaac	25	SN 5927
Capel Iwan	26	SN 2836
Capel le Ferne	15	TR 2439
Capel St. Mary	37	TM 0838
Capel-y-ffin	30	SO 2531
Capenhurst	50	SJ 3673
Capernwray	64	SD 5372
Capheaton	79	NZ 0380
Cappercleuch	77	NT 2423
Capstone	14	TQ 7865
Capton	5	SX 8353
Caputh	92	NO 0940
Carbis Bay	2	SW 5339
Carbost (Island of Skye)	100	NG 3731
Carbost (Island of Skye)	100	NG 4248
Carbrooke	46	TF 9402
Carburton	53	SK 6173
Carcary	99	NO 6455
Carclew	2	SW 7838
Car Colston	54	SK 7142
Carcroft	60	SE 5409
Cardenden	92	NT 2195
Cardeston	40	SJ 3912
Cardiff	28	ST 1877
Cardigan	26	SN 1846
Cardington (Beds.)	35	TL 0847
Cardington (Salop)	40	SO 5095
Cardinham	4	SX 1268
Cardow	104	NJ 1942
Cardrona	85	NT 3038
Cardross (Strath.)	82	NS 3477
Cardurnock	70	NY 1758
Careby	44	TF 0216
Careston	99	NO 5260
Carew	24	SN 0403
Carew Cheriton	24	SN 0402
Carew Newton	24	SN 0404
Carey	31	SO 5631
Carfrae	86	NT 5769
Cargen	70	NX 9672
Cargenbridge	69	NX 9474
Cargill	92	NO 1536
Cargo	70	NY 3659
Cargreen	4	SX 4262
Carham	87	NT 7938
Carhampton	16	ST 0042
Carharrack	2	SW 7241
Carie (Tays.)	97	NN 6157
Carie (Tays.)	90	NN 6437
Carinish	109	NF 8159
Carisbrooke	11	SZ 4888
Cark	64	SD 3676
Carlby	45	TF 0414
Carlecotes	59	SE 1703
Carleton (Cumbr.)	70	NY 4253
Carleton (Lancs.)	57	SD 3339
Carleton (N Yorks.)	58	SD 9749
Carleton Forehoe	47	TG 0805
Carleton Rode	47	TM 1192
Carlisle	70	NY 3955
Carlops	85	NT 1656
Carloway	109	NB 2042
Carlton (Beds.)	34	SP 9555
Carlton (Cambs.)	36	TL 6453
Carlton (Cleve.)	72	NZ 3921
Carlton (Leic.)	43	SK 3905
Carlton (Notts.)	53	SK 6141
Carlton (N Yorks.)	66	NZ 5004
Carlton (N Yorks.)	65	SE 0684
Carlton (N Yorks.)	66	SE 6086
Carlton (N Yorks.)	60	SE 6423
Carlton (Suff.)	37	TM 3864
Carlton (S Yorks.)	59	SE 3610
Carlton (W Yorks.)	59	SE 3327
Carlton Colville	47	TM 5190
Carlton Curlieu	43	SP 6997
Carlton Husthwaite	66	SE 4976
Carlton in Lindrick	53	SK 5984
Carlton-le-Moorland	54	SK 9058
Carlton Miniott	66	SE 3980
Carlton-on-Trent	54	SK 7963
Carlton Scroop	54	SK 9445
Carluke	84	NS 8450
Carmacoup	76	NS 7927
Carmarthen	25	SN 4120
Carmel (Clwyd)	50	SJ 1676
Carmel (Dyfed)	25	SN 5816
Carmel (Gwyn.)	48	SH 3882
Carmel (Gwyn.)	48	SH 4954
Carmunnock	84	NS 5957
Carmyle	84	NS 6461
Carmyllie	99	NO 5542
Carnaby	67	TA 1465
Carnach (Harris)	109	NG 2297
Carnbee	93	NO 5306
Carnbo	92	NO 0503
Carne	3	SW 9138
Carnell	82	NS 4632
Carnforth	64	SD 4970
Carnhell Green	2	SW 6137
Carnie	105	NJ 8105
Carno	39	SN 9696
Carnock	85	NT 0489
Carnon Downs	2	SW 7940
Carnousie	105	NJ 6650
Carnoustie	93	NO 5634
Carnwath	85	NS 9746
Carnyorth	2	SW 3733
Carperby	65	SE 0089
Carradale	81	NR 8138
Carrbridge	103	NH 9022
Carreglefn	48	SH 3889
Carrick (Fife.)	93	NO 4422
Carriden	85	NT 0181
Carrington (Gtr Mches.)	51	SJ 7492
Carrington (Lincs.)	55	TF 3155
Carrington (Lothian)	85	NT 3160
Carrog	50	SJ 1043
Carron (Central)	84	NS 8882
Carron (Grampn.)	104	NJ 2241
Carronbridge (Dumf. and Galwy.)	76	NX 8697
Carr Shield	71	NY 8047
Carrutherstown	70	NY 1071
Carr Vale	53	SK 4669
Carrville	72	NZ 3043
Carsaig	88	NM 5421
Carseriggan	68	NX 3167
Carsethorn	70	NX 9959
Carshalton	21	TQ 2764
Carsington	53	SK 2553
Carskiey	80	NR 6508
Carsluith	69	NX 4854
Carsphairn	75	NX 5693
Carstairs	84	NS 9345
Carstairs Junction	84	NS 9545
Carswell Marsh	19	SU 3198
Carter's Clay	11	SU 3024
Carterton	33	SP 2706
Carthew	4	SX 0055
Carthorpe	66	SE 3083
Cartington	79	NU 0304
Cartland	84	NS 8646
Cartmel	62	SD 3778
Cartmel Fell	62	SD 4188
Carway	25	SN 4606
Cashmoor	10	ST 9813
Cassington	33	SP 4510
Casswell's Bridge	45	TF 1627
Castell-y-bwch	29	ST 2792
Casterton	63	SD 6279
Castle Acre	46	TF 8115
Castle Ashby	34	SP 8659
Castle Bank	41	SJ 9021
Castlebay	109	NL 6698
Castle Bolton	65	SE 0391
Castle Bromwich	42	SP 1489
Castle Bytham	44	SK 9818
Castlebythe	24	SN 0229
Castle Caereinion	40	SJ 1605
Castle Camps	36	TL 6343
Castle Carrock	71	NY 5455
Castle Cary (Somer.)	17	ST 6332
Castlecary (Strath.)	84	NS 7878
Castle Combe	18	ST 8477
Castlecraig (Borders)	85	NT 1344
Castle Donington	43	SK 4427
Castle Douglas	69	NX 7662
Castle Eaton	18	SU 1495
Castle Eden	72	NZ 4338
Castleford	59	SE 4225
Castle Frome	31	SO 6645
Castle Green	63	SD 5292
Castle Gresley	43	SK 2718
Castle Heaton	87	NT 9041
Castle Hedingham	36	TL 7835
Castlehill (Strath.)	84	NS 8452
Castle Hill (Suff.)	37	TM 1646
Castle Kennedy	68	NX 1059
Castlemartin	24	SR 9198
Castle Morris	24	SM 9031
Castlemorton	32	SO 7937
Castle Pulverbatch	40	SJ 4202
Castle Rising	46	TF 6624
Castleside	72	NZ 0748
Castle Stuart	103	NH 7449
Castlethorpe	34	SP 7944
Castleton (Borders)	71	NY 5190
Castleton (Derby.)	52	SK 1582
Castleton (Gwent)	28	ST 2583
Castleton (N Yorks.)	66	NZ 6808
Castletown (Highld.)	112	ND 1967
Castletown (I. of M.)	56	SC 2667
Castletown (Tyne and Wear)	72	NZ 3558
Caston	46	TL 9598
Castor	45	TL 1298
Catacol	81	NR 9149
Catbrain	29	ST 5580
Catcliffe	53	SK 4288
Catcott	17	ST 3939
Caterham	21	TQ 3455
Catesby	33	SP 5159
Catfield	47	TG 3821
Catford	21	TQ 3872
Catforth	57	SD 4735
Cathcart	84	NS 5960
Cathedine	28	SO 1425
Catherington	11	SU 6914
Catherton	41	SO 6578
Catlodge	97	NN 6392
Catmore	19	SU 4579
Caton	64	SD 5364
Cator Court	5	SX 6877
Catrine	75	NS 5225
Cat's Ash	29	ST 3790
Catsfield	14	TQ 7213
Catshill	41	SO 9674
Cattal	66	SE 4454
Cattawade	37	TM 1033
Catterall	57	SD 4942
Catterick	66	SE 2397
Catterick Bridge	66	SE 2299
Catterick Camp	65	SE 1897
Catterlen	63	NY 4833
Catterline	99	NO 8678
Catterton	60	SE 5045
Catthorpe	43	SP 5578
Cattistock	9	SY 5999
Catton (Norf.)	47	TG 2312
Catton (Northum.)	71	NY 8257
Catton (N Yorks.)	66	SE 3778
Catwick	61	TA 1245
Catworth	45	TL 0873
Caulcott	33	SP 5024
Cauldcots	99	NO 6547
Cauldhame	91	NS 6494
Cauldon	52	SK 0749
Cauldside	71	NY 4480
Cauldwell	42	SK 2517
Caunsall	41	SO 8481
Caunton	54	SK 7460
Causewayhead	91	NS 8195
Causeyend	105	NJ 9419
Causey Park	79	NZ 1794
Cautley	63	SD 6994
Cavendish	36	TL 8046
Cavenham	36	TL 7669
Caversfield	33	SP 5824
Caversham	20	SU 7274
Caverswall	51	SJ 9442
Cawdor	103	NH 8450
Cawood	60	SE 5737
Cawsand	4	SX 4350
Cawston	47	TG 1324
Cawthorne	59	SE 2807

Cawton City Dulas

Cawton	66	SE 6476
Caxton	35	TL 3058
Caxton End	35	TL 3157
Caynham	40	SO 5473
Caythorpe (Lincs.)	54	SK 9348
Caythorpe (Notts.)	53	SK 6845
Cayton	67	TA 0583
Cefn-brith	49	SH 9350
Cefn Coch (Powys)	40	SJ 1026
Cefn-coed-y-cymmer	28	SO 0307
Cefn Cribwr	28	SS 8582
Cefn Cross	28	SS 8682
Cefn-ddwysarn	49	SH 9638
Cefn-Einion	40	SO 2886
Cefn-mawr (Clywd)	50	SJ 2842
Cefn-y-bedd	50	SJ 3156
Cefn-y-pant	24	SN 1925
Ceidio	48	SH 4085
Ceint	48	SH 4874
Cellan	27	SN 6149
Cellarhead (Staffs.)	51	SJ 9547
Cemaes	48	SH 3793
Cemmaes	39	SH 8306
Cemmaes Road	39	SH 8204
Cenarth	26	SN 2641
Cennin	48	SH 4645
Ceres	93	NO 4011
Cerne Abbas	9	ST 6601
Cerney Wick	18	SU 0796
Cerrigceinwen	48	SH 4273
Cerrigydrudion	49	SH 9548
Cessford	78	NT 7323
Chaceley	32	SO 8530
Chacewater	2	SW 7444
Chackmore	34	SP 6835
Chacombe	33	SP 4943
Chadderton	58	SD 9005
Chaddesden	53	SK 3737
Chaddesley Corbett	41	SO 8973
Chaddleworth	19	SU 4177
Chadlington	33	SP 3221
Chadshunt	33	SP 3453
Chad Valley	42	SP 0385
Chadwell St. Mary	22	TQ 6478
Chadwick End	42	SP 2073
Chaffcombe	8	ST 3510
Chagford	5	SX 7087
Chailey	13	TQ 3919
Chainhurst	14	TQ 7347
Chalbury Common	10	SU 0206
Chaldon	21	TQ 3155
Chaldon Herring or East Chaldon	10	SY 7983
Chale	11	SZ 4877
Chale Green	11	SZ 4879
Chalfont St. Giles	20	SU 9993
Chalfont St. Peter	20	SU 9990
Chalford	32	SO 8902
Chalgrove	19	SU 6396
Chalk	22	TQ 6772
Challacombe	7	SS 6941
Challoch	68	NX 3867
Challock Lees	15	TR 0050
Chalton (Beds.)	35	TL 0326
Chalvington	13	TQ 5109
Chandler's Cross	20	TQ 0698
Chandler's Ford	11	SU 4320
Chantry (Somer.)	18	ST 7146
Chantry (Suff.)	37	TM 1443
Chapel	92	NT 2593
Chapel Allerton (Somer.)	17	ST 4050
Chapel Allerton (W Yorks.)	59	SE 2936
Chapel Amble	4	SW 9975
Chapel Brampton	44	SP 7266
Chapel Chorlton	51	SJ 8037
Chapelend Way	36	TL 7039
Chapel-en-le-Frith	52	SK 0580
Chapelgate	45	TF 4124
Chapel Haddlesey	60	SE 5826
Chapelhall	84	NS 7862
Chapel Hill (Grampn.)	105	NK 0635
Chapel Hill (Gwent)	29	SO 5200
Chapelhill (Highld.)	108	NH 8273
Chapel Hill (Lincs.)	55	TF 2054
Chapelhill (Tays.)	92	NO 0030
Chapel Hill (Tays.)	92	NO 2021
Chapelknowe	70	NY 3173
Chapel Lawn	40	SO 3176
Chapel Le Dale	65	SD 7377
Chapel of Garioch	105	NJ 7124
Chapel Row	19	SU 5669
Chapel St. Leonards	55	TF 5572
Chapel Stile	62	NY 3205
Chapelton (Devon.)	6	SS 5826
Chapelton (Strath.)	84	NS 6848
Chapelton (Tays.)	99	NO 6247
Chapeltown (Grampn.)	104	NJ 2421
Chapeltown (Lancs.)	58	SD 7315
Chapeltown (S Yorks.)	53	SK 3596
Chapmanslade	18	ST 8247
Chappel	23	TL 8928
Chard	8	ST 3208
Chardstock	8	ST 3004
Charfield	18	ST 7292
Charing	15	TQ 9549
Charing Heath	15	TQ 9148
Charingworth	33	SP 1939
Charlbury	33	SP 3519
Charlcombe	18	ST 7467
Charlecote	33	SP 2656
Charles	7	SS 6832
Charleston	98	NO 3845
Charlestown (Corn.)	4	SX 0351
Charlestown (Dorset)	9	SY 6579
Charlestown (Fife.)	85	NT 0683
Charlestown (Grampn.)	99	NJ 9300
Charlestown (Highld.)	106	NG 8174
Charlestown (Highld.)	103	NH 6448
Charlestown of Aberlour	104	NJ 2642
Charles Tye	36	TM 0252
Charlesworth	52	SK 0092
Charlinch	16	ST 2337
Charlton (Gtr London)	21	TQ 4278
Charlton (Here. and Worc.)	32	SP 0045
Charlton (Northants.)	33	SP 5236
Charlton (Wilts.)	10	ST 9021
Charlton (Wilts.)	18	ST 9689
Charlton (Wilts.)	18	SU 1155
Charlton (Wilts.)	10	SU 1723
Charlton (W Susx)	12	SU 8812
Charlton Abbots	32	SP 0324
Charlton Adam	17	ST 5328
Charlton Horethorne	9	ST 6623
Charlton Kings	32	SO 9620
Charlton Mackrell	17	ST 5228
Charlton Marshall	10	ST 8903
Charlton Musgrove	17	ST 7229
Charlton-on-Otmoor	33	SP 5615
Charlwood	13	TQ 2441
Charminster	9	SY 6792
Charmouth	9	SY 3693
Charndon	34	SP 6724
Charney Bassett	19	SU 3894
Charnock Richard	57	SD 5415
Charsfield	37	TM 2556
Charterhouse	17	ST 4955
Chartershall	91	NS 7990
Charterville Allotments	33	SP 3110
Chartham	15	TR 1054
Chartham Hatch	15	TR 1056
Chartridge	34	SP 9303
Chart Sutton	14	TQ 8049
Charwelton	33	SP 5355
Chase Terrace	42	SK 0409
Chasetown	42	SK 0408
Chastleton	33	SP 2429
Chatburn	58	SD 7644
Chatcull	51	SJ 7934
Chatham	14	TQ 7567
Chathill	79	NU 1826
Chattenden	22	TQ 7672
Chatteris	45	TL 3986
Chattisham	37	TM 0942
Chatton	79	NU 0528
Chawleigh	7	SS 7112
Chawston	35	TL 1556
Chawton	12	SU 7037
Cheadle (Gtr Mches.)	51	SJ 8788
Cheadle (Staffs.)	52	SK 0043
Cheadle Hulme	51	SJ 8686
Cheam	21	TQ 2463
Chearsley	34	SP 7110
Chebsey	41	SJ 8528
Checkendon	19	SU 6682
Checkley (Ches.)	51	SJ 7245
Checkley (Staffs.)	52	SK 0237
Chedburgh	36	TL 7957
Cheddar	17	ST 4553
Cheddington	34	SP 9217
Cheddleton	51	SJ 9651
Cheddon Fitzpaine	16	ST 2427
Chedgrave	47	TM 3699
Chedington	9	ST 4805
Chediston	37	TM 3577
Chedworth	32	SP 0511
Chedzoy	17	ST 3337
Cheetham Hill	58	SD 8401
Cheldon	7	SS 7313
Chelford	51	SJ 8174
Chellaston	53	SK 3830
Chellington	34	SP 9656
Chelmarsh	41	SO 7187
Chelmondiston	37	TM 2037
Chelmorton	52	SK 1169
Chelmsford	22	TL 7006
Chelsfield	21	TQ 4864
Chelsworth	36	TL 9748
Cheltenham	32	SO 9422
Chelveston	44	SP 9969
Chelvey	29	ST 4668
Chelwood	17	ST 6361
Chelwood Gate	13	TQ 4130
Cheney Longville	40	SO 4184
Chenies	20	TQ 0198
Chepstow	29	ST 5393
Cherhill	18	SU 0370
Cherington (Glos.)	18	ST 9098
Cherington (Warw.)	33	SP 2936
Cheriton (Devon.)	7	SS 7346
Cheriton (Devon.)	8	ST 1001
Cheriton (Hants.)	11	SU 5828
Cheriton (Somer.)	17	ST 6825
Cheriton (W Glam.)	25	SS 4593
Cheriton Bishop	5	SX 7793
Cheriton Fitzpaine	7	SS 8606
Cherrington	41	SJ 6619
Cherry Burton	61	SE 9842
Cherry Hinton	35	TL 4857
Cherry Willingham	54	TF 0173
Chertsey	20	TQ 0466
Cheselbourne	9	SY 7699
Chesham	34	SP 9601
Chesham Bois	20	SU 9698
Cheshunt	35	TL 3502
Cheslyn Hay	41	SJ 9707
Chessington	21	TQ 1863
Chester	50	SJ 4066
Chesterblade	17	ST 6641
Chesterfield (Derby.)	53	SK 3871
Chesterfield (Staffs.)	42	SK 1005
Chester-le-Street	72	NZ 2751
Chesters (Borders)	78	NT 6210
Chesterton (Cambs.)	45	TL 1295
Chesterton (Cambs.)	35	TL 4560
Chesterton (Oxon.)	33	SP 5621
Chesterton (Staffs.)	51	SJ 8249
Chesterton Green	33	SP 3558
Chestfield	15	TR 1365
Cheswardine	41	SJ 7129
Cheswick	87	NU 0346
Chetnole	9	ST 6008
Chettiscombe	8	SS 9614
Chettisham	45	TL 5483
Chettle	10	ST 9513
Chetton	41	SO 6690
Chetwode	34	SP 6429
Chetwynd Aston	41	SJ 7517
Cheveley	36	TL 6760
Chevening	21	TQ 4857
Chevington	36	TL 7859
Chevington Drift	79	NZ 2699
Chevithorne	8	SS 9715
Chew Magna	17	ST 5763
Chew Stoke	17	ST 5561
Chewton Mendip	17	ST 5952
Chicheley	34	SP 9046
Chichester	12	SU 8605
Chickerell	9	SY 6480
Chicklade	10	ST 9134
Chidden	11	SU 6517
Chiddingfold	12	SU 9635
Chiddingly	13	TQ 5414
Chiddingstone	13	TQ 5045
Chiddingstone Causeway	21	TQ 5147
Chideock	9	SY 4292
Chidham	12	SU 7803
Chieveley	19	SU 4773
Chignall St. James	22	TL 6709
Chignall Smealy	22	TL 6611
Chigwell	21	TQ 4493
Chigwell Row	21	TQ 4693
Chilbolton	11	SU 3939
Chilcomb (Hants.)	11	SU 5028
Chilcombe (Dorset)	9	SY 5291
Chilcompton	17	ST 6452
Chilcote	43	SK 2811
Childer Thornton	50	SJ 3677
Child Okeford	10	ST 8312
Childrey	19	SU 3687
Child's Ercall	41	SJ 6625
Childswickham	32	SP 0738
Childwall	50	SJ 4089
Chilfrome	9	SY 5898
Chilgrove	12	SU 8314
Chilham	15	TR 0753
Chillaton	4	SX 4381
Chillenden	15	TR 2753
Chillerton	11	SZ 4883
Chillesford	37	TM 3852
Chillingham	79	NU 0625
Chillington (Devon.)	5	SX 7942
Chillington (Somer.)	9	ST 3811
Chilmark	10	ST 9632
Chilson	33	SP 3119
Chilsworthy (Corn.)	4	SX 4172
Chilsworthy (Devon.)	6	SS 3206
Chilthorne Domer	9	ST 5219
Chilton (Bucks.)	34	SP 6811
Chilton (Durham)	72	NZ 3031
Chilton (Oxon)	19	SU 4885
Chilton Cantelo	9	ST 5621
Chilton Foliat	19	SU 3170
Chilton Polden	17	ST 3739
Chilton Street	36	TL 7547
Chilton Trinity	11	ST 2939
Chilworth	11	SU 4018
Chimney	33	SP 3500
Chineham	19	SU 6554
Chingford	21	TQ 3893
Chinley	52	SK 0382
Chinnor	20	SP 7500
Chipnall	51	SJ 7231
Chippenham (Cambs.)	36	TL 6669
Chippenham (Wilts.)	18	ST 9173
Chipperfield	35	TL 0401
Chipping (Herts.)	35	TL 3532
Chipping (Lancs.)	58	SD 6243
Chipping Campden	32	SP 1539
Chipping Hill	22	TL 8215
Chipping Norton	33	SP 3127
Chipping Ongar	22	TL 5502
Chipping Sodbury	18	ST 7282
Chipping Warden	33	SP 4948
Chipstable	16	ST 0427
Chipstead (Kent)	21	TQ 5056
Chipstead (Surrey)	21	TQ 2756
Chirbury	40	SO 2598
Chirk	50	SJ 2937
Chirmorie	68	NX 2076
Chirnside	87	NT 8756
Chirnsidebridge	87	NT 8556
Chirton	18	SU 0757
Chisbury	18	SU 2766
Chiselborough	9	ST 4614
Chiseldon	18	SU 1879
Chislehampton	19	SU 5999
Chislehurst	21	TQ 4470
Chislet	15	TR 2264
Chiswellgreen	35	TL 1303
Chiswick	21	TQ 2077
Chisworth	52	SJ 9991
Chithurst	12	SU 8423
Chittering	45	TL 4970
Chitterne	18	ST 9843
Chittlehamholt	7	SS 6420
Chittlehampton	7	SS 6325
Chittoe	18	ST 9666
Chivelstone	5	SX 7838
Chobham	20	SU 9761
Cholderton	18	SU 2242
Cholesbury	34	SP 9307
Chollerton	78	NY 9372
Cholsey	19	SU 5886
Cholstrey	30	SO 4659
Choppington	79	NZ 2583
Chopwell	72	NZ 1158
Chorley (Ches.)	51	SJ 5650
Chorley (Lancs.)	57	SD 5817
Chorley (Salop)	41	SO 6983
Chorley (Staffs.)	42	SK 0711
Chorleywood	20	TQ 0396
Chorlton	51	SJ 7250
Chorlton Lane	50	SJ 4547
Chowley	50	SJ 4756
Chrishall	35	TL 4439
Christchurch (Cambs.)	45	TL 4996
Christchurch (Dorset)	11	SZ 1593
Christchurch (Glos.)	29	SO 5713
Christian Malford	18	ST 9678
Christleton	50	SJ 4365
Christmas Common	20	SU 7193
Christon	17	ST 3956
Christon Bank	79	NU 2122
Christow	5	SX 8385
Chudleigh	5	SX 8679
Chudleigh Knighton	5	SX 8477
Chulmleigh	7	SS 6814
Chunal	52	SK 0391
Church	58	SD 7428
Churcham	32	SO 7618
Church Brampton	44	SP 7165
Church Broughton	53	SK 2033
Church Crookham	20	SU 8152
Churchdown	32	SO 8819
Church Eaton	41	SJ 8417
Church End (Beds.)	34	SP 9921
Church End (Beds.)	35	TL 1937
Church End (Cambs.)	45	TF 3909
Church End (Cambs.)	35	TL 4857
Church End (Essex)	36	TL 5841
Churchend (Essex)	22	TL 6323
Churchend (Essex)	23	TR 0092
Church End (Hants.)	19	SU 6756
Church End (Warw.)	43	SP 2892
Church End (Wilts.)	18	SU 0278
Church Fenton	60	SE 5136
Church Gresley	43	SK 2918
Church Hanborough	33	SP 4212
Churchill (Avon)	17	ST 4359
Churchill (Here. and Worc.)	41	SO 8779
Churchill (Oxon.)	33	SP 2824
Churchingford	8	ST 2112
Church Knowle	10	SY 9481
Church Langton	44	SP 7293
Church Lawford	43	SP 4476
Church Lawton	51	SJ 8255
Church Leigh	52	SK 0235
Church Lench	32	SP 0251
Church Minshull	51	SJ 6660
Church Norton	12	SZ 8695
Churchover	43	SP 5080
Church Preen	40	SO 5398
Church Pulverbatch	40	SJ 4303
Churchstanton	8	ST 1914
Church Stoke	40	SO 2694
Churchstow (Devon.)	5	SX 7145
Church Stowe (Northants.)	34	SP 6357
Church Street	22	TQ 7174
Church Stretton	40	SO 4593
Churchtown (I. of M.)	56	SC 4294
Churchtown (Lancs.)	57	SD 4842
Churchtown (Mers.)	57	SD 3618
Church Warsop	53	SK 5668
Churt	12	SU 8538
Churton	50	SJ 4156
Churwell	59	SE 2729
Chwilog	48	SH 4338
Chyandour	2	SW 4731
Cilcain	50	SJ 1765
Cilcennin	26	SN 5160
Cilfor	48	SH 6237
Cilfrew	28	SN 7600
Cilfynydd	28	ST 0892
Cilgerran	26	SN 1943
Cilgwyn	25	SN 7430
Ciliau-Aeron	26	SN 5058
Cilmalieu	95	NM 8955
Cilmery	30	SO 0051
Cilrhedyn	26	SN 2734
Ciltalgarth	49	SH 8840
Cilycwm	27	SN 7540
Cinderford	29	SO 6513
Cirencester	32	SP 0201
City Dulas	48	SH 4687

Clachaig Conyer

Clachaig	89	NS 1181
Clachan (Lismore Island)	95	NM 8543
Clachan (Raasay)	100	NG 5436
Clachan (Strath.)	89	NM 7819
Clachan (Strath.)	81	NR 7656
Clachan Mor	94	NL 9847
Clachan of Campsie	84	NS 6179
Clachan of Glendaruel	89	NR 9984
Clachan-Seil	89	NM 7718
Clachbreck	89	NR 7675
Clachtoll	110	NC 0427
Clackavoid	98	NO 1463
Clackmannan	91	NS 9191
Clacton-on-Sea	23	TM 1715
Cladich	89	NN 0921
Claggan	95	NM 7049
Claigan	100	NG 2354
Claines	32	SO 8559
Clandown	17	ST 6955
Clanfield (Hants.)	11	SU 6916
Clanfield (Oxon.)	33	SP 2801
Clannaborough Barton	7	SS 7402
Clanville	19	SU 3148
Claonaig	81	NR 8656
Claonel	108	NC 5604
Clapgate	10	SU 0102
Clapham (Beds.)	35	TL 0252
Clapham (Gtr London)	21	TQ 2875
Clapham (N Yorks.)	65	SD 7469
Clapham (W Susx)	12	TQ 0906
Clappers	87	NT 9455
Clappersgate	62	NY 3603
Clapton (Glos.)	32	SP 1617
Clapton (Somer.)	9	ST 4106
Clapton-in-Gordano	29	ST 4774
Clapworthy	7	SS 6724
Clarbeston	24	SN 0421
Clarbeston Road	24	SN 0121
Clarborough	54	SK 7383
Clardon	112	ND 1468
Clare	36	TL 7645
Clarebrand	69	NX 7666
Clarencefield	70	NY 0968
Clarkston	84	NS 5757
Clashmore	108	NH 7489
Clashnessie	110	NC 0530
Clatt	104	NJ 5426
Clatter	39	SN 9994
Clatworthy	16	ST 0530
Claughton (Lancs.)	57	SD 5242
Claughton (Lancs.)	64	SD 5666
Claverdon	33	SP 1964
Claverham	29	ST 4566
Clavering	35	TL 4832
Claverley	41	SO 7993
Claverton	18	ST 7864
Clawdd-newydd	49	SJ 0852
Clawton	6	SX 3599
Claxby (Lincs.)	55	TF 1194
Claxby (Lincs.)	55	TF 4571
Claxton (Norf.)	47	TG 3303
Claxton (N Yorks.)	66	SE 6960
Claybrooke Magna	43	SP 4988
Clay Common	47	TM 4781
Clay Coton	43	SP 5977
Clay Cross	53	SK 3963
Claydon (Oxon.)	33	SP 4550
Claydon (Suff.)	37	TM 1350
Claygate	21	TQ 1563
Claygate Cross	14	TQ 6155
Clayhanger (Devon.)	8	ST 0223
Clayhanger (W Mids.)	42	SK 0404
Clayhidon	8	ST 1615
Claypole	54	SK 8449
Clayton (Staffs.)	51	SJ 8443
Clayton (S Yorks.)	60	SE 4507
Clayton (W Susx.)	13	TQ 3014
Clayton (W Yorks.)	59	SE 1131
Clayton-le-Moors	58	SD 7431
Clayton-le-Woods	57	SD 5722
Clayton West	59	SE 2511
Clayworth	54	SK 7288
Cleadale	95	NM 4789
Cleadon	72	NZ 3862
Clearwell	29	SO 5708
Cleasby	72	NZ 2713
Cleatlam	72	NZ 1118
Cleator	62	NY 0113
Cleator Moor	62	NY 0214
Cleckheaton	59	SE 1825
Cleedownton	41	SO 5880
Cleehill	41	SO 5975
Clee St. Margaret	40	SO 5684
Cleethorpes	61	TA 3008
Cleeton St. Mary	41	SO 6178
Cleeve	29	ST 4566
Cleeve Hill	32	SO 9827
Cleeve Prior	32	SP 0849
Clehonger	30	SO 4637
Cleigh	89	NM 8725
Cleish	92	NT 0998
Cleland	84	NS 7958
Clench Common	18	SU 1765
Clenchwarton	46	TF 5820
Clent	41	SO 9179
Cleobury Mortimer	41	SO 6775
Cleobury North	41	SO 6187
Cleongart	80	NR 6734
Clephanton	103	NH 8450
Clerklands	78	NT 5024
Clevancy	18	SU 0475
Clevedon	29	ST 4071
Cleveleys	57	SD 3142
Cleverton	18	ST 9785
Clewer	17	ST 4350
Cley next the Sea	47	TG 0444
Cliburn	63	NY 5824
Cliddesden	19	SU 6349
Cliffe (Kent)	22	TQ 7376
Cliffe (N Yorks.)	60	SE 6631
Cliff End	14	TQ 8813
Cliffe Woods	22	TQ 7373
Clifford (Here. and Worc.)	30	SO 2445
Clifford (W Yorks.)	59	SE 4244
Clifford Chambers	33	SP 1952
Clifford's Mesne	32	SO 7023
Cliffsend	15	TR 3464
Clifton (Avon)	29	ST 5673
Clifton (Beds.)	35	TL 1739
Clifton (Central)	90	NN 3230
Clifton (Cumbr.)	62	NY 0429
Clifton (Cumbr.)	63	NY 5326
Clifton (Derby.)	52	SK 1644
Clifton (Here. and Worc.)	32	SO 8446
Clifton (Lancs.)	57	SD 4630
Clifton (Notts.)	53	SK 5434
Clifton (Oxon.)	33	SP 4831
Clifton Campville	42	SK 2510
Clifton Hampden	19	SU 5495
Clifton Reynes	34	SP 9051
Clifton upon Dunsmore	43	SP 5276
Clifton upon Teme	32	SO 7161
Climping	12	TQ 0002
Clint	66	SE 2559
Clinterty	105	NJ 8311
Clint Green	46	TG 0210
Clippesby	47	TG 4214
Clipsham	44	SK 9616
Clipston (Northants.)	44	SP 7181
Clipston (Notts.)	53	SK 6333
Clipstone	53	SK 6064
Clitheroe	58	SD 7441
Clive	40	SJ 5124
Clocaenog	49	SJ 0854
Clochan	104	NJ 4060
Clock Face	50	SJ 5291
Clodock	29	SO 3227
Clola	105	NK 0043
Clophill	35	TL 0838
Clopton	45	TL 0680
Clopton Green	36	TL 7654
Closeburn	76	NX 8992
Close Clark	56	SC 2775
Clothall	35	TL 2732
Clotton	50	SJ 5263
Clough Foot	58	SD 9123
Cloughton	67	TA 0094
Cloughton Newlands	67	TA 0096
Clousta	113	HU 3157
Clova (Tays.)	98	NO 3273
Clovelly	6	SS 3124
Clovenfords	86	NT 4436
Clovenstone	105	NJ 7717
Clovulin	96	NN 0063
Clowne	53	SK 4975
Clows Top	41	SO 7171
Clun	40	SO 3081
Clunas	103	NH 8846
Clunbury	40	SO 3780
Clunes	96	NN 2088
Clungunford	40	SO 3978
Clunie (Grampn.)	104	NJ 6350
Clunie (Tays.)	98	NO 1043
Clunton	40	SO 3381
Cluny	92	NT 2495
Clutton (Avon)	17	ST 6159
Clutton (Ches.)	50	SJ 4654
Clydach (Gwent)	28	SO 2213
Clydach (W Glam.)	25	SN 6801
Clydach Vale	28	SS 9793
Clydebank	84	NS 5069
Clydey	26	SN 2535
Clyffe Pypard	18	SU 0776
Clynder	90	NS2484
Clynderwen	24	SN 1219
Clynelish	108	NC 8905
Clynnog-fawr	48	SH 4149
Clyro	30	SO 2143
Clyst Honiton	8	SX 9893
Clyst Hydon	8	ST 0301
Clyst St. George	8	SX 9888
Clyst St. Lawrence	8	ST 0200
Clyst St. Mary	8	SX 9890
Cnwch Coch	27	SN 6775
Coad's Green	4	SX 2976
Coal Aston	53	SK 3679
Coalbrookdale	41	SJ 6604
Coalburn	84	NS 8034
Coalcleugh	71	NY 8045
Coaley	32	SO 7701
Coalpit Heath	29	ST 6780
Coalport	41	SJ 6902
Coalsnaughton	91	NS 9195
Coaltown of Balgonie	93	NT 2999
Coaltown of Wemyss	93	NT 3295
Coalville	43	SK 4214
Coast	106	NG 9290
Coatbridge	84	NS 7265
Coatdyke	84	NS 7464
Coate (Wilts.)	18	SU 0361
Coate (Wilts.)	18	SU 1782
Coates (Cambs.)	45	TL 3097
Coates (Glos.)	32	SO 9700
Coatham	73	NZ 5925
Coatham Mundeville	72	NZ 2919
Cobbaton	6	SS 6127
Coberley	32	SO 9615
Cobham (Kent)	14	TQ 6768
Cobham (Surrey)	20	TQ 1060
Cobnash	30	SO 4560
Cockayne	66	SE 6298
Cockayne Hatley	35	TL 2549
Cockburnspath	87	NT 7770
Cock Clarks	22	TL 8102
Cockenzie and Port Seton	85	NT 4075
Cockerham	64	SD 4651
Cockerington	55	TF 3789
Cockermouth	62	NY 1230
Cockernhoe Green	35	TL 1223
Cockfield (Durham)	72	NZ 1224
Cockfield (Suff.)	36	TL 9054
Cockfosters	21	TQ 2896
Cocking	12	SU 8717
Cockington	5	SX 8964
Cocklake	17	ST 4349
Cockley Cley	46	TF 7904
Cockpole Green	20	SU 7981
Cockshutt	40	SJ 4329
Cockthorpe	46	TF 9842
Cockwood	8	SX 9780
Coddenham	37	TM 1354
Coddington (Ches.)	50	SJ 4455
Coddington (Here. and Worc.)	32	SO 7142
Coddington (Notts.)	54	SK 8354
Codford St. Mary	10	ST 9739
Codford St. Peter	18	ST 9640
Codicote	35	TL 2118
Codnor	53	SK 4149
Codrington	18	ST 7278
Codsall	41	SJ 8603
Codsall Wood	41	SJ 8405
Coedana	48	SH 4381
Coedely	28	ST 0285
Coedkernew	29	ST 2783
Coedpoeth	50	SJ 2850
Coed-y-paen	29	ST 3398
Coelbren	28	SN 8411
Coffinswell	5	SX 8868
Cofton Hackett	42	SP 0075
Cogenhoe	34	SP 8360
Coggeshall	22	TL 8522
Coillaig	89	NN 0120
Coille Mhorgil	96	NH 1001
Coity	28	SS 9281
Coker	9	ST 5312
Colaboll	108	NC 5610
Colan	3	SW 8661
Colaton Raleigh	8	SY 0787
Colby (Cumbr.)	63	NY 6620
Colby (I. of M.)	56	SC 2370
Colby (Norf.)	47	TG 2131
Colchester	23	TM 0025
Cold Ash	19	SU 5169
Cold Ashby	43	SP 6576
Cold Ashton	18	ST 7472
Coldbackie	111	NC 6160
Coldblow	21	TQ 5173
Cold Brayfield	34	SP 9252
Coldean	13	TQ 3408
Coldeast	5	SX 8274
Colden Common	11	SU 4822
Coldfair Green	37	TM 4361
Cold Hanworth	54	TF 0383
Coldharbour	12	TQ 1443
Cold Hesledon	72	NZ 4147
Cold Higham	34	SP 6653
Coldingham	87	NT 9065
Cold Kirby	66	SE 5384
Cold Newton	44	SK 7106
Cold Norton	22	TL 8500
Cold Overton	44	SK 8110
Coldrain	92	NO 0700
Coldred	15	TR 2747
Coldridge	7	SS 6907
Coldstream	84	NT 8439
Coldwaltham	12	TQ 0216
Coldwells	105	NK 1039
Cole	17	ST 6633
Colebatch	40	SO 3187
Colebrook	8	ST 0006
Colebrooke	7	SX 7799
Coleby (Humbs.)	60	SE 8919
Coleby (Lincs.)	54	SK 9760
Coleford (Devon.)	7	SS 7701
Coleford (Glos.)	29	SO 5710
Coleford (Somer.)	17	ST 6848
Colehill	10	SU 0300
Coleman's Hatch	13	TQ 4533
Colemere	50	SJ 4232
Colenden	92	NO 1029
Coleorton	43	SK 3917
Colerne	18	ST 8171
Colesbourne	32	SO 9913
Colesden	35	TL 1255
Coleshill (Bucks.)	20	SU 9495
Coleshill (Oxon.)	18	SU 2393
Coleshill (Warw.)	42	SP 1989
Colgate	13	TQ 2332
Colgrain	90	NS 3280
Colinsburgh	93	NO 4703
Colinton	85	NT 2169
Colintraive	89	NS 0374
Colkirk	46	TF 9126
Coll (Isle of Lewis)	109	NB 4739
Collace	92	NO 2032
Collafirth (Shetld.)	113	HU 3482
Collaton St. Mary	5	SX 8660
Collessie	93	NO 2813
Collier Row	21	TQ 4991
Collier's End	35	TL 3720
Collier Street	14	TQ 7145
Colliery Row	72	NZ 3449
Collieston	105	NK 0328
Collin	70	NY 0276
Collingbourne Ducis	18	SU 2453
Collingbourne Kingston	18	SU 2355
Collingham (Notts.)	54	SK 8261
Collingham (W Yorks.)	59	SE 3845
Collington	31	SO 6460
Collingtree	34	SP 7555
Colliston	99	NO 6045
Collynie	105	NJ 8436
Collyweston	44	SK 9903
Colmonell	68	NX 1586
Colmworth	35	TL 1058
Colnabaichin	104	NJ 2908
Colnbrook	20	TQ 0277
Colne (Cambs.)	45	TL 3776
Colne (Lancs.)	58	SD 8839
Colne Engaine	36	TL 8530
Colney	47	TG 1808
Colney Heath	35	TL 2005
Colney Street	35	TL 1502
Coln Rogers	32	SP 0809
Coln St. Aldwyns	32	SP 1405
Coln St. Dennis	32	SP 0810
Colp	105	NJ 7448
Colpy	104	NJ 6432
Colsterdale	65	SE 1280
Colsterworth	44	SK 9224
Colston Bassett	54	SK 7033
Coltfield	103	NJ 1163
Coltishall	47	TG 2619
Colton (Cumbr.)	62	SD 3186
Colton (Norf.)	47	TG 1009
Colton (N Yorks.)	60	SE 5444
Colton (Staffs.)	42	SK 0520
Colwall Green	32	SO 7541
Colwall Stone	32	SO 7542
Colwell	78	NY 9575
Colwich	42	SK 0121
Colwinston	28	SS 9475
Colworth	12	SU 9102
Colwyn Bay	49	SH 8478
Colyford	8	SY 2492
Colyton	8	SY 2493
Combe (Berks.)	19	SU 3760
Combe (Here. and Worc.)	30	SO 3463
Combe (Oxon.)	33	SP 4115
Combe Florey	16	ST 1531
Combe Hay	18	ST 7359
Combeinteignhead	8	SX 9071
Combe Martin	6	SS 5846
Combe Moor	30	SO 3663
Combe Raleigh	8	ST 1502
Comberbach	51	SJ 6477
Comberton	35	TL 3856
Combe St. Nicholas	8	ST 3011
Combrook	33	SP 3051
Combs (Derby.)	52	SK 0478
Combs (Suff.)	37	TM 0456
Combs Ford	37	TM 0457
Combwich	16	ST 2542
Comers	105	NJ 6707
Commins Coch	39	SH 8403
Commondale	73	NZ 6610
Common Edge	57	SD 3232
Common Moor	4	SX 2369
Common Side	53	SK 3375
Common, The	11	SU 2432
Compstall	51	SJ 9690
Compton (Berks.)	19	SU 5279
Compton (Devon.)	5	SX 8664
Compton (Hants.)	11	SU 4625
Compton (Surrey)	20	SU 9547
Compton (Wilts.)	18	SU 1352
Compton (W Susx.)	12	SU 7714
Compton Abbas	10	ST 8718
Compton Abdale	32	SP 0516
Compton Bassett	18	SU 0372
Compton Beauchamp	19	SU 2887
Compton Bishop	17	ST 3955
Compton Chamberlayne	10	SU 0229
Compton Dando	17	ST 6464
Compton Dundon	17	ST 4933
Compton Martin	17	ST 5456
Compton Pauncefoot	17	ST 6425
Compton Valence	9	SY 5993
Comrie	91	NN 7722
Conchra	89	NS 0288
Concraigie	98	NO 1044
Conderton	32	SO 9637
Condicote	32	SP 1528
Condorrat	84	NS 7373
Condover	40	SJ 4906
Coneyhurst Common	12	TQ 1024
Coneysthorpe	66	SE 7171
Coney Weston	36	TL 9578
Congerstone	43	SK 3605
Congham	46	TF 7123
Congleton	51	SJ 8562
Congresbury	17	ST 4363
Coningsby	55	TF 2258
Conington (Cambs.)	45	TL 1785
Conington (Cambs.)	45	TL 3266
Conisbrough	60	SK 5098
Conisholme	55	TF 3995
Coniston (Cumbr.)	62	SD 3097
Coniston (Humbs.)	61	TA 1535
Coniston Cold	65	SD 9054
Conistone	65	SD 9867
Connah's Quay	50	SJ 2869
Connel	89	NM 9134
Connor Downs	2	SW 5939
Conon Bridge	102	NH 5455
Cononley	59	SD 9846
Consall	51	SJ 9748
Consett	72	NZ 1150
Constable Burton	65	SE 1690
Constantine	2	SW 7229
Contin	102	NH 4555
Contlaw	99	NJ 8402
Conway	49	SH 7777
Conyer	15	TQ 9664

Cookbury Cross of Jackston

Cookbury	6	SS 4005
Cookham	20	SU 8985
Cookham Dean	20	SU 8785
Cookham Rise	20	SU 8884
Cookhill	32	SP 0558
Cookley (Here. and Worc.)	41	SO 8480
Cookley (Suff.)	37	TM 3475
Cookley Green	19	SU 6990
Cookney	99	NO 8793
Cooksbridge	13	TQ 4013
Cooksmill Green	22	TL 6306
Coolham	12	TQ 1222
Cooling	22	TQ 7575
Coombe (Corn.)	6	SS 2011
Coombe (Corn.)	3	SW 9551
Coombe Bissett	10	SU 1026
Coombe Hill	32	SO 8827
Coombe Keynes	10	SY 8484
Coombes	12	TQ 1908
Coopersale Common	35	TL 4702
Copdock	37	TM 1141
Copford Green	23	TL 9222
Cople	35	TL 1048
Copley	72	NZ 0825
Coplow Dale	52	SK 1679
Copmanthorpe	60	SE 5646
Coppathorne	6	SS 2000
Coppenhall	41	SJ 9019
Coppingford	45	TL 1680
Copplestone	7	SS 7702
Coppull	57	SD 5613
Copsale	12	TQ 1724
Copster Green	58	SD 6734
Copt Heath	42	SP 1778
Copt Hewick	66	SE 3371
Copthorne	13	TQ 3139
Copt Oak	43	SK 4812
Copythorne	11	SU 3014
Corbridge	72	NY 9964
Corby	44	SP 8988
Corby Glen	44	SK 9925
Coreley	41	SO 6173
Corfe	8	ST 2319
Corfe Castle	10	SY 9681
Corfe Mullen	10	SY 9798
Corfton	40	SO 4985
Corgarff	104	NJ 2708
Corhampton	11	SU 6120
Corley	43	SP 3085
Corley Ash	43	SP 2886
Corley Moor	43	SP 2884
Cornelly	28	SS 8281
Corney	62	SD 1191
Cornforth	72	NZ 3034
Cornhil!	104	NJ 5858
Cornhill-on-Tweed	87	NT 8639
Cornholme (W Yorks.)	58	SD 9025
Cornish Hall End	36	TL 6836
Cornquoy	113	ND 5299
Cornriggs	71	NY 8441
Cornsay	72	NZ 1443
Cornwell	33	SP 2727
Cornwood	5	SX 6059
Cornworthy	5	SX 8255
Corpach	96	NN 0976
Corpusty	47	TG 1129
Corran (Highld.)	101	NG 8509
Corran (Highld.)	96	NN 0163
Corrany	56	SC 4589
Corrie	81	NS 0243
Corrie Common	70	NY 2085
Corriemoillie	102	NH 3663
Corrimony	102	NH 3830
Corringham (Essex)	22	TQ 7183
Corringham (Lincs.)	54	SK 8691
Corris Uchaf	39	SH 7408
Corry	101	NG 6424
Corry of Ardnagrask	102	NH 5048
Corscombe	9	ST 5105
Corse	104	NJ 6040
Corse of Kinnoir	104	NJ 5443
Corsham	18	ST 8669
Corsindae	105	NJ 6808
Corsley	18	ST 8246
Corsley Heath	18	ST 8245
Corsock	69	NX 7576
Corston (Avon)	29	ST 6965
Corston (Wilts.)	18	ST 9284
Corstorphine	85	NT 1972
Cortachy	98	NO 3959
Corton (Suff.)	47	TM 5497
Corton (Wilts.)	10	ST 9340
Corton Denham	9	ST 6322
Corwen	49	SJ 0743
Coryton (Devon.)	5	SX 4583
Coryton (Essex)	22	TQ 7482
Cosby	43	SP 5495
Coseley	41	SO 9494
Cosgrove	34	SP 7942
Cosham	11	SU 6605
Cosheston	24	SN 0003
Cossall	53	SK 4842
Cossington (Leic.)	43	SK 6013
Cossington (Somer.)	17	ST 3540
Costessey	47	TG 1712
Costock	43	SK 5726
Coston	44	SK 8422
Cotebrook	51	SJ 5765
Cotehill	71	NY 4750
Cotes (Cumbr.)	63	SD 4886
Cotes (Leic.)	43	SK 5520
Cotes (Staffs.)	51	SJ 8434
Cotesbach	43	SP 5382
Cotgrave	53	SK 6435
Cothall	105	NJ 8716
Cotham	54	SK 7947
Cothelstone	16	ST 1831
Cotherstone	72	NZ 0119
Cothill	19	SU 4699
Cotleigh	8	ST 2002
Coton (Cambs.)	35	TL 4158
Coton (Northants.)	43	SP 6771
Coton (Staffs.)	51	SJ 9832
Coton Clanford	41	SJ 8723
Coton in the Elms	42	SK 2415
Cott	5	SX 7861
Cottam (Lancs.)	57	SD 4932
Cottam (Notts.)	54	SK 8179
Cottartown	103	NJ 0331
Cottenham	45	TL 4567
Cotterdale	65	SD 8393
Cottered	35	TL 3129
Cotterstock	45	TL 0490
Cottesbrooke	44	SP 7073
Cottesmore	44	SK 9013
Cottingham (Humbs.)	61	TA 0532
Cottingham (Northants.)	44	SP 8490
Cottisford	33	SP 5831
Cotton	37	TM 0667
Cotton End	35	TL 0845
Cot-town (Grampn.)	104	NJ 5026
Cottown (Grampn.)	105	NJ 7715
Cot-town (Grampn.)	105	NJ 8140
Cotwalton	51	SJ 9234
Coughton	32	SP 0760
Coulags	101	NG 9645
Coull	99	NJ 5102
Coulport	90	NS 2087
Coulsdon	21	TQ 3059
Coulter	85	NT 0233
Coulton	66	SE 6374
Cound	40	SJ 5504
Coundon	72	NZ 2329
Coundon Grange	72	NZ 2327
Countersett	65	SD 9287
Countess Wear	8	SX 9489
Countesthorpe	43	SP 5895
Countisbury	7	SS 7449
Coupar Angus	92	NO 2139
Coupland	87	NT 9331
Cour	81	NR 8248
Courteenhall	34	SP 7653
Court Henry	25	SN 5522
Courtsend	23	TR 0293
Courtway	16	ST 2033
Cousland	85	NT 3768
Cousley Wood	13	TQ 6533
Cove (Devon.)	8	SS 9519
Cove (Hants.)	20	SU 8555
Cove (Highld.)	106	NG 8190
Cove (Strath.)	90	NS 2281
Covehithe	47	TM 5281
Coven	41	SJ 9006
Coveney	45	TL 4882
Covenham St. Bartholomew	55	TF 3395
Covenham St. Mary	55	TF 3394
Coventry	43	SP 3379
Coverack	2	SW 7818
Coverham	65	SE 1086
Covington	45	TL 0570
Cowan Bridge	64	SD 6476
Cowbeech	13	TQ 6114
Cowbit	45	TF 2618
Cowbridge	28	SS 9974
Cowden	13	TQ 4640
Cowdenbeath	92	NT 1691
Cowes	11	SZ 4995
Cowesby	66	SE 4689
Cowfold	13	TQ 2122
Cowick	60	SE 6521
Cowie	84	NS 8389
Cowley (Devon.)	7	SX 9095
Cowley (Glos.)	32	SO 9614
Cowley (Gtr London)	20	TQ 0582
Cowley (Oxon.)	33	SP 5404
Cowling (N Yorks.)	58	SD 9743
Cowlinge	36	TL 7154
Cowpen Bewley	73	NZ 4824
Cowplain	11	SU 7011
Cowshill	71	NY 8540
Cowstrandburn	92	NT 0390
Coxbank	51	SJ 6541
Coxbench	53	SK 3743
Cox Common	47	TM 4082
Coxheath	14	TQ 7451
Coxhoe	72	NZ 3235
Coxley	17	ST 5343
Coxwold	66	SE 5377
Coychurch	28	SS 9379
Coylton	75	NS 4119
Coylumbridge	103	NH 9110
Coynach	104	NJ 4405
Crabbs Cross	32	SP 0464
Crabtree	13	TQ 2225
Crabtree Green	50	SJ 3344
Crackenthorpe	63	NY 6622
Crackington Haven	6	SX 1496
Crackleybank	41	SJ 7611
Crackpot	65	SD 9796
Cracoe	65	SD 9760
Cradley	32	SO 7347
Crafthole	4	SX 3654
Cragabus	80	NR 3345
Cragg	59	SE 0023
Craggan (Strath.)	90	NS 2699
Craghead	72	NZ 2150
Craibstone (Grampn.)	105	NJ 8611
Craichie	99	NO 5047
Craig (Dumf. and Galwy.)	69	NX 6875
Craig (Highld.)	101	NH 0349
Craigcefnparc	25	SN 6703
Craigdallie	92	NO 2428
Craigdam	105	NJ 8430
Craigearn	105	NJ 7214
Craigellachie (Grampn.)	104	NJ 2844
Craigend	92	NO 1120
Craigendoran	90	NS 3181
Craiggiecat	99	NO 8592
Craighat	90	NS 4984
Craighouse	80	NR 5267
Craigie (Grampn.)	105	NJ 9119
Craigie (Strath.)	82	NS 4232
Craigie (Tays.)	98	NO 1143
Craiglockhart	85	NT 2270
Craigmillar	85	NT 2871
Craignant	50	SJ 2535
Craigneuk (Strath.)	84	NS 7656
Craigneuk (Strath.)	84	NS 7764
Craignure	89	NM 7236
Craigo	99	NO 6864
Craigow	92	NO 0806
Craig Penllyn	28	SS 9777
Craigrothie	93	NO 3710
Craigruie	90	NN 5020
Craigton (Grampn.)	99	NJ 8301
Craigton (Tays.)	98	NO 3250
Craigton (Tays.)	93	NO 5138
Craigtown	111	NC 8856
Craig-y-nos	28	SN 8315
Craik	77	NT 3408
Crail	93	NO 6107
Crailing	78	NT 6824
Crailinghall	78	NT 6921
Crakehall	66	SE 2490
Crambe	66	SE 7364
Cramlington	79	NZ 2776
Cramond	85	NT 1876
Cramond Bridge	85	NT 1775
Cranage	51	SJ 7568
Cranberry	51	SJ 8236
Cranborne	10	SU 0513
Cranbourne	20	SU 9272
Cranbrook	14	TQ 7735
Cranbrook Common	14	TQ 7938
Cranfield	34	SP 9542
Cranford	20	TQ 1077
Cranford St. Andrew	44	SP 9277
Cranford St. John	44	SP 9276
Cranham (Essex)	21	TQ 5787
Cranham (Glos.)	32	SO 8912
Crank	50	SJ 5099
Cranleigh	12	TQ 0638
Cranmore (I. of W.)	11	SZ 3990
Cranmore (Somer.)	17	ST 6843
Cranna	104	NJ 6352
Crannach	104	NJ 4954
Cranoe	44	SP 7695
Cransford	37	TM 3164
Cranshaws	86	NT 6961
Cranstal	56	NX 4602
Crantock	2	SW 7860
Cranwell	54	TF 0349
Cranwich	46	TL 7795
Cranworth	46	TF 9804
Crapstone	5	SX 5067
Crarae	89	NR 9897
Craster	79	NU 2519
Cratfield	37	TM 3175
Crathes	99	NO 7596
Crathie (Grampn.)	98	NO 2695
Crathie (Highld.)	97	NN 5893
Crathorne	66	NZ 4407
Craven Arms	40	SO 4382
Crawcrook	72	NZ 1363
Crawford	76	NS 9520
Crawfordjohn	76	NS 8823
Crawick	76	NS 7710
Crawley (Hants.)	11	SU 4234
Crawley (Oxon.)	33	SP 3312
Crawley (W Susx)	13	TQ 2636
Crawley Down	13	TQ 3237
Crawley Side	72	NY 9940
Crawshawbooth	58	SD 8125
Crawton	99	NO 8779
Cray (N Yorks.)	65	SD 9479
Cray (Powys)	28	SN 8924
Crayford	21	TQ 5175
Crayke	66	SE 5670
Crays Hill	22	TQ 7192
Cray's Pond	19	SU 6380
Creacombe	7	SS 8119
Creagorry	109	NF 7948
Creaton	44	SP 7071
Credenhill	30	SO 4543
Crediton	7	SS 8300
Creech St. Michael	8	ST 2725
Creed	3	SW 9347
Creekmouth	21	TQ 4581
Creeting St. Mary	37	TM 0956
Creeton	44	TF 0120
Creetown	69	NX 4758
Creggans	89	NN 0802
Cregneish	56	SC 1967
Cregrina	30	SO 1252
Creich (Fife.)	93	NO 3221
Creigiau	28	ST 0881
Cressage	41	SJ 5904
Cresselly	24	SN 0606
Cressing	22	TL 7920
Cresswell (Dyfed)	24	SN 0506
Cresswell (Northum.)	79	NZ 2993
Cresswell (Staffs.)	51	SJ 9739
Creswell	53	SK 5274
Cretingham	37	TM 2260
Crewe (Ches.)	50	SJ 4253
Crewe (Ches.)	51	SJ 7055
Crew Green	40	SJ 3215
Crewkerne	9	ST 4409
Crianlarich	90	NN 3825
Cribyn	26	SN 5251
Criccieth	48	SH 4938
Crich	53	SK 3554
Crichie	105	NJ 9544
Crichton	85	NT 3862
Crick (Northants.)	43	SP 5872
Crickadarn	30	SO 0942
Cricket St. Thomas	9	ST 3708
Crickheath	40	SJ 2923
Crickhowell	28	SO 2118
Cricklade	18	SU 0993
Cridling Stubbs	60	SE 5221
Crieff	91	NN 8621
Criggion	40	SJ 2915
Crigglestone	59	SE 3116
Crimond	105	NK 0556
Crimplesham	46	TF 6503
Crinaglack	102	NH 4240
Crinan	89	NR 7894
Cringleford	47	TG 1905
Crinow	24	SN 1214
Cripplesease	2	SW 5036
Cripp's Corner	14	TQ 7821
Croachy	103	NH 6527
Crockenhill	21	TQ 5067
Crockernwell	5	SX 7592
Crockerton	18	ST 8642
Crocketford or Ninemile Bar	69	NX 8272
Crockey Hill	60	SE 6246
Crockham Hill	21	TQ 4450
Crockleford Heath	23	TM 0426
Croeserw	28	SS 8695
Croesgoch	24	SM 8330
Croesyceiliog (Gwent)	25	SN 4016
Croesyceiliog (Gwent)	29	ST 3196
Croes-y-mwyalch	29	ST 3092
Croft (Ches.)	51	SJ 6393
Croft (Leic.)	43	SP 5195
Croft (Lincs.)	55	TF 5162
Croftamie	90	NS 4786
Crofton	59	SE 3717
Croft-on-Tees	66	NZ 2909
Crofty	25	SS 5295
Croggan	89	NM 7027
Croglin	71	NY 5747
Croick	106	NH 4591
Cromarty	103	NH 7766
Cromdale	103	NJ 0728
Cromer (Herts.)	35	TL 2928
Cromer (Norf.)	47	TG 2142
Cromford	53	SK 2956
Cromhall	18	ST 6990
Cromhall Common	18	ST 6989
Cromore	109	NB 4021
Cromra	97	NN 5489
Cromwell	54	SK 7961
Cronberry	76	NS 6022
Crondall	20	SU 7948
Cronk, The	56	SC 3495
Cronk-y-Voddy	56	SC 3086
Cronton	50	SJ 4988
Crook (Cumbr.)	63	SD 4694
Crook (Durham)	72	NZ 1635
Crookham (Berks.)	19	SU 5364
Crookham (Northum.)	87	NT 9138
Crookham Village	20	SU 7952
Crooklands	63	SD 5383
Crook of Devon	92	NO 0301
Cropredy	33	SP 4646
Cropston	43	SK 5511
Cropthorne	32	SO 9944
Cropton	67	SE 7589
Cropwell Bishop	53	SK 6835
Cropwell Butler	53	SK 6837
Crosby (Cumbr.)	62	NY 0738
Crosby (I. of M.)	56	SC 3279
Crosby (Lincs.)	60	SE 8711
Crosby (Mers.)	50	SJ 3099
Crosby Garrett	65	NY 7309
Crosby Ravensworth	63	NY 6214
Croscombe	17	ST 5844
Cross (Somerset)	17	ST 4154
Cross (W Isles)	109	NB 5061
Crossaig	81	NR 8351
Crossapoll	94	NL 9943
Cross Ash	29	SO 4019
Crossbost	109	NB 3924
Crosscanonby	62	NY 0739
Crossdale Street	47	TG 2239
Crossens	57	SD 3719
Crossford (Fife.)	85	NT 0686
Crossford (Strath.)	84	NS 8246
Crossgates (Fife.)	85	NT 1488
Crossgates (Powys)	30	SO 0865
Crossgill	64	SD 5562
Cross Green (Devon.)	4	SX 3888
Cross Green (Suff.)	36	TL 9952
Cross Hands	25	SN 5612
Crosshill (Fife)	92	NT 1796
Crosshill (Strath.)	75	NS 3206
Crosshouse (Strath.)	82	NS 3938
Cross Houses (Salop)	40	SJ 5307
Crossings	71	NY 5177
Cross in Hand	13	TQ 5621
Cross Inn (Dyfed)	26	SN 3957
Cross Inn (Dyfed)	26	SN 5464
Cross Inn (Mid Glam.)	28	ST 0583
Crosskeys (Gwent)	28	ST 2292
Crosskirk	112	ND 0370
Cross Lanes (Clwyd)	50	SJ 3746
Crosslanes (N Yorks.)	66	SE 5264
Crosslanes (Salop.)	40	SJ 3218
Crosslee	77	NT 3018
Crossmichael	69	NX 7267
Crossmoor	57	SD 4438
Cross of Jackston	105	NJ 7432

Crossroads — Discoed

Crossroads	99	NO 7594
Cross Street	37	TM 1876
Crossway	29	SO 4419
Crossway Green	41	SO 8368
Crosswell	26	SN 1236
Crosthwaite	63	SD 4491
Croston	57	SD 4818
Crostwick	47	TG 2515
Crostwight	47	TG 3329
Crouch Hill	9	ST 7010
Croughton	33	SP 5433
Crovie	105	NJ 8065
Crowan	2	SW 6434
Crowborough	13	TQ 5130
Crowcombe	16	ST 1336
Crowfield (Northants.)	34	SP 6141
Crowfield (Suff.)	37	TM 1557
Crow Hill	29	SO 6326
Crowhurst (E Susx)	14	TQ 7512
Crowhurst (Surrey)	21	TQ 3947
Crowland	45	TF 2310
Crowlas	2	SW 5133
Crowle (Here. and Worc.)	32	SO 9256
Crowle (Humbs.)	60	SE 7713
Crowmarsh Gifford	19	SU 6189
Crownhill	5	SX 4857
Crownthorpe	47	TG 0803
Crowthorne	20	SU 8464
Crowton	51	SJ 5774
Croxall	42	SK 1913
Croxdale	72	NZ 2636
Croxden	52	SK 0639
Croxley Green	20	TQ 0795
Croxton (Cambs.)	35	TL 2459
Croxton (Humbs.)	61	TA 0912
Croxton (Norf.)	46	TL 8786
Croxton (Staffs.)	51	SJ 7832
Croxton Kerrial	44	SK 8329
Croy (Highld.)	103	NH 7949
Croy (Strath.)	84	NS 7275
Croyde	6	SS 4439
Croydon (Cambs.)	35	TL 3149
Croydon (Gtr London)	21	TQ 3365
Cruckmeole	40	SJ 4309
Cruckton	40	SJ 4210
Crudon Bay	105	NK 0936
Crudgington	41	SJ 6317
Crudwell	18	ST 9592
Crug	40	SO 1872
Crugmeer	3	SW 9076
Crulivig	109	NB 1733
Crumlin	28	ST 2198
Crundale (Dyfed.)	24	SM 9718
Crundale (Kent)	15	TR 0749
Crunwear	24	SN 1810
Cruwys Morchard	7	SS 8712
Crux Easton	19	SU 4256
Crwbin	25	SN 4713
Crymmych	26	SN 1833
Crynant	28	SN 7095
Crystal Palace	21	TQ 3470
Cuaig	101	NG 7057
Cubbington	43	SP 3368
Cubert	2	SW 7857
Cublington	34	SP 8422
Cuckfield	13	TQ 3024
Cucklington	17	ST 7527
Cuckney	53	SK 5671
Cuddesdon	33	SP 5902
Cuddington (Bucks.)	34	SP 7311
Cuddington (Ches.)	51	SJ 5971
Cuddington Heath	50	SJ 4646
Cuddy Hill	57	SD 4937
Cudham	21	TQ 4459
Cudliptown	5	SX 5278
Cudworth (Somer.)	8	ST 3810
Cudworth (S Yorks.)	59	SE 3808
Cuffley	35	TL 3002
Culbo	103	NH 6360
Culbokie	102	NH 6059
Culburnie	102	NH 4941
Culcabock	103	NH 6844
Culcharry	103	NH 8650
Culdrain	104	NJ 5133
Culduie	101	NG 7140
Culford	36	TL 8370
Culgaith	63	NY 6129
Culham	19	SU 5095
Culkein	110	NC 0333
Culkerton	18	ST 9296
Cullachie	103	NH 9720
Cullen	104	NJ 5166
Cullercoats	79	NZ 3571
Cullerlie	99	NJ 7603
Cullicudden	103	NH 6564
Cullingworth	59	SE 0636
Cullipool	89	NM 7313
Cullivoe	113	HP 5402
Culloch	91	NN 7818
Cullompton	8	ST 0207
Culmaily	108	NH 8099
Culmington	40	SO 4982
Culmstock	8	ST 1013
Culnacraig	106	NC 0603
Culrain	108	NH 5794
Culross	85	NS 9885
Culroy	75	NS 3114
Culsh (Grampn.)	105	NJ 8848
Culswick	113	HU 2745
Cultercullen	105	NJ 9124
Cults (Grampn.)	104	NJ 5331
Culverstone Green	14	TQ 6363
Culverthorpe	54	TF 0240
Culworth	33	SP 5447
Cumbernauld	84	NS 7676
Cumberworth	55	TF 5073
Cuminestown	105	NJ 8050
Cummersdale	70	NY 3952
Cummertrees	70	NY 1366
Cummingstown	103	NJ 1368
Cumnock	75	NS 5619
Cumnor	33	SP 4604
Cumrew	71	NY 5550
Cumwhinton	71	NY 4552
Cumwhitton	71	NY 5052
Cundall (N Yorks.)	66	SE 4272
Cunninghamhead	82	NS 3741
Cupar	93	NO 3714
Cupar Muir	93	NO 3613
Curbar	53	SK 2574
Curbridge (Hants.)	11	SU 5211
Curbridge (Oxon.)	33	SP 3208
Curdridge	11	SU 5313
Curdworth	42	SP 1892
Curland	8	ST 2716
Currie	85	NT 1867
Curry Mallet	8	ST 3221
Curry Rivel	9	ST 3824
Curtisden Green	14	TQ 7440
Cury	2	SW 6721
Cushnie	105	NJ 7962
Cushuish	16	ST 1930
Cusop	30	SO 2341
Cutiau	38	SH 6317
Cutnall Green	41	SO 8768
Cutsdean	32	SP 0830
Cutthorpe	53	SK 3473
Cuxham	19	SU 6695
Cuxton	14	TQ 7166
Cuxwold	61	TA 1701
Cwm (Clwyd)	49	SJ 0677
Cwm (Gwent)	28	SO 1805
Cwm (W Glam.)	25	SS 6895
Cwmaman	28	SS 9999
Cwmavon	28	SS 7892
Cwmbach (Dyfed)	25	SN 2525
Cwmbach (Mid Glam.)	28	SO 0201
Cwmbelan	39	SN 9481
Cwmbran	29	ST 2894
Cwmcarn	28	ST 2293
Cwmcarvan	29	SO 4707
Cwm-Cewydd	39	SH 8713
Cwmcoy	26	SN 2941
Cwmdare	28	SN 9803
Cwmdu (Dyfed)	27	SN 6330
Cwmdu (Powys)	28	SO 1823
Cwmduad	26	SN 3731
Cwmfelin Boeth	24	SN 1919
Cwmfelin Mynach	24	SN 2324
Cwmffrwd	25	SN 4217
Cwmgwrach	28	SN 8605
Cwm Irfon	27	SN 8549
Cwmisfael	25	SN 4915
Cwm-Llinau	39	SH 8407
Cwmllynfell	25	SN 7413
Cwmparc	28	SS 9496
Cwmpengraig	26	SN 3436
Cwmsychpant	26	SN 4746
Cwmtillery	28	SO 2106
Cwm-y-glo	48	SH 5562
Cwmyoy	29	SO 2923
Cwmystwyth	27	SN 7873
Cwrt-newydd	26	SN 4847
Cwrt-y-gollen	28	SO 2317
Cyffylliog	49	SJ 0557
Cymmer (Mid Glam.)	28	ST 0290
Cymmer (W Glam.)	28	SS 8696
Cynghordy	27	SN 8139
Cynwyd	49	SJ 0541
Cynwyl Elfed	25	SN 3727

D

Dacre (Cumbr.)	63	NY 4526
Dacre (N Yorks.)	65	SE 1960
Dacre Banks	65	SE 1961
Daddry Shield	63	NY 8937
Dadford	34	SP 6638
Dadlington	43	SP 4098
Dafen	25	SN 5201
Daffy Green	46	TF 9609
Dagenham	21	TQ 5084
Daglingworth	32	SO 9905
Dagnall	34	SP 9916
Dailly	75	NS 2701
Dairsie or Osnaburgh	93	NO 4117
Dalavich	89	NM 9612
Dalbeattie	69	NX 8361
Dalblair	76	NS 6419
Dalbog	99	NO 5871
Dalby	56	SC 2178
Dalcapon	98	NN 9755
Dalchalloch	97	NN 7264
Dalchenna	89	NN 0706
Dalchreichart	102	NH 2912
Dalcross	103	NH 7748
Dalderby	55	TF 2465
Dale (Derby.)	53	SK 4338
Dale (Dyfed)	24	SM 8005
Dale (Shetld.)	113	HU 1852
Dalelia	95	NM 7369
Dalgarven	82	NS 2945
Dalginross	91	NN 7721
Dalguise	98	NN 9947
Dalhalvaig	111	NC 8954
Dalham	36	TL 7261
Daliburgh	109	NF 7421
Dalkeith	85	NT 3367
Dall	97	NN 5956
Dallas	103	NJ 1252
Dalleagles	75	NS 5710
Dallinghoo	37	TM 2654
Dallington	13	TQ 6519
Dalmally	89	NN 1527
Dalmary	90	NS 5195
Dalmellington	75	NS 4705
Dalmeny	85	NT 1477
Dalmore (Highld.)	103	NH 6668
Dalnabreck	95	NM 7069
Dalnavie	108	NH 6483
Dalness	96	NN 1751
Dalqueich	92	NO 0704
Dalry	82	NS 2949
Dalrymple	75	NS 3514
Dalserf	84	NS 7950
Dalston	70	NY 3750
Dalswinton	69	NX 9385
Dalton (Dumf. and Galwy.)	70	NY 1173
Dalton (Lancs.)	57	SD 4907
Dalton (Northum.)	71	NY 9158
Dalton (Northum.)	79	NZ 1172
Dalton (N Yorks.)	65	NZ 1108
Dalton (N Yorks.)	66	SE 4376
Dalton (S Yorks.)	53	SK 4593
Dalton in Furness	64	SD 2374
Dalton-le-Dale	72	NZ 4047
Dalton-on-Tees	66	NZ 2908
Dalton Piercy	73	NZ 4631
Dalveich	90	NN 6124
Dalwhinnie	97	NN 6384
Dalwood	8	ST 2400
Damerham	10	SU 1015
Damgate	47	TG 3909
Damnaglaur	68	NX 1235
Danbury	22	TL 7805
Danby	66	NZ 7009
Danby Wiske	66	SE 3398
Dandaleith	104	NJ 2845
Danderhall	85	NT 3069
Danebridge	51	SJ 9665
Dane End	35	TL 3321
Danehill	13	TQ 4027
Dane Hills	43	SK 5605
Daren-felen	28	SO 2212
Darenth	21	TQ 5671
Daresbury	51	SJ 5782
Darfield	59	SE 4104
Dargate	15	TR 0861
Darite	4	SX 2569
Darlaston	41	SO 9796
Darlingscott	33	SP 2324
Darlington	72	NZ 2914
Darliston	51	SJ 5833
Darlochan	80	NR 6723
Darlton	54	SK 7773
Darowen	39	SH 8302
Darras Hall	79	NZ 1571
Darrington	60	SE 4919
Darsham	37	TM 4170
Dartford	21	TQ 5474
Dartington	5	SX 7862
Dartmeet	5	SX 6773
Dartmouth	5	SX 8751
Darton	59	SE 3110
Darvel	84	NS 5637
Darwen	58	SD 6922
Datchet	20	SU 9876
Datchworth	35	TL 2619
Dauntsey	18	ST 9882
Davenham	51	SJ 6570
Daventry	33	SP 5762
Davidstow	4	SX 1587
Davington	77	NT 2302
Daviot (Grampn.)	105	NJ 7528
Daviot (Highld.)	103	NH 7139
Davoch of Grange	104	NJ 4951
Dawes Heath	22	TQ 8188
Dawley	41	SJ 6807
Dawlish	8	SX 9676
Dawlish Warren	8	SX 9778
Dawn	49	SH 8672
Dawsmere	55	TF 4430
Daylesford	33	SP 2425
Deal	15	TR 3752
Dean (Cumbr.)	62	NY 0725
Dean (Devon.)	5	SX 7364
Dean (Hants.)	11	SU 5619
Dean (Somer.)	17	ST 6743
Deanburnhaugh	77	NT 3911
Deane	19	SU 5450
Deanland	10	ST 9918
Dean Prior	5	SX 7363
Dean Row	51	SJ 8781
Deanscale	62	NY 0926
Deanshanger	34	SP 7639
Deanston	91	NN 7101
Dearham	62	NY 0736
Debach	37	TM 2454
Debden	36	TL 5533
Debden Cross	36	TL 5832
Debenham	37	TM 1763
Dechmont	85	NT 0370
Deddington	33	SP 4631
Dedham	37	TM 0533
Deene	44	SP 9492
Deenethorpe	44	SP 9592
Deepcar	59	SK 2897
Deepcut	20	SU 9057
Deepdale (Cumbr.)	65	SD 7284
Deeping Gate	45	TF 1509
Deeping St. James	45	TF 1609
Deeping St. Nicholas	45	TF 2115
Deerhurst	32	SO 8729
Defford	32	SO 9143
Defynnog	28	SN 9227
Deganwy	49	SH 7779
Deighton (N Yorks.)	66	NZ 3801
Deighton (N Yorks.)	60	SE 6244
Deiniolen	48	SH 5863
Delabole	4	SX 0683
Delamere	51	SJ 5668
Dell	109	NB 4861
Delliefure	103	NJ 0731
Delph	59	SD 9807
Dembleby	54	TF 0437
Denaby	60	SK 4899
Denbigh	49	SJ 0566
Denbury	5	SX 8268
Denby	53	SK 3946
Denby Dale	59	SE 2208
Denchworth	19	SU 3891
Denend	104	NJ 6038
Denford	44	SP 9976
Dengie	23	TL 9801
Denham (Bucks.)	20	TQ 0386
Denham (Suff.)	36	TL 7561
Denham (Suff.)	37	TM 1974
Denham Green	20	TQ 0388
Denhead (Fife.)	93	NO 4613
Denhead (Grampn.)	105	NJ 9952
Denhead of Gray	93	NO 3431
Denholm	78	NT 5718
Denholme	59	SE 0633
Denmead	11	SU 6511
Dennington	37	TM 2866
Denny	84	NS 8182
Dennyloanhead	84	NS 8180
Denshaw	59	SD 9710
Denside	99	NO 8095
Densole	15	TR 2141
Denston	36	TL 7652
Denstone	52	SK 0940
Dent	63	SD 7087
Den, The	82	NS 3251
Denton (Cambs.)	45	TL 1487
Denton (Durham)	72	NZ 2118
Denton (E Susx.)	13	TQ 4502
Denton (Gtr Mches.)	51	SJ 9295
Denton (Kent)	15	TR 2146
Denton (Lincs.)	54	SK 8632
Denton (Norf.)	47	TM 2887
Denton (Northants.)	34	SP 8357
Denton (N Yorks.)	59	SE 1448
Denton (Oxon.)	33	SP 5902
Denver	46	TF 6101
Denwick (Northum.)	79	NU 2014
Deopham	47	TG 0400
Deopham Green	47	TM 0499
Depden Green	36	TL 7756
Deptford (Gtr London)	21	TQ 3676
Deptford (Wilts.)	10	SU 0038
Derby	53	SK 3435
Derbyhaven	56	SC 2867
Deri	28	SO 1202
Derringstone	15	TR 2049
Derrington	41	SJ 8822
Derry Hill	18	ST 9670
Derrythorpe	60	SE 8208
Dersingham	46	TF 6830
Dervaig	94	NM 4351
Derwen	49	SJ 0650
Desborough	44	SP 8083
Desford	43	SK 4703
Detchant	87	NU 0836
Detling	14	TQ 7958
Deuddwr	40	SJ 2317
Devauden	29	ST 4899
Devil's Bridge	27	SN 7477
Devizes	18	SU 0061
Devonport	5	SX 4554
Devonside	91	NS 9296
Devoran	2	SW 7939
Dewlish	9	SY 7798
Dewsbury	59	SE 2422
Dhoon	56	SC 4586
Dhoor	56	SC 4396
Dhowin	56	NX 4101
Dial Post	12	TQ 1519
Dibden	11	SU 3908
Dibden Purlieu	11	SU 4106
Dickleburgh	47	TM 1682
Didbrook	32	SP 0531
Didcot	19	SU 5290
Diddington	45	TL 1965
Diddlebury	40	SO 5085
Didley	30	SO 4432
Didmarton	18	ST 8287
Didsbury	51	SJ 8490
Didworthy	5	SX 6862
Digby	54	TF 0754
Diggle	59	SE 0008
Dihewyd	26	SN 4855
Dilham	47	TG 3325
Dilhorne	51	SJ 9743
Dilston	72	NY 9763
Dilton Marsh	18	ST 8449
Dilwyn	30	SO 4154
Dinas (Dyfed)	24	SN 0139
Dinas (Dyfed)	25	SN 2730
Dinas (Gwyn.)	48	SH 2736
Dinas-Mawddwy	39	SH 8514
Dinas Powis	28	ST 1571
Dinchope	49	SO 4583
Dinder	17	ST 5744
Dinedor	31	SO 5336
Dingley	44	SP 7687
Dingwall	102	NH 5458
Dinnet	98	NO 4698
Dinnington (Somer.)	9	ST 4012
Dinnington (S Yorks.)	53	SK 5386
Dinnington (Tyne and Wear)	79	NZ 2073
Dinorwic	48	SH 5961
Dinton	10	SU 0131
Dinwoodie Mains	77	NY 1090
Dinworthy	6	SS 3015
Dippen	81	NR 7937
Dippin	81	NS 0422
Dipple (Grampn.)	104	NJ 3258
Dipple (Strath.)	75	NS 2002
Diptford	5	SX 7256
Dipton	72	NZ 1554
Dirleton	86	NT 5183
Discoed	30	SO 2764

Diseworth **Earsdon**

Diseworth	43	SK 4524
Dishforth	66	SE 3873
Disley	51	SJ 9784
Diss	37	TM 1179
Distington	62	NY 0023
Ditcheat	17	ST 6236
Ditchingham	47	TM 3391
Ditchling	13	TQ 3215
Dittisham	5	SX 8655
Ditton (Ches.)	50	SJ 4986
Ditton (Kent)	14	TQ 7158
Ditton Green	36	TL 6658
Ditton Priors	41	SO 6089
Dixton (Glos.)	32	SO 9830
Dixton (Gwent)	29	SO 5114
Dobwalls	4	SX 2165
Doccombe	5	SX 7786
Dochgarroch	102	NH 6140
Docking	46	TF 7637
Docklow	31	SO 5657
Dockray	62	NY 3921
Doddinghurst	21	TQ 5998
Doddington (Cambs.)	45	TL 4090
Doddington (Kent)	15	TQ 9357
Doddington (Lincs.)	54	SK 8970
Doddington (Northum.)	87	NU 0032
Doddington (Salop)	41	SO 6176
Doddiscombsleigh	5	SX 8586
Dodford (Here. and Worc.)	41	SO 9273
Dodford (Northants.)	34	SP 6160
Dodington (Avon)	18	ST 7579
Dodleston	50	SJ 3661
Dodworth	59	SE 3105
Doe Lea	53	SK 4566
Dogdyke	55	TF 2055
Dogmersfield	20	SU 7852
Dog Village	8	SX 9896
Dolanog	39	SJ 0612
Dolau	40	SO 1367
Dolbenmaen	48	SH 5043
Dolfach	27	SN 9077
Dol-for (Powys)	39	SH 8006
Dolfor (Powys)	40	SO 1087
Dolgarrog	49	SH 7766
Dolgellau	39	SH 7217
Doll	108	NC 8803
Dollar	91	NS 9697
Dolphinholme	64	SD 5153
Dolphinton	85	NT 1046
Dolton	6	SS 5712
Dolwen (Clwyd)	49	SH 8874
Dolwen (Powys)	39	SH 9707
Dolwyddelan	49	SH 7352
Dolyhir	30	SO 2458
Domgay	40	SJ 2819
Doncaster	60	SE 5803
Donhead St. Andrew	10	ST 9124
Donhead St. Mary	10	ST 9024
Donibristle	85	NT 1688
Donington	55	TF 2135
Donington on Bain	55	TF 2382
Donisthorpe	43	SK 3114
Donkey Town	20	SU 9460
Donnington (Berks.)	19	SU 4668
Donnington (Glos.)	33	SP 1928
Donnington (Here. and Worc.)	32	SO 7034
Donnington (Salop)	41	SJ 5807
Donnington (Salop)	41	SJ 7114
Donnington (W Susx.)	12	SU 8502
Donyatt	8	ST 3313
Doonfoot	75	NS 3218
Dorchester (Dorset)	9	SY 6990
Dorchester (Oxon.)	19	SU 5794
Dordon	43	SK 2600
Dore	53	SK 3081
Dores	102	NH 5934
Dorking	21	TQ 1649
Dormans Land	13	TQ 4042
Dormanstown	73	NZ 5823
Dormington	31	SO 5840
Dorney	20	SU 9379
Dornie	101	NG 8826
Dornoch (Highld.)	108	NH 7989
Dornock (Dumf. and Galwy.)	70	NY 2366
Dorrery	112	ND 0754
Dorridge	42	SP 1774
Dorrington (Lincs.)	54	TF 0752
Dorrington (Salop)	40	SJ 4703
Dorsington	32	SP 1349
Dorstone	30	SO 3142
Dorton	34	SP 6714
Dosthill	42	SP 2199
Doublebois	4	SX 1964
Dougarie	81	NR 8837
Doughton	18	ST 8791
Douglas (I. of M.)	56	SC 3876
Douglas (Strath.)	76	NS 8330
Douglas and Angus	93	NO 4332
Douglas Hill	48	SH 6065
Douglastown	98	NO 4147
Doulting	17	ST 6443
Dounby	113	HY 2920
Doune (Tays.)	91	NN 7201
Douneside	104	NJ 4806
Doulting	108	NH 5590
Dounreay	112	NC 9966
Dousland	5	SX 5368
Dove Holes	52	SK 0778
Dovenby	62	NY 0933
Dover	15	TR 3141
Doverdale	32	SO 8566
Doveridge	52	SK 1134
Dowally	98	NO 0047
Dowdeswell	32	SO 9919
Dowland	6	SS 5610
Dowlish Wake	8	ST 3712
Down Ampney	18	SU 1097
Downderry	4	SX 3153
Downe	21	TQ 4361
Downend (Berks.)	19	SU 4775
Downend (I. of W.)	11	SZ 5387
Downfield	93	NO 3833
Downgate	4	SX 3772
Downham (Cambs.)	45	TL 5284
Downham (Essex)	22	TQ 7395
Downham (Lancs.)	58	SD 7844
Downham (Northum.)	87	NT 8633
Downham Market	46	TF 6003
Down Hatherley	32	SO 8622
Downhead	17	ST 6845
Downhill	3	SW 8669
Downholme	65	SE 1197
Downies	99	NO 9294
Downley	20	SU 8495
Down St. Mary	7	SS 7404
Downton (Hants.)	11	SZ 2693
Downton (Wilts.)	10	SU 1721
Downton on the Rock	40	SO 4273
Dowsby	45	TF 1129
Doynton	18	ST 7173
Draffan	84	NS 7945
Drakeland Corner	5	SX 5758
Drakemyre	82	NS 2850
Drakes Broughton	32	SO 9248
Draughton (Northants.)	44	SP 7676
Draughton (N Yorks.)	65	SE 0352
Drax	60	SE 6726
Draycote	43	SP 4469
Draycott (Derby)	53	SK 4433
Draycott (Glos.)	33	SP 1836
Draycott (Somer.)	17	ST 4750
Draycott in the Clay	42	SK 1528
Draycott in the Moors	51	SJ 9840
Drayton (Hants.)	11	SU 6605
Drayton (Here. and Worc.)	41	SO 9076
Drayton (Leic.)	44	SP 8392
Drayton (Norf.)	47	TG 1713
Drayton (Oxon.)	33	SP 4241
Drayton (Oxon.)	19	SU 4794
Drayton (Somer.)	9	ST 4042
Drayton Bassett	42	SK 1900
Drayton Parslow	34	SP 8428
Drayton St. Leonard	19	SU 5996
Drefach (Dyfed)	26	SN 3538
Drefach (Dyfed)	26	SN 5045
Drefach (Dyfed)	25	SN 5213
Dreghorn	82	NS 3538
Drem	86	NT 5079
Drewsteignton	5	SX 7391
Driby	55	TF 3874
Driffield	18	SU 0799
Drift	2	SW 4328
Drigg	62	SD 0698
Drighlington	59	SE 2229
Drimnin	95	NM 5553
Drimpton	9	ST 4104
Drinkstone	36	TL 9561
Drinkstone Green	36	TL 9660
Drointon	42	SK 0226
Droitwich	32	SO 8962
Dron	92	NO 1415
Dronfield	53	SK 3578
Dronfield Woodhouse	53	SK 3278
Drongan	75	NS 4418
Dronley	93	NO 3435
Droxford	11	SU 6018
Droylsden	51	SJ 9098
Druid	49	SJ 0343
Druidston	24	SM 8716
Druimarbin	96	NN 0861
Druimavuic	96	NN 0044
Drum (Grampn.)	105	NJ 8946
Drum (Tays.)	92	NO 0400
Drumbeg	110	NC 1232
Drumblade	104	NJ 5840
Drumbuie (Dumf. and Galwy.)	69	NX 5682
Drumbuie (Highld.)	101	NG 7730
Drumburgh	70	NY 2659
Drumchapel	84	NS 5270
Drumchardine	102	NH 5644
Drumclog	84	NS 6339
Drumeldrie	93	NO 4403
Drumelzier	85	NT 1333
Drumfearn	101	NG 6716
Drumgask	97	NN 6193
Drumgley	98	NO 4250
Drumguish	97	NN 7999
Drumhead	99	NO 6092
Drumlassie	104	NJ 6405
Drumlemble	80	NR 6619
Drumlithie	99	NO 7880
Drummore	68	NX 1336
Drumnadrochit	102	NH 5029
Drumnagorrach	104	NJ 5252
Drumrash	69	NX 6871
Drumsturdy	93	NO 4935
Drumuie	100	NG 4546
Drumuillie	103	NH 9420
Drumwhindle	105	NJ 9236
Drunkendub	99	NO 6646
Drury	50	SJ 2964
Drybeck	63	NY 6615
Drybridge (Grampn.)	104	NJ 4362
Drybridge (Strath.)	82	NS 3536
Drybrook	29	SO 6416
Dry Doddington	54	SK 8446
Dry Drayton	35	TL 3862
Dryhope	77	NT 2624
Drymen	90	NS 4788
Drymuir	105	NJ 9146
Drynoch	100	NG 4031
Dubford	105	NJ 7963
Dubton	99	NO 5652
Duckington	50	SJ 4851
Ducklington	33	SP 3507
Duck's Cross	35	TL 1156
Duddingston	85	NT 2972
Duddington	44	SK 9800
Duddleswell	13	TQ 4628
Duddo	87	NT 9342
Duddon	50	SJ 5164
Dudleston Heath	50	SJ 3636
Dudley	41	SO 9390
Duffield	53	SK 3443
Duffryn	28	SS 8495
Dufftown	104	NJ 3240
Duffus	104	NJ 1668
Dufton	63	NY 6925
Duggleby	67	SE 8766
Duirinish	101	NG 7831
Duisdalemore	101	NG 6913
Duisky	96	NN 0176
Dukestown	28	SO 1410
Dukinfield	51	SJ 9497
Dulas (Gwyn.)	48	SH 4789
Dulcote	17	ST 5644
Dulford	8	ST 0606
Dull	97	NN 8049
Dullatur	84	NS 7476
Dullingham	36	TL 6357
Dulnain Bridge	103	NH 9924
Duloe (Beds.)	35	TL 1560
Duloe (Corn.)	4	SX 2358
Dulsie	103	NH 9341
Dulverton	16	SS 9127
Dulwich	21	TQ 3373
Dumbarton	82	NS 4075
Dumbleton	32	SP 0135
Dumfries	70	NX 9775
Dummer	19	SU 5845
Dun (Tays.)	99	NO 6659
Dunalastair	97	NN 7159
Dunan (Isle of Skye)	100	NG 5828
Dunan (Strath.)	82	NS 1571
Dunans	89	NS 0491
Dunball	17	ST 3140
Dunbar	86	NT 6878
Dunbeath	112	ND 1629
Dunbeg	89	NM 8734
Dunblane	91	NN 7801
Dunbog	93	NO 2817
Duncaston (Grampn.)	104	NJ 5826
Duncanston (Highld.)	102	NH 5956
Dunchurch	43	SP 4871
Duncote	34	SP 6750
Duncow	70	NX 9683
Duncrievie	92	NO 1309
Duncton	12	SU 9516
Dundee	93	NO 4030
Dundon	17	ST 4732
Dundonald	82	NS 3634
Dundraw	70	NY 2149
Dundreggan	102	NH 3114
Dundrennan	69	NX 7447
Dundry	29	ST 5566
Dunecht	105	NJ 7509
Dunfermline	85	NT 0987
Dunham	54	SK 8174
Dunham-on-the-Hill	50	SJ 4772
Dunhampton	41	SO 8466
Dunham Town	51	SJ 7488
Dunholme	54	TF 0279
Dunino	93	NO 5311
Dunipace	84	NS 8083
Dunkeld	98	NO 0242
Dunkeswell	8	ST 1407
Dunkirk	15	TR 0758
Dunk's Green	21	TQ 6152
Dunlappie	99	NO 5967
Dunley	41	SO 7869
Dunlop	82	NS 4049
Dunmore (Central.)	84	NS 8989
Dunmore (Strath.)	81	NR 7961
Dunnet	112	ND 2171
Dunnichen	99	NO 5048
Dunning	92	NO 0114
Dunnington (Humbs.)	67	TA 1551
Dunnington (N Yorks.)	66	SE 6652
Dunnington (Warw.)	32	SP 0653
Dunnockshaw	58	SD 8127
Dunollie	89	NM 8532
Dunoon	82	NS 1777
Dunragit	68	NX 1557
Duns	87	NT 7853
Dunsby	45	TF 1026
Dunscore	69	NX 8684
Dunscroft	60	SE 6409
Dunsden Green	20	SU 7477
Dunsfold	12	TQ 0036
Dunsford	5	SX 8089
Dunshelt	93	NO 2410
Dunshillock	105	NJ 9848
Dunsley	73	NZ 8511
Dunsmore	34	SP 8605
Dunstable	35	TL 0221
Dunstall	42	SK 1920
Dunstall Green	36	TL 7460
Dunstan	79	NU 2419
Dunster	16	SS 9943
Duns Tew	33	SP 4528
Dunston (Lincs.)	54	TF 0663
Dunston (Norf.)	47	TG 2302
Dunston (Staffs.)	41	SJ 9217
Dunston (Tyne and Wear)	72	NZ 2263
Dunsville	60	SE 6407
Dunswell	61	TA 0735
Dunsyre	85	NT 0748
Dunterton	4	SX 3779
Duntisbourne Abbots	32	SO 9707
Duntisbourne Rouse	32	SO 9805
Duntish	9	ST 6906
Duntocher	82	NS 4972
Dunton (Beds.)	35	TL 2344
Dunton (Bucks.)	34	SP 8224
Dunton (Norf.)	46	TF 8730
Dunton Bassett	43	SP 5490
Dunton Green	21	TQ 5157
Dunton Wayletts	22	TQ 6590
Dunure	75	NS 2515
Dunvant	25	SS 5993
Dunvegan	100	NG 2548
Dunwich	37	TM 4770
Durdar	70	NY 4051
Durham	72	NZ 2742
Durisdeer	76	NS 8903
Durleigh	16	ST 2736
Durley (Hants.)	11	SU 5115
Durley (Wilts.)	18	SU 2364
Durley Street	11	SU 5217
Durnamuck	106	NH 0192
Durness	110	NC 4067
Durno	105	NJ 7128
Durran	108	ND 1863
Durrington (Wilts.)	18	SU 1544
Durrington (W Susx.)	12	TQ 1105
Dursley	18	ST 7597
Durston	17	ST 2828
Durweston	10	ST 8508
Duston	34	SP 7261
Duthil	103	NH 9324
Dutlas	40	SO 2077
Duton Hill	22	TL 6026
Dutton	51	SJ 5779
Duxford	35	TL 4846
Dwygyfylchi	49	SH 7377
Dwyran	48	SH 4466
Dyce	105	NJ 8812
Dyffryn	28	SS 8593
Dyffryn Ardudwy	38	SH 5822
Dyffryn Ceidrych	25	SN 7025
Dyffryn Cellwen	28	SN 8509
Dyke (Devon.)	6	SS 3123
Dyke (Grampn.)	103	NH 9858
Dyke (Lincs.)	45	TF 1022
Dykehead (Central)	90	NS 5997
Dykehead (Strath.)	84	NS 8759
Dykehead (Tays.)	98	NO 3860
Dykends	98	NO 2557
Dylife	39	SN 8594
Dymchurch	15	TR 1029
Dymock	31	SO 6931
Dyrham	18	ST 7375
Dysart	93	NT 3093
Dyserth	49	SJ 0579

E

Eagland Hill	57	SD 4345
Eagle	54	SK 8767
Eaglescliffe	72	NZ 4215
Eaglesfield (Cumbr.)	62	NY 0928
Eaglesfield (Dumf. and Galwy.)	70	NY 2374
Eaglesham	84	NS 5751
Eairy	56	SC 2977
Eakring	53	SK 6762
Ealand	60	SE 7811
Ealing	21	TQ 1781
Eamont Bridge	63	NY 5228
Earby	58	SD 9046
Earcroft	58	SD 6824
Eardington	41	SO 7290
Eardisland	30	SO 4158
Eardisley	30	SO 3149
Eardiston (Here. and Worc.)	41	SO 6968
Eardiston (Salop)	40	SJ 3725
Earith	45	TL 3875
Earle	79	NT 9826
Earlestown	51	SJ 5795
Earlish	100	NG 3861
Earls Barton	34	SP 8563
Earls Colne	22	TL 8528
Earl's Croome	32	SO 8642
Earlsdon	43	SP 3177
Earlsferry	93	NO 4800
Earlsford	105	NJ 8334
Earl's Green	36	TM 0366
Earl Shilton	43	SP 4697
Earl Soham	37	TM 2363
Earl Sterndale	52	SK 0967
Earlston (Borders)	86	NT 5738
Earlston (Strath.)	82	NS 4035
Earl Stonham	37	TM 1158
Earlswood	42	SP 1174
Earlswood Common	29	ST 4595
Earnley	12	SZ 8096
Earsdon	79	NZ 3272

Earshaig Elvington

Earshaig	76	NT 0402
Earsham	47	TM 3289
Earswick	66	SE 6157
Eartham	12	SU 9309
Easby	66	NZ 5708
Easdale (Strath.)	89	NM 7317
Easebourne	12	SU 8922
Easenhall	43	SP 4679
Easington (Bucks.)	34	SP 6810
Easington (Cleve.)	73	NZ 7418
Easington (Durham)	72	NZ 4143
Easington (Humbs.)	61	TA 3919
Easington (Northum.)	87	NU 1234
Easington (Oxon.)	19	SU 6697
Easington Lane	72	NZ 3646
Easingwold	66	SE 5269
Easole Street	15	TR 2652
Eassie and Nevay	98	NO 3345
East Aberthaw	28	ST 0367
East Allington	5	SX 7648
East Anstey	7	SS 8626
East Ashling	12	SU 8207
East Barming	14	TQ 7254
East Barnet	21	TQ 2794
East Barsham	46	TF 9133
East Beckham	47	TG 1640
East Bedfont	20	TQ 1074
East Bergholt	37	TM 0734
East Bilney	46	TF 9519
East Blatchington	13	TQ 4800
East Boldre	11	SU 3700
Eastbourne	13	TV 6199
East Bradenham	46	TF 9208
East Brent	17	ST 3452
East Bridge	37	TM 4566
East Bridgford	53	SK 6943
East Buckland	7	SS 6731
East Budleigh	8	SY 0684
East Burton	10	SY 8386
Eastbury (Berks.)	19	SU 3477
Eastbury (Gtr London)	20	TQ 0991
East Cairnbeg	99	NO 7076
East Calder	85	NT 0867
East Carleton (Norf.)	47	TG 1802
East Carlton (Northants.)	44	SP 8389
East Chaldon or Chaldon Herring	10	SY 7983
East Challow	19	SU 3988
East Chiltington	13	TQ 3715
East Chisenbury	18	SU 1352
Eastchurch	15	TQ 9871
East Clandon	20	TQ 0651
East Claydon	34	SP 7325
Eastcombe (Glos.)	32	SO 8804
East Combe (Somer.)	16	ST 1631
Eastcote (Gtr London)	20	TQ 1188
Eastcott (Corn.)	6	SS 2515
Eastcott (Wilts.)	18	SU 0255
East Cottingwith	60	SE 7042
East Coulston	18	ST 9454
Eastcourt	18	ST 9792
East Cowes	11	SZ 5095
East Cowton	66	NZ 3103
East Cramlington	79	NZ 2876
East Creech	10	SY 9282
Eastdean (E Susx.)	13	TV 5598
East Dean (Hants.)	11	SU 2726
East Dean (W Susx.)	12	SU 9013
East Dereham	46	TF 9913
East Down	6	SS 5941
East Drayton	54	SK 7775
East End (Avon)	29	ST 4770
East End (Dorset	10	SY 9998
Eastend (Essex)	23	TQ 9492
East End (Hants.)	19	SU 4161
East End (Hants.)	11	SZ 3697
East End (Herts.)	35	TL 4527
East End (Kent)	14	TQ 8335
East End (Oxon.)	33	SP 3914
Easter Ardross	108	NH 6373
Easter Balmoral	98	NO 2693
East Boleskine	102	NH 5122
Easter Compton	29	ST 5782
Easter Galcantray	103	NH 8147
Eastergate	12	SU 9405
Easter Lednathie	98	NO 3363
Easter Moniack	102	NH 5543
Easter Muckovie	103	NH 7044
Eastern Green	43	SP 2780
Easter Ord	99	NJ 8304
Easterton	18	SU 0154
Eastertown	17	ST 3454
East Farleigh	14	TQ 7353
East Farndon	44	SP 7185
East Ferry	60	SK 8199
Eastfield (N Yorks.)	67	TA 0484
Eastfield (Strath.)	84	NS 7574
Eastfield (Strath.)	84	NS 8964
Eastfield Hall	79	NU 2206
East Garston	19	SU 3676
Eastgate (Durham)	72	NY 9538
Eastgate (Norf.)	47	TG 1423
East Ginge	19	SU 4486
East Goscote	43	SK 6413
East Grafton	18	SU 2560
East Grimstead	11	SU 2227
East Grinstead	13	TQ 3938
East Guldeford	15	TQ 9321
East Haddon	43	SP 6668
East Hagbourne	19	SU 5388
East Halton	61	TA 1419
East Ham (Essex)	21	TQ 4283
Eastham (Mers.)	50	SJ 3580
Easthampstead	20	SU 8667
East Hanney	19	SU 4192
East Hanningfield	22	TL 7601
East Hardwick	60	SE 4618
East Harling	46	TL 9986
East Harlsey	66	SE 4299
East Harptree	17	ST 5655
East Hartford	79	NZ 2679
East Harting	12	SU 7919
East Hatley	35	TL 2850
East Hauxwell	65	SE 1693
East Heckington	55	TF 1944
East Hedleyhope	72	NZ 1540
East Hendred	19	SU 4588
East Heslerton	67	SE 9276
East Hoathly	13	TQ 5216
Easthope	40	SO 5695
Easthorpe	23	TL 9121
East Horrington	17	ST 5846
East Horsley	20	TQ 0952
Easthouses	85	NT 3465
East Huntspill	17	ST 3444
East Hyde	35	TL 1317
East Ilsley	19	SU 4981
Eastington (Glos.)	32	SO 7705
Eastington (Glos.)	32	SP 1213
East Kennett	18	SU 1167
East Keswick	59	SE 3544
East Kilbride	84	NS 6354
East Kirkby	55	TF 3362
East Knighton	10	SY 8185
East Knoyle	10	ST 8830
East Lambrook	9	ST 4319
East Langdon	15	TR 3346
East Langton	44	SP 7292
East Langwell	108	NC 7206
East Lavington	12	SU 9416
East Layton	72	NZ 1609
Eastleach Martin	33	SP 1905
Eastleach Turville	33	SP 1905
East Leake	43	SK 5526
East Leigh (Devon.)	7	SS 6905
Eastleigh (Hants.)	11	SU 4518
East Lexham	46	TF 8617
East Lilburn	79	NU 0423
Eastling	15	TQ 9656
East Linton	86	NT 5977
East Liss	12	SU 7827
East Looe	4	SX 2553
East Lound	60	SK 7899
East Lulworth	10	SY 8581
East Mains	99	NO 6797
East Malling	14	TQ 7057
East March	93	NO 4436
East Marden	12	SU 8014
East Markham	54	SK 7472
East Marton	65	SD 9050
East Meon	11	SU 6822
East Mersea	23	TM 0414
East Molesey	21	TQ 1568
East Morden	10	SY 9194
East Morton	59	SE 1042
Eastney	11	SZ 6698
Eastnor	32	SO 7337
East Norton	44	SK 7800
East Oakley	19	SU 5749
Eastoft	60	SE 8016
East Ogwell	5	SX 8370
Easton (Cambs.)	45	TL 1371
Easton (Cumbr.)	70	NY 4372
Easton (Devon.)	5	SX 7288
Easton (Dorset)	9	SY 6871
Easton (Hants.)	11	SU 5132
Easton (I. of W.)	11	SZ 3485
Easton (Lincs.)	44	SK 9226
Easton (Norf.)	47	TG 1311
Easton (Somer.)	17	ST 5147
Easton (Suff.)	37	TM 2858
Easton Grey	18	ST 8787
Easton-in-Gordano	29	ST 5175
Easton Maudit	34	SP 8858
Easton on the Hill	44	TF 0004
Easton Royal	18	SU 2060
East Ord	87	NT 9851
East Panson	4	SX 3692
East Peckham	14	TQ 6649
East Pennard	17	ST 5937
East Poringland	47	TG 2701
East Portlemouth	5	SX 7438
East Prawle	5	SX 7736
East Preston	12	TQ 0702
East Putford	6	SS 3616
East Quantoxhead	16	ST 1343
East Rainton	72	NZ 3347
East Ravendale	55	TF 2399
East Raynham	46	TF 8825
Eastrea	45	TL 2997
East Retford	54	SK 7080
Eastriggs	70	NY 2465
Eastrington	60	SE 7929
East Rudham	46	TF 8228
East Runton	47	TG 1942
East Ruston	47	TG 3427
Eastry	15	TR 3155
East Saltoun	86	NT 4767
East Shefford	19	SU 3974
East Sleekburn	79	NZ 2785
East Stoke (Dorset)	10	SY 8787
East Stoke (Notts.)	54	SK 7549
East Stour	10	ST 8022
East Stourmouth	15	TR 2662
East Stratton	19	SU 5440
East Studdal	15	TR 3149
East Taphouse	4	SX 1863
East Thirston	79	NZ 1999
East Tilbury	22	TQ 6877
East Tisted	12	SU 7032
East Torrington	55	TF 1483
East Tuddenham	47	TG 0811
East Tytherley	11	SU 2929
East Tytherton	18	ST 9674
East Village	7	SS 8405
Eastville	55	TF 4057
East Wall	40	SO 5293
East Walton	46	TF 7416
Eastwell	44	SK 7728
East Wellow	11	SU 3020
East Wemyss	93	NT 3396
East Whitburn	84	NS 9665
Eastwick	35	TL 4311
East Wickham	21	TQ 4576
East Williamston	24	SN 0905
East Winch	46	TF 6916
East Wittering	12	SZ 7996
East Witton	65	SE 1486
Eastwood (Essex)	22	TQ 8588
Eastwood (Notts.)	53	SK 4646
Eastwood (W Yorks.)	58	SD 9625
East Woodhay	19	SU 4061
East Worldham	12	SU 7538
East Wretham	46	TL 9190
Eathorpe	43	SP 3969
Eaton (Ches.)	51	SJ 5763
Eaton (Ches.)	51	SJ 8765
Eaton (Leic.)	44	SK 7929
Eaton (Norf.)	47	TG 2006
Eaton (Notts.)	54	SK 7077
Eaton (Oxon.)	33	SP 4403
Eaton (Salop)	40	SO 3789
Eaton (Salop)	40	SO 4989
Eaton Bishop	30	SO 4439
Eaton Bray	34	SP 9720
Eaton Constantine	41	SJ 5906
Eaton Hastings	18	SU 2698
Eaton Socon	35	TL 1658
Eaton upon Tern	41	SJ 6523
Ebberston	67	SE 8983
Ebbesborne Wake	10	ST 9824
Ebbw Vale (Gwent)	28	ST 2094
Ebchester	72	NZ 1055
Ebford	8	SX 9887
Ebrington	33	SP 1840
Ecchinswell	19	SU 5060
Ecclaw	86	NT 7568
Ecclefechan	70	NY 1974
Eccles (Borders)	87	NT 7641
Eccles (Gtr Mches.)	51	SJ 7798
Eccles (Kent)	14	TQ 7260
Ecclesfield	53	SK 3393
Eccleshall	41	SJ 8329
Ecclesmachan	85	NT 0573
Eccles Road	46	TM 0190
Eccleston (Ches.)	50	SJ 4162
Eccleston (Lancs.)	57	SD 5216
Eccleston (Mers.)	50	SJ 4895
Eccup	59	SE 2842
Echt	105	NJ 7305
Eckford	78	NT 7125
Eckington (Derby.)	53	SK 4379
Eckington (Here. and Worc.)	32	SO 9241
Ecton	34	SP 8263
Edale	52	SK 1285
Edburton	13	TQ 2311
Edderton	108	NH 7184
Eddleston	85	NT 2447
Edenbridge	21	TQ 4446
Edenfield	58	SD 8019
Edenhall	63	NY 5632
Edenham	45	TF 0621
Edensor	53	SK 2469
Edenthorpe	60	SE 6206
Ederline	89	NM 8702
Edern	48	SH 2739
Edgbaston	42	SP 0684
Edgcott	34	SP 6722
Edge	40	SJ 3908
Edgebolton	41	SJ 5721
Edge End	29	SO 5913
Edgefield	47	TG 0934
Edgeworth	32	SO 9406
Edgmond	41	SJ 7119
Edgmond Marsh	41	SJ 7120
Edgton	40	SO 3885
Edgware	21	TQ 2091
Edgworth	58	SD 7416
Edinample	90	NN 6022
Edinbane	100	NG 3451
Edinburgh	85	NT 2674
Edingale	42	SK 2112
Edingley	53	SK 6655
Edingthorpe	47	TG 3132
Edington (Somer.)	17	ST 3939
Edington (Wilts.)	18	ST 9252
Edington Burtle	17	ST 3943
Edithmead	17	ST 3249
Edith Weston	44	SK 9205
Edlesborough	34	SP 9719
Edlingham	79	NU 1108
Edlington	55	TF 2371
Edmonbyers	72	NZ 0150
Edmondsham	10	SU 0611
Edmondsley	72	NZ 2348
Edmondthorpe	44	SK 8517
Edmonton	21	TQ 3493
Ednam	86	NT 7337
Edradynate	97	NN 8852
Edrom	87	NT 8255
Edstaston	50	SJ 5131
Edstone	33	SP 1761
Edwalton	53	SK 5935
Edwardstone	36	TL 9442
Edwinsford	27	SN 6334
Edwinstowe	53	SK 6266
Edworth	35	TL 2241
Edwyn Ralph	31	SO 6457
Edzell	99	NO 5968
Efail Isaf	28	ST 0884
Efailnewydd	48	SH 3536
Efenechtyd	50	SJ 1155
Effingham	20	TQ 1253
Efford	7	SS 8901
Egerton (Gtr Mches.)	58	SD 7014
Egerton (Kent)	14	TQ 9047
Eggington	34	SP 9525
Egginton	52	SK 2628
Egglescliffe	72	NZ 4213
Eggleston	72	NZ 0023
Egham	20	TQ 0171
Egleton	44	SK 8707
Eglingham	79	NU 1019
Egloshayle	4	SX 0071
Egloskerry	4	SX 2786
Eglwysbach	49	SH 8070
Eglwys-Brewis	28	ST 0168
Eglwyswrw	26	SN 1438
Egmanton	54	SK 7368
Egremont	62	NY 0110
Egton	67	NZ 8006
Egton Bridge	67	NZ 8005
Eilanreach	101	NG 8017
Eilean Darach	106	NH 1087
Elan Village	27	SN 9365
Elberton (Avon)	29	ST 6088
Elburton (Devon.)	5	SX 5353
Elcombe	18	SU 1280
Eldernell	45	TL 3298
Eldersfield	32	SO 7931
Elderslie	82	NS 4462
Eldroth	65	SD 7665
Eldwick	59	SE 1240
Elford (Northum.)	87	NU 1830
Elford (Staffs.)	42	SK 1810
Elgin	104	NJ 2162
Elgol	100	NG 5214
Elham	15	TR 1744
Elie	93	NO 4900
Elim	48	SH 3584
Eling	11	SU 3612
Elishader	100	NG 5065
Elishaw	78	NY 8694
Elkesley	53	SK 6875
Elkstone	32	SO 9612
Elland	59	SE 1020
Ellastone	52	SK 1143
Ellemford	86	NT 7360
Ellenhall	41	SJ 8426
Ellen's Green	12	TQ 1035
Ellerbeck (N Yorks.)	66	SE 4396
Ellerby (Humbs.)	61	TA 1637
Ellerby (N Yorks.)	73	NZ 7914
Ellerdine Heath	41	SJ 6121
Ellerker	60	SE 9229
Ellerton (Humbs.)	60	SE 7039
Ellerton (Salop)	41	SJ 7126
Ellesborough	34	SP 8306
Ellesmere	50	SJ 3934
Ellesmere Port	50	SJ 4077
Ellingham (Norf.)	47	TM 3592
Ellingham (Northum.)	79	NU 1725
Ellingstring	65	SE 1783
Ellington (Cambs.)	45	TL 1671
Ellington (Northum.)	79	NZ 2792
Ellisfield	19	SU 6345
Ellistown	43	SK 4311
Ellon	105	NJ 9530
Ellough	47	TM 4486
Elloughton	61	SE 9428
Ellwood	29	SO 5808
Elm	45	TF 4607
Elmbridge	41	SO 8967
Elmdon (Essex)	35	TL 4639
Elmdon (W Mids)	42	SP 1783
Elmdon Heath	42	SP 1580
Elmesthorpe	43	SP 4696
Elmhurst	42	SK 1112
Elmley Castle	32	SO 9841
Elmley Lovett	41	SO 8669
Elmore	32	SO 7715
Elmore Back	32	SO 7716
Elm Park	21	TQ 5385
Elmscott	6	SS 2321
Elmsett	37	TM 0546
Elmstead Market	23	TM 0624
Elmsted Court	15	TR 1145
Elmstone	15	TR 2660
Elmstone Hardwicke	32	SO 9226
Elmswell	36	TL 9964
Elmton	53	SK 5073
Elphin	110	NC 2111
Elphinstone	85	NT 3970
Elrick	105	NJ 8206
Elrig	68	NX 3247
Elsdon	78	NY 9393
Elsecar	59	SE 3800
Elsenham	22	TL 5425
Elsfield	33	SP 5409
Elsham	61	TA 0312
Elsing	47	TG 0516
Elslack	58	SD 9349
Elsrickle	85	NT 0643
Elstead (Surrey)	12	SU 9043
Elsted (W Susx.)	12	SU 8119
Elston	54	SK 7548
Elstone	7	SS 6716
Elstow	35	TL 0547
Elstree	21	TQ 1895
Elstronwick	61	TA 2232
Elswick	57	SD 4138
Elsworth	35	TL 3163
Elterwater	62	NY 3204
Eltham	21	TQ 4274
Eltisley	35	TL 2759
Elton (Cambs.)	45	TL 0893
Elton (Ches.)	50	SJ 4575
Elton (Cleve.)	72	NZ 4017
Elton (Derby.)	53	SK 2261
Elton (Glos.)	29	SO 6914
Elton (Here. and Worc.)	40	SO 4571
Elton (Notts.)	54	SK 7638
Elvanfoot	76	NS 9517
Elvaston	53	SK 4132
Elveden	36	TL 8279
Elvingston	86	NT 4674
Elvington (Kent)	15	TR 2750
Elvington (N Yorks.)	60	SE 6947

Elwick Fitzhead

Elwick (Cleve.)	73	NZ 4532
Elwick (Northum.)	87	NU 1136
Elworth	51	SJ 7361
Elworthy	16	ST 0835
Ely (Cambs.)	45	TL 5380
Ely (S Glam.)	28	ST 1476
Emberton	34	SP 8849
Embleton (Cumbr.)	62	NY 1630
Embleton (Northum.)	79	NU 2322
Embo	108	NH 8192
Emborough	17	ST 6151
Embsay	65	SE 0053
Emery Down	11	SU 2808
Emley	59	SE 2413
Emmer Green	20	SU 7177
Emmington	34	SP 7402
Emneth	45	TF 4807
Emneth Hungate	45	TF 5107
Empingham	44	SK 9408
Empshott	12	SU 7731
Emsworth	12	SU 7405
Enborne	19	SU 4365
Enchmarsh	40	SO 4996
Enderby	43	SP 5399
End Moor	63	SD 5584
Endon	51	SJ 9253
Enfield	21	TQ 3296
Enford	18	SU 1351
Engine Common	18	ST 6984
Englefield	19	SU 6272
Englefield Green	20	SU 9870
English Bicknor	29	SO 5815
Englishcombe	18	ST 7162
English Frankton	40	SJ 4529
Enham-Alamein	19	SU 3648
Enmore	16	ST 2335
Ennerdale Bridge	62	NY 0615
Enoch	76	NS 8801
Enochdhu	98	NO 0662
Ensbury	10	SZ 0896
Ensdon	40	SJ 4016
Ensis	6	SS 5626
Enstone	33	SP 3725
Enterkinfoot	76	NS 8504
Enville	40	SO 8286
Eoropie	109	NB 5165
Epperstone	53	SK 6548
Epping	35	TL 4602
Epping Green (Essex)	35	TL 4305
Epping Green (Herts.)	35	TL 2906
Epping Upland	35	TL 4404
Eppleby	72	NZ 1713
Epsom	21	TQ 2160
Epwell	33	SP 3540
Epworth	60	SE 7803
Erbistock	50	SJ 3541
Erbusaig	101	NG 7629
Erdington	42	SP 1291
Eredine	89	NM 9609
Eriboll	110	NC 4356
Ericstane	77	NT 0710
Eridge Green	13	TQ 5535
Erines	89	NR 8575
Eriswell	36	TL 7278
Erith	21	TQ 5177
Erlestoke	18	ST 9853
Ermington	5	SX 6353
Erpingham	47	TG 1931
Errogie	102	NH 5622
Errol	93	NO 2522
Erskine	82	NS 4771
Ervie	68	NX 0067
Erwarton	37	TM 2234
Erwood	30	SO 0943
Eryholme	66	NZ 3208
Eryrys	50	SJ 2057
Escalls	2	SW 3627
Escrick	60	SE 6243
Esgairgeiliog	39	SH 7605
Esh	72	NZ 1944
Esher	20	TQ 1464
Eshott	79	NZ 2097
Eshton	65	SD 9356
Esh Winning	72	NZ 1942
Eskadale	102	NH 4539
Eskbank	85	NT 3266
Eskdale Green	62	NY 1400
Esprick	57	SD 4035
Essendine	44	TF 0412
Essendon	35	TL 2708
Essich	103	NH 6539
Essington	41	SJ 9603
Esslemont	105	NJ 9329
Eston	73	NZ 5518
Etal	87	NT 9339
Etchilhampton	18	SU 0460
Etchingham	14	TQ 7126
Etchinghill (Kent)	15	TR 1639
Etchinghill (Staffs.)	42	SK 0218
Eton	20	SU 9678
Etteridge	97	NN 6892
Ettington	33	SP 2649
Etton (Humbs.)	61	SE 9743
Etton (Northants.)	45	TF 1306
Ettrick	77	NT 2714
Ettrickbridge End	77	NT 3824
Etwall	53	SK 2732
Euston	36	TL 8978
Euxton	57	SD 5518
Evanton	102	NH 6066
Evedon	55	TF 0947
Evelix	108	NH 7690
Evenjobb	30	SO 2662
Evenley	33	SP 5834
Evenlode	33	SP 2229
Evenwood	72	NZ 1524
Evercreech	17	ST 6438
Everdon	33	SP 5957
Everingham	60	SE 8042
Everleigh	18	SU 1953
Everley	67	SE 9789
Eversholt	34	SP 9933
Evershot	9	ST 5704
Eversley	20	SU 7762
Eversley Cross	20	SU 7961
Everton (Beds.)	35	TL 2051
Everton (Hants.)	11	SZ 2993
Everton (Notts.)	53	SK 6891
Evertown	70	NY 3576
Evesbatch	31	SO 6848
Evesham	32	SP 0344
Evington	43	SK 6203
Ewden Village	53	SK 2796
Ewell	21	TQ 2262
Ewell Minnis	15	TR 2643
Ewelme	19	SU 6491
Ewen	18	SU 0097
Ewenny	28	SS 9077
Ewerby	55	TF 1247
Ewesley	79	NZ 0592
Ewhurst (E Susx)	14	TQ 7924
Ewhurst (Surrey)	12	TQ 0940
Ewloe	50	SJ 3066
Eworthy	5	SX 4494
Ewshot	20	SU 8149
Ewyas Harold	29	SO 3828
Exbourne	6	SS 6002
Exbury	11	SU 4200
Exebridge	8	SS 9324
Exelby	66	SE 2986
Exeter	8	SX 9292
Exford	7	SS 8538
Exhall	32	SP 1055
Exminster	8	SX 9487
Exmouth	8	SY 0080
Exning	36	TL 6265
Exton (Devon.)	8	SX 9886
Exton (Hants.)	11	SU 6121
Exton (Leic.)	44	SK 9211
Exton (Somer.)	16	SS 9233
Eyam	53	SK 2176
Eydon	33	SP 5450
Eye (Here. and Worc.)	30	SO 4963
Eye (Northants.)	45	TF 2202
Eye (Suffolk)	37	TM 1473
Eyemouth	87	NT 9464
Eyeworth	35	TL 2545
Eyhorne Street	14	TQ 8354
Eyke	37	TM 3151
Eynesbury	35	TL 1859
Eynsford	21	TQ 5365
Eynsham	33	SP 4309
Eype	9	SY 4491
Eythorne	15	TR 2849
Eyton (Here. and Worc.)	30	SO 4761
Eyton (Salop)	40	SO 3687
Eyton upon the Weald Moors	41	SJ 6414

F

Faccombe	19	SU 3857
Faceby	66	NZ 4903
Faddiley	51	SJ 5752
Fadmoor	66	SE 6789
Faifley	82	NS 5073
Failand	29	ST 5272
Failford	75	NS 4526
Failsworth	58	SD 9002
Fairbourne	38	SH 6113
Fairburn	60	SE 4727
Fairfield	41	SO 9475
Fairford	32	SP 1501
Fairlie	82	NS 2155
Fairlight	14	TQ 8612
Fairmile	8	SY 0997
Fairmilehead	85	NT 2567
Fair Oak (Hants.)	11	SU 4918
Fairoak (Staffs.)	51	SJ 7632
Fairseat	14	TQ 6261
Fairstead (Essex)	22	TL 7616
Fairstead (Norf.)	47	TG 2723
Fairwarp	13	TQ 4626
Fairy Cross	6	SS 4024
Fakenham	46	TF 9229
Fala	86	NT 4361
Fala Dam	86	NT 4261
Falahill	85	NT 3956
Faldingworth	54	TF 0684
Falfield	29	ST 6893
Falkenham	37	TM 2939
Falkirk	84	NS 8880
Falkland	92	NO 2507
Falla	78	NT 7013
Fallin	91	NS 8391
Falmer	13	TQ 3508
Falmouth	2	SW 8032
Falstone	78	NY 7287
Fanagmore	110	NC 1750
Fangdale Beck	66	SE 5694
Fangfoss	67	SE 7653
Fanmore	94	NM 4244
Fans	86	NT 6140
Farcet	45	TL 2094
Far Cotton	34	SP 7458
Farden	41	SO 5776
Fareham	11	SU 5806
Farewell	42	SK 0811
Faringdon	19	SU 2895
Farington	57	SD 5425
Farlam	71	NY 5558
Farleigh	21	TQ 3660
Farleigh Hungerford	18	ST 7957
Farleigh Wallop	19	SU 6246
Farlesthorpe	55	TF 4774
Farley (Salop)	40	SJ 3808
Farley (Staffs.)	52	SK 0644
Farley (Wilts.)	11	SU 2229
Farley Green	20	TQ 0645
Farley Hill	20	SU 7564
Farleys End	32	SO 7615
Farlington	66	SE 6167
Farlow	41	SO 6380
Farmborough	17	ST 6560
Farmcote	32	SP 0629
Farmers	27	SN 6444
Farmington	32	SP 1315
Farmoor	33	SP 4407
Farmtown	104	NJ 5051
Farnborough (Berks.)	19	SU 4381
Farnborough (Gtr London)	21	TQ 4464
Farnborough (Hants.)	20	SU 8753
Farnborough (Warw.)	33	SP 4349
Farncombe	20	SU 9755
Farndish	34	SP 9263
Farndon (Ches.)	50	SJ 4154
Farndon (Notts.)	54	SK 7651
Farnell	99	NO 6255
Farnham (Dorset)	10	ST 9514
Farnham (Essex)	35	TL 4724
Farnham (N Yorks.)	66	SE 3460
Farnham (Suff.)	37	TM 3660
Farnham (Surrey)	20	SU 8446
Farnham Common	20	SU 9584
Farnham Green	35	TL 4625
Farnham Royal	20	SU 9682
Farningham	21	TQ 5566
Farnley	59	SE 2147
Farnley Tyas	59	SE 1612
Farnsfield	53	SK 6456
Farnworth (Ches.)	50	SJ 5187
Farnworth (Gtr Mches.)	58	SD 7305
Farr (Highld.)	111	NC 7163
Farr (Highld.)	103	NH 6833
Farr (Highld.)	97	NH 8203
Farringdon	8	SY 0191
Farrington Gurney	17	ST 6255
Farsley	59	SE 2135
Farthinghoe	33	SP 5339
Farthingstone	34	SP 6155
Farway	8	SY 1895
Fasnacloich	96	NN 0247
Fasque	99	NO 6475
Fassfern	96	NN 0278
Fatfield	72	NZ 3053
Fattahead	105	NJ 6657
Faugh	71	NY 5154
Fauldhouse	84	NS 9260
Faulkbourne	22	TL 7917
Faulkland	18	ST 7354
Fauls	51	SJ 5933
Faversham	15	TR 0161
Favillar	104	NJ 2734
Fawfieldhead	52	SK 0763
Fawkham Green	21	TQ 5865
Fawler	33	SP 3717
Fawley (Berks.)	19	SU 3981
Fawley (Bucks.)	20	SU 7586
Fawley (Hants.)	11	SU 4503
Fawley Chapel	29	SO 5829
Faxfleet	60	SE 8624
Faygate	13	TQ 2134
Fazeley	42	SK 2001
Fearby	65	SE 1981
Fearnan	97	NN 7244
Fearnhead	51	SJ 6290
Fearnmore	101	NG 7260
Featherstone (Staffs.)	41	SJ 9305
Featherstone (W Yorks.)	59	SE 4222
Feckenham	32	SP 0061
Fedderate	105	NJ 8949
Feering	22	TL 8720
Feetham	65	SD 9898
Felbridge	13	TQ 3739
Felbrigg	47	TG 2039
Felcourt	13	TQ 3841
Felden	35	TL 0404
Felindre (Dyfed)	25	SN 7027
Felindre (Powys)	40	SO 1681
Felinfach	30	SO 0933
Felinfoel	25	SN 5202
Felingwm Uchaf	25	SN 5024
Felixkirk	66	SE 4684
Felixstowe	37	TM 3034
Felkington	87	NT 9444
Felling	72	NZ 2762
Felmersham	34	SP 9957
Felmingham	47	TG 2529
Felpham	12	SZ 9599
Felsham	36	TL 9457
Felsted	22	TL 6720
Feltham	20	TQ 1072
Felthorpe	47	TG 1618
Felton (Avon)	29	ST 5165
Felton (Here. and Worc.)	31	SO 5748
Felton (Northum.)	79	NU 1800
Felton Butler	40	SJ 3917
Feltwell	46	TL 7190
Feltwell Anchor	46	TL 6789
Fence	58	SD 8237
Fendike Corner	55	TF 4560
Fen Ditton	35	TL 4860
Fen Drayton	45	TL 3468
Fen End	42	SP 2274
Feniscowles	58	SD 6425
Feniton	8	SY 1199
Fenny Bentley	52	SK 1750
Fenny Bridges	8	SY 1198
Fenny Compton	33	SP 4152
Fenny Drayton	43	SP 3597
Fenny Stratford	34	SP 8834
Fenrother	79	NZ 1792
Fenstanton	45	TL 3168
Fenton (Cambs.)	45	TL 3279
Fenton (Lincs.)	54	SK 8476
Fenton (Lincs.)	54	SK 8750
Fenton (Staffs.)	51	SJ 8944
Fenton Town	87	NT 9733
Fenwick (Northum.)	87	NU 0639
Fenwick (Northum.)	79	NZ 0572
Fenwick (Strath.)	82	NS 4643
Fenwick (S Yorks.)	60	SE 5916
Feock	2	SW 8238
Feolin Ferry	80	NR 4469
Feriniquarrie	100	NG 1750
Fern	99	NO 4861
Ferndale	28	SS 9997
Ferndown	10	SU 0700
Ferness	103	NH 9645
Fernham	19	SU 2991
Fernhill Heath	32	SO 8659
Fernhurst	12	SU 9028
Fernie	93	NO 3115
Fernilee	52	SK 0178
Fernlea	100	NG 3732
Ferrensby	66	SE 3660
Ferring	12	TQ 0902
Ferrybridge	60	SE 4824
Ferryden	99	NO 7156
Ferryhill	72	NZ 2832
Ferryside	25	SN 3610
Fersfield	47	TM 0682
Feshiebridge	97	NH 8504
Fetcham	21	TQ 1555
Fetterangus	105	NJ 9850
Fettercairn	99	NO 6573
Fewston	65	SE 1954
Ffairfach	25	SN 6220
Ffestiniog	49	SH 7042
Fforest	25	SN 5804
Ffostrasol	26	SN 3747
Ffrith	50	SJ 2855
Ffrwdgrech	28	SO 0227
Ffynnonddrain	25	SN 4021
Ffynnongroew	50	SJ 1382
Fiddes	99	NO 8181
Fiddington (Glos.)	32	SO 9231
Fiddington (Somer.)	16	ST 2140
Fiddlers Hamlet	35	TL 4701
Field	52	SK 0233
Field Broughton	62	SD 3881
Field Dalling	46	TG 0039
Field Head	43	SK 4909
Fifehead Magdalen	9	ST 7721
Fifehead Neville	9	ST 7610
Fifield (Berks.)	20	SU 9076
Fifield (Oxon.)	33	SP 2318
Figheldean	18	SU 1547
Filby	47	TG 4613
Filey	67	TA 1180
Filgrave	34	SP 8748
Filkins	33	SP 2304
Filleigh (Devon.)	7	SS 6628
Filleigh (Devon.)	7	SS 7410
Fillingham	54	SK 9485
Fillongley	43	SP 2787
Filton	29	ST 6079
Fimber	67	SE 8960
Finavon	99	NO 4957
Fincham	46	TF 6806
Finchampstead	20	SU 7963
Finchdean	12	SU 7312
Finchingfield	36	TL 6832
Finchley	21	TQ 2890
Findern	53	SK 3030
Findhorn	103	NJ 0464
Findochty	104	NJ 4667
Findon (Grampn.)	99	NO 9397
Findon (W Susx)	12	TQ 1208
Findon Mains	102	NH 6060
Finedon	44	SP 9272
Fingal Street	37	TM 2169
Fingask	105	NJ 7827
Fingest	20	SU 7791
Finghall	65	SE 1889
Fingringhoe	23	TM 0220
Finmere	34	SP 6333
Finnart	97	NN 5157
Finningham	37	TM 0669
Finningly	60	SK 6699
Finnygaud	104	NJ 6054
Finsbay	109	NG 0786
Finsbury	21	TQ 3282
Finstall	41	SO 9869
Finsthwaite	62	SD 3687
Finstock	33	SP 3516
Finstown	113	HY 3514
Fintry (Central)	84	NS 6186
Fintry (Grampn.)	105	NJ 7554
Fionnphort (Island of Mull)	88	NM 2923
Firbeck	53	SK 5688
Firgrove	58	SD 9113
Firsby	55	TF 4563
Fir Tree	72	NZ 1334
Fishbourne (I of W)	11	SZ 5592
Fishbourne (W Susx)	12	SU 8304
Fishburn	72	NZ 3632
Fishcross	91	NS 8995
Fisherford	105	NJ 6635
Fisher's Pond	11	SU 4820
Fisherstreet	12	SU 9531
Fisherton (Highld.)	103	NH 7451
Fisherton (Strath.)	75	NS 2717
Fishguard	24	SM 9637
Fishlake	60	SE 6513
Fishpool	58	SD 8009
Fishtoft	55	TF 3642
Fishtoft Drove	55	TF 3148
Fishtown of Usan	99	NO 7254
Fishwick	87	NT 9151
Fiskavaig	100	NG 3234
Fiskerton (Lincs.)	54	TF 0472
Fiskerton (Notts.)	54	SK 7351
Fittleton	18	SU 1449
Fittleworth	12	TQ 0119
Fitton End	45	TF 4312
Fitz	40	SJ 4417
Fitzhead	16	ST 1228

Fitzwilliam	59	SE 4115
Five Ashes	13	TQ 5525
Fivehead	8	ST 3522
Five Oak Green	13	TQ 6445
Five Oaks	12	TQ 0928
Five Penny Borve	109	NB 4055
Five Penny Ness	109	NB 5364
Five Roads	25	SN 4905
Flackwell Heath	20	SU 8890
Fladbury	32	SO 9946
Fladdabister	113	HU 4332
Flagg	52	SK 1368
Flamborough	67	TA 2270
Flamstead	35	TL 0814
Flansham	12	SU 9601
Flasby	65	SD 9456
Flash	52	SK 0267
Flashader	100	NG 3553
Flatt, The	71	NY 5678
Flaunden	34	TL 0100
Flawborough	54	SK 7842
Flawith	66	SE 4865
Flax Bourton	29	ST 5069
Flaxby	66	SE 3957
Flaxley	29	SO 6915
Flaxpool	16	ST 1435
Flaxton	66	SE 6762
Fleckney	43	SP 6493
Flecknoe	33	SP 5163
Fleet (Hants.)	20	SU 8054
Fleet (Lincs.)	45	TF 3823
Fleetham	79	NU 1928
Fleet Hargate	45	TF 3925
Fleetwood	57	SD 3247
Flemingston	28	ST 0170
Flemington	84	NS 6559
Flempton	36	TL 8169
Fletching	13	TQ 4323
Flexford	20	SU 9350
Flimby	62	NY 0233
Flimwell	14	TQ 7131
Flint	50	SJ 2472
Flintham	54	SK 7446
Flint Mountain	50	SJ 2369
Flinton	61	TA 2136
Flitcham	46	TF 7226
Flitton	35	TL 0536
Flitwick	35	TL 0335
Flixborough	60	SE 8715
Flixton (Gtr Mches.)	51	SJ 7494
Flixton (N Yorks.)	67	TA 0479
Flixton (Suff.)	47	TM 3186
Flockton	59	SE 2314
Flodden	87	NT 9235
Flodigarry	100	NG 4671
Flookburgh	64	SD 3675
Flordon	47	TM 1897
Flore	34	SP 6460
Flotterton	79	NT 9902
Flowton	37	TM 0847
Flushing (Corn.)	2	SW 8034
Flushing (Grampn.)	105	NK 0546
Flyford Flavell	32	SO 9754
Fobbing	22	TQ 7183
Fochabers	104	NJ 3458
Fochriw	28	SO 1005
Fockerby	60	SE 8419
Fodderletter	104	NJ 1421
Fodderty	102	NH 5159
Foel	39	SH 9911
Foffarty	98	NO 4145
Foggathorpe	60	SE 7537
Fogo	87	NT 7749
Foindle	110	NC 1948
Folda	98	NO 1964
Fole	52	SK 0437
Foleshill	43	SP 3582
Folke	9	ST 6513
Folkestone	15	TR 2336
Folkingham	54	TF 0433
Folkington	13	TQ 5604
Folksworth	45	TL 1490
Folkton	67	TA 0579
Folla Rule	105	NJ 7333
Follifoot	66	SE 3452
Folly Gate	6	SX 5797
Fonthill Bishop	10	ST 9332
Fonthill Gifford	10	ST 9231
Fontmell Magna	10	ST 8616
Fontwell	12	SU 9407
Foolow	52	SK 1976
Foots Cray	21	TQ 4770
Forcett	72	NZ 1712
Ford (Bucks.)	34	SP 7709
Ford (Glos.)	32	SP 0829
Ford (Northum.)	87	NT 9437
Ford (Salop)	40	SJ 4113
Ford (Staffs.)	52	SK 0654
Ford (Strath.)	89	NM 8603
Ford (Wilts.)	18	ST 8475
Ford (W Susx)	12	TQ 0003
Fordcombe	13	TQ 5240
Fordell	85	NT 1588
Forden	40	SJ 2201
Ford End	22	TL 6716
Fordham (Cambs.)	36	TL 6370
Fordham (Essex)	23	TL 9228
Fordham (Norf.)	46	TL 6199
Fordingbridge	10	SU 1413
Fordon	67	TA 0475
Fordoun	99	NO 7475
Fordstreet (Essex)	23	TL 9227
Ford Street (Somer.)	8	ST 1518
Fordwells	33	SP 3013
Fordwich	15	TR 1859
Fordyce	104	NJ 5563
Foremark	43	SK 3326
Forestburn Gate	79	NZ 0696
Forestfield	84	NS 8566
Forest Gate	21	TQ 4085
Forest Green	12	TQ 1241
Forest Head	71	NY 5857
Forest Hill	33	SP 5807
Forest Mill	91	NS 9594
Forest Row	13	TQ 4235
Forestside	12	SU 7512
Forest Town	53	SK 5662
Forfar	98	NO 4550
Forgandenny	92	NO 0818
Forgie	104	NJ 3954
Formby	57	SD 2907
Forncett End	47	TM 1493
Forncett St. Mary	47	TM 1694
Forncett St. Peter	47	TM 1693
Forneth	98	NO 0945
Fornham All Saints	36	TL 8367
Fornham St. Martin	36	TL 8566
Forres	103	NJ 0358
Forsbrook	51	SJ 9641
Forse	112	ND 2234
Forsinard	111	NC 8842
Forstal, The	14	TQ 8946
Forston	9	SY 6695
Fort Augustus	102	NH 3709
Forter	98	NO 1864
Forteviot	92	NO 0517
Fort George	103	NH 7656
Forth	84	NS 9453
Forthampton	32	SO 8532
Fortingall	97	NN 7447
Forton (Lancs.)	64	SD 4851
Forton (Salop)	40	SJ 4216
Forton (Somer.)	8	ST 3306
Forton (Staffs.)	41	SJ 7521
Fortree	105	NJ 9640
Fortrie	105	NJ 6645
Fortrose	103	NH 7256
Fortuneswell	9	SY 6873
Fort William	96	NN 1074
Forty Hill	21	TQ 3398
Forward Green	37	TM 1059
Fosbury	19	SU 3157
Fosdyke	55	TF 3133
Foss	97	NN 7958
Fossebridge	32	SP 0811
Foss-y-ffin	26	SN 4460
Foster Street	35	TL 4909
Foston (Derby.)	52	SK 1831
Foston (Lincs.)	54	SK 8542
Foston on the Wolds	67	TA 1055
Fotherby	55	TF 3191
Fotheringhay	45	TL 0593
Foulden (Borders)	87	NT 9355
Foulden (Norf.)	46	TL 7699
Foul Mile	13	TQ 6215
Foulridge	58	SD 8942
Foulsham	47	TG 0324
Fountainhall	86	NT 4349
Four Ashes	36	TM 0070
Fourcrosses (Gwyn.)	48	SH 3939
Four Crosses (Powys)	39	SJ 0508
Four Crosses (Powys)	40	SJ 2718
Four Crosses (Staffs.)	41	SJ 9509
Four Elms	21	TQ 4648
Four Forks	16	ST 2336
Four Gotes	45	TF 4516
Four Lanes	2	SW 6838
Fourlanes End	51	SJ 8059
Four Marks	11	SU 6634
Four Mile Bridge	48	SH 2778
Four Oaks (E Susx)	14	TQ 8624
Four Oaks (W Mids)	42	SP 1198
Four Oaks (W Mids)	42	SP 2480
Fourstones	71	NY 8967
Four Throws	14	TQ 7729
Fovant	10	SU 0028
Foveran	105	NJ 9824
Fowey	4	SX 1251
Fowlis	93	NO 3133
Fowlis Wester	91	NN 9223
Fowlmere	35	TL 4245
Fownhope	31	SO 5734
Foxdale	56	SC 2878
Foxearth	36	TL 8344
Foxfield	62	SD 2085
Foxham	18	ST 9777
Foxhole (Corn.)	4	SW 9654
Foxholes (N Yorks.)	67	TA 0173
Fox Lane	20	SU 8557
Foxley (Norf.)	47	TG 0321
Foxley (Wilts.)	18	ST 8985
Foxt	52	SK 0348
Foxton (Cambs.)	35	TL 4148
Foxton (Leic.)	44	SP 7090
Foxup	65	SD 8676
Foy	29	SO 5928
Foyers	102	NH 4921
Fraddon	3	SW 9158
Fradley	42	SK 1513
Fradswell	51	SJ 9831
Fraisthorpe	67	TA 1561
Framfield	13	TQ 4920
Framingham Earl	47	TG 2702
Framingham Pigot	47	TG 2703
Framlingham	37	TM 2863
Frampton (Dorset)	9	SY 6294
Frampton (Lincs.)	55	TF 3239
Frampton Cotterell	29	ST 6582
Frampton Mansell	32	SO 9202
Frampton on Severn	32	SO 7407
Frampton West End	55	TF 3040
Framsden	37	TM 1959
Framwellgate Moor	72	NZ 2644
Franche	41	SO 8178
Frankby	50	SJ 2486
Frankley	41	SO 9980
Frankton	43	SP 4270
Frant	13	TQ 5835
Fraserburgh	105	NJ 9966
Frating Green	23	TM 0923
Fratton	11	SU 6600
Freathy	4	SX 3952
Freckenham	36	TL 6672
Freckleton	57	SD 4228
Freeby	44	SK 8020
Freeland	33	SP 4112
Freethorpe	47	TG 4105
Freethorpe Common	47	TG 4004
Freiston	55	TF 3743
Fremington	6	SS 5132
Frenchay	29	ST 6377
Frenchbeer	5	SX 6785
Frensham	12	SU 8441
Freshfield	36	SD 2807
Freshford	18	ST 7860
Freshwater	11	SZ 3487
Fressingfield	37	TM 2677
Freston	37	TM 1739
Freswick	112	ND 3667
Frettenham	47	TG 2417
Freuchie	93	NO 2806
Friar's Gate	13	TQ 4933
Friday Bridge	45	TF 4605
Fridaythorpe	67	SE 8759
Friern Barnet	21	TQ 2892
Friesthorpe	54	TF 0683
Frieth	20	SU 7990
Frilford	19	SU 4497
Frilsham	19	SU 5373
Frimley	20	SU 8758
Frindsbury	14	TQ 7369
Fring	46	TF 7334
Fringford	34	SP 6028
Frinsted	14	TQ 8957
Frinton-on-Sea	23	TM 2319
Friockheim	99	NO 5949
Frisby on the Wreake	43	SK 6917
Friskney	55	TF 4555
Friston (E Susx)	13	TV 5498
Friston (Suff.)	37	TM 4160
Fritchley	53	SK 3553
Fritham	11	SU 2413
Frith Bank	55	TF 3147
Frith Common	41	SO 6969
Frithelstock	6	SS 4619
Frithville	55	TF 3250
Frittenden	14	TQ 8141
Fritton (Norf.)	47	TG 4700
Fritton (Norf.)	47	TM 2293
Fritwell	33	SP 5229
Frizington	62	NY 0316
Frocester	32	SO 7803
Frodesley	40	SJ 5101
Frodsham	50	SJ 5177
Froggatt	53	SK 2476
Froghall	52	SK 0247
Frogmore	20	SU 8360
Frolesworth	43	SP 5090
Frome	18	ST 7747
Frome St. Quintin	9	ST 5902
Fromes Hill	31	SO 6846
Fron (Gwyn.)	48	SH 3539
Fron (Powys)	40	SJ 2203
Fron (Powys)	30	SO 0865
Fron Cysyllte	50	SJ 2741
Fron-goch	49	SH 9039
Frosterley	72	NZ 0237
Froxfield	19	SU 2967
Froxfield Green	11	SU 7025
Fryerning	22	TL 6400
Fryton	66	SE 6875
Fulbeck	54	SK 9450
Fulbourn	35	TL 5256
Fulbrook	33	SP 2513
Fulford (N Yorks.)	60	SE 6149
Fulford (Somer.)	16	ST 2129
Fulford (Staffs.)	51	SJ 9438
Fulham	21	TQ 2576
Fulking	13	TQ 2411
Fuller's Moor	50	SJ 4953
Fuller Street	22	TL 7415
Fullerton	11	SU 3739
Fulletby	55	TF 2973
Full Sutton	67	SE 7455
Fullwood	82	NS 4450
Fulmer	20	SU 9985
Fulmodeston	46	TF 9931
Fulnetby	55	TF 0979
Fulstow	55	TF 3297
Fulwell	72	NZ 3959
Fulwood (Lancs.)	57	SD 5331
Fulwood (S Yorks.)	53	SK 3085
Funtington	12	SU 7908
Funzie	113	HU 6689
Furnace	89	NN 0200
Furneux Pelham	35	TL 4327
Fyfett	8	ST 2314
Fyfield (Essex)	22	TL 5707
Fyfield (Glos.)	33	SP 2003
Fyfield (Hants.)	19	SU 2946
Fyfield (Oxon.)	19	SU 4298
Fyfield (Wilts.)	18	SU 1468
Fylingthorpe	67	NZ 9405
Fyvie	105	NJ 7637

G

Gabroc Hill	82	NS 4551
Gaddesby	43	SK 6813
Gaer	28	SO 1721
Gaerwen	48	SH 4871
Gagingwell	33	SP 4025
Gainford	72	NZ 1716
Gainsborough	54	SK 8189
Gainsford End	36	TL 7235
Gairloch	106	NG 8076
Gairlochy	96	NN 1784
Gairney Bank	92	NT 1299
Galashiels	86	NT 4936
Galby	43	SK 6901
Galgate	64	SD 4855
Galhampton	17	ST 6329
Gallatown	93	NT 2994
Galley Common	43	SP 3192
Galleyend	22	TL 7103
Galleywood	22	TL 7002
Gallowfauld	98	NO 4342
Galltair	101	NG 8120
Galmisdale	95	NM 4784
Galmpton (Devon.)	5	SX 6940
Galmpton (Devon.)	5	SX 8856
Galphay	66	SE 2572
Galston	82	NS 5036
Galtrigill	100	NG 1854
Gamblesby	63	NY 6039
Gamlingay	35	TL 2452
Gamrie	105	NJ 7962
Gamston (Notts.)	53	SK 6037
Gamston (Notts.)	54	SK 7076
Ganavan	89	NM 8632
Ganllwyd	39	SH 7224
Gannachy	99	NO 5970
Ganstead	61	TA 1434
Ganthorpe	66	SE 6870
Ganton	67	SE 9877
Garbhallt (Strath.)	89	NS 0295
Garboldisham	46	TM 0081
Gardenstown	105	NJ 7964
Gare Hill	18	ST 7840
Garelochhead	90	NS 2491
Garford	19	SU 4296
Garforth	59	SE 4033
Gargrave	65	SD 9354
Gargunnock	91	NS 7094
Garinin	109	NB 1944
Garlieston	69	NX 4746
Garlogie	105	NJ 7805
Garmond	105	NJ 8052
Garmouth	104	NJ 3364
Garn	48	SH 2734
Garnant	25	SN 6813
Garn-Dolbenmaen	48	SH 4944
Garnett Bridge	63	SD 5299
Garnkirk	84	NS 6768
Garrabost	109	NB 5133
Garraron	89	NM 8008
Garras	2	SW 7023
Garreg	48	SH 6141
Garreg Bank	40	SJ 2811
Garrick	91	NN 8412
Garrigill	71	NY 7441
Garros	100	NG 4963
Garrow	91	NN 8240
Garsdon	18	ST 9687
Garshall Green	51	SJ 9633
Garsington	33	SP 5802
Garstang	57	SD 4945
Garston	50	SJ 4083
Garswood	50	SJ 5599
Gartcosh	84	NS 6968
Garth (Clwyd)	50	SJ 2542
Garth (I. of M.)	56	SC 3177
Garth (Mid Glam.)	28	SS 8690
Garth (Powys)	27	SN 9549
Garthbrengy	30	SO 0433
Gartheli	27	SN 5956
Garthmyl	40	SO 1999
Garthorpe (Humbs.)	60	SE 8419
Garthorpe (Leic.)	44	SK 8320
Gartmore	90	NS 5297
Gartness (Central)	90	NS 5086
Gartness (Strath.)	84	NS 7864
Gartocharn	90	NS 4286
Garton	61	TA 2635
Garton-on-the-Wolds	67	SE 9859
Gartymore	112	ND 0114
Garvald	86	NT 5870
Garvan	96	NM 9777
Garvard	88	NR 3691
Garve	102	NH 3961
Garveston	46	TG 0207
Garvock	82	NS 2571
Garway	29	SO 4522
Garynahine	109	NB 2331
Gastard	18	ST 8868
Gasthorpe	46	TL 9780
Gatcombe	11	SZ 4885
Gatebeck	63	SD 5485
Gate Burton	54	SK 8382
Gateforth	60	SE 5528
Gatehead	82	NS 3936
Gate Helmsley	66	SE 6955
Gatehouse	78	NY 7988
Gatehouse of Fleet	69	NX 5956
Gatelawbridge	76	NX 9096
Gateley	46	TF 9624
Gatenby	66	SE 3287
Gateshead	72	NZ 2562
Gatesheath	50	SJ 4760
Gateside (Fife.)	92	NO 1809
Gateside (Strath.)	82	NS 3653
Gateside (Tays.)	98	NO 4344
Gathurst	57	SD 5307
Gatley	51	SJ 8387
Gattonside	86	NT 5435
Gatwick Airport—London	13	TQ 2841
Gauldry	93	NO 3723
Gaunt's Common	10	SU 0205
Gautby	55	TF 1772
Gavinton	87	NT 7652
Gawber	59	SE 3207
Gawcott	34	SP 6831
Gawsworth	51	SJ 8869
Gawthrop	63	SD 6987
Gawthwaite	62	SD 2784
Gaydon	33	SP 3654
Gayhurst	34	SP 8446
Gayles	65	NZ 1207
Gay Street	12	TQ 0820

Gayton Great Houghton

Gayton (Mers.)	50	SJ 2680
Gayton (Norf.)	46	TF 7219
Gayton (Northants.)	34	SP 7054
Gayton (Staffs.)	41	SJ 9728
Gayton le Marsh	55	TF 4284
Gayton Thorpe	46	TF 7418
Gaywood	46	TF 6320
Gazeley	36	TL 7264
Geary	100	NG 2661
Gedding	36	TL 9457
Geddington	44	SP 8983
Gedintailor	100	NG 5235
Gedney	45	TF 4024
Gedney Broadgate	45	TF 4022
Gedney Drove End	45	TF 4629
Gedney Dyke	45	TF 4126
Gedney Hill	45	TF 3311
Geise	112	ND 1064
Geldeston	47	TM 3891
Gell	49	SH 8569
Gelligaer	28	ST 1397
Gelli Gynan	50	SJ 1854
Gellilydan	49	SH 6839
Gellioedd	49	SH 9344
Gelly	24	SN 0819
Gellyburn	92	NO 0939
Gellywen	25	SN 2723
Gelston	69	NX 7758
Genoch Mains	68	NX 1356
Gentleshaw	42	SK 0511
Georgeham	6	SS 4639
George Nympton	7	SS 7023
Georgetown	82	NS 4567
Georgia	2	SW 4836
Germansweek	4	SX 4394
Germoe	2	SW 5829
Gerrans	3	SW 8735
Gerrards Cross	20	TQ 0088
Gestingthorpe	36	TL 8138
Geuffordd	40	SJ 2114
Gibraltar	55	TF 5558
Gidea Park	21	TQ 5390
Gidleigh	5	SX 6788
Gifford	86	NT 5368
Giggleswick	65	SD 8163
Gilberdyke	60	SE 8329
Gilcrux	62	NY 1138
Gildersome	59	SE 2429
Gildingwells	53	SK 5585
Gileston	28	ST 0167
Gilfach	28	ST 1598
Gilfach Goch	28	SS 9890
Gilfachrheda	26	SN 4058
Gillamoor	66	SE 6890
Gilling East	66	SE 6176
Gillingham (Dorset)	10	ST 8026
Gillingham (Kent)	14	TQ 7768
Gillingham (Norf.)	47	TM 4191
Gilling West	65	NZ 1805
Gillow Heath	51	SJ 8858
Gills	112	ND 3172
Gilmerton (Lothian)	85	NT 2968
Gilmerton (Tays.)	91	NN 8823
Gilmorton	43	SP 5787
Gilsland	71	NY 6366
Gilsland Spa	71	NY 6367
Gilston	86	NT 4456
Gilwern	28	SO 2414
Gimingham	47	TG 2836
Gipping	37	TM 0763
Gipsey Bridge	55	TF 2850
Girlsta	113	HU 4250
Girsby	66	NZ 3508
Girthon	69	NX 6053
Girton (Cambs.)	35	TL 4262
Girton (Notts.)	54	SK 8266
Girvan	75	NX 1897
Gisburn	58	SD 8248
Gisleham	47	TM 5188
Gislingham	37	TM 0771
Gissing	47	TM 1485
Gittisham	8	SY 1398
Glackossian	102	NH 5938
Gladestry	30	SO 2355
Gladsmuir	86	NT 4573
Glais	25	SN 7000
Glaisdale (N Yorks.)	67	NZ 7705
Glamis	98	NO 3846
Glanaber Terrace	49	SH 7547
Glanaman	25	SN 6713
Glan-Conwy	49	SH 8352
Glandford	47	TG 0441
Glandwr (Dyfed)	24	SN 1928
Glangrwyne	28	SO 2316
Glan-Mule	40	SO 1690
Glanrhyd	26	SN 1442
Glanton	79	NU 0714
Glanton Pike	79	NU 0514
Glanvilles Wootton	9	ST 6708
Glan-y-don	50	SJ 1679
Glan-yr-afon (Clwyd-Gwyn.)	49	SJ 0242
Glan-yr-afon (Gwyn.)	49	SH 9141
Glapthorn	44	TL 0290
Glapwell	53	SK 4766
Glasbury	30	SO 1739
Glascote	42	SK 2203
Glascwm	30	SO 1553
Glasdrum	96	NN 0046
Glasfryn	49	SH 9150
Glasgow	84	NS 5865
Glasinfryn	48	SH 5868
Glaspwll	39	SN 7397
Glasserton	68	NX 4238
Glassford	84	NS 7247
Glasshouse Hill	29	SO 7020
Glasshouses	65	SE 1764
Glasslaw	105	NJ 8659
Glasslie	92	NO 2305
Glasson (Cumbr.)	70	NY 2560
Glasson (Lancs.)	64	SD 4455
Glassonby	63	NY 5738
Glasterlaw	99	NO 6051
Glaston	44	SK 8900
Glastonbury	17	ST 4938
Glatton	45	TL 1586
Glazebury	51	SJ 6796
Glazeley	41	SO 7088
Gleadless Townend	53	SK 3883
Gleadsmoss	51	SJ 8469
Gleaston	64	SD 2570
Glemsford	36	TL 8247
Glenancross	95	NM 6691
Glen Auldyn	56	SC 4393
Glenbarr	80	NR 6736
Glenbervie	99	NO 7680
Glenboig	84	NS 7268
Glenbreck	77	NT 0521
Glenbuck	76	NS 7429
Glenburn	82	NS 4761
Glencaple	70	NX 9968
Glencarse	92	NO 1922
Glencloy	81	NS 0036
Glencoe (Highld.)	96	NN 1058
Glencraig	92	NT 1795
Glendevon (Tays.)	91	NN 9804
Glendoick	92	NO 2022
Glenduckie	93	NO 2818
Glenegedale	80	NR 3351
Glenelg	101	NG 8119
Glenfarg (Tays.)	92	NO 1310
Glenfield	43	SK 5306
Glenfinnan (Highld.)	95	NM 9080
Glenfoot	92	NO 1715
Glengarnock	82	NS 3252
Glengrasco	100	NG 4444
Glenkindie	104	NJ 4313
Glenlee (Dumf. and Galwy.)	69	NX 6080
Glenluce	68	NX 1957
Glenmaye	56	SC 2380
Glenmore (Skye)	100	NG 4340
Glen Parva	43	SP 5798
Glenridding	62	NY 3817
Glenrothes	92	NO 2600
Glensaugh	99	NO 6778
Glensluain	89	NS 0999
Glentham	54	TF 0090
Glentress	85	NT 2839
Glentrool Village	68	NX 3578
Glentworth	54	SK 9488
Glen Village	84	NS 8878
Glen Vine	56	SC 3378
Glespin	76	NS 8028
Gletness	113	HU 4651
Glewstone	29	SO 5522
Glinton	45	TF 1506
Glooston	44	SP 7596
Glossop	52	SK 0393
Gloster Hill	79	NU 2504
Gloucester	32	SO 8318
Gloup	113	HP 5004
Glusburn	59	SE 0344
Glympton	33	SP 4221
Glyn	49	SH 7457
Glynarthen	26	SN 3148
Glyn Ceiriog	50	SJ 2038
Glyncorrwg	28	SS 8799
Glyn-Cywarch	48	SH 6034
Glynde	13	TQ 4509
Glyndebourne	13	TQ 4510
Glyn Dyfrdwy	50	SJ 1542
Glyn-Neath	28	SN 8806
Glyntaff	28	ST 0889
Glynteg	26	SN 3637
Gnosall	41	SJ 8220
Gnosall Heath	41	SJ 8419
Goadby	44	SP 7598
Goadby Marwood	44	SK 7826
Goatacre	18	SU 0176
Goathill	9	ST 6717
Goathland	67	NZ 8301
Goathurst	16	ST 2534
Gobowen	50	SJ 3033
Godalming	12	SU 9743
Godmanchester	45	TL 2470
Godmanstone	9	SY 6697
Godmersham	15	TR 0650
Godney	17	ST 4842
Godolphin Cross	2	SW 6031
Godre'r-graig	25	SN 7507
Godshill (Hants.)	10	SU 1714
Godshill (I. of W.)	11	SZ 5281
Godstone	21	TQ 3551
Goetre	29	SO 3205
Goff's Oak	35	TL 3202
Gogar	85	NT 1672
Goginan	39	SN 6981
Golan	48	SH 5242
Golant	4	SX 1254
Golberdon	4	SX 3271
Golborne	51	SJ 6097
Golcar	59	SE 0915
Goldcliff	29	ST 3683
Golden Cross	13	TQ 5312
Golden Green	14	TQ 6348
Golden Grove	26	SN 5919
Goldenhill	51	SJ 8553
Golden Pot	12	SU 7143
Golden Valley (Glos.)	32	SO 9022
Golders Green	21	TQ 2488
Goldhanger	23	TL 9009
Golding	40	SJ 5403
Goldsborough (N Yorks.)	73	NZ 8314
Goldsborough (N Yorks.)	66	SE 3856
Goldsithney	2	SW 5430
Goldthorpe	60	SE 4604
Gollanfield	103	NH 8052
Golspie	108	NH 8399
Golval	111	NC 8962
Gomersal	59	SE 2026
Gomshall	20	TQ 0847
Gonalston	53	SK 6847
Good Easter	22	TL 6212
Gooderstone	46	TF 7602
Goodleigh	6	SS 5934
Goodmanham	60	SE 8842
Goodnestone (Kent)	15	TR 0461
Goodnestone (Kent)	15	TR 2554
Goodrich	29	SO 5719
Goodrington	5	SX 8958
Goodwick	24	SM 9438
Goodworth Clatford	19	SU 3642
Goodyers End	43	SP 3385
Goole	60	SE 7423
Goonbell	2	SW 7249
Goonhavern	2	SW 7953
Gooseham	6	SS 2316
Goosetrey	51	SJ 7769
Goosey	19	SU 3591
Goosnargh	57	SD 5536
Gordon	86	NT 6443
Gordonbush	108	NC 8409
Gordonstown (Grampn.)	104	NJ 5656
Gordonstown (Grampn.)	105	NJ 7138
Gorebridge	85	NT 3461
Gorefield	45	TF 4112
Goring	19	SU 6080
Goring-by-Sea	12	TQ 1102
Gorleston on Sea	47	TG 5203
Gorley	10	SU 1511
Gorrachie	105	NJ 7358
Gorran Haven	4	SX 0141
Gors	27	SN 6277
Gorsedd	50	SJ 1476
Gorseinon	25	SS 5998
Gorslas	25	SN 5713
Gorsley	29	SO 6826
Gorstan	102	NH 3862
Gorsty Common	30	SO 4537
Gorton	51	SJ 8996
Gosbeck	37	TM 1555
Gosberton	55	TF 2331
Gosfield	22	TL 7829
Gosforth (Cumbr.)	62	NY 0603
Gosforth (Tyne and Wear)	72	NZ 2467
Gosmore	35	TL 1927
Gosport	11	SZ 6199
Goswick	87	NU 0545
Gotham	53	SK 5330
Gotherington	32	SO 9629
Goudhurst	14	TQ 7337
Goulceby	55	TF 2579
Gourdas	105	NJ 7741
Gourdon	99	NO 8270
Gourock	82	NS 2477
Govan	84	NS 5464
Gowanhill	105	NK 0363
Gowdall	60	SE 6122
Gowerton	25	SS 5896
Gowkhall	85	NT 0589
Goxhill (Humbs.)	61	TA 1021
Goxhill (Humbs.)	61	TA 1844
Graffham (W Susx.)	12	SU 9216
Grafham (Cambs.)	45	TL 1669
Grafton (Here. and Worc.)	30	SO 4937
Grafton (Here. and Worc.)	31	SO 5761
Grafton (N Yorks.)	66	SE 4163
Grafton (Oxon.)	33	SP 2600
Grafton Flyford	32	SO 9655
Grafton Regis	34	SP 7546
Grafton Underwood	44	SP 9280
Grafty Green	14	TQ 8748
Graianrhyd	50	SJ 2156
Graig (Clwyd)	49	SJ 0872
Graig (Gwyn.)	49	SH 8071
Graig-fechan	50	SJ 1454
Grain	22	TQ 8876
Grainsby	55	TF 2799
Grainthorpe	55	TF 3896
Graizelound	54	SK 7798
Grampound	3	SW 9348
Grampound Road	3	SW 9150
Granborough	34	SP 7625
Granby	54	SK 7536
Grandborough	43	SP 4866
Grandtully	97	NN 9152
Grange (Cumbr.)	62	NY 2517
Grange (Mers.)	50	SJ 2286
Grange (N Yorks.)	66	SE 5796
Grange Hill	21	TQ 4492
Grange Moor	59	SE 2216
Grangemouth	84	NS 9281
Grange of Lindores	92	NO 2516
Grange-over-Sands-	64	SD 4077
Grangepans	85	NT 0282
Grangetown	73	NZ 5420
Grange Villa	72	NZ 2352
Granish	103	NH 8914
Gransmoor	67	TA 1259
Grantchester	35	TL 4355
Grantham	54	SK 9135
Grantlodge	105	NJ 7017
Granton (Dumf. and Galwy.)	77	NT 0709
Granton (Lothian)	85	NT 2277
Grantown-on-Spey	103	NJ 0327
Grantshouse	87	NT 8065
Grappenhall	51	SJ 6385
Grasby	61	TA 0804
Grasmere (Cumbr.)	62	NY 3307
Grassendale	50	SJ 3985
Grassholme	63	NY 9221
Grassington	65	SE 0064
Grassmoor	53	SK 4067
Grassthorpe	54	SK 7967
Grateley	19	SU 2741
Gratwich	52	SK 0231
Graveley (Cambs.)	35	TL 2564
Graveley (Herts.)	35	TL 2328
Gravelly Hill	42	SP 1090
Graveney	15	TR 0562
Gravesend	22	TQ 6473
Gravir	109	NB 3715
Grayingham	54	SK 9395
Grayrigg	63	SD 5797
Grays	22	TQ 6177
Grayshott	12	SU 8735
Grayswood	12	SU 9234
Grazeley	19	SU 6966
Greasbrough	53	SK 4195
Greasby	50	SJ 2587
Great Abington	35	TL 5348
Great Addington	44	SP 9575
Great Alne	32	SP 1159
Great Altcar	57	SD 3206
Great Amwell	35	TL 3712
Great Asby	63	NY 6813
Great Ashfield	36	TM 0068
Great Ayton	73	NZ 5510
Great Baddow	22	TL 7204
Great Badminton	18	ST 8082
Great Bardfield	36	TL 6730
Great Barford	35	TL 1352
Great Barr	42	SP 0495
Great Barrington	33	SP 2013
Great Barrow	50	SJ 4668
Great Barton	36	TL 8967
Great Barugh	67	SE 7478
Great Bavington	79	NY 9880
Great Bedwyn	18	SU 2764
Great Bentley	23	TM 1121
Great Billing	34	SP 8162
Great Bircham	46	TF 7632
Great Blakenham	37	TM 1150
Great Bolas	41	SJ 6421
Great Bookham	21	TQ 1454
Great Bosullow	2	SW 4133
Great Bourton	33	SP 4545
Great Bowden	44	SP 7488
Great Bradley	36	TL 6753
Great Braxted	22	TL 8614
Great Bricett	37	TM 0350
Great Brickhill	34	SP 9030
Great Bridgeford	41	SJ 8827
Great Brington	43	SP 6665
Great Bromley	23	TM 0826
Great Broughton	66	NZ 5406
Great Budworth	51	SJ 6677
Great Burdon	72	NZ 3116
Great Burstead	22	TQ 6892
Great Busby	66	NZ 5105
Great Canfield	22	TL 5917
Great Carlton	55	TF 4185
Great Casterton	44	TF 0009
Great Chart	15	TQ 9842
Great Chatwell	41	SJ 7914
Great Chesterford	35	TL 5042
Great Cheverell	18	ST 9858
Great Chishill	35	TL 4238
Great Clacton	23	TM 1716
Great Coates	61	TA 2310
Great Comberton	32	SO 9542
Great Corby	71	NY 4754
Great Cornard	36	TL 8840
Great Coxwell	18	SU 2693
Great Cransley	44	SP 8376
Great Cressingham	46	TF 8501
Great Crosby	50	SJ 3199
Great Cubley	52	SK 1637
Great Dalby	44	SK 7414
Great Doddington	34	SP 8864
Great Driffield	67	TA 0257
Great Dunham	46	TF 8714
Great Dunmow	22	TL 6221
Great Durnford	10	SU 1338
Great Easton (Essex)	22	TL 6125
Great Easton (Leic.)	44	SP 8493
Great Eccleston	57	SD 4240
Great Edstone	66	SE 7084
Great Ellingham	46	TM 0196
Great Elm	18	ST 7449
Great Eversden	35	TL 3653
Great Finborough	36	TM 0157
Greatford	45	TF 0811
Great Fransham	46	TF 8913
Great Gaddesden	34	TL 0211
Great Gidding	45	TL 1183
Great Givendale	67	SE 8153
Great Glemham	37	TM 3361
Great Glen	43	SP 6597
Great Gonerby	54	SK 8938
Great Gransden	35	TL 2756
Great Green (Norf.)	47	TM 2789
Great Green (Suff.)	36	TL 9155
Great Habton	67	SE 7576
Great Hallingbury	22	TL 5119
Greatham (Cleve.)	73	NZ 4927
Greatham (Hants.)	12	SU 7730
Greatham (W Susx)	12	TQ 0415
Great Hanwood	40	SJ 4309
Great Harrowden	44	SP 8871
Great Harwood	58	SD 7332
Great Haseley	34	SP 6401
Great Hatfield	61	TA 1842
Great Heck	60	SE 5920
Great Henny	36	TL 8738
Great Hinton	18	ST 9058
Great Hockham	46	TL 9592
Great Holland	23	TM 2119
Great Horkesley	36	TL 9731
Great Hormead	35	TL 4030
Great Horwood	34	SP 7731
Great Houghton (Northants.)	34	SP 7958

Great Houghton Handbridge

Great Houghton (S Yorks.)	59	SE 4206
Great Hucklow	52	SK 1777
Great Kelk	67	TA 1058
Great Kingshill	20	SU 8798
Great Langton	66	SE 2996
Great Leighs	22	TL 7317
Great Limber	61	TA 1308
Great Linford	34	SP 8542
Great Livermere	36	TL 8871
Great Longstone	53	SK 1971
Great Lumley	72	NZ 2949
Great Lyth	40	SJ 4507
Great Malvern	32	SO 7845
Great Maplestead	36	TL 8034
Great Marton	57	SD 3335
Great Massingham	46	TF 7922
Great Milton	34	SP 6302
Great Missenden	34	SP 8901
Great Mitton	58	SD 7138
Great Mongeham	15	TR 3451
Great Moulton	47	TM 1690
Great Musgrave	63	NY 7613
Great Ness	40	SJ 3918
Great Oakley (Essex)	23	TM 1927
Great Oakley (Northants.)	44	SP 8686
Great Offley	35	TL 1427
Great Ormside	63	NY 7017
Great Orton	70	NY 3254
Great Oxendon	44	SP 7383
Great Palgrave	46	TF 8312
Great Parndon	35	TL 4308
Great Paxton	35	TL 2164
Great Plumstead	47	TG 2910
Great Ponton	54	SK 9230
Great Postland	45	TF 2612
Great Preston	59	SE 4029
Great Raveley	45	TL 2581
Great Rissington	33	SP 1917
Great Rollright	33	SP 3231
Great Ryburgh	46	TF 9527
Great Ryle	79	NU 0212
Great Saling	22	TL 7025
Great Salkeld	63	NY 5536
Great Sampford	36	TL 6435
Great Sankey	51	SJ 5688
Great Saxham	36	TL 7862
Great Shefford	19	SU 3875
Great Shelford	35	TL 4652
Great Smeaton	66	NZ 3404
Great Snoring	46	TF 9434
Great Somerford	18	ST 9682
Great Soudley	41	SJ 7228
Great Stainton	72	NZ 3322
Great Stambridge	23	TQ 8991
Great Staughton	35	TL 1264
Great Steeping	55	TF 4364
Great Stonar	15	TR 3359
Greatstone-on-Sea	15	TR 0822
Great Strickland	63	NY 5522
Great Stukeley	45	TL 2275
Great Sturton	55	TF 2176
Great Swinburne	78	NY 9375
Great Tew	33	SP 3929
Great Tey	22	TL 8925
Great Torrington	6	SS 4919
Great Tosson	79	NU 0300
Great Totham (Essex)	22	TL 8511
Great Totham (Essex)	22	TL 8613
Great Wakering	23	TQ 9487
Great Waldingfield	36	TL 9143
Great Walsingham	46	TF 9437
Great Waltham	22	TL 6913
Great Warley	21	TQ 5890
Great Washbourne	32	SO 9834
Great Welnetham	36	TL 8759
Great Wenham	37	TM 0738
Great Whittington	79	NZ 0070
Great Wigborough	23	TL 9615
Great Wilbraham	36	TL 5557
Great Wishford	10	SU 0835
Great Witcombe	32	SO 9014
Great Witley	32	SO 7566
Great Wolford	33	SP 2434
Greatworth	33	SP 5542
Great Wratting	36	TL 6848
Great Wyrley	41	SJ 9907
Great Wytheford	41	SJ 5719
Great Yarmouth	47	TG 5207
Great Yeldham	36	TL 7638
Greenburn	84	NS 9360
Greendikes	79	NU 0628
Greenfield (Beds.)	35	TL 0534
Greenfield (Clwyd)	50	SJ 1977
Greenfield (Highld.)	96	NH 2000
Greenfield (Oxon.)	20	SU 7191
Greenford	21	TQ 1382
Greengairs	84	NS 7870
Greenham	19	SU 4865
Green Hammerton	66	SE 4656
Greenhaugh	78	NY 7987
Greenhead (Northum.)	71	NY 6665
Greenhill (Central)	84	NS 8278
Greenhill (Gtr London)	21	TQ 1688
Greenhill (S Yorks.)	53	SK 3481
Green Hill (Wilts.)	18	SU 0686
Greenhithe	21	TQ 5974
Greenholm	84	NS 5637
Greenhow Hill	65	SE 1164
Greenland	112	ND 2367
Greenlaw (Borders)	86	NT 7145
Greenloaning	91	NN 8307
Greenmount	58	SD 7714
Greenock	82	NS 2776
Greenodd	62	SD 3182
Green Ore	17	ST 5749
Greenside	72	NZ 1362
Greenskairs	105	NJ 7863
Greens Norton	34	SP 6649
Greenstead Green	22	TL 8227
Greensted	22	TL 5302
Green Street	21	TQ 1998
Green Street Green	21	TQ 4563
Green, The (Cumbr.)	62	SD 1784
Green, The (Wilts.)	10	ST 8731
Greenwich	21	TQ 4077
Greet	32	SP 0230
Greete	41	SO 5770
Greetham (Leic.)	44	SK 9214
Greetham (Lincs.)	55	TF 3070
Greetland	59	SE 0821
Greinton	17	ST 4136
Grendon (Northants.)	34	SP 8760
Grendon (Warw.)	43	SK 2800
Grendon Common	42	SP 2799
Grendon Green	31	SO 5957
Grendon Underwood	34	SP 6720
Grenoside	53	SK 3394
Gresford	50	SJ 3454
Gresham	47	TG 1738
Greshornish	100	NG 3454
Gress	109	NB 4842
Gressenhall	46	TF 9615
Gressenhall Green	46	TF 9616
Gressingham	64	SD 5769
Greta Bridge	72	NZ 0813
Gretna	70	NY 3167
Gretna Green	70	NY 3268
Gretton (Glos.)	32	SP 0030
Gretton (Northants.)	44	SP 8994
Gretton (Salop)	40	SO 5195
Grewelthorpe	66	SE 2276
Greysouthen	62	NY 0729
Greystoke	62	NY 4330
Greystone	99	NO 5343
Greywell	20	SU 7151
Griff	43	SP 3588
Griffithstown	28	ST 2999
Grigghall	63	SD 4691
Grimeford Village	58	SD 6112
Grimethorpe	59	SE 4109
Grimley	32	SO 8360
Grimoldby	55	TF 3988
Grimsargh	57	SD 5834
Grimsby	61	TA 2810
Grimscote	34	SP 6553
Grimscott	6	SS 2606
Grimshader	109	NB 4025
Grimsthorpe	44	TF 0423
Grimston (Leic.)	43	SK 6821
Grimston (Norf.)	46	TF 7221
Grimstone	9	SY 6393
Grindale	67	TA 1371
Grindle	41	SJ 7403
Grindleford	53	SK 2477
Grindleton	58	SD 7545
Grindlow	52	SK 1877
Grindon (Northum.)	87	NT 9144
Grindon (Staffs.)	52	SK 0854
Gringley on the Hill	54	SK 7390
Grinsdale	70	NY 3758
Grinshill	40	SJ 5223
Grinton	65	SE 0498
Gristhorpe	67	TA 0882
Griston	46	TL 9499
Grittenham	18	SU 0382
Grittleton	18	ST 8579
Grizebeck	62	SD 2384
Grizedale	62	SD 3394
Groby	43	SK 5207
Groes (Clwyd)	49	SJ 0064
Groes (W Glam.)	28	SS 7986
Groes-faen	28	ST 0780
Groesffordd Marli	49	SJ 0073
Groeslon	48	SH 4755
Grogport	81	NR 8044
Gronant	49	SJ 0883
Groombridge	13	TQ 5337
Grosebay	109	NG 1592
Grosmont (Gwent)	29	SO 4024
Grosmont (N Yorks.)	67	NZ 8205
Groton	36	TL 9641
Grove (Dorset)	9	SY 6972
Grove (Kent)	15	TR 2362
Grove (Notts.)	54	SK 7379
Grove (Oxon.)	19	SU 4090
Grove Park	21	TQ 4172
Grovesend	25	SN 5900
Gruids	108	NC 5604
Grula	100	NG 3826
Gruline	88	NM 5440
Grundisburgh	37	TM 2251
Gruting	113	HU 2748
Gualachulain	96	NN 1145
Guardbridge	93	NO 4519
Guarlford	32	SO 8145
Guay	98	NO 0049
Guestling Green	14	TQ 8513
Guestwick	47	TG 0627
Guide Post	79	NZ 2585
Guilden Morden	35	TL 2744
Guilden Sutton	50	SJ 4468
Guildford	20	TQ 0049
Guildtown	92	NO 1331
Guilsborough	43	SP 6773
Guilsfield	40	SJ 2111
Guisborough	73	NZ 6115
Guiseley	59	SE 1941
Guist	46	TF 9925
Guiting Power	32	SP 0924
Gullane	86	NT 4882
Gulval	2	SW 4831
Gumfreston	24	SN 1101
Gumley	43	SP 6890
Gunby (Lincs.)	44	SK 9021
Gundleton	11	SU 6133
Gunn	6	SS 6333
Gunnerside	65	SD 9598
Gunnerton	78	NY 9074
Gunness	60	SE 8411
Gunnislake	4	SX 4371
Gunnista	113	HU 5043
Gunthorpe (Norf.)	46	TG 0135
Gunthorpe (Notts.)	53	SK 6744
Gurnard	11	SZ 4795
Gurney Slade	17	ST 6249
Gurnos	28	SN 7709
Gussage All Saints	10	SU 0010
Gussage St. Michael	10	ST 9811
Guston	15	TR 3244
Gutcher	113	HU 5498
Guthrie	99	NO 5650
Guyhirn	45	TF 3903
Guy's Head	45	TF 4825
Guy's Marsh	10	ST 8420
Guyzance	79	NU 2103
Gwaenysgor	49	SJ 0780
Gwalchmai	48	SH 3975
Gwaun-Cae-Gurwen	25	SN 7011
Gwbert-on-Sea	26	SN 1650
Gweek	2	SW 7026
Gwehelog	29	SO 3804
Gwenddwr	30	SO 0643
Gwennap	2	SW 7340
Gwenter	2	SW 7418
Gwernaffield	50	SJ 2064
Gwernesney	29	SO 4101
Gwernogle	26	SN 5234
Gwernymynydd	50	SJ 2162
Gwespyr	50	SJ 1183
Gwinear	2	SW 5937
Gwithian	2	SW 5841
Gwyddelwern	49	SJ 0746
Gwyddgrug	26	SN 4635
Gwytherin	49	SH 8761

H

Habberley (Here. and Worc.)	41	SO 8077
Habberley (Salop)	40	SJ 3903
Habost (Isle of Lewis)	109	NB 5362
Habrough	61	TA 1514
Hacconby	45	TF 1025
Haceby	54	TF 0236
Hacheston	37	TM 3059
Hackenthorpe	53	SK 4183
Hacketts	35	TL 3208
Hackford	47	TG 0502
Hackforth	66	SE 2493
Hackleton	34	SP 8055
Hackness (N Yorks.)	67	SE 9690
Hackney	21	TQ 3585
Hackthorn	54	SK 9882
Hackthorpe	63	NY 5423
Hadden	87	NT 7836
Haddenham (Bucks.)	34	SP 7408
Haddenham (Cambs.)	45	TL 4675
Haddington	86	NT 5174
Haddiscoe	47	TM 4497
Haddon	45	TL 1392
Hademore	42	SK 1708
Hadfield	52	SK 0296
Hadham Cross	35	TL 4218
Hadham Ford	35	TL 4321
Hadleigh (Essex)	22	TQ 8087
Hadleigh (Suff.)	36	TM 0242
Hadley	41	SJ 6712
Hadley End	42	SK 1320
Hadlow	14	TQ 6349
Hadlow Down	13	TQ 5324
Hadnall	40	SJ 5120
Hadstock	36	TL 5645
Hadzor	32	SO 9162
Haffenden Quarter	14	TQ 8841
Hafod-Dinbych	49	SH 8953
Haggbeck	71	NY 4774
Hagley (Here. and Worc.)	31	SO 5641
Hagley (Here. and Worc.)	41	SO 9181
Hagworthingham	55	TF 3469
Haigh	58	SD 6108
Haighton Green	57	SD 5634
Haile	62	NY 0308
Hailes	32	SP 0530
Hailey (Herts.)	35	TL 3710
Hailey (Oxon.)	33	SP 3512
Hailsham	13	TQ 5909
Hail Weston	35	TL 1662
Hainault	21	TQ 4691
Hainford	47	TG 2218
Hainton	55	TF 1784
Haisthorpe	67	TA 1264
Halam	53	SK 6754
Halberton	8	ST 0012
Halcro	112	ND 2260
Hale (Ches.)	50	SJ 4682
Hale (Gtr Mches.)	51	SJ 7786
Hale (Hants.)	10	SU 1919
Hale (Lincs.)	55	TF 1443
Hale Bank	50	SJ 4784
Halebarns	51	SJ 7985
Hales (Norf.)	47	TM 3897
Hales (Staffs.)	51	SJ 7134
Halesowen	41	SO 9683
Hales Place	15	TR 1459
Hale Street	14	TQ 6749
Halesworth	37	TM 3877
Halewood	50	SJ 4585
Halford (Salop)	40	SO 4383
Halford (Warw.)	33	SP 2545
Halfpenny Green	41	SO 8292
Halfway (Berks.)	19	SU 4068
Halfway (Dyfed)	27	SN 6430
Halfway House	40	SJ 3411
Halfway Houses	23	TQ 9373
Halifax	59	SE 0825
Halistra	100	NG 2459
Halket	82	NS 4252
Halkirk	112	ND 1359
Halkyn	50	SJ 2071
Halland	13	TQ 5016
Hallaton	44	SP 7896
Hallatrow	17	ST 6356
Hallbankgate	71	NY 5859
Hallen	29	ST 5479
Hall Green	42	SP 1181
Hallin	100	NG 2559
Halling	14	TQ 7063
Hallington	79	NY 9875
Halloughton	53	SK 6851
Hallow	32	SO 8258
Hallrule	78	NT 5914
Hallsands	5	SX 8138
Hall's Green	35	TL 2728
Halltoft End	55	TF 3645
Hallworthy	4	SX 1787
Hallyne	85	NT 1940
Halmer End	51	SJ 7949
Halmore	32	SO 6902
Halmyre Mains	85	NT 1749
Halnaker	12	SU 9108
Halsall	57	SD 3710
Halse (Northants.)	33	SP 5640
Halse (Somer.)	16	ST 1327
Halsetown	2	SW 5038
Halsham	61	TA 2627
Halsinger	6	SS 5138
Halstead (Essex)	36	TL 8130
Halstead (Kent)	21	TQ 4961
Halstead (Leic.)	44	SK 7505
Halstock	9	ST 5308
Haltham	55	TF 2463
Halton (Bucks.)	34	SP 8710
Halton (Ches.)	50	SJ 5381
Halton (Clwyd)	50	SJ 3039
Halton (Lancs.)	64	SD 5065
Halton East	65	SE 0454
Halton Gill	65	SD 8876
Halton Holegate	55	TF 4165
Halton Lea Gate	71	NY 6558
Halton West	65	SD 8454
Haltwhistle	71	NY 7064
Halvergate	47	TG 4206
Halwell	5	SX 7753
Halwill	6	SX 4299
Halwill Junction	6	SS 4400
Ham (Glos.)	29	ST 6898
Ham (Gtr London)	21	TQ 1672
Ham (Highld.)	112	ND 2373
Ham (Kent)	15	TR 3354
Ham (Wilts.)	19	SU 3262
Hamble	11	SU 4806
Hambleden (Bucks.)	20	SU 7886
Hambledon (Hants.)	11	SU 6414
Hambledon (Surrey)	12	SU 9638
Hambleton (Lancs.)	57	SD 3742
Hambleton (N Yorks.)	60	SE 5430
Hambridge	9	ST 3921
Hambrook (Avon)	29	ST 6378
Hambrook (W Susx)	12	SU 7806
Hameringham	55	TF 3167
Hamerton	45	TL 1379
Ham Green (Here. and Worc.)	32	SP 0063
Hamilton	84	NS 7255
Hammersmith	21	TQ 2279
Hammerwich	42	SK 0707
Hammoon	10	ST 8114
Hamnavoe (Shetld.)	113	HU 4971
Hamnavoe (West Burra)	113	HU 3635
Hampden	34	SP 8603
Hampden Park	13	TQ 6002
Hampden Row	34	SP 8402
Hampnett	32	SP 0915
Hampole	60	SE 5010
Hampreston	10	SZ 0598
Hampstead	21	TQ 2485
Hampstead Norris	19	SU 5276
Hampsthwaite	66	SE 2558
Hampton (Gtr London)	20	TQ 1369
Hampton (Salop)	41	SO 7486
Hampton Bishop	31	SO 5538
Hampton Heath	50	SJ 4949
Hampton in Arden	42	SP 2081
Hampton Lovett	32	SO 8865
Hampton Lucy	33	SP 2557
Hampton on the Hill	33	SP 2564
Hampton Poyle	33	SP 5015
Hamsey	13	TQ 4112
Hamstall Ridware	42	SK 1019
Hamstead (I. of W.)	11	SZ 3991
Hamstead (W Mids)	42	SP 0593
Hamstead Marshall	19	SU 4165
Hamsterley (Durham)	72	NZ 1131
Hamsterley (Durham)	72	NZ 1156
Hamstreet (Kent)	15	TR 0034
Ham Street (Somer.)	17	ST 5534
Hamworthy	10	SY 9990
Hanbury (Here and Worc.)	32	SO 9663
Hanbury (Staffs.)	42	SK 1727
Hanchurch	51	SJ 8441
Handbridge	50	SJ 4164

Handcross Hengrave

Handcross	13	TQ 2630
Handforth	51	SJ 8883
Handley	50	SJ 4657
Handsacre	42	SK 0916
Handsworth (S Yorks.)	53	SK 4086
Handsworth (W Mids)	42	SP 0490
Hanford	51	SJ 8642
Hanging Langford	10	SU 0237
Hanham	29	ST 6372
Hankelow	51	SJ 6645
Hankerton	18	ST 9690
Hankham	13	TQ 6105
Hanley	51	SJ 8847
Hanley Castle	32	SO 8342
Hanley Swan	32	SO 8143
Hanley William	31	SO 6765
Hanlith	65	SD 9061
Hanmer	50	SJ 4540
Hannington (Hants.)	19	SU 5355
Hannington (Northants.)	44	SP 8171
Hannington (Wilts.)	18	SU 1793
Hannington Wick	18	SU 1795
Hanslope	34	SP 8046
Hanthorpe	45	TF 0824
Hanwell	33	SP 4343
Hanworth (Gtr London)	20	TQ 1271
Hanworth (Norf.)	47	TG 1935
Happendon	84	NS 8533
Happisburgh	47	TG 3731
Happisburgh Common	47	TG 3729
Hapsford	50	SJ 4774
Hapton (Lancs.)	58	SD 7931
Hapton (Norf.)	47	TM 1796
Harberton	5	SX 7758
Harbertonford	5	SX 7856
Harbledown	15	TR 1358
Harborne	42	SP 0384
Harborough Magna	43	SP 4779
Harbottle	78	NT 9304
Harbury	33	SP 3759
Harby (Leic.)	54	SK 7431
Harby (Notts.)	54	SK 8770
Harcombe	8	SY 1590
Harden	59	SE 0838
Hardenhuish	18	ST 9074
Hardgate	99	NJ 7801
Hardham	12	TQ 0317
Hardingham	46	TG 0403
Hardingstone	34	SP 7657
Hardings Wood	51	SJ 8054
Hardington	18	ST 7452
Hardington Mandeville	9	ST 5111
Hardington Marsh	9	ST 5009
Hardley	11	SU 4205
Hardley Street	47	TG 3801
Hardmead	34	SP 9347
Hardrow	65	SD 8691
Hardstoft	53	SK 4463
Hardway (Hants.)	11	SU 6101
Hardway (Somer.)	17	ST 7134
Hardwick (Bucks.)	34	SP 8019
Hardwick (Cambs.)	35	TL 3758
Hardwick (Norf.)	47	TM 2290
Hardwick (Northants.)	44	SP 8569
Hardwick (Oxon.)	33	SP 3706
Hardwick (Oxon.)	33	SP 5729
Hardwicke (Glos.)	32	SO 7912
Hardwicke (Glos.)	32	SO 9127
Hareby	55	TF 3365
Hareden	64	SD 6350
Harefield	20	TQ 0590
Hare Hatch	20	SU 8077
Harehope	79	NU 0920
Harescombe	32	SO 8410
Haresfield	32	SO 8110
Hare Street	35	TL 3929
Harewood	59	SE 3245
Harford	5	SX 6359
Hargrave (Ches.)	50	SJ 4862
Hargrave (Northants.)	44	TL 0370
Hargrave Green	36	TL 7759
Haringey	21	TQ 3290
Harker	70	NY 3960
Harkstead	37	TM 1935
Harlaston	42	SK 2111
Harlaxton	54	SK 8832
Harlech	48	SH 5831
Harlesden	21	TQ 2383
Harleston (Norf.)	47	TM 2483
Harleston (Suff.)	36	TM 0160
Harlestone	34	SP 7064
Harle Skye	58	SD 8634
Harley	41	SJ 5901
Harling Road	46	TL 9788
Harlington	35	TL 0330
Harlosh	100	NG 2841
Harlow	35	TL 4711
Harlow Hill	72	NZ 0768
Harlthorpe	60	SE 7337
Harlton	35	TL 3852
Harman's Cross	10	SY 9880
Harmby	65	SE 1289
Harmer Green	35	TL 2516
Harmer Hill	40	SJ 4822
Harmston	54	SK 9762
Harnhill	32	SP 0600
Harold Hill	21	TQ 5391
Haroldston West	24	SM 8615
Harold Wood	21	TQ 5590
Harome	66	SE 6482
Harpenden	35	TL 1314
Harpford	8	SY 0890
Harpham	67	TA 0961
Harpley (Here. and Worc.)	31	SO 6861
Harpley (Norf.)	46	TF 7826
Harpole	34	SP 6961
Harpsdale	112	ND 1256
Harpsden	20	SU 7680
Harpswell	54	SK 9389
Harpurhey	58	SD 8701
Harpur Hill	52	SK 0671
Harrapool	101	NG 6523
Harrietfield	91	NN 9829
Harrietsham	14	TQ 8753
Harrington (Cumbr.)	62	NX 9926
Harrington (Lincs.)	55	TF 3671
Harrington (Northants.)	44	SP 7780
Harringworth	44	SP 9197
Harriseahead	51	SJ 8656
Harrogate	66	SE 3055
Harrold	34	SP 9456
Harrow	20	TQ 1388
Harrowbarrow	4	SX 3969
Harrowden	35	TL 0646
Harrow on the Hill	21	TQ 1586
Harston (Cambs.)	35	TL 4251
Harston (Leic.)	54	SK 8331
Hart	73	NZ 4735
Hartburn	79	NZ 0886
Hartest	36	TL 8352
Hartfield	13	TQ 4735
Hartford (Cambs.)	45	TL 2572
Hartford (Ches.)	51	SJ 6372
Hartfordbridge	20	SU 7757
Hartford End	22	TL 6817
Harthill (Ches.)	50	SJ 4955
Harthill (Lothian)	84	NS 9064
Harthill (S Yorks.)	53	SK 4980
Hartington	52	SK 1360
Hartland	6	SS 2624
Hartlebury	41	SO 8470
Hartlepool	73	NZ 5032
Hartley (Cumbr.)	65	NY 7808
Hartley (Kent)	21	TQ 6166
Hartley (Kent)	14	TQ 7634
Hartley (Northum.)	79	NZ 3475
Hartley Wespall	19	SU 6958
Hartley Wintney	20	SU 7756
Hartlip	14	TQ 8364
Harton (N Yorks.)	66	SE 7061
Harton (Salop)	40	SO 4888
Harton (Tyne and Wear)	72	NZ 3864
Hartpury	32	SO 7924
Hartshill	43	SP 3293
Hartshorne	43	SK 3221
Hartwell	34	SP 7850
Hartwood	84	NS 8459
Harvel	14	TQ 6563
Harvington	32	SP 0548
Harvington Cross	32	SP 0549
Harwell	19	SU 4989
Harwich	37	TM 2431
Harwood (Durham)	63	NY 8133
Harwood (Gtr Mches.)	58	SD 7411
Harwood Dale	67	SE 9595
Harworth	53	SK 6291
Hascombe	12	TQ 0039
Haselbech	44	SP 7177
Haselbury Plucknett	9	ST 4711
Haseley	42	SP 2368
Haselor	32	SP 1257
Hasfield	32	SO 8227
Hasguard	24	SM 8509
Haskayne	57	SD 3507
Hasketon	37	TM 2550
Hasland	53	SK 3969
Haslemere	12	SU 9032
Haslingden	58	SD 7823
Haslingden Grane	58	SD 7523
Haslingfield	35	TL 4052
Haslington	51	SJ 7355
Hassall	51	SJ 7657
Hassall Green	51	SJ 7758
Hassell Street	15	TR 0946
Hassendean	78	NT 5420
Hassingham	47	TG 3605
Hassocks	13	TQ 3015
Hassop	53	SK 2272
Hastigrow	112	ND 2661
Hastingleigh	15	TR 0945
Hastings	14	TQ 8009
Hastingwood	35	TL 4807
Hastoe	34	SP 9209
Haswell	72	NZ 3743
Hatch (Beds.)	35	TL 1547
Hatch (Hants.)	19	SU 6752
Hatch (Wilts.)	10	ST 9228
Hatch Beauchamp	8	ST 3020
Hatch End	20	TQ 1391
Hatching Green	35	TL 1313
Hatchmere	50	SJ 5571
Hatcliffe	61	TA 2100
Hatfield (Here. and Worc.)	31	SO 5859
Hatfield (Herts.)	35	TL 2309
Hatfield (S Yorks.)	60	SE 6609
Hatfield Broad Oak	22	TL 5516
Hatfield Heath	22	TL 5215
Hatfield Peverel	22	TL 7911
Hatfield Woodhouse	60	SE 6708
Hatford	19	SU 3394
Hatherden	19	SU 3450
Hatherleigh	6	SS 5404
Hathern	43	SK 5022
Hatherop	32	SP 1505
Hathersage	53	SK 2381
Hatherton (Ches.)	51	SJ 6847
Hatherton (Staffs.)	41	SJ 9610
Hatley St. George	35	TL 2851
Hattingley	11	SU 6437
Hatton (Ches.)	51	SJ 5982
Hatton (Derby.)	53	SK 2130
Hatton (Grampn.)	105	NK 0537
Hatton (Gtr London)	20	TQ 1075
Hatton (Lincs.)	55	TF 1776
Hatton (Salop)	40	SO 4690
Hatton (Warw.)	42	SP 2367
Hattoncrook	105	NJ 8424
Hatton Heath	50	SJ 4561
Hatton of Fintray	105	NJ 8316
Haugham	55	TF 3381
Haugh Head	79	NU 0026
Haughley	36	TM 0262
Haughley Green	36	TM 0364
Haugh of Urr	69	NX 8066
Haughton (Notts.)	53	SK 6772
Haughton (Salop)	40	SJ 3727
Haughton (Salop)	40	SJ 5516
Haughton (Salop)	41	SO 6795
Haughton (Staffs.)	41	SJ 8620
Haughton Green	51	SJ 9393
Haughton Moss	51	SJ 5756
Haunton	42	SK 2411
Hauxley	79	NU 2703
Hauxton	35	TL 4351
Havant	12	SU 7106
Haven	30	SO 4054
Havenstreet	11	SZ 5690
Haverfordwest	24	SM 9515
Haverhill	36	TL 6745
Haverigg	62	SD 1578
Havering	21	TQ 5587
Havering-atte-Bower	21	TQ 5193
Havering's Grove	22	TQ 6594
Haversham	34	SP 8343
Haverthwaite	62	SD 3483
Hawarden	50	SJ 3165
Hawes	65	SD 8789
Hawford	32	SO 8460
Hawick (Borders)	78	NT 5014
Hawkchurch	8	ST 3400
Hawkedon	36	TL 7952
Hawkeridge	18	ST 8653
Hawkerland	8	SY 0588
Hawkesbury	18	ST 7687
Hawkesbury Upton	18	ST 7786
Hawkes End	43	SP 2983
Hawkhill	79	NU 2212
Hawkhurst	14	TQ 7630
Hawkinge	15	TR 2139
Hawkley	12	SU 7429
Hawkridge	7	SS 8630
Hawkshead	62	SD 3598
Hawkswick	65	SD 9570
Hawksworth (Notts.)	54	SK 7543
Hawksworth (W Yorks.)	59	SE 1641
Hawkwell	22	TQ 8691
Hawley (Hants.)	20	SU 8558
Hawley (Kent)	21	TQ 5571
Hawling	32	SP 0623
Hawnby	66	SE 5389
Haworth	59	SE 0337
Hawsker	67	NZ 9207
Hawstead	36	TL 8559
Hawthorn Hill	20	SU 8873
Hawton	54	SK 7851
Haxby	66	SE 6057
Haxey	60	SK 7699
Haydock	50	SJ 5696
Haydon	9	ST 6615
Haydon Bridge	71	NY 8464
Haydon Wick	18	SU 1388
Haye	4	SX 3570
Hayes (Gtr London)	20	TQ 0980
Hayes (Gtr London)	21	TQ 4165
Hayfield	52	SK 0386
Hayhillock	99	NO 5242
Hayle	2	SW 5537
Hayling Island	12	SU 7201
Haynes	35	TL 0841
Hay-on-Wye	30	SO 2342
Hayscastle Cross	24	SM 9125
Hayton (Cumbr.)	70	NY 1041
Hayton (Cumbr.)	71	NY 5057
Hayton (Humbs.)	60	SE 8145
Hayton (Notts.)	54	SK 7284
Hayton's Bent	40	SO 5280
Haytor Vale	5	SX 7677
Haywards Heath	13	TQ 3324
Haywood Oaks	53	SK 6055
Hazelbank	84	NS 8344
Hazelbury Bryan	9	ST 7408
Hazeley	20	SU 7459
Hazel Grove	51	SJ 9287
Hazelslade	42	SK 0212
Hazelton Walls	93	NO 3321
Hazelwood	53	SK 3245
Hazlemere	20	SU 8895
Hazlerigg	79	NZ 2472
Hazleton	32	SP 0718
Heacham	46	TF 6737
Headbourne Worthy	11	SU 4831
Headcorn	14	TQ 8344
Headington	33	SP 5407
Headlam	72	NZ 1818
Headley (Hants.)	19	SU 5162
Headley (Hants.)	12	SU 8236
Headley (Surrey)	21	TQ 2054
Head of Muir	84	NS 8080
Headon	54	SK 7476
Heads Nook	71	NY 4955
Heage	53	SK 3650
Healaugh (N Yorks.)	65	SE 0198
Healaugh (N Yorks.)	60	SE 4947
Heale	7	SS 6446
Healey (Lancs.)	58	SD 8817
Healey (Northum.)	72	NZ 0158
Healey (N Yorks.)	65	SE 1780
Healeyfield	72	NZ 0648
Healing	61	TA 2110
Heamoor	2	SW 4631
Heanish	94	NM 0343
Heanor	53	SK 4346
Heanton Punchardon	6	SS 5035
Heapham	54	SK 8788
Hearthstane	77	NT 1125
Heaste	100	NG 6417
Heath	53	SK 4467
Heath and Reach	34	SP 9228
Heathcote	52	SK 1460
Heath End (Hants.)	19	SU 5762
Heather	43	SK 3910
Heathfield (Devon.)	5	SX 8376
Heathfield (E Susx)	13	TQ 5821
Heathfield (Somer.)	16	ST 1526
Heath Hayes	42	SK 0110
Heath Hill	41	SJ 7614
Heath House	17	ST 4146
Heathrow Airport–London	20	TQ 0775
Heath, The	36	TL 9043
Heathton	41	SO 8192
Heatley	51	SJ 6988
Heaton (Lancs.)	64	SD 4460
Heaton (Staffs.)	51	SJ 9462
Heaton (Tyne and Wear)	72	NZ 2665
Heaverham	21	TQ 5758
Hebburn	72	NZ 3265
Hebden	65	SE 0263
Hebden Bridge	59	SD 9927
Hebden Green	51	SJ 6365
Hebron	79	NZ 1989
Heckfield	20	SU 7260
Heckfield Green	37	TM 1875
Heckington	55	TF 1444
Heckmondwike	59	SE 2123
Heddington	18	ST 9966
Heddon-on-the-Wall	72	NZ 1366
Hedenham	47	TM 3193
Hedge End	11	SU 4812
Hedgerley	20	SU 9787
Hedging	17	ST 3029
Hedley on the Hill	72	NZ 0759
Hednesford	42	SK 0012
Hedon	61	TA 1828
Hedsor	20	SU 9086
Hegdon Hill	31	SO 5854
Heighington (Durham)	72	NZ 2522
Heighington (Lincs.)	54	TF 0269
Heights of Brae	102	NH 5161
Heiton	86	NT 7130
Hele (Devon.)	6	SS 5347
Hele (Devon.)	8	SS 9902
Helensburgh	90	NS 2982
Helford	2	SW 7526
Helhoughton	46	TF 8626
Helions Bumpstead	36	TL 6541
Helland	4	SX 0770
Hellesdon	47	TG 1810
Hellidon	33	SP 5158
Hellifield	65	SD 8556
Hellingly	13	TQ 5812
Hellington	47	TG 3103
Helmdon	33	SP 5843
Helmingham	37	TM 1857
Helmsdale	112	ND 0215
Helmshore	58	SD 7821
Helmsley	66	SE 6183
Helperby	66	SE 4369
Helperthorpe	67	SE 9570
Helpringham	55	TF 1340
Helpston	45	TF 1205
Helsby	50	SJ 4875
Helston	2	SW 6527
Helstone	4	SX 0881
Helton	63	NY 5122
Hemblington	47	TG 3411
Hemel Hempstead	35	TL 0506
Hemingbrough	60	SE 6730
Hemingby	55	TF 2374
Hemingford Abbots	45	TL 2870
Hemingford Grey	45	TL 2970
Hemingstone	37	TM 1453
Hemington (Northants.)	45	TL 0985
Hemington (Somer.)	18	ST 7253
Hemley	37	TM 2842
Hempholme	67	TA 0850
Hempnall	47	TM 2494
Hempnall Green	47	TM 2593
Hempriggs	103	NJ 1064
Hempstead (Essex)	36	TL 6338
Hempstead (Norf.)	47	TG 4028
Hempsted (Glos.)	32	SO 8117
Hempsted (Norf.)	47	TG 1037
Hempton (Norf.)	46	TF 9129
Hempton (Oxon.)	33	SP 4431
Hemsby	47	TG 4917
Hemswell	54	SK 9290
Hemsworth	59	SE 4213
Hemyock	8	ST 1313
Henbury (Avon)	29	ST 5478
Henbury (Ches.)	51	SJ 8873
Hendon (Gtr London)	21	TQ 2389
Hendon (Tyne and Wear)	72	NZ 4055
Hendy	25	SN 5804
Heneglwys	48	SH 4276
Henfield	13	TQ 2116
Hengoed (Mid Glam.)	28	ST 1495
Hengoed (Powys)	30	SO 2253
Hengoed (Salop)	50	SJ 2833
Hengrave	36	TL 8268

Henham Hook

Henham 22 TL 5428
Heniarth 40 SJ 1108
Henley (Salop) 40 SO 5476
Henley (Somer.) 17 ST 4232
Henley (Suff.) 37 TM 1551
Henley (W Susx) 12 SU 8926
Henley-in-Arden 32 SP 1465
Henley on Thames 20 SU 7682
Henley Park 20 SU 9352
Henllan (Clwyd) 49 SJ 0268
Henllan (Dyfed) 26 SN 3540
Henllan Amgoed 24 SN 1820
Henllys 28 ST 2693
Henlow 35 TL 1738
Hennock 5 SX 8380
Henryd 49 SH 7674
Hensall 60 SE 5923
Henshaw 71 NY 7664
Henstead 47 TM 4986
Henstridge 9 ST 7219
Henstridge Marsh 9 ST 7420
Henton (Oxon.) 34 SP 7602
Henton (Somer.) 17 ST 4845
Henwick 32 SO 8354
Henwood 4 SX 2673
Heol Senni 28 SN 9223
Heol-y-Cyw 28 SS 9484
Hepburn 79 NU 0724
Hepple 79 NT 9800
Hepscott 79 NZ 2284
Heptonstall 59 SD 9827
Hepworth (Suff.) 36 TL 9874
Hepworth (W Yorks.) 59 SE 1606
Herbrandston 24 SM 8708
Hereford 31 SO 5040
Hergest 30 SO 2655
Heriot 85 NT 3952
Hermitage (Berks.) 19 SU 5072
Hermitage (Borders) 78 NY 5095
Hermitage (Dorset.) 9 ST 6306
Hermitage (Hants.) 12 SU 7505
Hermon (Dyfed) 26 SN 2032
Hermon (Dyfed) 26 SN 3630
Herne 15 TR 1866
Herne Bay 15 TR 1768
Herner 6 SS 5926
Hernhill 15 TR 0660
Herodsfoot 4 SX 2160
Herongate 22 TQ 6391
Heronsgate 20 TQ 0294
Herriard 19 SU 6645
Herringfleet 47 TM 4797
Herringswell 36 TL 7170
Herrington 72 NZ 3553
Hersden 15 TR 1961
Hersham 20 TQ 1164
Herstmonceux 13 TQ 6312
Hertford 35 TL 3212
Hertford Heath 35 TL 3510
Hertingfordbury 35 TL 3112
Hesketh Bank 57 SD 4323
Hesketh Lane 58 SD 6141
Hesket Newmarket 62 NY 3438
Heskin Green 57 SD 5315
Hesleden 73 NZ 4438
Hesleyside 78 NY 8183
Heslington 60 SE 6250
Hessay 66 SE 5253
Hessenford 4 SX 3057
Hessett 36 TL 9361
Hessle 61 TA 0326
Hest Bank 64 SD 4566
Heston 20 TQ 1277
Heswall 50 SJ 2682
Hethe 33 SP 5929
Hethersett 47 TG 1505
Hethersgill 71 NY 4767
Hethpool 78 NT 8928
Hett 72 NZ 2836
Hetton 65 SD 9658
Hetton-le-Hole 72 NZ 3548
Heugh 79 NZ 0873
Heugh-Head 104 NJ 3711
Heveningham 37 TM 3372
Hever 21 TQ 4744
Heversham 63 SD 4983
Hevingham 47 TG 2022
Hewelsfield 29 SO 5602
Hewish (Avon) 17 ST 4064
Hewish (Somer.) 9 ST 4108
Hexham 71 NY 9364
Hextable 21 TQ 5170
Hexton 35 TL 1030
Hexworthy 5 SX 6572
Heybridge (Essex) 22 TL 8508
Heybridge (Essex) 22 TQ 6498
Heybridge Basin 22 TL 8707
Heybrook Bay 5 SX 4948
Heydon (Cambs.) 35 TL 4340
Heydon (Norf.) 47 TG 1127
Heydour 54 TF 0039
Heyford 34 SP 6558
Heylipoll 94 NL 9643
Heylor 113 HU 2881
Heysham 64 SD 4161
Heyshott 12 SU 8918
Heytesbury 18 ST 9242
Heythrop 33 SP 3527
Heywood (Gtr Mches.) 58 SD 8510
Heywood (Wilts.) 18 ST 8753
Hibaldstow 61 SE 9702
Hickleton 60 SE 4805
Hickling (Norf.) 47 TG 4124
Hickling (Notts.) 43 SK 6929
Hickling Green 47 TG 4023
Hickling Heath 47 TG 4022
Hidcote Boyce 32 SP 1742
High Ackworth 59 SE 4317
Higham (Derby.) 53 SK 3959
Higham (Kent) 14 TQ 7171
Higham (Lancs.) 58 SD 8036
Higham (Suff.) 36 TL 7465
Higham (Suff.) 36 TM 0335
Higham Dykes 79 NZ 1375
Higham Ferrers 44 SP 9669
Higham Gobion 35 TL 1033
Higham on the Hill 43 SP 3895
Highampton 6 SS 4804
High Beach 21 TQ 4097
High Bentham 64 SD 6669
High Bickington 6 SS 5920
High Birkwith 65 SD 8076
High Blantyre 84 NS 6756
High Bonnybridge 84 NS 8378
Highbridge 17 ST 3147
Highbrook 13 TQ 3630
Highburton 59 SE 1813
Highbury 17 ST 6849
High Buston 79 NU 2308
High Callerton 79 NZ 1670
Highclere 19 SU 4360
Highcliffe 11 SZ 2193
High Cogges 33 SP 3709
High Coniscliffe 72 NZ 2215
High Cross (Hants.) 12 SU 7126
High Cross (Herts.) 35 TL 3618
High Cross Bank 43 SK 3018
High Easter 22 TL 6214
High Ellington 65 SE 1983
Higher Ansty 9 ST 7603
Higher Ballam 57 SD 3630
High Ercall 41 SJ 5917
Higher Penwortham 57 SD 5128
Higher Tale 8 ST 0601
Higher Walreddon 5 SX 4771
Higher Walton (Ches.) 51 SJ 5985
Higher Walton (Lancs.) 57 SD 5727
Higher Wych 50 SJ 4943
High Etherley 72 NZ 1628
Highfield (Strath.) 82 NS 3050
Highfield (Tyne and Wear) 72 NZ 1459
Highfields 35 TL 3559
High Garrett 22 TL 7726
High Grange 72 NZ 1731
High Green (Norf.) 47 TG 1305
High Green (S Yorks.) 59 SK 3397
High Halden 14 TQ 9037
High Halstow 22 TQ 7875
High Ham 17 ST 4231
High Hatton 41 SJ 6024
High Hesket 71 NY 4744
High Hoyland 59 SE 2710
High Hunsley 61 SE 9535
High Hurstwood 13 TQ 4926
High Lane 31 SO 6760
High Laver 22 TL 5208
Highleadon 32 SO 7623
High Legh 51 SJ 6984
Highleigh 12 SZ 8498
Highley 41 SO 7483
High Littleton 17 ST 6458
High Lorton 62 NY 1625
High Melton 60 SE 5001
Highmoor Cross 19 SU 7084
Highmoor Hill 29 ST 4689
Highnam 32 SO 7919
High Newton 62 SD 4082
High Newton-by-the-Sea 79 NU 2325
High Offley 41 SJ 7826
High Ongar 22 TL 5603
High Onn 41 SJ 8216
High Roding 22 TL 6017
High Salvington 12 TQ 1206
High Shaw 65 SD 8791
High Spen 72 NZ 1359
Highsted 14 TQ 9161
High Street (Corn.) 4 SW 9753
High Street (Suff.) 37 TM 4355
High Street Green 36 TM 0055
Hightae 70 NY 0979
Hightown (Ches.) 51 SJ 8762
Hightown (Mers.) 57 SD 2903
High Toynton 55 TF 2869
High Trewhitt 79 NU 0105
Highway 18 SU 0474
Highweek 5 SX 8472
Highworth 18 SU 2092
High Wray 62 SD 3799
High Wych 35 TL 4614
High Wycombe 20 SU 8593
Hilborough (Norf.) 46 TF 8200
Hildenborough 21 TQ 5648
Hildersham 36 TL 5448
Hilderstone 51 SJ 9434
Hilderthorpe 67 TA 1765
Hilgay 46 TL 6298
Hill 29 ST 6495
Hillam 60 SE 5028
Hillbeck 63 NY 7915
Hillberry 56 SC 3879
Hillborough (Kent) 15 TR 2168
Hillbrae (Grampn.) 104 NJ 6047
Hillbrae (Grampn.) 105 NJ 7923
Hill Brow 12 SU 7926
Hill Dyke 55 TF 3447
Hill End (Durham) 72 NZ 0135
Hill End (Fife.) 92 NT 0495
Hillend (Fife.) 85 NT 1483
Hillesden 34 SP 6828
Hillesley 18 ST 7689
Hillfarrance 8 ST 1624
Hillhead (Devon.) 5 SX 9053
Hill Head (Hants.) 11 SU 5402
Hillhead (Strath.) 75 NS 4219
Hillhead of Auchentumb 105 NJ 9258
Hillhead of Cocklaw 105 NK 0844
Hilliard's Cross 42 SK 1412
Hilliclay 112 ND 1764
Hillingdon 20 TQ 0882
Hillington 46 TF 7225
Hillmorton 43 SP 5374
Hillockhead 104 NJ 3809
Hill of Fearn 108 NH 8377
Hill Ridware 42 SK 0718
Hill Row 45 TL 4475
Hillside (Grampn.) 99 NO 9298
Hillside (Tays.) 99 NO 7061
Hillswick 113 HU 2877
Hill, The 62 SD 1783
Hill Top (Hants.) 11 SU 4002
Hill Top (W Yorks.) 59 SE 3315
Hilmarton 18 SU 0175
Hilperton 18 ST 8759
Hilsea 11 SU 6503
Hilton (Cambs.) 45 TL 2966
Hilton (Cleve.) 73 NZ 4611
Hilton (Cumbr.) 63 NY 7320
Hilton (Derby.) 53 SK 2430
Hilton (Dorset) 9 ST 7802
Hilton (Durham) 72 NZ 1621
Hilton (Grampn.) 105 NJ 9434
Hilton (Salop) 41 SO 7795
Hilton of Cadboll 108 NH 8776
Himbleton 32 SO 9458
Himley 41 SO 8891
Hincaster 63 SD 5184
Hinckley 43 SP 4294
Hinderclay 36 TM 0276
Hinderwell 73 NZ 7916
Hindford 50 SJ 3333
Hindhead 12 SU 8736
Hindley 58 SD 6104
Hindley Green 58 SD 6403
Hindlip 32 SO 8758
Hindolveston 46 TG 0329
Hindon 10 ST 9032
Hindringham 46 TF 9836
Hingham 46 TG 0202
Hinstock 41 SJ 6926
Hintlesham 37 TM 0843
Hinton (Avon) 18 ST 7376
Hinton (Hants.) 11 SZ 2095
Hinton (Northants.) 33 SP 5352
Hinton (Salop) 40 SJ 4008
Hinton Ampner 11 SU 5927
Hinton Blewett 17 ST 5956
Hinton Charterhouse 18 ST 7758
Hinton-in-the-Hedges 33 SP 5537
Hinton Marsh 11 SU 5827
Hinton Martell 10 SU 0106
Hinton on the Green 32 SP 0240
Hinton Parva 18 SU 2283
Hinton St. George 9 ST 4212
Hinton St. Mary 9 ST 7816
Hinton Waldrist 19 SU 3799
Hints (Salop) 41 SO 6175
Hints (Staffs.) 42 SK 1503
Hinwick 34 SP 9361
Hinxhill 15 TR 0442
Hinxton 35 TL 4945
Hinxworth 35 TL 2340
Hipperholme 59 SE 1225
Hirnant 39 SJ 0423
Hirst 79 NZ 2787
Hirst Courtney 60 SE 6124
Hirwaun 28 SN 9505
Hiscott 6 SS 5426
Histon 35 TL 4363
Hitcham 36 TL 9851
Hitchin 35 TL 1829
Hither Green 21 TQ 3874
Hittisleigh 7 SX 7395
Hixon 42 SK 0026
Hoaden 15 TR 2759
Hoaldalbert 29 SO 3923
Hoar Cross 42 SK 1223
Hoarwithy 29 SO 5429
Hoath 15 TR 2064
Hobarris 40 SO 3078
Hobkirk 78 NT 5810
Hobson 72 NZ 1755
Hoby 43 SK 6617
Hockering 47 TG 0713
Hockerton 54 SK 7156
Hockley 22 TQ 8293
Hockley Heath 42 SP 1572
Hockliffe 34 SP 9726
Hockwold cum Wilton 46 TL 7288
Hockworthy 8 ST 0319
Hoddesdon 35 TL 3709
Hoddlesden 58 SD 7122
Hodgeston 24 SS 0399
Hodnet 41 SJ 6128
Hodthorpe 53 SK 5476
Hoe 46 TF 9916
Hoe Gate 11 SU 6213
Hoggeston 34 SP 8025
Hoghton 58 SD 6125
Hognaston 53 SK 2350
Hogsthorpe 55 TF 5372
Holbeach 45 TF 3625
Holbeach Bank 45 TF 3627
Holbeach Drove 45 TF 3212
Holbeach Hurn 45 TF 3927
Holbeach St. Johns 45 TF 3418
Holbeach St. Marks 55 TF 3731
Holbeach St. Matthew 55 TF 4132
Holbeck 53 SK 5473
Holberrow Green 32 SP 0259
Holbeton 5 SX 6150
Holborn 21 TQ 3181
Holbrook (Derby.) 53 SK 3645
Holbrook (Suff.) 37 TM 1636
Holburn 87 NU 0436
Holbury 11 SU 4303
Holcombe (Devon.) 8 SX 9574
Holcombe (Somer.) 17 ST 6649
Holcombe Rogus 8 ST 0519
Holcot 44 SP 7969
Holden 58 SD 7749
Holdenby 43 SP 6967
Holdgate 40 SO 5589
Holdingham 54 TF 0547
Holestane 76 NX 8799
Holford 16 ST 1541
Holker 65 SD 3577
Holkham 46 TF 8944
Hollacombe 6 SS 3702
Holland Fen 55 TF 2445
Holland-on-Sea 23 TM 2016
Hollandstoun 113 HY 7553
Hollesley 37 TM 3544
Hollingbourne 14 TQ 8455
Hollington (Derby.) 53 SK 2239
Hollington (E Susx) 14 TQ 7911
Hollington (Staffs.) 52 SK 0538
Hollingworth 52 SK 0096
Hollins 58 SD 8108
Hollinsclough 52 SK 0666
Hollins Green 51 SJ 6990
Hollinswood 41 SJ 6909
Hollinwood 50 SJ 5236
Hollocombe 6 SS 6311
Holloway 53 SK 3256
Hollowell 43 SP 6972
Hollybush (Gwent) 28 SO 1603
Hollybush (Here. and Worc.) 32 SO 7636
Hollybush (Strath.) 75 NS 3914
Holly End 45 TF 4906
Hollym 61 TA 3425
Holmbury St. Mary 12 TQ 1144
Holme (Cambs.) 45 TL 1987
Holme (Cumbr.) 63 SD 5278
Holme (Notts.) 54 SK 8059
Holme (W Yorks.) 59 SE 1005
Holme Chapel 58 SD 8728
Holme Hale 46 TF 8807
Holme Lacy 31 SO 5535
Holme Marsh 30 SO 3354
Holme next the Sea 46 TF 7043
Holme on the Wolds 61 SE 9646
Holmer Green 20 SU 9097
Holmes Chapel 51 SJ 7667
Holmesfield 53 SK 3277
Holmeswood 57 SD 4316
Holme upon Spalding Moor 60 SE 8138
Holmewood 53 SK 4365
Holmfirth 59 SE 1408
Holmhead 75 NS 5620
Holmpton 61 TA 3623
Holmrook 62 SD 0799
Holne 5 SX 7069
Holnest 9 ST 6509
Holsworthy 6 SS 3403
Holsworthy Beacon 6 SS 3508
Holt (Clwyd) 50 SJ 4053
Holt (Dorset) 10 SU 0203
Holt (Here. and Worc.) 32 SO 8262
Holt (Norf.) 47 TG 0738
Holt (Wilts.) 18 ST 8661
Holtby 66 SE 6754
Holt End 42 SP 0769
Holt Heath 32 SO 8163
Holton (Lincs.) 55 TF 1181
Holton (Oxon.) 33 SP 6006
Holton (Somer.) 17 ST 6826
Holton (Suff.) 37 TM 4077
Holton Heath 10 SY 9491
Holton le Clay 61 TA 2802
Holton le Moor 54 TF 0797
Holton St. Mary 37 TM 0537
Holwell (Herts.) 35 TL 1633
Holwell (Leic.) 44 SK 7323
Holwell (Oxon.) 33 SP 2309
Holwick 63 NY 9026
Holybourne 12 SU 7341
Holy Cross 41 SO 9279
Holyhead 48 SH 2482
Holymoorside 53 SK 3369
Holyport 20 SU 8977
Holystone 78 NT 9502
Holytown 84 NS 7760
Holywell (Cambs.) 45 TL 3370
Holywell (Clwyd) 50 SJ 1875
Holywell (Corn.) 5 SW 7658
Holywell (Dorset) 9 ST 5904
Holywell Green 59 SE 0918
Holywell Lake 8 ST 1020
Holywell Row 36 TL 7077
Holywood 69 NX 9480
Homer 41 SJ 6101
Homersfield 47 TM 2885
Hom Green 29 SO 5822
Homington 10 SU 1226
Honeyborough 24 SM 9506
Honeybourne 32 SP 1144
Honeychurch 6 SS 6202
Honey Hill 15 TR 1161
Honiley 42 SP 2472
Honing 47 TG 3227
Honingham 47 TG 1011
Honington (Lincs.) 54 SK 9443
Honington (Suff.) 36 TL 9174
Honington (Warw.) 33 SP 2642
Honiton 8 ST 1600
Honley 59 SE 1311
Hoo (Kent) 22 TQ 7872
Hooe (Devon.) 5 SX 5052
Hooe (E Susx) 13 TQ 6809
Hoo Green 37 TM 2559
Hook (Dyfed) 24 SM 9811
Hook (Hants.) 20 SU 7254
Hook (Humbs.) 60 SE 7525

Hook Irby

Hook (Surrey)	21	TQ 1764
Hook (Wilts.)	18	SU 0784
Hooke (Dorset)	9	ST 5300
Hookgate	51	SJ 7435
Hook Norton	33	SP 3533
Hookway	7	SX 8598
Hookwood	13	TQ 2643
Hoole	50	SJ 4367
Hooton	50	SJ 3679
Hooton Levitt	53	SK 5291
Hooton Pagnell	60	SE 4808
Hooton Roberts	53	SK 4897
Hope (Clwyd)	50	SJ 3058
Hope (Derby.)	52	SK 1783
Hope (Devon.)	5	SX 6740
Hope (Powys)	40	SJ 2507
Hope (Salop)	40	SJ 3401
Hope Bagot	41	SO 5874
Hope Bowdler	40	SO 4792
Hopeman	104	NJ 1469
Hope Mansell	29	SO 6219
Hopesay	40	SO 3883
Hope under Dinmore	30	SO 5052
Hopton (Norf.)	47	TG 5200
Hopton (Salop)	41	SJ 5926
Hopton (Staffs.)	41	SJ 9426
Hopton (Suff.)	36	TL 9979
Hopton Cangeford	40	SO 5480
Hopton Castle	40	SO 3678
Hopton Wafers	41	SO 6476
Hopwas	42	SK 1705
Hopwood	42	SP 0375
Horam	13	TQ 5717
Horbling	55	TF 1135
Horbury	59	SE 2918
Horden	73	NZ 4441
Horderley	40	SO 4086
Hordle	11	SZ 2795
Hordley	40	SJ 3730
Horeb	26	SN 3942
Horham	37	TM 2172
Horkesley Heath	23	TL 9829
Horkstow	61	SE 9818
Horley (Oxon.)	33	SP 4143
Horley (W Susx)	13	TQ 2843
Hornblotton Green	17	ST 5833
Hornby (Lancs.)	64	SD 5868
Hornby (N Yorks)	66	NZ 3605
Horncastle	55	TF 2669
Hornchurch	21	TQ 5487
Horncliffe	87	NT 9249
Horndean	11	SU 7013
Horndon on the Hill	22	TQ 6683
Horne	13	TQ 3344
Horn Hill	20	TQ 0292
Horning	47	TG 3417
Horninghold	44	SP 8097
Horninglow	42	SK 2324
Horningsea	35	TL 4962
Horningsham	18	ST 8241
Horningtoft	46	TF 9323
Hornsby	71	NY 5150
Hornsea	61	TA 2047
Hornsey	21	TQ 3089
Hornton	33	SP 3945
Horrabridge	5	SX 5169
Horringer	36	TL 8261
Horsebridge (E Susx)	13	TQ 5911
Horsebridge (Hants.)	11	SU 3430
Horsebrook	41	SJ 8810
Horsehay	41	SJ 6707
Horseheath	36	TL 6147
Horsehouse	65	SE 0481
Horsell	20	SU 9959
Horseman's Green	50	SJ 4441
Horseway	45	TL 4287
Horsey	47	TG 4523
Horsford	47	TG 1915
Horsforth	59	SE 2337
Horsham (Here. and Worc.)	32	SO 7357
Horsham (W Susx)	12	TQ 1730
Horsham St. Faith	47	TG 2114
Horsington (Lincs.)	55	TF 1868
Horsington (Somer.)	9	ST 7023
Horsley (Derby.)	53	SK 3744
Horsley (Glos.)	18	ST 8398
Horsley (Northum.)	78	NY 8496
Horsley (Northum.)	72	NZ 0966
Horsley Cross	23	TM 1227
Horsleycross Street	23	TM 1228
Horsleyhill	78	NT 5319
Horsley Woodhouse	53	SK 3945
Horsmonden	14	TQ 7040
Horspath	33	SP 5704
Horstead	47	TG 2619
Horsted Keynes	13	TQ 3828
Horton (Avon)	18	ST 7684
Horton (Berks.)	20	TQ 0175
Horton (Bucks.)	34	SP 9219
Horton (Dorset)	10	SU 0307
Horton (Northants.)	34	SP 8254
Horton (Northum.)	87	NU 0230
Horton (Staffs.)	51	SJ 9457
Horton (W Glam.)	25	SS 4785
Horton (Wilts.)	18	SU 0463
Horton Green	50	SJ 4549
Horton Heath	11	SU 4916
Horton in Ribblesdale	65	SD 8172
Horton Kirby	21	TQ 5668
Horwich	58	SD 6311
Horwood	6	SS 5027
Hose	44	SK 7329
Hosh	91	NN 8523
Hotham	60	SE 8934
Hothfield	15	TQ 9644
Hoton	43	SK 5722
Hough	51	SJ 7151
Hougham	54	SK 8844
Hougharry	109	NF 7071
Hough Green	50	SJ 4885
Hough-on-the-Hill	54	SK 9246
Houghton (Cambs.)	45	TL 2871
Houghton (Cumbr.)	70	NY 4159
Houghton (Dyfed)	24	SM 9807
Houghton (Hants.)	11	SU 3331
Houghton (W Susx)	12	TQ 0111
Houghton Conquest	35	TL 0441
Houghton le Spring	72	NZ 3450
Houghton on the Hill	43	SK 6703
Houghton Regis	34	TL 0224
Houghton St. Giles	46	TF 9235
Houlsyke	67	NZ 7308
Hound Green	20	SU 7259
Houndslow	86	NT 6347
Houndwood	87	NT 8464
Hounslow	20	TQ 1276
Houston	82	NS 4067
Houstry	112	ND 1534
Hove	13	TQ 2805
Hoveringham	53	SK 6946
Hoveton	47	TG 3018
Hovingham	66	SE 6675
How	71	NY 5056
How Caple	31	SO 6030
Howden	60	SE 7428
Howden-le-Wear	72	NZ 1633
Howe (Cumbr.)	63	SD 4588
Howe (Highld.)	112	ND 3062
Howe (Norf.)	47	TM 2799
Howe Green	22	TL 7403
Howell	55	TF 1346
Howe of Teuchar	105	NJ 7947
Howe Street (Essex)	22	TL 6914
Howe Street (Essex)	36	TL 6934
Howe, The	56	SC 1967
Howey	30	SO 0558
Howgate	85	NT 2457
Howick	79	NU 2517
Howlaws	86	NT 7242
Howle	41	SJ 6823
Howlett End	36	TL 5834
Howmore	109	NF 7636
Hownam	78	NT 7719
Hownam Mains	78	NT 7820
Howsham (Humbs.)	61	TA 0404
Howsham (N Yorks.)	67	SE 7362
Howton	29	SO 4129
Howwood	82	NS 3960
Hoxne	37	TM 1877
Hoylake	50	SJ 2189
Hoyland Nether	59	SE 3600
Hoyland Swaine	59	SE 2604
Hubbert's Bridge	55	TF 2643
Huby	66	SE 5665
Hucclecote	32	SO 8717
Hucking	14	TQ 8358
Hucknall	53	SK 5349
Huddersfield	59	SE 1416
Huddington	32	SO 9457
Hudswell	65	NZ 1400
Huggate	67	SE 8855
Hughenden Valley	20	SU 8695
Hughley	40	SO 5697
Hugh Town	2	SV 9010
Hugmore	50	SJ 3752
Huish (Devon.)	6	SS 5311
Huish (Wilts.)	18	SU 1463
Huish Champflower	16	ST 0429
Huish Episcopi	17	ST 4226
Hulcott	34	SP 8516
Hulland	53	SK 2447
Hullavington	18	ST 8982
Hull	61	TA 0902
Hullbridge	22	TQ 8194
Hulme End	52	SK 1059
Hulme Walfield	51	SJ 8465
Hulver Street	47	TM 4686
Humber Court	31	SO 5356
Humberston	61	TA 3105
Humberstone	43	SK 6206
Humbie	86	NT 4562
Humbleton (Humbs.)	61	TA 2234
Humbleton (Northum.)	78	NT 9728
Hume	86	NT 7041
Humshaugh	78	NY 9171
Huna	112	ND 3573
Huncoat	58	SD 7730
Huncote	43	SP 5197
Hundalee	78	NT 6418
Hunderthwaite	72	NY 9821
Hundleby	55	TF 3966
Hundleton	24	SM 9600
Hundon	36	TL 7348
Hundred Acres	11	SU 5911
Hundred End	57	SD 4122
Hundred, The	31	SO 5264
Hungarton	43	SK 6807
Hungerford (Berks.)	19	SU 3368
Hungerford (Hants.)	10	SU 1612
Hungerford Newtown	19	SU 3571
Hunmanby	67	TA 0977
Hunningham	43	SP 3768
Hunsdon	35	TL 4114
Hunsingore	66	SE 4253
Hunsonby	63	NY 5835
Hunspow	112	ND 2172
Hunstanton	46	TF 6741
Hunstanworth	72	NY 9449
Hunston (Suff.)	36	TL 9768
Hunston (W Susx)	12	SU 8601
Hunstrete	17	ST 6462
Hunt End	32	SP 0364
Huntingdon	45	TL 2371
Huntingfield	37	TM 3374
Huntington (Here. and Worc.)	30	SO 2553
Huntington (Lothian)	86	NT 4875
Huntington (N Yorks.)	66	SE 6156
Huntington (Staffs.)	41	SJ 9713
Huntingtower	92	NO 0725
Huntley	32	SO 7219
Huntly	104	NJ 5339
Hunton (Kent)	14	TQ 7149
Hunton (N Yorks.)	65	SE 1892
Hunt's Cross	50	SJ 4385
Huntsham	8	ST 0020
Huntspill	17	ST 3045
Huntworth	17	ST 3134
Hunwick	72	NZ 1832
Hunworth	47	TG 0635
Hurdsfield	51	SJ 9274
Hurley (Berks.)	20	SU 8283
Hurley (Warw.)	42	SP 2495
Hurlford	82	NS 4536
Hurliness	113	ND 2888
Hurn	10	SZ 1296
Hursley	11	SU 4225
Hurst (Berks.)	20	SU 7972
Hurst (Gtr Mches.)	58	SD 9400
Hurstbourne Priors	19	SU 4346
Hurstbourne Tarrant	19	SU 3853
Hurst Green (E Susx)	14	TQ 7327
Hurst Green (Lancs.)	58	SD 6838
Hurst Green (Surrey)	21	TQ 3951
Hurstpierpoint	13	TQ 2816
Hurworth	72	NZ 3010
Hury	72	NY 9619
Husbands Bosworth	43	SP 6484
Husborne Crawley	34	SP 9535
Husinish	109	NA 9812
Husthwaite	66	SE 5175
Huthwaite	53	SK 4659
Huttoft	55	TF 5176
Hutton (Avon)	17	ST 3458
Hutton (Borders)	87	NT 9053
Hutton (Cumbr.)	62	NY 4326
Hutton (Essex)	22	TQ 6394
Hutton (Lancs.)	57	SD 4926
Hutton (N Yorks.)	67	SE 7667
Hutton Bonville	66	NZ 3300
Hutton Buscel	67	SE 9784
Hutton Conyers	66	SE 3273
Hutton Cranswick	67	TA 0252
Hutton End	63	NY 4538
Hutton Henry	72	NZ4236
Hutton-le-Hole	66	SE 7090
Hutton Magna	72	NZ 1212
Hutton Roof (Cumbr.)	62	NY 3734
Hutton Roof (Cumbr.)	63	SD 5777
Hutton Rudby	66	NZ 4606
Hutton Sessay	66	SE 4776
Hutton Wandesley	66	SE 5050
Huxley	50	SJ 5061
Huyton	50	SJ 4490
Hycemoor	62	SD 0989
Hyde (Glos.)	32	SO 8801
Hyde (Gtr. Mches.)	51	SJ 9294
Hyde Heath	34	SP 9300
Hydestile	12	SU 9740
Hynish	94	NL 9839
Hyssington	40	SO 3194
Hythe (Hants.)	11	SU 4207
Hythe (Kent)	15	TR 1635

I

Ibberton	9	ST 7807
Ible	53	SK 2457
Ibsley	10	SU 1509
Ibstock	43	SK 4010
Ibstone	20	SU 7593
Ibthorpe	19	SU 3753
Ibworth	19	SU 5654
Ickburgh	46	TL 8195
Ickenham	20	TQ 0786
Ickford	34	SP 6407
Ickham	15	TR 2258
Ickleford	35	TL 1831
Icklesham	14	TQ 8816
Ickleton	35	TL 4943
Icklingham	36	TL 7772
Ickwell Green	35	TL 1545
Icomb	33	SP 2122
Idbury	33	SP 2320
Iddesleigh	6	SS 5608
Ide	5	SX 8990
Ideford	5	SX 8977
Ide Hill	21	TQ 4851
Iden	14	TQ 9123
Iden Green	14	TQ 8031
Idlicote	33	SP 2844
Idmiston	11	SU 1937
Idridgehay	53	SK 2849
Idrigil	100	NG 3863
Idstone	18	SU 2584
Ifield (W Susx)	13	TQ 2537
Ifield or Singlewell (Kent)	22	TQ 6471
Ifold	12	TQ 0231
Iford	13	TQ 4007
Ifton Heath	50	SJ 3236
Ightfield	51	SJ 5938
Ightham	21	TQ 5956
Iken	37	TM 4155
Ilam	52	SK 1351
Ilchester	9	ST 5222
Ilderton	79	NU 0121
Ilford	21	TQ 4586
Ilfracombe	6	SS 5147
Ilkeston	53	SK 4642
Ilketshall St. Andrew	47	TM 3887
Ilketshall St. Margaret	47	TM 3485
Ilkley	59	SE 1147
Illey	41	SO 9881
Illingworth	59	SE 0728
Illogan	2	SW 6643
Illston on the Hill	44	SP 7099
Ilmer	34	SP 7605
Ilmington	33	SP 2143
Ilminster	8	ST 3614
Ilsington	5	SX 7876
Ilston	25	SS 5590
Ilton (N Yorks.)	65	SE 1878
Ilton (Somer.)	8	ST 3517
Imachar	81	NR 8640
Immingham	61	TA 1714
Impington	35	TL 4463
Ince	50	SJ 4476
Ince Blundell	57	SD 3203
Ince-in-Makerfield	58	SD 5903
Inchbare	99	NO 6065
Inchberry	104	NJ 3155
Inchinnan	82	NS 4768
Inchlaggan	96	NH 1801
Inchnacardoch	102	NH 3710
Inchnadamph	110	NC 2522
Inchture	93	NO 2728
Inchyra	92	NO 1820
Indian Queens	3	SW 9158
Ingatestone	22	TQ 6499
Ingbirchworth	59	SE 2205
Ingestre	41	SJ 9724
Ingham (Lincs.)	54	SK 9483
Ingham (Norf.)	47	TG 3825
Ingham (Suff.)	36	TL 8570
Ingleby Arncliffe	66	NZ 4400
Ingleby Greenhow	66	NZ 5806
Inglesbatch	18	ST 7061
Inglesham	18	SU 2098
Ingleton (Durham)	72	NZ 1720
Ingleton (N Yorks.)	64	SD 6972
Inglewhite	57	SD 5439
Ingoe	79	NZ 0374
Ingoldisthorpe	46	TF 6832
Ingoldmells	55	TF 5668
Ingoldsby	44	TF 0030
Ingram	79	NU 0116
Ingrave	22	TQ 6292
Ings	63	SD 4498
Ingst	29	ST 5887
Ingworth	47	TG 1929
Inkberrow	32	SP 0157
Inkhorn	105	NJ 9239
Inkpen	19	SU 3564
Inkstack	112	ND 2570
Innellan	82	NS 1469
Innerleithen	85	NT 3336
Innerleven	93	NO 3700
Innermessan	68	NX 0863
Innerwick (Lothian)	86	NT 7273
Innerwick (Tays.)	97	NN 5947
Insch	104	NJ 6327
Insh	97	NH 8101
Inskip	57	SD 4537
Instow	6	SS 4730
Inver (Grampn.)	98	NO 2393
Inver (Highld.)	108	NH 8682
Inverailort	95	NM 7681
Inveralligin	101	NG 8457
Inverallochy	105	NK 0464
Inveramsay	105	NJ 7424
Inveran	108	NH 5797
Inveraray	89	NN 0908
Inverarish	100	NG 5535
Inverarnan	90	NN 3118
Inverbervie	99	NO 8372
Invercreran	96	NN 0147
Inverdruie	103	NH 9010
Inverebrie	105	NJ 9233
Inveresk	85	NT 3471
Inverey	98	NO 0889
Inverfarigaig	102	NH 5224
Invergarry	96	NH 3101
Invergeldie	91	NN 7427
Invergordon	103	NH 7168
Invergowrie	93	NO 3430
Inverhadden	97	NN 6757
Inverharroch	104	NJ 3831
Inverinate	101	NG 9122
Inverkeilor	99	NO 6649
Inverkeithing	85	NT 1383
Inverkeithny	104	NJ 6246
Inverkip	82	NS 2071
Inverkirkaig	110	NC 0819
Inverlael	107	NH 1885
Inverlochlarig	90	NN 4318
Invermoriston	102	NH 4117
Invernaver	111	NC 7060
Inverness	103	NH 6645
Invernoaden	89	NS 1197
Inverquharity	98	NO 4057
Inverquhomery	105	NK 0246
Inverroy	96	NN 2581
Inverugie	105	NK 0947
Inveruglas	90	NN 3109
Inverurie	105	NJ 7721
Invervar	97	NN 6648
Inwardleigh	6	SX 5599
Inworth	22	TL 8717
Iping	12	SU 8522
Ipplepen	5	SX 8366
Ipsden	19	SU 6385
Ipstones	52	SK 0249
Ipswich	37	TM 1744
Irby	50	SJ 2584

Irby in the Marsh Kingston by Sea

Irby in the Marsh 55 TF 4763
Irby upon Humber 61 TA 1904
Irchester 34 SP 9265
Ireby (Cumbr.) 62 NY 2338
Ireby (Lancs.) 64 SD 6575
Ireleth 64 SD 2277
Ireshopeburn 63 NY 8638
Irlam 51 SJ 7194
Irnham 44 TF 0226
Iron Acton 29 ST 6783
Iron-Bridge 41 SJ 6703
Iron Cross 32 SP 0552
Ironside 105 NJ 8852
Ironville 53 SK 4351
Irstead 47 TG 3620
Irthington 71 NY 4961
Irthlingborough 44 SP 9470
Irton 67 TA 0084
Irvine 82 NS 3239
Isauld 111 NC 9765
Isfield 13 TQ 4417
Isham 44 SP 8873
Isle Abbotts 8 ST 3520
Isle Brewers 8 ST 3621
Isleham 36 TL 6474
Isle of Whithorn 69 NX 4736
Isleornsay 101 NG 6912
Isleworth 21 TQ 1675
Isley Walton 43 SK 4225
Islington 21 TQ 3085
Islip (Northants.) 44 SP 9879
Islip (Oxon.) 33 SP 5214
Islivig 109 NA 9927
Itchen Abbas 11 SU 5332
Itchen Stoke 11 SU 5532
Itchingfield 12 TQ 1328
Itchington 29 ST 6586
Itteringham 47 TG 1430
Itton (Devon.) 7 SX 6898
Itton (Gwent) 29 ST 4896
Ivegill 70 NY 4143
Iver 20 TQ 0381
Iver Heath 20 TQ 0283
Iveston 72 NZ 1350
Ivinghoe 34 SP 9416
Ivinghoe Aston 34 SP 9518
Ivington 30 SO 4756
Ivington Green 30 SO 4656
Ivybridge 5 SX 6356
Ivychurch 15 TR 0227
Ivy Hatch 21 TQ 5854
Iwade 14 TQ 9067
Iwerne Courtney or Shroton 10 ST 8512
Iwerne Minster 10 ST 8614
Ixworth 36 TL 9370
Ixworth Thorpe 36 TL 9172

J

Jack Hill 65 SE 1951
Jackstown 105 NJ 7531
Jackton 84 NS 5953
Jacobstow (Corn.) 6 SX 1995
Jacobstowe (Devon.) 6 SS 5801
Jameston 24 SS 0599
Jamestown (Dumf. and Galwy.) 77 NY 2996
Jamestown (Highld.) 102 NH 4756
Jamestown (Strath.) 90 NS 3981
Janetstown 112 ND 1932
Jarrow 72 NZ 3265
Jawcraig 84 NS 8475
Jaywick 23 TM 1513
Jedburgh 78 NT 6520
Jeffreyston 24 SN 0906
Jemimaville 103 NH 7165
Jevington 13 TQ 5601
Johnby 62 NY 4333
Johnshaven 99 NO 7966
Johnston (Dyfed) 24 SM 9310
Johnstone (Strath.) 82 NS 4263
Johnstonebridge 77 NY 1091
Jordans 20 SU 9791
Jump 59 SE 3701
Juniper Green 85 NT 2068
Jurby East 56 SC 3899
Jurby West 56 SC 3598

K

Kaber 63 NY 7911
Kaimes (Lothian) 85 NT 2767
Kames (Strath.) 89 NM 8211
Kames (Strath.) 81 NR 9771
Kames (Strath.) 76 NS 6926
Kea 2 SW 8042
Keadby 60 SE 8311
Keal 55 TF 3763
Keal Coates 55 TF 3661
Kearsley 58 SD 7504
Kearstwick 63 SD 6079
Kearton 65 SD 9999
Keasden 65 SD 7266
Keddington (Lincs.) 55 TF 3388
Kedington (Suff.) 36 TL 7046
Kedleston 53 SK 2941
Keelby 61 TA 1610
Keele 51 SJ 8045
Keeley Green 34 TL 0046
Keeston 24 SM 9019
Keevil 18 ST 9157
Kegworth 43 SK 4826
Kehelland 2 SW 6241
Keig 104 NJ 6119
Keighley 59 SE 0641
Keilarsbrae 91 NS 8993
Keilhill 105 NJ 7259
Keillor 93 NO 2640
Keillour 91 NN 9725
Keils 80 NR 5268
Keinton Mandeville 17 ST 5430
Keir Mill 76 NX 8593
Keisby 44 TF 0328
Keiss 112 ND 3461
Keith 104 NJ 4350
Keithock 99 NO 6063
Kelbrook 58 SD 9044
Kelby 54 TF 0041
Keld (Cumbr.) 63 NY 5514
Keld (N Yorks.) 65 NY 8901
Kelfield 60 SE 5938
Kelham 54 SK 7755
Kellas (Grampn.) 104 NJ 1654
Kellas (Tays.) 93 NO 4535
Kellaton 5 SX 8039
Kelleth 63 NY 6605
Kelling 47 TG 0942
Kellington 60 SE 5524
Kelloe 72 NZ 3435
Kelly 4 SX 3981
Kelly Bray 4 SX 3571
Kelmarsh 44 SP 7379
Kelmscot 18 SU 2499
Kelsale 37 TM 3865
Kelsall 50 SJ 5268
Kelshall 35 TL 3236
Kelso 86 NT 7333
Kelstern 55 TF 2590
Kelston 18 ST 6966
Keltneyburn (Tays.) 97 NN 7749
Kelty 92 NT 1494
Kelvedon 22 TL 8618
Kelvedon Hatch 21 TQ 5698
Kelynack 2 SW 3729
Kemback 93 NO 4115
Kemberton 41 SJ 7204
Kemble 18 ST 9897
Kemerton 32 SO 9437
Kemnay 105 NJ 7315
Kempley 29 SO 6729
Kempsey 32 SO 8549
Kempsford 18 SU 1596
Kempston 34 TL 0347
Kempston Hardwick 35 TL 0244
Kempton 40 SO 3582
Kemp Town 13 TQ 3303
Kemsing 21 TQ 5558
Kenardington 15 TQ 9732
Kenchester 30 SO 4343
Kencot 33 SP 2504
Kendal 63 SD 5192
Kenfig 28 SS 8081
Kenfig Hill 28 SS 8483
Kenilworth 43 SP 2872
Kenley (Gtr London) 21 TQ 3259
Kenley (Salop) 40 SJ 5600
Kenmore (Highld.) 101 NG 7557
Kenmore (Tays.) 97 NN 7745
Kenn (Avon) 29 ST 4168
Kenn (Devon.) 8 SX 9285
Kennacraig 81 NR 8262
Kennerleigh 7 SS 8107
Kennet 91 NS 9291
Kennethmont 104 NJ 5328
Kennett 36 TL 6968
Kennford 8 SX 9186
Kenninghall 47 TM 0386
Kennington (Kent) 15 TR 0245
Kennington (Oxon.) 33 SP 5202
Kennoway 93 NO 3402
Kennyhill 36 TL 6680
Kennythorpe 67 SE 7865
Kenovay 94 NL 9946
Kensaleyre 100 NG 4251
Kensington and Chelsea 21 TQ 2778
Kensworth 34 TL 0318
Kensworth Common 35 TL 0317
Kentallen 96 NN 0057
Kentford 36 TL 7066
Kentisbeare 8 ST 0608
Kentisbury 6 SS 6144
Kentmere 63 NY 4504
Kenton (Devon.) 8 SX 9583
Kenton (Suff.) 37 TM 1965
Kentra 95 NM 6568
Kents Bank 64 SD 3975
Kent's Green 32 SO 7423
Kent's Oak 11 SU 3224
Kenwick 40 SJ 4230
Kenwyn 2 SW 8145
Kenyon 51 SJ 6295
Keoldale 110 NC 3866
Keppanach 96 NN 0262
Keppoch 101 NG 9621
Kepwick 66 SE 4690
Keresley 43 SP 3182
Kerne Bridge 29 SO 5819
Kerridge 51 SJ 9376
Kerris 2 SW 4427
Kerry 40 SO 1490
Kerrycroy 82 NS 1061
Kerry's Gate 30 SO 3933
Kersall 54 SK 7162
Kersey 36 TM 0044
Kershader 109 NB 3419
Kersoe 32 SO 9939
Kerswell 8 ST 0806
Kerswell Green 32 SO 8646
Kesgrave 37 TM 2245
Kessingland 47 TM 5286
Kestle Mill 2 SW 8459
Keston 21 TQ 4164
Keswick (Cumbr.) 62 NY 2723
Keswick (Norf.) 47 TG 2004
Keswick (Norf.) 47 TG 3533
Kettering 44 SP 8778
Ketteringham 47 TG 1503
Kettins 92 NO 2338
Kettlebaston 36 TL 9650
Kettlebridge 93 NO 3007
Kettlebrook 42 SK 2103
Kettleburgh 37 TM 2660
Kettleshulme 51 SJ 9879
Kettlesing Bottom 66 SE 2257
Kettlestone 46 TF 9631
Kettlethorpe 54 SK 8475
Kettlewell 65 SD 9772
Ketton 44 SK 9704
Kew 21 TQ 1877
Kewstoke 17 ST 3363
Kexbrough 59 SE 3009
Kexby (Lincs.) 54 SK 8785
Kexby (N Yorks.) 66 SE 7050
Key Green 51 SJ 8963
Keyham 43 SK 6606
Keyhaven 11 SZ 3091
Keyingham 61 TA 2425
Keymer 13 TQ 3115
Keynsham 29 ST 6568
Keysoe 35 TL 0763
Keysoe Row 35 TL 0861
Keyston 44 TL 0475
Keyworth 53 SK 6130
Kibblesworth 72 NZ 2456
Kibworth Beauchamp 43 SP 6893
Kibworth Harcourt 43 SP 6894
Kidbrooke 21 TQ 4076
Kiddemore Green 41 SJ 8509
Kidderminster 41 SO 8376
Kiddington 33 SP 4122
Kidlington 33 SP 4913
Kidmore End 20 SU 6979
Kidsgrove 51 SJ 8354
Kidwelly 25 SN 4106
Kielder 78 NY 6293
Kiells 80 NR 4168
Kilbarchan 82 NS 4063
Kilbeg 95 NG 6506
Kilberry 81 NR 7164
Kilbirnie 82 NS 3154
Kilbride (Skye) 100 NG 5820
Kilbride (S. Uist) 109 NF 7514
Kilbride (Strath.) 89 NM 8525
Kilburn (Derby.) 53 SK 3845
Kilburn (N Yorks.) 66 SE 5179
Kilby 43 SP 6295
Kilcadzow 84 NS 8848
Kilchattan (Bute) 82 NS 1054
Kilchattan (Colonsay) 88 NR 3795
Kilchenzie 80 NR 6725
Kilchiaran 80 NR 2060
Kilchoan 95 NM 4963
Kilchoman 80 NR 2163
Kilchrenan 89 NN 0322
Kilconquhar 93 NO 4802
Kilcot 29 SO 6925
Kilcoy 102 NH 5751
Kilcreggan 90 NS 2380
Kildale 66 NZ 6009
Kildalloig 81 NR 7518
Kildonan (Island of Arran) 81 NS 0321
Kildrummy 104 NJ 4617
Kildwick 59 SE 0145
Kilfinan 89 NR 9378
Kilfinnan 96 NN 2795
Kilgetty 24 SN 1207
Kilgwrrwg Common 29 ST 4797
Kilham (Humbs.) 67 TA 0564
Kilham (Northum.) 87 NT 8832
Kilkhampton 6 SS 2511
Killamarsh 53 SK 4680
Killay 25 SS 6092
Killchianaig 88 NR 6486
Killean 81 NR 6944
Killearn 84 NS 5286
Killerby 72 NZ 1919
Killichonan 97 NN 5458
Killichronan 95 NM 5441
Killiechanate 96 NN 2481
Killiecrankie 97 NN 9162
Killilan 101 NG 9430
Killimster 112 ND 3156
Killin 90 NN 5732
Killinghall 66 SE 2858
Killingholme 61 TA 1416
Killington 63 SD 6188
Killochyett 86 NT 4545
Kilmacolm 82 NS 3569
Kilmahumaig 89 NR 7893
Kilmaluag 100 NG 4374
Kilmany 93 NO 3821
Kilmarie 100 NG 5417
Kilmarnock 82 NS 4237
Kilmartin 89 NR 8398
Kilmaurs 82 NS 4141
Kilmelfort 89 NM 8413
Kilmersdon 17 ST 6952
Kilmeston 11 SU 5825
Kilmichael Glassary 89 NR 8593
Kilmington (Devon.) 8 SY 2798
Kilmington (Wilts.) 17 ST 7736
Kilmorack 102 NH 4944
Kilmore (Island of Skye) 95 NG 6507
Kilmory (Highld.) 95 NM 5270
Kilmory (Island of Arran) 81 NR 9621
Kilmory (Strath.) 89 NR 7075
Kilmuir (Highld.) 103 NH 6749
Kilmuir (Highld.) 108 NH 7573
Kilmuir (Island of Skye) 100 NG 2547
Kilmun 89 NS 1781
Kilnave 80 NR 2871
Kilndown 13 TQ 7035
Kilninian 94 NM 3945
Kilninver 89 NM 8221
Kiln Pit Hill 72 NZ 0454
Kilnsea 61 TA 4015
Kilnsey 65 SD 9767
Kilnwick 61 SE 9949
Kiloran 88 NR 3996
Kilpatrick 81 NR 9027
Kilpeck 30 SO 4430
Kilphedir 112 NC 9818
Kilpin 60 SE 7726
Kilrenny 93 NO 5705
Kilsby 43 SP 5671
Kilspindie 92 NO 2225
Kilsyth 84 NS 7178
Kiltarlity 102 NH 5041
Kilton 16 ST 1644
Kilvaxter 100 NG 3869
Kilve 16 ST 1443
Kilvington 54 SK 7942
Kilwinning 82 NS 3043
Kimberley (Norf.) 47 TG 0704
Kimberley (Notts.) 53 SK 4944
Kimble 34 SP 8206
Kimblesworth 72 NZ 2547
Kimble Wick 34 SP 8007
Kimbolton (Cambs.) 45 TL 0967
Kimbolton (Here. and Worc.) 31 SO 5261
Kimcote 43 SP 5886
Kimmeridge 10 SY 9179
Kimmerston 87 NT 9535
Kimpton (Hants.) 19 SU 2746
Kimpton (Herts.) 35 TL 1718
Kinbrace 111 NC 8631
Kinbuck 91 NN 7905
Kincaple 93 NO 4518
Kincardine (Fife.) 84 NS 9387
Kincardine (Highld.) 108 NH 6089
Kincardine O'Neil 99 NO 5999
Kinclaven 92 NO 1538
Kincraig 103 NH 8305
Kincraigie 98 NN 9849
Kindallachan 98 NN 9950
Kineton (Glos.) 32 SP 0926
Kineton (Warw.) 33 SP 3351
Kinfauns 92 NO 1622
Kingarth 81 NS 0956
Kingcoed 29 SO 4205
Kingham 33 SP 2523
Kingholm Quay 70 NX 9773
Kinghorn 85 NT 2686
Kinglassie 92 NT 2298
Kingoodie 93 NO 3329
Kingsand 4 SX 4350
Kingsbarns 93 NO 5912
Kingsbridge (Devon.) 5 SX 7344
Kingsbridge (Somer.) 16 SS 9837
King's Bromley 42 SK 1216
Kingsburgh 100 NG 3955
Kingsbury (Gtr London) 21 TQ 1989
Kingsbury (Warw.) 42 SP 2196
Kingsbury Episcopi 9 ST 4320
Kings Caple 29 SO 5628
Kingsclere 19 SU 5258
King's Cliffe 44 TL 0097
Kingscote 18 ST 8196
Kingscott 6 SS 5318
King's Coughton 32 SP 0858
Kingscross 81 NS 0428
Kingsdon 17 ST 5126
Kingsdown 15 TR 3748
Kingseat 92 NT 1290
Kingsey 34 SP 7406
Kingsfold 12 TQ 1636
Kingsford 41 SO 8281
Kingshall Street 36 TL 9161
King's Heath 42 SP 0781
Kingshouse 90 NN 5620
Kingskerswell 5 SX 8767
Kingskettle 93 NO 3008
Kingsland 30 SO 4461
Kings Langley 35 TL 0702
Kingsley (Ches.) 50 SJ 5474
Kingsley (Hants.) 12 SU 7838
Kingsley (Staffs.) 52 SK 0047
Kingsley Green 12 SU 8930
King's Lynn 46 TF 6220
Kings Meaburn 63 NY 6221
Kings Muir (Borders) 85 NT 2539
Kingsmuir (Fife) 93 NO 5409
Kingsmuir (Tays.) 98 NO 4849
Kingsnorth 15 TR 0039
King's Norton (Leic.) 44 SK 6800
King's Norton (W Mids) 42 SP 0579
King's Nympton 7 SS 6819
King's Pyon 30 SO 4350
Kings Ripton 45 TL 2576
King's Somborne 11 SU 3631
King's Stag 9 ST 7210
King's Stanley 32 SO 8103
King's Sutton 33 SP 4936
Kingstanding 42 SP 0794
Kingsteignton 5 SX 8773
King Sterndale 52 SK 0972
Kingsthorne 30 SO 4932
Kingsthorpe 34 SP 7563
Kingston (Cambs.) 35 TL 3455
Kingston (Devon.) 5 SX 6347
Kingston (Dorset) 9 ST 7509
Kingston (Dorset) 10 SY 9579
Kingston (Grampn.) 104 NJ 3365
Kingston (Hants.) 10 SU 1401
Kingston (I. of W.) 11 SZ 4781
Kingston (Kent) 15 TR 1951
Kingston (Lothian) 86 NT 5482
Kingston Bagpuize 19 SU 4098
Kingston Blount 20 SU 7399
Kingston by Sea 13 TQ 2205

Langton Green Little Hucklow

Langton Green 13 TQ 5439
Langton Herring 9 SY 6182
Langton Matravers 10 SY 9978
Langtree 6 SS 4415
Langwathby 63 NY 5733
Langworth 54 TF 0676
Lanivet 4 SX 0364
Lanlivery 4 SX 0759
Lanner 2 SW 7139
Lanreath 4 SX 1756
Lansallos 4 SX 1751
Lanteglos Highway 4 SX 1453
Lanton (Borders) 78 NT 6221
Lanton (Northum.) 87 NT 9231
Lapford 7 SS 7308
Laphroaig 80 NR 3845
Lapley 41 SJ 8713
Lapworth 42 SP 1671
Larbert 84 NS 8582
Largie 104 NJ 6131
Largiemore 89 NR 9486
Largoward 93 NO 4607
Largs 82 NS 2058
Largybeg 81 NS 0423
Largymore 81 NS 0424
Larkfield 82 NS 2376
Larkhall 84 NS 7651
Larkhill 18 SU 1243
Larling 46 TL 9889
Larriston 78 NY 5494
Lartington 72 NZ 0117
Lasham 19 SU 6742
Lassodie 92 NT 1292
Lasswade 85 NT 3066
Lastingham 66 SE 7290
Latchingdon 22 TL 8800
Latchley 4 SX 4173
Lately Common 51 SJ 6797
Lathbury 34 SP 8745
Latheron 112 ND 1933
Lathones 93 NO 4708
Latimer 20 TQ 0099
Latteridge 29 ST 6684
Lattiford 17 ST 6926
Latton 18 SU 0995
Lauder 86 NT 5347
Laugharne 25 SN 3011
Laughterton 54 SK 8375
Laughton (E Susx) 13 TQ 4913
Laughton (Leic.) 53 SP 6589
Laughton (Lincs.) 54 SK 8497
Laughton-en-le-Morthen 53 SK 5188
Launcells 6 SS 2405
Launceston 4 SX 3384
Launton 34 SP 6022
Laurencekirk 99 NO 7171
Laurieston 69 NX 6864
Lavant 12 SU 8608
Lavendon 34 SP 9153
Lavenham 36 TL 9149
Laverhay 77 NY 1498
Laverstock 10 SU 1530
Laverstoke 19 SU 4948
Laverton (Glos.) 32 SP 0735
Laverton (N Yorks.) 66 SE 2273
Laverton (Somer.) 18 ST 7753
Law 84 NS 8252
Lawers (Tays.) 91 NN 6739
Lawford 37 TM 0830
Lawhitton 4 SX 3582
Lawkland 65 SD 7766
Lawley 41 SJ 6608
Lawnhead 41 SJ 8224
Lawrenny 24 SN 0107
Lawshall 36 TL 8654
Lawton 30 SO 4459
Laxay 109 NB 3321
Laxdale 109 NB 4234
Laxey 56 SC 4384
Laxfield 37 TM 2972
Laxo 113 HU 4463
Laxton (Humbs.) 60 SE 7825
Laxton (Northants.) 44 SP 9496
Laxton (Notts.) 54 SK 7266
Laycock 59 SE 0340
Layer Breton 23 TL 9417
Layer-de-la-Haye 23 TL 9620
Layham 36 TM 0340
Layland's Green 19 SU 3866
Laysters Pole 31 SO 5563
Laytham 60 SE 7439
Lazenby 73 NZ 5719
Lazonby 71 NY 5439
Lea (Derby.) 53 SK 3357
Lea (Here. and Worc.) 29 SO 6521
Lea (Lincs.) 54 SK 8286
Lea (Salop) 40 SJ 4108
Lea (Salop) 40 SO 3589
Lea (Wilts.) 18 ST 9586
Leachkin 103 NH 6344
Leadburn 85 NT 2355
Leadenham 54 SK 9452
Leaden Roding 22 TL 5913
Leadgate (Cumbr.) 71 NY 7043
Leadgate (Durham) 72 NZ 1251
Leadhills 76 NS 8814
Leafield 33 SP 3115
Leake Common Side 55 TF 3952
Leake Hurn's End 55 TF 4248
Lealholm 67 NZ 7607
Lealt (Island of Skye) 100 NG 5060
Lea Marston 42 SP 2093
Leamington Hastings 43 SP 4467
Leargybreck 80 NR 5371
Learmouth 87 NT 8537
Leasgill 63 SD 4984
Leasingham 54 TF 0548
Leask 105 NK 0232
Leatherhead 21 TQ 1656
Leathley 59 SE 2346
Leaton 50 SJ 4618
Lea Town 57 SD 4930
Leaveland 15 TQ 9854
Leavening 67 SE 7863
Leaves Green 21 TQ 4162
Lea Yeat 65 SD 7587
Lebberston 67 TA 0882
Lechlade 18 SU 2199
Leckford 11 SU 3737
Leckfurin 111 NC 7059
Leckgruinart 80 NR 2769
Leckhampstead (Berks.) 19 SU 4375
Leckhampstead (Bucks.) 34 SP 7237
Leckhampton 32 SO 9419
Leckmelm 106 NH 1690
Leconfield 61 TA 0143
Ledaig 89 NM 9037
Ledburn 34 SP 9022
Ledbury 32 SO 7037
Ledgemoor 30 SO 4150
Ledicot 30 SO 4162
Ledmore 110 NC 2412
Ledsham (Ches.) 50 SJ 3574
Ledsham (W Yorks.) 59 SE 4529
Ledston 59 SE 4328
Ledwell 33 SP 4128
Lee (Devon.) 6 SS 4846
Lee (Hants.) 11 SU 3517
Lee (Lancs.) 64 SD 5655
Lee (Salop) 50 SJ 4032
Leebotwood 40 SO 4798
Lee Brockhurst 40 SJ 5426
Leece 64 SD 2469
Lee Clump 34 SP 9004
Leeds (Kent) 14 TQ 8253
Leeds (W Yorks.) 59 SE 3034
Leedstown 2 SW 6034
Lee Green 51 SJ 6561
Leek 51 SJ 9856
Leek Wootton 43 SP 2868
Leeming 66 SE 2989
Leeming Bar 66 SE 2889
Lee Moor 5 SX 5862
Lee-on-the-Solent 11 SU 5600
Lees (Derby.) 53 SK 2637
Lees (Gtr Mches) 58 SD 9504
Leeswood 50 SJ 2759
Lee, The 34 SP 8904
Legbourne 55 TF 3684
Legerwood 86 NT 5843
Legsby 55 TF 1385
Leicester 53 SK 5904
Leigh (Dorset) 9 ST 6108
Leigh (Glos.) 32 SO 8725
Leigh (Gtr Mches) 58 SJ 6699
Leigh (Here. and Worc.) 32 SO 7853
Leigh (Kent) 21 TQ 5546
Leigh (Salop) 40 SJ 3303
Leigh (Surrey) 21 TQ 2246
Leigh (Wilts.) 18 SU 0692
Leigh Beck 22 TQ 8182
Leigh Common 17 ST 7329
Leigh Delamere 18 ST 8879
Leigh Green 14 TQ 8933
Leigh-on-Sea 22 TQ 8385
Leigh Sinton 32 SO 7750
Leighterton 18 ST 8290
Leighton (Powys) 40 SJ 2405
Leighton (Salop) 41 SJ 6105
Leighton Bromswold 45 TL 1175
Leighton Buzzard 34 SP 9225
Leigh upon Mendip 17 ST 6847
Leigh Woods 29 ST 5572
Leinthall Earls 40 SO 4467
Leinthall Starkes 40 SO 4369
Leintwardine 40 SO 4074
Leire 43 SP 5290
Leirinmore 110 NC 4267
Leishmore 102 NH 3940
Leiston 37 TM 4462
Leitfie 98 NO 2545
Leith 85 NT 2676
Leitholm 87 NT 7944
Lelant 2 SW 5437
Lelley 61 TA 2032
Lem Hill 41 SO 7274
Lempitlaw 87 NT 7832
Lemreway 109 NB 3711
Lendalfoot 75 NX 1390
Lenham 14 TQ 8952
Lenham Heath 14 TQ 9249
Lenie 102 NH 5127
Lennel 87 NT 8540
Lennoxtown 84 NS 6277
Lenton 54 TF 0230
Lenwade 47 TG 0918
Lenzie 84 NS 6571
Leoch 93 NO 3636
Leochel-Cushnie 104 NJ 5210
Leominster 30 SO 4959
Leonard Stanley 32 SO 8003
Lepe 11 SZ 4498
Lephin 100 NG 1749
Lephinmore 89 NR 9892
Leppington 67 SE 7661
Lepton 59 SE 2015
Lerryn 4 SX 1356
Lerwick (Shetld.) 113 HU 4741
Lesbury 79 NU 2311
Leslie (Fife.) 92 NO 2401
Leslie (Grampn.) 104 NJ 5924
Lesmahagow 84 NS 8139
Lesnewth 4 SX 1390
Lessingham 47 TG 3928
Lessonhall 70 NY 2250
Leswalt 68 NX 0263
Letchmore Heath 21 TQ 1597
Letchworth 35 TL 2132
Letcombe Bassett 19 SU 3785
Letcombe Regis 19 SU 3786
Letham (Fife.) 93 NO 3014
Letham (Tays.) 99 NO 5248
Lethenty 105 NJ 8041
Letheringham 37 TM 2757
Letheringsett 47 TG 0638
Lettaford 5 SX 7084
Letterfearn 101 NG 8823
Letters 106 NH 1687
Letterston 24 SM 9429
Lettoch (Grampn.) 103 NJ 0932
Letton (Here. and Worc.) 30 SO 3346
Letton (Here. and Worc.) 40 SO 3770
Letty Green 35 TL 2810
Letwell 53 SK 5587
Leuchars 93 NO 4521
Levedale 41 SJ 8916
Leven (Fife.) 93 NO 3700
Leven (Humbs.) 61 TA 1045
Levens 63 SD 4886
Levenshulme 51 SJ 8794
Leverburgh 109 NG 0186
Leverington 45 TF 4411
Leverton 55 TF 3947
Levington 87 TM 2339
Levisham 67 SE 8390
Lew 33 SP 3206
Lewannick 4 SX 2780
Lewdown 5 SX 4486
Lewes 13 TQ 4110
Leweston 24 SM 9422
Lewisham 21 TQ 3674
Lewiston 102 NH 5029
Lewknor 20 SU 7197
Leworthy 7 SS 6638
Lewtrenchard 5 SX 4586
Ley (Corn.) 4 SX 1766
Leybourne 14 TQ 6858
Leyburn 65 SE 1190
Leycett 51 SJ 7846
Leyland 57 SD 5421
Leylodge 105 NJ 7713
Leys (Grampn.) 105 NK 0052
Leys (Tays.) 93 NO 2537
Leysdown-on-Sea 15 TR 0370
Leysmill 99 NO 6047
Leys of Cossans 98 NO 3749
Leyton 21 TQ 3886
Lezant 4 SX 3378
Lhanbryde 104 NJ 2761
Lhen, The 56 NX 3801
Libberton 85 NS 9943
Liberton 85 NT 2769
Lichfield 42 SK 1209
Lickey 41 SO 9975
Lickey End 41 SO 9772
Lickfold 12 SU 9225
Liddington 18 SU 2081
Lidgate 36 TL 7258
Lidlington 34 SP 9939
Lidstone 33 SP 3524
Liff 93 NO 3332
Lifton 4 SX 3885
Lighthazles 59 SE 0220
Lighthorne 33 SP 3355
Lightwater 20 SU 9262
Lightwood 51 SJ 9041
Lightwood Green 50 SJ 3840
Lilbourne 43 SP 5677
Lilleshall 41 SJ 7315
Lilley 35 TL 1226
Lilliesleaf 78 NT 5325
Lillingstone Dayrell 34 SP 7039
Lillingstone Lovell 34 SP 7140
Lillington 9 ST 6212
Lilstock 16 ST 1644
Limbrick 58 SD 6016
Limefield 58 SD 8012
Limekilnburn 84 NS 7050
Limekilns 85 NT 0783
Limerigg 84 NS 8570
Limington 9 ST 5422
Limpenhoe 47 TG 3903
Limpley Stoke 18 ST 7760
Limpsfield 21 TQ 4152
Linby 53 SK 5350
Linchmere 12 SU 8630
Lincoln 54 SK 9771
Lincomb 41 SO 8268
Lincombe 5 SX 7458
Lindale 62 SD 4180
Lindal in Furness 64 SD 2575
Lindean 86 NT 4931
Lindfield 13 TQ 3425
Lindford 12 SU 8136
Lindores 93 NO 2616
Lindridge 41 SO 6769
Lindsell 22 TL 6427
Lindsey 36 TL 9744
Linford (Essex) 22 TQ 6779
Linford (Hants.) 10 SU 1707
Lingague 56 SC 2172
Lingdale 73 NZ 6716
Lingen 40 SO 3667
Lingfield 13 TQ 3943
Lingwood 47 TG 3609
Liniclett 109 NF 7949
Linicro 100 NG 3967
Linkenholt 19 SU 3657
Linkinhorne 4 SX 3173
Linktown 93 NT 2790
Linley 40 SO 3593
Linley Green 31 SO 6953
Linlithgow 85 NS 9977
Linsidemore 108 NH 5498
Linslade 34 SP 9125
Linstead Parva 37 TM 3377
Linstock 70 NY 4258
Linthwaite 59 SE 0913
Lintlaw 87 NT 8258
Lintmill 104 NJ 5165
Linton (Borders) 78 NT 7726
Linton (Cambs.) 36 TL 5646
Linton (Derby.) 43 SK 2716
Linton (Here. and Worc.) 29 SO 6625
Linton (Kent) 14 TQ 7550
Linton (N Yorks.) 65 SD 9962
Linton-on-Ouse 66 SE 4960
Linwood (Hants.) 10 SU 1809
Linwood (Lincs.) 55 TF 1186
Linwood (Strath.) 82 NS 4464
Lionel 109 NB 5263
Liphook 12 SU 8431
Liscombe 7 SS 8732
Liskeard 4 SX 2564
Liss 12 SU 7727
Lissett 67 TA 1458
Liss Forest 12 SU 7929
Lissington 55 TF 1083
Lisvane 28 ST 1983
Liswerry 29 ST 3487
Litcham 46 TF 8817
Litchborough 34 SP 6354
Litchfield 19 SU 4553
Litherland 50 SJ 3397
Litlington (Cambs.) 35 TL 3142
Litlington (E Susx) 13 TQ 5201
Little Abington 35 TL 5349
Little Addington 44 SP 9573
Little Alne 32 SP 1361
Little Amwell 35 TL 3511
Little Aston 42 SK 0900
Little Atherfield 11 SZ 4680
Little Ayre 113 ND 3091
Little Ayton 73 NZ 5710
Little Baddow 22 TL 7807
Little Badminton 18 ST 8084
Little Bardfield 36 TL 6530
Little Barford 35 TL 1857
Little Barningham 47 TG 1333
Little Barrington 33 SP 2012
Little Barugh 67 SE 7579
Little Bedwyn 19 SU 2966
Little Bentley 23 TM 1125
Little Berkhamsted 35 TL 2907
Little Billing 34 SP 8061
Little Birch 30 SO 5031
Little Blakenham 37 TM 1048
Littleborough (Gtr Mches) 58 SD 9316
Littleborough (Notts.) 54 SK 8282
Littlebourne 15 TR 2057
Little Bowden 44 SP 7487
Little Bradley 36 TL 6852
Little Brampton 40 SO 3681
Little Brechin 99 NO 5862
Littlebredy 9 SY 5888
Little Brickhill 34 SP 9032
Little Brington 34 SP 6663
Little Bromley 23 TM 0928
Little Budworth 51 SJ 5965
Little Burstead 22 TQ 6691
Littlebury 35 TL 5139
Littlebury Green 35 TL 4938
Little Bytham 44 TF 0118
Little Carlton 55 TF 3985
Little Casterton 44 TF 0109
Little Cawthorpe 55 TF 3583
Little Chalfont 20 SU 9997
Little Chart 15 TQ 9245
Little Chesterford 35 TL 5141
Little Cheverell 18 ST 9853
Little Chishill 35 TL 4237
Little Clacton 23 TM 1618
Little Comberton 32 SO 9643
Little Common 14 TQ 7107
Little Compton 33 SP 2530
Little Cowarne 31 SO 6051
Little Coxwell 19 SU 2893
Little Cressingham 46 TF 8600
Little Dalby 44 SK 7714
Littledean 29 SO 6713
Little Dens 105 NK 0744
Little Dewchurch 31 SO 5231
Little Dunham 46 TF 8613
Little Dunkeld 98 NO 0242
Little Dunmow 22 TL 6521
Little Easton 22 TL 6023
Little Eaton 53 SK 3641
Little Ellingham 46 TM 0099
Little Eversden 35 TL 3752
Little Fakenham 36 TL 9076
Little Faringdon 33 SP 2201
Little Fenton 60 SE 5135
Littleferry 108 NH 8095
Little Fransham 46 TF 9011
Little Gaddesden 34 SP 9913
Little Garway 29 SO 4424
Little Gidding 45 TL 1382
Little Glemham 37 TM 3458
Little Gransden 35 TL 2755
Little Gruinard 106 NG 9484
Little Hadham 35 TL 4422
Little Hallingbury 22 TL 5017
Littleham (Devon.) 6 SS 4323
Littleham (Devon.) 8 SY 0281
Littlehampton 12 TQ 0202
Little Harrowden 44 SP 8771
Little Haseley 34 SP 6400
Little Hautbois 47 TG 2521
Little Haven 24 SM 8513
Little Hay 42 SK 1202
Little Haywood 42 SK 0021
Littlehempston 5 SX 8162
Little Hereford 40 SO 5568
Little Horkesley 36 TL 9531
Little Horsted 13 TQ 4718
Little Horwood 34 SP 7930
Little Houghton (Northants.) 34 SP 8059
Littlehoughton (Northum.) 79 NU 2316
Little Hucklow 52 SK 1678

Llwynderw Madingley

Llwynderw	40	SJ 2004
Llwyndyrys	48	SH 3741
Llwyngwril	38	SH 5909
Llwynhendy	25	SS 5599
Llwynmawr	50	SJ 2236
Llwynypia	28	SS 9993
Llynclys	40	SJ 2924
Llynfaes	48	SH 4178
Llysfaen	49	SH 8977
Llyswen	30	SO 1337
Llysworney	28	SS 9674
Llys-y-fran	24	SN 0424
Llywel	27	SN 8630
Loan	84	NS 9575
Loanend	87	NT 9450
Loanhead	85	NT 2765
Loans	82	NS 3431
Lochailort (Highld.)	95	NM 7682
Lochaline (Highld.)	95	NM 6744
Lochans	68	NX 0656
Locharbriggs	70	NX 9980
Lochawe (Strath.)	89	NN 1227
Lochboisdale (S. Uist)	109	NF 7820
Lochbuie (Strath.)	88	NM 6125
Lochcarron (Highld.)	101	NG 9039
Lochdonhead	89	NM 7333
Lochearnhead	90	NN 5823
Lochee	93	NO 3631
Lochend (Highld.)	112	ND 2668
Lochend (Highld.)	102	NH 5937
Locheport (N. Uist)	109	NF 8563
Lochfoot	69	NX 8973
Lochgair	89	NR 9290
Lochgarthside	102	NH 5219
Lochgelly	92	NT 1893
Lochgilphead	89	NR 8687
Lochgoilhead	90	NN 1901
Lochhill	104	NJ 2964
Lochinver (Highld.)	110	NC 0922
Lochlane	91	NN 8320
Lochluichart	102	NH 3262
Lochmaben	70	NY 0882
Lochnaw	68	NW 9962
Lochore	92	NT 1796
Lochranza (Island of Arran)	81	NR 9350
Lochside (Grampn.)	99	NO 7464
Lochside (Highld.)	111	NC 8735
Lochton	99	NO 7592
Lochwinnoch	82	NS 3558
Lochwood (Strath.)	84	NS 6966
Lockengate	4	SX 0361
Lockerbie	70	NY 1381
Lockeridge	18	SU 1467
Lockerley	11	SU 2925
Locking	17	ST 3659
Lockington (Humbs.)	61	SE 9947
Lockington (Leic.)	43	SK 4628
Lockleywood	41	SJ 6828
Lockmaddy	109	NF 9168
Locks Heath	11	SU 5207
Lockton	67	SE 8489
Loddington (Leic.)	44	SK 7802
Loddington (Northants.)	44	SP 8178
Loddiswell	5	SX 7148
Loddon	47	TM 3698
Lode	35	TL 5362
Loders	9	SY 4994
Lodsworth	12	SU 9223
Lofthouse (N Yorks.)	65	SE 1073
Lofthouse (W Yorks.)	59	SE 3325
Loftus	73	NZ 7118
Logan	75	NS 5820
Loggerheads	51	SJ 7336
Logie (Fife.)	93	NO 4020
Logie (Grampn.)	105	NK 0356
Logie (Tays.)	99	NO 6963
Logie Coldstone	98	NJ 4304
Logie Hill	108	NH 7776
Logie Newton	105	NJ 6638
Logie Pert	99	NO 6664
Logierait	98	NN 9752
Login	24	SN 1623
Lolworth	35	TL 3664
Lonbain	101	NG 6853
Londesborough	60	SE 8645
London	21	TQ 3079
London Colney	35	TL 1603
Londonderry	66	SE 3087
Londonthorpe	54	SK 9537
Londubh	106	NG 8680
Long Ashton	29	ST 5470
Long Bennington	54	SK 8344
Longbenton	72	NZ 2668
Longborough	33	SP 1729
Long Bredy	9	SY 5690
Longbridge (Warw.)	33	SP 2662
Longbridge (W Mids.)	42	SP 0178
Longbridge Deverill	18	ST 8640
Long Buckby	43	SP 6267
Longburton	9	ST 6412
Long Clawson	44	SK 7227
Longcliffe	53	SK 2255
Long Common	11	SU 5014
Long Compton (Staffs.)	41	SJ 8522
Long Compton (Warw.)	33	SP 2832
Longcot	18	SU 2790
Long Crendon	34	SP 6908
Long Crichel	10	ST 9710
Longcroft	84	NS 7979
Longden	40	SJ 4306
Long Ditton	21	TQ 1666
Longdon (Here. and Worc.)	32	SO 8336
Longdon (Staffs.)	42	SK 0714
Longdon upon Tern	41	SJ 6215
Longdown	5	SX 8691
Longdowns	2	SW 7434
Long Drax	60	SE 6528
Long Duckmanton	53	SK 4371
Long Eaton	53	SK 4933
Longfield	14	TQ 6068
Longford (Derby.)	53	SK 2137
Longford (Glos.)	32	SO 8320
Longford (Gtr London)	20	TQ 0576
Longford (Salop)	51	SJ 6433
Longford (Salop)	41	SJ 7218
Longford (W Mids.)	43	SP 3583
Longforgan	93	NO 3129
Longformacus	86	NT 6957
Longframlington	79	NU 1201
Longham (Dorset)	10	SZ 0697
Longham (Norf.)	46	TF 9415
Long Hanborough	33	SP 4114
Long Hermiston	85	NT 1770
Longhirst	79	NZ 2289
Longhope (Glos.)	29	SO 6819
Longhorsley	79	NZ 1494
Longhoughton	79	NU 2414
Long Itchington	33	SP 4165
Long Lawford	43	SP 4775
Longley Green	32	SO 7350
Long Load	9	ST 4623
Longmanhill	105	NJ 7462
Long Marston (Herts.)	34	SP 8915
Long Marston (N Yorks.)	66	SE 4951
Long Marston (Warw.)	32	SP 1548
Long Marton	63	NY 6624
Long Melford	36	TL 8646
Longmoor Camp	12	SU 7930
Longmorn	104	NJ 2358
Long Newnton (Glos.)	18	ST 9092
Longnewton (Bord)	78	NT 5827
Longnewton (Cleve.)	72	NZ 3816
Longney	32	SO 7612
Longniddry	86	NT 4476
Longnor (Salop)	40	SJ 4800
Longnor (Staffs.)	52	SK 0864
Longparish	19	SU 4344
Long Preston	65	SD 8357
Longridge (Lancs.)	57	SD 6037
Longridge (Lothian)	84	NS 9462
Longriggend	84	NS 8270
Long Riston	61	TA 1242
Longsdon	51	SJ 9554
Longside	105	NK 0347
Longslow	51	SJ 6535
Longstanton	45	TL 3966
Longstock	11	SU 3536
Longstowe	35	TL 3054
Long Stratton	47	TM 1992
Long Street	34	SP 7947
Long Sutton (Hants.)	20	SU 7347
Long Sutton (Lincs.)	45	TF 4322
Long Sutton (Somer.)	9	ST 4625
Longthorpe	45	TL 1698
Longton (Lancs.)	57	SD 4725
Longton (Staffs.)	51	SJ 9043
Longtown (Cumbr.)	70	NY 3768
Longtown (Here. and Worc.)	29	SO 3228
Longville in the Dale	40	SO 5393
Long Whatton	43	SK 4723
Longwick	34	SP 7805
Long Wittenham	19	SU 5493
Longwitton	79	NZ 0788
Longwood	41	SJ 6007
Longworth	19	SU 3899
Longyester	86	NT 5465
Lonmore	100	NG 2646
Loose	14	TQ 7552
Loosley Row	34	SP 8100
Lootcherbrae	104	NJ 6054
Lopcombe Corner	11	SU 2435
Lopen	9	ST 4214
Loppington	40	SJ 4629
Lorbottle	79	NU 0306
Lornty	98	NO 1746
Loscoe	53	SK 4247
Lossiemouth	104	NJ 2370
Lossit	80	NR 1856
Lostock Gralam	51	SJ 6874
Lostwithiel	4	SX 1059
Lothbeg	108	NC 9410
Lothersdale	58	SD 9545
Lothmore	111	NC 9611
Loudwater	20	SU 8990
Loughborough	43	SK 5319
Loughor	25	SS 5898
Loughton (Bucks.)	34	SP 8337
Loughton (Essex)	21	TQ 4296
Loughton (Salop)	41	SO 6183
Lound (Lincs.)	45	TF 0618
Lound (Notts.)	53	SK 6986
Lound (Suff.)	47	TM 5099
Lount	43	SK 3819
Louth	55	TF 3287
Love Clough	58	SD 8126
Lover	11	SU 2120
Loversall	60	SK 5798
Loves Green	22	TL 6404
Loveston	24	SN 0808
Lovington	17	ST 5931
Low Bradfield	53	SK 2691
Low Bradley	59	SE 0048
Low Braithwaite	70	NY 4242
Low Brunton	78	NY 9269
Low Burnham	60	SE 7702
Lowca	62	NX 9821
Low Catton	66	SE 7053
Low Crosby	71	NY 4459
Lowdham	53	SK 6646
Low Dinsdale	72	NZ 3411
Low Eggborough	60	SE 5522
Lower Aisholt	16	ST 2035
Lower Assendon	20	SU 7484
Lower Beeding	13	TQ 2227
Lower Benefield	44	SP 9888
Lower Bentham	64	SD 6469
Lower Boddington	33	SP 4752
Lower Bullingham	30	SO 5038
Lower Cam	32	SO 7401
Lower Chapel	30	SO 0235
Lower Chute	19	SU 3153
Lower Cwmtwrch	28	SN 7710
Lower Darwen	58	SD 6824
Lower Down	40	SO 3384
Lower Dunsforth	66	SE 4464
Lower Farringdon	12	SU 7035
Lower Frankton	50	SJ 3732
Lower Froyle	12	SU 7544
Lower Gledfield	108	NH 5990
Lower Green	46	TF 9837
Lower Greenbank	64	SD 5254
Lower Halstow	14	TQ 8567
Lower Hardres	15	TR 1453
Lower Heyford	33	SP 4824
Lower Higham	22	TQ 7172
Lower Hordley	40	SJ 3929
Lower Killeyan	80	NR 2743
Lower Langford	17	ST 4660
Lower Largo	93	NO 4102
Lower Lemington	33	SP 2134
Lower Lye	30	SO 4067
Lower Maes-coed	30	SO 3431
Lower Mayland	23	TL 9101
Lower Moor	32	SO 9847
Lower Nazeing	35	TL 3906
Lower Penarth	28	ST 1869
Lower Penn	41	SO 8696
Lower Pennington	11	SZ 3193
Lower Peover	51	SJ 7474
Lower Pitcalzean	108	NH 8070
Lower Quinton	33	SP 1847
Lower Shader	109	NB 3854
Lower Shelton	34	SP 9942
Lower Shiplake	20	SU 7779
Lower Shuckburgh	33	SP 4862
Lower Slaughter	32	SP 1622
Lower Stanton St. Quintin	18	ST 9180
Lower Sundon	35	TL 0526
Lower Swanwick	11	SU 4909
Lower Swell	32	SP 1725
Lower Tysoe	33	SP 3445
Lower Upham	11	SU 5219
Lower Vexford	16	ST 1135
Lower Weare	17	ST 4053
Lower Wield	19	SU 6340
Lower Winchendon	34	SP 7312
Lower Woodend	20	SU 8088
Lower Woodford	10	SU 1235
Lowesby	44	SK 7207
Lowestoft	47	TM 5493
Lowestoft End	47	TM 5394
Loweswater	62	NY 1421
Low Gate	71	NY 9064
Lowgill (Lancs.)	64	SD 6564
Low Ham	17	ST 4329
Low Hesket	71	NY 4646
Low Hesleyhurst	79	NZ 0997
Lowick (Cumbr.)	62	SD 2985
Lowick (Northants.)	44	SP 9781
Lowick (Northum.)	87	NU 0139
Low Moor	58	SD 7241
Lownie Moor	99	NO 4848
Low Redford	72	NZ 0731
Low Row (Cumbr.)	71	NY 5863
Low Row (N Yorks.)	65	SD 9897
Low Santon	61	SE 9312
Lowsonford	42	SP 1867
Low Street	47	TG 3424
Lowthorpe	67	TA 0860
Low Thurlton	47	TM 4299
Lowton	51	SJ 6197
Lowton Common	51	SJ 6397
Low Torry	85	NT 0086
Low Worsall	66	NZ 3909
Loxbeare	8	SS 9116
Loxhill	12	TQ 0037
Loxhore	6	SS 6138
Loxley	33	SP 2553
Loxton	17	ST 3755
Loxwood	12	TQ 0431
Lubenham	44	SP 7087
Luccombe	16	SS 9144
Luccombe Village	11	SZ 5880
Lucker	79	NU 1530
Luckett	4	SX 3873
Luckington	18	ST 8383
Lucklawhill	93	NO 4222
Luckwell Bridge	7	SS 9038
Lucton	30	SO 4364
Ludborough	55	TF 2995
Ludchurch	24	SN 1411
Luddenden	59	SE 0425
Luddesdown	14	TQ 6766
Luddington	60	SE 8216
Ludford (Lincs.)	55	TF 1989
Ludford (Salop)	40	SO 5173
Ludgershall (Bucks.)	34	SP 6617
Ludgershall (Wilts.)	18	SU 2650
Ludgvan	2	SW 5033
Ludham	47	TG 3818
Ludlow	40	SO 5175
Ludwell	10	ST 9122
Ludworth	72	NZ 3641
Luffincott	4	SX 3394
Luffness	86	NT 4780
Lugar	75	NS 5821
Luggiebank	84	NS 7672
Lugton	82	NS 4152
Lugwardine	31	SO 5441
Luib	100	NG 5628
Lulham	30	SO 4041
Lullington (Derby.)	42	SK 2513
Lullington (Somer.)	18	ST 7851
Lulsgate Bottom	29	ST 5065
Lulsley	32	SO 7455
Lumb	59	SE 0221
Lumby	60	SE 4830
Lumloch	84	NS 6369
Lumphanan	104	NJ 5804
Lumphinnans	92	NT 1692
Lumsden	104	NJ 4722
Lunan	99	NO 6851
Lunanhead	99	NO 4752
Luncarty	92	NO 0929
Lund (Humbs.)	61	SE 9648
Lund (N Yorks.)	60	SE 6532
Lundie (Tays.)	93	NO 2836
Lundin Links	93	NO 4002
Lunning	113	HU 5066
Lunsford's Cross	14	TQ 7210
Lunt	57	SD 3401
Luntley	30	SO 3955
Luppitt	8	ST 1606
Lupton	63	SD 5581
Lurgashall	12	SU 9326
Lurgmore	102	NH 5937
Lusby	55	TF 3367
Luss	90	NS 3592
Lusta	100	NG 2756
Lustleigh	5	SX 7881
Luston	30	SD 4863
Luthermuir	99	NO 6568
Luthrie	93	NO 3219
Luton (Beds.)	35	TL 0821
Luton (Devon.)	8	SX 9076
Luton (Kent)	14	TQ 7766
Lutterworth	43	SP 5484
Lutton (Devon.)	5	SX 5959
Lutton (Lincs.)	45	TF 4325
Lutton (Northants.)	45	TL 1187
Luxborough	16	SS 9738
Luxulyan	4	SX 0458
Lybster	112	ND 2435
Lydbury North	40	SO 3486
Lydcott	7	SS 6936
Lydd	15	TR 0421
Lydden	15	TR 2645
Lyddington	44	SP 8797
Lydd-on Sea	15	TR 0819
Lydeard St. Lawrence	16	ST 1232
Lydford (Devon.)	5	SX 5084
Lydford (Somer.)	17	ST 5731
Lydgate	58	SD 9225
Lydham	40	SO 3391
Lydiard Millicent	18	SU 0986
Lydiate	57	SD 3604
Lydlinch	9	ST 7413
Lydney	29	SO 6203
Lydstep	24	SS 0898
Lye	41	SO 9284
Lye Green	34	SP 9703
Lyford	19	SU 3994
Lymbridge Green	15	TR 1243
Lyme Regis	8	SY 3492
Lyminge	15	TR 1641
Lymington	11	SZ 3295
Lyminster	12	TQ 0204
Lymm	51	SJ 6786
Lymore	11	SZ 2992
Lympne	15	TR 1235
Lympsham	17	ST 3454
Lympstone	8	SX 9984
Lynchat	97	NH 7801
Lyndhurst	11	SU 2907
Lyndon	44	SK 9004
Lyne	20	TQ 0166
Lyneal	50	SJ 4433
Lyneham (Oxon.)	33	SP 2720
Lyneham (Wilts.)	18	SU 0179
Lynemouth	79	NZ 2991
Lyne of Gorthleck	102	NH 5420
Lyne of Skene	105	NJ 7610
Lyness	113	ND 3094
Lyng (Norf.)	47	TG 0617
Lyng (Somer.)	17	ST 3328
Lynmouth	7	SS 7249
Lynsted	15	TQ 9461
Lynton	7	SS 7149
Lyon's Gate	9	ST 6605
Lyonshall	30	SO 3356
Lytchett Matravers	10	SY 9495
Lytchett Minster	10	SY 9593
Lyth	112	ND 2763
Lytham	57	SD 3727
Lytham St. Anne's	57	SD 3427
Lythe	73	NZ 8413

M

Mabe Burnthouse	2	SW 7634
Mablethorpe	55	TF 5085
Macclesfield	51	SJ 9173
Macduff	105	NJ 7064
Macharioch	81	NR 7309
Machen	28	ST 2189
Machrihanish	80	NR 6220
Machynlleth	39	SH 7401
Mackworth	53	SK 3137
Macmerry	86	NT 4372
Madderty	91	NN 9522
Maddiston	84	NS 9476
Madehurst	12	SU 9810
Madeley (Salop)	41	SJ 6904
Madeley (Staffs.)	51	SJ 7744
Madingley	35	TL 3960

Madresfield **Midbea**

Madresfield	*32*	SO 8047
Madron	*2*	SW 4532
Maenclochog	*24*	SN 0827
Maendy	*28*	ST 0176
Maentwrog	*49*	SH 6640
Maer	*51*	SJ 7938
Maerdy (Clwyd)	*49*	SJ 0144
Maerdy (Mid Glam.)	*28*	SS 9798
Maesbrook	*40*	SJ 3121
Maesbury Marsh	*40*	SJ 3125
Maes-glas	*29*	ST 2985
Maesgwynne	*24*	SN 2024
Maeshafn	*50*	SJ 2061
Maesllyn	*26*	SN 3644
Maesmynis	*30*	SO 0148
Maesteg	*28*	SS 8591
Maesybont	*25*	SN 5616
Maes-y-cwmmer	*28*	ST 1794
Magdalen Laver	*22*	TL 5108
Maggieknockater	*104*	NJ 3145
Magham Down	*13*	TQ 6111
Maghull	*57*	SD 3702
Magor	*29*	ST 4287
Maiden Bradley	*77*	ST 8038
Maidencombe	*8*	SX 9268
Maidenhead	*20*	SU 8881
Maiden Law	*72*	NZ 1749
Maiden Newton	*9*	SY 5997
Maidens	*75*	NS 2107
Maidford	*34*	SP 6052
Maids' Moreton	*34*	SP 7035
Maidstone	*14*	TQ 7656
Maidwell	*44*	SP 7477
Mains	*102*	NH 4239
Mains of Ardestie	*93*	NO 5034
Mains of Balhall	*99*	NO 5163
Mains of Ballindarg	*98*	NO 4051
Mains of Dalvey	*103*	NJ 1132
Mains of Drum	*99*	NO 8099
Mains of Thornton	*99*	NO 6871
Mains of Throsk	*91*	NS 8690
Mainstone	*40*	SO 2687
Maisemore	*32*	SO 8121
Malborough	*5*	SX 7039
Malden	*21*	TQ 2166
Maldon	*22*	TL 8506
Malham	*65*	SD 9062
Mallaig	*95*	NM 6796
Malleny Mills	*85*	NT 1665
Mallwyd	*39*	SH 8612
Malmesbury	*18*	ST 9387
Malpas (Ches.)	*50*	SJ 4847
Malpas (Cornwall)	*2*	SW 8442
Maltby (Cleve.)	*73*	NZ 4613
Maltby (S Yorks.)	*53*	SK 5392
Maltby le Marsh	*55*	TF 4681
Malting Green	*23*	TL 9720
Maltman's Hill	*14*	TQ 9043
Malton	*67*	SE 7871
Malvern Link	*32*	SO 7848
Malvern Wells	*32*	SO 7742
Mamble	*41*	SO 6871
Manaccan	*2*	SW 7625
Manafon	*40*	SJ 1102
Manaton	*5*	SX 7481
Manby	*55*	TF 3986
Mancetter	*43*	SP 3196
Manchester	*51*	SJ 8397
Mancot	*50*	SJ 3267
Mandally	*96*	NH 2900
Manea	*45*	TL 4789
Manfield	*72*	NZ 2213
Mangotsfield	*29*	ST 6676
Mankinholes	*58*	SD 9523
Manley	*50*	SJ 5071
Manmoel	*28*	SO 1703
Mannel	*94*	NL 9840
Manningford Bohune	*18*	SU 1357
Manningford Bruce	*18*	SU 1359
Manning's Heath	*12*	TQ 2028
Mannington	*10*	SU 0605
Manningtree	*37*	TM 1031
Mannofield	*105*	NJ 9104
Manorbier	*24*	SS 0698
Manorhill	*86*	NT 6632
Manorowen	*24*	SM 9336
Mansell Gamage	*30*	SO 3944
Mansell Lacy	*30*	SO 4245
Mansergh	*63*	SD 6082
Mansfield (Notts.)	*53*	SK 5361
Mansfield (Strath.)	*76*	NS 6214
Mansfield Woodhouse	*53*	SK 5363
Mansriggs	*62*	SD 2880
Manston	*10*	ST 8115
Manthorpe	*45*	TF 0616
Manton (Humbs.)	*61*	SE 9302
Manton (Leic.)	*44*	SK 8704
Manton (Wilts.)	*18*	SU 1768
Manuden	*35*	TL 4926
Maplebeck	*54*	SK 7160
Maple Cross	*20*	TQ 0392
Mapledurham	*19*	SU 6776
Mapledurwell	*19*	SU 6851
Maplehurst	*12*	TQ 1924
Mapleton	*52*	SK 1648
Mapperley	*53*	SK 4343
Mapperton	*9*	SY 5099
Mappleborough Green	*32*	SP 0866
Mappleton	*61*	TA 2244
Mappowder	*9*	ST 7105
Marazion	*2*	SW 5130
Marbury	*51*	SJ 5545
March	*45*	TL 4197
Marcham	*19*	SU 4596
Marchamley	*41*	SJ 5929
Marchbankwood	*77*	NY 0899
Marchington	*52*	SK 1330
Marchinton Woodlands	*42*	SK 1128
Marchwiel	*50*	SJ 3547
Marchwood	*11*	SU 3809
Marcross	*28*	SS 9269
Marden (Here. and Worc.)	*30*	SO 5247
Marden (Kent)	*14*	TQ 7444
Marden (Wilts.)	*18*	SU 0857
Mardy	*29*	SO 3016
Marefield	*44*	SK 7408
Mare Green	*17*	ST 3326
Mareham le Fen	*55*	TF 2761
Mareham on the Hill	*55*	TF 2867
Maresfield	*13*	TQ 4624
Marfleet	*61*	TA 1329
Margam	*28*	SS 7887
Margaret Marsh	*10*	ST 8218
Margaret Roding	*22*	TL 5912
Margaretting	*22*	TL 6601
Margate	*15*	TR 3670
Margnaheglish	*81*	NS 0331
Marham	*46*	TF 7110
Marhamchurch	*6*	SS 2203
Marholm	*45*	TF 1402
Marian-glas	*48*	SH 5084
Mariansleigh	*7*	SS 7422
Marishader	*100*	NG 4963
Maristow	*5*	SX 4764
Mariveg	*109*	NB 4119
Mark	*17*	ST 3747
Markbeech	*13*	TQ 4842
Markby	*55*	TF 4878
Mark Causeway	*17*	ST 3547
Mark Cross	*13*	TQ 5831
Market Bosworth	*43*	SK 4003
Market Deeping	*45*	TF 1310
Market Drayton	*51*	SJ 6734
Market Harborough	*44*	SP 7387
Markethill	*92*	NO 2239
Market Lavington	*18*	SU 0154
Market Overton	*44*	SK 8816
Market Rasen	*55*	TF 1089
Market Stainton	*55*	TF 2279
Market Street	*47*	TG 2921
Market Weighton	*60*	SE 8741
Market Weston	*36*	TL 9877
Markfield	*43*	SK 4810
Markham	*28*	SO 1600
Markinch	*93*	NO 2901
Markington	*66*	SE 2864
Marksbury	*17*	ST 6662
Marks Tey	*23*	TL 9123
Markwell	*4*	SX 3658
Markyate	*35*	TL 0616
Marlborough	*18*	SU 1869
Marlcliff	*32*	SP 0950
Marldon	*5*	SX 8663
Marlesford	*37*	TM 3258
Marley Green	*51*	SJ 5745
Marlingford	*47*	TG 1208
Marloes	*24*	SM 7908
Marlow	*20*	SU 8587
Marlpit Hill	*21*	TQ 4447
Marnhull	*9*	ST 7718
Marnoch	*104*	NJ 5950
Marple	*51*	SJ 9588
Marr	*60*	SE 5105
Marrick	*65*	SE 0798
Marros	*24*	SN 2008
Marsden	*59*	SE 0411
Marsh	*8*	ST 2410
Marshall's Heath	*35*	TL 1515
Marsham	*47*	TG 1924
Marsh Baldon	*19*	SU 5699
Marshborough	*15*	TR 2958
Marshbrook	*40*	SO 4389
Marshchapel	*55*	TF 3598
Marshfield (Avon)	*18*	ST 7773
Marshfield (Gwent)	*29*	ST 2582
Marshgate	*4*	SX 1592
Marsh Gibbon	*34*	SP 6423
Marsh Green (Devon.)	*8*	SY 0493
Marsh Green (Kent)	*13*	TQ 4344
Marsh Green (Salop)	*41*	SJ 6014
Marshside	*57*	SD 3419
Marsh, The	*40*	SO 3197
Marshwood	*9*	SY 3899
Marske	*65*	NZ 1000
Marske-by-the-Sea	*73*	NZ 6322
Marston (Ches.)	*51*	SJ 6474
Marston (Here. and Worc.)	*30*	SO 3657
Marston (Lincs.)	*54*	SK 8943
Marston (Oxon.)	*33*	SP 5208
Marston (Staffs.)	*41*	SJ 8314
Marston (Staffs.)	*41*	SJ 9227
Marston (Warw.)	*42*	SP 2095
Marston (Wilts.)	*18*	ST 9656
Marston Green	*42*	SP 1685
Marston Magna	*9*	ST 5922
Marston Meysey	*18*	SU 1297
Marston Montgomery	*52*	SK 1338
Marston Moretaine	*34*	SP 9941
Marston on Dove	*42*	SK 2329
Marston St. Lawrence	*33*	SP 5342
Marston Trussell	*43*	SP 6986
Marstow	*29*	SO 5519
Marsworth	*34*	SP 9214
Marten	*19*	SU 2860
Marthall	*51*	SJ 8076
Martham	*47*	TG 4518
Martin (Hants.)	*10*	SU 0719
Martin (Lincs.)	*55*	TF 1259
Martinhoe	*7*	SS 6648
Martin Hussingtree	*32*	SO 8860
Martinscroft	*51*	SJ 6589
Martinstown	*9*	SY 6488
Martlesham	*37*	TM 2547
Martletwy	*24*	SN 0310
Martley	*32*	SO 7559
Martock	*9*	ST 4619
Marton (Ches.)	*51*	SJ 8468
Marton (Cleve.)	*73*	NZ 5115
Marton (Lincs.)	*54*	SK 8381
Marton (N Yorks.)	*66*	SE 4162
Marton (N Yorks.)	*66*	SE 7383
Marton (Salop)	*40*	SJ 2802
Marton (Warw.)	*43*	SP 4069
Marwood	*6*	SS 5437
Marybank	*102*	NH 4753
Maryburgh	*102*	NH 5456
Marygold	*87*	NT 8160
Maryhill	*105*	NJ 8245
Marykirk	*99*	NO 6865
Marylebone	*57*	SD 5807
Marypark	*104*	NJ 1938
Maryport	*68*	NX 1434
Maryport	*62*	NY 0336
Marystow	*4*	SX 4382
Mary Tavy	*5*	SX 5079
Maryton	*99*	NO 6856
Marywell (Grampn.)	*99*	NO 5896
Marywell (Tays.)	*99*	NO 6544
Masham	*66*	SE 2280
Mashbury	*22*	TL 6511
Mastrick	*105*	NJ 9007
Matching	*22*	TL 5212
Matching Green	*22*	TL 5311
Matching Tye	*22*	TL 5111
Matfen	*79*	NZ 0371
Matfield	*13*	TQ 6541
Mathern	*29*	ST 5291
Mathon	*32*	SO 7345
Mathry	*24*	SM 8832
Matlaske	*47*	TG 1534
Matlock	*53*	SK 3060
Matlock Bath	*53*	SK 2958
Matson	*32*	SO 8316
Matterdale End	*62*	NY 3923
Mattersey	*53*	SK 6889
Mattingley	*20*	SU 7357
Mattishall	*47*	TG 0510
Mattishall Burgh	*47*	TG 0511
Mauchline	*75*	NS 4927
Maud	*105*	NJ 9247
Maugersbury	*33*	SP 1925
Maughold	*56*	SC 4991
Maulden	*35*	TL 0538
Maulds Meaburn	*63*	NY 6216
Maunby	*66*	SE 3486
Maund Bryan	*31*	SO 5550
Mautby	*47*	TG 4712
Mavesyn Ridware	*42*	SK 0817
Mavis Enderby	*55*	TF 3666
Mawbray	*70*	NY 0846
Mawdesley	*57*	SD 4914
Mawgan	*2*	SW 7024
Maw Green	*42*	SP 0197
Mawla	*2*	SW 6945
Mawnan	*2*	SW 7827
Mawnan Smith	*2*	SW 7728
Maxey	*45*	TF 1208
Maxstoke	*42*	SP 2386
Maxton	*86*	NT 6129
Maxwellheugh	*86*	NT 7333
Maxwellston	*75*	NS 2600
Maybole	*75*	NS 3009
Mayfield (E Susx)	*13*	TQ 5827
Mayfield (Staffs.)	*52*	SK 1545
Mayford	*20*	SU 9956
Maypole	*29*	SO 4716
Maypole Green	*47*	TM 4195
Meadle	*34*	SP 8005
Meadowtown	*40*	SJ 3101
Meal Bank	*63*	SD 5495
Mealsgate	*70*	NY 2141
Mearbeck	*65*	SD 8160
Meare	*17*	ST 4541
Mears Ashby	*44*	SP 8366
Measham	*43*	SK 3312
Meathop	*63*	SD 4380
Meaux	*61*	TA 0939
Meavy	*5*	SX 5467
Medbourne	*44*	SP 7993
Meddon	*6*	SS 2717
Medmenham	*20*	SU 8084
Medstead	*11*	SU 6537
Meerbrook	*51*	SJ 9860
Meer End	*42*	SP 2474
Meesden	*35*	TL 4432
Meeth	*6*	SS 5408
Meidrim	*25*	SN 2820
Meifod	*40*	SJ 1513
Meigle	*98*	NO 2844
Meikle Earnock	*84*	NS 7253
Meikleour	*92*	NO 1539
Meikle Strath	*99*	NO 6471
Meikle Tarty	*105*	NJ 9928
Meikle Wartle	*105*	NJ 7230
Meinciau	*25*	SN 4610
Meir	*51*	SJ 9342
Melbourn (Cambs.)	*35*	TL 3844
Melbourne (Derby.)	*43*	SK 3825
Melbourne (Humbs.)	*60*	SE 7543
Melbury Bubb	*9*	ST 5906
Melbury Osmond	*9*	ST 5707
Melbury Sampford	*9*	ST 5705
Melchbourne	*44*	TL 0265
Melcombe Bingham	*9*	ST 7602
Meldon (Devon)	*5*	SX 5592
Meldon (Northum.)	*79*	NZ 1284
Meldreth	*35*	TL 3746
Melfort	*89*	NM 8314
Meliden	*49*	SJ 0580
Melin Court	*28*	SN 8201
Melin-y-coed	*49*	SH 8160
Melin-y-ddol	*39*	SJ 0807
Melin-y-grug	*39*	SJ 0507
Melin-y-wig	*49*	SJ 0448
Melkinthorpe	*63*	NY 5525
Melkridge	*71*	NY 7363
Melksham	*18*	ST 9063
Melldalloch	*89*	NR 9375
Melling (Lancs.)	*64*	SD 5970
Melling (Mers.)	*57*	SD 3800
Mellis	*37*	TM 0974
Mellon Charles	*106*	NG 8491
Mellor (Gtr Mches.)	*51*	SJ 9888
Mellor (Lancs.)	*58*	SD 6530
Mellor Brook	*58*	SD 6331
Mells	*18*	ST 7249
Melmerby (Cumbr.)	*63*	NY 6137
Melmerby (N Yorks.)	*65*	SE 0785
Melmerby (N Yorks.)	*66*	SE 3376
Melplash	*9*	SY 4797
Melrose	*86*	NT 5433
Melsonby	*65*	NZ 1908
Meltham	*59*	SE 0910
Melton	*37*	TM 2850
Meltonby	*67*	SE 7952
Melton Constable	*47*	TG 0433
Melton Mowbray	*44*	SK 7518
Melton Ross	*61*	TA 0610
Melvaig	*106*	NG 7486
Melverley	*40*	SJ 3316
Melvich	*111*	NC 8864
Membury	*8*	ST 2703
Memsie	*105*	NJ 9762
Memus	*98*	NO 4258
Menabilly	*4*	SX 0951
Menai Bridge	*48*	SH 5572
Mendham	*47*	TM 2783
Mendlesham	*37*	TM 1065
Mendlesham Green	*37*	TM 0963
Menheniot	*4*	SX 2862
Mennock	*76*	NS 8008
Menston	*59*	SE 1743
Menstrie	*91*	NS 8596
Mentmore	*34*	SP 9019
Meole Brace	*40*	SJ 4811
Meonstoke	*11*	SU 6119
Meopham	*14*	TQ 6466
Meopham Station	*14*	TQ 6467
Mepal	*45*	TL 4481
Meppershall	*35*	TL 1336
Mere (Ches.)	*51*	SJ 7281
Mere (Wilts.)	*10*	ST 8132
Mere Brow	*57*	SD 4118
Mereclough	*58*	SD 8730
Mere Green	*42*	SP 1298
Mereworth	*14*	TQ 6553
Mergie	*99*	NO 7988
Meriden	*42*	SP 2482
Merkadale	*100*	NG 3831
Merkland	*75*	NX 2491
Merlin's Bridge	*24*	SM 9414
Merrington	*40*	SJ 4621
Merriott	*9*	ST 4412
Merrivale	*5*	SX 5475
Merrymeet	*4*	SX 2766
Mersham	*15*	TR 0539
Merstham	*21*	TQ 2953
Merston	*12*	SU 8903
Merstone	*11*	SZ 5285
Merther	*3*	SW 8644
Merthyr	*25*	SN 3520
Merthyr Cynog	*27*	SN 9837
Merthyr Dyfan	*28*	ST 1169
Merthyr Mawr	*28*	SS 8877
Merthyr Tydfil	*28*	SO 0406
Merthyr Vale	*28*	ST 0899
Merton (Devon.)	*6*	SS 5212
Merton (Gtr London)	*21*	TQ 2569
Merton (Norf.)	*46*	TL 9098
Merton (Oxon.)	*33*	SP 5717
Mervinslaw	*78*	NT 6713
Meshaw	*7*	SS 7519
Messing	*23*	TL 8918
Messingham	*60*	SE 8904
Metfield	*37*	TM 2980
Metheringham	*54*	TF 0661
Methil	*93*	NT 3699
Methley	*59*	SE 3826
Methlick	*105*	NJ 8537
Methven	*92*	NO 0225
Methwold	*46*	TL 7394
Methwold Hithe	*46*	TL 7195
Mettingham	*47*	TM 3689
Mevagissey	*4*	SX 0144
Mexborough	*60*	SK 4799
Mey	*112*	ND 2872
Meysey Hampton	*18*	SU 1199
Miavaig	*109*	NB 0834
Michaelchurch	*29*	SO 5125
Michaelchurch Escley	*30*	SO 3134
Michaelchurch-on-Arrow	*30*	SO 2450
Michaelston-le-Pit	*28*	ST 1573
Michaelston-y-Vedw	*28*	ST 2484
Michaelstow	*4*	SX 0778
Micheldever	*11*	SU 5138
Michelmersh	*11*	SU 3426
Mickfield	*37*	TM 1361
Mickleby	*73*	NZ 8013
Micklefield	*59*	SE 4433
Mickleham	*21*	TQ 1753
Mickleover	*53*	SK 3034
Mickleton (Durham)	*72*	NY 9623
Mickleton (Glos.)	*32*	SP 1543
Mickle Trafford	*50*	SJ 4469
Mickley	*66*	SE 2576
Mickley Square	*72*	NZ 0761
Mid Ardlaw	*105*	NJ 9464
Midbea	*113*	HY 4444

Mid Beltie Mountgerald

Mid Beltie	99	NJ 6200
Mid Cairncross	99	NO 4979
Middle Assendon	20	SU 7385
Middle Aston	33	SP 4726
Middle Barton	33	SP 4326
Middlebie	70	NY 2176
Middle Claydon	34	SP 7125
Middle Drums	99	NO 5957
Middleham	65	SE 1287
Middlehope	40	SO 4988
Middle Littleton	32	SP 0747
Middle Maes-coed	30	SO 3334
Middlemarsh	9	ST 6707
Middle Rasen	54	TF 0889
Middlesbrough	73	NZ 4920
Middlesmoor	65	SE 0974
Middlestone Moor	72	NZ 2532
Middlestown	59	SE 2617
Middleton (Cumbr.)	63	SD 6286
Middleton (Derby.)	53	SK 1963
Middleton (Derby.)	53	SK 2755
Middleton (Essex)	36	TL 8639
Middleton (Gtr Mches.)	58	SD 8606
Middleton (Hants.)	19	SU 4243
Middleton (Here. and Worc.)	40	SO 5469
Middleton (Lancs.)	64	SD 4258
Middleton (Lothian)	85	NT 3657
Middleton (Norf.)	46	TF 6616
Middleton (Northants.)	44	SP 8489
Middleton (Northum.)	79	NU 0024
Middleton (Northum.)	87	NU 1035
Middleton (Northum.)	79	NZ 0585
Middleton (N Yorks.)	67	SE 7885
Middleton (N Yorks.-W Yorks.)	59	SE 1249
Middleton (Salop)	40	SJ 3128
Middleton (Salop)	40	SO 5377
Middleton (Suff.)	37	TM 4267
Middleton (Tays.)	98	NO 1206
Middleton (Tiree)	94	NL 9443
Middleton (Warw.)	42	SP 1798
Middleton (W Yorks.)	59	SE 3027
Middleton Cheney	33	SP 4941
Middleton Green	51	SJ 9935
Middleton Hall	79	NT 9825
Middleton in Teesdale	63	NY 9425
Middleton-on-Sea	12	SU 9800
Middleton-on-the-Wolds	61	SE 9449
Middleton Priors	41	SO 6290
Middleton St. George	72	NZ 3412
Middleton Scriven	41	SO 6787
Middleton Stoney	33	SP 5323
Middleton Tyas	66	NZ 2205
Middletown	40	SJ 3012
Middle Tysoe	33	SP 3344
Middle Wallop	11	SU 2937
Middlewich	51	SJ 7066
Middle Winterslow	11	SU 2432
Middle Witchyburn	104	NJ 6356
Middle Woodford	10	SU 1136
Middlewood Green	37	TM 0961
Middleyard	82	NS 5132
Middlezoy	17	ST 3733
Middridge	72	NZ 2526
Midfield	111	NC 5864
Midge Hall	57	SD 5123
Midgeholme	71	NY 6458
Midgham	19	SU 5567
Midgley	59	SE 0226
Midhopestones	59	SK 2399
Midhurst	12	SU 8821
Midlem	78	NT 5227
Mid Sannox	81	NS 0145
Midsomer Norton	17	ST 6654
Mid Thundergay	81	NR 8846
Midtown	106	NG 8285
Midville	55	TF 3857
Mid Yell	113	HU 4991
Migvie	104	NJ 4306
Milborne Port	9	ST 6718
Milborne St. Andrew	10	SY 7997
Milborne Wick	9	ST 6620
Milbourne	79	NZ 1175
Milburn (Cumbr.)	63	NY 6529
Milbury Heath	29	ST 6690
Milcombe	33	SP 4134
Milden	36	TL 9546
Mildenhall (Suff.)	36	TL 7074
Mildenhall (Wilts.)	18	SU 2069
Milebrook	40	SO 3172
Milebush	14	TQ 7546
Mile Elm	18	ST 9968
Mile End	23	TL 9827
Mileham	46	TF 9119
Milesmark	85	NT 0688
Milfield	87	NT 9333
Milford (Derby.)	53	SK 3445
Milford (Staffs.)	41	SJ 9721
Milford (Surrey)	12	SU 9442
Milford Haven (Dyfed)	24	SM 9006
Milford on Sea	11	SZ 2891
Milkwall	29	SO 5809
Milland	12	SU 8228
Milland Marsh	12	SU 8326
Mill Bank	59	SE 0321
Millbreck	105	NK 0045
Millbridge	12	SU 8542
Millbrook (Beds.)	34	TL 0138
Millbrook (Corn.)	4	SX 4252
Millbrook (Hants.)	11	SU 4012
Millburn (Strath.)	75	NS 4429
Millcorner	14	TQ 8223
Mill End (Bucks.)	20	SU 7885
Mill End (Herts.)	35	TL 3332
Millerhill	85	NT 3269
Miller's Dale	52	SK 1373
Mill Green (Essex)	22	TL 6400
Millgreen (Salop)	41	SJ 6727
Millheugh	84	NS 7551
Mill Hill	21	TQ 2292
Millholme	63	SD 5690
Millhouse	81	NR 9570
Millikenpark	82	NS 4162
Millington	67	SE 8351
Mill Lane	20	SU 7850
Millmeece	51	SJ 8333
Mill of Kingoodie	105	NJ 8425
Millom	62	SD 1780
Millport	82	NS 1655
Mill Street	46	TG 0118
Millthrop	63	SD 6691
Milltimber	99	NJ 8501
Millton of Auchriachan	104	NJ 1718
Milltown (Derby.)	53	SK 3561
Milltown (Dumf. and Galwy.)	70	NY 3375
Milltown (Grampn.)	104	NJ 4616
Milltown (Grampn.)	104	NJ 5447
Milltown of Aberdalgie	92	NO 0720
Milltown of Auchindown	104	NJ 3540
Milltown of Campfield	99	NJ 6400
Milltown of Craigston	105	NJ 7655
Milltown of Edinvillie	104	NJ 2639
Milltown of Towie	104	NJ 4612
Milnathort	92	NO 1204
Milngavie	84	NS 5574
Milnrow	58	SD 9212
Milnthorpe	63	SD 4981
Milovaig	100	NG 1550
Milson	41	SO 6372
Milstead	14	TQ 9058
Milston	18	SU 1645
Milton (Cambs.)	35	TL 4762
Milton (Central)	90	NN 5001
Milton (Central)	90	NS 4490
Milton (Cumbr.)	71	NY 5560
Milton (Dumf. and Galwy.)	68	NX 2154
Milton (Dumf. and Galwy.)	69	NX 8470
Milton (Grampn.)	104	NJ 5163
Milton (Highld.)	112	ND 3451
Milton (Highld.)	102	NH 3055
Milton (Highld.)	102	NH 4930
Milton (Highld.)	102	NH 5749
Milton (Highld.)	108	NH 7674
Milton (Highld.)	103	NH 9553
Milton (Oxon.)	33	SP 4535
Milton (Oxon.)	19	SU 4892
Milton (Staffs.)	51	SJ 9050
Milton (Strath.)	82	NS 4274
Milton (Tays.)	91	NN 9138
Milton (Tays.)	98	NO 3843
Milton Abbas	10	ST 8001
Milton Abbot	4	SX 4079
Milton Bridge	85	NT 2363
Milton Bryan	34	SP 9730
Milton Clevedon	17	ST 6637
Milton Coldwells	105	NJ 9538
Milton Combe	5	SX 4866
Milton Damerel	6	SS 3810
Miltonduff	104	NJ 1760
Milton Ernest	34	TL 0156
Milton Green	50	SJ 4558
Milton Hill	19	SU 4790
Milton Keynes	34	SP 8939
Milton Lilbourne	18	SU 1860
Milton Malsor	34	SP 7355
Milton Morenish	90	NN 6135
Milton of Auchinhove	99	NJ 5503
Milton of Balgonie	93	NO 3100
Milton of Campsie	84	NS 6576
Milton of Cushnie	104	NJ 5111
Milton of Lesmore	104	NJ 4628
Milton of Noth	104	NJ 5028
Milton of Potterton	105	NJ 9415
Milton of Tullich	98	NO 3897
Milton on Stour	17	ST 7928
Milton Regis	14	TQ 9064
Milton-under-Wychwood	33	SP 2618
Milverton	16	ST 1225
Milwich	51	SJ 9632
Milwr	50	SJ 1974
Minard	89	NR 9796
Minchinhampton	32	SO 8600
Mindrum	87	NT 8432
Minehead	16	SS 9746
Minera	50	SJ 2651
Minety	18	SU 0290
Minffordd	48	SH 5938
Miningsby	55	TF 3264
Minions	4	SX 2671
Minishant	75	NS 3314
Minnes	105	NJ 9423
Minnigaff	68	NX 4166
Minskip	66	SE 3864
Minstead	11	SU 2811
Minster (Kent)	15	TQ 9573
Minster (Kent)	15	TR 3164
Minsteracres	72	NZ 0255
Minsterley	40	SJ 3705
Minster Lovell	33	SP 3111
Minsterworth	32	SO 7717
Minterne Magna	9	ST 6504
Minting	55	TF 1873
Mintlaw	105	NK 0048
Minto	78	NT 5620
Minton	40	SO 4290
Minwear	24	SN 0413
Minworth	42	SP 1592
Mireland	112	ND 3160
Mirfield	59	SE 2019
Miserden	32	SO 9308
Miskin	28	ST 0481
Misson	53	SK 6895
Misterton (Leic.)	43	SP 5584
Misterton (Notts.)	54	SK 7694
Misterton (Somer.)	9	ST 4508
Mistley	37	TM 1231
Mitcham	21	TQ 2868
Mitcheldean	29	SO 6618
Mitchell	3	SW 8554
Mitchel Troy	29	SO 4910
Mitford	79	NZ 1786
Mithian	2	SW 7450
Mitton	41	SJ 8815
Mixbury	34	SP 6033
Mobberley	51	SJ 7880
Moccas	30	SO 3542
Mochdre (Clwyd)	49	SH 8278
Mochdre (Powys)	39	SO 0788
Mochrum	68	NX 3446
Mockerkin	62	NY 0823
Modbury	5	SX 6551
Moddershall	51	SJ 9236
Moelfre (Clwyd)	40	SJ 1828
Moelfre (Gwyn.)	48	SH 5186
Moffat	77	NT 0805
Mogerhanger	35	TL 1349
Moira	43	SK 3216
Molash	15	TR 0251
Mold	50	SJ 2363
Molehill Green	22	TL 5624
Molescroft	61	TA 0140
Molesworth	45	TL 0775
Molland	7	SS 8028
Mollington (Ches.)	50	SJ 3870
Mollington (Northants.)	33	SP 4347
Mollinsburn	84	NS 7171
Monachty	26	SN 5062
Mondynes	99	NO 7879
Monewden	37	TM 2358
Moneydie	92	NO 0629
Moniaive	76	NX 7791
Monikie	93	NO 4938
Monimail	93	NO 2914
Monington	26	SN 1344
Monken Hadley	21	TQ 2497
Monk Fryston	60	SE 5029
Monkhopton	41	SO 6293
Monkland	30	SO 4557
Monkleigh	6	SS 4520
Monknash	28	SS 9270
Monkokehampton	6	SS 5805
Monks Eleigh	36	TL 9647
Monks' Heath	51	SJ 8873
Monk Sherborne	19	SU 6056
Monkshill	105	NJ 7941
Monksilver	16	ST 0737
Monks Kirby	43	SP 4683
Monk Soham	37	TM 2165
Monkswood	29	SO 3403
Monkton (Devon.)	8	ST 1803
Monkton (Kent)	15	TR 2865
Monkton (Strath.)	75	NS 3527
Monkton (Tyne and Wear)	72	NZ 3463
Monkton Combe	18	ST 7761
Monkton Deverill	10	ST 8537
Monkton Farleigh	18	ST 8065
Monkton Heathfield	16	ST 2526
Monkton Up Wimborne	10	SU 0113
Monkwood	11	SU 6730
Monmouth	29	SO 5113
Monnington on Wye	30	SO 3743
Monreith	68	NX 3641
Monreith Mains	68	NX 3643
Montacute	9	ST 4916
Montford	40	SJ 4114
Montgarrie	104	NJ 5717
Montgomery	40	SO 2296
Montgreenan	82	NS 3343
Montrave	93	NO 3706
Montrose	99	NO 7157
Monxton	19	SU 3144
Monyash	52	SK 1566
Monymusk	105	NJ 6815
Monzie	91	NN 8725
Moonzie	93	NO 3317
Moorby	55	TF 2964
Moorcot	30	SO 3555
Moor Crichel	10	ST 9908
Moordown	10	SZ 0994
Moore	51	SJ 5584
Moorends	60	SE 6915
Moorhall	53	SK 3175
Moorhampton	30	SO 3846
Moorhouse (Cumbr.)	70	NY 3356
Moorhouse (Notts.)	54	SK 7566
Moorland or Northmoor Green	17	ST 3332
Moorlinch	17	ST 3936
Moor Monkton	66	SE 5056
Moor Nook	58	SD 6537
Moorsholm	73	NZ 6814
Moorside	58	SD 9507
Moor, The	14	TQ 7529
Moortown (Hants.)	11	SZ 4283
Moortown (Lincs.)	54	TF 0699
Morborne	45	TL 1391
Morchard Bishop	7	SS 7607
Morcombelake	8	SY 4093
Morcott	44	SK 9200
Morda	40	SJ 2827
Morden (Dorset)	10	SY 9195
Morden (Gtr London)	21	TQ 2567
Mordiford	31	SO 5637
Mordon	72	NZ 3326
More	40	SO 3491
Morebath	8	SS 9525
Morebattle	78	NT 7724
Morecambe	64	SD 4364
Morefield	106	NH 1195
Moreleigh	5	SX 7652
Morenish	90	NN 6035
Moresby	62	NX 9821
Morestead	11	SU 5125
Moreton (Dorset)	10	SY 8089
Moreton (Essex)	22	TL 5307
Moreton (Mers.)	50	SJ 2689
Moreton (Oxon.)	34	SP 6904
Moreton Corbet	40	SJ 5523
Moretonhampstead	5	SX 7586
Moreton-in-Marsh	33	SP 2032
Moreton Jeffries	31	SO 6048
Moreton Morrell	33	SP 3155
Moreton on Lugg	30	SO 5045
Moreton Pinkney	33	SP 5749
Moreton Say	51	SJ 6234
Moreton Valence	32	SO 7809
Morfa Bychan	48	SH 5437
Morfa Glas	28	SN 8606
Morfa Nefyn	48	SH 2840
Morgan's Vale	11	SU 1921
Morland	63	NY 6022
Morley (Derby.)	53	SK 3941
Morley (Durham)	72	NZ 1227
Morley (W Yorks.)	59	SE 2627
Morley Green	51	SJ 8282
Morley St. Botolph	47	TM 0799
Morningside	85	NT 2471
Morningthorpe	47	TM 2192
Morpeth	79	NZ 2085
Morphie	99	NO 7164
Morrey	42	SK 1218
Morriston	25	SS 6698
Morston	46	TG 0043
Mortehoe	6	SS 4545
Mortimer	19	SU 6564
Mortimer's Cross	30	SO 4263
Mortimer West End	19	SU 6363
Mortlake	21	TQ 2075
Morton (Avon)	29	ST 6491
Morton (Derby.)	53	SK 4060
Morton (Lincs.)	54	SK 8091
Morton (Lincs.)	45	TF 0924
Morton (Norf.)	47	TG 1217
Morton (Salop)	40	SJ 2824
Morton Bagot	32	SP 1164
Morton-on-Swale	66	SE 3292
Morvah	2	SW 4035
Morval	4	SX 2556
Morvich	101	NG 9621
Morville	41	SO 6694
Morwenstow	6	SS 2015
Mosborough	53	SK 4281
Moscow	82	NS 4840
Mosedale	62	NY 3532
Moseley (Here. and Worc.)	32	SO 8159
Moseley (W Mids)	42	SP 0883
Moss (Clwyd)	50	SJ 3052
Moss (S Yorks.)	60	SE 5914
Moss (Tiree)	94	NL 9644
Mossat	104	NJ 4719
Moss Bank (Cumbr.)	50	SJ 5198
Mossbank (Shetld.)	113	HU 4475
Mossburnford	78	NT 6616
Mossdale	69	NX 6571
Mossend	84	NS 7460
Mosside	98	NO 4252
Mossley	58	SD 9702
Moss Nook	51	SJ 8385
Moss of Barmuckity	104	NJ 2461
Moss Side	57	SD 3830
Mosston	99	NO 5444
Mosterton	9	ST 4505
Mostyn	50	SJ 1680
Motcombe	10	ST 8425
Motherwell	84	NS 7557
Mottingham	21	TQ 4272
Mottisfont	11	SU 3226
Mottistone	11	SZ 4083
Mottram in Logdendale	51	SJ 9995
Mouldsworth	50	SJ 5171
Moulin	97	NN 9459
Moulsecoomb	13	TQ 3307
Moulsford	19	SU 5984
Moulsoe	34	SP 9041
Moulton (Ches.)	51	SJ 6569
Moulton (Lincs.)	45	TF 3023
Moulton (Northants.)	44	SP 7866
Moulton (N Yorks.)	66	NZ 2303
Moulton (Suff.)	36	TL 6964
Moulton Chapel	45	TF 2918
Moulton Seas End	45	TF 3227
Mount (Corn.)	2	SW 7856
Mount (Corn.)	4	SX 1467
Mountain Ash	28	ST 0498
Mountain Cross	85	NT 1446
Mountain Water	24	SM 9224
Mountbenger	77	NT 3125
Mount Bures	36	TL 9032
Mountfield	14	TQ 7320
Mountgerald	102	NH 5661

Mount Hawke Newport

Mount Hawke 2 SW 7147
Mountjoy 3 SW 8760
Mountnessing 22 TQ 6297
Mounton 29 ST 5193
Mount Pleasant 37 TM 5077
Mountsorrel 43 SK 5814
Mousehole 2 SW 4626
Mouswald 70 NY 0672
Mow Cop 51 SJ 8557
Mowhaugh 78 NT 8120
Mowsley 43 SP 6489
Mowtie 99 NO 8388
Moy 96 NN 4282
Moylgrove 26 SN 1244
Muasdale 81 NR 6840
Muchalls 99 NO 9091
Much Birch 30 SO 5030
Much Cowarne 31 SO 6147
Much Dewchurch 30 SO 4831
Muchelney 9 ST 4224
Much Hadham 35 TL 4319
Much Hoole 57 SD 4723
Muchlarnick 4 SX 2156
Much Marcle 31 SO 6533
Much Wenlock 41 SO 6199
Mucking 22 TQ 6881
Mucklestone 51 SJ 7237
Muckleton 41 SJ 5821
Muckletown 104 NJ 5621
Muckton 55 TF 3781
Muddiford 6 SS 5638
Mudeford 10 SZ 1892
Mudford 9 ST 5719
Mudgley 17 ST 4445
Mugdock 84 NS 5576
Mugeary 100 NG 4438
Mugginton 53 SK 2843
Muggleswick 72 NZ 0450
Muie 108 NC 6704
Muirdrum 93 NO 5637
Muirhead (Fife.) 93 NO 2805
Muirhead (Strath.) 93 NS 3530
Muirhead (Strath.) 84 NS 6869
Muirhead (Tays.) 93 NO 3434
Muirhouses 85 NT 0180
Muirkirk 76 NS 6927
Muir of Fowlis 104 NJ 5612
Muir of Ord 102 NH 5250
Muirshearlich 96 NN 1380
Muirskie 99 NO 8295
Muirtack (Grampn.) 105 NJ 8146
Muirtack (Grampn.) 105 NJ 9937
Muirton 103 NH 7463
Muirton of Ardblair 98 NO 1743
Muirton of Ballochy 99 NO 6462
Muirtown 91 NN 9211
Muiryfold 105 NJ 7651
Muker 65 SD 9198
Mulbarton 47 TG 1901
Mulben 104 NJ 3450
Mullion 2 SW 6719
Mumbles, The 25 SS 6287
Mumby 55 TF 5174
Munderfield Row 31 SO 6451
Munderfield Stocks 31 SO 6550
Mundesley 47 TG 3136
Mundford 46 TL 8093
Mundham (Norf.) 47 TM 3298
Mundham (W Susx) 12 SU 8701
Mundon Hill 22 TL 8702
Mundurno 105 NJ 9413
Munerigie 96 NH 2602
Mungrisdale 62 NY 3630
Munlochy 103 NH 6453
Munsley 31 SO 6640
Munslow 40 SO 5187
Munslow Aston 40 SO 5086
Murcott 33 SP 5815
Murkle 112 ND 1668
Murlaggan (Highld.) 96 NN 3181
Murrow 45 TF 3707
Mursley 34 SP 8128
Murthill 98 NO 4657
Murthly 92 NO 0938
Murton (Cumbr.) 63 NY 7221
Murton (Durham) 72 NZ 3947
Murton (Northum.) 87 NT 9748
Murton (N Yorks.) 66 SE 6452
Musbury 8 SY 2794
Muscoates 66 SE 6880
Musselburgh 85 NT 3472
Muston (Leic.) 54 SK 8237
Muston (N Yorks.) 67 TA 0979
Mustow Green 41 SO 8774
Mutford 47 TM 4888
Muthill 91 NN 8616
Mutterton 8 ST 0304
Mybster 112 ND 1652
Myddfai 28 SN 7730
Myddle 40 SJ 4623
Mydroilyn 26 SN 4555
Mylor Bridge 2 SW 8036
Mynachlog-ddu 26 SN 1430
Myndtown 40 SO 3889
Mynytho 48 SH 3031
Myrebird 99 NO 7498
Mytchett 20 SU 8855
Mytholm 58 SD 9827
Mytholmroyd 59 SE 0125
Myton-on-Swale 66 SE 4366

N

Naburn 60 SE 5945
Nackington 15 TR 1554
Nacton 37 TM 2240
Nafferton 67 TA 0559
Nailsea 29 ST 4670
Nailstone 43 SK 4107
Nailsworth 18 ST 8499
Nairn 103 NH 8756
Nancegollan 2 SW 6632
Nanhoron 48 SH 2831
Nannau 39 SH 7420
Nannerch 50 SJ 1669
Nanpantan 43 SK 5017
Nanpean 4 SW 9556
Nant-ddu 28 SO 0015
Nanternis 26 SN 3756
Nantgaredig 25 SN 4921
Nantgarw 28 ST 1285
Nant-glas 27 SN 9965
Nantglyn 49 SJ 0061
Nantlle 48 SH 5053
Nantmawr 40 SJ 2424
Nantmel 30 SO 0366
Nantwich 51 SJ 6552
Nant-y-derry 29 SO 3306
Nantyffyllon 28 SS 8492
Nantyglo 28 SO 1911
Nant-y-moel 28 SS 9393
Naphill 20 SU 8496
Napton on the Hill 33 SP 4661
Narberth 24 SN 1114
Narborough (Leic.) 43 SP 5497
Narborough (Norf.) 46 TF 7413
Nasareth 48 SH 4749
Naseby 43 SP 6878
Nash (Bucks.) 34 SP 7734
Nash (Gwent) 29 ST 3483
Nash (Here. and Worc.) 30 SO 3062
Nash (Salop) 41 SO 6071
Nash Lee 34 SP 8408
Nassington 45 TL 0696
Nasty 35 TL 3624
Nateby (Cumbr.) 65 NY 7706
Nateby (Lancs.) 57 SD 4644
Natland 63 SD 5289
Naughton 36 TM 0249
Naunton (Glos.) 32 SP 1123
Naunton (Here. and Worc.) 32 SO 8739
Naunton Beauchamp 32 SO 9652
Naust 106 NG 8283
Navenby 54 SK 9857
Navestock 21 TQ 5397
Navestock Side 21 TQ 5697
Nawton 66 SE 6584
Nayland 36 TL 9734
Nazeing 35 TL 4106
Neacroft 10 SZ 1897
Neal's Green 43 SP 3384
Neap 113 HU 5060
Near Cotton 52 SK 0646
Neasham 72 NZ 3210
Neath 28 SS 7597
Neatishead 47 TG 3421
Nebo (Dyfed) 26 SN 5465
Nebo (Gwyn.) 48 SH 4750
Nebo (Gwyn.) 49 SH 8356
Necton 46 TF 8709
Nedd 110 NC 1332
Nedging Tye 36 TM 0149
Needham 47 TM 2281
Needham Market 37 TM 0855
Needingworth 45 TL 3472
Neen Savage 41 SO 6777
Neen Sollars 41 SO 6572
Neenton 41 SO 6487
Nefyn 48 SH 3040
Neilston 82 NS 4657
Nelson (Lancs.) 58 SD 8737
Nelson (Mid Glam.) 28 ST 1195
Nelson Village 79 NZ 2577
Nemphlar 84 NS 8544
Nempnett Thrubwell 17 ST 5360
Nenthead 71 NY 7743
Nenthorn 86 NT 6837
Nercwys 50 SJ 2260
Nereabolls 80 NR 2255
Nerston 84 NS 6457
Nesbit 87 NT 9833
Ness (Ches.) 50 SJ 3075
Ness (N Yorks.) 66 SE 6878
Nesscliffe 40 SJ 3819
Neston (Ches.) 50 SJ 2877
Neston (Wilts.) 18 ST 8667
Nether Alderley 51 SJ 8476
Netheravon 18 SU 1448
Nether Blainslie 86 NT 5443
Netherbrae 105 NJ 7959
Nether Broughton 44 SK 6925
Netherburn 84 NS 7947
Nether Burrow 64 SD 6174
Netherbury 9 SY 4799
Netherby 70 NY 3971
Nether Cerne 9 SY 6698
Nether Compton 9 ST 5907
Nether Crimond 105 NJ 8222
Nether Dallachy 104 NJ 3663
Netherend 29 SO 5900
Nether Exe 8 SS 9300
Netherfield 14 TQ 7018
Netherhampton 10 SU 1029
Nether Handwick 98 NO 3641
Nether Haugh 53 SK 4196
Nether Howecleuch 76 NT 0312
Nether Kellet 64 SD 5067
Nether Kinmundy 105 NK 0444
Nether Kirkton 82 NS 4757
Nether Langwith 53 SK 5371
Netherlaw 69 NX 7445
Netherley 99 NO 8593
Nethermill 70 NY 0487
Nethermuir 105 NJ 9143
Nether Padley 53 SK 2478
Netherplace 82 NS 5155
Nether Poppleton 66 SE 5654
Netherseal 43 SK 2813
Nether Silton 66 SE 4592
Nether Stowey 16 ST 1939
Netherstreet 18 ST 9764
Netherthird 75 NS 5818
Netherthong 59 SE 1309
Netherton (Devon.) 5 SX 8971
Netherton (Here. and Worc.) 32 SO 9941
Netherton (Northum.) 79 NT 9907
Netherton (Tays.) 98 NO 1452
Netherton (Tays.) 99 NO 5457
Netherton (W Yorks.) 59 SE 2716
Nethertown (Cumbr.) 62 NX 9807
Nether Wallop 11 SU 3036
Nether Whitacre 42 SP 2393
Netherwitton 79 NZ 1090
Nether Worton 33 SP 4230
Nethy Bridge 103 NJ 0020
Netley 11 SU 4508
Netley Marsh 11 SU 3312
Nettlebed 19 SU 7086
Nettlebridge 17 ST 6448
Nettlecombe 9 SY 5195
Nettleden 34 TL 0210
Nettleham 54 TF 0075
Nettlestead 14 TQ 6852
Nettlestead Green 14 TQ 6850
Nettlestone 11 SZ 6290
Nettleton (Lincs.) 55 TA 1000
Nettleton (Wilts.) 18 ST 8178
Neuk, The 99 NO 7397
Nevendon 22 TQ 7390
Nevern 24 SN 0840
New Abbey 70 NX 9665
New Aberdour 105 NJ 8863
New Addington 21 TQ 3863
New Alresford 11 SU 5832
New Alyth 98 NO 2447
New Annesley 53 SK 5153
Newark (Northants.) 45 TF 2100
Newark-on-Trent 54 SK 7953
Newarthill 84 NS 7859
Newbald 60 SE 9136
New Bewick 79 NU 0620
Newbiggin (Cumbr.) 71 NY 5649
Newbiggin (Cumbr.) 63 NY 6228
Newbiggin (Cumbr.) 64 SD 2669
Newbiggin (Durham) 63 NY 9127
Newbiggin (N Yorks.) 65 SD 9591
Newbiggin (N Yorks.) 65 SD 9985
Newbiggin-by-the Sea 79 NZ 3187
Newbigging (Strath.) 85 NT 0145
Newbigging (Tays.) 98 NO 2841
Newbigging (Tays.) 93 NO 4237
Newbigging (Tays.) 93 NO 4936
Newbiggin on Lune 65 NY 7005
Newbold (Derby.) 53 SK 3773
Newbold (Leic.) 43 SK 4018
Newbold on Avon 43 SP 4877
Newbold on Stour 33 SP 2446
Newbold Pacey 33 SP 2957
Newbold Verdon 43 SK 4403
New Bolingbroke 55 TF 3058
Newborough (Gwyn.) 48 SH 4265
Newborough (Northants.) 45 TF 2006
Newborough (Staffs.) 42 SK 1325
Newbottle 33 SP 5236
Newbourn 37 TM 2743
Newbridge (Clwyd) 50 SJ 2841
Newbridge (Corn.) 2 SW 4231
Newbridge (Gwent) 28 ST 2197
Newbridge (Hants.) 11 SU 2915
Newbridge (I. of W.) 11 SZ 4187
Newbridge (Lothian) 85 NT 1272
Newbridge-on-Usk 29 ST 3894
Newbridge on Wye 27 SO 0158
New Brighton 50 SJ 3093
New Brinsley 53 SK 4550
Newbrough 71 NY 8767
New Buckenham 47 TM 0890
Newburgh (Fife) 92 NO 2318
Newburgh (Grampn.) 105 NJ 9925
Newburgh (Lancs.) 57 SD 4810
Newburn 72 NZ 1765
Newbury 19 SU 4666
Newby (Cumbr.) 63 NY 5921
Newby (N Yorks.) 73 NZ 5012
Newby (N Yorks.) 65 SD 7269
Newby Bridge 62 SD 3686
Newby East 71 NY 4758
New Byth 105 NJ 8254
Newby West 70 NY 3653
Newby Wiske 66 SE 3687
Newcastle (Gwent) 29 SO 4417
Newcastle (Salop) 40 SO 2482
Newcastle Emlyn 26 SN 3040
Newcastleton 71 NY 4887
Newcastle-under-Lyme 51 SJ 8445
Newcastle upon Tyne 72 NZ 2464
Newchapel (Dyfed) 26 SN 2239
Newchapel (Staffs.) 51 SJ 8654
Newchapel (Surrey) 13 TQ 3642
Newchurch (Dyfed) 37 SN 3724
Newchurch (Gwent) 29 ST 4597
Newchurch (I. of W.) 11 SZ 5585
Newchurch (Kent) 15 TR 0531
Newchurch (Powys) 30 SO 2150
Newchurch in Pendle 58 SD 8239
New Clipstone 53 SK 5863
New Costessey 47 TG 1710
Newcott 8 ST 2309
New Cross 27 SN 6376
New Cumnock 76 NS 6113
New Deer 105 NJ 8846
Newdigate 12 TQ 2042
New Duston 34 SP 7162
New Earswick 66 SE 6155
New Edlington 60 SK 5399
New Ellerby 61 TA 1639
Newell Green 20 SU 8771
New Eltham 21 TQ 4573
New End 32 SP 0560
Newenden 14 TQ 8327
Newent 32 SO 7226
New Farnley 59 SE 2431
New Ferry 50 SJ 3385
Newfield (Durham) 72 NZ 2033
Newfield (Highld.) 108 NH 7877
New Fryston 60 SE 4526
Newgale 24 SM 8422
New Galloway 69 NX 6377
Newgate 47 TG 0443
Newgate Street 35 TL 3005
New Gilston 93 NO 4207
Newhall (Ches.) 51 SJ 6045
Newhall (Derby.) 43 SK 2821
Newham (Gtr London) 21 TQ 4082
Newham (Northum.) 79 NU 1728
Newham Hall 79 NU 1729
New Hartley 79 NZ 3076
Newhaven 13 TQ 4401
New Hedges 24 SN 1302
New Holland 61 TA 0724
Newholm 73 NZ 8610
New Houghton (Derby.) 53 SK 4965
New Houghton (Norf.) 46 TF 7827
Newhouse 84 NS 7961
New Houses 65 SD 8073
New Hutton 63 SD 5691
New Hythe 14 TQ 7159
Newick 13 TQ 4121
Newington (Kent) 14 TQ 8665
Newington (Kent) 15 TR 1737
Newington (Oxon.) 19 SU 6196
New Inn (Gwent) 29 SO 4800
New Inn (Gwent) 29 ST 3099
New Inn (N Yorks.) 65 SD 8072
New Invention 40 SO 2976
New Kelso 101 NG 9442
New Lanark 84 NS 8742
Newland (Glos.) 29 SO 5509
Newland (Here. and Worc.) 32 SO 7948
Newland (N Yorks.) 60 SE 6824
Newlandrig 85 NT 3662
Newlands (Grampn.) 104 NJ 3051
Newlands (Northum.) 72 NZ 0955
Newlands of Geise 112 ND 0865
New Lane 57 SD 4212
New Leake 55 TF 4057
New Leeds 105 NJ 9954
New Longton 57 SD 5125
New Luce 68 NX 1764
Newlyn 2 SW 4628
Newlyn East 2 SW 8256
Newmachar 105 NJ 8819
Newmains 84 NS 8256
New Mains of Ury 99 NO 8787
Newmarket (Isle of Lewis) 109 NB 4235
Newmarket (Suff.) 36 TL 6463
New Marton 50 SJ 3334
Newmill (Borders) 77 NT 4510
New Mill (Corn.) 3 SW 4534
Newmill (Grampn.) 104 NJ 4352
New Mill (Herts.) 34 SP 9212
New Mill (W Yorks.) 59 SE 1608
Newmill of Inshewan 98 NO 4260
New Mills (Corn.) 2 SW 8952
New Mills (Derby.) 52 SK 0085
Newmills (Lothian) 85 NT 1667
New Mills (Powys) 39 SJ 0901
Newmiln 92 NO 1230
Newmilns 82 NS 5337
New Milton 11 SZ 2495
New Moat 24 SN 0625
Newnham (Glos.) 29 SO 6911
Newnham (Hants.) 20 SU 7054
Newnham (Herts.) 35 TL 2437
Newnham (Kent) 15 TQ 9557
Newnham (Northants.) 33 SP 5859
Newnham Bridge 41 SO 6469
New Pitsligo 105 NJ 8855
New Polzeath 3 SW 9379
Newport (Devon.) 6 SS 5631
Newport (Dyfed) 24 SN 0639
Newport (Essex) 35 TL 5234

Newport **Nunwick**

Newport (Glos.)	*29*	ST 7097
Newport (Gwent)	*29*	ST 3187
Newport (Highld.)	*112*	ND 1224
Newport (Humbs.)	*60*	SE 8530
Newport (I. of W.)	*11*	SZ 4989
Newport (Norf.)	*47*	TG 5017
Newport (Salop)	*41*	SJ 7419
Newport-on-Tay	*93*	NO 4228
Newport Pagnell	*34*	SP 8743
Newpound Common	*12*	TQ 0627
New Prestwick	*75*	NS 3424
Newquay (Corn.)	*2*	SW 8161
New Quay (Dyfed)	*26*	SN 3859
New Rackheath	*47*	TG 2812
New Radnor	*30*	SO 2161
New Rent	*63*	NY 4536
New Romney	*15*	TR 0624
New Rossington	*60*	SK 6198
New Sauchie	*91*	NS 8993
New Scone	*92*	NO 1325
Newseat (Grampn.)	*105*	NJ 7033
Newsham (Northum.)	*79*	NZ 3079
Newsham (N Yorks.)	*65*	NZ 1010
Newsholme (Humbs.)	*60*	SE 7229
Newsholme (Lancs.)	*65*	SD 8451
New Silksworth	*72*	NZ 3853
Newstead (Borders)	*86*	NT 5634
Newstead (Northum.)	*79*	NU 1526
Newstead (Notts.)	*53*	SK 5252
New Stevenston	*84*	NS 7659
Newthorpe	*60*	SE 4632
Newtimber Place	*13*	TQ 2613
New Tolsta	*109*	NB 5348
Newton (Borders)	*78*	NT 6020
Newton (Cambs.)	*45*	TF 4314
Newton (Cambs.)	*35*	TL 4349
Newton (Ches.)	*50*	SJ 5059
Newton (Ches.)	*50*	SJ 5274
Newton (Cumbr.)	*64*	SD 2371
Newton (Dumf. and Galwy.)	*77*	NY 1194
Newton (Grampn.)	*104*	NJ 1663
Newton (Hants.)	*11*	SU 2322
Newton (Here. and Worc.)	*30*	SO 3433
Newton (Here. and Worc.)	*30*	SO 5054
Newton (Highld.)	*110*	NC 2331
Newton (Highld.)	*112*	ND 3449
Newton (Highld.)	*103*	NH 7448
Newton (Highld.)	*103*	NH 7866
Newton (Lancs.)	*64*	SD 5974
Newton (Lancs.)	*58*	SD 6950
Newton (Lincs.)	*54*	TF 0436
Newton (Lothian)	*85*	NT 0877
Newton (Mid Glam.)	*28*	SS 8377
Newton (Norf.)	*46*	TF 8315
Newton (Northants.)	*44*	SP 8883
Newton (Northum.)	*72*	NZ 0364
Newton (Notts.)	*53*	SK 6841
Newton (Staffs.)	*42*	SK 0325
Newton (Strath.)	*84*	NS 6560
Newton (Strath.)	*84*	NS 9331
Newton (Suff.)	*36*	TL 9140
Newton (Warw.)	*43*	SP 5378
Newton (W Glam.)	*25*	SS 6088
Newton (W Yorks.)	*59*	SE 4427
Newton Abbot	*5*	SX 8671
Newton Arlosh	*70*	NY 1955
Newton Aycliffe	*72*	NZ 2824
Newton Bewley	*73*	NZ 4626
Newton Blossomville	*34*	SP 9251
Newton Bromswold	*44*	SP 9966
Newton Burgoland	*43*	SK 3609
Newton by Toft	*54*	TF 0487
Newton Ferrers	*5*	SX 5447
Newton Flotman	*47*	TM 2198
Newtongarry Croft	*104*	NJ 5735
Newtongrange	*85*	NT 3364
Newton Harcourt	*43*	SP 6397
Newtonill	*99*	NO 9193
Newton Kyme	*60*	SE 4644
Newton-le-Willows (Mers.)	*51*	SJ 5894
Newton-le-Willows (N Yorks.)	*65*	SE 2189
Newton Longville	*34*	SP 8431
Newton Mearns	*84*	NS 5456
Newtonmill	*99*	NO 6064
Newtonmore	*97*	NN 7199
Newton Mountain	*24*	SM 9807
Newton of Balcanquhal	*92*	NO 1510
Newton-on-Ouse	*66*	SE 5059
Newton-on-Rawcliffe	*67*	SE 8090
Newton-on-the-Moor	*79*	NU 1605
Newton on Trent	*54*	SK 8374
Newton Poppleford	*8*	SY 0889
Newton Purcell	*34*	SP 6230
Newton Regis	*43*	SK 2707
Newton Reigny	*63*	NY 4731
Newton St. Cyres	*7*	SX 8797
Newton St. Faith	*47*	TG 2117
Newton St. Loe	*18*	ST 7064
Newton St. Petrock	*6*	SS 4112
Newton Solney	*43*	SK 2825
Newton Stacey	*19*	SU 4040
Newton Stewart	*68*	NX 4165
Newton Toney	*18*	SU 2140
Newton Tracey	*6*	SS 5226
Newton under Roseberry	*73*	NZ 5613
Newton upon Derwent	*60*	SE 7149
Newton Valence	*12*	SU 7232
Newtown (Ches.)	*51*	SJ 6247
Newtown (Ches.)	*51*	SJ 9784
Newtown (Corn.)	*2*	SW 7323
Newtown (Cumbr.)	*71*	NY 5062
Newtown (Dorset)	*10*	SZ 0393
Newtown (Hants.)	*11*	SU 2710
Newtown (Hants.)	*11*	SU 3023
Newtown (Hants.)	*19*	SU 4763
Newtown (Hants.)	*11*	SU 6013
Newtown (Here. and Worc.)	*31*	SO 6145
Newtown (Highld.)	*96*	NH 3504
Newtown (I. of M.)	*56*	SC 3273
Newtown (I. of W.)	*11*	SZ 4290
New Town (Lothian)	*86*	NT 4470
Newtown (Northum.)	*87*	NT 9731
Newtown (Northum.)	*79*	NU 0300
Newtown (Northum.)	*79*	NU 0425
Newtown (Powys)	*40*	SO 1091
Newtown (Salop)	*50*	SJ 4831
Newtown (Staffs.)	*51*	SJ 9060
Newtown (Wilts.)	*10*	ST 9128
Newtown Linford	*43*	SK 5110
Newtown St. Boswells	*86*	NT 5731
New Tredegar	*28*	SO 1403
New Tupton	*53*	SK 3966
Newtyle	*98*	NO 2941
New Walsoken	*45*	TF 4709
New Waltham	*61*	TA 2804
New Wimpole	*35*	TL 3450
New Winton	*86*	NT 4271
New Yatt	*33*	SP 3713
New York (Lincs.)	*55*	TF 2455
New York (Tyne and Wear)	*72*	NZ 3270
Neyland	*24*	SM 9605
Nibley	*29*	ST 6882
Nicholashayne	*8*	ST 1015
Nigg (Grampn.)	*99*	NJ 9402
Nigg (Highld.)	*108*	NH 8071
Nightcott	*7*	SS 8925
Nine Ashes	*22*	TL 5902
Ninebanks	*71*	NY 7853
Ninfield	*14*	TQ 7012
Ningwood	*11*	SZ 3989
Nisbet	*78*	NT 6725
Niton	*11*	SZ 5076
Nitshill	*84*	NS 5160
Noak Hill	*21*	TQ 5493
Nobottle	*34*	SP 6763
Nocton	*54*	TF 0564
Noke	*33*	SP 5413
Nolton	*24*	SM 8718
No Man's Heath (Ches.)	*50*	SJ 5148
No Man's Heath (Warw.)	*43*	SK 2709
Nomansland (Devon)	*7*	SS 8313
Nomansland (Wilts.)	*11*	SU 2517
Noneley	*40*	SJ 4727
Nonington	*15*	TR 2552
Nook	*71*	NY 4679
Norbury (Ches.)	*51*	SJ 5547
Norbury (Derby.)	*52*	SK 1242
Norbury (Salop)	*40*	SO 3693
Norbury (Staffs.)	*41*	SJ 7823
Nordelph	*46*	TF 5501
Norden (Dorset)	*10*	SY 9483
Norden (Gtr Mches)	*58*	SD 8514
Nordley	*41*	SO 6998
Norham	*87*	NT 9047
Norley	*51*	SJ 5672
Norleywood	*11*	SZ 3597
Normanby (Humbs.)	*60*	SE 8716
Normanby (Lincs.)	*54*	SK 9988
Normanby (N Yorks.)	*66*	SE 7381
Normanby le Wold	*55*	TF 1294
Norman Cross	*45*	TL 1691
Normandy	*20*	SU 9251
Norman's Green	*8*	ST 0503
Normanton (Derby.)	*53*	SK 3433
Normanton (Lincs.)	*54*	SK 9446
Normanton (Notts.)	*54*	SK 7054
Normanton (W Yorks.)	*59*	SE 3822
Normanton le Heath	*43*	SK 3712
Normanton on Soar	*43*	SK 5123
Normanton on the Wolds	*53*	SK 6232
Normanton on Trent	*54*	SK 7868
Normoss	*57*	SD 3437
Norrington Common	*18*	ST 8864
Norris Hill	*43*	SK 3216
Northallerton	*66*	SE 3793
Northam (Devon.)	*6*	SS 4429
Northam (Hants.)	*11*	SU 4312
Northampton	*34*	SP 7561
North Aston	*33*	SP 4728
Northaw	*35*	TL 2802
North Baddesley	*11*	SU 3920
North Ballachulish	*96*	NN 0560
North Barrow	*17*	ST 6029
North Barsham	*46*	TF 9135
North Benfleet	*22*	TQ 7590
North Berwick	*86*	NT 5485
North Boarhunt	*11*	SU 6010
Northborough	*45*	TF 1508
Northbourne	*15*	TR 3352
North Bovey	*5*	SX 7483
North Bradley	*18*	ST 8554
North Brentor	*5*	SX 4781
North Buckland	*6*	SS 4740
North Burlingham	*47*	TG 3610
North Cadbury	*17*	ST 6327
North Cairn	*68*	NW 9770
North Carlton	*54*	SK 9477
North Cave	*60*	SE 8832
North Cerney	*32*	SP 0208
Northchapel	*12*	SU 9529
North Charford	*11*	SU 1919
North Charlton	*79*	NU 1622
Northchurch	*34*	SP 9708
North Cliffe	*60*	SE 8737
North Clifton	*54*	SK 8272
North Cotes	*61*	TA 3400
Northcott	*4*	SX 3392
North Cove	*47*	TM 4689
North Cowton	*66*	NZ 2803
North Crawley	*34*	SP 9244
North Cray	*21*	TQ 4972
North Creake	*46*	TF 8538
North Curry	*8*	ST 3125
North Dalton	*67*	SE 9352
North Deighton	*66*	SE 3851
North Duffield	*60*	SE 6837
North Elkington	*55*	TF 2890
North Elmham	*46*	TF 9820
North End (Avon)	*29*	ST 4167
Northend (Avon)	*18*	ST 7867
North End (Berks.)	*19*	SU 4063
Northend (Bucks.)	*20*	SU 7392
North End (Hants.)	*11*	SU 6502
Northend (Warw.)	*33*	SP 3852
North End (W Susx)	*12*	TQ 1209
North Erradale	*106*	NG 7481
North Fearns	*100*	NG 5835
North Ferriby	*61*	SE 9826
Northfield (Borders)	*87*	NT 9167
Northfield (Grampn.)	*105*	NJ 9008
Northfield (W Mids.)	*42*	SP 0179
Northfleet	*22*	TQ 6274
North Frodingham	*67*	TA 1053
North Green	*47*	TM 2288
North Grimston	*67*	SE 8467
North Hayling	*12*	SU 7203
North Heasley	*7*	SS 7333
North Heath	*12*	TQ 0621
North Hill (Corn.)	*4*	SX 2776
North Hinksey	*33*	SP 4806
North Holmwood	*21*	TQ 1646
North Huish	*5*	SX 7156
North Hykeham	*54*	SK 9465
Northiam	*14*	TQ 8324
Northill (Beds.)	*35*	TL 1446
Northington	*11*	SU 5637
North Kelsey	*61*	TA 0401
North Kessock	*103*	NH 6548
North Kilvington	*66*	SE 4285
North Kilworth	*43*	SP 6183
North Kingennie	*93*	NO 4736
North Kyme	*55*	TF 1452
North Lancing	*12*	TQ 1805
Northlands	*55*	TF 3453
Northleach	*32*	SP 1114
North Lee (Bucks.)	*34*	SP 8309
Northleigh (Devon.)	*8*	SY 1995
North Leigh (Oxon.)	*33*	SP 3813
North Leverton with Habblesthorpe	*54*	SK 7882
Northlew	*6*	SX 5099
North Littleton	*32*	SP 0847
North Lopham	*47*	TM 0383
North Luffenham	*44*	SK 9303
North Marden	*12*	SU 8015
North Marston	*34*	SP 7722
North Middleton	*85*	NT 3559
North Molton	*7*	SS 7329
Northmoor	*33*	SP 4202
Northmoor Green or Moorland	*17*	ST 3332
North Moreton	*19*	SU 5689
Northmuir	*98*	NO 3855
North Muskham	*54*	SK 7958
North Newington	*33*	SP 4139
North Newnton	*18*	SU 1257
North Newton	*17*	ST 2931
North Nibley	*18*	ST 7396
North Oakley	*19*	SU 5354
North Ockendon	*21*	TQ 5984
Northolt	*21*	TQ 1285
Northop	*50*	SJ 2468
Northop Hall	*50*	SJ 2767
North Ormsby	*55*	TF 2893
Northorpe (Lincs.)	*54*	SK 8996
Northorpe (Lincs.)	*45*	TF 0917
North Otterington	*66*	SE 3589
Northover	*9*	ST 5223
North Owersby	*54*	TF 0594
Northowram	*59*	SE 1127
North Perrott	*9*	ST 4709
North Petherton	*17*	ST 2832
North Petherwin	*4*	SX 2889
North Pickenham	*46*	TF 8606
North Piddle	*32*	SO 9654
North Poorton	*9*	SY 5197
North Queensferry	*85*	NT 1380
Northrepps	*47*	TG 2439
North Rigton	*59*	SE 2749
North Rode	*51*	SJ 8866
North Runcton	*46*	TF 6416
North Scale	*64*	SD 1769
North Scarle	*54*	SK 8466
North Seaton	*79*	NZ 2986
North Shian	*95*	NM 9143
North Shields	*72*	NZ 3468
North Shoebury	*23*	TQ 9286
North Side	*45*	TL 2799
North Somercotes	*55*	TF 4296
North Stainley	*66*	SE 2876
North Stainmore	*63*	NY 8215
North Stifford	*22*	TQ 6080
North Stoke (Avon)	*29*	ST 7068
North Stoke (Oxon.)	*19*	SU 6186
North Stoke (W Susx)	*12*	TQ 0211
North Street (Berks.)	*19*	SU 6372
North Street (Hants.)	*11*	SU 6433
North Sunderland	*87*	NU 2131
North Tamerton	*6*	SX 3197
North Tawton	*7*	SS 6601
North Thoresby	*55*	TF 2998
North Tidworth	*18*	SU 2248
North Tolsta	*109*	NB 5347
Northton	*109*	NF 9889
North Tuddenham	*47*	TG 0413
North Walsham	*47*	TG 2730
North Waltham	*19*	SU 5546
North Warnborough	*20*	SU 7351
North Watten	*112*	ND 2458
Northway	*32*	SO 9234
North Weald Basset	*22*	TL 4904
Northwich	*51*	SJ 6573
Northwick (Avon)	*29*	ST 5586
North Wick (Avon)	*29*	ST 5865
North Widcombe	*17*	ST 5758
North Willingham	*55*	TF 1688
North Wingfield	*53*	SK 4064
North Witham	*44*	SK 9221
Northwold	*46*	TL 7596
Northwood (Gtr London)	*20*	TQ 1090
Northwood (I. of W.)	*11*	SZ 4992
Northwood (Salop)	*50*	SJ 4633
Northwood Green	*32*	SO 7216
North Wootton (Dorset)	*9*	ST 6614
North Wootton (Norf.)	*46*	TF 6424
North Wootton (Somer.)	*17*	ST 5641
North Wraxall	*18*	ST 8174
North Wroughton	*18*	SU 1581
Norton (Ches.)	*51*	SJ 5581
Norton (Cleve.)	*73*	NZ 4421
Norton (Glos.)	*32*	SO 8624
Norton (Here. and Worc.)	*32*	SO 8750
Norton (Here. and Worc.)	*32*	SP 0447
Norton (Herts.)	*35*	TL 2234
Norton (I. of W.)	*11*	SZ 3489
Norton (Northants.)	*34*	SP 6063
Norton (Notts.)	*53*	SK 5772
Norton (N Yorks.)	*67*	SE 7971
Norton (N Yorks.)	*53*	SK 3581
Norton (Powys)	*40*	SO 3067
Norton (Salop)	*40*	SJ 5609
Norton (Salop)	*41*	SJ 7200
Norton (Salop)	*40*	SO 4581
Norton (Suff.)	*36*	TL 9565
Norton (S Yorks.)	*60*	SE 5415
Norton (Wilts.)	*18*	ST 8884
Norton (W Susx)	*12*	SU 9306
Norton Bavant	*18*	ST 9043
Norton Canes	*42*	SK 0108
Norton Canon	*30*	SO 3847
Norton Disney	*54*	SK 8859
Norton Ferris	*17*	ST 7936
Norton Fitzwarren	*16*	ST 1925
Norton Green	*11*	SZ 3388
Norton Hawkfield	*17*	ST 5964
Norton Heath	*22*	TL 6004
Norton in Hales	*51*	SJ 7038
Norton-Juxta-Twycross	*43*	SK 3207
Norton-le-Clay	*66*	SE 4071
Norton Lindsey	*33*	SP 2263
Norton Malreward	*17*	ST 6064
Norton St. Philip	*18*	ST 7755
Norton Subcourse	*47*	TM 4098
Norton sub Hamdon	*9*	ST 4615
Norwell	*54*	SK 7661
Norwell Woodhouse	*54*	SK 7462
Norwich	*47*	TG 2308
Norwick (Unst)	*113*	HP 6414
Norwood Green	*20*	TQ 1378
Norwood Hill	*13*	TQ 2443
Noseley	*44*	SP 7398
Noss Mayo	*5*	SX 5447
Nosterfield	*66*	SE 2780
Nostie	*101*	NG 8527
Notgrove	*32*	SP 1020
Nottage	*28*	SS 8278
Nottingham	*53*	SK 5741
Notton (Wilts.)	*18*	ST 9169
Notton (W Yorks.)	*59*	SE 3413
Nounsley	*22*	TL 7910
Noutard's Green	*41*	SO 7966
Nox	*40*	SJ 4010
Nuffield	*19*	SU 6687
Nunburnholme	*60*	SE 8548
Nuneaton	*43*	SP 3592
Nuneham Courtenay	*19*	SU 5599
Nun Monkton	*66*	SE 5057
Nunney	*18*	ST 7345
Nunnington	*66*	SE 6679
Nunthorpe	*73*	NZ 5313
Nunton (Wilts.)	*10*	SU 1525
Nunwick	*78*	NY 8774

Peasmarsh Port Ellen

Peasmarsh	14	TQ 8822
Peaston Bank	86	NT 4466
Peathill (Grampn.)	105	NJ 9365
Peat Inn	93	NO 4509
Peatling Magna	43	SP 5992
Peatling Parva	43	SP 5889
Peaton	40	SO 5385
Pebmarsh	36	TL 8533
Pebworth	32	SP 1347
Pecket Well	59	SD 9929
Peckforton	50	SJ 5356
Peckleton	43	SK 4701
Pedmore	41	SO 9182
Pedwell	17	ST 4236
Peebles	85	NT 2540
Peel	56	SC 2484
Pegswood	79	NZ 2287
Peinchorran	100	NG 5233
Peinlich	100	NG 4158
Pelaw	72	NZ 2962
Peldon	23	TL 9816
Pelsall	42	SK 0103
Pelton	72	NZ 2553
Pelutho	70	NY 1249
Pelynt	4	SX 2055
Pembrey	25	SN 4201
Pembridge	30	SO 3858
Pembroke	24	SM 9901
Pembroke Dock	24	SM 9603
Pembury	13	TQ 6240
Penallt	29	SO 5210
Penally	24	SS 1199
Penant	26	SN 5163
Penare	4	SW 9940
Penarth	28	ST 1871
Pen-bont Rhydybeddau	39	SN 6783
Penbryn	26	SN 2952
Pencader	26	SN 4436
Pencaitland	86	NT 4468
Pencarreg	26	SN 5345
Pencelli	28	SO 0925
Penclawdd	25	SS 5495
Pencoed (Mid Glam.)	28	SS 9581
Pencombe	31	SO 5952
Pencoyd	29	SO 5126
Pencraig (Powys)	39	SJ 0427
Pendeen	2	SW 3834
Penderyn	28	SN 9408
Pendine	24	SN 2308
Pendlebury	58	SD 7802
Pendleton	58	SD 7539
Pendock	32	SO 7832
Pendoggett	4	SX 0279
Pendoylan	28	ST 0576
Penegoes	39	SH 7701
Pen-ffordd	24	SN 0722
Pengam	28	ST 1797
Penge	21	TQ 3570
Penhalvean	2	SW 7037
Penhow	29	ST 4290
Penhurst	13	TQ 6916
Peniarth	38	SH 6105
Penicuik	85	NT 2359
Penifiler	100	NG 4841
Peninver	81	NR 7524
Pen-isa'r-cwm	39	SJ 0018
Penisar Waun	48	SH 5564
Penistone	59	SE 2402
Penjerrick	2	SW 7730
Penketh	51	SJ 5687
Penkill	75	NX 2398
Penkridge	41	SJ 9214
Penley	50	SJ 4039
Pen-llyn (Gwyn.)	48	SH 3482
Penllyn (S Glam.)	28	SS 9776
Penmachno	49	SH 7950
Penmaen	25	SS 5288
Penmaenmawr	49	SH 7176
Penmaenpool	39	SH 6918
Penmark	28	ST 0568
Penmon	48	SH 6381
Penmorfa	48	SH 5440
Penmynydd	48	SH 5174
Penn	20	SU 9193
Pennal	39	SH 6900
Pennan	105	NJ 8465
Pennant	39	SN 8897
Pennant-Melangell	39	SJ 0226
Pennard	25	SS 5688
Pennerley	40	SO 3599
Pennington	64	SD 2577
Penn Street	20	SU 9296
Penny Bridge	62	SD 3082
Pennycross	88	NM 5025
Pennygown	95	NM 6042
Pennymoor	7	SS 8611
Penparc	26	SN 2148
Penparcau	26	SN 5980
Penperlleni	29	SO 3204
Penpillick	4	SX 0756
Penpol	2	SW 8139
Penpoll	4	SX 1454
Penpont (Dumf. and Galwy.)	76	NX 8494
Penpont (Powys)	28	SN 9728
Penrherber	26	SN 2839
Penrhiwceiber	28	ST 0597
Penrhiwllan	26	SN 3742
Penrhiwpal	26	SN 3445
Penrhos (Gwent)	29	SO 4111
Penrhos (Gwyn.)	48	SH 2781
Penrhos (Gwyn.)	48	SH 3433
Penrhos (Powys)	28	SN 8011
Penrhyn Bay	49	SH 8281
Penrhyncoch	39	SN 6484
Penrhyndeudraeth	48	SH 6139
Penrhyn-side	49	SH 8181
Penrice	25	SS 4988
Penrith	63	NY 5130
Penrose	3	SW 8770
Penruddock	62	NY 4227
Penryn	2	SW 7834
Pensarn (Clwyd)	49	SH 9478
Pen-Sarn (Gwyn.)	48	SH 4344
Pen-Sarn (Gwyn.)	38	SH 5728
Pensax	41	SO 7269
Pensby	50	SJ 2683
Penselwood	17	ST 7531
Pensford	17	ST 6163
Penshaw	72	NZ 3253
Penshurst	13	TQ 5243
Pensilva	4	SX 2969
Pentewan	4	SX 0147
Pentir	48	SH 5767
Pentire	2	SW 7961
Pentney	46	TF 7213
Penton Mewsey	19	SU 3247
Pentraeth	48	SH 5278
Pentre (Clwyd)	49	SJ 0862
Pentre (Clwyd)	50	SJ 2840
Pentre (Powys)	39	SO 0686
Pentre (Powys)	30	SO 2466
Pentre (Salop)	40	SJ 3617
Pentrebach (Mid Glam.)	28	SO 0604
Pentre-bach (Powys)	27	SN 9033
Pentrebeirdd	40	SJ 1913
Pentre Berw	48	SH 4772
Pentre-celyn (Clwyd)	50	SJ 1453
Pentre-cwrt	26	SN 3938
Pentre-Dolau-Honddu	27	SN 9943
Pentre-dwr	25	SS 6996
Pentrefelin	48	SH 5239
Pentrefoelas	49	SH 8751
Pentregat	26	SN 3551
Pentre-Gwenlais	25	SN 6116
Pentre Halkyn	50	SJ 2072
Pentre-poeth	28	ST 2686
Pentre'r-felin	27	SN 9130
Pentre-tafarn-y-fedw	49	SH 8162
Pentre ty gwyn	27	SN 8135
Pentrich	53	SK 3852
Pentridge	10	SU 0317
Pen-twyn	29	SO 5209
Pentyrch	28	ST 1082
Penuwch	27	SN 5962
Penwithick	4	SX 0256
Penybanc	25	SN 6124
Pen-y-bont (Clwyd)	40	SJ 2123
Penybont (Powys)	30	SO 1164
Penybontfawr	39	SJ 0824
Pen-y-bryn	39	SH 6919
Penycae (Clwyd)	50	SJ 2745
Pen-y-cae (Powys)	28	SN 8413
Pen-y-cefn	50	SJ 1175
Pen-y-coedcae	28	ST 0587
Penyffordd	50	SJ 3061
Pen-y-garn	26	SN 5731
Penygraig	28	SS 9991
Penygroes (Dyfed)	25	SN 5813
Penygroes (Gwyn.)	48	SH 4753
Penysarn	48	SH 4690
Penywaun	28	SN 9704
Penzance	2	SW 4730
Peopleton	32	SO 9350
Peover Heath	51	SJ 7973
Peper Harow	12	SU 9344
Peplow	41	SJ 6324
Percie	99	NO 5991
Percyhorner	105	NJ 9565
Perivale	21	TQ 1682
Perranarworthal	2	SW 7738
Perranporth	2	SW 7554
Perranuthnoe	2	SW 5329
Perranzabuloe	2	SW 7752
Perry	45	TL 1466
Perry Barr	42	SP 0791
Perry Green	35	TL 4317
Pershore	32	SO 9446
Pert	99	NO 6565
Pertenhall	35	TL 0865
Perth	92	NO 1123
Perthy	50	SJ 3633
Perton	41	SO 8598
Peterborough	45	TL 1999
Peterchurch	30	SO 3438
Peterculter	99	NJ 8400
Peterhead	105	NK 1346
Peterlee	72	NZ 4440
Petersfield	12	SU 7423
Peter's Green	35	TL 1419
Peters Marland	6	SS 4713
Peterstone Wentlooge	29	ST 2680
Peterston-super Ely	28	ST 0876
Peterstow	29	SO 5624
Peter Tavy	5	SX 5177
Petham	15	TR 1251
Petrockstow	6	SS 5109
Pett	14	TQ 8714
Pettaugh	37	TM 1659
Pettinain	84	NS 9542
Pettistree	37	TM 2954
Petton (Devon.)	8	ST 0024
Petton (Salop)	40	SJ 4326
Petty	105	NJ 7636
Pettycur	85	NT 2686
Pettymuk	105	NJ 9024
Petworth	12	SU 9721
Pevensey	13	TQ 6405
Pewsey	18	SU 1761
Philham	6	SS 2522
Philiphaugh	77	NT 4427
Phillack	2	SW 5539
Philleigh	3	SW 8639
Philpstoun	85	NT 0577
Phoenix Green	20	SU 7655
Pica	62	NY 0222
Piccotts End	35	TL 0509
Pickering	67	SE 7983
Picket Piece	19	SU 3947
Picket Post	10	SU 1905
Pickhill	66	SE 3483
Picklescott	40	SO 4399
Pickmere	51	SJ 6876
Pickwell (Devon.)	6	SS 4540
Pickwell (Leic.)	44	SK 7811
Pickworth (Leic.)	44	SK 9913
Pickworth (Lincs.)	54	TF 0433
Picton (N Yorks.)	66	NZ 4107
Piddinghoe	13	TQ 4303
Piddington (Northants.)	34	SP 8054
Piddington (Oxon.)	34	SP 6317
Piddlehinton	9	SY 7197
Piddletrenthide	9	SY 7099
Pidley	45	TL 3377
Piercebridge	72	NZ 2115
Pierowall	113	HY 4348
Pigdon	79	NZ 1588
Pilgrims Hatch	21	TQ 5895
Pilham	54	SK 8693
Pill	29	ST 5275
Pillaton	4	SX 3664
Pillerton Hersey	33	SP 2948
Pillerton Priors	33	SP 2947
Pilleth	40	SO 2568
Pilley	59	SE 3300
Pilling	57	SD 4048
Pilling Lane	57	SD 3749
Pilning	29	ST 5585
Pilsbury	52	SK 1163
Pilsdon	9	SY 4199
Pilsley (Derby.)	53	SK 2471
Pilsley (Derby.)	53	SK 4262
Pilton (Leic.)	44	SK 9102
Pilton (Northants.)	44	TL 0284
Pilton (Somer.)	17	ST 5940
Pimperne	10	ST 9009
Pinchbeck	45	TF 2425
Pinchbeck West	45	TF 2024
Pinfold	57	SD 3811
Pinhoe	8	SX 9694
Pinmore	68	NX 2090
Pinner	20	TQ 1289
Pinvin	32	SO 9548
Pinwherry	68	NX 1987
Pinxton	53	SK 4555
Pipe and Lyde	30	SO 5044
Piperhill	103	NH 8650
Pipewell	44	SP 8385
Pippacott	6	SS 5237
Pirbright	20	SU 9455
Pirnmill	81	NR 8744
Pirton (Here. and Worc.)	32	SO 8847
Pirton (Herts.)	35	TL 1431
Pishill	20	SU 7289
Pistyll	48	SH 3242
Pitagowan	97	NN 8266
Pitblae	105	NJ 9865
Pitcairngreen	92	NO 0627
Pitcaple	105	NJ 7225
Pitcarity	98	NO 3265
Pitchcombe	32	SO 8408
Pitchcott	34	SP 7720
Pitchford	40	SJ 5303
Pitch Green	34	SP 7703
Pitch Place	20	SU 9752
Pitcombe	17	ST 6732
Pitcox	86	NT 6475
Pitcur	92	NO 2536
Pitfichie	105	NJ 6716
Pitforthie	99	NO 8079
Pitfour Castle	92	NO 1921
Pitgrudy	108	NH 7990
Pitkennedy	99	NO 5454
Pitlessie	93	NO 3309
Pitlochry	97	NN 9458
Pitmedden	105	NJ 8927
Pitminster	8	ST 2119
Pitmuies	99	NO 5649
Pitmunie	104	NJ 6615
Pitney	17	ST 4428
Pitroddie	92	NO 2224
Pitscottie	93	NO 4113
Pitsea	22	TQ 7488
Pitsford	44	SP 7568
Pitstone	34	SP 9415
Pittendreich	104	NJ 1961
Pittentrail	108	NC 7202
Pittenweem	93	NO 5402
Pittington	72	NZ 3245
Pitton	11	SU 2131
Pixey Green	37	TM 2475
Plains	84	NS 7966
Plaish	40	SO 5296
Plaistow	12	TQ 0030
Plaitford	11	SU 2719
Plas Gogerddan	38	SN 6283
Plas Gwynant	48	SH 6250
Plas Isaf	49	SJ 0442
Plas Llwyngwern	39	SH 7504
Plas Llysyn	39	SN 9597
Plastow Green	19	SU 5361
Plas-yn-Cefn	49	SJ 0171
Platt	14	TQ 6257
Plawsworth	72	NZ 2647
Plaxtol	14	TQ 6053
Playden	14	TQ 9121
Playford	37	TM 2148
Play Hatch	20	SU 7376
Playing Place	2	SW 8141
Plealey	40	SJ 4206
Plean	84	NS 8386
Pleasington	58	SD 6425
Pleasley	53	SK 5064
Plenmeller	71	NY 7162
Pleshey	22	TL 6614
Plockton	101	NG 8033
Ploughfield	30	SO 3841
Plowden	40	SO 3888
Ploxgreen	40	SJ 3604
Pluckley	14	TQ 9045
Plumbland	62	NY 1438
Plumley	51	SJ 7275
Plumpton (E Susx)	13	TQ 3613
Plumpton (Lancs.)	57	SD 3732
Plumpton Green	13	TQ 3616
Plumpton Head	63	NY 5035
Plumpton Wall	63	NY 4937
Plumstead	47	TG 1335
Plumtree	53	SK 6133
Plungar	54	SK 7633
Plush	9	ST 7102
Plwmp	26	SN 3652
Plymouth	5	SX 4755
Plympton	5	SX 5356
Plymstock	5	SX 5152
Plymtree	8	ST 0502
Pockley	66	SE 6385
Pocklington	60	SE 8048
Pode Hole	45	TF 2122
Podimore	9	ST 5424
Podington	34	SP 9462
Podmore	51	SJ 7835
Pointon	55	TF 1131
Pokesdown	10	SZ 1292
Polapit Tamar	4	SX 3389
Polbain	106	NB 9910
Polbathic	4	SX 3456
Polbeth	85	NT 0364
Polchar	103	NH 8909
Polebrook	45	TL 0687
Polegate	13	TQ 5805
Polesworth	42	SK 2602
Polglass	106	NC 0307
Polgooth	4	SW 9950
Poling	12	TQ 0405
Polkerris	4	SX 0952
Pollington	60	SE 6119
Polloch	95	NM 7968
Pollokshaws	84	NS 5560
Pollokshields	84	NS 5663
Polmassick	4	SW 9745
Polnessan	75	NS 4111
Polperro	4	SX 2051
Polruan	4	SX 1250
Polsham	17	ST 5142
Polstead	36	TL 9938
Poltimore	8	SX 9696
Polton	85	NT 2964
Polwarth	86	NT 7450
Polyphant	4	SX 2682
Polzeath	3	SW 9378
Pondersbridge	45	TL 2691
Ponders End	21	TQ 3695
Ponsanooth	2	SW 7336
Ponsworthy	5	SX 7073
Pontamman	25	SN 6312
Pontantwn	25	SN 4412
Pontardawe	25	SN 7204
Pontardulais	25	SN 5903
Pontarsais	25	SN 4428
Pont Cyfyng	49	SH 7357
Pontefract	60	SE 4522
Ponteland	79	NZ 1672
Ponterwyd	39	SN 7481
Pontesbury	40	SJ 3905
Pontfadog	50	SJ 2338
Pontfaen (Dyfed)	24	SN 0234
Pont-faen (Powys)	30	SN 9934
Ponthenry	25	SN 4709
Ponthirwaun	26	SN 2645
Pontllanfraith	28	ST 1895
Pontlliw	25	SN 6101
Pont-Llogel	39	SJ 0315
Pontlottyn	28	SO 1206
Pontlyfni	48	SH 4352
Pontnewydd	29	ST 2896
Pont Pen-y-benglog	48	SH 6460
Pontrhydfendigaid	27	SN 7366
Pont Rhyd-y-cyff	28	SS 8788
Pont-rhyd-y-fen	28	SS 7994
Pontrhydygroes	27	SN 7472
Pontrilas	29	SO 3927
Pontrobert	40	SJ 1112
Pont-rug	48	SH 5163
Ponts Green	13	TQ 6717
Pontshaen	26	SN 4346
Pontshill	29	SO 6321
Pontsticill	28	SO 0511
Pontyates	25	SN 4708
Pontyberem	25	SN 4911
Pontybodkin	50	SJ 2759
Pontyclun	28	ST 0381
Pontycymer	28	SS 9091
Pont-y-pant	49	SH 7554
Pontypool	29	SO 2701
Pontypridd	28	ST 0690
Pontywaun	28	ST 2293
Pooksgreen	11	SU 3710
Pool (W Yorks.)	59	SE 2445
Poole (Dorset)	10	SZ 0190
Poole Green	51	SJ 6355
Poole Keynes	18	ST 9995
Poolewe	106	NG 8580
Pooley Bridge	63	NY 4724
Poolhill (Glos.)	32	SO 7329
Pool of Muckhart	91	NO 0001
Pool Quay	40	SJ 2512
Pool Street	36	TL 7637
Popeswood	20	SU 8469
Popham	19	SU 5543
Poplar	21	TQ 3781
Porchfield	11	SZ 4491
Porin	102	NH 3155
Porkellis	2	SW 6933
Porlock	7	SS 8846
Port Ann	89	NR 9086
Port Appin	95	NM 9045
Port Askaig	80	NR 4369
Portavadie	81	NR 9369
Port Bannatyne	81	NS 0867
Portbury	29	ST 4975
Port Carlisle	70	NY 2461
Port Charlotte	80	NR 2558
Portchester	11	SU 6105
Port Dinorwic	48	SH 5267
Port Driseach	89	NR 9973
Port Ellen	80	NR 3645

Port Elphinstone Redmile

Port Elphinstone	105	NJ 7719
Portencross	82	NS 1748
Port Erin	56	SC 1969
Portesham	9	SY 6085
Port e Vullen	56	SC 4793
Port-Eynon	25	SS 4685
Portfield Gate	24	SM 9115
Portgate	4	SX 4185
Port Gaverne	4	SX 0080
Port Glasgow	82	NS 3274
Portgordon	104	NJ 3964
Portgower	112	ND 0013
Porth	28	ST 0291
Porthallow	2	SW 7923
Porthcawl	28	SS 8176
Porthcurno	2	SW 3822
Port Henderson	106	NG 7573
Porthgain	24	SM 8132
Porthleven	2	SW 6225
Porthmadog	48	SH 5638
Porth Mellin	2	SW 6618
Porthmeor	2	SW 4337
Porth Navas	2	SW 7428
Portholland	3	SW 9541
Porthoustock	2	SW 8021
Porthpean	4	SX 0350
Porthtowan	2	SW 6847
Porthyrhyd (Dyfed)	25	SN 5115
Porthyrhyd (Dyfed)	27	SN 7137
Portincaple	90	NS 2393
Portington	60	SE 7830
Portinnisherrich	89	NM 9711
Port Isaac	4	SW 9980
Portishead	29	ST 4676
Portknockie	104	NJ 4868
Portlethen	99	NO 9396
Portloe	3	SW 9339
Port Logan	68	NX 0940
Portmahomack	108	NH 9184
Portmeirion	48	SH 5937
Portmore (Hants)	11	SZ 3397
Port Mulgrave	73	NZ 7917
Portnacroish	95	NM 9247
Portnaguiran	109	NB 5537
Portnahaven	80	NR 1652
Portnalong	100	NG 3434
Portnancon	110	NC 4260
Portobello (Lothian)	85	NT 3073
Port of Menteith	90	NN 5801
Port of Ness	109	NB 5363
Porton	10	SU 1836
Portpatrick	68	NX 0054
Port Quin	4	SW 9780
Portreath	2	SW 6545
Portree	100	NG 4843
Port St. Mary	56	SC 2067
Portscatho	3	SW 8735
Portsea	11	SU 6300
Portskerra	111	NC 8765
Portskewett	29	ST 4988
Portslade	13	TQ 2506
Portslade-by-Sea	13	TQ 2604
Portsmouth	11	SU 6501
Portsoy	104	NJ 5865
Port Sunlight	50	SJ 3483
Portswood	11	SU 4314
Port Talbot	25	SS 7690
Portuairk	95	NM 4468
Portway (Warw.)	42	SP 0872
Port Wemyss	80	NR 1751
Port William	68	NX 3343
Portwrinkle	4	SX 3553
Poslingford	36	TL 7648
Postbridge	5	SX 6579
Postcombe	34	SU 7099
Postling	15	TR 1439
Postwick	47	TG 2907
Potarch	99	NO 6097
Potsgrove	34	SP 9529
Potten End	34	TL 0108
Potterhanworth	54	TF 0566
Potter Heigham	47	TG 4119
Potterne	18	ST 9958
Potterne Wick	18	ST 9957
Potters Bar	35	TL 2501
Potter's Cross	41	SO 8484
Potterspury	34	SP 7543
Potter Street	35	TL 4608
Potto	66	NZ 4703
Potton	35	TL 2249
Pott Row	46	TF 7021
Poughill (Corn.)	6	SS 2207
Poughill (Devon.)	7	SS 8508
Poulshot	18	ST 9659
Poulton	32	SP 1001
Poulton-le-Fylde	57	SD 3439
Pound Bank	41	SO 7373
Pound Hill	13	TQ 2937
Poundon	34	SP 6425
Poundsgate	5	SX 7072
Poundstock	6	SX 2099
Powburn (Northum.)	79	NU 0616
Powderham	8	SX 9784
Powerstock	9	SY 5196
Powfoot	70	NY 1465
Powick	32	SO 8351
Powmill	92	NT 0197
Poxwell	9	SY 7484
Poyle	20	TQ 0376
Poynings	13	TQ 2612
Poyntington	9	ST 6419
Poynton	51	SJ 9283
Poynton Green	40	SJ 5618
Poys Street	37	TM 3570
Poystreet Green	36	TL 9858
Praa Sands	2	SW 5828
Pratt's Bottom	21	TQ 4762
Praze-an-Beeble	2	SW 6336
Predannack Wollas	2	SW 6616
Prees	51	SJ 5533
Preesall	57	SD 3646
Prees Green	51	SJ 5631
Preesgweene	50	SJ 3135
Prees Higher Heath	51	SJ 5636
Prendwick	79	NU 0012
Pren-gwyn	26	SN 4244
Prenteg	48	SH 5841
Prenton	50	SJ 3184
Prescot (Mers.)	50	SJ 4692
Prescott (Salop)	40	SJ 4221
Pressen	87	NT 8335
Prestatyn	49	SJ 0682
Prestbury (Ches.)	51	SJ 8976
Presteigne	30	SO 3164
Presthope	41	SO 5897
Prestleigh	17	ST 6340
Preston (Borders)	87	NT 7957
Preston (Devon.)	5	SX 8574
Preston (Dorset)	9	SY 7082
Preston (E Susx)	13	TQ 3107
Preston (Glos.)	31	SO 6734
Preston (Glos.)	32	SP 0400
Preston (Herts.)	35	TL 1724
Preston (Humbs.)	61	TA 1830
Preston (Kent)	15	TR 0060
Preston (Kent)	15	TR 2561
Preston (Lancs.)	57	SD 5329
Preston (Leic.)	44	SK 8602
Preston (Lothian)	86	NT 5977
Preston (Northum.)	79	NU 1825
Preston (Suff.)	36	TL 9450
Preston (Wilts.)	18	SU 0377
Preston Bagot	32	SP 1766
Preston Bissett	34	SP 6530
Preston Brockhurst	40	SJ 5324
Preston Brook	51	SJ 5680
Preston Candover	19	SU 6041
Preston Capes	33	SP 5754
Preston Gubbals	40	SJ 4819
Preston on Stour	33	SP 2049
Preston on Wye	30	SO 3842
Prestonpans	85	NT 3874
Preston-under-Scar	65	SE 0791
Preston upon the Weald Moors	41	SJ 6815
Preston Wynne	31	SO 5646
Prestwich	58	SD 8103
Prestwick (Northum.)	79	NZ 1872
Prestwick (Strath.)	75	NS 3525
Prestwood	20	SP 8700
Price Town	28	SS 9392
Prickwillow	46	TL 5982
Priddy	17	ST 5250
Priest Hutton	64	SD 5273
Priestweston	40	SO 2997
Primethorpe	43	SP 5293
Primrose Green	47	TG 0616
Primrose Hill (Cambs.)	45	TL 3889
Primrosehill (Herts.)	35	TL 0803
Princes Risborough	34	SP 8003
Princethorpe	43	SP 3970
Princetown	5	SX 5873
Prior Muir	93	NO 5213
Priors Hardwick	33	SP 4756
Priors Marston	33	SP 4857
Priory Wood	30	SO 2545
Priston	17	ST 6960
Prittlewell	22	TQ 8787
Privett	11	SU 6726
Probus	3	SW 8947
Prudhoe	72	NZ 0962
Puckeridge	35	TL 3823
Puckington	8	ST 3718
Pucklechurch	29	ST 6976
Puddington (Ches.)	50	SJ 3273
Puddington (Devon)	7	SS 8310
Puddledock	47	TM 0592
Puddletown	9	SY 7594
Pudleston	31	SO 5659
Pudsey	59	SE 2232
Pulborough	12	TQ 0418
Puleston	41	SJ 7322
Pulford	50	SJ 3758
Pulham	9	ST 7008
Pulham Market	47	TM 1986
Pulham St. Mary	47	TM 2185
Pulloxhill	35	TL 0634
Pumpherston	85	NT 0669
Pumsaint	27	SN 6540
Puncheston	24	SN 0029
Puncknowle	9	SY 5388
Punnett's Town	13	TQ 6220
Purbrook	11	SU 6707
Purfleet	21	TQ 5578
Puriton	17	ST 3241
Purleigh	22	TL 8301
Purley (Berks.)	19	SU 6676
Purley (Gtr Lon.)	21	TQ 3161
Purlogue	40	SO 2877
Purls Bridge	45	TL 4787
Purse Caundle	9	ST 6917
Purslow	40	SO 3680
Purston Jaglin	59	SE 4319
Purton (Glos.)	29	SO 6605
Purton (Glos.)	29	SO 6904
Purton (Wilts.)	18	SU 0887
Purton Stoke	18	SU 0890
Pury End	34	SP 7045
Pusey	19	SU 3596
Putley	31	SO 6437
Putney	21	TQ 2274
Puttenham (Herts.)	34	SP 8814
Puttenham (Surrey)	20	SU 9347
Puxton	17	ST 4063
Pwll	25	SN 4801
Pwllcrochan	24	SM 9202
Pwlldefaid	38	SH 1526
Pwllheli	48	SH 3735
Pwllmeyric	29	ST 5192
Pwll-y-glaw	28	SS 7993
Pyecombe	13	TQ 2912
Pye Corner	29	ST 3485
Pyle (I. of W.)	11	SZ 4879
Pyle (Mid Glam.)	28	SS 8282
Pylle	17	ST 6038
Pymore	45	TL 4986
Pyrford	20	TQ 0458
Pyrton	19	SU 6895
Pytchley	44	SP 8574
Pyworthy	6	SS 3102

Q

Quabbs	40	SO 2080
Quadring	55	TF 2233
Quainton	34	SP 7419
Quarff	113	HU 4235
Quarley	18	SU 2743
Quarndon	53	SK 3340
Quarrier's Homes	82	NS 3666
Quarrington	54	TF 0544
Quarrington Hill	72	NZ 3337
Quarrybank (Ches.)	50	SJ 5465
Quarry Bank (W Mids.)	41	SO 9386
Quarrywood	104	NJ 1864
Quarter	84	NS 7251
Quatford	41	SO 7390
Quatt	41	SO 7588
Quebec	72	NZ 1743
Quedgeley	32	SO 8114
Queen Adelaide	46	TL 5681
Queenborough	23	TQ 9471
Queen Camel	9	ST 5924
Queen Charlton	29	ST 6366
Queensbury	59	SE 1030
Queensferry (Clwyd)	50	SJ 3168
Queensferry (Lothian)	85	NT 1278
Queenzieburn	84	NS 6977
Quendale	113	HU 3713
Quendon	35	TL 5130
Queniborough	43	SK 6412
Quenington	32	SP 1404
Quernmore	64	SD 5160
Quethiock	4	SX 3164
Quidenham	46	TM 0287
Quidhampton (Hants.)	19	SU 5150
Quidhampton (Wilts.)	10	SU 1030
Quilquox	105	NJ 9038
Quinton	34	SP 7754
Quoditch	6	SX 4097
Quoig	91	NN 8222
Quorndon	43	SK 5616
Quothquan	85	NS 9939

R

Raby	50	SJ 3179
Rachub	48	SH 6268
Rackenford	7	SS 8418
Rackham	12	TQ 0514
Rackheath	47	TG 2814
Racks	70	NY 0374
Rackwick (Hoy)	113	ND 1999
Radcliffe (Gtr Mches)	58	SD 7806
Radcliffe (Northum.)	79	NU 2602
Radcliffe on Trent	53	SK 6439
Radclive	34	SP 6734
Radernie	93	NO 4609
Radford Semele	33	SP 3464
Radlett	20	TL 1600
Radley	19	SU 5398
Radnage	20	SU 7897
Radstock	18	ST 6854
Radstone	33	SP 5840
Radway	33	SP 3648
Radway Green	51	SJ 7754
Radwell	35	TL 2335
Radwinter	36	TL 6037
Radyr	28	ST 1380
Rafford	103	NJ 0656
Ragdale	43	SK 6619
Raglan	29	SO 4107
Ragnall	54	SK 8073
Rahane	90	NS 2386
Rainford	57	SD 4700
Rainham (Gtr London)	21	TQ 5282
Rainham (Kent)	14	TQ 8165
Rainhill	50	SJ 4990
Rainhill Stoops	50	SJ 5090
Rainow	51	SJ 9575
Rainton	66	SE 3775
Rainworth	53	SK 5958
Raisbeck	66	NY 6407
Rait	92	NO 2226
Raithby (Lincs.)	55	TF 3084
Raithby (Lincs.)	55	TF 3767
Rake	12	SU 8027
Ramasaig	100	NG 1644
Rame (Corn.)	2	SW 7233
Rame (Corn.)	4	SX 4249
Ram Lane	15	TQ 9646
Rampisham	9	ST 5502
Rampside	64	SD 2366
Rampton (Cambs.)	45	TL 4268
Rampton (Notts.)	54	SK 7978
Ramsbottom	58	SD 7916
Ramsbury	18	SU 2771
Ramscraigs	112	ND 1427
Ramsdean	12	SU 7021
Ramsdell	19	SU 5957
Ramsden	33	SP 3515
Ramsden Bellhouse	22	TQ 7194
Ramsden Heath	22	TQ 7195
Ramsey (Cambs.)	45	TL 2885
Ramsey (Essex)	37	TM 2130
Ramsey (I. of M.)	56	SC 4594
Ramsey Forty Foot	45	TL 3187
Ramsey Mereside	45	TL 2889
Ramsey St. Mary's	45	TL 2588
Ramsgate	15	TR 3865
Ramsgate Street	47	TG 0933
Ramsgill	65	SE 1170
Ramshorn	52	SK 0845
Ranby	53	SK 6480
Rand	55	TF 1078
Randwick	32	SO 8206
Ranfurly	82	NS 3865
Rangemore	42	SK 1822
Rangeworthy	18	ST 6886
Rankinston	75	NS 4514
Ranskill	53	SK 6587
Ranton	41	SJ 8524
Ranworth	47	TG 3514
Rascarrel	69	NX 7948
Raskelf	66	SE 4971
Rassau	28	SO 1411
Rastrick	59	SE 1321
Ratagan	101	NG 9220
Ratby	43	SK 5105
Ratcliffe Culey	43	SP 3299
Ratcliffe on the Wreake	43	SK 6314
Rathen	105	NK 0060
Rathillet	93	NO 3620
Rathmell	65	SD 8059
Ratho	85	NT 1370
Rathven	104	NJ 4465
Ratley	33	SP 3847
Ratlinghope	40	SO 4096
Rattar	112	ND 2672
Ratten Row	57	SD 4241
Rattery	5	SX 7361
Rattlesden	36	TL 9758
Rattray	98	NO 1745
Rauceby	54	TF 0146
Raughton Head	70	NY 3745
Raunds	44	SP 9972
Ravenfield	53	SK 4895
Ravenglass	62	SD 0896
Raveningham	47	TM 3996
Ravenscar	67	NZ 9801
Ravensdale	56	SC 3592
Ravensden	35	TL 0754
Ravenshead	53	SK 5654
Ravensmoor	51	SJ 6250
Ravensthorpe (Northants.)	43	SP 6670
Ravensthorpe (W Yorks.)	59	SE 2220
Ravenstone (Bucks.)	34	SP 8450
Ravenstone (Leic.)	43	SK 4013
Ravenstonedale	65	NY 7203
Ravenstruther	84	NS 9245
Ravensworth	65	NZ 1407
Raw	67	NZ 9305
Rawcliffe (Humbs.)	60	SE 6822
Rawcliffe (N Yorks.)	66	SE 5855
Rawcliffe Bridge	60	SE 6921
Rawdon	37	SE 2139
Rawmarsh	53	SK 4396
Rawreth	22	TQ 7793
Rawridge	8	ST 2006
Rawtenstall	58	SD 8122
Raydon	37	TM 0438
Raylees	78	NY 9291
Rayleigh	22	TQ 8090
Rayne	22	TL 7222
Reach	36	TL 5666
Read	58	SD 7634
Reading	20	SU 7272
Reading Street	14	TQ 9230
Reagill	63	NY 6017
Rearquhar	108	NH 7492
Rearsby	43	SK 6514
Rease Heath	51	SJ 6454
Reaster	112	ND 2565
Reawick	113	HU 3244
Reay	111	NC 9664
Reculver	15	TR 2269
Redberth	24	SN 0804
Redbourn	35	TL 1012
Redbourne	54	SK 9699
Redbridge	21	TQ 4389
Redbrook	29	SO 5310
Redbrook Street	15	TQ 9336
Redburn (Highld.)	102	NH 5767
Redburn (Highld.)	103	NH 9447
Redcar	73	NZ 6024
Redcastle (Highld.)	102	NH 5849
Redcastle (Tays.)	99	NO 6850
Redcliff Bay	29	ST 4475
Red Dial	70	NY 2545
Redding	84	NS 9178
Reddingmuirhead	84	NS 9177
Reddish	51	SJ 8993
Redditch	42	SP 0468
Rede	36	TL 8055
Redenhall	47	TM 2684
Redford	99	NO 5644
Redgrave	37	TM 0478
Redheugh	98	NO 4463
Redhill (Avon)	17	ST 4962
Redhill (Grampn.)	105	NJ 6837
Redhill (Grampn.)	99	NJ 7704
Redhill (Surrey)	21	TQ 2850
Redisham	47	TM 4084
Redland (Avon)	29	ST 5875
Redland (Orkney)	113	HY 3724
Redlingfield	37	TM 1871
Redlynch (Somer.)	17	ST 6933
Redlynch (Wilts.)	10	SU 2020
Redmarley D'Abitot	32	SO 7531
Redmarshall	72	NZ 3821
Redmile	54	SK 7935

Scartho Sissinghurst

Scartho	*61*	TA 2606
Scaur or Kippford	*69*	NX 8355
Scawby	*61*	SE 9605
Scawton	*66*	SE 5483
Scayne's Hill	*13*	TQ 3723
Scethrog	*28*	SO 1025
Scholes (W Yorks.)	*59*	SE 1507
Scholes (W Yorks.)	*59*	SE 3736
Scleddau	*24*	SM 9434
Scole	*37*	TM 1579
Scolton	*24*	SM 9922
Sconser	*100*	NG 5232
Scopwick	*54*	TF 0658
Scorborough	*61*	TA 0145
Scorrier	*2*	SW 7244
Scorton (Lancs.)	*57*	SD 5048
Scorton (N Yorks.)	*66*	NZ 2400
Sco Ruston	*47*	TG 2821
Scotby	*71*	NY 4454
Scotforth	*64*	SD 4759
Scothern	*54*	TF 0377
Scotland Gate	*79*	NZ 2584
Scotlandwell	*92*	NO 1801
Scotsburn	*108*	NH 7275
Scotscraig	*93*	NO 4428
Scots' Gap	*79*	NZ 0486
Scotstown	*95*	NM 8263
Scotter	*60*	SE 8800
Scotterthorpe	*60*	SE 8701
Scotton (Lincs.)	*54*	SK 8899
Scotton (N Yorks.)	*65*	SE 1895
Scotton (N Yorks.)	*66*	SE 3259
Scottow	*47*	TG 2623
Scoughall	*86*	NT 6183
Scoulton	*46*	TF 9800
Scourie	*110*	NC 1544
Scousburgh	*113*	HU 3717
Scrabster	*112*	ND 0970
Scrainwood	*79*	NT 9909
Scrane End	*55*	TF 3841
Scraptoft	*43*	SK 6405
Scratby	*47*	TG 5115
Scrayingham	*66*	SE 7360
Scredington	*55*	TF 0940
Scremby	*55*	TF 4467
Scremerston	*87*	NU 0049
Screveton	*54*	SK 7343
Scriven	*66*	SE 3458
Scrooby	*53*	SK 6590
Scropton	*52*	SK 1930
Scrub Hill	*55*	TF 2355
Scruton	*66*	SE 2992
Sculthorpe	*46*	TF 8931
Scunthorpe	*60*	SE 8910
Seaborough	*9*	ST 4205
Seacombe	*50*	SJ 3190
Seacroft	*55*	TF 5660
Seafield	*85*	NT 0066
Seaford	*13*	TV 4899
Seaforth	*50*	SJ 3297
Seagrave	*43*	SK 6117
Seaham	*72*	NZ 4149
Seahouses	*87*	NU 2132
Seal	*21*	TQ 5556
Sealand	*50*	SJ 3268
Seamer (N Yorks.)	*66*	NZ 4910
Seamer (N Yorks.)	*67*	TA 0183
Seamill	*82*	NS 2047
Sea Palling	*47*	TG 4327
Searby	*61*	TA 0605
Seasalter	*15*	TR 0864
Seascale	*62*	NY 0301
Seathwaite (Cumbr.)	*62*	SD 2296
Seaton (Corn.)	*4*	SX 3054
Seaton (Cumbr.)	*62*	NY 0130
Seaton (Devon.)	*8*	SY 2490
Seaton (Durham)	*72*	NZ 4049
Seaton (Humbs.)	*61*	TA 1646
Seaton (Leic.)	*44*	SP 9098
Seaton (Northum.)	*79*	NZ 3276
Seaton Delaval	*79*	NZ 3075
Seaton Ross	*60*	SE 7741
Seaton Sluice	*79*	NZ 3376
Seave Green	*66*	NZ 5600
Seaview	*11*	SZ 6291
Seavington St. Mary	*9*	ST 3914
Seavington St. Michael	*9*	ST 4015
Sebergham	*70*	NY 3541
Seckington	*42*	SK 2607
Sedbergh	*63*	SD 6592
Sedbusk	*65*	SD 8891
Sedgeberrow	*32*	SP 0238
Sedgebrook	*54*	SK 8537
Sedgefield	*72*	NZ 3528
Sedgeford	*46*	TF 7136
Sedgehill	*10*	ST 8627
Sedgley	*41*	SO 9193
Sedgwick	*63*	SD 5186
Sedlescombe	*14*	TQ 7818
Seend	*18*	ST 9460
Seend Cleeve	*18*	ST 9260
Seer Green	*20*	SU 9691
Seething	*47*	TM 3197
Sefton	*57*	SD 3500
Seghill	*79*	NZ 2874
Seighford	*41*	SJ 8725
Seisdon	*41*	SO 8394
Selattyn	*50*	SJ 2633
Selborne	*12*	SU 7433
Selby	*60*	SE 6132
Selham	*12*	SU 9320
Selkirk	*77*	NT 4728
Sellack	*29*	SO 5627
Sellindge	*15*	TR 0938
Selling	*15*	TR 0356
Sells Green	*18*	ST 9462
Selly Oak	*42*	SP 0482
Selmeston	*13*	TQ 5007
Selsdon	*21*	TQ 3562
Selsey	*12*	SZ 8593
Selsfield Common	*13*	TQ 3434
Selston	*53*	SK 4553
Selworthy	*16*	SS 9146
Semer	*36*	TL 9946
Semington	*18*	ST 8960
Semley	*10*	ST 8926
Send	*20*	TQ 0155
Senghenydd	*28*	ST 1191
Sennen	*2*	SW 3525
Sennen Cove	*2*	SW 3425
Sennybridge	*28*	SN 9228
Sessay	*66*	SE 4575
Setchey	*46*	TF 6313
Setley	*11*	SU 3000
Settle	*65*	SD 8263
Settrington	*67*	SE 8370
Sevenhampton (Glos.)	*32*	SP 0321
Sevenhampton (Wilts.)	*18*	SU 2090
Seven Kings	*21*	TQ 4586
Sevenoaks	*21*	TQ 5355
Sevenoaks Weald	*21*	TQ 5351
Seven Sisters	*28*	SN 8108
Severn Beach	*29*	ST 5384
Severn Stoke	*32*	SO 8544
Sevington	*15*	TR 0340
Sewards End	*36*	TL 5738
Sewerby	*67*	TA 2068
Seworgan	*2*	SW 7030
Sewstern	*44*	SK 8821
Sezincote	*33*	SP 1731
Shabbington	*34*	SP 6606
Shackerstone	*43*	SK 3706
Shackleford	*20*	SU 9345
Shadforth	*72*	NZ 3441
Shadingfield	*47*	TM 4383
Shadoxhurst	*15*	TQ 9737
Shaftesbury	*10*	ST 8622
Shafton	*59*	SE 3810
Shalbourne	*19*	SU 3163
Shalcombe	*11*	SZ 3985
Shalden	*20*	SU 6941
Shaldon	*8*	SX 9272
Shalfleet	*11*	SZ 4189
Shalford (Essex)	*22*	TL 7229
Shalford (Surrey)	*20*	TQ 0047
Shalford Green	*22*	TL 7127
Shallowford	*7*	SS 7144
Shalstone	*34*	SP 6436
Shamley Green	*12*	TQ 0344
Shandon	*90*	NS 2586
Shandwick	*108*	NH 8574
Shangton	*44*	SP 7196
Shanklin	*11*	SZ 5881
Shap	*63*	NY 5615
Shapwick (Dorset)	*10*	ST 9301
Shapwick (Somer.)	*17*	ST 4137
Shardlow	*53*	SK 4330
Shareshill	*41*	SJ 9406
Sharlston	*59*	SE 3818
Sharnbrook	*34*	SP 9959
Sharnford	*43*	SP 4891
Sharoe Green	*57*	SD 5332
Sharow	*66*	SE 3271
Sharpenhoe	*35*	TL 0630
Sharperton	*79*	NT 9503
Sharpness	*29*	SO 6702
Sharpthorne	*13*	TQ 3732
Sharrington	*47*	TG 0337
Shatterford	*41*	SO 7980
Shaughlaige-e-Quiggin	*56*	SC 3187
Shaugh Prior	*5*	SX 5463
Shavington	*51*	SJ 6951
Shaw (Gtr Mches.)	*58*	SD 9308
Shaw (Wilts.)	*18*	ST 8865
Shawbost	*109*	NB 2646
Shawbury	*40*	SJ 5521
Shawell	*43*	SP 5480
Shawford	*11*	SU 4624
Shawforth	*58*	SD 8920
Shawhead	*69*	NX 8675
Shaw Mills	*66*	SE 2562
Shawwood	*75*	NS 5325
Shear Cross	*18*	ST 8642
Shearsby	*43*	SP 6291
Shebbear	*6*	SS 4309
Shebdon	*41*	SJ 7525
Shebster	*112*	ND 0164
Shedfield	*11*	SU 5512
Sheen	*52*	SK 1161
Sheepscombe	*32*	SO 8910
Sheepstor	*5*	SX 5567
Sheepwash	*6*	SS 4806
Sheepy Magna	*43*	SK 3201
Sheepy Parva	*43*	SK 3301
Sheering	*22*	TL 5013
Sheerness	*23*	TQ 9274
Sheet	*12*	SU 7524
Sheffield	*53*	SK 3587
Sheffield Bottom	*19*	SU 6469
Shefford	*35*	TL 1439
Sheinton	*41*	SJ 6104
Shelderton	*40*	SO 4077
Sheldon (Derby.)	*52*	SK 1768
Sheldon (Devon.)	*8*	ST 1208
Sheldon (W Mids.)	*42*	SP 1584
Sheldwich	*15*	TR 0156
Shelf	*59*	SE 1228
Shelfanger	*47*	TM 1083
Shelfield	*42*	SK 0302
Shelford	*53*	SK 6642
Shelley	*59*	SE 2011
Shellingford	*19*	SU 3193
Shellow Bowells	*22*	TL 6108
Shelsley Beauchamp	*32*	SO 7362
Shelsley Walsh	*32*	SO 7263
Shelton (Beds.)	*34*	TL 0368
Shelton (Norf.)	*47*	TM 2191
Shelton (Notts.)	*54*	SK 7744
Shelton Green	*47*	TM 2390
Shelve	*40*	SO 3399
Shelwick	*31*	SO 5243
Shenfield	*22*	TQ 6094
Shenington	*33*	SP 3642
Shenley	*35*	TL 1900
Shenley Brook End	*34*	SP 8335
Shenleybury	*35*	TL 1802
Shenley Church End	*34*	SP 8336
Shenmore	*30*	SO 3938
Shenstone (Here. and Worc.)	*41*	SO 8673
Shenstone (Staffs.)	*42*	SK 1004
Shenton	*43*	SK 3800
Shenval	*104*	NJ 2129
Shepherd's Green	*20*	SU 7183
Shepherdswell or Sibertswold	*15*	TR 2548
Shepley	*59*	SE 1909
Shepperdine	*29*	ST 6195
Shepperton	*20*	TQ 0867
Shepreth	*35*	TL 3947
Shepshed	*43*	SK 4719
Shepton Beauchamp	*9*	ST 4016
Shepton Mallet	*17*	ST 6143
Shepton Montague	*17*	ST 6731
Shepway	*14*	TQ 7753
Sheraton	*73*	NZ 4334
Sherborne (Dorset)	*9*	ST 6316
Sherborne (Glos.)	*33*	SP 1714
Sherborne St. John	*19*	SU 6155
Sherbourne	*33*	SP 2661
Sherburn (Durham)	*72*	NZ 3142
Sherburn (N Yorks.)	*67*	SE 9577
Sherburn in Elmet	*60*	SE 4933
Shere	*20*	TQ 0747
Shereford	*46*	TF 8829
Sherfield English	*11*	SU 2922
Sherfield on Loddon	*19*	SU 6757
Sherford	*5*	SX 7744
Sheriffhales	*41*	SJ 7512
Sheriff Hutton	*66*	SE 6566
Sheringham	*47*	TG 1543
Sherington	*34*	SP 8846
Shernborne	*46*	TF 7132
Sherrington	*10*	ST 9638
Sherston	*18*	ST 8585
Sherwood Green	*6*	SS 5520
Shettleston	*84*	NS 6464
Shevington	*57*	SD 5408
Shevington Moor	*57*	SD 5410
Sheviock	*4*	SX 3655
Shiel Bridge	*101*	NG 9318
Shieldaig	*101*	NG 8154
Shieldhill (Central)	*84*	NS 8976
Shielfoot	*95*	NM 6669
Shifnal	*41*	SJ 7407
Shilbottle	*79*	NU 1908
Shildon	*72*	NZ 2226
Shillingford (Devon.)	*8*	SS 9723
Shillingford (Oxon.)	*19*	SU 5992
Shillingford St. George	*8*	SX 9087
Shillingstone	*10*	ST 8211
Shillington	*35*	TL 1234
Shillmoor (Northum.)	*78*	NT 8807
Shilton (Oxon.)	*33*	SP 2608
Shilton (Warw.)	*43*	SP 4084
Shimpling (Norf.)	*47*	TM 1583
Shimpling (Suff.)	*36*	TL 8551
Shimpling Street	*36*	TL 8652
Shiney Row	*72*	NZ 3252
Shinfield	*20*	SU 7368
Shinness	*111*	NC 5314
Shipbourne	*21*	TQ 5952
Shipdham	*46*	TF 9607
Shipham	*17*	ST 4457
Shiphay	*5*	SX 8965
Shiplake	*20*	SU 7678
Shipley (Salop)	*41*	SO 8095
Shipley (W Susx.)	*12*	TQ 1422
Shipley (W Yorks.)	*59*	SE 1337
Shipmeadow	*47*	TM 3789
Shippon	*19*	SU 4898
Shipston on Stour	*33*	SP 2540
Shipton (Glos.)	*32*	SP 0318
Shipton (N Yorks.)	*66*	SE 5558
Shipton (Salop)	*40*	SO 5591
Shipton Bellinger	*18*	SU 2345
Shipton Gorge	*9*	SY 4991
Shipton Green	*12*	SU 8000
Shipton Moyne	*18*	ST 8889
Shipton-on-Cherwell	*33*	SP 4716
Shiptonthorpe	*60*	SE 8543
Shipton-under-Wychwood	*33*	SP 2717
Shirburn	*20*	SU 6995
Shirdley Hill	*57*	SD 3612
Shirebrook	*53*	SK 5267
Shirehampton	*29*	ST 5276
Shiremoor	*79*	NZ 3171
Shirenewton	*29*	ST 4793
Shire Oak	*42*	SK 0504
Shirland	*53*	SK 3958
Shirley (Derby.)	*53*	SK 2141
Shirley (Hants.)	*11*	SU 4114
Shirley (W Mids.)	*42*	SP 1277
Shirl Heath	*30*	SO 4359
Shirrell Heath	*11*	SU 5714
Shirwell	*6*	SS 5937
Shiskine	*81*	NR 9129
Shobdon	*30*	SO 3961
Shobrooke	*7*	SS 8600
Shocklach	*50*	SJ 4348
Shoeburyness (Essex)	*23*	TQ 9384
Sholden	*15*	TR 3552
Sholing	*11*	SU 4511
Shop (Corn.)	*6*	SS 2214
Shop (Corn.)	*3*	SW 8773
Shoreditch	*21*	TQ 3284
Shoreham	*21*	TQ 5261
Shoreham-by-Sea	*13*	TQ 2105
Shoresdean	*87*	NT 9546
Shoreswood	*87*	NT 9446
Shoretown	*102*	NH 6161
Shorncote	*18*	SU 0296
Shorne	*14*	TQ 6970
Shortgate	*13*	TQ 4915
Short Heath (Leic)	*43*	SK 3014
Short Heath (W Mids.)	*42*	SP 0992
Shortlanesend	*2*	SW 8047
Shortless	*82*	NS 4335
Shorwell	*11*	SZ 4582
Shoscombe	*18*	ST 7156
Shotesham	*47*	TM 2599
Shotgate	*22*	TQ 7692
Shotley Bridge	*72*	NZ 0752
Shotley Gate	*37*	TM 2433
Shotley Street	*37*	TM 2335
Shottenden	*15*	TR 0454
Shottermill	*12*	SU 8732
Shottery	*32*	SP 1854
Shotteswell	*33*	SP 4245
Shottisham	*37*	TM 3144
Shottle	*53*	SK 3149
Shotton (Clwyd)	*50*	SJ 3069
Shotton (Durham)	*72*	NZ 4139
Shotton (Northum.)	*87*	NT 8430
Shotton Colliery	*72*	NZ 3941
Shotts	*84*	NS 8760
Shotwick	*50*	SJ 3371
Shouldham	*46*	TF 6708
Shouldham Thorpe	*46*	TF 6607
Shoulton	*32*	SO 8058
Shrawley	*32*	SO 8064
Shrewley	*42*	SP 2167
Shrewsbury	*40*	SJ 4912
Shrewton	*18*	SU 0643
Shripney	*12*	SU 9302
Shrivenham	*18*	SU 2489
Shropham	*46*	TL 9893
Shroton or Irwerne Courtney	*10*	ST 8512
Shrub End	*23*	TL 9723
Shucknall	*31*	SO 5842
Shudy Camps	*36*	TL 6244
Shurdington	*32*	SO 9118
Shurlock Row	*20*	SU 8374
Shurrery	*112*	ND 0458
Shurton	*16*	ST 2044
Shustoke	*42*	SP 2290
Shute	*8*	SY 2597
Shut End	*41*	SO 9089
Shutford	*33*	SP 3840
Shuthonger	*32*	SO 8935
Shutlanger	*34*	SP 7249
Shuttington	*42*	SK 2505
Shuttlewood	*53*	SK 4672
Sibbertoft	*43*	SP 6782
Sibdon Carwood	*40*	SO 4083
Sibertswold or Shepherdswell	*15*	TR 2548
Sibford Ferris	*33*	SP 3537
Sibford Gower	*33*	SP 3537
Sible Hedingham	*36*	TL 7734
Sibsey	*55*	TF 3551
Sibson (Cambs.)	*45*	TL 0997
Sibson (Leic.)	*43*	SK 3500
Sibthorpe	*54*	SK 7645
Sicklesmere	*36*	TL 8760
Sicklinghall	*59*	SE 3548
Sidbury (Devon.)	*8*	SY 1491
Sidbury (Salop)	*41*	SO 6885
Sidcup	*21*	TQ 4672
Siddington (Ches.)	*51*	SJ 8470
Siddington (Glos.)	*18*	SU 0399
Sidestrand	*47*	TG 2539
Sidford	*8*	SY 1390
Sidlesham	*12*	SZ 8599
Sidley	*14*	TQ 7409
Sidmouth	*8*	SY 1287
Siefton	*40*	SO 4883
Sigford	*5*	SX 7773
Sigglesthorne	*61*	TA 1545
Silchester	*19*	SU 6462
Sileby	*43*	SK 6015
Silecroft	*62*	SD 1281
Silian	*27*	SN 5751
Silkstone	*59*	SE 2904
Silk Willoughby	*54*	TF 0542
Silloth	*70*	NY 1153
Sillyearn	*104*	NJ 5254
Silpho	*67*	SE 9692
Silsden	*59*	SE 0446
Silsoe	*35*	TL 0835
Silverburn	*85*	NT 2060
Silverdale (Lancs.)	*64*	SD 4674
Silverdale (Staffs.)	*51*	SJ 8146
Silver End (Beds.)	*35*	TL 0942
Silver End (Essex)	*22*	TL 8019
Silverford	*105*	NJ 7764
Silverley's Green	*37*	TM 2976
Silverstone	*34*	SP 6644
Silverton	*8*	SS 9502
Simonburn	*78*	NY 8773
Simonsbath	*7*	SS 7739
Simonstone	*58*	SD 7734
Simprim	*87*	NT 8545
Simpson	*34*	SP 8836
Sinclairston	*75*	NS 4716
Sinderby	*66*	SE 3481
Sinderhope	*71*	NY 8452
Sindlesham	*20*	SU 7769
Singleton (Lancs.)	*57*	SD 3838
Singleton (W Susx)	*12*	SU 8713
Singlewell or Ifield	*22*	TQ 6471
Sinnahard	*104*	NJ 4713
Sinnington	*67*	SE 7485
Sinton Green	*32*	SO 8160
Sipson	*20*	TQ 0877
Sirhowy	*28*	SO 1410
Sissinghurst	*14*	TQ 7937

Siston	29	ST 6875
Sithney	2	SW 6329
Sittenham	108	NH 6574
Sittingbourne	14	TQ 9163
Six Ashes	41	SO 6988
Sixhills	55	TF 1787
Six Mile Bottom	36	TL 5756
Sixpenny Handley	10	ST 9917
Sizewell	37	TM 4762
Skaill (Orkney)	113	HY 5806
Skares	75	NS 5217
Skateraw	86	NT 7375
Skeabost	100	NG 4148
Skeeby	65	NZ 1902
Skeffington	44	SK 7402
Skeffling	61	TA 3619
Skegby	53	SK 4961
Skegness	55	TF 5663
Skeldyke	55	TF 3337
Skellingthorpe	54	SK 9272
Skelmanthorpe	59	SE 2210
Skelmersdale	57	SD 4605
Skelmonae	105	NJ 8839
Skelmorlie	82	NS 1967
Skelmuir	105	NJ 9842
Skelpick	111	NC 7355
Skelton (Cleve.)	73	NZ 6518
Skelton (Cumbr.)	63	NY 4335
Skelton (N Yorks.)	65	NZ 0900
Skelton (N Yorks.)	66	SE 3568
Skelton (N Yorks.)	66	SE 5656
Skelwith Bridge	62	NY 3503
Skendleby	55	TF 4369
Skenfrith	29	SO 4520
Skerne	67	TA 0455
Skerray	111	NC 6563
Skewen	25	SS 7297
Skewsby	66	SE 6270
Skeyton	47	TG 2425
Skidbrooke	55	TF 4393
Skidby	61	TA 0133
Skigersta	109	NB 5461
Skilgate	16	SS 9827
Skillington	44	SK 8925
Skinburness	70	NY 1255
Skinidin	100	NG 2247
Skinningrove	73	NZ 7119
Skipness	81	NR 8957
Skipsea	67	TA 1655
Skipton	65	SD 9851
Skipton-on-Swale	66	SE 3679
Skipwith	60	SE 6538
Skirling	85	NT 0739
Skirmett	20	SU 7789
Skirpenbeck	67	SE 7457
Skirwith (Cumbr.)	63	NY 6132
Skirwith (N Yorks.)	65	SD 7073
Skirza	112	ND 3868
Skulamus	101	NG 6722
Skullomie	111	NC 6161
Skye of Curr	103	NH 9924
Slackhall	52	SK 0781
Slackhead	104	NJ 4063
Slad	32	SO 8707
Slade	6	SS 5046
Slade Green	21	TQ 5276
Slaggyford	71	NY 6752
Slaidburn	65	SD 7152
Slaithwaite	59	SE 0714
Slaley	72	NY 9757
Slamannan	84	NS 8573
Slapton (Bucks.)	34	SP 9320
Slapton (Devon.)	5	SX 8244
Slapton (Northants.)	34	SP 6346
Slaugham	13	TQ 2528
Slawston	44	SP 7794
Sleaford (Hants.)	12	SU 8037
Sleaford (Lincs.)	54	TF 0645
Sleagill	63	NY 5919
Sleapford	41	SJ 6315
Sledge Green	32	SO 8134
Sledmere	67	SE 9364
Sleights	67	NZ 8607
Slickly	112	ND 2966
Sliddery	81	NR 9322
Sliemore	103	NJ 0320
Sligachan	100	NG 4829
Slimbridge	32	SO 7303
Slindon (Staffs.)	51	SJ 8232
Slindon (W Susx)	12	SU 9608
Slinfold	12	TQ 1131
Slingsby	66	SE 6974
Slioch (Grampn.)	104	NJ 5638
Slip End	35	TL 0818
Slipton	44	SP 9479
Slockavullin	89	NR 8297
Sloley	47	TG 2924
Sloothby	55	TF 4970
Slough	20	SU 9779
Slyne	64	SD 4765
Smailholm	86	NT 6436
Smallbridge	58	SD 9114
Smallburgh	47	TG 3324
Smallburn (Grampn.)	105	NK 0141
Smallburn (Strath.)	76	NS 6827
Small Dole	13	TQ 2112
Smalley	53	SK 4044
Smallfield	13	TQ 3243
Small Hythe	14	TQ 8930
Smallridge	8	ST 3001
Smarden	14	TQ 8842
Smeatharpe	8	ST 1910
Smeeth	15	TR 0739
Smeeton Westerby	43	SP 6792
Smerral	112	ND 1733
Smethwick	42	SP 0288
Smisby	43	SK 3419
Smithfield	71	NY 4465
Smithincott	8	ST 0611
Smithton	103	NH 7145
Snailbeach	40	SJ 3702
Snailwell	36	TL 6467
Snainton	67	SE 9182
Snaith	60	SE 6422
Snape (N Yorks.)	66	SE 2684
Snape (Suff.)	37	TM 3959
Snape Street	37	TM 3958
Snarestone	43	SK 3409
Snarford	54	TF 0482
Snargate	15	TQ 9928
Snave	15	TR 0130
Snead	40	SO 3191
Sneaton	67	NZ 8907
Sneaton Thorpe	67	NZ 9006
Snelland	54	TF 0780
Snelston	52	SK 1543
Snettisham	46	TF 6834
Snitter	79	NU 0203
Snitterby	54	SK 9894
Snitterfield	33	SP 2159
Snitton	40	SO 5575
Snodhill	30	SO 3140
Snodland	14	TQ 7061
Snowshill	32	SP 0933
Soberton	11	SU 6016
Soberton Heath	11	SU 6014
Soham	36	TL 5973
Soldon Cross	6	SS 3210
Soldridge	11	SU 6534
Sole Street	15	TR 0949
Solihull	42	SP 1479
Sollas	109	NF 8074
Sollers Dilwyn	30	SO 4255
Sollers Hope	31	SO 6033
Sollom	57	SD 4518
Solva	24	SM 8024
Somerby	44	SK 7710
Somercotes	53	SK 4253
Somerford Keynes	18	SU 0195
Somerley	12	SZ 8198
Somerleyton	47	TM 4897
Somersal Herbert	52	SK 1335
Somersby	55	TF 3472
Somersham (Cambs.)	45	TL 3677
Somersham (Suff.)	37	TM 0848
Somerton (Norf.)	47	TG 4719
Somerton (Oxon.)	33	SP 4928
Somerton (Somer.)	17	ST 4828
Sompting	12	TQ 1605
Sonning	20	SU 7575
Sonning Common	19	SU 7080
Sopley	10	SZ 1596
Sopworth	18	ST 8286
Sorbie	69	NX 4346
Sordale	112	ND 1462
Sorisdale	94	NM 2763
Sorn	75	NS 5526
Sornhill	82	NS 5134
Sortat	112	ND 2863
Sotby	55	TF 2078
Sots Hole	55	TF 1164
Sotterly	47	TM 4584
Soughton	50	SJ 2466
Soulbury	34	SP 8827
Soulby	63	NY 7410
Souldern	33	SP 5231
Souldrop	34	SP 9861
Soundwell	29	ST 6574
Sourhope	78	NT 8420
Sourton	5	SX 5390
Soutergate	62	SD 2281
South Acre	46	TF 8014
Southall	20	TQ 1280
South Alloa	91	NS 8791
Southam (Glos.)	32	SO 9725
Southam (Warw.)	33	SP 4161
South Ambersham	12	SU 9120
Southampton	11	SU 4212
South Ballachulish	96	NN 0559
South Bank	73	NZ 5220
South Barrow	17	ST 6027
South Benfleet	22	TQ 7785
Southborough	13	TQ 5842
Southbourne (Dorset)	10	SZ 1491
Southbourne (W Susx)	12	SU 7705
South Brent	5	SX 6960
Southburgh	46	TG 0004
South Burlingham	47	TG 3708
South Cadbury	9	ST 6325
South Cairn	68	NW 9768
South Carlton	54	SK 9476
South Cave	60	SE 9231
South Cerney	18	SU 0497
South Chard	8	ST 3205
South Charlton	79	NU 1620
Southchurch	23	TQ 9186
South Cliffe	60	SE 8736
South Clifton	54	SK 8270
Southcott	5	SX 5495
South Cove	47	TM 5081
South Creake	46	TF 8536
South Croxton	43	SK 6810
South Dalton	61	SE 9645
South Darenth	21	TQ 5669
South Duffield	60	SE 6733
Southease	13	TQ 4205
South Elkington	55	TF 2988
South Elmsall	60	SE 4711
South End (Berks.)	19	SU 5970
South End (Cumbr.)	64	SD 2063
Southend (Strath.)	81	NR 6908
Southend-on-Sea	22	TQ 8885
Southerndown	28	SS 8874
Southerness	70	NX 9754
Southery	46	TL 6294
South Fambridge	22	TQ 8694
South Fawley	19	SU 3979
South Ferriby	61	SE 9820
Southfleet	14	TQ 6171
Southgate (Gtr London)	21	TQ 3093
Southgate (Norf.)	46	TF 6833
Southgate (Norf.)	47	TG 1324
South Green	22	TQ 6893
South-haa	113	HU 3688
South Hanningfield	22	TQ 7497
South Harting	12	SU 7819
South Hayling	12	SZ 7299
South Heath	34	SP 9102
South Heighton	13	TQ 4503
South Hetton	72	NZ 3745
South Hiendley	59	SE 3812
South Hill	4	SX 3272
South Hole	6	SS 2219
South Holmwood	12	TQ 1745
South Hornchurch	21	TQ 5283
South Hylton	72	NZ 3556
Southill	35	TL 1442
South Kelsey	54	TF 0398
South Kilvington	66	SE 4283
South Kilworth	43	SP 6082
South Kirkby	60	SE 4410
South Kirkton	105	NJ 7405
South Kyme	55	TF 1749
South Lancing	12	TQ 1804
Southleigh (Devon)	8	SY 2093
South Leigh (Oxon.)	33	SP 3908
South Leverton	54	SK 7881
South Littleton	32	SP 0746
South Lopham	47	TM 0481
South Luffenham	44	SK 9402
South Malling	13	TQ 4211
South Marston	18	SU 1987
South Milford	60	SE 4931
South Milton	5	SX 7042
South Mimms	35	TL 2200
Southminster	23	TQ 9599
South Molton	7	SS 7125
South Moor	72	NZ 1952
South Moreton	19	SU 5688
South Muskham	54	SK 7957
South Newington	33	SP 4033
South Newton	10	SU 0834
South Normanton	53	SK 4456
South Norwood	21	TQ 3468
South Nutfield	21	TQ 3048
South Ockendon	21	TQ 5982
Southoe	35	TL 1864
Southolt	37	TM 1968
South Ormsby	55	TF 3675
Southorpe	45	TF 0803
South Otterington	66	SE 3787
Southowram	59	SE 1123
South Oxhey	20	TQ 1193
South Perrott	9	ST 4706
South Petherton	9	ST 4316
South Petherwin	4	SX 3182
South Pickenham	46	TF 8504
South Pool	5	SX 7740
Southport	57	SD 3316
South Radworthy	7	SS 7432
South Raynham	46	TF 8723
Southrepps	47	TG 2536
South Reston	55	TF 4082
Southrey	55	TF 1366
Southrop	33	SP 1903
Southrope	19	SU 6744
South Runcton	46	TF 6308
South Scarle	54	SK 8463
Southsea	11	SZ 6498
South Shields	72	NZ 3667
South Skirlaugh	61	TA 1439
South Somercotes	55	TF 4193
South Stainley	66	SE 3063
South Stoke (Avon)	18	ST 7461
South Stoke (Oxon.)	19	SU 6083
South Stoke (W Susx)	12	TQ 0210
South Street	13	TQ 3918
South Tawton	5	SX 6594
South Thoresby	55	TF 4077
South Tidworth	18	SU 2347
South Town (Hants.)	11	SU 6536
Southwaite	71	NY 4445
South Walsham	47	TG 3613
South Warnborough	20	SU 7247
Southwater	12	TQ 1526
Southway	17	ST 5142
South Weald	21	TQ 5793
Southwell (Dorset)	9	SY 6870
Southwell (Notts.)	53	SK 7053
South Weston	19	SU 7098
South Wheatley	4	SX 2492
Southwick (Hants.)	11	SU 6208
Southwick (Northants.)	44	TL 0192
Southwick (Tyne and Wear)	72	NZ 3758
Southwick (Wilts.)	18	ST 8354
Southwick (W Susx)	13	TQ 2405
South Widcombe	17	ST 5756
South Wigston	43	SP 5898
South Willingham	55	TF 1983
South Wingfield	53	SK 3755
South Witham	44	SK 9219
Southwold	37	TM 5076
South Wonston	11	SU 4635
Southwood (Norf.)	47	TG 3905
Southwood (Somer.)	17	ST 5533
South Woodham Ferrers	22	TQ 8097
South Wootton	46	TF 6422
South Wraxall	18	ST 8364
South Zeal	5	SX 6593
Soutra Mains	86	NT 4559
Sowerby (N Yorks.)	66	SE 4381
Sowerby (W Yorks.)	59	SE 0423
Sowerby Bridge	59	SE 0523
Sowerby Row	70	NY 3940
Sowton	8	SX 9792
Spa Common	47	TG 2930
Spalding	45	TF 2422
Spaldington	60	SE 7533
Spaldwick	45	TL 1272
Spalford	54	SK 8369
Sparham	47	TG 0619
Spark Bridge	62	SD 3084
Sparkford	17	ST 6026
Sparkwell	5	SX 5757
Sparrowpit	52	SK 0980
Sparsholt (Hants.)	11	SU 4331
Sparsholt (Oxon.)	19	SU 3487
Spaunton	66	SE 7289
Spaxton	16	ST 2236
Spean Bridge	96	NN 2281
Speen (Berks.)	19	SU 4568
Speen (Bucks.)	20	SU 8499
Speeton	67	TA 1574
Speke	50	SJ 4383
Speldhurst	13	TQ 5541
Spellbrook	35	TL 4817
Spelsbury	33	SP 3421
Spencers Wood	20	SU 7166
Spennithorne	65	SE 1489
Spennymoor	72	NZ 2533
Spetchley	32	SO 8953
Spettisbury	10	ST 9002
Spexhall	37	TM 3780
Spey Bay	104	NJ 3866
Spilsby	55	TF 4066
Spindlestone	87	NU 1533
Spinningdale	108	NH 6789
Spirthill	18	ST 9975
Spital	112	ND 1654
Spithurst	13	TQ 4217
Spittal (Dyfed)	24	SM 9723
Spittal (Lothian)	86	NT 4677
Spittal (Northum.)	87	NU 0051
Spittalfield	98	NO 1040
Spittal of Glenmuick	98	NO 3184
Spittal of Glenshee	98	NO 1070
Spixworth	47	TG 2415
Spofforth	66	SE 3650
Spondon	53	SK 3935
Spooner Row	47	TM 0997
Sporle	46	TF 8411
Spott	86	NT 6775
Spratton	44	SP 7170
Spreakley	12	SU 8341
Spreyton	7	SX 6996
Spridlington	54	TF 0084
Springburn	84	NS 5968
Springfield (Fife.)	93	NO 3411
Springfield (Grampn.)	103	NJ 0559
Springfield (W Mids.)	42	SP 1082
Springholm	69	NX 8070
Springside	82	NS 3639
Springthorpe	54	SK 8789
Sproatley	61	TA 1934
Sproston Green	51	SJ 7367
Sprotbrough	60	SE 5302
Sproughton	37	TM 1244
Sprouston	86	NT 7535
Sprowston	47	TG 2412
Sproxton (Leic.)	44	SK 8524
Sproxton (N Yorks.)	66	SE 6181
Spurstow	51	SJ 5556
Stackhouse	65	SD 8165
Stacksteads	58	SD 8421
Staddiscombe	5	SX 5151
Staddlethorpe	60	SE 8428
Stadhampton	19	SU 6098
Staffield	71	NY 5442
Staffin	100	NG 4967
Stafford	41	SJ 9223
Stagsden	34	SP 9849
Stainburn	59	SE 2448
Stainby	44	SK 9022
Staincross	59	SE 3210
Staindrop	72	NZ 1220
Staines	20	TQ 0471
Stainfield (Lincs.)	45	TF 0724
Stainfield (Lincs.)	55	TF 1173
Stainforth (N Yorks.)	65	SD 8267
Stainforth (S Yorks.)	60	SE 6411
Staining	57	SD 3435
Stainland	59	SE 0719
Stainsacre	67	NZ 9108
Stainton (Cleve.)	73	NZ 4714
Stainton (Cumbr.)	63	NY 4827
Stainton (Cumbr.)	63	SD 5285
Stainton (Durham)	72	NZ 0718
Stainton (N Yorks.)	65	SE 1096
Stainton (S Yorks.)	53	SK 5593
Stainton by Langworth	54	TF 0577
Staintondale	67	SE 9898
Stainton le Vale	55	TF 1794
Stainton with Adgarley	64	SD 2472
Stair (Cumbr.)	62	NY 2321
Stair (Strath.)	75	NS 4323
Staithes	73	NZ 7818
Stake Pool	57	SD 4148
Stalbridge	9	ST 7317
Stalbridge Weston	9	ST 7216
Stalham	47	TG 3725
Stalham Green	47	TG 3824
Stalisfield Green	15	TQ 9652
Stallingborough	61	TA 2011
Stalling Busk	65	SD 9185
Stalmine	57	SD 3745
Stalybridge	51	SJ 9698
Stambourne	36	TL 7238
Stamford	44	TF 0207

Stamford Bridge Stromness

Stamford Bridge	66	SE 7155
Stamfordham	79	NZ 0772
Stanborough	35	TL 2210
Stanbridge (Beds.)	34	SP 9623
Stanbridge (Dorset)	10	SU 0003
Stand	84	NS 7668
Standburn	84	NS 9274
Standeford	41	SJ 9107
Standen	14	TQ 8539
Standford	12	SU 8134
Standish	57	SD 5609
Standlake	33	SP 3902
Standon (Hants.)	11	SU 4227
Standon (Herts.)	35	TL 3922
Standon (Staffs.)	51	SJ 8134
Stane	84	NS 8859
Stanfield	46	TF 9320
Stanford (Beds.)	35	TL 1641
Stanford (Kent)	15	TR 1238
Stanford Bishop	31	SO 6851
Stanford Bridge	32	SO 7165
Stanford Dingley	19	SU 5771
Stanford in the Vale	19	SU 3493
Stanford le Hope	22	TQ 6882
Stanford on Avon	43	SP 5878
Stanford on Soar	43	SK 5422
Stanford on Teme	31	SO 7065
Stanford Rivers	22	TL 5301
Stanghow	73	NZ 6715
Stanhoe	46	TF 8036
Stanhope	72	NY 9939
Stanion	44	SP 9187
Stanley (Derby.)	53	SK 4140
Stanley (Durham)	72	NZ 1953
Stanley (Staffs.)	51	SJ 9252
Stanley (Tays.)	92	NO 1033
Stanley (W Yorks.)	59	SE 3422
Stanmer	13	TQ 3309
Stanmore (Berks.)	19	SU 4778
Stanmore (Gtr London)	21	TQ 1692
Stannington (Northum.)	79	NZ 2179
Stannington (S Yorks.)	53	SK 2988
Stansbatch	30	SO 3461
Stansfield	36	TL 7852
Stanstead	36	TL 8449
Stanstead Abbots	35	TL 3811
Stansted	14	TQ 6062
Stansted Mountfitchet	22	TL 5124
Stanton (Glos.)	32	SP 0634
Stanton (Northum.)	79	NZ 1390
Stanton (Staffs.)	52	SK 1246
Stanton (Suff.)	36	TL 9673
Stanton by Bridge	43	SK 3627
Stanton by Dale	53	SK 4637
Stanton Drew	17	ST 5963
Stanton Fitzwarren	18	SU 1790
Stanton Harcourt	33	SP 4105
Stanton Hill	53	SK 4860
Stanton in Peak	53	SK 2464
Stanton Lacy	40	SO 4978
Stanton Long	41	SO 5690
Stanton on the Wolds	53	SK 6330
Stanton Prior	17	ST 6762
Stanton St. Bernard	18	SU 0962
Stanton St. John	33	SP 5709
Stanton St. Quintin	18	ST 9079
Stanton Street	36	TL 9566
Stanton under Bardon	43	SK 4610
Stanton upon Hine Heath	40	SJ 5624
Stanton Wick	17	ST 6162
Stanwardine in the Fields	40	SJ 4124
Stanway (Essex)	23	TL 9324
Stanway (Glos.)	32	SP 0532
Stanwell	20	TQ 0574
Stanwell Moor	20	TQ 0474
Stanwick	44	SP 9871
Stape	67	SE 7993
Stapehill	10	SU 0500
Stapeley	51	SJ 6749
Staple	15	TR 2756
Staple Cross	14	TQ 7822
Staplefield	13	TQ 2728
Staple Fitzpaine	8	ST 2618
Stapleford (Cambs.)	35	TL 4751
Stapleford (Herts.)	35	TL 3117
Stapleford (Leic.)	44	SK 8018
Stapleford (Lincs.)	54	SK 8757
Stapleford (Notts.)	53	SK 4837
Stapleford (Wilts.)	10	SU 0637
Stapleford Abbots	21	TQ 5096
Stapleford Tawney	21	TQ 5098
Staplegrove	16	ST 2126
Staplehurst	14	TQ 7843
Staplers	11	SZ 5189
Stapleton (Avon)	29	ST 6175
Stapleton (Cumbr.)	71	NY 5071
Stapleton (Here. and Worc.)	30	SO 3265
Stapleton (Leic.)	43	SP 4398
Stapleton (N Yorks.)	72	NZ 2612
Stapleton (Salop)	40	SJ 4604
Stapleton (Somer.)	9	ST 4621
Stapley	8	ST 1813
Staploe	35	TL 1460
Star (Dyfed)	26	SN 2435
Star (Fife.)	93	NO 3103
Star (Somer.)	17	ST 4358
Starbotton	65	SD 9574
Starcross	8	SX 9781
Starston	47	TM 2384
Startforth	72	NZ 0416
Startley	18	ST 9482
Stathe	17	ST 3728
Stathern	54	SK 7731
Station Town	72	NZ 4036
Staughton Highway	35	TL 1364
Staunton (Glos.)	29	SO 5412
Staunton (Glos.)	32	SO 7929
Staunton on Arrow	30	SO 3660
Staunton on Wye	30	SO 3645
Staveley (Cumbr.)	62	SD 3786
Staveley (Cumbr.)	63	SD 4698
Staveley (Derby.)	53	SK 4374
Staveley (N Yorks.)	66	SE 3662
Staverton (Devon.)	5	SX 7964
Staverton (Glos.)	32	SO 8923
Staverton (Northants.)	33	SP 5461
Staverton (Wilts.)	18	ST 8560
Stawell	17	ST 3638
Staxigoe	112	ND 3852
Staxton	67	TA 0179
Staylittle	39	SN 8892
Staythorpe	54	SK 7554
Stean	65	SE 0873
Stearsby	66	SE 6171
Steart	17	ST 2745
Stebbing	22	TL 6624
Stedham	12	SU 8622
Steele Road	78	NY 5292
Steen's Bridge	31	SO 5457
Steep	12	SU 7525
Steeple (Dorset)	10	SY 9080
Steeple (Essex)	23	TL 9303
Steeple Ashton	18	ST 9056
Steeple Aston	33	SP 4725
Steeple Barton	33	SP 4424
Steeple Bumpstead	36	TL 6741
Steeple Claydon	34	SP 7027
Steeple Gidding	45	TL 1381
Steeple Langford	10	SU 0337
Steeple Morden	35	TL 2842
Steeton	59	SE 0344
Steinmanhill	105	NJ 7642
Stelling Minnis	15	TR 1446
Stenalees	4	SX 0157
Stenhousemuir	84	NS 8682
Stenness	113	HU 2176
Stenton	86	NT 6274
Steppingley	34	TL 0135
Stepps	84	NS 6668
Sternfield	37	TM 3861
Stert	18	SU 0259
Stetchworth	36	TL 6458
Stevenage	35	TL 2325
Stevenston	82	NS 2642
Steventon (Hants.)	19	SU 5547
Steventon (Oxon.)	19	SU 4691
Stevington	34	SP 9853
Stewartby	35	TL 0242
Stewarton	82	NS 4246
Stewkley	34	SP 8525
Stewton	55	TF 3687
Steyning	12	TQ 1711
Steynton	24	SM 9108
Stibb	6	SS 2210
Stibbard	46	TF 9828
Stibb Cross	6	SS 4314
Stibb Green	18	SU 2262
Stibbington	45	TL 0898
Stichill	86	NT 7138
Sticker	4	SW 9750
Stickford	55	TF 3560
Sticklepath	5	SX 6394
Stickney	55	TF 3456
Stiffkey	46	TF 9743
Stifford's Bridge	32	SO 7348
Stilligarry	109	NF 7638
Stillingfleet	60	SE 5940
Stillington (Cleve. Durham)	72	NZ 3723
Stillington (N Yorks.)	66	SE 5867
Stilton	45	TL 1689
Stinchcombe	18	ST 7298
Stinsford	9	SY 7191
Stirchley	41	SJ 6906
Stirling	91	NS 7993
Stisted	22	TL 8024
Stithians	2	SW 7336
Stivichall	43	SP 3376
Stixwould	55	TF 1765
Stoak	50	SJ 4273
Stobo	85	NT 1837
Stoborough	10	SY 9286
Stoborough Green	10	SY 9184
Stock	22	TQ 6998
Stockbridge	11	SU 3535
Stockbriggs	84	NS 7936
Stockbury	14	TQ 8461
Stockcross	19	SU 4368
Stockdalewath	70	NY 3845
Stockerston	44	SP 8397
Stock Green	32	SO 9859
Stockingford	43	SP 3391
Stocking Pelham	35	TL 4529
Stockland	8	ST 2404
Stockland Bristol	16	ST 2443
Stockleigh English	7	SS 8406
Stockleigh Pomeroy	7	SS 8703
Stockley	18	SU 0067
Stockport	51	SJ 8989
Stocksbridge	59	SK 2798
Stocksfield	72	NZ 0561
Stockton (Here. and Worc.)	30	SO 5161
Stockton (Norf.)	47	TM 3894
Stockton (Salop)	41	SO 7299
Stockton (Warw.)	33	SP 4363
Stockton (Wilts.)	10	ST 9738
Stockton Heath	51	SJ 6185
Stockton-on-Tees	72	NZ 4419
Stockton on Teme	41	SO 7167
Stockton on the Forest	66	SE 6556
Stockwith	54	SK 7994
Stock Wood	32	SP 0058
Stodmarsh	15	TR 2160
Stody	47	TG 0535
Stoer	110	NC 0428
Stoford (Somer.)	9	ST 5613
Stoford (Wilts.)	10	SU 0835
Stogumber	16	ST 0937
Stogursey	16	ST 2042
Stoke (Devon.)	6	SS 2324
Stoke (Hants.)	19	SU 4051
Stoke (Hants.)	12	SU 7202
Stoke (Kent)	22	TQ 8275
Stoke Abbott	9	ST 4500
Stoke Albany	44	SP 8088
Stoke Ash	37	TM 1170
Stoke Bardolph	53	SK 6441
Stoke Bliss	31	SO 6562
Stoke Bruerne	34	SP 7450
Stoke by Clare	36	TL 7443
Stoke-by-Nayland	36	TL 9836
Stoke Canon	8	SX 9397
Stoke Charity	11	SU 4839
Stoke Climsland	4	SX 3574
Stoke D'Abernon	20	TQ 1259
Stoke Doyle	44	TL 0286
Stoke Dry	44	SP 8597
Stoke Ferry	46	TF 7000
Stoke Fleming	5	SX 8648
Stokeford	10	SY 8787
Stoke Gabriel	5	SX 8457
Stoke Gifford	29	ST 6280
Stoke Golding	43	SP 3997
Stoke Goldington	34	SP 8348
Stokeham	54	SK 7876
Stoke Hammond	34	SP 8829
Stoke Holy Cross	47	TG 2301
Stokeinteignhead	8	SX 9170
Stoke Lacy	31	SO 6149
Stoke Lyne	33	SP 5628
Stoke Mandeville	34	SP 8310
Stokenchurch	20	SU 7596
Stoke Newington	21	TQ 3286
Stokenham	5	SX 8042
Stoke-on-Trent	51	SJ 8745
Stoke Orchard	32	SO 9128
Stoke Poges	20	SU 9884
Stoke Prior (Here. and Worc.)	30	SO 5256
Stoke Prior (Here. and Worc.)	41	SO 9467
Stoke Rivers	6	SS 6335
Stoke Rochford	44	SK 9127
Stoke Row	19	SU 6883
Stoke St. Gregory	17	ST 3426
Stoke St. Mary	8	ST 2622
Stoke St. Michael	17	ST 6646
Stoke St. Milborough	40	SO 5682
Stokesay	40	SO 4381
Stokesby	47	TG 4310
Stokesley	66	NZ 5208
Stoke sub Hamdon	9	ST 4717
Stoke Talmage	19	SU 6799
Stoke Trister	17	ST 7328
Stoke upon Tern	41	SJ 6327
Stolford	16	ST 2245
Stondon Massey	22	TL 5800
Stone (Bucks.)	34	SP 7812
Stone (Glos.)	29	ST 6895
Stone (Here. and Worc.)	41	SO 8675
Stone (Kent)	21	TQ 5774
Stone (Kent)	15	TQ 9427
Stone (Staffs.)	51	SJ 9034
Stone Allerton	17	ST 3950
Ston Easton	17	ST 6253
Stonebroom	53	SK 4159
Stone Cross	13	TQ 6104
Stonefield	84	NS 6957
Stonegate	13	TQ 6628
Stonegate Crofts	105	NK 0339
Stonegrave	66	SE 6577
Stonehaugh	78	NY 7976
Stonehaven	99	NO 8685
Stone House (Cumbr.)	65	SD 7785
Stonehouse (Glos.)	32	SO 8005
Stonehouse (Northum.)	71	NY 6958
Stonehouse (Strath.)	76	NS 7546
Stoneleigh	43	SP 3272
Stonely	45	TL 1067
Stonesby	44	SK 8224
Stonesfield	33	SP 3917
Stones Green	23	TM 1626
Stoneybridge	109	NF 7433
Stoneyburn	85	NS 9762
Stoney Cross	11	SU 2511
Stoneygate	43	SK 6102
Stoneyhills	23	TQ 9497
Stoneykirk	68	NX 0853
Stoney Middleton	53	SK 2275
Stoney Stanton	43	SP 4894
Stoney Stratton	17	ST 6539
Stoney Stretton	40	SJ 3809
Stoneywood	105	NJ 8910
Stonham Aspal	37	TM 1359
Stonnall	42	SK 0603
Stonor	20	SU 7388
Stonton Wyville	44	SP 7395
Stony Stratford	34	SP 7840
Stoodleigh	8	SS 9218
Stopham	12	TQ 0219
Stopsley	35	TL 1023
Storeton	50	SJ 3084
Stornoway	109	NB 4333
Storridge	32	SO 7448
Storrington	12	TQ 0814
Storth	63	SD 4780
Stotfold	35	TL 2136
Stottesdon	41	SO 6782
Stoughton (Leic.)	43	SK 6402
Stoughton (Surrey)	20	SU 9851
Stoughton (W Susx)	12	SU 8011
Stoulton	32	SO 9049
Stourbridge	41	SO 8984
Stourpaine	10	ST 8509
Stourport-on-Severn	41	SO 8171
Stour Provost	10	ST 7921
Stour Row	10	ST 8220
Stourton (Here. and Worc.)	41	SO 8585
Stourton (Warw.)	33	SP 2936
Stourton (Wilts.)	17	ST 7733
Stourton Caundle	9	ST 7114
Stoven	47	TM 4481
Stow (Borders)	86	NT 4644
Stow (Lincs.)	54	SK 8781
Stow Bardolph	46	TF 6205
Stow Bedon	46	TL 9596
Stowbridge	46	TF 6007
Stow cum Quy	35	TL 5260
Stowe (Salop)	40	SO 3173
Stowe (Staffs.)	42	SK 0027
Stowell	9	ST 6822
Stowford	4	SX 4386
Stowlangtoft	36	TL 9568
Stow Longa	45	TL 1171
Stow Maries	22	TQ 8399
Stowmarket	37	TM 0458
Stow-on-the-Wold	33	SP 1925
Stowting	15	TR 1241
Stowupland	37	TM 0659
Straad	81	NS 0462
Strachan	99	NO 6792
Strachur	89	NN 0901
Stradbroke	37	TM 2373
Stradishall	36	TL 7452
Stradsett	46	TF 6605
Stragglethorpe	54	SK 9152
Straiton (Lothian)	85	NT 2766
Straiton (Strath.)	75	NS 3804
Straloch (Grampn.)	105	NJ 8621
Straloch (Tays.)	98	NO 0463
Stramshall	52	SK 0735
Strands	62	NY 1204
Stranraer	68	NX 0660
Strata Florida	27	SN 7465
Stratfield Mortimer	19	SU 6764
Stratfield Saye	19	SU 6961
Stratfield Turgis	19	SU 6959
Stratford St. Andrew	37	TM 3560
Stratford St. Mary	37	TM 0434
Stratford Tony	10	SU 0926
Stratford-upon-Avon	33	SP 2055
Strathan (Highld.)	110	NC 0821
Strathaven	84	NS 7044
Strathblane (Central)	84	NS 5679
Strathcarron (Highld.)	101	NG 9442
Strathdon	104	NJ 3513
Strath Gairloch	106	NG 7977
Strathkanaird (Highld.)	106	NC 1501
Strathkinness	93	NO 4516
Strathmiglo	92	NO 2109
Strathpeffer	102	NH 4858
Strathwhillan	81	NS 0235
Strathy	111	NC 8465
Strathyre	90	NN 5617
Stratton (Corn.)	6	SS 2306
Stratton (Dorset)	9	SY 6593
Stratton (Glos.)	32	SP 0103
Stratton Audley	34	SP 6026
Stratton-on-the-Fosse	17	ST 6550
Stratton St. Margaret	18	SU 1787
Stratton St. Michael	47	TM 2093
Stratton Strawless	47	TG 2220
Stravithie	93	NO 5311
Streat	13	TQ 3515
Streatham	21	TQ 2972
Streatley (Beds.)	35	TL 0728
Streatley (Berks.)	19	SU 5980
Street (Lancs.)	64	SD 5252
Street (Somer.)	17	ST 4836
Street End	12	SZ 8599
Streethay	42	SK 1410
Streetly	42	SP 0898
Strefford	40	SO 4485
Strensall	66	SE 6360
Strensham	32	SO 9040
Stretcholt	17	ST 2943
Strete	5	SX 8447
Stretford	51	SJ 7894
Stretford Court	30	SO 4455
Strethall	35	TL 4939
Stretham	45	TL 5174
Strettington	12	SU 8807
Stretton (Ches.)	50	SJ 4452
Stretton (Ches.)	51	SJ 6182
Stretton (Derby.)	53	SK 3961
Stretton (Leic.)	44	SK 9415
Stretton (Staffs.)	41	SJ 8811
Stretton (Staffs.)	42	SK 2526
Stretton en le Field	43	SK 3012
Stretton Grandison	31	SO 6344
Stretton Heath	40	SJ 3610
Stretton-on-Dunsmore	43	SP 4072
Stretton on Fosse	33	SP 2238
Stretton under Fosse	43	SP 4581
Stretton Westwood	41	SO 5998
Strichen	105	NJ 9455
Stringston	16	ST 1742
Strixton	34	SP 9061
Stroat	29	ST 5798
Stromeferry	101	NG 8634
Stromness (Orkney)	113	HY 2509

Stronachlachar Thirsk

Stronachlachar	90	NN 4010
Strone (Highld.)	102	NH 5228
Strone (Strath.)	96	NS 1880
Stronenaba	96	NN 2084
Stronmilchan	89	NN 1528
Strontian	95	NM 8161
Strood	14	TQ 7369
Stroud (Glos.)	32	SO 8504
Stroud (Hants.)	12	SU 7223
Struan	100	NG 3438
Strubby	55	TF 4582
Strumpshaw	47	TG 3507
Strutherhill	84	NS 7650
Struy	102	NH 4039
Stuartfield	105	NJ 9745
Stubbington	11	SU 5503
Stubbins	58	SD 7918
Stubhampton	10	ST 9113
Stubton	54	SK 8748
Stuckton	10	SU 1613
Studham	34	TL 0215
Studland	10	SZ 0382
Studley (Oxon.)	34	SP 5912
Studley (Warw.)	32	SP 0763
Studley (Wilts.)	18	ST 9671
Studley Roger	66	SE 2970
Stump Cross	35	TL 5044
Stuntney	36	TL 5578
Sturbridge	51	SJ 8330
Sturmer	36	TL 6944
Sturminster Common	9	ST 7812
Sturminster Marshall	10	SY 9499
Sturminster Newton	9	ST 7813
Sturry	15	TR 1760
Sturton by Stow	54	SK 8980
Sturton le Steeple	54	SK 7884
Stuston	37	TM 1378
Stutton (N Yorks.)	60	SE 4741
Stutton (Suff.)	37	TM 1434
Styal	51	SJ 8383
Suckley	32	SO 7151
Sudborough	44	SP 9682
Sudbourne	37	TM 4153
Sudbrook	29	ST 5087
Sudbrooke	54	TF 0276
Sudbury (Derby.)	52	SK 1631
Sudbury (Suff.)	36	TL 8741
Suddie	103	NH 6654
Sudgrove	32	SO 9307
Suffield	47	TG 2332
Sulby	56	SC 3994
Sulgrave	33	SP 5545
Sulham	19	SU 6474
Sulhamstead	19	SU 6368
Sullington	12	TQ 0913
Sullom	113	HU 3573
Sully	28	ST 1568
Summer Bridge	65	SE 1962
Summercourt	3	SW 8856
Summerleaze	29	ST 4284
Summerseat	58	SD 7914
Summit	58	SD 9418
Sunadale	81	NR 8145
Sunbury	20	TQ 1069
Sunderland (Cumbr.)	62	NY 1735
Sunderland (Tyne and Wear)	72	NZ 3957
Sunderland Bridge	72	NZ 2637
Sundhope	77	NT 3324
Sundon Park	35	TL 0525
Sundridge	21	TQ 4854
Sunk Island	61	TA 2619
Sunningdale	20	SU 9567
Sunninghill	20	SU 9367
Sunningwell	33	SP 4900
Sunniside (Durham)	72	NZ 1438
Sunniside (Tyne and Wear)	72	NZ 2159
Sunny Bank	62	SD 2992
Sunnylaw	91	NS 7998
Sunnyside	13	TQ 3937
Surbiton	21	TQ 1867
Surfleet	45	TF 2528
Surfleet Seas End	45	TF 2628
Surlingham	47	TG 3106
Sustead	47	TG 1837
Susworth	60	SE 8302
Sutcombe	6	SS 3411
Sutterton	55	TF 2835
Sutton (Beds.)	35	TL 2247
Sutton (Cambs.)	45	TL 4479
Sutton (Gtr London)	21	TQ 2463
Sutton (Kent)	15	TR 3349
Sutton (Norf.)	47	TG 3823
Sutton (Northants.)	45	TL 0998
Sutton (Notts.)	53	SK 6784
Sutton (Notts.)	54	SK 7637
Sutton (Oxon.)	33	SP 4106
Sutton (Salop)	51	SJ 6631
Sutton (Salop)	40	SO 5082
Sutton (Salop)	41	SO 7286
Sutton (Staffs.)	41	SJ 7622
Sutton (Suff.)	37	TM 3046
Sutton (Surrey)	20	TQ 1046
Sutton (W Susx)	12	SU 9715
Sutton at Hone	21	TQ 5570
Sutton Bassett	44	SP 7790
Sutton Benger	18	ST 9478
Sutton Bonington	43	SK 5025
Sutton Bridge	45	TF 4821
Sutton Cheney	43	SK 4100
Sutton Coldfield	42	SP 1296
Sutton Courtenay	19	SU 5093
Sutton Crosses	45	TF 4321
Sutton Grange	66	SE 2874
Sutton Howgrave	66	SE 3179
Sutton in Ashfield	53	SK 5058
Sutton-in-Craven	59	SE 0044
Sutton Lane Ends	51	SJ 9270
Sutton Maddock	41	SJ 7201
Sutton Mallet	17	ST 3736
Sutton Mandeville	10	ST 9828
Sutton Montis	9	ST 6224
Sutton-on-Hull	61	TA 1132
Sutton on Sea	55	TF 5282
Sutton-on-the-Forest	66	SE 5864
Sutton on the Hill	53	SK 2333
Sutton on Trent	54	SK 7965
Sutton St. Edmund	45	TF 3613
Sutton St. James	45	TF 3918
Sutton St. Nicholas	31	SO 5345
Sutton Scotney	11	SU 4539
Sutton-under-Brailes	33	SP 2937
Sutton-under-Whitestonecliffe	66	SE 4882
Sutton upon Derwent	60	SE 7046
Sutton Valence	14	TQ 8148
Sutton Veny	18	ST 9041
Sutton Waldron	10	ST 8615
Sutton Weaver	50	SJ 5479
Swaby	55	TF 3877
Swadlincote	43	SK 3019
Swaffham	46	TF 8109
Swaffham Bulbeck	36	TL 5562
Swaffham Prior	36	TL 5764
Swafield	47	TG 2832
Swainby	66	NZ 4701
Swainsthorpe	47	TG 2101
Swainswick	18	ST 7568
Swalcliffe	33	SP 3738
Swalecliffe	15	TR 1367
Swallow	61	TA 1703
Swallowcliffe	10	ST 9626
Swallowfield	20	SU 7264
Swanage	10	SZ 0278
Swanbourne	34	SP 8027
Swanland	61	SE 9927
Swanley	21	TQ 5168
Swanmore	11	SU 5815
Swannington (Leic.)	43	SK 4116
Swannington (Norf.)	47	TG 1319
Swanscombe	21	TQ 6074
Swansea	25	SS 6593
Swanton Abbot	47	TG 2625
Swanton Morley	46	TG 0117
Swanton Novers	46	TG 0132
Swanwick (Derby.)	53	SK 4053
Swanwick (Hants.)	11	SU 5109
Swarby	54	TF 0440
Swardeston	47	TG 2002
Swarkestone	43	SK 3728
Swarland	79	NU 1601
Swarland Estate	79	NU 1603
Swaton	55	TF 1337
Swavesey	45	TL 3669
Sway	11	SZ 2798
Swayfield	44	SK 9822
Swaythling	11	SU 4315
Swefling	37	TM 3463
Swepstone	43	SK 3610
Swerford	33	SP 3731
Swettenham	51	SJ 8067
Swilland	37	TM 1853
Swillington	59	SE 3830
Swimbridge	6	SS 6230
Swinbrook	33	SP 2812
Swinderby	54	SK 8662
Swindon (Glos.)	32	SO 9325
Swindon (Staffs.)	41	SO 8690
Swindon (Wilts.)	18	SU 1484
Swine	61	TA 1335
Swinefleet	60	SE 7621
Swineshead (Beds.)	45	TL 0565
Swineshead Bridge	55	TF 2142
Swiney	112	ND 2335
Swinford (Leic.)	43	SP 5679
Swinford (Oxon.)	33	SP 4408
Swingfield Minnis	15	TR 2142
Swinhill	84	NS 7748
Swinhoe	79	NU 2028
Swinhope	55	TF 2196
Swinithwaite	65	SE 0489
Swinscoe	52	SK 1347
Swinstead	44	TF 0122
Swinton (Borders)	87	NT 8447
Swinton (Gtr Mches.)	58	SD 7701
Swinton (N Yorks.)	65	SE 2179
Swinton (N Yorks.)	67	SE 7573
Swinton (S Yorks.)	60	SK 4499
Swintonmill	87	NT 8145
Swithland	43	SK 5413
Swordale	102	NH 5765
Swordly	111	NC 7363
Sworton Heath	51	SJ 6784
Swyddffynnon	27	SN 6966
Swynnerton	51	SJ 8435
Swyre	9	SY 5288
Syde	32	SO 9411
Sydenham (Gtr London)	21	TQ 3571
Sydenham (Oxon.)	34	SP 7301
Sydenham Damerel	4	SX 4075
Syderstone	46	TF 8332
Sydling St. Nicholas	9	SY 6399
Sydmonton	19	SU 4857
Syerston	54	SK 7447
Syke	58	SD 8915
Sykehouse	60	SE 6216
Sylen	25	SN 5107
Symbister	113	HU 5362
Symington (Strath.)	82	NS 3831
Symington (Strath.)	85	NS 9935
Symondsbury	9	SY 4493
Synod Inn	26	SN 4054
Syre	111	NC 6843
Syreford	32	SP 0320
Syresham	34	SP 6241
Syston (Leic.)	43	SK 6211
Syston (Lincs.)	54	SK 9240
Sytchampton	32	SO 8466
Sywell	44	SP 8267

T

Tackley	33	SP 4720
Tacolneston	47	TM 1395
Tadcaster	60	SE 4843
Tadden	10	ST 9801
Taddington	52	SK 1471
Tadley	19	SU 6060
Tadlow	35	TL 2847
Tadmarton	33	SP 3937
Tadworth	21	TQ 2356
Tafarnaubach	28	SO 1110
Tafarn-y-Gelyn	50	SJ 1861
Taff's Well	28	ST 1283
Tafolwern	39	SH 8902
Tai-bach (Clwyd)	40	SJ 1528
Taibach (W Glam.)	28	SS 7789
Tain (Highld.)	112	ND 2266
Tain (Highld.)	108	NH 7782
Tai'r Bull	28	SN 9926
Tai'r-lon	48	SH 4450
Takeley	22	TL 5421
Talachddu	30	SO 0733
Talacre	50	SJ 1083
Talaton	8	SY 0699
Talbenny	24	SM 8412
Talerddig	39	SH 9300
Talgarreg	26	SN 4251
Talgarth	30	SO 1534
Taliesin	39	SN 6591
Talisker	100	NG 3230
Talke	51	SJ 8253
Talkin	71	NY 5557
Talladale	106	NG 9270
Tallentire	62	NY 1035
Talley	27	SN 6332
Tallington	45	TF 0908
Talmine	111	NC 5862
Talog	25	SN 3325
Talsarn	26	SN 5456
Talsarnau	48	SH 6135
Talskiddy	3	SW 9165
Talwrn	48	SH 4876
Talybont (Dyfed)	39	SN 6589
Tal-y-bont (Gwyn.)	38	SH 5921
Tal-y-Bont (Gwyn.)	49	SH 7668
Talybont (Powys)	28	SO 1122
Tal-y-cafn	49	SH 7971
Tal-y-llyn (Gwyn.)	39	SH 7109
Tal-y-llyn (Powys)	28	SO 1127
Talysarn	48	SH 4852
Talywern	39	SH 8200
Tamerton Foliot	5	SX 4761
Tamworth	42	SK 2004
Tandridge	21	TQ 3750
Tanfield	72	NZ 1855
Tangley	19	SU 3352
Tangmere	12	SU 9006
Tankersley	59	SK 3499
Tannach	112	ND 3247
Tannadice	99	NO 4758
Tannington	37	TM 2467
Tansley	53	SK 3259
Tansor	45	TL 0590
Tantobie	72	NZ 1754
Tanton	73	NZ 5210
Tanworth in Arden	42	SP 1170
Tan-y-fron	49	SH 9564
Tanygrisiau	49	SH 6845
Tan-y-groes	26	SN 2849
Taplow	20	SU 9182
Tarbert (Harris)	109	NB 1500
Tarbert (Jura)	88	NR 6082
Tarbert (Strath.)	81	NR 8668
Tarbet (Highld.)	110	NC 1648
Tarbet (Strath.)	90	NN 3104
Tarbock Green	50	SJ 4687
Tarbolton	75	NS 4327
Tarbrax	85	NT 0255
Tardebigge	41	SO 9969
Tarfside	99	NO 4979
Tarland	99	NJ 4804
Tarleton	57	SD 4420
Tarlscough	57	SD 4313
Tarlton	18	ST 9599
Tarnbrook	64	SD 5855
Tarporley	50	SJ 5562
Tarr	16	ST 1030
Tarrant Crawford	10	ST 9203
Tarrant Gunville	10	ST 9212
Tarrant Hinton	10	ST 9310
Tarrant Keynston	10	ST 9204
Tarrant Launceston	10	ST 9409
Tarrant Monkton	10	ST 9408
Tarrant Rawston	10	ST 9306
Tarrant Rushton	10	ST 9305
Tarring Neville	13	TQ 4404
Tarrington	31	SO 6140
Tarsappie	92	NO 1220
Tarskavaig	100	NG 5810
Tarves	105	NJ 8631
Tarvin	50	SJ 4867
Tasburgh	47	TM 2096
Tasley	41	SO 6994
Taston	33	SP 3521
Tatenhill	42	SK 2022
Tathwell	55	TF 3282
Tatsfield	21	TQ 4156
Tattenhall	50	SJ 4858
Tatterford	46	TF 8628
Tattersett	46	TF 8429
Tattershall	55	TF 2157
Tattershall Bridge	55	TF 1956
Tattershall Thorpe	55	TF 2159
Tattingstone	37	TM 1337
Taunton	8	ST 2324
Taverham	47	TG 1513
Tavernspite	24	SN 1812
Tavistock	5	SX 4774
Taw Green	7	SX 6597
Tawstock	6	SS 5529
Taxal	52	SK 0079
Tayinloan	81	NR 6945
Taynton (Glos.)	32	SO 7221
Taynton (Oxon.)	33	SP 2313
Taynuilt	89	NN 0031
Tayport	93	NO 4528
Tayvallich	89	NR 7386
Tealby	55	TF 1590
Teangue	101	NG 6609
Tebay	63	NY 6104
Tebworth	34	SP 9926
Tedburn St. Mary	5	SX 8194
Teddington (Glos.)	32	SO 9632
Teddington (Gtr London)	21	TQ 1671
Tedstone Delamere	31	SO 6958
Tedstone Wafre	31	SO 6759
Teeton	43	SP 6970
Teffont Evias	10	ST 9831
Teffont Magna	10	ST 9832
Tegryn	26	SN 2233
Teigh	44	SK 8616
Teigngrace	5	SX 8474
Teignmouth	8	SX 9473
Telford	41	SJ 6909
Tellisford	18	ST 8055
Telscombe	13	TQ 4003
Templand	70	NY 0886
Temple (Corn.)	4	SX 1473
Temple (Lothian)	85	NT 3158
Temple (Strath.)	84	NS 5469
Temple Bar	26	SN 5354
Temple Cloud	17	ST 6157
Templecombe	9	ST 7022
Temple Ewell	15	TR 2844
Temple Grafton	32	SP 1254
Temple Guiting	32	SP 0928
Temple Hirst	60	SE 6025
Temple Normanton	53	SK 4167
Temple Sowerby	63	NY 6127
Templeton (Devon.)	7	SS 8813
Templeton (Dyfed)	24	SN 1111
Tempsford	35	TL 1653
Tenbury Wells	41	SO 5968
Tenby	24	SN 1300
Tendring	23	TM 1424
Ten Mile Bank	46	TL 6097
Tenterden	14	TQ 8833
Terling	22	TL 7715
Ternhill	51	SJ 6332
Terrington	66	SE 6670
Terrington St. Clement	45	TF 5520
Terrington St. John	45	TF 5416
Teston	14	TQ 7053
Testwood	11	SU 3514
Tetbury	18	ST 8993
Tetbury Upton	18	ST 8795
Tetchill	50	SJ 3832
Tetcott	6	SX 3396
Tetford	55	TF 3374
Tetney	61	TA 3101
Tetney Lock	61	TA 3402
Tetsworth	34	SP 6802
Teversal	53	SK 4661
Teversham	35	TL 4958
Teviothead	77	NT 4005
Tewin	35	TL 2714
Tewkesbury	32	SO 8933
Teynham	15	TQ 9663
Thakeham	12	TQ 1017
Thame	34	SP 7006
Thames Ditton	21	TQ 1567
Thames Haven	22	TQ 7581
Thaneston	99	NO 6375
Thanington	15	TR 1356
Thankerton	85	NS 9737
Tharston	47	TM 1894
Thatcham	19	SU 5167
Thatto Heath	50	SJ 5093
Thaxted	36	TL 6131
Theakston	66	SE 3085
Thealby	60	SE 8917
Theale (Berks.)	19	SU 6371
Theale (Somer.)	17	ST 4646
Thearne	61	TA 0736
Theberton	37	TM 4365
Theddingworth	43	SP 6685
Theddlethorpe All Saints	55	TF 4688
Theddlethorpe St. Helen	55	TF 4788
Thelbridge Barton	7	SS 7812
Thelnetham	36	TM 0178
Thelwall	51	SJ 6587
Themelthorpe	47	TG 0524
Thenford	33	SP 5141
Therfield	35	TL 3337
Thetford	46	TL 8783
Theydon Bois	21	TQ 4598
Thickwood	18	ST 8272
Thimbleby (Lincs.)	55	TF 2369
Thimbleby (N Yorks.)	66	SE 4495
Thirkleby	66	SE 4778
Thirlby	66	SE 4884
Thirlestane	86	NT 5647
Thirn	65	SE 2185
Thirsk	66	SE 4282

Toynton Fen Side Upton

Toynton Fen Side	*55*	TF 3961
Toynton St. Peter	*55*	TF 4063
Toy's Hill	*21*	TQ 4751
Trabboch	*75*	NS 4321
Traboe	*2*	SW 7421
Tradespark (Highld.)	*103*	NH 8656
Tradespark (Orkney)	*113*	HY 4408
Tranent	*86*	NT 4072
Trantlemore	*111*	NC 8853
Tranwell	*79*	NZ 1883
Trapp	*25*	SN 6519
Traprain	*86*	NT 5975
Traquair	*85*	NT 3334
Trawden	*58*	SD 9138
Trawsfynydd	*49*	SH 7035
Trealaw	*28*	SS 9992
Treales	*57*	SD 4432
Trearddur Bay	*48*	SH 2478
Treaslane	*100*	NG 3953
Trebartha	*4*	SX 2677
Trebarwith	*4*	SX 0585
Trebetherick	*3*	SW 9377
Treborough	*16*	ST 0036
Trebudannon	*3*	SW 8961
Treburley	*4*	SX 3477
Trecastle	*28*	SN 8729
Trecwn	*24*	SM 9632
Trecynon	*28*	SN 9903
Tredavoe	*2*	SW 4528
Tre-ddiog	*24*	SM 8928
Tredegar	*28*	SO 1409
Tredington	*33*	SP 2543
Tredinnick	*3*	SW 9270
Tredomen	*30*	SO 1231
Tredunnock	*29*	ST 3795
Treen	*2*	SW 3923
Treeton	*53*	SK 4387
Trefdraeth	*48*	SH 4070
Trefecca	*30*	SO 1431
Trefeglwys	*39*	SN 9690
Trefenter	*27*	SN 6068
Treffgarne	*24*	SM 9523
Treffynnon	*24*	SM 8428
Trefil	*28*	SO 1212
Trefilan	*26*	SN 5457
Trefnannau	*40*	SJ 2015
Trefnant	*49*	SJ 0570
Trefonen	*40*	SJ 2526
Trefor	*48*	SH 3779
Trefriw	*49*	SH 7763
Tregadillett	*4*	SX 2983
Tregaian	*48*	SH 4579
Tregare	*29*	SO 4110
Tregaron	*27*	SN 6759
Tregarth	*48*	SH 6067
Tregeare	*4*	SX 2486
Tregeiriog	*50*	SJ 1733
Tregele	*48*	SH 3592
Tregidden	*2*	SW 7523
Treglemais	*24*	SM 8229
Tregole	*6*	SX 1998
Tregonetha	*3*	SW 9563
Tregony	*3*	SW 9244
Tregoyd	*30*	SO 1937
Tre-groes	*26*	SN 4044
Tregurrian	*2*	SW 8465
Tregynon	*39*	SO 0999
Trehafod	*28*	ST 0491
Treharris	*28*	ST 1097
Treherbert	*28*	SS 9398
Trelawnyd	*49*	SJ 0879
Trelech	*26*	SN 2830
Trelech a'r Betws	*25*	SN 3026
Treleddyd-fawr	*24*	SM 7528
Trelewis	*28*	ST 1197
Trelights	*4*	SW 9879
Trelill	*4*	SX 0477
Trelleck	*29*	SO 5005
Trelleck Grange	*29*	SO 4901
Trelogan	*50*	SJ 1180
Trelystan	*40*	SJ 2603
Tremadog	*48*	SH 5640
Tremail	*4*	SX 1686
Tremain	*26*	SN 2348
Tremaine	*4*	SX 2388
Tremar	*4*	SX 2568
Trematon	*4*	SX 3959
Tremerichion	*49*	SJ 0773
Trenance	*2*	SW 8567
Trenarren	*4*	SX 0348
Trench	*41*	SJ 6913
Treneglos	*4*	SX 2088
Trenewan	*4*	SX 1753
Trent	*9*	ST 5918
Trentham	*51*	SJ 8640
Trentishoe	*7*	SS 6448
Treoes	*28*	SS 9478
Treorchy	*28*	SS 9596

Tre'r-ddol	*39*	SN 6592
Tresaith	*26*	SN 2751
Trescott	*41*	SO 8497
Trescowe	*2*	SW 5731
Tresham	*18*	ST 7991
Tresillian	*3*	SW 8646
Tresmeer	*4*	SX 2387
Tressait	*97*	NN 8160
Tresta (Fetlar)	*113*	HU 6190
Tresta (Shetld.)	*113*	HU 3650
Treswell	*54*	SK 7779
Trethurgy	*4*	SX 0355
Tretio	*24*	SM 7829
Tretire	*29*	SO 5124
Tretower	*28*	SO 1821
Treuddyn	*50*	SJ 2458
Trevalga	*4*	SX 0889
Trevanson	*4*	SW 9772
Trevarren	*3*	SW 9160
Trevarrick	*4*	SW 9843
Trevellas	*2*	SW 7452
Treverva	*2*	SW 7631
Trevethin	*29*	SO 2802
Trevigro	*4*	SX 3369
Trevine	*24*	SM 8432
Treviscoe	*3*	SW 9455
Trevone	*3*	SW 8975
Trevor	*48*	SH 3746
Trewarmett	*4*	SX 0686
Trewarthenick	*3*	SW 9044
Trewassa	*4*	SX 1486
Trewellard	*2*	SW 3733
Trewen	*4*	SX 2583
Trewidland	*4*	SX 2560
Trewint	*6*	SX 1897
Trewithian	*3*	SW 8737
Trewoon	*4*	SW 9952
Treyford	*12*	SU 8218
Trickett's Cross	*10*	SU 0801
Trimdon	*72*	NZ 3634
Trimdon Colliery	*72*	NZ 3835
Trimdon Grange	*72*	NZ 3735
Trimingham	*47*	TG 2738
Trimley	*37*	TM 2736
Trimley Heath	*37*	TM 2737
Trimpley	*41*	SO 7978
Trimsaran	*25*	SN 4504
Trimstone	*6*	SS 5043
Trinant	*28*	SO 2000
Tring	*34*	SP 9211
Trinity	*99*	NO 6061
Trislaig	*96*	NN 0874
Trispen	*2*	SW 8450
Tritlington	*79*	NZ 2092
Trochry	*91*	NN 9740
Troedyraur	*26*	SN 3245
Troedyrhiw	*28*	SO 0702
Trofarth	*49*	SH 8571
Troon (Corn.)	*2*	SW 6638
Troon (Strath.)	*82*	NS 3230
Troston	*36*	TL 8972
Trottiscliffe	*14*	TQ 6460
Trotton	*12*	SU 8322
Troutbeck	*62*	NY 4103
Troutbeck Bridge	*62*	NY 4000
Trowbridge	*18*	ST 8557
Trow Green	*29*	SO 5706
Trowle Common	*18*	ST 8358
Trows	*86*	NT 6932
Trowse Newton	*47*	TG 2406
Trudoxhill	*18*	ST 7443
Trull	*8*	ST 2122
Trumpan	*100*	NG 2261
Trumpet	*31*	SO 6539
Trumpington	*35*	TL 4455
Trunch	*47*	TG 2834
Truro	*2*	SW 8244
Trusham	*5*	SX 8582
Trusley	*53*	SK 2535
Trusthorpe	*55*	TF 5183
Trysull	*41*	SO 8494
Tubney	*19*	SU 4498
Tuckenhay	*5*	SX 8156
Tuddenham (Suff.)	*36*	TL 7371
Tuddenham (Suff.)	*37*	TM 1948
Tudeley	*13*	TQ 6245
Tudhoe	*72*	NZ 2635
Tudweiloig	*48*	SH 2336
Tuffley	*32*	SO 8315
Tugby	*44*	SK 7601
Tugford	*40*	SO 5587
Tullibody	*91*	NS 8595
Tullich (Highld.)	*108*	NH 8576
Tullich (Strath.)	*89*	NN 0815
Tullich Muir	*108*	NH 7373
Tulliemet	*98*	NN 9952
Tulloch (Grampn.)	*99*	NO 7671
Tullochgorm	*89*	NR 9695
Tulloes	*99*	NO 5145
Tullybannocher	*91*	NN 7521

Tullyfergus	*98*	NO 2149
Tullynessle	*104*	NJ 5519
Tumble	*25*	SN 5411
Tumby	*55*	TF 2359
Tumby Woodside	*55*	TF 2657
Tunstall (Humbs.)	*61*	TA 3032
Tunstall (Kent)	*14*	TQ 8961
Tunstall (Lancs.)	*64*	SD 6073
Tunstall (Norf.)	*47*	TG 4107
Tunstall (N Yorks.)	*65*	SE 2195
Tunstall (Staffs.)	*51*	SJ 8551
Tunstall (Suff.)	*37*	TM 3655
Tunstead	*47*	TG 3022
Tunworth	*19*	SU 6748
Tupsley	*31*	SO 5340
Turgis Green	*19*	SU 6959
Turin	*99*	NO 5352
Turkdean	*32*	SP 1017
Tur Langton	*44*	SP 7194
Turnastone	*30*	SO 3536
Turnberry	*75*	NS 2005
Turnditch	*53*	SK 2946
Turner's Hill	*13*	TQ 3435
Turners Puddle	*10*	SY 8293
Turnworth	*10*	ST 8107
Turriff	*105*	NJ 7249
Turton Bottoms	*58*	SD 7315
Turvey	*34*	SP 9452
Turville	*20*	SU 7691
Turville Heath	*20*	SU 7391
Turweston	*34*	SP 6037
Tushingham cum Grindley	*50*	SJ 5246
Tutbury	*42*	SK 2129
Tutnall	*41*	SO 9870
Tutshill	*29*	ST 5394
Tuttington	*47*	TG 2227
Tuxford	*54*	SK 7370
Twatt (Orkney)	*113*	HY 2624
Twechar	*84*	NS 6975
Tweedmouth	*87*	NT 9952
Tweedsmuir	*77*	NT 1024
Twelveheads	*2*	SW 7642
Twenty	*45*	TF 1520
Twerton	*18*	ST 7263
Twickenham	*21*	TQ 1473
Twigworth	*32*	SO 8421
Twineham	*13*	TQ 2519
Twinhoe	*18*	ST 7359
Twinstead	*36*	TL 8637
Twiss Green	*51*	SJ 6595
Twitchen (Devon)	*7*	SS 7830
Twitchen (Salop)	*40*	SO 3679
Two Bridges	*5*	SX 6075
Two Dales	*53*	SK 2762
Two Gates	*42*	SK 2101
Twycross	*43*	SK 3305
Twyford (Berks.)	*20*	SU 7975
Twyford (Bucks.)	*34*	SP 6626
Twyford (Hants.)	*11*	SU 4724
Twyford (Leic.)	*44*	SK 7210
Twyford (Norf.)	*46*	TG 0124
Twyford Common	*30*	SO 5135
Twynholm	*69*	NX 6654
Twyning	*32*	SO 8936
Twyning Green	*32*	SO 9037
Twynllanan	*28*	SN 7524
Twyn-y-Sheriff	*29*	SO 4005
Twywell	*44*	SP 9578
Tyberton	*30*	SO 3739
Tyburn	*42*	SP 1490
Tycroes	*25*	SN 6010
Tycrwyn	*40*	SJ 1018
Tydd Gote	*45*	TF 4518
Tydd St. Giles	*45*	TF 4216
Tydd St. Mary	*45*	TF 4418
Ty-hen	*48*	SH 1731
Tyldesley	*58*	SD 6902
Tyler Hill	*15*	TR 1460
Tylers Green	*20*	SU 9094
Tylorstown	*28*	ST 0195
Tylwch	*39*	SN 9780
Ty-nant (Clwyd)	*49*	SH 9944
Ty-nant (Gwyn.)	*39*	SH 9026
Tyndrum	*90*	NN 3330
Tyneham	*10*	SY 8880
Tynehead	*86*	NT 3959
Tynemouth (Tyne and Wear)	*72*	NZ 3468
Tynewydd	*28*	SS 9399
Tyninghame	*86*	NT 6179
Tynribbie	*95*	NM 9446
Tynron	*76*	NX 8093
Tyn-y-ffridd	*40*	SJ 1230
Tyn-y-graig	*30*	SO 0149
Ty'n-y-groes	*49*	SH 7771
Tyringham	*34*	SP 8547
Tythegston	*28*	SS 8578
Tytherington (Avon)	*29*	ST 6788

Tytherington (Ches.)	*51*	SJ 9175
Tytherington (Somer.)	*18*	ST 7744
Tytherington (Wilts.)	*18*	ST 9140
Tytherleigh	*8*	ST 3203
Tywardreath	*4*	SX 0854
Tywyn (Gwyn)	*38*	SH 5800
Tywyn (Gwyn)	*49*	SH 7878

U

Ubbeston Green	*37*	TM 3271
Ubley	*17*	ST 5257
Uckerby	*66*	NZ 2402
Uckfield	*13*	TQ 4721
Uckington	*32*	SO 9224
Uddingston	*84*	NS 6960
Uddington	*84*	NS 8633
Udimore	*14*	TQ 8718
Udny Green	*105*	NJ 8726
Uffcott	*18*	SU 1277
Uffculme	*8*	ST 0612
Uffington (Lincs.)	*45*	TF 0608
Uffington (Oxon.)	*19*	SU 3089
Uffington (Salop)	*40*	SJ 5313
Ufford (Northants.)	*45*	TF 0904
Ufford (Suff.)	*37*	TM 2953
Ufton	*33*	SP 3762
Ufton Nervet	*19*	SU 6367
Ugborough	*5*	SX 6755
Uggeshall	*37*	TM 4580
Ugglebarnby	*67*	NZ 8707
Ugley	*22*	TL 5128
Ugley Green	*22*	TL 5227
Ugthorpe	*73*	NZ 7911
Uig (Isle of Lewis)	*109*	NB 0534
Uig (Isle of Skye)	*100*	NG 1952
Uig (Isle of Skye)	*100*	NG 3963
Ulbster	*112*	ND 3241
Ulceby (Humbs.)	*61*	TA 1014
Ulceby (Lincs.)	*55*	TF 4272
Ulcombe	*14*	TQ 8449
Uldale	*62*	NY 2536
Uley	*18*	ST 7898
Ulgham	*79*	NZ 2392
Ullapool	*106*	NH 1294
Ullenhall	*42*	SP 1267
Ullenwood	*32*	SO 9416
Ulleskelf	*60*	SE 5140
Ullesthorpe	*43*	SP 5087
Ulley	*53*	SK 4687
Ullingswick	*31*	SO 5950
Ullinish	*100*	NG 3237
Ullock	*62*	NY 0724
Ulpha	*62*	SD 1993
Ulrome	*67*	TA 1656
Ulsta	*113*	HU 4680
Ulverston	*62*	SD 2878
Umberleigh	*6*	SS 6023
Unapool	*110*	NC 2333
Underbarrow	*63*	SD 4692
Under River	*21*	TQ 5552
Underwood	*53*	SK 4750
Undy	*29*	ST 4386
Union Mills	*56*	SC 3578
Unstone	*53*	SK 3777
Upavon	*18*	SU 1354
Up Cerne	*9*	ST 6502
Upchurch	*14*	TQ 8467
Upcott	*30*	SO 3250
Upend	*36*	TL 7058
Up Exe	*8*	SS 9302
Uphall	*85*	NT 0571
Upham (Devon.)	*7*	SS 8808
Upham (Hants.)	*11*	SU 5320
Up Hatherley	*32*	SO 9120
Uphill (Avon)	*17*	ST 3158
Up Holland	*57*	SD 5105
Uplawmoor	*82*	NS 4355
Upleadon	*32*	SO 7527
Upleatham	*73*	NZ 6319
Uplees	*15*	TQ 9964
Uplowman	*8*	ST 0115
Uplyme	*8*	SY 3293
Upminster	*21*	TQ 5686
Up Nately	*20*	SU 6951
Upnor	*14*	TQ 7470
Upottery	*8*	ST 2007
Uppark	*12*	SU 7717
Upper Ardchronie	*108*	NH 6188
Upper Arley	*41*	SO 7680
Upper Astrop	*33*	SP 5137
Upper Basildon	*19*	SU 5976

Upper Beeding	*12*	TQ 1910
Upper Benefield	*44*	SP 9789
Upper Boddington	*33*	SP 4853
Upper Borth	*38*	SN 6088
Upper Breinton	*30*	SO 4640
Upper Broughton	*43*	SK 6826
Upper Bucklebury	*19*	SU 5368
Upper Caldecote	*35*	TL 1645
Upper Chapel	*30*	SO 0040
Upper Chute	*19*	SU 2953
Upper Clatford	*19*	SU 3543
Upper Clynnog	*48*	SH 4746
Upper Cokeham	*12*	TQ 1605
Upper Cwmtwrch	*28*	SN 7611
Upper Dallachy	*104*	NJ 3662
Upper Dean	*45*	TL 0467
Upper Denby	*59*	SE 2207
Upper Derraid	*103*	NJ 0233
Upper Dicker	*13*	TQ 5510
Upper Elkstone	*52*	SK 0559
Upper End	*52*	SK 0876
Upper Ethie	*103*	NH 7663
Upper Farringdon	*12*	SU 7135
Upper Framilode	*32*	SO 7510
Upper Froyle	*12*	SU 7542
Upper Gravenhurst	*35*	TL 1136
Upper Green	*19*	SU 3663
Upper Hackney	*53*	SK 2961
Upper Hale	*20*	SU 8448
Upper Hambleton	*44*	SK 8907
Upper Hardres Court	*15*	TR 1550
Upper Hartfield	*13*	TQ 4634
Upper Heath	*40*	SO 5685
Upper Helmsley	*66*	SE 6956
Upper Heyford	*33*	SP 4926
Upper Hill	*30*	SO 4753
Upper Hopton	*59*	SE 1918
Upper Hulme	*52*	SK 0160
Upper Inglesham	*18*	SU 2096
Upper Killay	*25*	SS 5892
Upper Knockando	*104*	NJ 1843
Upper Lambourn	*19*	SU 3180
Upper Langwith	*53*	SK 5169
Upper Lochton	*99*	NO 6997
Upper Longdon	*42*	SK 0614
Upper Lydbrook	*29*	SO 6015
Upper Maes-coed	*30*	SO 3335
Uppermill	*59*	SD 9906
Upper Minety	*18*	SU 0091
Upper North Dean	*20*	SU 8598
Upper Poppleton	*66*	SE 5554
Upper Quinton	*33*	SP 1746
Upper Sapey	*31*	SO 6863
Upper Scoulag	*82*	NS 1059
Upper Seagry	*18*	ST 9580
Upper Shelton	*34*	SP 9943
Upper Sheringham	*47*	TG 1441
Upper Skelmorlie	*82*	NS 1968
Upper Slaughter	*32*	SP 1523
Upper Soudley	*29*	SO 6610
Upper Stondon	*35*	TL 1535
Upper Stowe	*34*	SP 6456
Upper Street (Hants.)	*10*	SU 1418
Upper Street (Norf.)	*47*	TG 3516
Upper Sundon	*35*	TL 0527
Upper Swell	*32*	SP 1726
Upper Tasburgh	*47*	TM 2095
Upper Tean	*52*	SK 0139
Upperthong	*59*	SE 1208
Upper Tillyrie	*92*	NO 1006
Upperton	*12*	SU 9522
Upper Tooting	*21*	TQ 2772
Upper Town (Avon)	*29*	ST 5265
Upper Tysoe	*33*	SP 3343
Upper Upham	*18*	SU 2277
Upper Wardington	*33*	SP 4946
Upper Weald	*34*	SP 8037
Upper Weedon	*34*	SP 6258
Upper Wield	*11*	SU 6238
Upper Winchendon	*34*	SP 7414
Upper Woodford	*10*	SU 1237
Uppingham	*44*	SP 8699
Uppington	*41*	SJ 5909
Upsall	*66*	SE 4587
Upshire	*35*	TL 4100
Up Somborne	*11*	SU 3932
Upstreet	*15*	TR 2262
Up Sydling	*9*	ST 6201
Upton (Berks.)	*20*	SU 9879
Upton (Bucks.)	*34*	SP 7711
Upton (Cambs.)	*45*	TL 1778
Upton (Ches.)	*50*	SJ 4069
Upton (Dorset)	*10*	SY 9893
Upton (Hants.)	*19*	SU 3555
Upton (Hants.)	*11*	SU 3716
Upton (Lincs.)	*54*	SK 8686

Upton

Wem

Upton (Mers.) *50* SJ 2687
Upton (Norf.) *47* TG 3912
Upton (Northants.) *34* SP 7160
Upton (Northants.) *45* TF 1000
Upton (Notts.) *54* SK 7354
Upton (Notts.) *54* SK 7476
Upton (Oxon.) *19* SU 5186
Upton (Somer.) *16* SS 9928
Upton (W Yorks.) *60* SE 4713
Upton Bishop *29* SO 6427
Upton Cheyney *18* ST 6969
Upton Cressett *41* SO 6592
Upton Cross *4* SX 2872
Upton Grey *19* SU 6948
Upton Hellions *7* SS 8303
Upton Lovell *18* ST 9440
Upton Magna *40* SJ 5512
Upton Noble *17* ST 7139
Upton Pyne *8* SX 9197
Upton St. Leonards *32* SO 8615
Upton Scudamore *18* ST 8647
Upton Snodsbury *32* SO 9454
Upton upon Severn *32* SO 8540
Upton Warren *41* SO 9267
Upwaltham *12* SU 9413
Upware *45* TL 5370
Upwell *45* TF 5002
Upwey *9* SY 6684
Upwood *45* TL 2582
Urchal *103* NH 7544
Urchany *103* NH 8849
Urchfont *18* SU 0356
Urdimarsh *31* SO 5249
Urmston *51* SJ 7695
Urquhart *104* NJ 2863
Urra *66* NZ 5702
Urray *102* NH 5053
Urswick *64* SD 2674
Ushaw Moor *72* NZ 2342
Usk *29* SO 3701
Usselby *55* TF 0993
Utley *59* SE 0542
Uton *7* SX 8298
Utterby *55* TF 3093
Uttoxeter *52* SK 0933
Uwchmynydd (Gwyn.) *38* SH 1425
Uxbridge *20* TQ 0583
Uyeasound (Unst) *113* HP 5901
Uzmaston *24* SM 9714

V

Valley *48* SH 2979
Valleyfield *85* NT 0086
Valtos (Island of Skye) *100* NG 5163
Valtos (Isle of Lewis) *109* NB 0936
Vange *22* TQ 7287
Vardre *25* SN 6902
Varteg *28* SO 2506
Vatten *100* NG 2843
Vauld, The *31* SO 5349
Vaynor *28* SO 0410
Veensgarth *26* HU 4244
Velindre (Dyfed) *26* SN 1039
Velindre (Dyfed) *26* SN 3538
Velindre (Powys) *30* SO 1836
Vennington *40* SJ 3309
Venn Ottery *8* SY 0791
Ventnor *11* SZ 5677
Vernham Dean *19* SU 3356
Vernham Street *19* SU 3457
Vernolds Common *40* SO 4780
Verwig *26* SN 1849
Verwood *10* SU 0908
Veryan *3* SW 9139
Vicarage *8* SY 2088
Vickerstown *64* SD 1868
Victoria *4* SW 9961
Vidlin *113* HU 4765
Viewpark *84* NS 7161
Villavin *6* SS 5816
Vinehall Street *14* TQ 7520
Vine's Cross *13* TQ 5917
Virginia Water *20* SU 9967
Virginstow *4* SX 3792
Vobster *18* ST 7048
Voe (Shetld.) *113* HU 4062
Vowchurch *30* SO 3636

W

Wackerfield *72* NZ 1522
Wacton *47* TM 1891
Wadborough *32* SO 8947
Waddesdon *34* SP 7416
Waddingham *54* SK 9896
Waddington (Lancs.) *58* SD 7243
Waddington (Lincs.) *54* SK 9764
Wadebridge *4* SW 9972
Wadeford *8* ST 3110
Wadenhoe *44* TL 0083
Wadesmill *35* TL 3517
Wadhurst *13* TQ 6431
Wadshelf *53* SK 3171
Wadworth *53* SK 5697
Waen Fach *40* SJ 2017
Wainfleet All Saints *55* TF 4959
Wainfleet Bank *55* TF 4759
Wainhouse Corner *4* SX 1895
Wainscott *22* TQ 7471
Wainstalls *59* SE 0428
Waitby *65* NY 7507
Wakefield *59* SE 3320
Wakerley *44* SP 9599
Wakes Colne *22* TL 8928
Walberswick *37* TM 4974
Walberton *12* SU 9705
Walcot (Lincs.) *54* TF 0535
Walcot (Lincs.) *55* TF 1256
Walcot (Salop) *41* SJ 5912
Walcot (Warw.) *32* SP 1258
Walcote *43* SP 5683
Walcott (Norf.) *47* TG 3632
Walden Head *65* SD 9880
Walden Stubbs *60* SE 5516
Walderslade *14* TQ 7563
Walderton *12* SU 7910
Walditch *9* SY 4892
Waldridge *72* NZ 2549
Waldringfield *37* TM 2744
Waldron *13* TQ 5419
Wales *53* SK 4782
Walesby (Lincs.) *55* TF 1392
Walesby (Notts.) *53* SK 6870
Walford (Here. and Worc.) *40* SO 3872
Walford (Here. and Worc.) *29* SO 5820
Walford (Salop) *40* SJ 4320
Walgherton *51* SJ 6948
Walgrave *44* SP 8071
Walkden *58* SD 7303
Walker *72* NZ 2864
Walkerburn *85* NT 3637
Walker Fold *58* SD 6742
Walkeringham *54* SK 7692
Walkerith *54* SK 7892
Walkern *35* TL 2926
Walker's Green *31* SO 5248
Walkhampton *5* SX 5369
Walkington *61* SE 9936
Walk Mill *58* SD 8629
Wall (Northum.) *71* NY 9168
Wall (Staffs.) *42* SK 0906
Wallacetown *75* NS 3422
Wallasey *50* SJ 2992
Wall Bank *40* SO 5092
Wallend *22* TQ 8775
Wallingford *19* SU 6089
Wallington (Gtr London) *21* TQ 2863
Wallington (Hants.) *11* SU 5806
Wallington (Herts.) *35* TL 2933
Wallis *24* SN 0125
Walliswood *12* TQ 1138
Walls *113* HU 2449
Wallsend *72* NZ 2766
Wallyford *85* NT 3671
Walmer *15* TR 3750
Walmer Bridge *57* SD 4724
Walmersley *58* SD 8013
Walmley *42* SP 1393
Walpole *37* TM 3674
Walpole Highway *45* TF 5113
Walpole St. Andrew *45* TF 5017
Walpole St. Peter *45* TF 5016
Walsall *42* SP 0198
Walsall Wood *42* SK 0403
Walsden *58* SD 9322
Walsgrave on Sowe *43* SP 3781
Walsham le Willows *36* TM 0071
Walsoken *45* TF 4710
Walston *85* NT 0545
Walterstone *29* SO 3425
Waltham (Humbs.) *61* TA 2503
Waltham (Kent) *15* TR 1148
Waltham Abbey *21* TL 3800
Waltham Chase *11* SU 5614
Waltham on the Wolds *44* SK 8025
Waltham St. Lawrence *20* SU 8276
Walthamstow *21* TQ 3788
Walton (Bucks.) *34* SP 8936
Walton (Cumbr.) *71* NY 5264
Walton (Derby.) *53* SK 3569
Walton (Leic.) *43* SP 5987
Walton (Powys) *30* SO 2559
Walton (Salop) *41* SJ 5818
Walton (Somer.) *17* ST 4636
Walton (Suff.) *37* TM 2935
Walton (Warw.) *33* SP 2853
Walton (W Yorks.) *59* SE 3516
Walton (W Yorks.) *59* SE 4447
Walton Cardiff *32* SO 9032
Walton East *24* SN 0123
Walton-in-Gordano *29* ST 4273
Walton-le-Dale *57* SD 5627
Walton-on-Thames *20* TQ 1066
Walton-on-the-Hill (Staffs.) *41* SJ 9520
Walton on the Hill (Surrey) *21* TQ 2255
Walton on the Naze *23* TM 2521
Walton on the Wolds *43* SK 5919
Walton-on-Trent *42* SK 2118
Walton West *24* SM 8713
Walworth *72* NZ 2218
Wambrook *8* ST 2907
Wanborough *18* SU 2082
Wandsworth *21* TQ 2673
Wangford *37* TM 4679
Wanlip *43* SK 5910
Wanlockhead *76* NS 8712
Wansford (Cambs.) *45* TL 0799
Wansford (Humbs.) *67* TA 0656
Wanstead *21* TQ 4087
Wanstrow *18* ST 7141
Wanswell *29* SO 6801
Wantage *19* SU 4087
Wapley *18* ST 7179
Wappenbury *43* SP 3769
Wappenham *34* SP 6245
Warbleton *13* TQ 6018
Warborough *19* SU 6093
Warboys *45* TL 3080
Warbstow *4* SX 2090
Warburton *51* SJ 7089
Warcop *63* NY 7415
Warden *15* TR 0271
Ward Green *37* TM 0564
Wardington *33* SP 4946
Wardle (Ches.) *51* SJ 6057
Wardle (Gtr Mches.) *58* SD 9116
Wardley *44* SK 8300
Wardlow *52* SK 1874
Wardy Hill *45* TL 4782
Ware *35* TL 3614
Wareham *10* SY 9287
Warehorne *15* TQ 9832
Warenford *79* NU 1328
Waren Mill *87* NU 1534
Warenton *87* NU 1030
Wareside *35* TL 3915
Waresley *35* TL 2454
Warfield *20* SU 8872
Wargrave *20* SU 7878
Warham All Saints *46* TF 9441
Warham St. Mary *46* TF 9441
Wark (Northum.) *87* NT 8238
Wark (Northum.) *78* NY 8576
Warkleigh *7* SS 6422
Warkton *44* SP 8980
Warkworth *79* NU 2406
Warlaby *66* SE 3591
Warland *58* SD 9419
Warleggan *4* SX 1569
Warley *42* SP 0086
Warlingham *21* TQ 3658
Warmfield *59* SE 3720
Warmingham *51* SJ 7161
Warmington (Northants.) *45* TL 0791
Warmington (Warw.) *33* SP 4147
Warminster *18* ST 8644
Warmsworth *60* SE 5400
Warmwell *9* SY 7585
Warndon *32* SO 8856
Warnford *11* SU 6223
Warnham *12* TQ 1633
Warninglid *13* TQ 2526
Warren (Ches.) *51* SJ 8870
Warren (Dyfed) *24* SR 9397
Warren Row *20* SU 8180
Warren Street *14* TQ 9253
Warrington (Bucks.) *34* SP 8954
Warrington (Ches.) *51* SJ 6088
Warsash *11* SU 4905
Warslow *52* SK 0858
Warsop *53* SK 5667
Warter *67* SE 8750
Warthill *66* SE 6755
Wartling *13* TQ 6509
Wartnaby *44* SK 7123
Warton (Lancs.) *57* SD 4028
Warton (Lancs.) *64* SD 4972
Warton (Northum.) *79* NU 0002
Warton (Warw.) *42* SK 2803
Warwick (Cumbr.) *71* NY 4656
Warwick (Warw.) *33* SP 2865
Warwick Bridge *71* NY 4756
Washaway *4* SX 0369
Washbourne *5* SX 7954
Washfield *8* SS 9315
Washfold *65* NZ 0502
Washford *16* ST 0441
Washford Pyne *7* SS 8111
Washingborough *54* TF 0170
Washington (Tyne and Wear) *72* NZ 3356
Washington (W Susx) *12* TQ 1212
Wasing *19* SU 5764
Waskerley *72* NZ 0545
Wasperton *33* SP 2659
Wass *66* SE 5579
Watchet *16* ST 0743
Watchfield (Oxon.) *18* SU 2490
Watchfield (Somer.) *17* ST 3446
Watchgate *63* SD 5399
Water *58* SD 8425
Waterbeach *45* TL 4965
Waterbeck *70* NY 2477
Waterden *46* TF 8835
Water End (Herts.) *35* TL 0310
Water End (Herts.) *35* TL 2304
Waterfall *52* SK 0851
Waterfoot (Lancs.) *58* SD 8321
Waterfoot (Strath.) *84* NS 5654
Waterford *35* TL 3114
Waterheads *85* NT 2451
Waterhouses (Durham) *72* NZ 1841
Waterhouses (Staffs.) *52* SK 0850
Wateringbury *14* TQ 6853
Wateringhouse *113* ND 3090
Waterloo (Dorset) *10* SZ 0194
Waterloo (Mers.) *50* SJ 3297
Waterloo (Norf.) *47* TG 2219
Waterloo (Strath.) *84* NS 8153
Waterloo (Tays.) *92* NO 0636
Waterlooville *11* SU 6809
Water Meetings *76* NS 9513
Water Newton *45* TL 1097
Water Orton *42* SP 1791
Waterperry *34* SP 6206
Waterrow *16* ST 0525
Watersfield *12* TQ 0115
Waterside (Strath.) *75* NS 4308
Waterside (Strath.) *82* NS 4843
Waterside (Strath.) *82* NS 5160
Waterside (Strath.) *84* NS 6773
Waterstock *34* SP 6305
Waterston *24* SM 9306
Water Stratford *34* SP 6534
Waters Upton *41* SJ 6319
Water Yeat *62* SD 2889
Watford (Herts.) *20* TQ 1196
Watford (Northants.) *43* SP 6069
Wath (N Yorks.) *65* SE 1467
Wath (N Yorks.) *66* SE 3277
Wath Upon Dearne *59* SE 4300
Watlington (Norf.) *46* TF 6211
Watlington (Oxon.) *19* SU 6994
Watnall Chaworth *53* SK 4946
Watten *112* ND 2454
Wattisfield *36* TM 0174
Wattisham *36* TM 0151
Watton (Humbs.) *67* TA 0150
Watton (Norf.) *46* TF 9100
Watton-at-Stone *35* TL 3019
Wattston *84* NS 7770
Wattstown *28* ST 0194
Waunarlwydd *25* SS 6095
Waunfawr *48* SH 5259
Wavendon *34* SP 9137
Waverton (Ches.) *50* SJ 4663
Waverton (Cumbr.) *70* NY 2247
Wawne *61* TA 0836
Waxham *47* TG 4326
Waxholme *61* TA 3229
Wayford *9* ST 4006
Way Village *7* SS 8810
Wealdstone *21* TQ 1689
Weare *17* ST 4152
Weare Giffard *6* SS 4721
Weasenham All Saints *46* TF 8421
Weasenham St. Peter *46* TF 8522
Weaverham *51* SJ 6173
Weaverthorpe *67* SE 9670
Webheath *32* SP 0266
Weddington *43* SP 3693
Wedhampton *18* SU 0557
Wedmore *17* ST 4347
Wednesbury *42* SP 0095
Wednesfield *41* SJ 9400
Weedon *34* SP 8118
Weedon Bec *34* SP 6259
Weedon Lois *33* SP 6047
Weeford *42* SK 1404
Week *7* SS 7316
Weekley *44* SP 8880
Week St. Mary *6* SX 2397
Weeley *23* TM 1422
Weeley Heath *23* TM 1520
Weem *97* NN 8449
Weeping Cross *41* SJ 9421
Weeting *46* TL 7788
Weeton (Lancs.) *57* SD 3834
Weeton (W Yorks.) *59* SE 2846
Weir *58* SD 8724
Welbeck Colliery Village *53* SK 5869
Welborne *47* TG 0610
Welbourn *54* SK 9654
Welburn *66* SE 7168
Welbury *66* NZ 3902
Welby *54* SK 9738
Welches Dam *45* TL 4786
Welcombe *6* SS 2218
Weldon *44* SP 9289
Welford (Berks.) *19* SU 4073
Welford (Northants.) *43* SP 6480
Welford-on-Avon *32* SP 1552
Welham *44* SP 7692
Welham Green *35* TL 2305
Well (Hants.) *20* SU 7646
Well (Lincs.) *55* TF 4473
Well (N Yorks.) *66* SE 2682
Welland *32* SO 7940
Wellesbourne Hastings *33* SP 2755
Wellesbourne Mountford *33* SP 2755
Well Hill (Kent) *21* TQ 4963
Welling *21* TQ 4575
Wellingborough *44* SP 8968
Wellingham *46* TF 8722
Wellingore *54* SK 9856
Wellington (Here. and Worc.) *30* SO 4948
Wellington (Salop) *41* SJ 6411
Wellington (Somer.) *8* ST 1320
Wellington Heath *32* SO 7140
Wellow (Avon) *18* ST 7358
Wellow (I. of W.) *11* SZ 3887
Wellow (Notts.) *53* SK 6666
Wells *17* ST 5445
Wellsborough *43* SK 3602
Wells-Next-The-Sea *46* TF 9143
Wells of Ythan *104* NJ 6338
Wellwood *85* NT 0888
Welney *45* TL 5294
Welshampton *50* SJ 4334
Welsh End *50* SJ 5035
Welsh Frankton *50* SJ 3633
Welsh Hook *24* SM 9327
Welsh Newton *29* SO 4918
Welshpool (Trallwng) *40* SJ 2207
Welsh St. Donats *28* ST 0276
Welton (Cumbr.) *70* NY 3544
Welton (Humbs.) *61* SE 9527
Welton (Lincs.) *54* TF 0079
Welton (Northants.) *43* SP 5865
Welton le Marsh *55* TF 4768
Welton le Wold *55* TF 2787
Welwick *61* TA 3421
Welwyn *35* TL 2316
Welwyn Garden City *35* TL 2412
Wem *40* SJ 5129

Place	No.	Grid
Wolferlow	31	SO 6661
Wolferton	46	TF 6528
Wolfhill	92	NO 1533
Wolf's Castle	24	SM 9627
Wolfsdale	24	SM 9321
Wollaston (Northants.)	34	SP 9062
Wollaston (Salop)	40	SJ 3212
Wollerton	41	SJ 6229
Wolsingham	72	NZ 0737
Wolston	43	SP 4175
Wolvercote	33	SP 4809
Wolverhampton	41	SO 9198
Wolverley (Here. and Worc.)	41	SO 8279
Wolverley (Salop)	40	SJ 4631
Wolverton (Bucks.)	34	SP 8141
Wolverton (Hants.)	19	SU 5557
Wolverton (Warw.)	33	SP 2062
Wolvey	43	SP 4387
Wolviston	73	NZ 4525
Wombleton	66	SE 6683
Wombourne	41	SO 8793
Wombwell	59	SE 3902
Womenswold	15	TR 2250
Womersley	60	SE 5319
Wonastow	29	SO 4811
Wonersh	20	TQ 0145
Wonston	11	SU 4739
Wooburn	20	SU 9187
Wooburn Green	20	SU 9188
Woodale	65	SE 0279
Woodbastwick	47	TG 3315
Woodbeck	54	SK 7777
Woodborough (Notts.)	53	SK 6347
Woodborough (Wilts.)	18	SU 1059
Woodbridge	37	TM 2749
Woodbury	8	SY 0087
Woodbury Salterton	8	SY 0189
Woodchester	32	SO 8302
Woodchurch	15	TQ 9434
Woodcote (Oxon.)	19	SU 6481
Woodcote (Salop)	41	SJ 7715
Woodcroft	29	ST 5495
Wood Dalling	47	TG 0927
Woodditton	36	TL 6559
Woodeaton	33	SP 5311
Wood End (Herts.)	35	TL 3225
Woodend (Northants.)	34	SP 6149
Wood End (Warw.)	42	SP 1071
Wood End (Warw.)	42	SP 2498
Woodend (W Susx)	12	SU 8108
Wood Enderby	55	TF 2764
Woodfalls	10	SU 1920
Woodford (Corn.)	6	SS 2113
Woodford (Gtr Mches.)	51	SJ 8982
Woodford (Northants.)	44	SP 9676
Woodford Bridge	21	TQ 4291
Woodford Green	21	TQ 4192
Woodford Halse	33	SP 5452
Woodgate (Here. and Worc.)	41	SO 9666
Woodgate (Norf.)	46	TG 0215
Woodgate (W Mids.)	41	SO 9982
Woodgate (W Susx)	12	SU 9304
Wood Green (Gtr London)	21	TQ 3191
Woodgreen (Hants.)	10	SU 1717
Woodhall	65	SD 9790
Woodhall Spa	55	TF 1963
Woodham	20	TQ 0261
Woodham Ferrers	22	TQ 7999
Woodham Mortimer	22	TL 8205
Woodham Walter	22	TL 8006
Woodhaven	93	NO 4127
Wood Hayes	41	SJ 9501
Woodhead (Grampn.)	105	NJ 7938
Woodhill	41	SO 7384
Woodhorn	79	NZ 2988
Woodhouse (Leic.)	43	SK 5315
Woodhouse (S Yorks.)	53	SK 4184
Woodhouse Eaves	43	SK 5214
Woodhouselee	85	NT 2364
Woodhurst	45	TL 3176
Woodingdean	13	TQ 3605
Woodland (Devon)	5	SX 7968
Woodland (Durham)	72	NZ 0726
Woodlands (Dorset)	10	SU 0508
Woodlands (Grampn.)	99	NO 7895
Woodlands (Hants.)	11	SU 3111
Woodlands Park	20	SU 8578
Woodleigh	5	SX 7348
Woodlesford	59	SE 3629
Woodley	20	SU 7973
Woodmancote (Glos.)	32	SP 0008
Woodmancote (W Susx)	12	SU 7707
Woodmancott	19	SU 5642
Woodmansey	61	TA 0537
Woodmansterne	21	TQ 2760
Woodminton	10	SU 0122
Woodnesborough	15	TR 3156
Woodnewton	44	TL 0394
Wood Norton	46	TG 0128
Woodplumpton	57	SD 4934
Woodrising	46	TF 9803
Woodseaves (Salop)	41	SJ 6830
Woodseaves (Staffs.)	41	SJ 7925
Woodsend	18	SU 2275
Woodsetts	53	SK 5483
Woodsford	9	SY 7690
Woodside (Berks.)	20	SU 9371
Woodside (Herts.)	35	TL 2506
Woodside (Tays.)	92	NO 2037
Woodstock	33	SP 4416
Wood Street	20	SU 9551
Woodthorpe (Derby.)	53	SK 4574
Woodthorpe (Leic.)	43	SK 5417
Woodton	47	TM 2894
Woodtown	6	SS 4926
Woodville	43	SK 3119
Wood Walton	45	TL 2180
Woodyates	10	SU 0219
Woofferton	40	SO 5168
Wookey	17	ST 5145
Wookey Hole	17	ST 5347
Wool	10	SY 8486
Woolacombe	6	SS 4543
Woolage Green	15	TR 2449
Woolaston	29	ST 5999
Woolavington	17	ST 3441
Woolbeding	12	SU 8722
Wooler	79	NT 9928
Woolfardisworthy (Devon)	6	SS 3321
Woolfardisworthy (Devon)	7	SS 8208
Woolhampton	19	SU 5766
Woolhope	31	SO 6135
Woolland	9	ST 7706
Woolley (Cambs.)	45	TL 1474
Woolley (W Yorks.)	59	SE 3113
Woolmer Green	35	TL 2518
Woolpit	36	TL 9762
Woolscott	43	SP 4968
Woolstaston	40	SO 4498
Woolsthorpe	54	SK 8334
Woolston (Ches.)	51	SJ 6589
Woolston (Hants.)	11	SU 4410
Woolston (Salop)	40	SJ 3224
Woolston (Salop)	40	SO 4287
Woolstone (Bucks.)	34	SP 8738
Woolstone (Oxon.)	19	SU 2987
Woolton	50	SJ 4286
Woolton Hill	19	SU 4261
Woolverstone	37	TM 1838
Woolverton	18	ST 7853
Woolwich	21	TQ 4478
Wooperton	79	NU 0420
Woore	51	SJ 7242
Wootton (Beds.)	34	TL 0045
Wootton (Hants.)	11	SZ 2498
Wootton (Humbs.)	61	TA 0815
Wootton (Kent)	15	TR 2246
Wootton (Northants.)	34	SP 7656
Wootton (Oxon.)	33	SP 4319
Wootton (Oxon.)	33	SP 4701
Wootton (Staffs.)	41	SJ 8227
Wootton (Staffs.)	52	SK 1045
Wootton Bassett	11	SU 0682
Wootton Bridge	11	SZ 5491
Wootton Common	11	SZ 5390
Wootton Courtenay	16	SS 9343
Wootton Fitzpaine	8	SY 3695
Wootton Rivers	18	SU 1962
Wootton St. Lawrence	19	SU 5953
Wootton Wawen	32	SP 1563
Worcester	32	SO 8555
Worcester Park	21	TQ 2266
Wordsley	41	SO 8887
Worfield	41	SO 7595
Workington	62	NX 9928
Worksop	53	SK 5879
Worlaby	61	TA 0113
World's End (Berks.)	19	SU 4876
Worle	17	ST 3562
Worleston	51	SJ 6856
Worlingham	47	TM 4489
Worlington (Devon.)	7	SS 7713
Worlington (Suff.)	36	TL 6973
Worlingworth	37	TM 2368
Wormbridge	30	SO 4230
Wormegay	46	TF 6611
Wormhill	52	SK 1274
Wormiehills	93	NO 6239
Wormingford	36	TL 9332
Worminghall	34	SP 6408
Wormington	32	SP 0336
Worminster	17	ST 5742
Wormit	93	NO 3925
Wormleighton	33	SP 4453
Wormley	35	TL 3605
Wormshill	14	TQ 8857
Wormsley	30	SO 4248
Worplesdon	20	SU 9753
Worrall	53	SK 3092
Worsbrough	59	SE 3503
Worsley	58	SD 7400
Worstead	47	TG 3026
Worsthorne	58	SD 8732
Worston	58	SD 7642
Worth (Kent)	15	TR 3356
Wortham	37	TM 0777
Worthen	40	SJ 3204
Worthenbury	50	SJ 4146
Worthing (Norf.)	46	TF 9919
Worthing (W Susx)	12	TQ 1402
Worthington	43	SK 4020
Worth Matravers	10	SY 9777
Wortley	59	SK 3099
Worton	18	ST 9757
Wortwell	47	TM 2784
Wotherton	40	SJ 2800
Wotton	20	TQ 1348
Wotton Under Edge	18	ST 7593
Wotton Underwood	34	SP 6815
Woughton on the Green	34	SP 8737
Wouldham	14	TQ 7164
Wrabness	37	TM 1731
Wragby	55	TF 1378
Wramplingham	47	TG 1106
Wrangham	104	NJ 6331
Wrangle	55	TF 4250
Wrangway	8	ST 1217
Wrantage	8	ST 3022
Wrawby	61	TA 0108
Wraxall (Avon)	29	ST 4872
Wraxall (Somer.)	17	ST 5936
Wray	64	SD 6067
Wraysbury	20	TQ 0173
Wrea Green	57	SD 3931
Wreay (Cumbr.)	71	NY 4349
Wreay (Cumbr.)	63	NY 4423
Wrekenton	72	NZ 2758
Wrelton	67	SE 7686
Wrenbury	51	SJ 5947
Wreningham	47	TM 1699
Wrentham	47	TM 4982
Wressle	60	SE 7031
Wrestlingworth	35	TL 2547
Wretton	46	TF 6800
Wrexham	50	SJ 3349
Wribbenhall	41	SO 7975
Wrightington Bar	57	SD 5313
Wrinehall	51	SJ 7546
Wrington	22	ST 4662
Writtle	22	TL 6606
Wrockwardine	41	SJ 6212
Wroot	60	SE 7102
Wrotham	14	TQ 6159
Wrotham Heath	14	TQ 6258
Wroughton	18	SU 1480
Wroxall (I. of W.)	11	SZ 5579
Wroxall (Warw.)	42	SP 2271
Wroxeter	40	SJ 5608
Wroxham	47	TG 3017
Wroxton	33	SP 4141
Wyaston	52	SK 1842
Wyberton	55	TF 3240
Wyboston	35	TL 1656
Wybunbury	51	SJ 6949
Wychbold	32	SO 9166
Wych Cross	13	TQ 4231
Wyche	32	SO 7643
Wyck	12	SU 7539
Wycombe Marsh	20	SU 8992
Wyddial	35	TL 3731
Wye	15	TR 0546
Wyke (Dorset)	17	ST 7926
Wyke (Salop)	41	SJ 6402
Wyke (W Yorks.)	59	SE 1526
Wykeham (N Yorks.)	67	SE 9683
Wyke Regis	9	SY 6677
Wyke, The (Salop)	41	SJ 7306
Wykey	40	SJ 3925
Wylam	72	NZ 1164
Wylde Green	42	SP 1293
Wylye	10	SU 0037
Wymering	11	SU 6405
Wymeswold	43	SK 6023
Wymington	34	SP 9564
Wymondham (Leic.)	44	SK 8518
Wymondham (Norf.)	47	TG 1101
Wymondley	35	TL 2128
Wyndham	28	SS 9391
Wynford Eagle	9	SY 5895
Wyre Piddle	32	SO 9647
Wysall	43	SK 6027
Wythall	42	SP 0775
Wytham	33	SP 4708
Wyverstone	37	TM 0468
Wyverstone Street	36	TM 0367

Y

Place	No.	Grid
Yaddlethorpe	60	SE 8806
Yafford	11	SZ 4581
Yafforth	66	SE 3494
Yalding	14	TQ 7050
Yanworth	32	SP 0713
Yapham	67	SE 7851
Yapton	12	SU 9703
Yarburgh	55	TF 3493
Yarcombe	8	ST 2408
Yardley	42	SP 1385
Yardley Gobion	34	SP 7644
Yardley Hastings	34	SP 8656
Yardro	30	SO 2258
Yarkhill	31	SO 6042
Yarlet	41	SJ 9129
Yarlington	17	ST 6529
Yarm	72	NZ 4111
Yarmouth	11	SZ 3589
Yarnfield	51	SJ 8632
Yarnscombe	6	SS 5523
Yarnton	33	SP 4711
Yarpole	30	SO 4665
Yarrow	77	NT 3527
Yarrow Feus	77	NT 3325
Yarwell	45	TL 0697
Yate	18	ST 7082
Yateley	20	SU 8160
Yatesbury	18	SU 0671
Yattendon	19	SU 5474
Yatton (Avon)	29	ST 4265
Yatton (Here. and Worc.)	30	SO 4367
Yatton (Here. and Worc.)	31	SO 6330
Yatton Keynell	18	ST 8676
Yaverland	11	SZ 6185
Yaxham	46	TG 0010
Yaxley (Cambs.)	45	TL 1892
Yaxley (Suff.)	37	TM 1173
Yazor	30	SO 4046
Yeading	20	TQ 1182
Yeadon	59	SE 2040
Yealand Conyers	64	SD 5074
Yealand Redmayne	64	SD 5075
Yealmpton	5	SX 5751
Yearsley	66	SE 5874
Yeaton	40	SJ 4319
Yeaveley	52	SK 1840
Yedingham	67	SE 8979
Yelford	33	SP 3564
Yelling	35	TL 2562
Yelvertoft	43	SP 5975
Yelverton (Devon)	5	SX 5267
Yelverton (Norf.)	47	TG 2901
Yenston	9	ST 7120
Yeoford	7	SX 7898
Yeolmbridge	4	SX 3187
Yeovil	9	ST 5515
Yeovil Marsh	9	ST 5418
Yeovilton	9	ST 5422
Yerbeston	24	SN 0609
Yesnaby	113	OY 2215
Yetlington	79	NU 0209
Yetminster	9	ST 5910
Yetton	17	SY 0585
Yetts o'Muckhart	91	NO 0001
Y Fan	39	SN 9487
Yielden	44	TL 0167
Yieldshields	84	NS 8750
Yiewsley	20	TQ 0680
Ynysboeth	28	ST 0696
Ynysddu	28	ST 1892
Ynyshir	28	ST 0292
Ynyslas	38	SN 6092
Ynysybwl	28	ST 0594
Yockenthwaite	65	SD 9079
Yockleton	40	SJ 3910
Yokefleet	60	SE 8124
Yoker	82	NS 5168
Yonder Bognie	104	NJ 5946
York	66	SE 6052
Yorkletts	15	TR 0963
Yorkley	29	SO 6306
Yorton	40	SJ 4923
Youlgreave	53	SK 2164
Youlstone	6	SS 2715
Youlthorpe	67	SE 7655
Youlton	66	SE 4863
Young's End	22	TL 7319
Yoxall	42	SK 1419
Yoxford	37	TM 3968
Y Rhiw	38	SH 2228
Ysbyty Ifan	49	SH 8448
Ysbyty Ystwyth	27	SN 7371
Ysceifiog	50	SJ 1571
Ysgubor-y-coed	39	SN 6895
Ystalyfera	28	SN 7608
Ystrad	28	SS 9796
Ystrad Aeron	26	SN 5256
Ystradfellte	28	SN 9313
Ystradgynlais	28	SN 7910
Ystrad Meurig	27	SN 7067
Ystrad-Mynach	28	ST 1493
Ystradowen (Dyfed)	28	SN 7512
Ystradowen (S Glam.)	28	ST 0177
Ythanbank	105	NJ 9034
Ythsie	105	NJ 8830

Z

Place	No.	Grid
Zeal Monachorum	7	SS 7103
Zeals	17	ST 7731
Zelah	2	SW 8051
Zennor	2	SW 4538